table broth ziti with and izzes
atmeal cookies chinese
urora sauce dashi pine nu
and beans soup chickpea an
nut cake hearty minestron
asta dough sweet potato pi
paghetti and t-balls almon
bbiata golden beet soup wit
eggplant stew chocolate
ed bean and bulgur chili sicilia
plant root vegetable brot
lla walnut cookies marinar
and broccoli rabe brazilia
ttanesca chocolate–peanu
portobellos parmasio chile
nut brownies orecchiett
ean chili chai spice cooki

# 1,000 VEGAN RECIPES

# 1,000 VEGAN RECIPES

## ROBIN ROBERTSON

WILEY

John Wiley & Sons, Inc.

Library of Congress Cataloging-in-Publication Data:

Robertson, Robin (Robin G.)
  1,000 vegan recipes / Robin Robertson.
    p. cm.
  Includes index.
  ISBN 978-0-470-08502-8 (cloth)
  1. Vegan cookery. I. Title. II. Title: One thousand vegan recipes.
  TX837.R62365 2009
  641'5'636—dc22
                              2008055898

All decorative spot art: © Vallentin/Dreamstime.com
Border under chapter titles: © Jamey Ekins/istockphoto.com
Leaf borders of chapter openers: © Heidi Kalyani/istockphoto.com

Printed in the United States of America

10 9 8 7 6 5

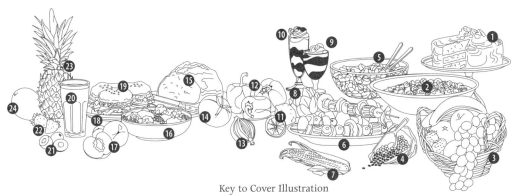

Key to Cover Illustration

| | | | |
|---|---|---|---|
| 1. | Vegan Chocolate Mousse Cake | 13. | garlic |
| 2. | Tempeh and Vegetable Stir-Fry | 14. | tomato |
| 3. | basket of fruit | 15. | Sunflower Artisan Bread |
| 4. | cranberry and cannellini beans | 16. | Broccoli and White Beans with Potatoes and Walnuts |
| 5. | Spinach Salad with Almonds, Fuji Apples, and Figs | 17. | peaches |
| 6. | Grilled Seitan and Vegetable Kabobs | 18. | plum |
| 7. | corn | 19. | Golden Veggie Burgers |
| 8. | artichoke | 20. | Tropical Smoothie |
| 9. | Vegan Tiramisu | 21. | kiwi |
| 10. | Strawberry Parfait with Cashew Crème | 22. | strawberries |
| 11. | lemons | 23. | pineapple |
| 12. | bell peppers | 24. | mango |

FOR JON

# CONTENTS

# ACKNOWLEDGMENTS

Writing a book this comprehensive has required the assistance and support of family, friends, and experts that I am privileged to know.

For generously sharing recipes with me, I want to give special thanks to Tal Ronnen and Francis Janes, as well as Nava Atlas, Peter Kumar, Corey Portalatin-Berrien, Christine Waltermyer, Tami Noyes, Lisa Dahlmeier, Toni Dahlmeier, Laura Yanne, Lori Kettler, Mylie Thompson, Melissa Ling, Robin Dempsey, and Ann Swissdorf.

For diligently testing recipes for this book, I'm grateful to Tami Noyes, Tina Matlock, Cassandra Greenwald, Jenna Patton, Russell Patton, Andrea Weaver, Melanie Baker, Becca Bennett, Linda Evans, Chessa Hickox, Lea Jacobson, Lisa Dahlmeier, Toni Dalhmeier, Linda Levy, Sandy Boss, Karen Taggart, Kim Hammond, Rebecca Fischer, Laura Frisk, Edie Fidler, Robin Dempsey, Martha Crofts, Leigh Hudson, Melissa Ling, Nancy Shafran, Sarah Ryczek, Cathy Frisinger, Gina Meyers, Mary Janskey, John Barstow, Janet Aaronson, and Anna West.

I am also grateful to the staff at John Wiley & Sons, especially my editor, Linda Ingroia, for inviting me to write this book and for shepherding the book throughout the process, and assistant editor Charleen Barila for her daily editorial support and diligence on the project. I appreciate the careful work of production editor Amy Zarkos; cover designer Jeff Faust; interior designer Holly Wittenberg; art director Tai Blanche, and copyeditor Justine Gardner. Thanks also to Jana Nordstrand for all her publicity support.

I also want to thank my agent, Stacey Glick of Dystel & Goderich Literary Management, and, most of all, my husband, Jon Robertson, for his support, encouragement, and assistance throughout the writing of this book.

# INTRODUCTION

## A VEGAN KITCHEN

From a certain perspective, vegan cooking can be truly magical: you can make roasts without meat, sandwiches without cold cuts, cream sauces without cream, cheesecakes without cheese, and cakes without eggs. It's a celebration of the world's diverse cultures, an homage to good health, and a way to honor and respect all life. It's the wave of the future, a future that is already well begun.

Filling any cookbook with a thousand recipes would seem to be a daunting task, but especially so when those recipes are vegan. Some may wonder how one could manage to fill such a comprehensive book without using meat, fish, poultry, eggs, cheese, dairy, or honey—no animal products of any kind. This book is a testimonial to all the rich and versatile ways to eat vegan. It may surprise you to know that the bigger challenge was how to limit the number of recipes to one thousand. (And you will likely find ways to vary my recipes, expanding the possibilities further.)

I've been happily vegan for more than twenty years, and it's astonishing how often people have asked me: "So what do you eat?" The short answer is: everything and anything, as long as it is plant-based. With the recipes in this volume, however, I now have a new tangible response to that question.

I've devoted much of my life to developing new ways to prepare classic recipes without using animal products and helping others experience the versatility, ease, and excitement of plant-based cooking. My years of being immersed in the cooking (and eating) of rich foods of all kinds actually helped my transition to a vegan diet. I realized that much of what I liked about certain dishes was the sauces or the seasonings, and it didn't make sense to me that, just because I chose not to eat meat, I should deprive myself of the flavors and textures of traditional dishes. I didn't skip a beat in figuring out ways to adapt many of my favorite meat- and dairy-centered recipes into vegan versions. *1,000 Vegan Recipes* is the result of more than twenty-five years of experience as a former restaurant chef, cooking instructor, and author of more than fifteen cookbooks. The recipes in this book reflect a broad range of cooking styles and the wide variety of global cuisines that I have grown to love. Readers familiar with my previous cookbooks will no doubt find some familiar tried-and-true favorite recipes that are a part of most vegan cooking repertoire, such as vegan lasagna and cheesecake, as well as basics such as marinara sauce, pesto, and hummus. However, as with anyone who loves to cook, my own cooking style has evolved over the years, so even within the realm of certain familiar recipes, you'll find new twists, tweaks, and nuances along the way. In addition, this book contains hundreds of totally new recipes that I've developed especially for this book, resulting in the most wide-ranging and inclusive collection of vegan recipes ever assembled in a single volume.

While vegetarian cooking grew in popularity from the 1970s to the 1990s, in recent years, "vegan" has become the new "vegetarian." The need for a comprehensive volume of great vegan recipes has never been more timely. To fill that need, *1,000 Vegan Recipes* is the one-stop source for a whole new generation of people interested in going all the way with healthy, ethical, and environmentally responsible eating. *1,000 Vegan Recipes* is the first comprehensive book of vegan recipes, containing not only hundreds of flavorful recipes for every occasion and taste, but also informative notes, useful nutrition and cooking charts, and helpful kitchen tips.

Not just for vegans, *1,000 Vegan Recipes* also serves as a valuable resource for the millions of vegetarians, as well as others trying to eat a healthier diet, and for whom cooking creative and tasty meals every day may be a challenge. For anyone who loves to eat, *1,000 Vegan Recipes* comes to the rescue with a diverse collection of delicious international recipes for breakfast, lunch, dinner, and everything in between.

The recipes are designed to appeal to cooks of all skill levels and abilities, from novices to seasoned cooks. With easy-to-follow instructions, *1,000 Vegan Recipes* delivers delicious dishes to satisfy a variety of tastes and occasions. The recipes include global ethnic favorites, such as Pad Thai (page 236) and Paella (page 320), family-style comfort foods such as Millet-Topped Lentil Shepherd's Pie (page 266), and elegant show-stoppers such as Seitan en Croute (page 314) and Roasted Vegetable Strudel (page 333). With this much variety, there are recipes to appeal to everyone, including children who will adore kid-friendly recipes such as Baked Mac and Cheeze (page 222) and Rustic Cottage Pie (page 316). Even meat-eaters will enjoy flavorful and satisfying dishes such as Corn and Potato Chowder (page 165), Tagliatelle with Porcini Bolognese Sauce (page 200), and Brazilian Black Bean Stew (page 252).

With an emphasis on fresh whole foods, the recipes in *1,000 Vegan Recipes* are also a dieter's dream because they are cholesterol-free, low in saturated fat, and high in fiber and complex carbohydrates. Most important, these delicious recipes offer endless variety, and there's a collection of menus at the back that will help make menu planning a breeze. Many of the recipes also feature a "FAST" icon, indicating quick and easy recipes that can be ready in 30 minutes or less. You'll find a list of all the FAST recipes on page 578.

Within these pages you will find tempting appetizers such as Spicy Chipotle Potato Quesadillas (page 361), Shiitakes in Puff Pastry (page 36), and Smoky Chipotle-Pinto Hummus (page 4), as well as a variety of soothing soups and refreshing salads. A wealth of hearty main-dish recipes feature pasta, beans, and grains, as well as fabulous ways to prepare tofu, tempeh, and seitan ("wheat-meat"). There are also recipes for side dishes, beverages, condiments, sauces, and tempting desserts, such as Peach Crumb Pie (page 463), Spice Cake with Mango and Lime (page 451), and Chocolate Swirl Tofu Cheezecake (page 454), as well as recipes that are ideal for buffets and cocktail parties such as Pinto-Pecan Fireballs (page 31), Mushroom Croustades (page 33), and Tempeh Taco Bites (page 37).

When hosting a get-together, it can be difficult to know who eats meat and dairy and who doesn't, but sumptuous dishes such as Chard-Stuffed Manicotti with Creamy Cashew Sauce (page 208) and Seitan and Potato Torta (page 315) can take the guesswork out of entertaining. In *1,000 Vegan Recipes,* the seductive flavors of these and many of the other tantalizing recipes are perfect for company and family meals alike.

## WHY WE GO VEGAN

Vegans have been around for thousands of years, and plant-based eating has been known by various names. Some people call the vegan diet "strict vegetarian," but it is more accurately "pure vegetarian," the original name and meaning of "vegetarian." As the word "vegetarian" drifted to include eggs and dairy (lacto-ovo vegetarians), a new term was needed for the purists. "Vegan" was coined in 1944 by Donald Watson, founder of The Vegan Society in the U.K. As more people seek healthy alternatives to meat and dairy, vegans are the fastest growing segment because many vegetarians are now shifting to pure plant-based diets. People who choose vegan do so chiefly for three reasons: ethics, environment, and health, or a combination of all three.

## ETHICS

What do ethics have to do with what you eat for dinner? People who go vegan by way of conscience believe it is wrong to kill animals for food. Supporting that belief is clear proof, documented by responsible investigators, of the cruel conditions of factory farms and routine, inhumane slaughtering practices. The brutal evidence spans the full spectrum of the beef, veal, pork, and poultry industries.

The commitment of ethical vegans doesn't stop with diet, but extends to avoiding all animal-related products, such as leather, silk, fur, and wool products. They even avoid products such as soaps and cosmetics that contain animal products, purchasing only those labeled "cruelty-free" or "vegan," as well as avoiding products made by companies who use animal testing. (See Resources, page 585, for books and Web sites containing more information on this aspect of veganism). In terms of ethics, choosing vegan food is choosing a diet of compassion.

## ENVIRONMENT

Aside from the ethical and health issues, meat production has a well known deleterious effect on the environment, ranging from deforestation, to pollution, to the waste of fresh water. The fact is that meat production is the most inefficient and wasteful use of land and water one could devise. Over half of the water consumed in the United States is used for animal feed. The amount of water needed to produce an entire day of food for a human requires only a fraction of the water needed for the production of one pound of meat. Much of the rain forest being cleared in South America is not for human food but for feed for cattle for beef exports. The pollution from meat consumption is devastating and includes mountains of animal waste and chemical run-off that spoils the rivers, lakes, and oceans. The plant-based diet may become especially important in the light of the coming water crisis, which was acknowledged by the federal government in October 2007.

## HEALTH

Do you want to look younger, trim down, have clearer skin, and enjoy more energy? If this sounds like a pitch, it is. A well-balanced vegan diet that includes lots of fresh produce, beans, and whole grains, can actually improve health, beautify the skin, minimize the symptoms of seasonal illnesses, colds, and flu, and also provide more energy. Fresh whole foods are loaded with vitamins, nutrients, and, yes, even protein (see page xi), as well as anti-oxidants, minerals, and calcium. At the same time, they contain no cholesterol and are low in saturated fats.

When I first began writing cookbooks back in the mid-1990s, it was difficult to find reliable research on the benefits of a vegan diet. Since then, dozens of books have been published by medical experts and researchers extolling the plant-based diet. Medical doctors such as Neal Barnard, Michael Klaper, John A.

McDougall, Joel Furman, and others have written books and maintain informative Web sites (see Resources, page 585). Numerous food companies have placed their prepared vegan food products on grocery store shelves nationwide.

Vegan celebrities abound, too—some, such as Moby and Chrissie Hynde, even opened their own vegan restaurants. Actors such as Alicia Silverstone, Forrest Whitaker, Natalie Portman, and James Cromwell, among many others, as well as sports figures such as marathoner Scott Jurek, and scores of musicians, including the iconic Paul McCartney, know that a vegan diet will keep them healthier and looking younger. In 2008, popular vegan diet books made headlines, with *Skinny Bitch* by Rory Freedman and Kim Barnouin a runaway *New York Times* bestseller. That same year, author Kathy Freston's *Quantum Wellness* became the inspiration for TV talk show host Oprah Winfrey to explore a vegan diet on her show and Web site.

The end result of a diet of animal products, fast foods, and processed ingredients has actually earned a name for itself—"lifestyle disease." The long-term effect produces cardiovascular disease, stroke, diabetes, and cancer not only because of the inherent fat and cholesterol in meats and dairy products, but because of the artificial additives, hormones, and antibiotics regularly added to the animal feed to accelerate production.

To keep healthy, vegans must learn to eat properly. If even the most committed vegan neglects to maintain a proper balance of nutrients, ill health can be the result—a diet of potato chips and celery may be vegan, but it's never going to make you healthy. Poor health can occur particularly with people who choose to become vegan but don't take the time to adapt their daily menu. As with any style of cooking, a common-sense understanding of basic nutrition is important. The key for a plant-based diet is eating a variety of fresh vegetables, whole grains, legumes, nuts, seeds, and fruits each day, in order to acquire the nutrients necessary for good health, including protein, calcium, fat, and iron. The only elements of the vegan diet requiring supplements are omega-3s (obtained from ground flaxseed) and vitamin B-12. (You should check with your doctor regarding your personal nutrient needs.)

The topic of vegan health and nutrition can fill shelves of books and tackling it comprehensively is beyond the scope of this cookbook. However, if you are new to the vegan diet or have interest in learning more, I urge you to turn to page 588 for a helpful reference called The New Four Food Groups, as well as to consult the books and Web sites listed in the Resources section (page 585).

## PROTEIN

After "What do you eat?" the next most common question asked of vegans is: "Where do you get your protein?" In order to have robust health, our bodies require protein. Animal products provide these, although meat-eaters sometimes consume too much protein, which can damage bones and bodily organs. The fact is, you can get all the protein you need from plant foods, as they are naturally cholesterol-free, low in fat, and high in fiber and complex carbohydrates.

Most plant foods, such as whole grains, beans, and vegetables, contain various amounts and qualities of protein and essential amino acids.

Not all beans provide complete protein, but soybeans surpass other food plants in the amount of protein they deliver. Many vegan meals pair grains and beans, so this is an ideal way to get the protein and other nutrients you need. If you eat a variety of wholesome plant-based ingredients every day, it will go a long way to helping you maintain good health.

### Vegan Protein Sources

Protein is found in a wide variety of whole foods including beans, whole grains, fruits, vegetables, nuts, and seeds, along with products derived from them, such as tofu, tempeh, and quality meat-alternative products. A good rule of thumb is that if you eat a reasonably varied vegan diet and ingest enough calories, you will get enough protein. Refer to the Resources section (page 585) for books and Web sites containing detailed information and studies regarding this topic.

Among all the nondairy milks, soy milk contains the highest concentration of protein at 7 grams per cup. Per ounce, soy nuts contain 10 grams of protein; tahini (from sesame seeds) 5 grams; almonds 6 grams; peanuts 5 grams; and cashews 4 grams.

The plant-based diet provides calcium from tofu, dark leafy greens, sesame seeds, almonds, and cooked beans. For iron, look no further than tofu, lentils, beans, tahini, and grains. Vitamin B-12 can be found in nutritional yeast, fortified cereals, fortified soy milk, tempeh, miso. Omega-3s are found in adequate amounts in vegetables, fruits, beans, and most notably, flax seeds. Finding a comfortable mix and balance of delicious foods containing these ingredients and nutrients is the key, rather than following a checklist.

# SOME INGREDIENTS USED IN THIS BOOK

My goal with this cookbook is to present a collection of recipes that provide people of every taste a master source for satisfying recipes and menus that range from vegan standbys of grain and bean dishes to new plant-based interpretations of traditional fare. For longtime vegans, this is a comprehensive palette from which to choose exciting meals. For newcomers to the healthful plant-based world and seasoned vegans of compassionate dining, you will discover all the delicious ways you can prepare memorable vegan dishes that you will want to make again and again. Here is a list to help you become familiar with some of the ingredients vegans enjoy.

## TOFU

One of the best protein sources on earth, versatile tofu lends itself well to a variety of dishes and cooking methods because it absorbs the flavors of the food with which it is cooked. Also known as "bean curd," tofu is curdled soy milk, extracted from ground, cooked soybeans, and made in a process similar to cheese. Tofu is available in two main types: regular (Chinese) and silken (Japanese). Both types come in three textures: soft, firm, and extra-firm, each of which lends itself well to various types of dishes.

Extra-firm regular tofu is the sturdiest of the two main types. The firm and extra-firm lend themselves to stir-fries and other dishes in which the tofu must retain its shape. Soft regular tofu is used in recipes where a softer texture is desired, such as in lasagna, where it functions like ricotta, but in which silken tofu would be too soft. Silken tofu, or "Japanese-style," is used when the desired result is smooth and creamy, such as in smoothies, sauces, and puddings.

| type | texture | used in |
|---|---|---|
| Regular or Chinese Tofu | Extra-firm | Stir-fries and other dishes in which the tofu must retain its shape |
| | Firm | A casserole filling such as lasagna |
| | Soft | For a pudding or sauce requiring a smooth consistency |
| Silken or Japanese Tofu | Firm | Diced into Asian soups |
| | Soft | Sauces, puddings, and creams |

Tofu is most often packed in water-filled tubs, so, before using it in a recipe, it is essential to drain, blot, and press out the excess water. (It is not necessary to rinse it.) To squeeze tofu dry, cut the block into slabs and place the slabs on a baking sheet lined with paper towels. Weigh down the slabs with a baking sheet topped with heavy canned goods and let it sit for an hour.

Regular tofu can be frozen. Its texture will become chewy and more porous, which works well for marinating or sautéing. Freezing also makes tofu easier to crumble for use in recipes such as chili. To freeze tofu, cut the drained and pressed tofu into slices and either place in an airtight container or wrap it in plastic wrap. When needed for a recipe, thaw the tofu and squeeze again to remove excess water. Once defrosted, tofu should be used within two or three days. Freezing is a good way to preserve tofu, especially as the expiration date approaches. Frozen, tofu will keep for several months.

Regular tofu is also sold as "marinated and baked" and can be used as it is without additional seasoning. You can find it in a variety of flavors, including lemon-pepper, Mediterranean, and teriyaki. It is firm and delicious and since it can be eaten right out of the package, I think of it as a protein-rich convenience food. Cube it and add to salads and stir-fries, or slice it and add to sandwiches and wraps.

## TEMPEH

Not to be outdone by tofu's versatility and nutrition, tempeh, which originated in Indonesia, is made from fermented, compressed soybeans and is especially well suited to stews, stir-fries, and sautés because, like tofu, it absorbs the surrounding flavors. Tempeh turns a crisp, golden brown when fried and it marinates well. Tempeh is high in protein with a chewy texture and a distinct nutty flavor.

Tempeh can be found in the refrigerated or freezer sections of natural foods stores, Asian markets, and some supermarkets, and is usually sold in 8-ounce slabs, depending on the brand. The slabs can be cut lengthwise to make thin slices and can also be cut into strips, cubed, or grated. Tempeh requires refrigeration, where it will keep, unopened, for several weeks (when purchasing, always check the expiration date). Once it is opened, however, it should be wrapped tightly and used within three days. Tempeh will keep for a month or so frozen. I recommend poaching or steaming tempeh for thirty minutes before using to mellow the flavor and aid digestibility.

## Seitan or "Wheat-meat"

Seitan, as it is known in Japan, is the gluten that remains after washing the starch and bran from whole wheat flour. It is perhaps the most versatile ingredient owing to its chewy texture and the many forms it can take. It can be diced, cut into strips for stir-fries, cubed for stews and soups, shredded or ground, stuffed like a roast, or thinly sliced and sautéed. Dining on a meal of seitan, meat consumers may have a change of heart about plant-based dishes.

Making seitan from scratch is fairly easy and a recipe for doing so is included in this book. To save time, you can purchase precooked seitan in natural food stores and Asian markets. Always read the label, as commercial seitan sometimes comes marinated and the flavors may be incompatible with your recipe. Also, be sure to drain and rinse marinated seitan.

## Meat-Alternative Products

In addition to the natural vegan meat alternatives, tofu, seitan, and tempeh, there are a number of commercial products made with plant-based ingredients that are made to mimic, in taste and texture, actual meat products such as burgers and sausages. Some vegans avoid commercial meat- and dairy-alternative products because they don't want to eat anything that even resembles meat. Others avoid processed foods in general and still others refuse to buy products if the producer's company also manufactures animal products. On the other hand, some vegans find these products useful, especially for their convenience, when making the transition to a plant-based diet, or cooking for finicky children.

While I personally enjoy the convenience of an occasional commercially produced veggie burger, in these recipes I do not call for commercial meat alternative products. A handful of recipes reference ingredients such as vegan sausage links as an optional ingredient when I feel that they would be a particularly good inclusion, such as in jambalaya.

## A Word About Dairy and Alternatives

During the 1950s, the dairy industry created an "education" program to promote its products in American classrooms. Ever since, people have believed that consuming calcium in milk is the only way to grow "big and strong." The secret that was not shared was that better sources of calcium can be found in tofu, nuts, broccoli, dark leafy greens, and sea vegetables. And what about added vitamin D? This vitamin, which is actually a hormone that the body creates when exposed to sunlight, doesn't occur naturally in cow's milk and must be added later (the same is true of vitamin D added to soy milk).

Contrary to popular belief, milk consumption does not prevent osteoporosis and is not necessary for bone development. (Calcium, which does contribute to bone development, can be found in other foods listed above.) Humans are the only animals that drink the milk of other species and continue to drink milk after infancy. Recent studies show that milk consumption in some people can actually contribute to heart disease, some forms of cancer, psoriasis, allergies, and a host of other ailments. The highest incidences of osteoporosis occur in countries where milk consumption is high.

People who have difficulty making the transition to a plant-based diet often remain vegetarian because it's difficult for them to part with their beloved dairy products. Fortunately a variety of plant-based alternatives are now available that facilitate cooking all our favorite creamy dishes.

A variety of "milks" can be made from soy, rice, oats, and various nuts to replace the cow's milk once used in cooking and baking. These milks are available in most supermarkets and natural foods stores. Some even come flavored with vanilla or chocolate. Vegan mayonnaise, such as Vegenaise or Nayonaise brands, is also available, as well as dairy-free sour cream, cream cheese, and other kinds of "cheese," which are made from soy, rice, or other plant-based ingredients. (Note: recipes for homemade vegan mayonnaise (page 573) and sour cream (page 574) are provided.) In the place of butter, choose high-quality expeller- or cold-pressed oils, which are made without the use of heat and harsh solvents. When only a solid butter alternative will do, use nonhydrogenated vegan margarine, such as the Earth Balance brand. On your morning toast, consider using nut butters. While they contain about the same amount of calories as butter, they contain no cholesterol yet provide plenty of protein and essential fatty acids.

## Beans

People around the world rely on beans as their main source of protein. They are inexpensive, easy to use, low in fat, and a vital component of any well-balanced plant-based diet. Whether you're cooking chickpeas, black-eyed peas, lentils, black beans, pintos, kidney beans, limas or cannellini, beans are high in protein, fiber, complex carbohydrates, and B vitamins. Beans find their way onto the dinner table throughout North America in stews, burgers, loaves, spreads, and more. As dried beans

require soaking before they can be used, you can dramatically shorten your preparation time by using organic, canned beans. If you want to use dried beans, however, follow the basic instructions on page xv.

Beans are widely used in recipes throughout this book. Most of the recipes calling for specific beans were developed with a particular bean in mind, however in many of the recipes, you will find that one variety is easily interchanged for another. For example, in recipes calling for kidney beans, you can probably substitute pintos or black beans, if you prefer them. If you're not a fan of chickpeas, for example, but like a recipe that calls for them, another cooked bean in equal measure would probably be fine. The only caveat would be if the color and texture is an important factor in the recipe, such as white beans for a white bean dip, although within the realm of white beans, you could certainly use Great Northern, navy, and cannellini beans interchangeably.

### Soaking and Cooking Beans

In most of the recipes using beans in this book, canned or cooked dried beans can be used interchangeably. I use canned organic beans whenever I want to save time, however, if you prefer to cook your own dried beans for use in the recipes, follow these procedures.

With the exception of lentils and split peas, all dried beans require soaking. Soaking rehydrates the beans and shortens their cooking time. It also dissolves some of the complex sugars that cause digestive gas. It's always a good idea to begin by picking through them first in order to remove small stones and other debris.

To soak the beans, place them in a bowl with enough water to cover them by 3 inches. Soak overnight and drain before cooking. To quick-soak beans, put them in a pot with 2 to 3 inches of water and boil for 2 minutes. Remove the pot from the stove, cover it, and let it stand for 2 hours. Drain the beans, and they're ready for cooking.

A simple formula for cooking beans is: bring them to a boil, then reduce the heat to low and simmer them until tender. The general ratio is 1 cup of dried beans for 3 cups of water. Add 1 teaspoon of salt to the water during the last 15 minutes of cooking time, as salt will toughen the beans if added in the early stages of cooking. Generally, 1 cup of dried beans yields 2 to 2$\frac{1}{2}$ cups of cooked beans. Cooking time may vary, depending on the type, quality, and age of the beans. Altitude and even water quality can vary the results, so check for doneness about two-thirds of the way through so you don't overcook the beans. Since cooked beans freeze well, consider making a double batch and freezing half for a future use.

The cooking times below apply to conventional stovetop cooking.

## stovetop cooking times for soaked beans

| bean (1 cup dried) | water | cooking time |
| --- | --- | --- |
| Adzuki beans | 3 cups | 1 hour |
| Black beans | 3½ cups | 2 hours |
| Black-eyed peas | 3 cups | 1 hour |
| Cannellini beans | 3½ cups | 2 hours |
| Chickpeas | 3½ cups | 2½ hours |
| Great Northern beans | 3½ cups | 2 hours |
| Kidney beans | 3½ cups | 2 hours |
| Navy beans | 3 cups | 1½ hours |
| Pinto beans | 3½ cups | 2 hours |

## GRAINS

What is more wholesome and delicious than freshly cooked whole grains? A dependable staple throughout the world, grains are abundant, inexpensive, great sources of protein, fiber, and have more complex carbohydrates than any other food. From breakfast cereal to daily bread, grains find their way into every diet. In vegan cooking, however, we draw from the entire global pantry of whole grains for their high nutritional value and variety of textures and flavors.

In addition to many varieties of rice including basmati, jasmine, and Arborio, this book also includes recipes using other nutritious grains such as quinoa, millet, barley, and bulgur. Here are brief descriptions of some of the less familiar grains:

amaranth—this tiny grain is actually a small super-nutritious seed. It has a slightly sweet, nutty flavor and contains higher essential amino acids than any other grain. Since it can be a bit sticky when cooked, it is best used as an ingredient in patties and loaves.

barley—a chewy texture and nutty flavor make this nutritious grain an interesting alternative to rice as a side dish, in a pilaf, or in a soup. The pearled variety, which has been hulled and polished, is the quickest cooking.

bulgur—steamed and dried wheat kernels with a tender but chewy texture and a mild wheat-like flavor. Good as an alternative to rice or used in salads.

kasha—this brown angular grain is roasted hulled buckwheat groats. It has a deep nutty flavor and is traditionally used in Eastern European cooking.

millet—a small yellow-beige non-glutinous grain with a mild, nutlike flavor. It makes a good side dish or a component in patties or loaves.

quinoa—this compact disc-shaped "super-grain of the Incas" is especially notable for being a complete protein. It has a nutty flavor and comes in red and brown varieties. Use as a side dish or in a pilaf. Also good in salads or used in loaves and patties. It is important to thoroughly rinse quinoa before using to remove a bitter coating called saponin.

spelt—this member of the wheat family has a low gluten level; consequently spelt flour is often used by those who are gluten sensitive. (Check with your doctor before eating if you are gluten sensitive.) The whole grain takes a long time to cook (usually several hours). Spelt is often confused with farro (or emmer wheat), an Italian wheat-like grain that takes only about 45 minutes to cook. Farro has a chewy texture and nutty flavor that is especially good in soups.

Each grain has its own unique flavor, texture, and nutritional profile. If you want to experiment with grains that are new to you, a grain cooking chart is provided below. One way to become familiar with a grain is to cook up a small batch as a side dish or as a bed for a stew or other recipe.

### Cooking Grains

Before you cook any grain, be sure to rinse it to remove loose hulls, dust, and other impurities. To intensify the flavor of grains, toast them briefly in a dry skillet before cooking.

STOVETOP METHOD: Pour the grain into a pot and cover with twice as much water. Bring the water to a boil, add about $\frac{1}{4}$ teaspoon of salt, then reduce the heat to low, simmering until tender, for the time specified in the chart below. The grain is finished cooking when the water is entirely absorbed. After cooking, let the pot stand, covered, for 5 minutes before serving. If any liquid is remaining, drain it off. When ready to serve, fluff the grain with a fork. One cup of uncooked grain makes about 3 cups of cooked grain. For extra flavor, grains can be cooked in vegetable broth instead of water.

OTHER METHODS: Grains can also be baked in the oven in a tightly covered pot, cooked in a pressure cooker, or, as in the case of pilaf, prepared in a skillet on top of the stove. For the pilaf method, sauté the grains in oil first, then add the liquid, and cook until tender.

The following table of average cooking times pertains to the stovetop method.

## stovetop cooking times for whole grains

| grain (1 cup dried) | water | cooking time |
| --- | --- | --- |
| Amaranth | 1½ cups | 15 minutes |
| Barley (pearled) | 3 cups | 25 minutes |
| Basmati rice (brown) | 2 cups | 35 minutes |
| Brown rice (short grain) | 2½ cups | 45 minutes |
| Brown rice (long grain) | 2 cups | 30 minutes |
| Cornmeal (polenta) | 4 cups | 25 minutes |
| Kasha (buckwheat) | 2½ cups | 20 minutes |
| Millet | 2¼ cups | 30 minutes |
| Rolled oats | 2 cups | 10 minutes |
| Quinoa | 2 cups | 20 minutes |
| White rice (long grain) | 1½ cups | 20 minutes |
| Wild rice | 3 cups | 1 hour |

Not included in the chart are bulgur or couscous. Since they are both already partially cooked, they only need to be soaked, not cooked. For bulgur: combine 1 cup of bulgur with $1\frac{1}{2}$ cups boiling water and $\frac{1}{4}$ teaspoon of salt. Cover and set aside for 30 minutes. For couscous: combine 1 cup of couscous with $1\frac{1}{4}$ cups water and $\frac{1}{4}$ teaspoon salt. Cover and set aside for 10 minutes. (Note: couscous, made from semolina, isn't, in fact, a "whole" grain.)

## VEGETABLES

The key to enjoying nutritious, satisfying vegan dishes is to serve protein-rich beans, grains, nuts, and soy foods combined with fresh, preferably organic produce. Whenever possible, use fresh, locally grown vegetables, and be sure to take advantage of the variety that may be native to your region. In vegan dining, vegetables are the featured stars, rather than the side-dish bit players, so choose them at their peak of freshness. To make sure you are getting the full spectrum of vitamins and minerals in your diet, be adventurous and creative. Combine veggies in pleasing color combinations, and be sure to include leafy greens, root vegetables, and squashes, too, when planning your menus.

## NUTS AND SEEDS

In addition to being great snack foods, nuts and seeds can be enjoyed in both sweet and savory dishes. Important sources of protein for vegans (see chart on page xi), nuts and seeds can be found in and out of the shell, whole, halved, sliced, chopped, raw, roasted, or made into nut butter (see below). Due to their high oil content, nuts and seeds go rancid quickly once the shells are removed, unless properly

## toasting nuts and seeds

Toasting nuts and seeds enhances their flavor and can be done either in the oven or on top of the stove.

OVEN: Preheat the oven to 350°F. Arrange nuts or seeds in a single layer on a baking sheet and toast until golden brown and fragrant, 5 to 10 minutes depending on the variety, stirring occasionally. The smaller the seed or nut, the faster they will be done, so watch closely and don't let them burn. Set aside to cool.

STOVETOP: Spread a single layer of seeds or nuts in a dry skillet over medium heat. Toast for 5 to 10 minutes, shaking the pan and stirring until they are golden brown and fragrant. As soon as they are toasted, take them out of the pan so they do not continue to cook. Set aside to cool.

packaged. If buying large quantities of nuts or seeds in bulk, they should be refrigerated in airtight containers. Properly stored, they will keep for several months. Many types of nuts are available in smaller quantities in sealed packages that will last several weeks at room temperature.

## NUT AND SEED BUTTERS

It used to be that the only nut butter you could buy was highly processed peanut butter. Today, a wide variety of nut butters are available, including almond, cashew, hazelnut, macadamia, pistachio, tahini (sesame paste), and even soy (which is not really a nut, but the butter can be used like nut and seed butters). Rich in protein, fiber, and essential fatty acids, at least half the fat in nuts is monounsaturated, which can be good for blood cholesterol.

Nut butters work well in vegan cooking because they can be used to make sauces, enrich soups and stews, and replace animal fat in baking. They are easier to digest than whole nuts and can be made at home with a blender. They should be kept in covered jars in the refrigerator, where they will keep as long as a month or more. Try to buy only natural nut butters that do not contain stabilizers and other additives.

## OILS

The best oils for cooking are organic oils labeled either "cold-pressed," "unrefined," or "expeller-pressed."

Even though it's relatively expensive, extra-virgin olive oil is my preferred option because of its pleasant flavor and health benefits. It's especially good on salads and pasta dishes, and can be used in moderate-temperature cooking. I never use olive oil for higher-temperature cooking, such as in an Asian stir-fry, because it has a relatively low smoking point. Moreover, the olive flavor may compete with other ingredients. I reserve a pricier extra-virgin olive oil for salads or to drizzle on a cooked dish for added flavor, and use a less expensive brand of extra-virgin olive oil for cooking.

When I want a flavorless oil that is stable at higher temperatures, I use either canola or grapeseed oil—again, organic, unrefined, cold- or expeller-pressed are best. Both canola and grapeseed oil have a mild bland flavor. Grapeseed or another neutral oil can be used in salads where the distinctive flavor of olive oil won't do.

To impart an Asian flavor to salads and other recipes, use dark toasted sesame oil. This oil has a rich toasted sesame flavor and is used for flavoring a dish, not cooking, since it becomes unstable at high temperatures.

Flaxseed oil, a great source of omega-3 fatty acids, provides heart-healthy properties and various other nutritional benefits. Flaxseed oil has a mild nutty flavor. Don't use it for cooking since the heat will destroy the oil's nutritional benefits. Instead, add flaxseed oil to salads and smoothies, or drizzled on cooked foods, to benefit from its omega-3s.

## SALT

Salt can be the deciding factor between a flavorful or bland dish. I use sea salt for cooking and seasoning, because it is natural, balances flavors, and contributes to nutrition. Ordinary table salt tastes bitter, has no nutrition, and contains chemicals to prevent caking. Although sea salt costs more than regular table salt, the flavor and nutritional benefits make it worthwhile.

It's well known that the more processed the food, the higher the sodium content. Since too much salt isn't good for anyone, try to cook only with natural whole foods, use a low-sodium soy sauce, and when using canned beans, look for an organic variety since they contain less sodium. Add salt to a dish while it is cooking rather than afterwards, as the body absorbs uncooked salt from the food instead of simply passing it out.

## SOY SAUCE

In many dishes in which soy sauce is used, the sauce itself provides the salt content, so be careful not to add salt until you taste the dish. Some soy sauces are very high in sodium and additives, which can result in a bitter or harsh flavor. For best results and nutritional value, I recommend cooking with high-quality, reduced-sodium soy sauces, as well as the naturally fermented tamari and shoyu.

Thicker and more flavorful than other soy sauces, shoyu and tamari are generally fermented from one to three years, which contributes to their mellow flavor. Shoyu is a blend of soybeans, wheat, and sea salt. Tamari is made with soybeans and sea salt, and traditionally contains no wheat, although if you are wheat-sensitive, read the label to be sure. Tamari and shoyu are available at natural food stores, specialty stores, and well stocked supermarkets.

## VEGETABLE BROTH

A good vegetable broth is a cornerstone of many great vegan soups and sauces. Broth enriches the flavor of any of the recipes that call for either broth or water and boosts nutrition, too. It's not difficult to make a quick simple broth. Just fill a pot with water, add washed, rough-chopped vegetables, and let it simmer for an hour. Strain out the vegetables, and the result is a good, simple broth. Even an all-purpose broth made with some basics such as carrots, celery, onions, and water will add dimension to your cooking. For a richer broth, I rough-chop the vegetables, with their leaves, skins, peels, and stems, and sweat them in a little oil to bring out their flavors. Then I add the water.

If you don't have time to make homemade broth, but you want the added flavor and nutrition, you can buy vegetable broth in cans or aseptic containers. As a substitute, you can use powdered vegetable soup base or vegetable bouillon cubes. The salt content in these products varies, so find one you like and adjust seasonings accordingly. (These variables are why many recipes say "salt to taste.") Certain commercial broths are so rich and intense, I cut them with water by half and freeze what I don't use. If you don't have time to make broth or buy commercial products, you can simply add some soy sauce or miso paste (a concentrated and fermented soybean paste) to the water. (For more information and several broth recipes, see pages 140–143.)

## ABOUT SWEETENERS

Whether you use refined, white cane sugar or a natural sweetener in your cooking is a matter of personal preference, though many people avoid refined sugar because some of it is filtered using charred animal bones. Another reason is that it's devoid of nutritional value and difficult for the body to metabolize.

In cooking, I prefer to use an unrefined sugar, or naturally processed granulated cane sugar, which is sold under various brand names, including Sucanat or Florida Crystals. These can be substituted in equal measure for white table sugar, although they are a little darker in color than white granulated sugar and have a slight molasses flavor. If the filtering issue is important to you but you want to use a white granulated sugar, you can use beet sugar, which is more expensive than cane sugar, but does not use bone char for filtration. There are also some companies that make granulated cane sugar using other filtration methods.

Since honey is not vegan, you'll want a reliable substitute when a liquid sweetener is desired. Two good substitutes for honey are agave nectar and pure maple syrup, though maple will always add a bit of its distinct flavor to whatever you're cooking. Both have a similar sweetness level as honey.

## VEGAN BAKING

Just as most people associate vegetarians with "no meat," vegans extend the association to "and no eggs, dairy, or other animal products." And that's precisely what causes vegans to think twice before stopping at a bakery or accepting a cookie at a holiday gathering.

Everyone loves desserts, but having to ask or be asked the question: "Is it vegan?" can be a source of frustration to many. Learning to make your own baked goods is the best defense in the wide world of breads, cakes, and cookies, and other tasty treats where eggs and dairy have long held reign.

In traditional baking, most types of baked goods can easily be made vegan by replacing the dairy and eggs with plant-based ingredients. Some of the obvious substitutions are: soy milk or rice milk to replace dairy milk; nonhydrogenated vegan margarine or oil instead of butter; and agave nectar or pure maple syrup to replace honey. Various companies now make vegan semisweet chocolate.

There are also a number of ways to replace eggs in baking. Here is a list of some of the most common. Use any of these techniques to replace 1 egg in a baking recipe:

### hidden animal ingredients

As with anything we buy today, it's especially important to read the labels of any products that purport to be vegan. Watch out for:

- Gelatin and lard, for example, in the labels of marshmallows, cookies, candies, and pastries.
- Some seemingly nondairy cheese products are made with casein, which is obtained from cow's milk and is used to facilitate melting.
- Animal-based ingredients such as albumin, whey, and lactose, as well as isinglass, lanolin, and suet.

As a rule, the more processed a food item is, the more likely it is to contain some form of animal product whose true nature is disguised in the technical lingo.

Fortunately, for virtually every animal ingredient, there is a plant-based alternative. Look carefully, and you will find vegan versions of:

- Worcestershire sauce (the regular product contains anchovies)
- Gelatin-like desserts and puddings that use agar-agar or carrageen (sea vegetables) as gelling agents instead of gelatin, which is made from animal skin and bones.

The safest bet is to avoid processed foods as much as possible and go for fresh, whole foods, such as vegetables, grains, beans, and fruits.

- In a blender, grind 1 tablespoon flax seeds to a powder, add $2^1/_2$ tablespoons water, and blend until thick.
- Combine $1^1/_2$ teaspoons Ener-G Egg Replacer with 2 tablespoons water.
- Blend together 3 tablespoons applesauce, mashed banana, or soft tofu, and $^1/_2$ teaspoon baking powder. (Keep the desired flavor of your finished recipe in mind when deciding which is best.)

It is helpful to know that many "short cut" baking products are often vegan as well. Commercially produced phyllo dough is vegan as is the Pepperidge Farm brand frozen puff pastry. Many prepared pie crusts are vegan, but be sure to check the label as some brands contain lard. If you prefer to bake something "almost from scratch," there are also a number of vegan baking mixes available. Check online for sources.

## A WELL-STOCKED PANTRY

To make plant-based cooking convenient and fun, equip your kitchen with a vegan pantry. In the list below, you will find a variety of items that are especially important for plant-based cooking. It includes beans, grains, pastas, and tomato products, along with ingredients such as tahini, salsa, peanut butter, and chutney, all of which add to your creativity in the kitchen.

Certain perishable ingredients are vital to a vegan pantry. These include seeds, nuts, whole grain flours, and oils, which can turn rancid. So, after being opened, it's best to get these out of the pantry and into the refrigerator.

Other ingredients to keep on hand are dried herbs, spices, vinegars, sea salt, and other basic seasonings, as well as baking items such as baking powder, baking soda, extracts, and thickeners.

Fresh ingredients are also important to the list, so if you are not already in the habit, keep onions, celery, and carrots in the fridge drawer, along with fresh lettuce and other salad fixings, and a variety of vegetables and fruits. Have on hand lemons, limes, garlic, fresh ginger, olives, and fresh herbs whenever available. Also keep handy tofu, tempeh, seitan, veggie burgers, and other products you may use such as vegan sour cream, vegan cream cheese, and vegan mayonnaise. There is no need to stock every item all the time, but choose the items you will regularly use, and purchase others as you need them.

## ABOUT THE RECIPES

My goal in this book is to make the recipes as user friendly as possible. To accomplish this, I have simplified certain steps without diminishing the integrity of the dish, using ingredients that are easy to find, and listing ingredient substitutions for those that may be difficult to find or not in season. There is also a "Fast" icon noting each recipe that can be made within 30 minutes. Still, there are a few points to clarify in order for you to get the best results from these recipes.

### CAN SIZES

When ingredients such as beans or tomatoes list a can size, I've used the size that I find in my local supermarket. Since brands can vary from store to store, you should use whatever is close in size to that listed. For example, the canned beans I buy are almost all 15.5-ounce

## vegan pantry

Below is a list of many of the basic items common to a vegan pantry.

### DRIED ITEMS

- beans (black, white, pinto, kidney, chickpeas, lentils, split peas, etc.)
- chiles (mild and hot)
- fruits (raisins, cranberries, apricots, etc.)
- mushrooms (shiitake, porcini, etc.)
- sun-dried tomatoes

### WHOLE GRAINS

- rice, millet, barley, bulgur, couscous, old-fashioned oats, etc.
- cereals
- flours (unbleached all-purpose, whole wheat, spelt, wheat gluten flour, chickpea flour, etc.)
- cornmeal

### PASTAS AND NOODLES

- whole grain spaghetti, linguine, fettuccine, penne, ziti, etc.
- rice noodles
- soba (buckwheat) noodles

### NUTS AND SEEDS

- peanuts, pecans, walnuts, cashews, almonds, macadamias, pine nuts, etc.
- sesame seeds, pumpkin seeds, flaxseeds

### CANNED ITEMS

- beans: chickpeas, kidney beans, Great Northern beans, pintos, black beans, etc.
- tomatoes: whole, diced, crushed, puree, paste
- artichoke hearts
- roasted red peppers
- unsweetened coconut milk
- diced green chiles: hot or mild

### SWEETENERS

- unrefined sugar
- agave nectar
- pure maple syrup

### OILS

- extra-virgin olive
- unrefined canola
- grapeseed
- flaxseed
- dark (toasted) sesame

### BREAD PRODUCTS

- whole grain breads
- pita, bagels
- flour tortillas

### OTHER ITEMS

- nondairy milk (soy, rice, oat, almond)
- silken tofu (aseptic package)
- miso paste
- capers
- Asian chili paste
- soy sauce (tamari or shoyu are best)
- nutritional yeast
- mirin
- vegetable broth base
- vinegars (balsamic, cider, sherry, rice, etc.)
- unsweetened coconut milk
- ener-G egg replacer
- chutney
- mustard
- salsa
- peanut butter, tahini, almond butter
- vegan mayonnaise (such as Vegenaise)

## travel tips for vegans

Whenever I'm traveling, I always make the Internet my first stop, where I research restaurants located in my destination. Many restaurants post their menus online, so it's easy to determine the vegan-friendly options. If there are no vegan-specific restaurants in the area, I usually head for ethnic eateries, such as Thai, Vietnamese, Italian, or Indian. I also read online restaurant reviews. A little advance preparation can eliminate the stress of searching for a suitable restaurant and leave more time for relaxation.

If you're going to a restaurant or an event when there are no vegan choices listed, you can still request a vegan meal. Many chefs are happy to prepare vegan meals, especially if notified in advance. It's important to specify what you can't eat—sometimes asking if a dish is "vegan" isn't enough as the restaurant staff may not be clear on what it means. You'll want to ask specifically whether a menu item contains eggs, dairy, or meat broths, and so on.

While on the road, it's always a good idea to bring along some energy bars, nuts, or other non-perishable high-energy food to help you get by between exits on the interstate. When visiting non-vegan friends or family, you might want to offer to cook during your stay. You can plan to prepare some easy dishes that everyone can enjoy and either bring along a few ingredients you may need or plan to shop for groceries after you arrive.

cans, (about $1\frac{1}{2}$ cups when drained). If your cans are 16-ounces and yield closer to 2 cups, go ahead and use them—such a small difference in volume will be insignificant to the success of the recipes. Similarly, other ingredients, from pasta to tofu, are sold with varying weights depending on the brand. The same rule applies—other than in baking recipes, of course, where exact measurements are important.

## SALT TO TASTE

When a recipe says "salt to taste" rather than an actual measurement, it usually has to do with the relative saltiness of other ingredients in the recipe such as vegetable broth, which can range from unsalted to very salty. The key here is: "to taste"—tasting as you prepare a recipe is an important element of good cooking because it allows you to keep the seasonings in check.

## SUBSTITUTING INGREDIENTS
### Food Allergies and Sensitivities

What we choose to eat is a personal matter, but sometimes dinner can be dictated by food allergies and sensitivities and, of course, you should always follow the advice of your healthcare professional in these matters. If you must avoid gluten, soy, or fat in recipes, here are some general pointers to help navigate around them.

GLUTEN: Seitan is made from wheat gluten flour, so if you're allergic to wheat or gluten, you can instead substitute extra-firm tofu or tempeh in recipes. In baking, however, substituting gluten-free flours for wheat flour in recipes can be tricky, since it is the gluten that binds the dough in baking. There are gluten-free flour blends available, if you want to experiment, but the best strategy is to consult a gluten-free cookbook for guidelines and suggestions.

SOY: For allergies to soy, you can replace the soy milk in recipes with other nondairy milks, such as rice milk, almond milk, or oat milk. In recipes where tempeh or extra-firm tofu is used in a sauté or stir-fry, seitan can be substituted. Where tofu is blended with other ingredients, such as in puddings or sauces, it is often possible to substitute non-soy ingredients, such as pureed cooked rice or millet, but this would depend on the recipe and involve experimentation. If you are allergic to soy, it would be best to consult soy-free cookbooks for specific substitution guidelines.

FATS: If you avoid fats in your diet, you may choose to modify the amount of oil used in certain recipes simply by using less of it. For example, in salad dressings, a thickened fruit or vegetable juice may be used to replace all or part of the oil. For recipes that call for sautéing ingredients in oil, the oil can be eliminated by simply using a nonstick cooking spray or by sautéing the ingredients in a small amount of water, vegetable broth, or wine. There are numerous cookbooks and Web sites available that address this issue.

### As You Like It

A recipe is like a road map because it helps you find your way to a destination, in this case, great-tasting food. After you familiarize yourself with a recipe, you can truly make it your own by personalizing it. Whether you take the direct route (following the recipe exactly) or try some side roads (by substituting ingredients or changing the recipe in some way to suit your taste) matters little, as long as the results are pleasing to you and your family.

In many of my recipes, you can substitute ingredients without affecting the integrity of the dish. For example, if a recipe calls for cilantro and you don't like cilantro, leave it out or use parsley instead. If you're not a fan of chickpeas, use a bean that you do enjoy, and so on. You'll enjoy cooking more if you can learn to be flexible, creative, and relaxed. The exception to this, of course, is in baking, which requires precise measurements to succeed. However, even in baking, you can modify certain ingredients, such as swapping out walnuts for pecans in a brownie recipe, or leaving them out entirely. I offer simple variations in many of the recipes to help guide you to do just that, so be sure to read the headnotes and sidebars as you use this book.

### YIELDS

In most cases, you'll find that the recipes yields are "makes 4 servings" or "makes 4 to

6 servings." I've come to consider the serving yield to be a general guideline since there are so many variables that may come into play. The main variables are the relative appetites of the people eating (or the appetites of your relatives), as well as whatever else is being served (or not served) with the dish. Similarly, as regards soups and salads, the serving yield will vary, depending on the size of your bowls and whether you are serving the soup or salad as a first course of a larger meal or as the main dish.

## INGREDIENT SPECIFICS

As a space-saving measure, some of the more frequently used ingredients in the recipes are listed in as brief a way as possible—for example, "sugar" and "soy sauce." However, there are particular adjectives that, although not stated in each recipe, should be understood when that particular ingredient is called for.

- WHEN YOU SEE: "CANOLA OIL" IT MEANS: "organic, unrefined, cold-pressed/expeller-pressed canola oil." You can, instead, use grapeseed oil or other light flavorless oil. "Olive oil" means extra-virgin olive oil.

- WHEN YOU SEE: "SOY SAUCE" IT MEANS: "high-quality, low-sodium soy sauce, or naturally-brewed tamari or shoyu."

- WHEN YOU SEE: "SALT" IT MEANS: "sea salt."

- WHEN YOU SEE "SUGAR" IT CAN MEAN: "unrefined, naturally processed sugar or other natural sweetener." It can also mean "regular granulated sugar" if that's what you want to use. When superfine sugar is called for, if you're using a natural unrefined sugar, then you can make it finer by whizzing it in a blender or spice mill.

- WHEN YOU SEE "ALL-PURPOSE FLOUR" IT MEANS: "unbleached all-purpose flour" but it can also mean spelt flour or another type of whole grain flour that you may prefer to use.

- WHEN YOU SEE "SOY MILK" IT CAN ALSO MEAN rice milk, oat milk, or another variety of nondairy milk. Feel free to use whichever you prefer.

- WHEN YOU SEE "VEGAN MARGARINE" IT MEANS a non-hydrogenated product such as the Earth Balance brand.

## WASHING YOUR PRODUCE

In every case, the recipes in this book assume that you have thoroughly washed, scrubbed, or trimmed all the produce before using in the recipes. Fruits and vegetables should be well scrubbed in general before using them in order to rinse off pesticides and bacteria. Leafy greens need to be thoroughly washed to remove sand and grit. Potatoes and root vegetables should be well scrubbed, as well, and any wilted or damaged areas should be removed before using them.

## KITCHEN EQUIPMENT

With so many choices available, kitchen equipment can be costly and confusing. As much as I like the newest, latest gadgets, I also know that you can cook up a storm with a minimum of basic reliable equipment.

Where cookware is concerned, quality is definitely better than quantity. If you're short on space or cash, it's better to have a few good multipurpose saucepans and pots, a good skillet, and a few good knives than a kitchen full of trendy gadgets. A good 12-inch skillet, for example, can be used to sauté, braise, and stir-fry. A large pot can be used for soups and stews or as a pasta pot. One or two saucepans can take care of the rest.

If you can't afford a full set of knives, opt for a good chef's knife, a paring knife, and a serrated bread knife. Add to that list a colander, mixing bowls, baking pans, a good cutting board, and a food processor or blender, and you can cook your way through just about any culinary scenario.

If baking is of special interest, you will also need to add to the list bread pans, cake pans, cookie sheets, pie plate, springform pan, muffin tin, and so forth. Add a set of measuring spoons and cups, metal and rubber spatulas, and you're on your way.

## HOW TO MAKE SIMPLY GREAT FOOD

For some cooks, approaching a new recipe is intimidating, but it shouldn't be. Here are some tricks to simplify the process. The first step is getting the recipe in your head before you begin.

Before starting any recipe, read the recipe through like it's a newspaper article, and then read it again, making notes on any ingredients you do not have on hand. This becomes your shopping list.

### MIS-EN-PLACE

Once you have all the ingredients you need, gather them together along with any equipment you may need. This process, *mis-en-place*, includes preheating your oven as well as chopping and premeasuring ingredients in the quantities required. Then, you are ready

to cook. This way, you won't be scrambling for a spatula or chopping an onion while your oil is burning. It can also help you avoid discovering missing ingredients, and will allow you to get done faster, and enjoy the cooking process.

### PRESENTATION

For the time it takes, the food you prepare needs to smell good and look good on the plate, in addition to being delicious. It's true that we eat with our eyes and noses as well as with our mouths. So, when you cook, pay special attention to combining textures, colors, and flavors to turn any meal into a memorable dining experience. This also includes paying attention to garnishes and tableware.

People who are new to plant-based cooking often discover, once they take the first step, that the world is suddenly bigger, not smaller. They find a whole new range of exciting ingredients, such as tofu, tempeh, and seitan, and a previously overlooked vast new world of beans and grains. They are also pleased to discover the naturally vegan dishes of other cultures, such as India, the Middle East, Mexico, Indonesia, the Mediterranean, and Asia, where plant-based ingredients have been used for centuries for good taste and good health.

In this book, I've attempted to provide recipes that are as delicious and satisfying as anything in the non-vegan world, prepared in a way so that anyone can enjoy them. Vegan cooks tend to relish the opportunity to demonstrate just how good their food can be, and with these one thousand carefully chosen recipes, I believe I have provided the ultimate master guide to help you do it.

# APPETIZERS AND SNACKS

## SNACKS

ragin' cajun popcorn

asian fusion party mix

sesame pita chips

tortilla chips

black sesame wonton chips

roasted chickpeas

fiery pumpkin seeds

personalized trail mix

agave-glazed pecans

five-spiced walnuts

curried cashews

edamame with coarse salt

jerk-spiced soy jerky

flower power granola squares

## DIPS AND SPREADS

green-green guacamole

black and green olive tapenade

back-to-basics hummus

roasted red pepper hummus

white bean and dill hummus

smoky chipotle-pinto hummus

baba ghanoush

three-bean dip

black bean and sun-dried tomato dip

mylie's secret queso dip

layered bean dip

cucumber and green olive dip

lemony edamame dip

sushi-inspired edamame-avocado dip

creamy spinach-tahini dip

sassy spinach dip with roasted garlic

salsa and pinto bean spread

four-seed bread spread

golden sunshine roasted veg spread

eggplant walnut spread

za'atar-spiced roasted red pepper spread

white bean and artichoke spread

tempeh-pimiento cheeze ball

smooth and savory mushroom pâté

## Cold Appetizers

marinated olives

sesame-shiitake wonton crisps

cheezy cashew–roasted
red pepper toasts

jicama-guacamole bites

lemon and garlic marinated
mushrooms

cherry tomatoes stuffed
with whirled peas

snow peas stuffed with
sun-dried tomato hummus

artichoke-and-walnut-stuffed
belgian endive

lentil-pecan country-style pâté

mushroom-walnut pâté

mango-avocado spring rolls

lemongrass tofu and snow pea
spring rolls

sesame seitan and spinach
spring rolls

vietnamese-style lettuce rolls

lemony rice-stuffed
grape leaves

couscous dolmas

rainbow sushi

avocado and asparagus
sushi rolls

## Hot Appetizers

asparagus wrapped in phyllo

pinto-pecan fireballs

mushrooms stuffed with
spinach and walnuts

spicy chipotle potato
quesadillas

baby potatoes stuffed
with roasted bell pepper
and walnuts

mushroom croustades

cherry peppers stuffed
with sun-dried tomatoes
and pine nuts

cajun tofu crunchies

basic bruschetta

classic crostini

french onion pastry puffs

shiitakes in puff pastry

tempeh taco bites

savory artichoke squares

chickpea pancake
with rosemary

sesame-cilantro scallion
pancakes

ginger-lime–glazed
bean curd skewers

tempeh satay

in-lieu-of-crab wontons

steamed vegetable dumplings

artichoke-mushroom
phyllo packets

vegetable pakoras

potato samosas

chickpea kofta with chutney
dipping sauce

ppetizers encompass a wide range of flavors, ingredients, and preparations. They include a number of global traditions, such as antipasti, tapas, meze, and hors d'oeuvres, but good old American dips, chips, and other munchies fit in, too.

From the French, "hors d'oeuvres" translates to "outside the main work" and are often dramatic, richly seasoned bites of savory, oven-baked nibbles or dips and spreads ideally suited to cocktail parties or a buffet table. When served as the first course of a meal, appetizers are often enjoyed while seated at the dinner table with a knife and fork, but more casual pickup food is often eaten out of hand. People may also be willing to try new things when offered in "small bites," so it is inspiring both for the cook and those being fed.

The chapter begins with a tasty collection of snacks and munchies, from party mix, to popcorn, to chips, followed by a savory selection of dips and spreads, including favorites like hummus and tapenade. The next section is filled with a tempting selection of cold appetizers—recipes like spring rolls and dolmas that can be made ahead of time and then refrigerated until needed. Hot appetizers can be found in the final section of this chapter. These include tasty bites such as dumplings and samosas, as well as crostini and vegetables in puff pastry. Since these recipes are served warm or hot, they need last-minute attention.

# SNACKS

## ragin' cajun popcorn

makes 8 to 10 cups

*Adding spices to popcorn transforms it from an ordinary snack food to party fare. The Cajun seasoning in this recipe is guaranteed to wake up your taste buds, but why stop here? Experiment with other flavors, such as curry spices or jerk spice seasonings.*

1 tablespoon dried oregano
1 tablespoon smoked paprika
1 teaspoon ground cumin
½ teaspoon garlic powder
½ teaspoon onion powder
½ teaspoon celery salt
¼ teaspoon ground cayenne
¼ cup olive oil
⅓ cup popcorn kernels

1. In a small bowl, combine the oregano, paprika, cumin, garlic powder, onion powder, celery salt, and cayenne. Mix well and set aside.

2. In a large saucepan, combine the oil and popcorn. Cover tightly and place over high heat, shaking the pan occasionally. Once popping begins, continue shaking the pan until the popping almost stops. Transfer the hot popcorn to a large bowl. Sprinkle with the spice mixture and mix well. Serve immediately.

## asian fusion party mix

makes about 11 cups

*Wasabi peas, soy sauce, and the use of rice cereal give this party mix an Asian nuance. For more Asian flavor, use scissors to cut a sheet of nori into 1-inch strips and then cut those strips into thin matchstick-size strips. Just before serving, toss the prepared nori into the party mix.*

6 cups popped popcorn
2 cups bite-size crisp rice breakfast cereal squares
1 cup unsalted roasted cashews or peanuts
1 cup small pretzels
1 cup wasabi peas
¼ cup vegan margarine
1 tablespoon soy sauce
½ teaspoon garlic salt
½ teaspoon seasoned salt

1. Preheat the oven to 250°F. In a 9 × 13-inch baking pan, combine the popcorn, cereal, cashews, pretzels, and peas.

2. In a small saucepan, combine the margarine, soy sauce, garlic salt, and seasoned salt. Cook, stirring, over medium heat until margarine is melted, about 2 minutes. Pour over the popcorn mixture, stirring to mix well. Bake for 45 minutes, stirring occasionally. Cool completely before serving.

## sesame pita chips

makes 64 chips

*Sure, you can buy pita chips in the store, but making your own is easy and economical. This recipe is easily halved or doubled, according to your needs.*

4 (7-inch) pita breads
Toasted sesame oil
⅓ cup sesame seeds
Salt

1. Preheat the oven to 350°F. Carefully slice each pita bread into two circles with a serrated knife. Lightly brush oil onto the inner side of each circle.

2. Cut the pita circles into eighths and arrange the pieces on a baking sheet in a single layer, oil side up. Sprinkle with sesame seeds and salt to taste. Bake until golden brown, about 10 minutes. Serve warm or at room temperature. These are best eaten on the day they are made but, once cooled, they can be covered and stored at room temperature for 1 to 2 days.

## tortilla chips  🅕

makes 32 chips

*Homemade tortillas taste great fresh from the oven—an advantage you don't get with commercial chips. You can also season these chips to suit your own taste—adding more or less salt and even spicing things up by sprinkling on some chili powder and cayenne.*

4 (6-inch) flour tortillas
Olive oil or nonstick cooking spray
Salt

1. Preheat the oven to 350°F. Lightly brush both sides of the tortillas with oil. Cut each tortilla into eighths and place the triangles on a baking sheet.

2. Sprinkle with salt to taste, and bake until crisp and lightly browned, 8 to 10 minutes. Cool completely before serving. These are best eaten on the day they are made but, once cooled, they can be covered and stored at room temperature for 1 to 2 days.

## black sesame wonton chips  🅕

makes 24 chips

*Black sesame seeds give these chips an exotic, sophisticated look, but if they are unavailable, regular white sesame seeds can be used instead.*

12 Vegan Wonton Wrappers, (page 41)
Toasted sesame oil
⅓ cup black sesame seeds
Salt

1. Preheat the oven to 450°F. Lightly oil a baking sheet and set aside. Cut the wonton wrappers in half crosswise, brush them with sesame oil, and arrange them in a single layer on the prepared baking sheet.

2. Sprinkle wonton wrappers with the sesame seeds and salt to taste, and bake until crisp and golden brown, 5 to 7 minutes. Cool completely before serving. These are best eaten on the day they are made but, once cooled, they can be covered and stored at room temperature for 1 to 2 days.

## roasted chickpeas  *3*

makes about 1½ cups

*This crunchy high-protein snack is a nice change from nuts and chips. I sometimes toss a few in my salad, too. For a spicy version, sprinkle crushed red pepper or ground cayenne on the chickpeas.*

1½ cups cooked or 1 (15.5-ounce) can chickpeas, drained and rinsed
2 tablespoons olive oil
Salt

1. Preheat the oven to 375°F. In a small bowl, combine the chickpeas and oil. Toss to coat. Spread the chickpeas in a 9 × 13-inch baking pan and sprinkle with salt to taste. Roast until the chickpeas are crisp and browned, about 30 minutes.

2. Cool completely before serving. These are best eaten on the day they are made but, once cooled, they can be covered and stored at room temperature for 2 to 3 days.

# fiery pumpkin seeds  2½

makes about 2 cups

*Shelled pumpkin seeds, sometimes called pepitas, are available in Latin American groceries and natural food stores.*

1 teaspoon sweet paprika
½ teaspoon ground cumin
¼ cup olive oil
1 teaspoon Tabasco sauce
2 cups shelled pumpkin seeds (pepitas)
Salt

1. Preheat the oven to 400°F. In a small bowl, combine the paprika and cumin. Whisk in the oil and Tabasco. Add the pumpkin seeds and toss to coat.

2. Spread the seeds on a baking sheet and bake until fragrant, about 5 minutes. Remove from oven, sprinkle with salt to taste, and cool completely before serving. These are best eaten on the day they are made but, once cooled, they can be covered and stored at room temperature for 2 to 3 days.

*Pie Pumkin seeds are too small.*

# personalized trail mix

makes about 3 cups

*The best part about making your own trail mix is that you get to decide what goes in it. Don't like coconut? Leave it out. Want more cashews? Put them in. Brimming with nuts and fruit, it's also a nutritious snack to keep on hand for children.*

½ cup unsweetened flaked coconut
½ cup unsalted roasted cashews
½ cup slivered blanched almonds
½ cup vegan semisweet chocolate chips
½ cup sweetened dried cranberries
⅓ cup chopped dried pineapple
¼ cup unsalted roasted sunflower seeds

1. In a small skillet, toast the coconut over medium heat, stirring, until lightly browned, 2 to 3 minutes. Set aside to cool.

2. In a large bowl, combine the cashews, almonds, chocolate chips, cranberries, pineapple, and sunflower seeds. Stir in the toasted coconut. Cool completely before serving. This is best when served on the same day that it is made.

# agave-glazed pecans

makes about 2 cups

*A delicious party munchie, these crunchy pecans also make a nice hostess gift—place them in a clear bag or jar and tie with a ribbon. Look for agave nectar in natural food stores. If unavailable, brown rice syrup or pure maple syrup may be used instead.*

⅓ cup agave nectar
1½ tablespoons vegan margarine
½ teaspoon ground cinnamon
⅛ teaspoon salt
1 teaspoon pure vanilla extract
2 cups pecan halves

1. In a medium skillet, combine the agave nectar, margarine, cinnamon, and salt. Cook over medium heat, stirring until the mixture turns an amber color and thickens. Add the vanilla and the pecans, stirring gently until the nuts are coated with the glaze.

2. Quickly transfer the nuts to a nonstick baking sheet and spread in a single layer to cool completely before serving. These are best eaten on the day they are made but, once cooled, they can be covered and stored at room temperature for 2 to 3 days.

# five-spiced walnuts

makes about 2 cups

*In addition to being a great snack bursting with flavor, these zesty walnuts make a rich addition to Asian salads or stir-fries. If five-spice powder is unavailable, use a combination of ¼ teaspoon ground fennel seed, ¼ teaspoon ground cinnamon, ¼ teaspoon ground star anise, ¼ teaspoon ground Szechuan peppercorns, and ¼ teaspoon ground cloves instead.*

2 tablespoons vegan margarine
1 tablespoon canola or grapeseed oil
1 tablespoon soy sauce
1¼ teaspoons five-spice powder (see headnote)
2 cups walnut halves
Salt (optional)

1. Preheat the oven to 325°F. In a medium saucepan, combine the margarine and oil and cook over low heat, stirring until the margarine is melted. Stir in the soy sauce and the five-spice powder and cook for 1 to 2 minutes to blend the flavors. Add the walnuts and toss to coat well.

2. Spread the walnuts on a baking sheet in a single layer and bake for 15 minutes, stirring occasionally. Sprinkle lightly with salt, if using, and cool to room temperature before serving. These are best eaten on the day they are made but, once cooled, they can be covered and stored at room temperature for 2 to 3 days.

# curried cashews

makes about 2 cups

*The natural sweetness of cashews is a delightful complement to the spicy curry seasoning. Eat as a snack or sprinkle on top of your favorite curried dish.*

2 tablespoons vegan margarine
2 tablespoons canola or grapeseed oil
2 tablespoons hot or mild curry powder
½ teaspoon salt
2 cups unsalted roasted cashews

1. In a large skillet over medium heat, combine the margarine and oil, stirring until the margarine is melted. Add the curry powder and salt and stir to blend. Add the cashews and cook, stirring until the nuts are coated with the seasoning and lightly browned, about 10 minutes

2. Transfer to a baking sheet and spread in a single layer to cool to room temperature before serving. These are best eaten on the day they are made but, once cooled, they can be covered and stored at room temperature for 2 to 3 days.

# edamame with coarse salt

makes 6 servings

*Edamame are green soybeans in the pod, sold both fresh and frozen. They make a nourishing snack and are a great way to begin a Japanese meal. They're fun to eat, too, with the beans slipping out of the pods directly into your mouth. Be sure to have a bowl handy for the discarded pods.*

1 (16-ounce) bag unshelled frozen edamame
Coarse salt

1. In a large saucepan of boiling salted water, cook the edamame until tender, 10 minutes. Drain well and pat dry.

2. Transfer to a bowl and season with coarse salt to taste. Serve hot or warm.

# jerk-spiced soy jerky

makes 8 servings

*This tasty and economical jerky can also be made in a dehydrator, if you have one.*

2 teaspoons allspice

2 teaspoons dried thyme

1 teaspoon garlic powder

1 teaspoon sugar

½ teaspoon freshly ground black pepper

3 tablespoons soy sauce

2 tablespoons ketchup

1 tablespoon pure maple syrup

1 tablespoon olive oil

½ teaspoon liquid smoke

1 (16-ounce) package extra-firm tofu, drained, cut into ¼-inch slices, and pressed (page xiv)

1. In a shallow bowl, combine the allspice, thyme, garlic powder, sugar, and pepper. Stir in the soy sauce, ketchup, maple syrup, oil, and liquid smoke, stirring until well blended.

2. Dip the tofu slices into the sauce to coat on both sides and place on a nonstick baking sheet. Refrigerate for 1 hour to allow the sauce to soak into the tofu.

3. Place the oven rack in the lowest position of the oven. Preheat the oven to 200°F. Transfer the baking sheet to the oven and bake for about 8 hours, turning the tofu slices every few hours. The jerky is done when it is very firm and a deep reddish brown color. Cool to room temperature. If not using right away, cover and refrigerate until needed. Properly stored, it will keep for up to 5 days.

# flower power granola squares

makes 16 squares

*Powered by sunflower seeds, as well as cranberries, chocolate chips, and coconut, these granola squares make a yummy snack for flower children of all ages.*

1 cup shelled sunflower seeds, lightly crushed

2 cups quick-cooking oats

1 cup vegan semisweet chocolate chips

¾ cup sweetened dried cranberries

½ cup unsweetened flaked coconut

1 cup soy milk

2 tablespoons vegan margarine, melted

2 tablespoons agave nectar or maple syrup

1. Preheat the oven to 350°F. Lightly oil an 8-inch square baking pan and set aside.

2. In a large bowl, combine the sunflower seeds, oats, chocolate chips, cranberries, and coconut. Mix well.

3. In a small bowl, combine the soy milk, melted margarine, and agave nectar and pour over the dry mixture. Mix until thoroughly blended.

4. Transfer the mixture to the prepared pan and press it evenly into the pan. Bake until lightly browned around the edges, about 25 minutes. Cool for 5 minutes on a wire rack before cutting into 2-inch squares. Cool completely before serving. These are best eaten on the day they are made but, once cooled, they can be covered and stored at room temperature for 2 to 3 days.

# DIPS AND SPREADS

## green-green guacamole 🅕

makes about 2½ cups

*Since avocados are high in fat, some people limit their intake, which can be difficult for card-carrying guacamole lovers. This lighter, lower fat version comes to the rescue with zucchini and protein-rich edamame replacing some of the avocado.*

1 tablespoon olive oil
1 small zucchini, peeled and cut into ¼-inch slices
2 garlic cloves, minced
Salt
¾ cup shelled fresh or frozen edamame
1 ripe Hass avocado
1 tablespoon fresh lemon juice

1. In a large skillet, heat the oil over medium heat. Add the zucchini and garlic, and season with salt to taste. Cover and cook until soft and liquid is evaporated, about 10 minutes. Set aside to cool for 15 minutes.

2. In a medium saucepan of boiling salted water, cook the edamame until soft, 10 minutes. Drain well and set aside to cool. Transfer the cooled zucchini mixture to a food processor. Add the edamame and puree.

3. Pit and peel the avocado and transfer to the food processor along with the lemon juice and salt to taste. Pulse to combine, if you like a little texture in your guacamole, otherwise process until smooth and well blended. Taste, adjusting seasonings if necessary. Cover and refrigerate until ready to serve. This dip is best if used on the same day that it is made.

**basic guacamole:** For an all-avocado guacamole, simply mash 2 or 3 ripe avocados in a bowl with lemon or lime juice and salt to taste, adding minced garlic, tomato, cilantro, or other seasonings according to your own preferences.

## black and green olive tapenade 🅕

makes about 1½ cups

*Tapenade is a classic olive and caper spread from Provence. It can be made entirely with black or green olives instead of both, if you prefer. Just don't omit the capers since that's what makes it tapenade (*tapeno *means "caper" in Provençal). Be sure to use good quality olives such as the black niçoise or kalamata and the green gorda or picholine. Tapenade is delicious spread on crackers or toasted bread.*

¼ cup capers
1 cup pitted black olives
½ cup pitted green olives
1 teaspoon fresh lemon juice
Pinch dried thyme
Freshly ground black pepper
¼ cup olive oil

In a food processor, combine the capers with the black and green olives and process until finely chopped. Add the lemon juice, thyme, and pepper to taste. With the machine running, stream in the oil and blend to a smooth paste. Transfer the tapenade to a small bowl and serve. If not using right away, cover and refrigerate until needed. Properly stored, it will keep for up to 5 days.

# back-to-basics hummus 5 🅕

makes about 2 cups

*This tried-and-true hummus recipe can be the foundation for myriad variations, such as the addition of chipotle chiles, tapenade, roasted garlic, or marinated artichokes. On the other hand, it's pretty darn good just the way it is, too. Tahini is made from ground sesame seeds and is widely available in natural food stores, specialty grocers, and well-stocked supermarkets.*

3 to 4 garlic cloves
1½ cups cooked or 1 (15.5-ounce) can chickpeas, drained and rinsed
¼ cup tahini (sesame paste)
Juice of 1 lemon
½ teaspoon salt
⅛ teaspoon ground cayenne
2 tablespoons olive oil
Sweet or smoked paprika, for garnish

1. In a food processor, process the garlic until finely minced. Add the chickpeas and tahini and process until smooth. Add the lemon juice, salt to taste, and cayenne and process until well combined.

2. With the machine running, stream in the oil and process until smooth. Taste, adjusting seasonings if necessary. Transfer to a medium bowl and sprinkle with paprika to serve. If not using right away, cover and refrigerate until needed. Properly stored it will keep in the refrigerator for up to 4 days.

# roasted red pepper hummus 🅕

makes about 1½ cups

*Roasted red pepper gives a vibrant color and flavor to hummus, making it an ideal inclusion on a holiday party buffet, especially when served with green dippers such as celery sticks and blanched green beans and broccoli florets.*

2 garlic cloves, crushed
1½ cups cooked or 1 (15.5-ounce) can chickpeas, drained and rinsed
2 roasted red peppers*
1 tablespoon fresh lime juice
Salt
Ground cayenne

1. In a food processor, process the garlic until finely minced. Add the chickpeas and red pepper and process until smooth. Add the lime juice and salt and cayenne to taste. Process until well blended. Taste, adjusting seasonings if necessary.

2. Transfer to a medium bowl and serve. If not using right away, cover and refrigerate until needed. Properly stored, it will keep for up to 3 days.

*Roasting Bell Peppers: Roast the peppers over an open flame or under the broiler, about 4 inches from the heat, turning until the skins are completely blackened. Put the charred peppers into a paper bag and set aside for 5 minutes to allow the steam to loosen the skins. Scrape off the blackened skin and remove the seeds and stems. The peppers are now ready to use in recipes.*

## white bean and dill hummus 🅕

makes about 2 cups

*Dillweed adds a nice flavor nuance to this hummus, giving it a refreshing taste that sets it apart from the traditional hummus flavor. Serve with rice crackers or crisp cucumber slices for dipping. Try different herbs, too, such as rosemary.*

2 garlic cloves, crushed

1½ cups cooked or 1 (15.5-ounce) can white beans, such as Great Northern, drained and rinsed

¼ cup tahini (sesame paste)

2 tablespoons fresh lemon juice

¼ cup fresh dillweed or 2 tablespoons dried

½ teaspoon salt

⅛ teaspoon ground cayenne

2 tablespoons olive oil

1. In a food processor, process the garlic until finely minced. Add the chickpeas and tahini and process until smooth. Add the lemon juice, dillweed, salt, and cayenne and process until well blended.

2. With the machine running, stream in the oil and process until smooth. Taste, adjusting seasonings if necessary. Transfer to a medium bowl and cover and refrigerate 2 hours before serving. The flavors improve and intensify if made ahead. Properly stored, it will keep for up to 3 days.

## smoky chipotle-pinto hummus 🅕

makes about 1½ cups

*Pinto bean's and spicy chipotle chiles combine to create a hummus-inspired dip that goes great with tortilla chips.*

1 garlic clove, crushed

1½ cups cooked or 1 (15.5-ounce) can pinto beans, drained and rinsed

1½ teaspoons canned chipotle chile in adobo

2 teaspoons fresh lime juice

Salt and freshly ground black pepper

1 tablespoon finely minced green onions, for garnish

1. In a food processor, process the garlic until finely minced. Add the beans and chipotle and process until smooth. Add the lime juice and salt and pepper to taste. Process until well blended.

2. Transfer to a medium bowl and sprinkle with the green onions. Serve right away or cover and refrigerate for 1 to 2 hours to allow the flavors to intensify. Properly stored, it will keep for up to 3 days.

# baba ghanoush

makes about 2 cups

*This classic Middle Eastern eggplant spread is wonderful as a dip for pita chips or as a spread on pita bread or wrap sandwiches. The tahini is added in increments—how much you use will depend on the size of your eggplant as well as personal taste.*

1 large eggplant, halved lengthwise

3 garlic cloves, slivered

¼ cup tahini (sesame paste), plus more if needed

2 tablespoons fresh lemon juice

½ teaspoon salt

⅛ teaspoon ground cayenne

¼ teaspoon dried oregano (optional)

1 tablespoon chopped fresh parsley, for garnish

1 tablespoon pomegranate seeds, for garnish (optional)

1. Preheat the oven to 425°F. Lightly oil a 9 × 13-inch baking pan and set aside. Make small slits in the cut sides of the eggplant and press the garlic into the slits. Transfer the eggplant halves, cut-side down, to the prepared baking pan and bake until soft, about 30 minutes. Set aside to cool.

2. Scoop the cooked eggplant flesh into a food processor. Add about ¼ cup of the tahini, the lemon juice, salt, cayenne, and oregano, if using, and process until smooth. Taste, adjusting seasonings if necessary, adding more tahini, if needed.

3. Transfer to a medium bowl and sprinkle with the parsley and pomegranate seeds, if using. Serve at room temperature. If not using right away, cover and refrigerate until needed. Properly stored, it will keep for up to 3 days.

# three-bean dip

makes about 3 cups

*This dip lends itself to lots of variation. Change the number and quantity of beans according to personal preference. If you substitute kidney beans or pintos for the edamame, for example, it will give it a pinkish hue. Adding more garlic and some hot chiles will spice it up. A sprinkle of cilantro or basil instead of parsley changes the character in yet another way. Beans freeze well, so if you have leftover beans from an opened can, you can store them in a sealed container in the freezer for later use.*

1 garlic clove, crushed

1 tablespoon chopped green onions

1 cup cooked or canned Great Northern or other white beans, drained and rinsed

1 cup cooked or canned chickpeas, drained and rinsed

1 cup cooked shelled edamame

1 tablespoon fresh lemon juice

Salt and freshly ground black pepper

1 tablespoon minced fresh parsley, for garnish

1. In a food processor, process the garlic and green onions until minced. Add beans, chickpeas, edamame, lemon juice, and salt and black pepper to taste, and process until smooth. Taste, adjusting seasonings if necessary.

2. Transfer to a medium bowl and sprinkle with the parsley. Serve right away or cover and refrigerate for 1 hour to allow the flavors to intensify. If not using right away, cover and refrigerate. Properly stored, it will keep for up to 3 days.

# black bean and sun-dried tomato dip 🅕

makes about 1½ cups

*Sun-dried tomatoes and balsamic vinegar add a complexity to the flavor of this robust dip. Serve with whole grain crackers or toasted coarse bread.*

¼ cup oil-packed sun-dried tomatoes
1½ cups cooked or 1 (15.5-ounce) can black
    beans, drained and rinsed
1 tablespoon balsamic vinegar
2 tablespoons chopped fresh parsley
¼ teaspoon dried marjoram or basil
Salt and freshly ground black pepper

1. In a food processor, process the tomatoes until finely chopped. Add the beans and pulse until combined. Add the vinegar, parsley, marjoram, and salt and pepper to taste. Process until just blended, leaving some texture.

2. Transfer to a medium bowl and serve. If not using right away, cover and refrigerate. Properly stored, it will keep for up to 3 days.

# mylie's secret queso dip 🅕

makes about 2½ cups

*This cheesy dip is too good to keep a secret any longer. Adapted from a recipe shared with me by my friend and vegan queso dip lover Mylie Thompson, it's great for nachos as well as on baked potatoes, cooked veggies,* or even soft pretzels. Try spooning a little over some veggie chili.

1 tablespoon olive oil
½ cup minced onion
¼ cup oat flour or finely ground old-fashioned
    oats
2 tablespoons tahini (sesame paste)
½ cup nutritional yeast
⅓ cup unsweetened soy milk, plus more if needed
1 teaspoon pure maple syrup
1 (14.5-ounce) can diced tomatoes, drained and
    finely chopped
1 (4-ounce) can diced hot or mild green chiles,
    drained
1½ teaspoons chili powder
1½ teaspoons sweet or smoked paprika
½ teaspoon ground cumin
¼ teaspoon ground cayenne
½ teaspoon salt
1½ tablespoons fresh lemon juice

1. In a large saucepan, heat the oil over medium heat. Add the onion, cover, and cook until softened, about 5 minutes. Stir in the flour, tahini, nutritional yeast, soy milk, and maple syrup. Stir in the tomatoes and mix well.

2. Lower heat, and cook, stirring constantly. When the mixture starts to bubble, add the chiles, chili powder, paprika, cumin, cayenne, and salt. Continue to cook, stirring for about 10 minutes. Stir in the lemon juice. If the mixture is too thick, add a bit more soy milk. Taste, adjusting seasonings if necessary. Transfer to a medium bowl and serve warm. If not using right away, cover and refrigerate. Properly stored, it will keep for up to 4 days.

# layered bean dip

makes about 6 cups

*This recipe makes a lot, so keep it in mind when you need something easy and delicious to serve a crowd. Serve with tortilla chips.*

1 (15.5-ounce) can pinto beans, drained and rinsed

1½ cups tomato salsa, homemade (page 567) or store-bought

½ cup vegan sour cream, homemade (page 574) or store-bought

1 cup guacamole, homemade (page 9) or store-bought

4 green onions, chopped

1 ripe tomato, chopped

½ cup sliced pitted black olives

1 (4-ounce) can diced hot or mild green chiles

¼ cup chopped fresh cilantro

1. In a medium bowl, mash the beans well. Add ½ cup of the salsa and mix well to combine.

2. Spread the bean mixture in a glass bowl or on a platter. Spread the sour cream on top, followed by the guacamole. Spread a layer of the remaining salsa on top of the guacamole and sprinkle with the green onions, tomato, olives, chiles, and cilantro.

3. Cover and refrigerate for at least 1 hour before serving. This dip is best if eaten on the same day that it is made.

# cucumber and green olive dip

makes about 1½ cups

*This light, refreshing, pale green dip can be served with crackers, chips, or cut-up vegetables. If you prefer a dip with texture, stir in some extra chopped green olives and minced green onion to the finished dip.*

½ medium English cucumber, peeled, halved, seeded, and chopped

¾ cup pitted green olives

1 garlic clove, crushed

4 ounces firm tofu, well drained and crumbled

¼ cup chopped fresh parsley

2 tablespoons fresh lemon juice

½ teaspoon salt

⅛ teaspoon ground cayenne

1. In a food processor, combine the cucumber, olives, and garlic. Process until finely chopped. Add the tofu, parsley, lemon juice, salt, and cayenne and process until smooth.

2. Transfer to a medium bowl. Cover and chill for 1 hour before serving. This dip is best if used on the same day that it is made.

# lemony edamame dip

makes about 2½ cups

*Edamame, or fresh soybeans, are now widely available in and out of the pod and sold fresh and frozen. The vibrant color is surpassed only by the fresh taste derived by combining edamame with frozen green peas and a touch of lemon. This dip lends itself to lots of variation—you can add chiles or different herbs to change the flavor.*

1¼ cups shelled fresh or frozen edamame

¾ cup frozen peas

1 garlic clove, crushed

1 tablespoon chopped green onions

2 tablespoons fresh lemon juice

1 tablespoon olive oil

½ teaspoon salt

¼ teaspoon ground cayenne

½ cup water

2 tablespoons minced fresh parsley or cilantro, for garnish

1. In a large saucepan of salted boiling water, cook the edamame until soft, about 10 minutes. During the last minute, add the peas. Drain well and set aside.

2. In a food processor, process the garlic and green onions until finely minced. Add the cooked edamame and peas, lemon juice, oil, salt, and cayenne, and process until smooth. Add up to $1/2$ cup of water and process until smooth. Taste, adjusting seasonings if necessary. Transfer to a medium bowl and sprinkle with the parsley. Serve right away or cover and refrigerate for 1 hour to allow flavors to intensify. This dip is best if used on the same day that it is made.

# sushi-inspired edamame-avocado dip 🄵

makes about 2 cups

*Two of my favorite Japanese treats, avocado sushi rolls and edamame, were the inspiration for this dip. Serve it with Black Sesame Wonton Chips (page 5). If black sesame seeds are unavailable, regular toasted sesame seeds can be used.*

¾ cup shelled fresh or frozen edamame
1 ripe Hass avocado
1 tablespoon fresh lime juice, plus more if needed
Salt
1 tablespoon minced pickled ginger, for garnish
1 tablespoon black sesame seeds, for garnish

1. In a medium saucepan of salted boiling water, cook the edamame until soft, about 10 minutes. Drain well and set aside to cool.

2. Pit and peel the avocado and transfer to a food processor. Add the lime juice and salt to taste, and the cooked edamame and process until smooth. Taste, adjusting seasonings, adding a bit more lime juice if needed. Transfer to a medium bowl and sprinkle with the pickled ginger and sesame seeds. This dip is best if used on the same day that it is made.

# creamy spinach-tahini dip 🄵

makes about 1 cup

*The delectable Japanese sesame-spinach dish called* gomai *is the inspiration for this delightful fresh-tasting spinach dip made with tahini (sesame paste).*

1 (10-ounce) package fresh baby spinach
1 to 2 garlic cloves
½ teaspoon salt
⅓ cup tahini (sesame paste)
Juice of 1 lemon
Ground cayenne
2 teaspoons toasted sesame seeds, for garnish

1. Lightly steam the spinach until wilted, about 3 minutes. Squeeze dry and set aside.

2. In a food processor, process the garlic and salt until finely chopped. Add the steamed spinach, tahini, lemon juice, and cayenne to taste. Process until well blended and taste, adjusting seasonings if necessary. Transfer the dip to a medium bowl and sprinkle with the sesame seeds. If not using right away, cover and refrigerate until needed. Properly stored, it will keep for up to 3 days.

# sassy spinach dip with roasted garlic

makes about 2½ cups

*Thanks to vegan sour cream and mayo, no one has to be without their favorite spinach dip. This version, developed by my friend and recipe tester Toni Dahlmeier, has the added flavor dimension of roasted garlic. Serve with crackers, chips, veggies, or Great Garlic Bread (page 397).*

5 to 7 garlic cloves

1 (10-ounce) package frozen chopped spinach, thawed

½ cup vegan mayonnaise, homemade (page 573) or store-bought

½ cup vegan sour cream, homemade (page 574) or store-bought

2 teaspoons fresh lime juice

¼ cup minced green onions

¼ cup shredded carrot

2 tablespoons minced fresh cilantro or parsley

½ teaspoon celery salt

Salt and freshly ground black pepper

1. Preheat the oven to 350° F. Roast the garlic on a small baking sheet until golden, 12 to 15 minutes. Press or crush the roasted garlic and mash to a paste. Set aside.

2. While the garlic is roasting, steam the spinach until tender, 5 minutes. Squeeze dry and finely chop. Set aside.

3. In a medium bowl, combine the mayonnaise, sour cream, lime juice, and roasted garlic. Stir to combine. Add the green onions, carrot, and cilantro. Stir in the steamed spinach and season with the celery salt and salt and pepper to taste. Mix well. Chill at least 1 hour before serving to allow flavors to intensify. If not using right away, cover and refrigerate. Properly stored, it will keep for up to 3 days.

# salsa and pinto bean spread

makes about 2½ cups

*Pinto beans add protein and substance to this zesty spread. Make it with hot or mild salsa, depending on your preference. Serve with corn chips.*

1½ cups cooked or 1 (15.5-ounce) can pinto beans, drained and rinsed

1 cup tomato salsa, homemade (page 567) or store-bought

¼ cup minced fresh parsley or cilantro

1 teaspoon fresh lime juice

½ teaspoon ground cumin

½ teaspoon chili powder

Salt and freshly ground black pepper

In a food processor, combine all of the ingredients. Pulse until well mixed, but still slightly coarse. Taste, adjusting seasonings if necessary. Transfer the mixture to a medium a bowl. Cover and refrigerate for at least 1 hour before serving. Properly stored, it will keep for up to 3 days.

# four-seed bread spread

makes about 1¼ cups

*I like to spread this high-protein spread on toasted Sunflower Artisan Bread (page 398). To vary the texture and flavor, try adding some minced onion, green onion, celery, or tomato.*

½ cup sunflower seeds

¼ cup shelled pumpkin seeds (pepitas)

3 tablespoons sesame seeds

1 tablespoon ground flax seed

1 garlic clove, minced

3 tablespoons tahini (sesame paste)

3 tablespoons water

2 tablespoons olive oil

1 tablespoon soy sauce

2 teaspoons fresh lemon juice

1 tablespoon minced fresh parsley

1 teaspoon minced fresh chives (optional)

½ teaspoon salt

⅛ teaspoon ground cayenne

1. Lightly toast the sunflower seeds, pumpkin seeds, and sesame seeds (see page xix), then transfer them to a food processor.

2. Add the flax seeds and garlic, and process until finely ground. Add the tahini, water, oil, soy sauce, lemon juice, parsley, chives, if using, salt, and cayenne and process until smooth. Taste, adjusting seasonings if necessary. Transfer the spread to a medium bowl. If not using right away, cover and refrigerate until needed. Properly stored, it will keep for up to 4 days.

# golden sunshine roasted veg spread

makes about 2 cups

*This recipe was one of those happy accidents that began as a way to use up leftover roasted vegetables. After I spread it on some toasted coarse bread, it was love at first bite. This spread is also great served with the Walnut Oat Crackers (page 421) or your favorite crackers.*

1 medium sweet potato, peeled and diced

1 medium carrot, sliced

½ medium yellow bell pepper, diced

½ small yellow onion, chopped

2 tablespoons olive oil

Salt and freshly ground black pepper

¼ cup tahini (sesame paste)

1. Preheat the oven to 400°F. In a large bowl, toss the sweet potato, carrot, bell pepper, and onion with the oil and spread on a baking sheet. Season with salt and pepper to taste and roast, stirring occasionally, until the vegetables are soft, about 30 minutes. Set aside to cool.

2. Transfer the cooled vegetable mixture to a food processor. Add the tahini and process until smooth. Season with salt and pepper to taste. Transfer the mixture to a medium bowl. Cover and refrigerate until needed. Properly stored, it will keep for up to 3 days.

# eggplant walnut spread

makes about 2½ cups

*Walnuts and eggplant combine to make a versatile, rich-tasting spread that can be used as a dip, a spread for crackers or bread, or as a flavorful addition to a wrap sandwich.*

2 tablespoons olive oil

1 small onion, chopped

1 small eggplant, peeled and cut into ½-inch dice

2 garlic cloves, chopped

½ teaspoon salt

⅛ teaspoon ground cayenne

½ cup chopped walnuts

1 tablespoon fresh minced basil

2 tablespoons vegan mayonnaise, homemade (page 573) or store-bought

2 tablespoons chopped fresh parsley, for garnish

1. In a large skillet, heat the oil over medium heat. Add the onion, eggplant, garlic, salt, and cayenne. Cover and cook until soft, about 15 minutes. Stir in the walnuts and basil and set aside to cool.

2. Transfer the cooled eggplant mixture to a food processor. Add the mayonnaise and process until smooth. Taste, adjusting seasonings if necessary, and then transfer to a medium bowl and garnish with the parsley. If not using right away, cover and refrigerate until needed. Properly stored, it will keep for up to 3 days.

## za'atar-spiced roasted red pepper spread ⦿

makes about 1½ cups

*Za'atar is Arabic for "thyme." The name is given to the herb Syrian marjoram, as well as a spice blend containing thyme, marjoram, and sumac. The latter is what is called for in this recipe. If za'atar spice blend is unavailable, use dried thyme mixed with a pinch of marjoram.*

⅔ cup toasted walnuts
2 jarred roasted red peppers (or see page 10)
1 tablespoon fresh lemon juice
1 tablespoon olive oil
½ teaspoon za'atar spice blend
½ teaspoon salt
¼ teaspoon ground cayenne
Chopped fresh parsley, for garnish

1. In a food processor, process the walnuts until finely ground. Add the red peppers and lemon juice and process until smooth. Add the oil, za'atar, salt, and cayenne and blend until smooth. Taste, adjusting seasonings if necessary.

2. Transfer the spread to a small bowl and garnish with the parsley. If not using right away, cover and refrigerate until needed. Properly stored, it will keep for up to 3 days.

## white bean and artichoke spread ⦿

makes about 2½ cups

*Creamy white beans are an ideal complement for the piquant artichoke hearts in this tasty spread festooned with chopped kalamata olives. It's great spread on pita triangles or used as a base for wrap sandwiches.*

1 (6-ounce) jar marinated artichoke hearts, drained
1½ cups cooked or 1 (15.5-ounce) Great Northern or other white beans, drained and rinsed
1 tablespoon chopped fresh parsley
1 tablespoon olive oil
2 teaspoons fresh lemon juice
½ teaspoon salt
¼ teaspoon ground cayenne
2 tablespoons pitted chopped kalamata olives

1. In a food processor, combine the artichoke hearts, beans, parsley, oil, lemon juice, salt, and cayenne. Process until well blended. Taste, adjusting seasonings if necessary.

2. Transfer to a medium bowl and top with the chopped olives. If not using right away, cover and refrigerate until needed. Properly stored, it will keep for up to 3 days.

# tempeh-pimiento cheeze ball

makes 8 servings

*This totally retro appetizer gets a thoroughly modern makeover with the help of tempeh and nutritional yeast. Serve with crackers and one of those little cheese-spread knives you thought you'd never use again.*

8 ounces tempeh, cut into ½-inch pieces

1 (2-ounce) jar chopped pimientos, drained

¼ cup nutritional yeast

¼ cup vegan mayonnaise, homemade (page 573) or store-bought

2 tablespoons soy sauce

¾ cup chopped pecans

1. In a medium saucepan of simmering water, cook the tempeh for 30 minutes. Set aside to cool. In a food processor, combine the cooled tempeh, pimientos, nutritional yeast, mayo, and soy sauce. Process until smooth.

2. Transfer the tempeh mixture to a bowl and refrigerate until firm and chilled, at least 2 hours or overnight.

3. In a dry skillet, toast the pecans over medium heat until lightly toasted, about 5 minutes. Set aside to cool.

4. Shape the tempeh mixture into a ball, and roll it in the pecans, pressing the nuts slightly into the tempeh mixture so they stick. Refrigerate for at least 1 hour before serving. If not using right away, cover and keep refrigerated until needed. Properly stored, it will keep for 2 to 3 days.

# smooth and savory mushroom pâté

makes about 2 cups

*Ground cashews give this luxurious pâté a buttery richness that will make it disappear in a crowd. Serve with a selection of crackers or breads for slathering.*

1 tablespoon olive oil

½ cup chopped onion

1 garlic clove, minced

2 cups thinly sliced white mushrooms

½ teaspoon dried savory

1 tablespoon brandy or cognac (optional)

2 teaspoons soy sauce

Salt and freshly ground black pepper

½ cup raw cashews

Chopped fresh parsley, for garnish

1. In a large skillet, heat the oil over medium heat. Add the onion and garlic, cover, and cook until softened, about 5 minutes. Add the mushrooms and savory. Stir in the brandy, if using, soy sauce, and salt and pepper to taste. Cook, uncovered, stirring occasionally, until the mushrooms are soft and the liquid is evaporated, about 5 minutes. Set aside to cool.

2. In a food processor, grind the cashews to a fine powder. Add the cooled mushroom mixture and process until smooth. Spoon the pâté into a small crock or serving bowl. Smooth the top and sprinkle with parsley. Cover and refrigerate for at least 1 hour before serving. Properly stored, it will keep for up to 5 days.

# COLD APPETIZERS

## marinated olives

makes 4 servings

*A bowl of marinated olives makes a great appetizer before dinner or a zesty (and easy) addition to a buffet table. While many supermarkets now have olive bars where marinated olives are available, I prefer making my own marinade so I can customize the flavors to my own taste. For a refreshing variation, make a citrus marinade by using orange or lemon juice in place of the vinegar and adding a tablespoon of orange or lemon zest. Instead of the oregano, use thyme, fennel, or rosemary.*

¼ cup olive oil

2 garlic cloves, crushed

½ teaspoon dried oregano

¼ teaspoon crushed red pepper

1½ tablespoons white wine vinegar

1 cup brine-cured black olives, drained

2 teaspoons minced fresh parsley

1. In a small saucepan, heat the oil over low heat. Add the garlic, oregano, crushed red pepper, and vinegar and cook for 2 minutes. Remove from heat and stir in the olives.

2. Transfer to a bowl. Cover and refrigerate overnight. Remove the olives from the marinade and place in a small serving bowl. Sprinkle with parsley and serve. Cover and refrigerate any unused olives. Properly stored, they will keep for several weeks. To intensify flavor, remaining olives can be stored in the leftover marinade; otherwise, the remaining marinade can be discarded.

## sesame-shiitake wonton crisps

makes 12 crisps

*Chewy, earthy shiitakes and crisp, refreshing snow peas and carrot are anointed with a light sesame-lime dressing for a delicious and easy topping for toasted wontons. This is a great way to use homemade wrappers, but if you don't have the time to make them, you can use pita chips or rice crackers as a base for the topping, or spoon the mixture into thawed frozen phyllo cups, which can be found in supermarket freezers.*

12 Vegan Wonton Wrappers, (page 41)

2 tablespoons toasted sesame oil

2 teaspoons canola or grapeseed oil

12 shiitake mushrooms, lightly rinsed, patted dry, stemmed, and cut into ¼-inch slices

4 snow peas, trimmed and cut crosswise into thin slivers

1 teaspoon soy sauce

1 tablespoon fresh lime juice

½ teaspoon sugar

1 medium carrot, shredded

Toasted sesame seeds or black sesame seeds, if available

1. Preheat the oven to 350°F. Lightly oil a baking sheet and set aside. Brush the wonton wrappers with 1 tablespoon of the sesame oil and arrange on the baking sheet. Bake until golden brown and crisp, about 5 minutes. Set aside to cool. (Alternately, you can tuck the wonton wrappers into mini-muffin tins to create cups for the filling. Brush with sesame oil and bake them until crisp.)

2. In a large skillet, heat the canola oil over medium heat. Add the mushrooms and cook until softened, 3 to 5 minutes. Stir in the snow peas and the soy sauce and cook 30 seconds. Set aside to cool.

3. In a large bowl, combine the lime juice, sugar, and remaining 1 tablespoon sesame oil. Stir in the carrot and cooled shiitake mixture. Top each wonton crisp with a spoonful of the shiitake mixture. Sprinkle with sesame seeds and arrange on a platter to serve.

# cheezy cashew–roasted red pepper toasts

makes 16 to 24 toasts

*A tangy flavor and bright color give these cute canapés a festive appeal and a retro look. A soft white sourdough or wheat bread works best, since coarser breads may be too crumbly to cut attractively.*

8 thin soft bread slices
2 jarred roasted red peppers (or see page 10)
1 cup unsalted cashews
¼ cup water
1 tablespoon soy sauce
2 tablespoons chopped green onions
¼ cup nutritional yeast
2 tablespoons balsamic vinegar
2 tablespoons olive oil

1. Use canapé or cookie cutters to cut the bread into desired shapes about 2 inches wide. If you don't have a cutter, use a knife to cut the bread into squares, triangles, or rectangles. You should get 2 to 4 pieces out of each slice of bread. Toast the bread and set aside to cool.

2. Coarsely chop 1 red pepper and set aside. Cut the remaining pepper into thin strips or decorative shapes and set aside for garnish.

3. In a blender or food processor, grind the cashews to a fine powder. Add the water and soy sauce and process until smooth. Add the chopped red pepper and puree. Add the green onions, nutritional yeast, vinegar, and oil and process until smooth and well blended.

4. Spread a spoonful of the pepper mixture onto each of the toasted bread pieces and top decoratively with the reserved pepper strips. Arrange on a platter or tray and serve.

# jicama-guacamole bites 🅕

makes about 24 bites

*Jicama is used here as a fresh, crisp, and surprising canapé bottom that complements the guacamole topping. For a more casual presentation, serve the guacamole in a bowl and cut the jicama into strips to use as dippers.*

2 ripe Hass avocados, pitted and peeled
2 garlic cloves, minced
2 tablespoons minced green onions
2 tablespoons fresh lime juice
Salt and freshly ground black pepper
1 large jicama
Cilantro leaves, for garnish

1. In a medium bowl, combine the avocado, garlic, green onions, and 1 tablespoon of the lime juice. Season with salt and pepper to taste. Mash with a fork until smooth but still slightly chunky. Set aside.

2. Peel the jicama and cut it into ¼-inch slices. Use canapé or cookie cutters to cut the slices into desired shapes, or use a knife to cut the jicama into 2-inch triangles. Toss the jicama with the remaining lime juice to prevent discoloration.

3. Top each slice of jicama with a heaping teaspoonful of the guacamole. Garnish each canapé with a cilantro leaf and arrange on a platter to serve.

# lemon and garlic marinated mushrooms

makes 4 servings

*Once you discover how fresh-tasting and delicious these mushrooms are (and easy to prepare), you'll never go back to buying those tired deli mushrooms. Serve on a buffet with a slotted spoon or toothpicks for easy pickup. They make a great addition to an antipasto platter as well.*

3 tablespoons olive oil

2 tablespoons fresh lemon juice

2 garlic cloves, crushed

1 teaspoon dried marjoram

½ teaspoon coarsely ground fennel seed

½ teaspoon salt

¼ teaspoon freshly ground black pepper

8 ounces small white mushrooms, lightly rinsed, patted dry, and stemmed

1 tablespoon minced fresh parsley

1. In a medium bowl, whisk together the oil, lemon juice, garlic, marjoram, fennel seed, salt, and pepper. Add the mushrooms and parsley and stir gently until coated.

2. Cover and refrigerate for at least 2 hours or overnight. Stir well before serving.

# cherry tomatoes stuffed with whirled peas 🅕

makes 24 tomatoes

*Not many recipes have been inspired by bumper stickers, but it's easy to visualize "whirled peas" when it's a tasty stuffing for cherry tomatoes. Pass a platter of them at your next gathering and ask guests to "give peas a chance."*

24 ripe cherry tomatoes

2 teaspoons olive oil

2 medium shallots, finely chopped

¾ cup frozen peas, thawed

1 teaspoon chopped fresh basil or mint

1 tablespoon vegan cream cheese or vegan sour cream, homemade (page 574) or store-bought

Salt and freshly ground black pepper

1. Cut a very thin slice off the bottoms of the tomatoes. Use a small melon baller or a teaspoon to scoop out seeds and juice. Discard seeds and juice. Set aside scooped-out tomatoes, cut side down to drain.

2. In a small skillet, heat the oil over medium heat. Add the shallots, cover, and cook until softened, about 3 minutes. Add the peas, and cook, covered, 2 minutes longer. Remove from the heat and set aside to cool.

3. Transfer the shallot and pea mixture to a food processor and add the basil, cream cheese, and salt and pepper to taste. Puree until smooth. Use a pastry bag to pipe the mixture into the tomatoes and arrange on a platter to serve.

# snow peas stuffed with sun-dried tomato hummus ⓕ

makes about 24 snow peas

*Crisp-tender snow peas stuffed with a flavorful sun-dried tomato hummus look lovely on a platter, especially when the hummus is piped into the snow peas using a pastry bag with a decorative tip. You can also use a plastic bag with one corner snipped off.*

24 large firm snow peas, trimmed

3 garlic cloves, crushed

2 tablespoons chopped oil-packed sun-dried tomatoes

½ teaspoon salt

1½ cups cooked or 1 (15.5-ounce) can chickpeas, drained and rinsed

¼ cup tahini (sesame paste)

2 tablespoons water

⅛ teaspoon ground cayenne (optional)

1. Immerse the snow peas in a medium saucepan of simmering water just long enough to turn them bright green, about 30 seconds. Drain and run under cold water. Pat dry and set aside.

2. In a food processor, combine the garlic, tomatoes, and salt, and process to a thick paste. Add the chickpeas, tahini, water, and cayenne, if using, and process until smooth. Taste, adjusting seasonings if necessary. Spoon or pipe the mixture onto the snow peas and arrange decoratively on a platter to serve.

# artichoke-and-walnut-stuffed belgian endive ⓕ

makes 6 servings

*When the endive leaves are arranged concentrically on a round platter, they look like a large flower or starburst. To add a bit of color to the presentation, fill the center of the circle with a small bowl filled with cherry tomatoes. If frozen artichoke hearts are unavailable, substitute a 15-ounce can (not marinated) and proceed with the recipe after the frozen-artichoke cooking instructions.*

1 (10-ounce) package frozen artichoke hearts

½ cup walnut pieces

1 garlic clove, crushed

2 tablespoons chopped green onions

½ teaspoon salt

⅛ teaspoon freshly ground black pepper

1 tablespoon olive oil

2 teaspoons fresh lemon juice

½ teaspoon minced fresh thyme

2 medium Belgian endive, leaves separated

1. In a medium saucepan of boiling salted water, cook the artichoke hearts until tender, about 10 minutes. Drain well and set aside to cool.

2. In a food processor, combine the walnuts, garlic, green onions, salt, and pepper and process until chopped. Add the oil, lemon juice, thyme, and cooled artichoke hearts and process until well mixed. Transfer to a medium bowl.

3. Use a small spoon to stuff the artichoke mixture into each of the endive leaves. Arrange the filled endive leaves decoratively on a platter to serve.

# lentil-pecan country-style pâté

makes 6 to 8 servings

*Serve this hearty and flavorful pâté on a platter surrounded by breads and crackers, or slice and plate for an elegant first course. Garnish with fresh thyme sprigs or chopped parsley or pecans.*

1 cup brown lentils, picked over, rinsed, and drained

1 tablespoon olive oil

1 medium yellow onion, chopped

2 garlic cloves, chopped

1¼ teaspoons dried thyme

¼ teaspoon ground allspice

1 teaspoon salt

¼ teaspoon freshly ground black pepper

2 tablespoons sherry or brandy (optional)

2 tablespoon sherry vinegar

½ cup toasted chopped pecan pieces

2 tablespoons chopped fresh parsley

2 tablespoons all-purpose flour

1. In a saucepan of boiling salted water, cook the lentils until soft, about 40 minutes. Drain well and set aside. Preheat the oven to 375°F. Lightly oil a 9-inch loaf pan and set aside.

2. In a medium skillet, heat the oil over medium heat. Add the onion and garlic and cook until soft, about 5 minutes. Stir in the thyme, allspice, salt, pepper, and sherry, if using. Cook 1 minute longer and set aside.

3. In a food processor, combine the cooked lentils with the onion mixture. Add the vinegar, pecans, and parsley and process until mixed, but not pureed. Add the flour and pulse to combine. Taste, adjusting seasonings

if necessary, then spoon into the prepared pan and bake until firm, 30 to 40 minutes.

4. Cool the pâté to room temperature, then refrigerate until chilled, 3 to 4 hours. When ready to serve, run a knife along the edge of the pan and invert onto a plate. Garnish decoratively and serve at room temperature.

# mushroom-walnut pâté

makes 6 to 8 servings

*You can use regular white mushrooms in this savory pâté, but if you want a deeper mushroom flavor, consider using a mix of wild mushrooms. This pâté tastes better the day after it is made, so if possible make it a day ahead of when you need it.*

1 tablespoon olive oil

1 medium yellow onion, chopped

3 garlic cloves, chopped

2 cups chopped mushrooms, any variety

2 tablespoons brandy (optional)

¼ cup tahini (sesame paste)

1 teaspoon dried savory

1 teaspoon salt

⅛ teaspoon ground cayenne

1 cup toasted walnut pieces

2 tablespoons chopped fresh parsley

3 tablespoons all-purpose flour

1. Preheat the oven to 350°F. Lightly oil a 9-inch loaf pan and set aside. In a large skillet, heat the oil over medium heat. Add the onion and garlic and cover and cook until softened, about 5 minutes. Add the mushrooms and cook, uncovered, until the mushrooms are soft and the liquid has evaporated, 5 to 7 minutes. Add the brandy, if using. Stir in the tahini,

savory, salt, and cayenne and cook, stirring for 1 to 2 minutes more. Set aside.

2. In a food processor, chop the walnuts. Add the parsley and flour and pulse to combine. Add the mushroom mixture and process until combined. Taste, adjusting seasonings if necessary, then spoon the mixture into the prepared pan. Bake until firm, about 40 minutes. Cool the pâté to room temperature, then refrigerate until chilled. When ready to serve, run a knife along the edge of the pan and invert onto a plate. Serve at room temperature.

# mango-avocado spring rolls 🅕

makes 10 to 12 rolls

*These delightful spring rolls are especially good with Spicy Mango Sauce (page 558). Rice vermicelli, extremely thin and brittle dried noodles made from rice, are available at Asian markets, natural food stores, and well-stocked supermarkets. Don't confuse them with cellophane noodles, which are made from mung bean starch.*

3 ounces rice vermicelli

12 rice paper wrappers

2 ripe Hass avocados

1 tablespoon fresh lemon juice

1 ripe mango, peeled, pitted, and cut into ¼-inch slices

1 medium English cucumber, peeled, halved lengthwise, seeded, and cut into thin strips

2 cups finely chopped romaine or iceberg lettuce

Salt and freshly ground black pepper

½ cup fresh cilantro leaves

1. Soak the vermicelli in a medium bowl of hot water until soft, about 1 minute, and drain well. Cut the noodles into 4- or 5-inch lengths and set aside.

2. Fill a large shallow bowl with warm water and add one rice paper wrapper at a time, soaking it in the water for a few seconds until soft. Remove it from the water and lay it on a dry work surface. Pit and peel the avocados and cut into ¼-inch strips. Toss the avocado strips with the lemon juice to prevent discoloration, then place 2 or 3 avocado strips down the center of each the wrapper, leaving a 1-inch margin at each end. Add a few strips of mango, followed by a layer of cucumber strips. Top with some of the rice noodles and a layer of lettuce strips. Season with salt and pepper, to taste, and sprinkle with some of the cilantro leaves.

3. Pull one side of the rice paper over the filling, folding over the two short ends, rolling up tightly to enclose the filling. Transfer to a serving plate and repeat with the remaining ingredients. Serve immediately or cover the rolls with a damp cloth for no more than 1 hour before serving.

# lemongrass tofu and snow pea spring rolls

makes 12 rolls

*Serve these spring rolls with Sesame-Scallion Dipping Sauce (page 560) or another dipping sauce of your choice. Rice paper wrappers, available in Asian markets, are sometimes labeled "banh trang" or "galettes de riz."*

1 pound extra-firm tofu, drained, cut into
　　¼-inch slices, and pressed (page xiv)

2 tablespoons soy sauce

1 tablespoon mirin

1 tablespoon minced lemongrass

4 ounces snow peas, trimmed

2 tablespoons canola or grapeseed oil

12 rice paper wrappers

1 large carrot, shredded

1 cup fresh Thai basil or cilantro leaves

1. Cut the tofu into ¼-inch strips. Transfer to a shallow bowl and add the soy sauce, mirin, and lemongrass. Cover and refrigerate for 1 to 2 hours to marinate.

2. In a small saucepan of salted boiling water, cook the snow peas for 1 minute. Drain and rinse under cold water. Pat the snow peas dry and slice them lengthwise into thin strips. Set aside.

3. In a large skillet, heat the oil over medium heat. Drain the marinade from the tofu and discard. Add the tofu to the hot skillet and cook, turning gently, until golden brown, about 7 minutes. Transfer the tofu to a plate and set aside to cool.

4. Fill a large shallow bowl with warm water and add 1 rice paper wrapper at a time, soaking it in the water for a few seconds until soft.

Remove it from the water and lay it on a dry work surface. Place 2 or 3 strips of tofu down the center of each wrapper, leaving a 1-inch margin at each end. Top with a few strips of the cooked snow peas, followed by some shredded carrot and basil leaves.

5. Fold the bottom of the rice paper over the filling, fold over the two short ends, then roll up tightly to enclose the filling. Transfer to a serving plate. Repeat with the remaining ingredients. Serve immediately or cover the rolls with a damp cloth for no more than 1 hour before serving.

# sesame seitan and spinach spring rolls

makes 8 rolls

*Seitan makes a hearty addition to these spring rolls that are especially good served with Ginger-Soy Dipping Sauce (page 559).*

3 tablespoons hoisin sauce

1 tablespoon soy sauce

1 tablespoon toasted sesame oil

8 ounces seitan, homemade (page 305) or
　　store-bought, cut into ¼-inch thin strips

3 tablespoons sesame seeds

1 tablespoon canola or grapeseed oil

8 rice paper wrappers

2 medium carrots, shredded

4 ounces fresh baby spinach

1. In a shallow bowl, combine the hoisin sauce, soy sauce, and sesame oil. Add the seitan, spooning the marinade over the seitan to coat thoroughly. Cover and refrigerate for 1 hour.

2. Spread the sesame seeds on a plate. Drain the marinade from the seitan and discard. Add

the seitan strips to the sesame seeds, turning to coat. In a large skillet, heat the canola oil over medium heat. Add the seitan and cook until browned, 5 minutes. Remove from the skillet and set aside to cool.

3. Fill a large shallow bowl with warm water and add 1 rice paper wrapper at a time, soaking it for a few seconds until soft. Remove it from the water and lay it on a dry work surface. Place 2 or 3 strips of seitan down the center of each wrapper, leaving a 1-inch margin at each end. Top the seitan with some of the carrots followed by a few spinach leaves.

4. Fold the bottom of the rice paper over the filling, then fold over the two short ends and roll up to enclose the filling. Repeat with the remaining ingredients. Serve immediately or cover the rolls with a damp cloth for no more than 1 hour before serving.

# vietnamese-style lettuce rolls

makes 4 servings

*Crisp vegetables and a lettuce leaf wrapper make these rolls especially light and refreshing—ideal for a spring or summer gathering. Variation: substitute strips of baked marinated tofu for the rice noodles in the filling. Instead of the scallion-soy dipping sauce in this recipe, try serving them with Apricot and Chile Dipping Sauce (page 560).*

2 green onions
2 tablespoons soy sauce
2 tablespoons rice vinegar
1 teaspoon sugar
⅛ teaspoon crushed red pepper
3 tablespoons water
3 ounces rice vermicelli
4 to 6 soft green leaf lettuce leaves
1 medium carrot, shredded
½ medium English cucumber, peeled, seeded, and cut lengthwise into ¼-inch strips
½ medium red bell pepper, cut into ¼-inch strips
1 cup loosely packed fresh cilantro or basil leaves

1. Cut the green part off the green onions and cut them lengthwise into thin slices and set aside. Mince the white part of the green onions and transfer to a small bowl. Add the soy sauce, rice vinegar, sugar, crushed red pepper, and water. Stir to blend and set aside.

2. Soak the vermicelli in medium bowl of hot water until softened, about 1 minute. Drain the noodles well and cut them into 3-inch lengths. Set aside.

3. Place a lettuce leaf on a work surface and arrange a row of noodles in the center of the leaf, followed by a few strips of scallion greens, carrot, cucumber, bell pepper, and cilantro. Bring the bottom edge of the leaf over the filling and fold in the two short sides. Roll up gently but tightly. Place the roll seam side down on a serving platter. Repeat with remaining ingredients. Serve with the dipping sauce.

# lemony rice-stuffed grape leaves

makes about 30 grape leaves

*Called* dolmades *or* dolmas, *these moist leaf-wrapped packages make a great addition to a meze platter or a buffet. Their diminutive size makes them an ideal finger food. Look for grape leaves in well-stocked supermarkets, gourmet grocers, or Greek or Middle Eastern markets.*

2 cups cooked basmati or other rice*

3 tablespoons finely minced green onions

3 tablespoons fresh lemon juice

1 teaspoon finely minced lemon zest

2 tablespoons minced dillweed

Salt

¼ teaspoon freshly ground black pepper

1 (16-ounce) jar grape leaves, drained, rinsed, and patted dry

2 tablespoons olive oil

1. In a large bowl, combine the rice, green onions, 1 tablespoon of the lemon juice, lemon zest, dillweed, about ½ teaspoon of salt (less if your rice is well seasoned), and pepper. Mix well.

2. Trim the stems from the grape leaves. Place one grape leaf at a time on a work surface, shiny side down. Place about 1 tablespoon of the rice mixture near the stem end and fold the sides of the leaf over the filling. Beginning at the stem end, roll up the leaf firmly into a neat roll. Repeat with the remaining ingredients.

3. Place the stuffed leaves in a large skillet. Add the oil, remaining 2 tablespoons lemon juice, and just enough water to come about halfway up the stuffed leaves. Cover and heat to a simmer. Cook over low heat until tender, 20 to 30 minutes. Uncover, remove from the heat, and set aside to cool. Use a slotted spoon to transfer to a platter. Serve at room temperature.

*Any variety of rice may be used in the stuffing, but I prefer fragrant basmati rice.*

# couscous dolmas

makes about 20 grape leaves

*Tired of the same old rice-filled stuffed grape leaves? Try this nontraditional version made with couscous and chopped cashews for an interesting contrast of textures and flavors.*

2 tablespoons olive oil

½ cup minced onion

1 cup couscous

1½ cups vegetable broth, homemade (page 141) or store-bought

¼ cup chopped golden raisins

¼ cup chopped cashews

2 tablespoons minced fresh parsley

Salt and freshly ground black pepper

1 (16-ounce) jar grape leaves, drained, rinsed, and patted dry

2 tablespoons fresh lemon juice

1. In a medium saucepan, heat 1 tablespoon oil over medium heat. Add the onion, cover, and cook until softened, about 5 minutes. Add the couscous and stir in the broth, raisins, cashews, parsley, and salt and pepper to taste. Cover and remove from the heat. Set aside for 5 minutes.

2. Trim the stems from the grape leaves. Place one grape at a time leaf on a cutting board, shiny side down. Place about 1 tablespoon of the couscous mixture near the stem end and fold the sides of the leaf over the filling. Beginning at the stem end, roll up the leaf firmly into a neat roll. Repeat with the remaining ingredients and grape leaves.

3. Place the stuffed leaves in a large skillet. Add enough water to cover along with the remaining 1 tablespoon of oil and the lemon juice. Cover and heat to a simmer. Cook over low heat until tender, about 30 minutes. Uncover, remove from the heat, and set aside to cool. Use a slotted spoon to transfer to a serving plate. Serve at room temperature.

# rainbow sushi

makes 6 rolls

*These days, you can find sushi ingredients in nearly every supermarket, as well as in natural food stores and, of course, Asian markets. Feel free to add other ingredients such as thin strips of baked marinated tofu, minced green onions, or toasted sesame seeds.*

1½ cups sushi rice

3 cups water

¼ cup rice vinegar

2 teaspoons sugar

½ teaspoon salt

6 nori sheets

1 medium English cucumber, peeled, halved lengthwise, seeded, and cut into thin strips

1 medium red bell pepper, cut lengthwise into thin strips

1 medium carrot, shredded

1 tablespoon wasabi powder

1 tablespoon warm water

Pickled ginger, for garnish

Soy sauce, for dipping

1. Rinse and drain the rice until the water runs clear. Transfer the drained rice to a medium saucepan. Add the 3 cups water, soak for 30 minutes, then cover and bring to a boil over high heat. Reduce the heat to low and simmer until the water is absorbed, about 15 minutes. Remove from the heat and let stand for 10 to 15 minutes.

2. In a small bowl, combine the vinegar, sugar, and salt, then stir the mixture into the rice. Transfer the rice to a shallow bowl and cool to room temperature.

3. Place a sheet of nori on a bamboo sushi mat. Spread about ½ cup of the rice evenly over the nori, leaving a 2-inch border along the top edge. Place strips of cucumber and bell pepper on top of the rice, along the edge nearest you. Top the vegetable strips with shredded carrot.

4. Roll the mat away from you, pressing firmly against the nori to enclose the ingredients. Continue rolling slowly up to the top edge. Moisten the exposed edge of the nori with a small amount of water to seal the roll. Gently squeeze the mat around the sushi roll and remove. Repeat with the remaining ingredients to make a total of 6 filled rolls.

5. Using a sharp knife, cut the sushi roll into 6 pieces. Wipe the knife clean with a damp cloth after each cut. Turn the pieces upright and place on a platter.

6. In a small bowl, combine the wasabi powder with the 1 tablespoon warm water to form a paste. Shape the wasabi paste into a small mound and place it on the sushi platter, along with a mound of pickled ginger. Serve with dipping bowls of soy sauce.

# avocado and asparagus sushi rolls

makes 6 rolls

*Asparagus and avocado join forces in these luxurious sushi rolls. For added crunch and color, sprinkle some grated carrot alongside the asparagus spears.*

1½ cups sushi rice

3 cups water

¼ cup rice vinegar

2 teaspoons sugar

½ teaspoon salt

1 ripe Hass avocado

6 nori sheets

2 tablespoons black sesame seeds

12 thin asparagus spears, tough ends trimmed and lightly steamed until crisp-tender

1 tablespoon wasabi powder

1 tablespoon warm water

Pickled ginger, for garnish

Soy sauce, for dipping

1. Rinse and drain the rice until the water runs clear. Transfer the drained rice to a medium saucepan. Add the 3 cups water, soak for 30 minutes, then cover and bring to a boil over high heat. Reduce the heat to low and simmer until the water is absorbed, about 15 minutes. Remove from the heat and let stand for 10 to 15 minutes.

2. In a small bowl, combine the vinegar, sugar, and salt, then stir the mixture into the rice. Transfer the rice to a shallow bowl and cool to room temperature. Pit and peel the avocado and cut into ¼-inch strips. Set aside.

3. Place a sheet of nori on a bamboo sushi mat. Spread about ½ cup of the rice evenly over the nori, leaving a 2-inch border along the top edge.

4. Sprinkle the sesame seeds over the rice. At the edge nearest to you, place 2 strips of avocado and 2 asparagus spears end to end on top of the rice. Roll the mat away from you, pressing firmly against the nori to enclose the ingredients. Continue rolling slowly up to the top edge. Moisten the exposed edge of the nori with a small amount of water to seal the roll. Gently squeeze the mat around the sushi roll and remove the mat. Repeat with the remaining ingredients to make a total of 6 filled rolls.

5. Using a sharp knife, cut the sushi roll into 6 pieces. Wipe the knife clean with a damp cloth after each cut. Turn the pieces upright and place on a platter.

6. In a small bowl, combine the wasabi powder with the 1 tablespoon warm water to form a paste. Shape the wasabi paste into a small mound and place it on the sushi platter, along with a mound of pickled ginger. Serve with dipping bowls of soy sauce.

# Hot Appetizers

## asparagus wrapped in phyllo

makes 24 pieces

*This easy and elegant appetizer is best made with asparagus spears that are cut to be no more than five inches in length. Select spears that are of uniform thickness—slender to medium ones work best, but if using thick asparagus, peel the spears with a vegetable peeler so they are more tender. For a flavor variation, sprinkle the asparagus with lemon pepper and garlic salt instead of regular pepper and salt. Dried herbs, such as basil or tarragon, are also good additions. Instead of asparagus, you can use steamed green beans or roasted spiced carrot sticks.*

24 asparagus spears, tough ends trimmed
4 sheets frozen phyllo pastry, thawed
¼ cup olive oil
Salt and freshly ground black pepper

1. Steam the asparagus until just tender, about 3 minutes, then run the spears under cold water and drain. Pat dry and set aside.

2. Preheat the oven to 400°F. Lightly oil a baking sheet and set aside. Spread the phyllo sheets on a work surface and cut them in half lengthwise. Cut the phyllo halves crosswise into thirds. You should end up with 24 6-inch squares. Cover them with a slightly damp clean dish towel to keep them from drying out.

3. Working with 1 phyllo square at a time, brush with oil, and arrange 1 asparagus spear on the square, about 1 inch from the edge closest to you. Sprinkle the asparagus and phyllo

with salt and pepper, to taste. Brush the edges of the phyllo with a bit more oil, if necessary, and fold the short edges up onto the asparagus. Tightly roll the asparagus and phyllo into a cigar-shaped packet. Arrange on the prepared baking sheet. Repeat with the remaining ingredients.

4. When all of the rolls are prepared, bake them until browned, 12 to 15 minutes. Allow to cool for 2 to 3 minutes before serving.

## pinto-pecan fireballs

makes about 20 pieces

*Spicy food lovers will make short work of these zesty tidbits at your next get-together, so you may want to make a double batch and set out some toothpicks for skewering. They're also great tucked into a pita pocket. For a milder version, omit the cayenne and decrease the amount of hot sauce in the fireballs; for extra spice, add a little extra hot sauce to the sauce.*

1½ cups cooked or 1 (15.5-ounce) can pinto beans, drained and rinsed
½ cup chopped pecans
¼ cup minced green onions
1 garlic clove, minced
3 tablespoons wheat gluten flour (vital wheat gluten)
3 tablespoons unseasoned dry bread crumbs
4 tablespoons Tabasco or other hot sauce
¼ teaspoon salt
⅛ teaspoon ground cayenne
¼ cup vegan margarine

1. Preheat the oven to 350°F. Lightly oil a 9 × 13-inch baking pan and set aside. Blot the drained beans well with a paper towel, pressing out any excess liquid. In a food

continues on next page

processor, combine the pinto beans, pecans, green onions, garlic, flour, bread crumbs, 2 tablespoons of the Tabasco, salt, and cayenne. Pulse until well combined, leaving some texture. Use your hands to roll the mixture firmly into 1-inch balls.

2. Place the balls in the prepared baking pan and bake until nicely browned, about 25 to 30 minutes, turning halfway through.

3. Meanwhile, in small saucepan, combine the remaining 2 tablespoons Tabasco and the margarine and melt over low heat. Pour the sauce over the fireballs and bake 10 minutes longer. Serve immediately.

# mushrooms stuffed with spinach and walnuts

makes 4 to 6 servings

*These juicy mushrooms, stuffed with a tasty mixture of spinach, walnuts, and garlic, are delicious and easy to make. They can be arranged on a platter as a pickup food or nestled on small plates in groups of three to serve as a first course for a sit-down dinner.*

2 tablespoons olive oil
8 ounces white mushroom, lightly rinsed, patted dry, and stems reserved
1 garlic clove, minced
1 cup cooked spinach
1 cup finely chopped walnuts
½ cup unseasoned dry bread crumbs
Salt and freshly ground black pepper

1. Preheat the oven to 400°F. Lightly oil a large baking pan and set aside. In a large skillet, heat the oil over medium heat. Add the mushroom caps and cook for 2 minutes to soften slightly. Remove from the skillet and set aside.

2. Chop the mushroom stems and add to the same skillet. Add the garlic and cook over medium heat until softened, about 2 minutes. Stir in the spinach, walnuts, bread crumbs, and salt and pepper to taste. Cook for 2 minutes, stirring well to combine.

3. Fill the reserved mushroom caps with the stuffing mixture and arrange in the baking pan. Bake until the mushrooms are tender and the filling is hot, about 10 minutes. Serve hot.

# spicy chipotle potato quesadillas

makes 4 servings

*Guacamole makes a good accompaniment to these flavorful and fiery quesadillas. If you want to beat the heat, cut back on the chipotle or substitute some canned minced mild green chiles instead. To make them kid-friendly, leave out the chiles altogether. If you don't have cooked potatoes on hand, you can bake potatoes in the microwave in a matter of minutes.*

1 tablespoon olive oil
½ cup chopped onion
2 baked or boiled medium potatoes, coarsely mashed
1 to 1½ teaspoons chopped canned chipotle chile in adobo
Salt and freshly ground black pepper
4 (10-inch) flour tortillas

1. In a large skillet, heat the oil over medium heat. Add the onion, cover, and cook until softened, about 5 minutes. Add the potatoes to the skillet and stir in the chipotle and salt and pepper to taste.

2. Spread a layer of the potato mixture evenly over each of the tortillas and fold them in half. Arrange two of the quesadillas in a large

nonstick skillet or griddle over medium-heat and cook until lightly browned on both sides, turning once. Keep warm while you cook the remaining quesadillas. Cut the quesadillas into quarters and serve warm.

## baby potatoes stuffed with roasted bell pepper and walnuts

makes 12 potatoes

*The crunchy filling plays nicely against the soft potato in this hearty appetizer. For the most appealing presentation, try to find small potatoes that are uniform in size.*

12 small white- or red-skinned potatoes, about 2 inches in diameter
1 jarred roasted red pepper (or see page 10)
½ cup chopped walnuts
¼ cup chopped fresh parsley
2 tablespoons olive oil
Salt and freshly ground black pepper
1 tablespoon vegan Parmesan or Parmasio (page 193, optional)

1. In a large saucepan of boiling water, cook the potatoes until just tender, about 12 minutes. Drain and set aside to cool.

2. Meanwhile, in a food processor, combine the red pepper, walnuts, parsley, oil, and salt and black pepper to taste. Process until well mixed. Set aside.

3. Preheat the oven to 350°F. Lightly oil a baking sheet and set aside. When the potatoes are cool enough to handle, gently cut a thin sliver off each potato to make a flat bottom. Cut off a third of each potato and scoop out the inside of the potato with a small melon baller or a small spoon. Spoon the pepper-walnut

mixture into the potato shell and arrange on the baking sheet. Sprinkle with Parmesan, if using, and bake until hot, about 15 minutes. Serve warm.

## mushroom croustades

makes 12 croustades

*A croustade is an edible container, usually made from bread or pastry, that is used to hold a filling—in this case, a savory mushroom mixture. Be sure your bread slices are thin and soft for best results. Try cremini or porcini mushrooms instead of, or in combination with, the white mushrooms for a deeper mushroom flavor.*

12 thin slices soft white bread
1 tablespoon olive oil, plus more for brushing bread
2 medium shallots, chopped
2 garlic cloves, minced
12 ounces white mushrooms, chopped
¼ cup chopped fresh parsley
1 teaspoon dried thyme
1 tablespoon soy sauce

1. Preheat the oven to 400°F. Using a 3-inch round pastry cutter or a drinking glass, cut a circle from each bread slice. Brush the bread circles with oil and press them firmly but gently into a mini-muffin tin. Bake until the bread is toasted, about 10 minutes.

2. Meanwhile, in a large skillet, heat the 1 tablespoon oil over medium heat. Add the shallots, garlic, and mushrooms and sauté for 5 minutes to soften the vegetables. Stir in the parsley, thyme, and soy sauce and cook until the liquid is absorbed, about 5 minutes longer. Spoon the mushroom mixture into the croustade cups and return to the oven for 3 to 5 minutes to heat through. Serve warm.

# cherry peppers stuffed with sun-dried tomatoes and pine nuts

makes 8 to 12 peppers

*The cherry pepper is a small round pepper that is most often found pickled in jars labeled "mild" or "hot." Its lively flavor and diminutive size make it an ideal finger food. The number of peppers in a jar will vary depending on the size (usually 1 to 2 inches in diameter), so plan accordingly—the stuffing is easily doubled. Look for cherry peppers in well-stocked supermarkets or Italian grocery stores.*

1 (16-ounce) jar hot or mild cherry peppers, drained
2 tablespoons olive oil
2 garlic cloves, minced
½ cup pine nuts
½ cup chopped sun-dried tomatoes
½ cup fresh unseasoned bread crumbs
1 teaspoon chopped fresh basil or ½ teaspoon dried
Salt and freshly ground black pepper

1. Preheat the oven to 400°F. Lightly oil a 9 × 13-inch baking pan and set aside. Slice the tops off the cherry peppers, scrape out the seeds, and set aside. In a large skillet, heat the oil over medium heat. Add garlic and pine nuts and cook to soften the garlic and lightly toast the pine nuts, 2 to 3 minutes.

2. Transfer the pine nut mixture to a food processor and add the sun-dried tomatoes, bread crumbs, basil, and salt and pepper to taste. Pulse until well combined. Stuff the cherry peppers with the pine nut–tomato mixture and place them in the prepared baking dish. Cover and bake until the filling is hot, about 15 minutes. Serve warm.

# cajun tofu crunchies

makes 6 to 8 servings

*These crisp and chewy tofu strips make a great high-protein snack. Instead of cutting them into strips, you can cube them and serve with toothpicks and a dipping sauce. They can also be tossed into salads. Change the seasonings according to your preference—try an Asian version by eliminating the Cajun spices and salt and splashing on soy sauce before baking.*

1 pound extra-firm tofu, well drained, cut into ¼-inch slices, and pressed (page xiv)
2 tablespoons olive oil
1 teaspoon Cajun seasoning
½ teaspoon salt
¼ teaspoon freshly ground black pepper

1. Preheat the oven to 350° F. Lightly oil a baking sheet and set aside. Cut the tofu slices into ¼-inch strips.

2. In a medium bowl, gently toss the tofu strips with the oil, Cajun spice blend, salt, and pepper, until well coated. Arrange in a single layer on the prepared baking sheet, and bake until firm and nicely browned, about 45 minutes, turning once with a metal spatula about halfway through. Set aside to let them cool and firm up. Serve at room temperature.

# basic bruschetta

makes 4 to 6 servings

*Bruschetta is toasted bread that has been brushed with olive oil and rubbed with garlic. It can be served alone or with any number of delicious toppings. Chopped fresh tomatoes are the most traditional topping, but try any flavor combination that inspires you. In addition to toasting the bread on a grill or under a broiler, you can toast it in a hot oven, as done in the Classic Crostini recipe below.*

4 to 6 thick slices Italian bread
Olive oil, for brushing the bread
1 large garlic clove, halved
Coarse salt
Topping of choice (see sidebar)

1. Preheat the grill or broiler. Lightly brush the bread slices with oil and place on a hot grill or under the broiler until golden brown on both sides, turning once, 1 to 2 minutes per side.

2. When the bread is toasted, rub the garlic halves onto one side of each bread slice and sprinkle with coarse salt. Serve as is or top each slice with topping of choice.

## classic crostini

makes 6 servings

*Crostini are the diminutive siblings of the bruschetta, the main difference being that crostini are usually made with smaller bread, such as a French baguette. Because crostini bread is more delicate, it is usually not rubbed with garlic. Crostini can be topped with the same toppings used for bruschetta.*

1 small French baguette, cut into ½-inch-thick slices
Topping of choice (see sidebar)

Preheat the oven to 400°F. Arrange the bread slices in a single layer on a baking sheet and toast, turning once, until lightly browned, 6 to 8 minutes. Serve immediately with topping of choice.

## bruschetta and crostini toppings

The most traditional bruschetta topping, beyond the requisite olive oil and garlic, is chopped ripe tomatoes. For the smaller crostini, I prefer a more assertive topping, such as tapenade. Below are some of my favorite toppings that can be used on either bruschetta or crostini. In addition to the individual toppings, you can mix and match many of them for even more variety and great flavor combinations.

Chopped fresh tomatoes
Green or black olive tapenade
Roasted garlic
Roasted red pepper
Basil pesto with chopped fresh tomato
Pureed white beans with sage
Garlicky sautéed spinach, chard, or other greens
Sautéed mushrooms

FLAVOR COMBOS

Chopped tomatoes with black olive tapenade
Pureed white beans with garlicky sautéed greens
Roasted garlic with sautéed mushrooms
Sautéed mushrooms with roasted red pepper
Pureed white beans with basil pesto
Garlicky sautéed greens with sautéed mushrooms
Roasted garlic with chopped fresh tomatoes

# french onion pastry puffs

makes 24 puffs

*These elegant little appetizers are inspired by the onion-topped pastry tart of southern France known as* pissaladière. *Onions play a starring role in this recipe, so be sure to use flavorful sweet onions such as Vidalia or Walla Walla. When cooking the onions, the goal is to get them meltingly soft to bring out their flavor.*

2 tablespoons olive oil

2 medium sweet yellow onions, thinly sliced

1 garlic clove, minced

1 teaspoon chopped fresh rosemary

Salt and freshly ground black pepper

1 tablespoon capers

1 sheet frozen vegan puff pastry, thawed

18 pitted black olives, quartered

1. In a medium skillet, heat the oil over medium heat. Add the onions and garlic, season with rosemary and salt and pepper to taste. Cover and cook until very soft, stirring occasionally, about 20 minutes. Stir in the capers and set aside.

2. Preheat the oven to 400°F. Roll out the puff pastry and cut into 2- to 3-inch circles using a lightly floured pastry cutter or drinking glass. You should get about 2 dozen circles.

3. Arrange the pastry circles on baking sheets and top each with a heaping teaspoon of onion mixture, patting down to smooth the top. Top with 3 olive quarters, arranged decoratively—either like flower petals emanating from the center or parallel to each other like 3 bars.

4. Bake until pastry is puffed and golden brown, about 15 minutes. Serve hot.

# shiitakes in puff pastry

makes 4 to 6 servings

*Although classic puff pastry is traditionally made with butter, the Pepperidge Farm brand found in the freezer section of your supermarket is not, making it a vegan's best friend for quick and easy appetizers. This brand of puff pastry contains two sheets to a box and has thawing, handling, and storage instructions on the box. If shiitakes are unavailable, any type of mushroom may be used instead.*

2 tablespoons olive oil

2 cups finely chopped fresh shiitake mushrooms

3 garlic cloves, minced

1 medium bunch green onions, finely chopped

1 teaspoon minced fresh thyme or ½ teaspoon dried

½ teaspoon salt

¼ teaspoon freshly ground black pepper

1 sheet frozen vegan puff pastry, thawed

1. Preheat the oven to 400°F. In a large skillet, heat the oil over medium heat. Add the mushrooms, garlic, and green onions. Season with thyme, salt, and pepper. Cook until the vegetables are soft and the liquid has evaporated, about 10 minutes. Remove from the heat and set aside to cool.

2. Unfold the pastry sheet onto a lightly floured work surface and roll into a rectangle about 12 × 15 inches. Cut the pastry into 3-inch squares and press them into the bottoms of nonstick mini-muffin tins. Spoon about 1 tablespoon of the mushroom mixture into the center of each pastry cup. Bake until golden brown, about 15 minutes. Serve warm.

# tempeh taco bites

makes 3 dozen

*Recipe tester Tami Noyes was kind enough to share her recipe for these tempting tempeh taco bites. She made them when she hosted an international appetizer party. It turned out to be the hit of the evening! Miniature phyllo pastry cups are widely available in supermarket freezer cases. They are prebaked and easy to use in a variety of ways, both savory and sweet. Keep some on hand for impromptu entertaining.*

8 ounces tempeh

3 tablespoons soy sauce

2 teaspoons ground cumin

1 teaspoon chili powder

1 teaspoon dried oregano

1 tablespoon olive oil

½ cup finely minced onion

2 garlic cloves, minced

Salt and freshly ground black pepper

2 tablespoons tomato paste

1 chipotle chile in adobo, finely minced

¼ cup hot water or vegetable broth, homemade (page 141) or store-bought, plus more if needed

36 phyllo pastry cups, thawed

½ cup basic guacamole, homemade (page 9) or store-bought

18 ripe cherry tomatoes, halved

1. In a medium saucepan of simmering water, cook the tempeh for 30 minutes. Drain well, then finely mince and place it in a bowl. Add the soy sauce, cumin, chili powder, and oregano. Mix well and set aside.

2. In a medium skillet, heat the oil over medium heat. Add the onion, cover, and cook for 5 minutes. Stir in the garlic, then add the tempeh mixture and cook, stirring, for 2 to 3 minutes. Season with salt and pepper to taste. Set aside.

3. In a small bowl, combine the tomato paste, chipotle, and the hot water or broth. Return tempeh mixture to heat and in stir tomato-chile mixture and cook for 10 to 15 minutes, stirring occasionally, until the liquid is absorbed. The mixture should be fairly dry, but if it begins to stick to the pan, add a little more hot water, 1 tablespoon at a time. Taste, adjusting seasonings if necessary. Remove from the heat.

4. To assemble, fill the phyllo cups to the top with the tempeh filling, using about 2 teaspoons of filling in each. Top with a dollop of guacamole and a cherry tomato half and serve.

# savory artichoke squares

makes 9 squares

*Imbued with the flavors of artichoke and walnuts, these tasty squares can be made ahead and reheated in a moderate oven. If cooking for a crowd, this recipe is easily doubled. If frozen artichoke hearts are unavailable, substitute a 15-ounce can (not the marinated kind) and proceed with the recipe after the frozen-artichoke cooking instructions.*

1 (10-ounce) package frozen artichoke hearts

¼ cup plus 2 tablespoons olive oil

1 large yellow onion, chopped

1 cup all-purpose flour

1 teaspoon baking powder

½ teaspoon salt

3 tablespoons finely chopped fresh parsley

½ teaspoon dried thyme

½ cup unsweetened soy milk

Salt and freshly ground black pepper

2 tablespoons vegan Parmesan or Parmasio (page 193)

½ cup chopped walnuts

1. Preheat the oven to 425°F. Lightly oil an 8-inch square baking pan and set aside. If using frozen artichoke hearts, in a medium saucepan of boiling salted water, cook the artichoke hearts until tender, about 10 minutes. Drain and set aside to cool.

2. In a medium skillet, heat 2 tablespoons of the oil over medium heat. Add the onion, cover, and cook until soft, about 7 minutes. Set aside to cool.

3. In a medium bowl, combine the flour, baking powder, and salt. Add the remaining ¼ cup oil and stir until the mixture resembles coarse crumbs. Add 2 tablespoons parsley, thyme, and soy milk and stir to combine. Stir in about half the onion and spread the mixture evenly into the bottom of the prepared pan.

4. Chop the cooked artichoke hearts and combine with the remaining cooked onion. Add salt and pepper, to taste. Spread the artichoke and onion mixture on top of the dough and sprinkle with the Parmesan and walnuts. Bake until hot and cooked through, about 20 minutes. Cut into squares. Serve immediately sprinkled with the remaining 1 tablespoon parsley.

# chickpea pancake with rosemary

makes 6 servings

*Served in Northern Italy and Southern France, the chickpea pancake is called fari-nata in Liguria and socca in Nice. It is a sublime treat that can be enjoyed as an appetizer or served as part of the main meal. Chickpea flour is a rich silky flour made from ground chickpeas. Look for it in gourmet grocers, natural food stores, Indian markets (where it's called "gram flour"), or in Italian markets (where it's known as "ceci flour"). Add ¼ cup finely chopped pitted kalamata olives to the batter to give it even more Mediterranean flavor.*

1 cup water
1 cup chickpea flour
2 tablespoons olive oil
1 teaspoon salt
2 teaspoons chopped fresh rosemary
Freshly ground black pepper

1. In a large mixing bowl, whisk together the water and the chickpea flour until the mixture is very smooth. Add the oil, salt, and rosemary and mix until smooth and well blended. Set aside at room temperature for at least 30 minutes or up to 4 hours. (Cover if leaving out for longer than an hour.)

2. Preheat the oven to 425°F. Lightly oil a 12-inch pizza pan or large cast-iron skillet and heat in the oven until hot. Carefully remove the pan from the oven and pour the batter into the pan. Bake until the top is firm and the edges are golden brown, about 15 minutes. Be sure that the pan lies very flat in the oven, or the mixture will be too thick and undercooked on one side and too thin and overcooked on the other. If the top seems undercooked, cook it in the broiler for a minute to brown it lightly.

3. To serve, sprinkle with freshly ground pepper to taste and cut into slices. Serve immediately.

# sesame-cilantro scallion pancakes

makes 4 servings

*These crisp and flavorful pancakes are delicious when served with Ginger-Soy Dipping Sauce (page 559). They also make a good soup accompaniment—I especially enjoy them served alongside a steamy bowl of Vietnamese-Style Noodle Soup (page 151).*

2 cups all-purpose flour
½ cup chopped green onions (scallions)
¼ cup minced fresh cilantro
1½ tablespoons white or black sesame seeds
¾ teaspoon salt
1 cup water
2 tablespoons toasted sesame oil
Canola or grapeseed oil, for frying

1. In a medium bowl, combine the flour, green onions, cilantro, sesame seeds, and salt. Add the water and sesame oil and mix to form dough, adding more water if necessary. Transfer the dough to a lightly floured surface and divide into 4 pieces. Roll each piece of dough into circles, about ¼ inch thick.

2. In a large skillet, heat a thin layer of oil over medium heat. Fry the pancakes in batches until golden brown on both sides, turning once, about 3 minutes per side. Drain on paper towels and keep warm while you cook the rest, adding more oil as needed. To serve, cut the pancakes into wedges and serve hot.

# ginger-lime–glazed bean curd skewers

makes 4 servings

*The heady ginger-lime marinade complements the tofu, which soaks it up readily. Remember to immerse bamboo skewers in water for 30 minutes prior to using, to prevent them from burning. Note: You can strain the reserved marinade to remove the bits of ginger and garlic before serving in small dipping bowls. For added interest, sprinkle some crushed peanuts on top of the dipping sauce.*

½ cup soy sauce

1½ tablespoons grated fresh ginger

2 tablespoons fresh lime juice

2 tablespoons rice wine vinegar

1 garlic clove, minced

1 tablespoon light brown sugar

1 pound extra-firm tofu, drained and cut into
    1½-inch cubes

1. In a small bowl, combine the soy sauce, ginger, lime juice, vinegar, garlic, and sugar and set aside. Thread the tofu onto presoaked bamboo skewers and arrange them in a single layer on a baking pan. Pour the marinade over the tofu, turning to coat. Marinate at least 30 minutes at room temperature, or up to 2 hours in the refrigerator.

2. Preheat the grill or broiler. Remove the tofu skewers from the pan and reserve the marinade. Place the skewers on an oiled grill or under the broiler until browned, about 5 minutes per side. While the tofu skewers are browning, heat the reserved marinade in a small saucepan and serve with the tofu.

# tempeh satay

makes 4 servings

*A popular street food in many Asian countries, satay—grilled, skewered foods—originated in Indonesia and is usually made with chicken or other meats. Here it is made with tempeh, which, coincidentally, also came from Indonesia. This recipe can also be made with seitan or extra-firm tofu. Be sure to soak bamboo skewers in water for 30 minutes before using to prevent burning.*

8 ounces tempeh

2 teaspoons sugar

½ teaspoon ground coriander

½ teaspoon ground cumin

½ teaspoon turmeric

¼ teaspoon salt

⅛ teaspoon freshly ground black pepper

¼ cup unsweetened coconut milk

2 tablespoons soy sauce

2 teaspoons fresh lime juice

2 tablespoons canola or grapeseed oil

Satay Sauce (recipe follows)

Lime wedges, for garnish

Cilantro sprigs, for garnish

1. Cut the tempeh into ½-inch-thick pieces, 1 inch wide by 2 inches long. In a medium saucepan of simmering water, cook the tempeh for 30 minutes, then place in a shallow bowl and set aside.

2. In a small bowl, combine the sugar, coriander, cumin, turmeric, salt, and pepper. Stir in the coconut milk, soy sauce, and lime juice. Spoon the coconut mixture over the tempeh, turning to coat. Set aside for 30 minutes or cover and refrigerate overnight.

3. Preheat a grill or broiler. Thread the tempeh onto presoaked bamboo skewers, brush with the oil, and cook until browned and heated through, turning frequently, 10 to 15 minutes. Meanwhile, heat the satay sauce. To serve, arrange the tempeh skewers on a platter and garnish with lime wedges and cilantro, alongside a bowl of warm satay sauce.

## satay sauce

makes about 1¼ cups

1 medium shallot, chopped
1 garlic clove, chopped
1 teaspoon Asian chili paste
⅓ cup creamy peanut butter
1½ tablespoons rice vinegar
1 teaspoon soy sauce
1 tablespoon sugar
¾ cup unsweetened coconut milk

1. In a blender or food processor, combine the shallot, garlic, and chili paste and blend to a paste. Add the peanut butter, rice vinegar, soy sauce, sugar, and coconut milk. Blend until smooth.

2. Transfer the mixture to a small saucepan and bring to a boil. Reduce heat to low and cook, stirring, for 5 minutes. Add a little water if the sauce becomes too thick. Transfer to a small bowl and serve warm. If not using right away cover and refrigerate until needed. Properly stored, the sauce will keep 2 to 3 days. When ready to use, heat in a saucepan over low heat until warm.

## wanted: vegan wontons

Since commercial wonton wrappers generally contain eggs, making homemade vegan wonton wrappers is a matter of necessity for those who want to enjoy the versatility of this Asian staple. Use the recipe below to make the Steamed Vegetable Dumplings (page 42) or the In-Lieu-of-Crab Wontons (page 42).

## vegan wonton wrappers

makes about 20 wrappers

1 cup all-purpose flour
½ teaspoon salt
½ cup hot water

1. In a food processor, combine the flour, salt, and hot water. Process into a smooth dough. The dough can be mixed by hand in a bowl, if you prefer. When a dough ball is formed, dust it with flour and cover it with plastic wrap. Set aside for 30 minutes or up to an hour.

2. Place the dough on a lightly floured board, and knead for 2 minutes. Roll into a log, about 1 inch in diameter. Cut the log crosswise into 1-inch pieces. Flatten the pieces of dough on a lightly floured work surface. Use a rolling pin to roll each piece into a very thin round wrapper, about 3½ inches in diameter. Repeat with remaining dough. If not using right away, stack each wrapper between pieces of plastic wrap, then wrap them together. Properly stored the wrappers will keep in the refrigerator for up to a week or in the freezer for up to a month.

# in-lieu-of-crab wontons

makes 4 to 6 servings

*There's something magical about a hot appe-tizer that delivers a crisp pastry outside and a creamy savory filling. The taste of the sea comes from nori seaweed and oyster mush-rooms, although the flavor is still quite good when made with regular white mushrooms. Vegan cream cheese is available in natural food stores and well-stocked supermarkets. My favorite brand is Tofutti Better Than Cream Cheese (the nonhydrogenated kind).*

1 tablespoon canola or grapeseed oil, plus more for frying

1 garlic clove, minced

¼ cup minced green onions

8 ounces oyster mushrooms or other mushrooms, trimmed and chopped

1 teaspoon soy sauce

Splash of Tabasco sauce

4 ounces vegan cream cheese

16 to 20 Vegan Wonton Wrappers (page 41)

2 nori sheets, cut into 2-inch squares

1. In a small skillet, heat 1 tablespoon of the oil over medium heat. Add the garlic and green onions and cook until softened, about 45 sec-onds. Add the mushrooms and cook, stirring occasionally, until tender. Add the soy sauce and Tabasco, and remove from heat. Stir in the cream cheese until well blended. Set aside to cool completely.

2. Arrange the wonton wrappers on a work surface. Place a piece of the nori on top of each wonton wrapper and top with a small teaspoonful of the filling mixture. Fold the wontons over to make a semicircle and seal the edges with a bit of water. Repeat until all the filling mixture is used up.

3. In a large skillet, heat a thin layer of oil over medium-high heat. Add the wontons in batches and cook, turning gently, until crisp and golden brown, about 5 minutes. Keep the cooked wontons warm while you fry the rest. Serve warm.

# steamed vegetable dumplings

makes 4 to 6 servings

*These soft yet chewy dumplings can be enjoyed as an appetizer with a soy dipping sauce, but they are also delicious when served as a soup in a light Asian broth, such as Dashi (page 143).*

2 cups fresh baby spinach

2 cups finely chopped napa cabbage

1 cup chopped white or shiitake mushrooms

½ cup shredded carrot

¼ cup minced green onions

1 garlic clove, minced

1 tablespoon grated fresh ginger

1 teaspoon toasted sesame oil

¾ teaspoon cornstarch

½ teaspoon salt

16 to 20 Vegan Wonton Wrappers (page 41)

1. Steam the spinach, cabbage, mushrooms, and carrot just long enough to soften, about 2 min-utes. Blot dry to remove any liquid. Transfer the vegetables to a food processor and add the green onions, garlic, ginger, sesame oil, corn-starch, and salt. Process until well combined.

2. Working with 1 wonton wrapper at a time, place on a work surface and spoon 1 table-spoon of the filling mixture onto the wrap-per. Fold the wrapper over the filling to form a semicircle. Moisten the edges of the wrapper with water to seal. Repeat with the remaining wrappers and filling.

**3.** Steam the dumplings until cooked through, about 10 minutes. Serve immediately.

# artichoke-mushroom phyllo packets
makes about 24 packets

*The earthy flavors of artichokes and mush-rooms combine beautifully in this tasty fill-ing that also makes a yummy topping for bruschetta. If not used right away, these tasty pastry packages can be assembled ahead and frozen for baking at another time. This can be especially helpful when planning a party so you can get some of the work done ahead of time. If frozen artichoke hearts are unavail-able, substitute a 15-ounce can (not the marinated kind) and proceed with the recipe from Step 2. Variation: Instead of artichokes, substitute 2 (10-ounce) packages of frozen spinach.*

2 (10-ounce) packages frozen artichoke hearts
½ cup plus 1 tablespoon olive oil
1 small yellow onion, chopped
8 ounces white mushrooms, chopped
2 garlic cloves, chopped
1 tablespoon minced fresh parsley
½ teaspoon Dijon mustard
½ teaspoon dried thyme
½ teaspoon salt
¼ teaspoon freshly ground black pepper
1 (16-ounce) package frozen phyllo pastry,
   thawed

**1.** In a medium saucepan of boiling salted water, cook the artichoke hearts until tender, about 10 minutes. Drain well and set aside.

**2.** In a large skillet, heat 1 tablespoon of the oil over medium heat. Add the onion, cover, and cook until softened, about 5 minutes. Stir in the mushrooms and garlic and cook uncov-ered until the mushrooms soften and the liquid is absorbed, about 7 minutes.

**3.** Transfer the mixture to a food processor and add the cooked artichokes, parsley, mus-tard, thyme, salt, and pepper. Process until the artichokes are finely chopped and the mixture is well blended.

**4.** Preheat the oven to 375°F. Lightly oil a baking sheet. Divide the phyllo sheets in half. Tightly wrap half the sheets and reserve for another use. Cut the remaining sheets length-wise into thirds.

**5.** Place one strip of phyllo on a flat surface. Cover the remaining phyllo with a clean damp cloth. Lightly brush the strip of phyllo with oil. Top with another strip and brush with more oil. Spoon a small amount of the filling mixture across one short end of the pastry, about 2 inches from the end. Fold the end up over the filling. Fold the side in and continue folding the filled end of the pastry until you come to the end of the strip. You should end up with a small rectangular packet.

**6.** Place the packet on the prepared baking sheet and brush the top with oil. Repeat with the remaining phyllo strips until the filling is used up. Bake until golden brown, about 15 minutes. Serve hot.

# vegetable pakoras

makes 4 pakoras

*Pakoras are small crisp fried fritters, usually made with one or more vegetables. In addition to the vegetables suggested below, sliced carrots, potatoes, and cauliflower are good choices. Serve with your favorite chutney or with Tamarind Sauce (page 555). Look for chickpea flour in Indian markets (where it is called "gram" or "besan"). It can also be found at Italian markets (where it is called "ceci flour") and specialty grocers.*

1 cup chickpea flour

1 teaspoon salt

½ teaspoon baking powder

1 teaspoon hot or mild curry powder
    or garam masala

½ teaspoon ground cumin

½ teaspoon ground coriander

¼ teaspoon turmeric

¼ teaspoon ground cayenne

1 tablespoon canola or grapeseed oil,
    plus more for frying

¾ cup warm water

1 cup broccoli florets, blanched

1 cup peeled and sliced sweet potatoes,
    steamed until just tender

½ large yellow onion, cut into ½-inch slices

1. In a large bowl, combine the flour, salt, baking powder, curry powder, cumin, coriander, turmeric, and cayenne. Stir in the 1 tablespoon of oil and the water and mix well to make a smooth batter. Set aside to rest.

2. In a large skillet, heat a thin layer of oil over medium-high heat. Dip the broccoli, sweet potato slices, and onion slices in the batter to coat, then place them in the hot oil and fry until lightly browned, 4 to 5 minutes. Drain on paper towels and serve hot.

# potato samosas

makes 4 samosas

*Samosas are crisp pastry pillows filled with a savory blend. In this case the filling is a yummy potato and onion mixture that is good enough to eat right out of the bowl, so make sure you save enough to make the samosas. Some thawed frozen green peas or cooked chopped spinach or cauliflower can be added to the filling mixture, if desired. Serve the samosas with Tamarind Sauce (page 555) or a dipping sauce of your choice. Leftover samosa filling can be shaped into small patties and fried in a small amount of oil for crisp and tasty fritters.*

2 cups all-purpose flour

Salt

¾ cup water, or as needed

2 tablespoons unsweetened soy milk

4 tablespoons canola or grapeseed oil,
    plus more for frying

1 pound baking potatoes, peeled and cut into
    ½-inch dice

1 large yellow onion, chopped

1 teaspoon grated fresh ginger

2 teaspoons hot or mild curry powder
    or garam masala

½ teaspoon ground coriander

½ teaspoon turmeric

¼ teaspoon ground cayenne

1. In a large bowl, combine the flour, 1 teaspoon salt, water, soy milk, and 2 tablespoons oil and mix until crumbly. Knead into a dough, adding more water if needed. Cover and set aside for 20 minutes.

2. Steam the potatoes until tender, about 15 minutes. In a large skillet, heat 1 tablespoon of the remaining oil over medium heat. Add the onion, cover, and cook until soft, about

7 minutes. Stir in the ginger, curry powder, coriander, turmeric, cayenne, and salt to taste. Add the potatoes, stirring to mix well and mash the potatoes slightly. Remove from heat and set aside to cool.

3. Roll out the dough into a large rectangle on a floured board. Use a pastry cutter or a knife to cut the dough into 5-inch squares. Place a spoonful of the filling mixture into the center and fold the dough over, sealing the sides together with a small amount of water. Repeat with remaining ingredients.

4. In a deep skillet, heat a thin layer of oil over medium heat. Fry the samosas, turning once, until golden brown, 2 to 3 minutes per side. Drain on paper towels. If not using right away, the samosas can be reheated in a 350° F oven until hot.

# chickpea kofta with chutney dipping sauce

makes about 24 kofta

*Kofta are spiced Indian dumplings or "meatballs" usually served as a main dish in a creamy gravy. Transform them into an appetizer by flattening them and arranging them on a platter served with a dipping sauce. You can make them ahead and then reheat them when ready to serve.*

1¼ cups water
½ cup medium-grind bulgur
Salt
½ cup mango chutney, homemade (page 561) or store-bought
1 tablespoon fresh lime juice

¼ cup plus 1 tablespoon minced fresh cilantro
1½ cups cooked or 1 (15.5-ounce) can chickpeas, drained and rinsed
1 garlic clove, crushed
1 teaspoon ground coriander
½ teaspoon ground cardamom
¼ teaspoon ground cumin
Freshly ground black pepper
Canola or grapeseed oil, for frying

1. In a small saucepan, bring the water to boil over high heat. Add the bulgur and salt the water. Cover, and remove from heat. Set aside until the bulgur is tender, 15 to 20 minutes.

2. In a blender or food processor, combine the chutney, lime juice, and the 1 tablespoon of cilantro and blend until smooth. Transfer to a small bowl and set aside.

3. In a food processor, combine the chickpeas, garlic, remaining ¼ cup cilantro, coriander, cardamom, cumin, and salt and pepper to taste. Process until smooth.

4. Combine the chickpea mixture with the reserved bulgur and form into balls, about 1 inch in diameter. Flatten the balls until they are ½-inch patties.

5. In a large skillet, heat a thin layer of oil over medium heat. Add the kofta and cook, in batches if necessary, turning gently, until golden brown all over, about 15 minutes. Serve hot, accompanied by the sauce.

**baked chickpea kofta:** Instead of frying the kofta, they may be lightly brushed with oil and baked in a 400°F oven in a nonstick baking pan until golden brown, about 10 minutes.

# SALADS

## LEAFY GREEN SALADS

butterhead lettuce and walnut salad with raspberry-walnut vinaigrette

romaine and grape tomato salad with avocado and baby peas

arugula and apple salad with creamy mustard dressing

mixed lettuces with white radish, snow peas, and yuzu dressing

strawberry field greens with black olives and toasted pine nuts

watercress, fennel, and avocado salad with dried cherries and macadamias

leaf lettuce and grilled radicchio salad with lemony dressing

baby greens with pear, pecans, and ginger dressing

greek goddess salad

spinach salad with almonds, fuji apple, and figs

spinach salad with orange-dijon dressing

## VEGETABLE SALADS

chopped salad

carrot and orange salad with cashews and cilantro

dazzling vegetable salad

cucumber-radish salad with tarragon vinaigrette

mango and snow pea salad

autumn harvest salad

indonesian green bean salad with cabbage and carrots

giardiniera

chilled cucumber salad

daikon salad

sesame-cucumber salad

eggplant and bell pepper salad

corn and red bean salad

caponata salad

yellow mung bean salad with broccoli and mango

green bean and pear salad with almonds

cranberry-carrot salad with citrus-walnut vinaigrette

fennel-orange salad with black olives and pine nuts

yellow beet salad with pears and pecans

endive and orange salad with toasted pecans

fresh tomato salad

tuscan bread and tomato salad

syrian bread salad

edamame and snow pea salad with lime-ginger dressing

## Potato Salads and Slaws

retro potato salad redux

french-style potato salad

three-alarm potato salad

roasted potato salad
with chickpeas and sun-dried
tomatoes

potato and white bean salad
with roasted red pepper

german-style potato salad

potato salad with artichoke
hearts and grape tomatoes

potato salad with seitan strips
and tarragon-mustard
vinaigrette

indonesian-style potato salad

sweet potato and broccoli
salad with pomegranate-peanut
dressing

creamy coleslaw

german-style kool-sla

red cabbage slaw with
black-vinegar dressing

asian slaw

crunchy sesame slaw

rainbow slaw

broccoli slaw with apple
and walnuts

tahini broccoli slaw

spicy southwestern-style
coleslaw

## Bean, Grain, and Pasta Salads

tropical black bean salad
with mango

white bean salad with
fennel and avocado

warm lentil salad with walnuts

lentil salad with chiles

southwestern three-bean salad

black bean and corn salad
with cilantro dressing

grilled vegetable antipasto
salad with chickpeas

provençal white bean salad

white bean and broccoli
salad with parsley-walnut pesto

chickpea "tuna" salad
in avocados

puttanesca seitan
and spinach salad

curried walnut "chicken" salad

chinese "chicken" salad

rice salad with cashews
and dried papaya

roasted cauliflower and rice
salad with dijon vinaigrette

white and wild rice salad
with walnuts, cranberries,
and figs

brown rice salad with
black-eyed peas

eight treasure barley salad

pistachio-pear couscous salad

golden couscous salad

 = fast

classic tabbouleh

garden variety couscous
tabbouleh

quinoa salad with black beans
and tomatoes

southwestern quinoa salad
with pinto beans and corn

mediterranean quinoa salad

pasta salad with grilled summer
vegetables

winter pasta salad with creamy
mustard vinaigrette

tarragon pasta salad
with red and green grapes

california pasta salad

farfalle with crunchy crucifers
and creamy poppy seed
dressing

last-minute italian-style
pasta salad

macaroni salad

creamy curry pasta and
vegetable salad

rotini remoulade

asian noodle salad with tempeh

sesame udon salad
with adzuki beans and
baby spinach

chilled glass noodles
with snow peas and baked tofu

## FRUIT SALADS

mango-avocado salad
with macadamias and
pomegranate seeds

blazing sunset salad

fruit salad in winter

summer berries with fresh mint

curried fruit salad

"mixed grill" fruit platter

fruit salad with a hint of heat

orange and fig salad with
walnuts and dried cherries

strawberry, mango,
and pineapple salad with
banana-lime dressing

cherry berry watermelon salad

## SALAD DRESSINGS

basic balsamic vinaigrette

dijon vinaigrette

oh-my-goddess dressing

tarragon-chive vinaigrette

carrot-ginger dressing

green olive herb dressing

creamy cucumber dressing

creamy artichoke dressing

sesame-orange dressing

lemony white miso vinaigrette

creamy avocado dressing

creamy tahini dressing

lime-cilantro dressing

citrus vinaigrette

ginger soy vinaigrette

Today's supermarkets offer an amazing array of lettuce varieties and salad greens, from mesclun mix, field greens, and baby spinach, to crunchy romaine, assertive arugula, and soft leaf lettuces like Bibb and Boston. But, as this chapter attests, there is a lot more to salads than just greens.

In addition to light and leafy salads, this chapter includes many globally inspired vegetable-centric dishes, such as Mango and Snow Pea Salad, Eggplant and Bell Pepper Salad, and Tuscan Bread and Tomato Salad. There are also numerous hearty main dish salads made with grains, pasta, and beans, such as Lentil Salad with Chiles, Mediterranean Quinoa Salad, and Tropical Black Bean Salad with Mango.

Rounding out the collection are recipes for delicious potato salads, slaws, and fruit salads, including Potato Salad with Seitan Strips and Tarragon-Mustard Vinaigrette, Spicy Southwestern-Style Coleslaw, and Cherry Berry Watermelon Salad.

A good dressing is a vital part of any salad. The chapter concludes with several recipes for delicious salad dressings that add a personal touch to any salad. The basic dressing of a green salad can be as simple as oil and vinegar, but with so many fragrant oils and aged vinegars, the flavor combinations are seemingly endless. Citrus, lemon juice in particular, is sometimes used to replace the vinegar in salad dressings. And while the basic oil-and-vinegar combination requires little more than a bit of salt, you can, in fact, enhance these simple ingredients with the addition of garlic, shallots, herbs, and spices.

# LEAFY GREEN SALADS

## butterhead lettuce and walnut salad with raspberry-walnut vinaigrette ●

makes 4 servings

*This elegant salad is an ideal first course for a special dinner. Olive oil can be used to replace the walnut oil if desired.*

1 tablespoon raspberry jam
2 tablespoons sherry vinegar
¼ cup walnut oil
Salt and freshly ground black pepper
1 medium head butterhead lettuce, torn into bite-size pieces
⅓ cup toasted coarsely chopped walnuts
2 tablespoons coarsely chopped red onion
½ cup fresh raspberries

1. In a blender or food processor, combine the jam, vinegar, oil, and salt and pepper to taste. Blend until smooth.

2. In a large bowl, combine the lettuce, walnuts, and onion. Add the dressing and toss gently to combine. Divide among salad plates and garnish with fresh raspberries.

## romaine and grape tomato salad with avocado and baby peas ●

makes 4 servings

*This flavorful salad, made with crisp romaine lettuce, can easily be transformed into a main dish by adding a can of chickpeas or diced baked tofu and served with toasted garlic bread.*

1 garlic clove, chopped
1 tablespoon chopped shallot
½ teaspoon dried basil
½ teaspoon salt
⅛ teaspoon freshly ground black pepper
¼ teaspoon sugar
3 tablespoons white wine vinegar
⅓ cup olive oil
1 medium head romaine lettuce, cut into ¼-inch strips
12 ripe grape tomatoes, halved
½ cup frozen baby peas, thawed
8 kalamata olives, pitted
1 ripe Hass avocado

1. In a blender or food processor, combine the garlic, shallot, basil, salt, pepper, sugar, and vinegar until smooth. Add the oil and blend until emulsified. Set aside.

2. In a large bowl, combine the lettuce, tomatoes, peas, and olives. Pit and peel the avocado and cut into ½-inch dice. Add to the bowl, along with enough dressing to lightly coat. Toss gently to combine and serve.

## arugula and apple salad with creamy mustard dressing ●

makes 4 servings

*The sweetness of the apple balances nicely with the assertive flavors of arugula, red onion, and the tangy mustard dressing.*

2 tablespoons white wine vinegar
1 tablespoon Dijon mustard
1 tablespoon minced fresh parsley

# salad basics

With bagged lettuce blends and bottled dressings widely available, putting a salad together can be as simple as toss and serve. But bagged salads can be expensive and less than fresh, and bottled dressings can be hit or miss in terms of flavor (not to mention expensive).

Sometimes less really is more. Take the classic French green salad, which consists of butterhead lettuce dressed with a simple vinaigrette. When the lettuce is fresh, and the vinaigrette made with high-quality oil and vinegar, the flavor is beyond comparison.

A salad doesn't have to be complicated or contain a mile-long list of ingredients, but the lettuce and other ingredients do need to be the freshest possible and the dressing of good quality.

While a simple green salad with a light vinaigrette is lovely, most of us enjoy some variety. There are no hard-and-fast rules to salad making: you can combine a variety of greens, soft tender leaves such as Boston or Bibb, bitter ones like arugula or chicory, and crunchy ones such as romaine.

Embellishments such as raw or cooked vegetables, fresh or dried fruit, toasted nuts, or cooked beans can add flavor, color, and texture to salads. Infuse your vinaigrette with garlic, mustard, and/or fresh herbs such as basil, parsley, or tarragon.

Also, experiment with oils and vinegars. If you don't want the pronounced flavor of olive oil, substitute grapeseed oil. If you want a distinctive nutty flavor, consider adding some walnut or toasted sesame oil. For variety, be sure to keep an array of vinegars on hand, including balsamic, sherry, rice, and cider. Use lemon or lime juice instead of vinegar when it seems appropriate. Rich creamy dressings are usually best on crisp lettuces, while lighter dressings do better on softer leaves.

⅓ cup olive oil

½ teaspoon salt

¼ teaspoon freshly ground black pepper

2 cups arugula leaves

3 cups chopped leaf lettuce

½ small red onion, cut into ¼-inch slices

1 apple, such as Gala or Fuji, halved, cored, and cut into ¼-inch slices

1. In a small bowl, combine the vinegar, mustard, parsley, oil, salt, and pepper. Whisk until emulsified. Set aside to allow flavors to blend, 10 to 15 minutes.

2. In a large bowl, combine the arugula, leaf lettuce, onion, and apple. Add enough dressing to lightly coat. Toss gently to combine and serve.

## mixed lettuces with white radish, snow peas, and yuzu dressing 🅕

makes 4 servings

*Yuzu vinegar is made from the juice of the yuzu, a sour Japanese citrus fruit. If yuzu vinegar is unavailable, substitute 1½ tablespoons rice vinegar plus 1 tablespoon fresh lemon juice.*

2½ tablespoons Japanese yuzu vinegar
    (see headnote)

1 tablespoon minced shallot

½ teaspoon agave nectar

½ teaspoon salt

¼ teaspoon freshly ground black pepper

⅓ cup olive oil

5 cups mixed lettuce leaves (torn or chopped
    if large)

3 small white radishes, cut into ⅛-inch slices

12 snow peas, trimmed, blanched, and cut
    diagonally into thirds

1. In a small bowl, combine the vinegar, shallot, agave nectar, salt, and pepper. Whisk in the oil, and taste, adjusting seasonings if necessary.

2. In a large bowl, combine the lettuce, radishes, and snow peas. Add enough dressing to lightly coat. Toss gently to combine and serve.

## strawberry field greens with black olives and toasted pine nuts 🅕

makes 4 servings

*The texture and flavor harmonies created by combining black olives, strawberries, and pine nuts will make you want to serve strawberry field greens—forever. Field greens are sold in bags or in bulk in well-stocked supermarkets and specialty grocers. If unavailable under that moniker, any mixed baby lettuces will do. Olive oil may be used instead of walnut oil, if you prefer.*

1 tablespoon chopped green onions

¼ cup chopped fresh parsley

¼ cup walnut oil

1½ tablespoons fresh lemon juice

½ teaspoon sugar

½ teaspoon salt

Freshly ground black pepper

5 cups mixed field greens

¼ cup chopped pitted kalamata olives

¾ cup sliced hulled fresh strawberries

2 tablespoons toasted pine nuts

1. In a blender or food processor, combine the green onions, parsley, oil, lemon juice, sugar, salt, and pepper to taste, and process until smooth. Set aside.

2. In a large bowl, combine the field greens, olives, strawberries, and pine nuts. Add enough dressing to lightly coat. Toss gently to combine and serve.

# watercress, fennel, and avocado salad with dried cherries and macadamias ⓕ

makes 4 servings

*This gorgeous salad is one of my favorites—whenever I make it, I find myself humming "these are a few of my favorite things." What's not to love about a colorful salad made with peppery watercress, fragrant fennel, and creamy avocado, teamed up with sweet dried cherries, crunchy macadamia nuts, and a light sherry vinaigrette? Since dried cherries can be pricey, you can substitute the more economical dried cranberries, if you wish. If watercress is unavailable, substitute one or more of your favorite salad greens and start humming.*

1 tablespoon chopped shallot
⅓ cup olive oil
3 tablespoons sherry vinegar
¾ teaspoon salt
¼ teaspoon sugar
⅛ teaspoon freshly ground black pepper
2 medium bunches watercress, tough stems removed
1 fennel bulb, cut into ¼-inch slices
⅓ cup dried cherries or sweetened dried cranberries
¼ cup macadamia nuts, coarsely chopped
1 ripe Hass avocado, pitted, peeled, and
    cut into ¼-inch dice

1. In a blender or food processor, combine the shallot, oil, vinegar, salt, sugar, and pepper and blend until smooth. Set aside.

2. In a large bowl, combine the watercress, fennel, cherries, and macadamias. Add the avocado to the salad, along with enough dressing to coat. Toss gently to combine and serve.

# leaf lettuce and grilled radicchio salad with lemony dressing ⓕ

makes 4 servings

*Grilling mellows the slightly bitter flavor of radicchio, a member of the chicory family. The creamy sweet-tart dressing is an ideal complement.*

1 medium head radicchio, quartered
¼ cup olive oil, plus more to coat the radicchio
1 medium head leaf lettuce, torn into bite-size
    pieces
1 small red or yellow bell pepper, cut into matchsticks
¼ cup raw cashews
¼ cup chopped green onions
¼ cup water
3 tablespoons fresh lemon juice
1 teaspoon pure maple syrup
½ teaspoon salt
⅛ teaspoon ground cayenne

1. Preheat the grill or broiler. Coat the radicchio with oil and grill or broil until the leaves begin to char around the edges, turning and brushing with more oil, as necessary, about 6 minutes total.

2. Cut the radicchio halves in half lengthwise, then cut crosswise into 1-inch strips and place in a large bowl. Add the leaf lettuce and bell pepper and set aside.

3. In a blender, grind the cashews to a fine powder. Add the green onions and water and blend until smooth. Add the lemon juice, maple syrup, salt, cayenne, and the remaining ¼ cup of oil. Blend until smooth and creamy. Add enough dressing to the salad to coat. Toss gently to combine and serve.

# baby greens with pear, pecans, and ginger dressing

makes 4 servings

*The natural affinity of ginger and pear are further enhanced by the crunchy texture of pecans in this delicious salad. Baby greens are used for their delicate taste and visual appeal, but other salad greens, alone or in combination, may be used instead.*

3 tablespoons sherry vinegar

1 medium shallot, minced

2 teaspoons grated fresh ginger

½ teaspoon sugar

⅛ teaspoon dry mustard

⅛ teaspoon ground cayenne

½ teaspoon salt

⅓ cup olive oil

5 cups mixed baby greens

2 celery ribs, cut into ¼-inch slices

½ cup toasted pecan pieces

1 ripe pear, such as Bosc or Anjou

1. In a small bowl, combine the vinegar, shallot, ginger, sugar, mustard, cayenne, and salt. Whisk in the oil and set aside.

2. In a large bowl, combine the greens, celery, and pecans. Core the pear and cut into ¼-inch dice. Add the pear to the salad and add enough dressing to lightly coat. Toss gently to combine and serve.

# greek goddess salad

makes 4 servings

*A tangy "goddess" dressing combined with crisp romaine lettuce, olives, and tofu feta creates a heavenly Greek salad.*

1 medium head romaine lettuce, torn into bite-size pieces

1 medium English cucumber, peeled, seeded, and chopped

1 ripe tomato, cut into bite-size pieces

3 canned artichoke hearts, drained and quartered

½ small red onion, cut into ¼-inch slices

½ cup kalamata olives, pitted and halved

¼ cup toasted pine nuts

¼ cup chopped fresh parsley

½ cup Oh-My-Goddess Dressing (page 99)

8 ounces Tofu Feta (page 358)

In a large bowl, combine the lettuce, cucumber, tomato, artichoke hearts, onion, olives, pine nuts, and parsley. Add the dressing and toss gently to combine. Top with the tofu feta and serve.

# spinach salad with almonds, fuji apple, and figs 🅕

makes 4 servings

*This salad, resplendent with delicious bits of almonds, figs, and apple, makes a great first course for a winter meal. If a Fuji apple is unavailable, substitute a Gala, Delicious, or other good eating apple.*

¼ cup olive oil
2 tablespoons white balsamic vinegar
½ teaspoon sugar
Salt and freshly ground black pepper
5 cups fresh baby spinach
1 cup toasted slivered almonds
½ cup sliced or chopped figs
1 Fuji apple, peeled, cored, and cut into ¼-inch dice

1. In a small bowl, combine the oil, vinegar, sugar, and salt and pepper to taste. Blend well and set aside.

2. In a large bowl, combine the spinach, almonds, and figs. Add the apple along with the dressing. Toss gently to combine and serve.

# spinach salad with orange-dijon dressing 🅕

makes 4 servings

*The refreshing taste of orange adds sparkle to this lovely salad made with tender baby spinach.*

2 tablespoons Dijon mustard
2 tablespoons olive oil
¼ cup fresh orange juice
1 teaspoon agave nectar
½ teaspoon salt
¼ teaspoon freshly ground black pepper
2 tablespoons minced fresh parsley
1 tablespoon minced green onions
5 cups fresh baby spinach, torn into bite-size pieces
1 navel orange, peeled and segmented
½ small red onion, sliced paper thin

1. In a blender or food processor combine the mustard, oil, orange juice, agave nectar, salt, pepper, parsley, and green onions. Blend well and set aside.

2. In a large bowl, combine the spinach, orange, and onion. Add the dressing, toss gently to combine, and serve.

# Vegetable Salads

## chopped salad 🅕

makes 4 servings

*The classic chopped salad has almost endless variations. It is basically lettuce and a dressing with whatever additional salad ingredients you enjoy—feel free to add some chopped red bell pepper, artichoke hearts, baked tofu, or other ingredients, according to your personal preference. Depending on what ingredients you add, this salad can be hearty enough to serve as a main dish.*

¾ cup olive oil

¼ cup white wine vinegar

2 teaspoons Dijon mustard

1 garlic clove

1 tablespoon minced green onions

½ teaspoon salt

¼ teaspoon ground black pepper

½ small head romaine lettuce, chopped

½ small head iceberg lettuce, chopped

1½ cups cooked or 1 (15.5-ounce) can chickpeas, drained and rinsed

2 ripe tomatoes, cut into ½-inch dice

1 medium English cucumber, peeled, halved lengthwise, and chopped

2 celery ribs, chopped celery

1 medium carrot, chopped

½ cup halved pitted kalamata olives

3 small red radishes, chopped

2 tablespoons chopped fresh parsley

1 ripe Hass avocado, pitted, peeled, and cut into ½-inch dice

1. In a blender or food processor, combine the oil, vinegar, mustard, garlic, green onions, salt, and pepper. Blend well and set aside.

2. In a large bowl, combine the romaine and iceberg lettuces. Add the chickpeas, tomatoes, cucumber, celery, carrot, olives, radishes, parsley, and avocado. Add enough dressing to lightly coat. Toss gently to combine and serve.

## carrot and orange salad with cashews and cilantro 🅕

makes 4 servings

*I've always loved the flavor combination of carrot and orange, whether in a juice blend, cooked side dish, or muffin, so when I wanted to develop a great-tasting carrot salad, I reached for the oranges. Further complemented by crunchy cashews, aromatic cilantro, and a touch of lime, the result is a delightful merging of color, texture, and flavor and a refreshing and flavorful way to get your vitamin C and beta-carotene.*

1 pound carrots, shredded

2 oranges, peeled, segmented, and chopped

½ cup unsalted roasted cashews

¼ cup chopped fresh cilantro

2 tablespoons fresh orange juice

2 tablespoons fresh lime juice

2 teaspoons sugar

Salt and freshly ground black pepper

⅓ cup olive oil

1. In a large bowl, combine the carrots, oranges, cashews, and cilantro and set aside.

2. In a small bowl, combine the orange juice, lime juice, sugar, and salt and pepper to taste. Whisk in the oil until blended. Pour the dressing over the carrot mixture, stirring to lightly coat. Taste, adjusting seasonings if necessary. Toss gently to combine and serve.

## dazzling vegetable salad 🅕

makes 4 servings

*Colorful vegetables with a variety of flavor and textural elements add up to one dazzling—and delicious—salad. If watercress is unavailable, coarsely chopped romaine works well in this salad.*

3 cups watercress, tough stems removed and coarsely chopped

1 medium carrot, shredded

1 cup finely shredded red cabbage

1 cup ripe grape or cherry tomatoes, halved

1 medium yellow bell pepper, cut into matchsticks

1½ cups cooked or 1 (15.5-ounce) can chickpeas, rinsed and drained

¼ cup halved pitted kalamata olives

1 ripe Hass avocado, pitted, peeled, and cut into ½-inch dice

¼ cup olive oil

1½ tablespoons fresh lemon juice

½ teaspoon salt

⅛ teaspoon freshly ground black pepper

Pinch sugar

1. In a large bowl, combine the watercress, carrot, cabbage, tomatoes, bell pepper, chickpeas, olives, and avocado and set aside.

2. In a small bowl, combine the oil, lemon juice, salt, black pepper, and sugar. Blend well and add to the salad. Toss gently to combine and serve.

## cucumber-radish salad with tarragon vinaigrette 🅕

makes 4 servings

*The peppery bite of radish combines nicely with the refreshing taste of cucumbers, unified by a light tarragon vinaigrette. This salad needs to be enjoyed within a few hours, otherwise the cucumbers will lose their crispness.*

2 medium English cucumbers, peeled, halved, seeded, cut into ¼-inch slices

6 small red radishes, cut into ⅛-inch slices

2½ tablespoons tarragon vinegar

½ teaspoon dried tarragon

¼ teaspoon sugar

Salt and freshly ground black pepper

¼ cup olive oil

1. In a large bowl, combine the cucumbers and the radishes and set aside.

2. In a small bowl, combine the vinegar, tarragon, sugar, and salt and pepper to taste. Whisk in the oil until well blended, then add the dressing to the salad. Toss gently to combine and serve.

# mango and snow pea salad 🅕

makes 4 servings

*A spicy peanut dressing provides a rich flavor accent to the crunchy snow peas and juicy sweet mangos in this gorgeous salad. Add some cooked noodles to transform it into a main dish meal—if you do, be sure to make a double batch of the dressing so you have enough to coat the noodles.*

½ teaspoon minced garlic

½ teaspoon grated fresh ginger

¼ cup creamy peanut butter

1 tablespoon plus 1 teaspoon light brown sugar

¼ teaspoon crushed red pepper

3 tablespoons rice vinegar

3 tablespoons water

1 tablespoon soy sauce

2 cups snow peas, trimmed and lightly blanched

2 ripe mangos, peeled, pitted, cut into ½-inch dice

1 large carrot, shredded

1 medium cucumber, peeled, halved lengthwise, and seeded

3 cups shredded romaine lettuce

½ cup chopped unsalted roasted peanuts, for garnish

1. In a small bowl, combine the garlic, ginger, peanut butter, sugar, and crushed red pepper. Stir in the vinegar, water, and soy sauce. Taste, adjusting seasonings, if necessary, and set aside.

2. Cut the snow peas diagonally into a thin matchsticks and place in a large bowl. Add the mangos and carrot. Cut the cucumber into ¼-inch slices and add to the bowl.

3. Pour the dressing onto the salad and toss gently to combine. Spoon the salad onto a bed of shredded lettuce, sprinkle with peanuts, and serve.

# autumn harvest salad

makes 4 servings

*The colors of autumn leaves and the vibrant produce of the season were the inspiration for this beautiful salad. For a dramatic presentation, serve it on a bed of shredded red cabbage and romaine lettuce, tossed with a little additional dressing.*

1 pound sweet potatoes, peeled and cut into ½-inch dice

1 tablespoon pure maple syrup

½ teaspoon Dijon mustard

½ teaspoon salt

2 tablespoons apple cider vinegar

⅓ cup grapeseed oil

1 ripe Bosc pear

1 crisp red-skinned apple, such as Red Delicious, Fuji, or Gala

2 celery ribs, chopped

½ cup toasted walnuts or pecans

¼ cup sweetened dried cranberries

2 green onions, minced

1. In a large saucepan of boiling salted water, cook the sweet potatoes until just tender, about 20 minutes. Drain well, place in a large bowl, and set aside.

2. In a separate large bowl, combine the maple syrup, mustard, salt, and vinegar. Whisk in the oil until well blended. Set aside.

3. Core the pear and apple and cut into ½-inch dice. Add them to the bowl with the dressing, and toss to coat. Add the pear and apple mixture to the sweet potatoes. Add the celery, walnuts, cranberries, and green onions. Toss gently to combine and serve.

# indonesian green bean salad with cabbage and carrots 🅕

makes 4 servings

*This tasty salad, loaded with flavor and crunch appeal, was inspired by gado gado, an Indonesian vegetable salad with a rich peanut dressing. Equally good served chilled or at room temperature, this salad can be made ahead and kept in the refrigerator for a day or two, a plus for busy people.*

2 cups green beans, trimmed and cut into 1-inch pieces

2 medium carrots, cut into ¼-inch slices

2 cups finely shredded cabbage

⅓ cup golden raisins

¼ cup unsalted roasted peanuts

1 garlic clove, minced

1 medium shallot, chopped

1½ teaspoons grated fresh ginger

⅓ cup creamy peanut butter

2 tablespoons soy sauce

2 tablespoons fresh lemon juice

1 teaspoon sugar

¼ teaspoon salt

⅛ teaspoon ground cayenne

¾ cup unsweetened coconut milk

1. Lightly steam the green beans, carrots, and cabbage for about 5 minutes, then place them in a large bowl. Add the raisins and peanuts and set aside to cool.

2. In a food processor or blender, puree the garlic, shallot, and ginger. Add the peanut butter, soy sauce, lemon juice, sugar, salt, and cayenne, and process until blended. Add the coconut milk and blend until smooth. Pour the dressing over the salad, toss gently to combine, and serve.

# giardiniera

makes 6 servings

*I find most commercial brands of this classic Italian vegetable salad to be too vinegary and expensive. Making your own is more cost-effective, and you can adjust the dressing to suit your taste.*

1 medium carrot, cut into ¼-inch rounds

1 medium red bell pepper, cut into ½-inch dice

1 cup small cauliflower florets

2 celery ribs, finely chopped

½ cup chopped onion

2 tablespoons salt

¼ cup sliced pimiento-stuffed green olives

1 garlic clove, minced

½ teaspoon sugar

½ teaspoon crushed red pepper

¼ teaspoon freshly ground black pepper

3 tablespoons white wine vinegar

⅓ cup olive oil

1. In a large bowl, combine the carrot, bell pepper, cauliflower, celery, and onion. Stir in the salt and add enough cold water to cover. Tightly cover the bowl and refrigerate for 4 to 6 hours.

2. Drain and rinse the vegetables and place them in a large bowl. Add the olives and set aside.

3. In a small bowl, combine the garlic, sugar, crushed red pepper, black pepper, vinegar, and oil, and mix well. Pour the dressing over the vegetables and toss gently to combine. Cover and refrigerate overnight before serving.

# chilled cucumber salad

makes 6 servings

*Thin slices of red onion add a lovely color contrast and burst of flavor to this versatile cucumber salad. By using a different herb or swapping out other ingredients, you can transform this simple salad into a range of flavors. See Variations below for some delicious options.*

2 medium English cucumbers, peeled and cut into ¼-inch slices

½ small red onion, cut into ⅛-inch slices

3 tablespoons fresh lemon juice

¼ cup olive oil

2 tablespoons chopped fresh dillweed

¼ teaspoon salt

⅛ teaspoon freshly ground black pepper

Pinch sugar

1. In a large bowl, combine the cucumbers and onion. Set aside.

2. In a small bowl, whisk together the lemon juice, oil, dillweed, salt, pepper, and sugar. Pour the dressing over the salad mixture and toss gently to coat. Refrigerate for 1 hour, until chilled and serve.

## variations:

- Instead of dillweed, use fresh basil and swap the red onion for garlic.
- Use cilantro instead of the dillweed and lime juice in place of the lemon.
- Replace the red onion with 3 or 4 minced green onions.
- Use sherry vinegar instead of the lemon juice.
- Instead of olive oil, use equal amounts of walnut oil and canola or grapeseed oil.
- Use parsley instead of the dillweed, and sprinkle with toasted chopped walnuts.

# daikon salad

makes 4 servings

*Black sesame seeds provide a dramatic garnish to this light and lovely Asian-style salad made with two kinds of radish. If black sesame seeds are unavailable, substitute toasted white sesame seeds or simply omit them. Mirin is a sweet Japanese cooking wine made from rice. Look for it in natural food stores, Asian markets, or well-stocked supermarkets.*

1 medium daikon radish, cut into ¼-inch slices

3 small red radishes, cut into ¼-inch slices

¼ cup rice vinegar

1 tablespoon sugar

2 teaspoons mirin (see headnote)

1 teaspoon toasted sesame oil

½ teaspoon salt

1 tablespoon black sesame seeds, for garnish

1. In a small bowl, combine the daikon and red radishes and set aside.

2. In a separate small bowl, combine the vinegar, sugar, mirin, oil, and salt, and mix well. Pour the dressing over the radishes. Set aside for at least 15 minutes before serving.

3. Spoon the radish salad into 4 small bowls, sprinkle with sesame seeds, and serve.

# sesame cucumber salad

makes 4 to 6 servings

*The light, delicate flavors of this Asian-flavored salad offer a sweet compliment to a sushi meal.*

2 medium English cucumbers, peeled and cut into ¼-inch slices

2 tablespoons chopped fresh parsley

3 tablespoons toasted sesame oil

2 tablespoons soy sauce

1 tablespoon mirin

2 teaspoons rice vinegar

1 teaspoon sugar

2 tablespoons toasted sesame seeds

1. In a small bowl, combine the cucumbers and parsley and set aside.

2. In a separate small bowl, combine the oil, soy sauce, mirin, vinegar, and sugar, stirring to blend. Pour the dressing over the cucumbers. Set aside for at least 10 minutes.

3. Spoon the cucumber salad into small bowls, sprinkle with sesame seeds, and serve.

# eggplant and bell pepper salad

makes 4 servings

*This recipe is inspired by a salad I enjoyed in a Moroccan restaurant. I like to use Japanese or Asian eggplants here because they have fewer seeds and a more delicate flavor than the Western globe eggplants. If Japanese eggplants are unavailable, use 1 medium globe eggplant instead. This salad tastes best when allowed to marinate for a bit.*

2 medium Japanese eggplants, cut into ½-inch dice

2 medium red bell peppers, cut into ½-inch dice

¼ cup olive oil

2 tablespoons white balsamic vinegar

1 garlic clove, minced

½ teaspoon sugar

½ teaspoon salt

¼ teaspoon crushed red pepper

1 small head romaine lettuce, torn into bite-size pieces

½ cup toasted walnut pieces, for garnish

1. Preheat the oven to 375°F. Lightly oil a 9 × 13-inch baking pan. Place the eggplants and bell peppers in the prepared pan, and bake until tender, 15 to 20 minutes. Transfer the eggplants and peppers to a large bowl and set aside to cool for 10 minutes.

2. In a small bowl, combine the oil, vinegar, garlic, sugar, salt, and crushed red pepper. Mix well and pour over the cooled vegetables. Cover and refrigerate for at least 30 minutes.

3. Spread the romaine on a serving platter. Spoon the eggplant and pepper mixture onto the romaine and top with the remaining marinade. Garnish with walnuts and serve.

# corn and red bean salad 🅕

makes 4 servings

*This hearty and colorful salad is a great accompaniment for the Seared Portobello Fajitas (page 125) or the Beer-Marinated Seitan Fajitas (page 125). To transform this salad into a tempting one-dish meal, combine it with about 3 cups of cooked long-grain brown rice.*

1 (10-ounce) package frozen corn kernels, cooked

1½ cups cooked or 1 (15.5-ounce) can dark red kidney beans, drained and rinsed

1 celery rib, cut into ¼-inch slices

2 green onions, minced

2 tablespoons chopped fresh cilantro or parsley

¼ cup olive oil

2 tablespoons white wine vinegar

½ teaspoon ground cumin

¼ teaspoon sugar

½ teaspoon salt

⅛ teaspoon freshly ground black pepper

1. In a large bowl, combine the corn, beans, celery, green onions, and cilantro, and set aside.

2. In a small bowl, combine the oil, vinegar, cumin, sugar, salt, and pepper. Mix well and pour the dressing over the vegetables. Toss gently to combine and serve.

# caponata salad

makes 6 servings

*This classic sweet-tart Sicilian eggplant salad can be enjoyed on its own or as part of an antipasto platter. It also makes a delicious bruschetta topping when served at room temperature.*

¼ cup olive oil

1 medium eggplant, peeled and cut into ¼-inch dice

1 small red onion, chopped

1 celery rib, chopped

2 garlic cloves, minced

2 cups chopped fresh or drained canned plum tomatoes

2 tablespoons capers

3 tablespoons red wine vinegar

2 teaspoons sugar

1 tablespoon minced fresh basil or 1 teaspoon dried

½ teaspoon salt

1. In a large saucepan, heat the oil over medium heat. Add the eggplant, onion, celery, and garlic. Cover and cook until the vegetables are softened, about 15 minutes. Add the tomatoes, cover, and cook 5 minutes longer. Stir in the capers, vinegar, sugar, basil, and salt and simmer, uncovered, for 5 minutes to allow flavors to develop.

2. Remove from heat and allow to cool slightly, then transfer to a large bowl and refrigerate until chilled, about 2 hours. Taste, adjusting seasonings if necessary. Serve chilled or at room temperature.

# yellow mung bean salad with broccoli and mango

makes 4 servings

*Diverse ingredients come together in this salad of vivid colors and flavors. Yellow mung beans, also called* moong dal, *are mung beans that have been hulled and split. They cook up quickly and don't require soaking. Look for them at gourmet grocers or Indian markets.*

½ cup yellow mung beans, picked over, rinsed, and drained

3 cups small broccoli florets, blanched

1 ripe mango, peeled, pitted, and chopped

1 small red bell pepper, chopped

1 jalapeño or other hot green chile, seeded and minced

2 tablespoons chopped fresh cilantro

1 teaspoon grated fresh ginger

2 tablespoons fresh lemon juice

3 tablespoons grapeseed oil

Salt

¼ teaspoon sugar

⅓ cup unsalted roasted cashews, for garnish

1. In a saucepan of boiling salted water, cook the mung beans until just tender, 18 to 20 minutes. Drain and run under cold water to cool. Transfer the beans to a large bowl. Add the broccoli, mango, bell pepper, chile, and cilantro. Set aside.

2. In a small bowl, combine the ginger, lemon juice, oil, salt to taste, and sugar. Stir to mix well, then pour the dressing over the vegetables and toss to combine. Sprinkle with cashews and serve.

# green bean and pear salad with almonds ⑤

makes 4 servings

*A creamy sesame-almond dressing is the crowning glory on this luscious salad made with tender cooked green beans, juicy pears, and crunchy almonds.*

¼ cup toasted sesame oil

3 tablespoons rice vinegar

2 tablespoons almond butter

2 tablespoons soy sauce

1 tablespoon agave nectar

1 teaspoon grated fresh ginger

⅛ teaspoon ground cayenne

8 ounces green beans, trimmed and cut into 1-inch pieces

1 carrot, cut on the diagonal into ¼-inch slices

¼ cup minced red onion

2 ripe pears, cored and cut into ½-inch dice

½ cup toasted slivered almonds

¼ cup golden raisins

4 to 6 cups mixed salad greens

1. In a blender or food processor, combine the oil, vinegar, almond butter, soy sauce, agave nectar, ginger, and cayenne. Process to blend. Set aside.

2. In a saucepan of boiling water, immerse the green beans and carrot and cook until crisp-tender, about 5 minutes. Drain and transfer to a large bowl. Add the onion, pears, almonds, and raisins. Add the dressing and toss gently to combine. Line a serving platter or individual plates with the salad greens, spoon the salad mixture on top, and serve.

# cranberry-carrot salad with citrus-walnut vinaigrette 🍴

makes 4 servings

*I set out to come up with a lighter alternative to the traditional mayo-based carrot-raisin salad. What began as an experiment developed into a salad that is not only light and delicious but also visually stunning.*

1 pound carrots, shredded
1 cup sweetened dried cranberries
½ cup toasted walnut pieces
2 tablespoons fresh lemon juice
3 tablespoons toasted walnut oil
½ teaspoon sugar
¼ teaspoon salt
⅛ teaspoon freshly ground black pepper

1. In a large bowl, combine the carrots, cranberries, and walnuts. Set aside.

2. In a small bowl, whisk together the lemon juice, walnut oil, sugar, salt, and pepper. Pour the dressing over the salad, toss gently to combine and serve.

# fennel-orange salad with black olives and pine nuts 🍴

makes 4 servings

*This refreshing salad is inspired by an old family favorite that my mother used to make. It generally accompanied pasta meals to aid in digestion, ostensibly because oranges are alkaline-forming in the system and fennel contains a compound that has been believed since ancient times to promote good digestion.*

1 medium fennel bulb, cut into ¼-inch slices
2 oranges, peeled, quartered, and cut into ¼-inch slices
¼ cup kalamata olives, pitted and halved
2 tablespoons chopped fresh parsley
2 tablespoons olive oil
1 tablespoon lemon juice
½ teaspoon sugar
Salt and freshly ground black pepper
4 large or 8 small Boston lettuce leaves
¼ cup toasted pine nuts

1. In a large bowl, combine the fennel, oranges, olives, and parsley. Set aside.

2. In a small bowl, whisk together the oil, lemon juice, sugar, and salt and pepper to taste. Pour the dressing over the salad and toss gently to combine.

3. Arrange a layer of the lettuce leaves on a serving platter or individual plates. Spoon the salad on top of the lettuce, sprinkle with the pine nuts, and serve.

# yellow beet salad with pears and pecans

makes 4 servings

*This hearty winter salad showcases yellow beets, once only seen at farmer's markets and specialty grocers, but now available in many supermarkets. If you can't find yellow beets, red beets may be used instead, taking care that juice from the red beets doesn't run and detract from the appearance of the salad.*

3 to 4 medium yellow beets
2 tablespoons white balsamic vinegar
3 tablespoons vegan mayonnaise, homemade (page 573) or store-bought
3 tablespoons vegan sour cream, homemade (page 574) or store-bought

1 tablespoon soy milk

1½ tablespoons minced fresh dillweed

1 tablespoon minced shallot

½ teaspoon salt

⅛ teaspoon freshly ground black pepper

2 ripe Bosc pears

Juice of 1 lemon

1 small head red leaf lettuce, torn into bite-size
    pieces

½ cup toasted pecan pieces

1. Steam the beets until tender, then cool and peel them. Cut the beets into matchsticks and place them in a shallow bowl. Add the vinegar and toss to coat. Set aside.

2. In a small bowl, combine the mayonnaise, sour cream, soy milk, dillweed, shallot, salt, and pepper. Set aside.

3. Core the pears and cut them into ¼-inch dice. Place the pears in a medium bowl, add the lemon juice, and toss gently to combine. Divide the lettuce among 4 salad plates and spoon the pears and the beets on top. Drizzle the dressing over the salad, sprinkle with pecans, and serve.

# endive and orange salad with toasted pecans

makes 4 servings

*This light and lovely salad is an elegant way to start a meal. If fig-infused balsamic vinegar is unavailable, use a white wine or tarragon vinegar instead.*

2 medium heads Belgian endive, leaves separated

2 navel oranges, peeled, halved, and cut into
    ¼-inch slices

¼ cup chopped toasted pecans

2 tablespoons minced red onion

3 tablespoons olive oil

1½ tablespoons fig-infused balsamic vinegar

¼ teaspoon sugar

Salt and freshly ground black pepper

1 tablespoon fresh pomegranate seeds (optional)

1. In a large bowl, combine the endive, oranges, pecans, and onion. Set aside.

2. In a small bowl, combine the oil, vinegar, sugar, and salt and pepper to taste. Stir until blended. Pour the dressing over the salad and toss gently to combine. Sprinkle with pomegranate seeds, if using, and serve.

# fresh tomato salad

makes 4 servings

*This salad is a celebration of the tomato and should be reserved for the summer months when fresh ripe tomatoes are at their peak.*

2 garlic cloves, crushed

¼ cup olive oil

2 tablespoons tarragon vinegar

½ teaspoon salt

⅛ teaspoon freshly ground black pepper

4 large ripe tomatoes, cut into ¼-inch slices

4 to 8 Boston lettuce leaves

2 tablespoons chopped fresh parsley

1 tablespoon torn fresh basil leaves

1. In a small bowl, combine the garlic, oil, vinegar, salt, and pepper. Stir until blended. Set aside.

2. Arrange the sliced tomatoes on a large platter or individual plates lined with the lettuce leaves. Sprinkle parsley and basil over the tomatoes and drizzle with dressing. Let the salad rest at room temperature to allow the flavors to mingle, about 10 minutes, and then serve.

# tuscan bread and tomato salad

makes 4 servings

*This hearty salad, called* panzanella, *has many variations, but good bread, olive oil, and tomatoes are essential, so plan to make this only when tomatoes are in season.*

½ pound day-old crusty Italian bread, cut into ½-inch cubes

1 garlic clove, minced

2 tablespoons red wine vinegar

½ teaspoon sugar

½ teaspoon salt

½ teaspoon freshly ground black pepper

½ cup olive oil

2 or 3 large ripe tomatoes, chopped

½ medium English cucumber, peeled and cut into ¼-inch dice

½ cup chopped red onion

⅓ cup brine-cured black olives, pitted and halved

1 tablespoon capers

¼ cup chopped fresh basil leaves

¼ cup chopped fresh flat-leaf parsley

1. Preheat the oven to 350°F. Arrange the bread cubes on baking sheet in single layer. Bake until lightly toasted, about 10 minutes, tossing once. Set aside to cool.

2. In a small bowl, combine the garlic, vinegar, sugar, salt, and pepper. Whisk in the oil until blended. Set aside.

3. In a large bowl, combine the tomatoes, cucumber, onion, olives, capers, basil, and parsley, and the toasted bread cubes. Add the dressing, toss gently to combine, and serve.

# syrian bread salad

makes 4 servings

*Similar to the Tuscan* panzanella, *this Syrian bread salad, called* fattoush, *is made with pita bread and a variety of vegetables. Like* panzanella, *good tomatoes and olive oil are essential.*

3 (6-inch) pita breads, torn into bite-size pieces

2 large ripe tomatoes, cut into ¼-inch dice

1 small red onion, chopped

1 medium English cucumber, peeled and cut into ½-inch dice

⅓ cup chopped green bell pepper

¼ cup pitted brine-cured black olives

¼ cup chopped fresh parsley

2 garlic cloves, minced

Juice of 1 lemon

½ teaspoon salt

Pinch ground cayenne

⅓ cup olive oil

1. Preheat the oven to 350°F. Arrange the pita pieces on a baking sheet in a single layer. Bake until lightly toasted, about 10 minutes, then transfer to a large bowl.

2. Add the tomatoes, onion, cucumber, bell pepper, olives, and parsley. Set aside.

3. In a small bowl, combine the garlic, lemon juice, salt, cayenne, and oil. Mix well and pour over the salad. Toss gently to combine and serve.

# edamame and snow pea salad with lime-ginger dressing

makes 4 servings

*A fragrant dressing of sesame oil, ginger, and lime anoints this refreshing salad made with protein-rich edamame, crisp snow peas, and other flavorful vegetables.*

2 tablespoons fresh lime juice

1 teaspoon grated fresh ginger

½ teaspoon sugar

¼ teaspoon salt

2 tablespoons grapeseed oil

2 tablespoons toasted sesame oil

3 ounces snow peas, trimmed and blanched

1½ cups cooked fresh or frozen shelled edamame

1 large carrot, shredded

1 medium yellow bell pepper, cut into matchsticks

3 green onions, minced

1 tablespoon minced fresh parsley or cilantro

1. In a small bowl, combine the lime juice, ginger, sugar, salt, grapeseed oil, and sesame oil. Mix well and set aside.

2. In a large bowl, combine the snow peas, edamame, carrot, bell pepper, green onions, and parsley. Add the dressing, toss gently to combine, and serve.

# POTATO SALADS AND SLAWS

## retro potato salad redux

makes 4 to 6 servings

*If you're longing for a vegan version of the classic potato salad, like the recipe most of us grew up with, this recipe is the one for you, complete with celery and sweet pickle relish. Vegan mayonnaise and a splash of soy milk make it vegan. It's a hit with children of all ages.*

1½ pounds small white potatoes, unpeeled

2 celery ribs, cut into ¼-inch slices

¼ cup sweet pickle relish

3 tablespoons minced green onions

½ to ¾ cup vegan mayonnaise, homemade (page 573) or store-bought

1 tablespoon soy milk

1 tablespoon tarragon vinegar

1 teaspoon Dijon mustard

½ teaspoon salt

Freshly ground black pepper

1. In a large pot of salted boiling water, cook the potatoes until just tender, about 30 minutes. Drain and set aside to cool. When cool enough to handle, peel the potatoes and cut them into 1-inch dice. Transfer the potatoes to a large bowl and add the celery, pickle relish, and green onions. Set aside.

2. In a small bowl, combine the mayonnaise, soy milk, vinegar, mustard, salt, and pepper to taste. Mix until well blended. Pour the dressing onto the potato mixture, toss gently to combine, and serve.

# french-style potato salad

makes 4 to 6 servings

*The slightly anise scent of tarragon permeates this salad made the French way—with a vinaigrette rather than mayonnaise dressing. A few thinly sliced French cornichons are a delicious addition. If you don't like tarragon, just omit it—you'll still have a delicious salad. You can also add a little fresh or dried dillweed instead, if you enjoy the flavor.*

1½ pounds small white potatoes, unpeeled

2 tablespoons minced fresh parsley

1 tablespoon minced fresh chives

1 teaspoon minced fresh tarragon or ½ teaspoon dried

⅓ cup olive oil

2 tablespoons white wine or tarragon vinegar

½ teaspoon salt

⅛ teaspoon freshly ground black pepper

⅛ teaspoon sugar

1. In a large pot of boiling salted water, cook the potatoes until tender but still firm, about 30 minutes. Drain and cut into ¼-inch slices. Transfer to a large bowl and add the parsley, chives, and tarragon. Set aside.

2. In a small bowl, combine the oil, vinegar, salt, pepper, and sugar. Pour the dressing onto the potato mixture and toss gently to combine. Taste, adjusting seasonings if necessary. Chill for 1 to 2 hours before serving.

# three-alarm potato salad

makes 4 to 6 servings

*This is one hot potato salad, perfect for all those spicy food lovers in your crowd. The creamy richness of the avocado offers a flavorful respite from the heat.*

2 pounds small white potatoes, unpeeled

1 small red onion, minced

½ medium red bell pepper, chopped

2 celery ribs, chopped

1 or 2 small fresh hot chiles, seeded and minced

¼ cup minced fresh parsley

½ cup vegan mayonnaise, homemade (page 573) or store-bought

⅓ cup hot tomato salsa

Salt and freshly ground black pepper

1 ripe Hass avocado

1. In a large pot of boiling salted water, cook the potatoes until tender but still firm, about 30 minutes. Drain well and let cool. Cut the potatoes into bite-size chunks and transfer to a large bowl. Add the onion, bell pepper, celery, chiles, and parsley and set aside.

2. In a blender or food processor, blend the mayonnaise, salsa, and salt and black pepper to taste.

3. Pour the dressing over the salad and toss gently to combine. Chill for 1 to 2 hours. Pit, peel, and cut the avocado into ½-inch dice and add to the salad, stirring gently to combine, and serve.

# roasted potato salad with chickpeas and sun-dried tomatoes

makes 4 to 6 servings

*Roasting gives the potatoes loads of extra flavor in this hearty salad that is filling enough to serve as a main dish, thanks to the addition of protein-rich chickpeas. Since this recipe uses mostly pantry ingredients (except the potatoes and parsley), it makes a good winter salad.*

1½ pounds Yukon Gold potatoes, cut into ½-inch dice

1 medium shallot, halved lengthwise and cut into ¼-inch slices

¼ cup olive oil

Salt and freshly ground black pepper

3 tablespoons white wine vinegar

1½ cups cooked or 1 (15.5-ounce) can chickpeas, drained and rinsed

⅓ cup chopped drained oil-packed sun-dried tomatoes

¼ cup green olives, pitted and halved

¼ cup chopped fresh parsley

1. Preheat the oven to 425°F. In a large bowl, combine the potatoes, shallot, and 1 tablespoon of the oil. Season with salt and pepper to taste and toss to coat. Transfer the potatoes and shallot to a baking sheet and roast, turning once, until tender and golden brown, about 20 minutes. Transfer to a large bowl and set aside to cool.

2. In a small bowl, combine the remaining 3 tablespoons oil with the vinegar and salt and pepper to taste. Add the chickpeas, tomatoes, olives, and parsley to the cooked potatoes and shallots. Drizzle with the dressing and toss gently to combine. Taste, adjusting seasonings if necessary. Serve warm or at room temperature.

# potato and white bean salad with roasted red pepper

makes 4 servings

*Capers and a sprightly mustard vinaigrette adds a tangy flavor to this hearty and colorful potato salad.*

1½ pounds small white potatoes, unpeeled

1 medium red bell pepper

1 (15.5-ounce) can cannellini or other white beans, drained and rinsed

3 green onions, minced

1 tablespoon capers

⅓ cup olive oil

3 tablespoons white wine vinegar

1 teaspoon Dijon mustard

½ teaspoon salt

⅛ teaspoon freshly ground black pepper

1. In a large pot of boiling salted water, cook the potatoes until tender, about 30 minutes. Drain well and set aside to cool.

2. Roast the bell pepper over an open flame or under the broiler until charred and blackened on all sides. Place the pepper inside a paper for 10 minutes. Peel, halve, and seed the pepper, scraping off any black bits. Cut into thin 1-inch strips and set aside.

3. When the potatoes are cool, cut into 1-inch chunks. Transfer to a large bowl. Add the roasted peppers along with the beans, green onions, and capers and toss gently to combine.

4. In a small bowl, combine the oil, vinegar, mustard, salt, and black pepper and stir to blend. Add the dressing to the potato salad and mix gently to combine. Taste, adjusting seasonings if necessary, and serve.

# german-style potato salad

makes 4 to 6 servings

*Tempeh bacon adds its smoky flavor to this hearty sweet-and-sour potato salad inspired by the German classic.*

1½ pounds white potatoes, unpeeled

½ cup olive oil

4 slices tempeh bacon, homemade (page 525) or store-bought

1 medium bunch green onions, chopped

1 tablespoon all-purpose flour

2 tablespoons sugar

⅓ cup white wine vinegar

¼ cup water

½ teaspoon salt

⅛ teaspoon freshly ground black pepper

1. In a large pot of boiling salted water, cook the potatoes until just tender, about 30 minutes. Drain well and set aside to cool.

2. In a large skillet, heat the oil over medium heat. Add the tempeh bacon and cook until browned on both sides, about 5 minutes total. Remove from skillet, and set aside to cool.

3. Cut the cooled potatoes into 1-inch chunks and place in a large bowl. Crumble or chop the cooked tempeh bacon and add to the potatoes.

4. Reheat the skillet over medium heat. Add the green onions and cook for 1 minute to soften. Stir in the flour, sugar, vinegar, water, salt, and pepper, and bring to a boil, stirring until smooth. Pour the hot dressing onto the potatoes. Stir gently to combine and serve.

# potato salad with artichoke hearts and grape tomatoes

makes 4 to 6 servings

*I love pairing potatoes and artichokes in gratins and other hot dishes, so it is no surprise that they're also compatible in this sophisticated salad. Grape tomatoes are generally flavorful all year round, or substitute cherry tomatoes or diced plum tomatoes. If frozen artichoke hearts are unavailable, substitute a 15-ounce can (not marinated).*

1½ pounds Yukon Gold potatoes, peeled and cut into 1-inch dice

1 (10-ounce) package frozen artichoke hearts, cooked

2 cups halved ripe grape tomatoes

½ cup frozen peas, thawed

3 green onions, minced

1 tablespoon minced fresh parsley

⅓ cup olive oil

2 tablespoons fresh lemon juice

1 garlic clove, minced

½ teaspoon sugar

Salt and freshly ground black pepper

1. In a large pot of boiling salted water, cook the potatoes until just tender but still firm, about 15 minutes. Drain well and transfer to a large bowl.

2. Quarter the artichokes and add them to the potatoes. Add the tomatoes, peas, green onions, and parsley and set aside.

3. In a small bowl, combine the oil, lemon juice, garlic, sugar, and salt and pepper to taste. Mix well, pour the dressing over potato salad, and toss gently to combine. Set aside at room temperature to allow flavors to blend, about 20 minutes. Taste, adjusting seasonings if necessary, and serve.

# potato salad with seitan strips and tarragon-mustard vinaigrette

makes 4 to 6 servings

*Serve this hearty salad to the meat and potato lovers in your crowd. If you're not a fan of tarragon, use white wine vinegar instead and omit the tarragon, using parsley or another herb that you enjoy.*

1½ pounds small red potatoes, unpeeled and halved or quartered

½ cup minced red onion

2 celery ribs, chopped

⅓ cup plus 1 tablespoon olive oil

6 ounces seitan, homemade (page 305) or store-bought, cut into ¼-inch strips

1 tablespoon Dijon mustard

1 garlic clove, minced

2 tablespoons tarragon vinegar

1 teaspoon minced fresh tarragon or ¼ teaspoon dried

½ teaspoon salt

¼ teaspoon freshly ground black pepper

1. In a large pot of boiling salted water, cook the potatoes until tender, about 20 minutes. Drain well and place in a large bowl. Add the onion and celery and set aside.

2. In a large skillet, heat 1 tablespoon of the oil over medium-high heat. Add the seitan and cook until browned on all sides, about 5 minutes. Add to the potato mixture.

3. In a small bowl, combine the remaining ⅓ cup oil with the mustard, garlic, vinegar, tarragon, salt, and pepper. Blend well. Pour the dressing over the potato salad, toss gently to combine, and serve.

# indonesian-style potato salad

makes 4 to 6 servings

*Inspired by the Indonesian vegetable salad called* gado gado, *this flavorful dish is made rich and creamy by the addition of peanut butter and coconut milk.*

1½ pounds small white potatoes, unpeeled

1 cup frozen peas, thawed

½ cup shredded carrot

4 green onions, chopped

1 tablespoon grapeseed oil

1 garlic clove, minced

⅓ cup creamy peanut butter

2 teaspoons sugar

½ teaspoon Asian chili paste

2 tablespoons soy sauce

1 tablespoon rice vinegar

¾ cup unsweetened coconut milk

3 tablespoons chopped unsalted roasted peanuts, for garnish

1. In a large pot of boiling salted water, cook the potatoes until tender, 20 to 30 minutes. Drain well and set aside to cool.

2. When cool enough to handle, cut the potatoes into 1-inch chunks and transfer to a large bowl. Add the peas, carrot, and green onions, and set aside.

3. In a small saucepan, heat the oil over medium heat. Add the garlic and cook until fragrant, about 30 seconds. Stir in the peanut butter, sugar, chili paste, soy sauce, vinegar, and about half of the coconut milk. Simmer over medium heat for 5 minutes, stirring frequently to make a smooth sauce. Add as much of the remaining coconut milk as needed for a creamy consistency. Pour the dressing over the salad and toss well to combine. Garnish with peanuts and serve.

# sweet potato and broccoli salad with pomegranate-peanut dressing

makes 4 to 6 servings

*This gorgeous salad is definitely not your mother's potato salad—but even Mom would have to agree that it is one delicious and beautiful dish. If pomegranate seeds are unavailable, add sweetened dried cranberries instead to add that touch of scarlet.*

3 sweet potatoes, unpeeled

2 cups lightly steamed broccoli florets

2 celery ribs, cut into ¼-inch slices

2 green onions, minced

2 tablespoons chopped fresh parsley

¼ cup creamy peanut butter

1 teaspoon minced fresh ginger

¼ cup grapeseed oil

¼ cup fresh lemon juice

½ teaspoon sugar

Salt and freshly ground black pepper

¼ cup crushed unsalted roasted peanuts, for garnish

2 tablespoons fresh pomegranate seeds or ¼ cup sweetened dried cranberries, for garnish

1. In a large saucepan, bring the sweet potatoes and enough water to cover to boil over high heat. Reduce heat to medium and simmer until tender, but still firm, about 30 minutes. Drain and cool, then peel them and cut into ½-inch chunks and transfer to a large bowl. Add the broccoli, celery, green onions, and parsley. Set aside.

2. In a small bowl, combine the peanut butter, ginger, oil, lemon juice, sugar, and salt and pepper to taste. Pour the dressing over the salad and toss gently to combine. Garnish with peanuts and pomegranate seeds and serve.

# creamy coleslaw

makes 4 servings

*This close-to-classic coleslaw uses vegan soy products to make the creamy dressing.*

1 small head green cabbage, finely shredded

1 large carrot, shredded

¾ cup vegan mayonnaise, homemade (page 573) or store-bought

¼ cup soy milk

2 tablespoons cider vinegar

1 teaspoon sugar

½ teaspoon dry mustard

¼ teaspoon celery seeds

½ teaspoon salt

Freshly ground black pepper

1. In a large bowl, combine the cabbage and carrot and set aside.

2. In a small bowl, combine the mayonnaise, soy milk, vinegar, sugar, mustard, celery seeds, salt, and pepper to taste. Mix until smooth and well blended. Add the dressing to the slaw and mix well to combine. Taste, adjusting seasonings if necessary, and serve.

# german-style kool-sla

makes 8 servings

*Like German potato salad, German-style cabbage salad (kool sla) is sweet and sour rather than creamy. This recipe makes a lot, but is easily halved.*

1 medium head green cabbage, shredded
1 small yellow onion, minced
½ medium green bell pepper, minced
¾ cup sugar
¾ cup cider vinegar
¾ cup grapeseed oil
1 teaspoon celery seeds
1 teaspoon dry mustard
1 teaspoon salt

1. In a large bowl, combine the cabbage, onion, and bell pepper and set aside.

2. In a small saucepan combine the sugar, vinegar, oil, celery seeds, mustard, and salt, and cook over medium heat, stirring until the sugar dissolves and the dressing is hot. Pour the hot dressing over the cabbage mixture and toss to combine. Cover and refrigerate at least 30 minutes before serving.

# red cabbage slaw with black-vinegar dressing

makes 6 servings

*Chinese black vinegar and black sesame seeds team up with red cabbage to produce a bold and vibrant slaw that tastes as good as it looks. Szechuan peppercorns are not actually a member of the peppercorn family, but rather a distinctive spice from the prickly ash tree. If unavailable, you can omit them and still have a yummy slaw. If napa cabbage is unavailable, use regular green cabbage. Chinese black vinegar is a complex vinegar similar to balsamic vinegar and is available in Asian markets and gourmet grocers. If you can't find it, use balsamic vinegar instead and the slaw will still taste great.*

4 cups shredded red cabbage
2 cups thinly sliced napa cabbage
1 cup shredded daikon radish
¼ cup fresh orange juice
2 tablespoons Chinese black vinegar
    (see headnote)
1 tablespoon soy sauce
1 tablespoon grapeseed oil
1 tablespoon toasted sesame oil
1 teaspoon grated fresh ginger
1 teaspoon sugar
½ teaspoon ground Szechuan peppercorns
    (see headnote)
1 tablespoon black sesame seeds, for garnish

1. In a large bowl, combine the red cabbage, napa, and daikon and set aside.

2. In a small bowl, combine the orange juice, vinegar, soy sauce, grapeseed oil, sesame oil, ginger, sugar, and peppercorns. Blend well. Pour the dressing onto the slaw, stirring to coat. Taste, adjusting seasonings if necessary. Cover and refrigerate to allow flavors to blend, about 2 hours. Sprinkle with sesame seeds and serve.

# asian slaw

makes 4 servings

*Similar to the Red Cabbage Slaw with Black-Vinegar Dressing (page 73) but made with less exotic ingredients, this is a quick and easy slaw to whip up as an accompaniment to the Vietnamese Po'Boys (page 117) or Teriyaki Tofu Wraps (page 115). To save time, substitute bagged shredded cabbage (coleslaw mix) for the napa and carrot.*

8 ounces napa cabbage, cut crosswise into
    ¼-inch strips
1 cup grated carrot
1 cup grated daikon radish
2 green onions, minced
2 tablespoons chopped fresh parsley
2 tablespoons rice vinegar
1 tablespoon grapeseed oil
2 teaspoons toasted sesame oil
1 tablespoon soy sauce
1 teaspoon grated fresh ginger
1 teaspoon sugar
½ teaspoon dry mustard
Salt and freshly ground black pepper
2 tablespoons chopped unsalted roasted peanuts,
    for garnish (optional)

1. In a large bowl, combine the napa cabbage, carrot, daikon, green onions, and parsley. Set aside.

2. In a small bowl, combine the vinegar, grapeseed oil, sesame oil, soy sauce, ginger, sugar, mustard, and salt and pepper to taste. Stir until well blended. Pour the dressing over the vegetables and toss gently to coat. Taste, adjusting seasonings if necessary. Cover and refrigerate to allow flavors to blend, about 2 hours. Sprinkle with peanuts, if using, and serve.

# crunchy sesame slaw

makes 4 servings

*The optional addition of chow mein noodles adds a delicious and surprising crunch to this tasty slaw.*

¼ cup tahini (sesame paste)
2 tablespoons rice vinegar
1 tablespoon soy sauce
1 tablespoon toasted sesame oil
½ teaspoon sugar
Salt and freshly ground black pepper
3 cups shredded green cabbage
1 medium carrot, shredded
12 snow peas, trimmed and cut diagonally into
    thin matchsticks
2 green onions, minced
2 tablespoons toasted sesame seeds, for garnish
1 cup crispy chow mein noodles (optional)

1. In a small bowl, combine the tahini, vinegar, soy sauce, sesame oil, sugar, and salt and pepper to taste. Stir well to blend and set aside.

2. In a large bowl, combine the cabbage, carrot, snow peas, and green onions. Pour the dressing over the vegetables and toss gently to coat. Taste, adjusting seasonings if necessary. Sprinkle with toasted sesame seeds and chow mein noodles, if using. Refrigerate, covered, until ready to serve.

# rainbow slaw

makes 6 servings

*A variety of colors, textures, and flavors, makes this unusual slaw pretty to look at and fun to eat. If Asian pears are unavailable, substitute an apple or a ripe Bosc pear.*

½ small head green cabbage, finely shredded

1 large carrot, shredded

1 cup shredded fennel bulb

1 Asian pear, halved, cored, and cut into
    ¼-inch slices

½ cup dried sweetened cranberries

2 tablespoons minced green onions

1 cup vegan vanilla yogurt

1 tablespoon fresh lemon juice

½ teaspoon sugar

Salt and freshly ground black pepper

**1.** In a large bowl, combine the cabbage, carrot, fennel, pear, cranberries, and green onions and set aside.

**2.** In a small bowl, combine the yogurt, lemon juice, and sugar and blend until smooth. Add the dressing to the slaw, stirring well to coat. Season with salt and pepper to taste, and set aside, covered, to allow flavors to blend, about 20 minutes. If not serving right away, cover and refrigerate until needed.

# broccoli slaw with apple and walnuts

makes 4 to 6 servings

*Shredded broccoli stems, called "broccoli slaw," can be found in supermarkets, and make a nice change from the usual cabbage slaw. This hearty slaw, made with walnut and apple, is a decidedly winter dish.*

1 Fuji or Gala apple, halved, cored, and cut into
    ¼-inch slices

1 teaspoon fresh lemon juice

1 (12-ounce) bag broccoli slaw

½ cup toasted walnut pieces

1 tablespoon sugar

¼ cup white balsamic vinegar

¼ cup walnut oil

½ teaspoon salt

¼ teaspoon freshly ground black pepper

**1.** In a large bowl, combine the apples and lemon juice and toss to prevent discoloration. Add the broccoli slaw and walnut pieces and set aside.

**2.** In a small bowl, combine the sugar, vinegar, walnut oil, salt, and pepper. Mix well and pour the dressing over the slaw mixture. Toss well to combine and serve.

# tahini broccoli slaw

makes 4 to 6 servings

*Make your own broccoli slaw by shredding the broccoli stalks with the shredding disc on your food processor. The creamy tahini dressing complements the broccoli nicely for a tasty slaw loaded with calcium and vitamin C.*

¼ cup tahini (sesame paste)

2 tablespoons white miso

1 tablespoon rice vinegar

1 tablespoon toasted sesame oil

2 teaspoons soy sauce

1 (12-ounce) bag broccoli slaw

2 green onions, minced

¼ cup toasted sesame seeds

**1.** In a large bowl, whisk together the tahini, miso, vinegar, oil, and soy sauce. Add the broccoli slaw, green onions, and sesame seeds and toss to coat.

**2.** Set aside for 20 minutes before serving.

## spicy southwestern-style coleslaw

makes 4 servings

*Shredded red and green cabbages are tossed in a spicy vinaigrette for a light and flavorful slaw that makes a great accompaniment for chili or a Mexican casserole.*

2 cups shredded green cabbage

2 cups shredded red cabbage

1 medium red bell pepper, cut into matchsticks

2 tablespoons minced fresh parsley

¼ cup olive oil

2 tablespoons cider vinegar

½ teaspoon sugar

½ teaspoon salt

¼ teaspoon ground cumin

¼ teaspoon chili powder

⅛ teaspoon ground cayenne

1. In a large bowl, combine the green and red cabbage, bell pepper, and parsley. Set aside.

2. In a small bowl, combine the oil, vinegar, sugar, salt, cumin, chili powder, and cayenne. Blend well. Pour the dressing over the vegetables and toss to combine. Taste, adjusting seasonings if necessary. Cover and refrigerate to allow flavors to blend, about 2 hours, and serve.

## tropical black bean salad with mango 🅕

makes 4 to 6 servings

*This colorful and flavorful salad can be transformed into a hearty main-dish salad with the addition of 2 or 3 cups of cooked long-grain brown rice.*

3 cups cooked or 2 (15.5-ounce) cans black beans, drained and rinsed

1 ripe mango, peeled, pitted, and cut into a ½-inch dice

½ cup chopped red bell pepper

¼ cup minced red onion

¼ cup minced fresh cilantro

1 jalapeño, seeded and minced (optional)

3 tablespoons grapeseed oil

2 tablespoons fresh lime juice

2 teaspoons agave nectar

¼ teaspoon salt

⅛ teaspoon ground cayenne

1. In a large bowl, combine the beans, mango, bell pepper, onion, cilantro, and jalapeño if using, and set aside.

2. In a small bowl, whisk together the oil, lime juice, agave nectar, salt, and cayenne. Pour the dressing onto the salad and mix well. Refrigerate for 20 minutes and serve.

# white bean salad with fennel and avocado 🅕

makes 4 to 6 servings

*Creamy cannellini beans are the star of this salad, combined with a dazzling array of contrasting textures and complementary flavors, including fragrant fennel, piquant olives, and buttery avocado. Add 3 cups of cold cooked brown rice and turn this into a one-dish meal.*

3 cups cooked or 2 (15.5-ounce) cans cannellini beans or other white beans, drained and rinsed

1 small fennel bulb, shredded

1 cup ripe grape tomatoes, halved

¼ cup minced red onion

¼ cup minced fresh parsley

¼ cup kalamata olives, pitted and sliced

¼ cup olive oil

2 tablespoons fresh lemon juice

½ teaspoon sugar

½ teaspoon dried basil

¼ teaspoon dried marjoram

½ teaspoon salt

¼ teaspoon freshly ground black pepper

1 ripe Hass avocado

1. In a large bowl, combine the beans, fennel, tomatoes, onion, parsley, and olives. Set aside.

2. In a small bowl, combine the oil, lemon juice, sugar, basil, marjoram, salt, and pepper. Set aside.

3. Pit and peel the avocado and cut into ½-inch dice. Add the avocado to the salad and drizzle with the dressing. Toss gently to combine and serve.

## grain and bean salads

Whole grains and beans are the foundation of a healthful vegan diet, so it's no surprise they have become popular salad ingredients as well. From rice in its many varieties, including basmati, jasmine, and the basic brown, to quinoa, bulgur, and couscous, cooked cold grains are a nutritious component to a satisfying salad.

When paired with beans such as lentils, cannellini, kidney, pinto, and black, you have the makings of a satisfying dish that transcends a simple salad and can become a meal in itself. Add cooked or raw vegetables, nuts, seeds, or fruit, and a complementary dressing, then serve over your favorite salad greens.

Quick, easy, nutritious, and great tasting—what more could you ask for? Best of all, when you use these ingredient components in different combinations, you create an astonishing variety of salads. Next time you have a small amount of cooked leftover grains or beans in the refrigerator, think about using them as a basis for a salad.

# warm lentil salad with walnuts

makes 4 servings

*Tiny green lentils, or French lentils, are the most flavorful variety of lentils. In this salad, they are complemented by the crunch of toasted walnuts and dressed in a zesty Dijon vinaigrette. For extra flavor, drizzle with a small amount of walnut oil when ready to serve or omit the olive oil and use half walnut oil and half grapeseed oil in the dressing.*

1 cup green lentils, picked over, rinsed, and drained

1 medium shallot, halved

1 garlic clove, crushed

2 tablespoons white wine vinegar

1 tablespoon Dijon mustard

¼ cup olive oil

½ teaspoon dried oregano

½ teaspoon salt

¼ teaspoon freshly ground black pepper

½ cup finely chopped red bell pepper

⅓ cup chopped toasted walnuts

¼ cup finely chopped red onion

2 tablespoons minced fresh parsley

1. Bring a medium saucepan of salted water to a boil. Add the lentils and return to a boil, then reduce the heat to low. Cover and cook until lentils are tender, about 45 minutes.

2. In a blender or food processor, mince the shallot and garlic. Add the vinegar, mustard, oil, oregano, salt, and black pepper and process until well blended. Set aside.

3. When the lentils are tender, drain well and transfer to a serving bowl. Add the bell pepper, walnuts, onion, and parsley. Add enough dressing to coat and toss gently to combine. Serve warm.

# lentil salad with chiles

makes 4 servings

*Earthy brown lentils make a great salad— as long as you don't overcook them. The heat level of this salad depends on the amount and type of chiles used—from super-hot to mildly flavorful.*

1 cup brown lentils, picked over, rinsed, and drained

4 ripe plum tomatoes, chopped

2 celery ribs, cut into ¼-inch slices

1 or 2 hot or mild chiles, seeded and minced

⅓ cup chopped green onions

2 tablespoons chopped fresh parsley

4 tablespoons olive oil

2 tablespoons sherry or balsamic vinegar

Salt and freshly ground black pepper

1. Bring a medium saucepan of salted water to boil over high heat. Add the lentils, return to a boil, then reduce to low. Cover and cook until the lentils are tender, about 40 minutes.

2. Drain the lentils well and transfer to a large bowl. Add the tomatoes, celery, chiles, green onions, parsley, oil, and vinegar. Season with salt and pepper to taste, toss well to combine, and serve.

# southwestern three-bean salad

makes 6 to 8 servings

*Three kinds of beans combined with a variety of vegetables results in a beautiful salad filled with great flavors and textures. Best of all, this recipe yields generous portions, so it's great to feed a crowd.*

1½ cups cooked or 1 (15.5-ounce) can pinto beans, drained and rinsed

1½ cups cooked or 1 (15.5-ounce) can dark red kidney beans, drained and rinsed

1½ cups cooked or 1 (15.5-ounce) can black beans, drained and rinsed

1 medium red bell pepper, chopped

1 cup frozen corn kernels, thawed

2 green onions, minced

2 tablespoons finely chopped fresh cilantro

2 ripe plum tomatoes, chopped

1 garlic clove, crushed

1 teaspoon minced canned jalapeño

¼ teaspoon chili powder

¼ teaspoon ground cumin

2 tablespoons apple cider vinegar

¼ cup olive oil

Salt and freshly ground black pepper

1 ripe Hass avocado (optional)

1. In a large bowl, combine all the beans, the bell pepper, corn, green onions, and cilantro. Set aside.

2. In a blender or food processor, combine the tomatoes, garlic, jalapeño, chili powder, cumin, vinegar, oil, and salt and black pepper to taste. Process until well blended. Pour the dressing onto the salad. Toss to combine. Taste, adjusting seasonings if necessary.

3. Cover and set aside for 30 minutes. Pit, peel, and cut the avocado into ½-inch dice, if using. Add to the salad and serve.

# black bean and corn salad with cilantro dressing 🔵

makes 4 servings

*This attractive salad contains favorite flavors of Mexican and Southwestern cuisine. Serve it on a bed of lettuce or cold cooked rice—or both.*

2 cups frozen corn, thawed

3 cups cooked or 2 (15.5-ounce) cans black beans, rinsed and drained

½ cup chopped red bell pepper

¼ cup minced red onion

1 (4-ounce) can chopped mild green chiles, drained

2 garlic cloves, crushed

¼ cup chopped fresh cilantro

1 teaspoon ground cumin

½ teaspoon salt

¼ teaspoon freshly ground black pepper

2 tablespoons fresh lime juice

2 tablespoons water

¼ cup olive oil

1. In a large bowl, combine the corn, beans, bell pepper, onion, and chiles. Set aside.

2. In a blender or food processor, mince the garlic. Add the cilantro, cumin, salt, and black pepper and pulse to blend. Add the lime juice, water, and oil and process until well blended. Pour the dressing over the salad and toss to combine. Taste, adjusting seasonings if necessary, and serve.

# grilled vegetable antipasto salad with chickpeas

makes 4 to 6 servings

*This celebration of summer produce makes an ideal outdoor meal. While you have the grill on, make some grilled garlic bread to serve with it.*

½ cup olive oil

3 tablespoons balsamic vinegar

1 garlic clove, minced

1 tablespoon chopped fresh basil

½ teaspoon salt

¼ teaspoon freshly ground black pepper

1 small eggplant, halved lengthwise and cut into ½-inch slices

1 medium red onion, cut into ½-inch slices

1 medium fennel bulb, quartered

2 large portobello mushroom caps, thickly sliced

2 medium zucchini or yellow squash, trimmed and halved lengthwise

2 medium red bell peppers, halved lengthwise and seeded

1 (9-ounce) jar marinated artichoke hearts, drained and chopped

1½ cups cooked or 1 (15.5-ounce) can chickpeas, drained and rinsed

1 cup ripe cherry tomatoes, halved

⅓ cup Gaeta or kalamata olives, pitted

3 tablespoons minced fresh parsley

1. In a small bowl, combine the oil, vinegar, garlic, basil, salt, and black pepper. Mix well and set aside. Preheat the grill.

2. In a large bowl, combine the eggplant, onion, fennel, mushrooms, zucchini, and bell peppers, and drizzle with the marinade. Transfer the vegetables to the hot grill, brushing with some of the marinade as they grill. Grill for 4 to 5 minutes, then flip the vegetables over and grill on the other side until tender, about 5 minutes more. Arrange the grilled vegetables on a platter and set aside.

3. In a medium bowl, combine the artichoke hearts, chickpeas, tomatoes, olives, and parsley. Pour on as much of the remaining marinade as needed to moisten. Toss to combine and then spoon the chickpea mixture on top of the grilled vegetables and serve.

# provençal white bean salad 🅕

makes 4 servings

*Creamy white beans play nicely against the steamed green beans and other salad ingredients. A tangy vinaigrette brings it all together. Though delicious on its own, the addition of cooked pasta or sliced potatoes turns this salad into a hearty one-dish meal.*

4 ounces green beans, trimmed and cut into
   1-inch pieces
3 cups cooked or 2 (15.5-ounce) cans
   Great Northern or other white beans,
   drained and rinsed
⅓ cup minced red onion
1 cup ripe cherry tomatoes, halved
¼ cup pitted niçoise olives
⅓ cup olive oil
3 tablespoons tarragon vinegar
1 teaspoon Dijon mustard
2 garlic cloves, minced
2 tablespoons minced fresh parsley
¼ teaspoon sugar
¼ teaspoon salt
¼ teaspoon freshly ground black pepper

1. Steam the green beans until just tender, about 7 minutes, and transfer them to a large bowl. Add the white beans, onion, tomatoes, and olives and set aside.

2. In a small bowl, combine the oil, vinegar, mustard, garlic, parsley, sugar, salt, and pepper. Whisk until blended and pour over the salad. Toss gently until well mixed. Taste, adjusting seasonings if necessary, and serve.

# white bean and broccoli salad with parsley-walnut pesto 🅕

makes 4 to 6 servings

*This satisfying salad combines creamy cannellini beans and buttery Yukon Gold potatoes with fresh broccoli and kalamata olives. The rich full-bodied flavor of the walnut dressing unifies the ingredients into a delightful whole.*

1 pound Yukon Gold potatoes, peeled and cut into
   1-inch chunks
3 cups broccoli florets
1½ cups cooked or 1 (15.5-ounce) can cannellini
   or other white beans, drained and rinsed
½ cup kalamata olives, pitted and halved
½ cup walnut pieces
2 garlic cloves, finely minced
½ cup chopped fresh parsley
¼ cup walnut oil
¼ cup olive oil
¼ cup white wine vinegar
½ teaspoon salt
½ teaspoon sugar
¼ teaspoon crushed red pepper

1. Steam the potatoes until almost tender, about 10 minutes. Steam the broccoli until just tender, about 5 minutes. Drain the potatoes and broccoli and place them in a large bowl. Add the beans, olives, and ¼ cup of the walnuts and set aside.

2. In a blender or food processor, combine the remaining ¼ cup walnuts with the garlic and process until well minced. Add the parsley, walnut oil, olive oil, vinegar, salt, sugar, and crushed red pepper and process until blended. Pour the dressing over the salad, toss gently to combine, and serve.

# chickpea "tuna" salad in avocados

makes 2 to 4 servings

*This salad, reminiscent of tuna, looks and tastes great, especially when mounded onto avocado halves. Chopped chickpeas supply the texture and kelp powder provides the taste of the sea. Serve one or two avocado halves per person, depending on whether the salad is a first course or main dish, for a light lunch.*

1½ cups cooked or 1 (15.5-ounce) can chickpeas, drained and rinsed

2 celery ribs, minced

¼ cup minced red bell pepper

2 green onions, minced

⅓ cup vegan mayonnaise, homemade (page 573) or store-bought, plus more if needed

1 tablespoon plus 1 teaspoon fresh lemon juice

1 teaspoon Dijon mustard

1 teaspoon kelp powder

Salt and freshly ground black pepper

2 ripe Hass avocados

Lettuce leaves, to serve

1. In a food processor, pulse the chickpeas until chopped, then transfer to a large bowl. Add the celery, bell pepper, green onions, mayonnaise, 1 tablespoon of the lemon juice, mustard, kelp powder, and salt and black pepper to taste. Mix well, adding a little more mayonnaise if the mixture seems dry. Cover and refrigerate at least 30 minutes.

2. Halve and pit the avocados and brush the exposed flesh with the remaining 1 teaspoon lemon juice to prevent discoloration. Divide the chickpea mixture among the avocado halves, pressing gently with a spoon to mound the salad onto the avocados. Arrange the filled avocados on salad plates lined with the lettuce leaves, and serve.

# puttanesca seitan and spinach salad 🅕

makes 4 servings

*You don't need a plate of pasta to enjoy the tantalizing flavors of puttanesca—notably olives, garlic, tomatoes, and capers—when they can be savored in this hearty salad. On the other hand, tossing in 2 or 3 cups of cooked pasta isn't a bad idea, and it easily transforms this salad into a hearty one-dish meal.*

4 tablespoons olive oil

8 ounces seitan, homemade (page 305) or store-bought, cut into ½-inch strips

3 garlic cloves, minced

½ cup kalamata olives, pitted and halved

½ cup green olives, pitted and halved

2 tablespoons capers

3 cups fresh baby spinach, cut into strips

1½ cups ripe cherry tomatoes, halved

2 tablespoons balsamic vinegar

½ teaspoon sugar

¼ teaspoon salt

¼ teaspoon freshly ground black pepper

2 tablespoons torn fresh basil leaves

2 tablespoons minced fresh parsley

1. In a large skillet, heat 1 tablespoon of the oil over medium heat. Add the seitan and cook until browned on both sides, about 5 minutes. Add the garlic and cook until fragrant, about 30 seconds. Transfer to a large bowl and set aside to cool, about 15 minutes.

2. When the seitan has cooled to room temperature, add the kalamata and green olives, capers, spinach, and tomatoes. Set aside.

3. In a small bowl, combine the remaining 3 tablespoons oil with the vinegar, sugar, salt, and pepper. Whisk until blended, then pour the dressing over the salad. Add the basil and parsley, toss gently to combine, and serve.

## curried walnut "chicken" salad 🄵

makes 4 servings

*Instead of using seitan as the vegan "chicken" in this recipe, try baked marinated tofu, extra-firm tofu, or simmered tempeh. Serve this salad "luncheon-style," scooped onto a lettuce leaf or use it as a filling for wrap sandwiches.*

1 tablespoon olive oil

3 cups chopped seitan, homemade (page 305) or store-bought

¾ cup chopped toasted walnuts

2 celery ribs, finely chopped

⅓ cup shredded carrot

3 tablespoons minced green onions

¼ cup golden raisins

⅓ cup vegan mayonnaise, homemade (page 573) or store-bought

⅓ cup plain vegan yogurt

2 teaspoons hot or mild curry powder

½ teaspoon salt

1. In a large skillet, heat the oil over medium heat. Add the seitan and cook until browned, about 7 minutes. Transfer to a large bowl. Add the walnuts, celery, carrot, green onions, and raisins.

2. In a small bowl, combine the mayonnaise, yogurt, curry powder, and salt. Taste, adjusting

seasonings if necessary, adding more curry powder if desired. Add the dressing to the salad, toss to combine, and serve.

## chinese "chicken" salad 🄵

makes 4 servings

*I like using an Asian-flavored baked marinated tofu in this recipe, but seitan or tempeh can be used instead, if you prefer. You can omit the lettuce from the salad and wrap the "chicken" salad in soft lettuce leaves to enjoy as lettuce roll-ups.*

2 cups finely shredded romaine lettuce or cabbage

½ cup shredded carrot

¼ cup minced green onions

2 tablespoons chopped fresh cilantro

1 garlic clove, crushed

1 teaspoon grated fresh ginger

3 tablespoons creamy peanut butter

1 tablespoon hot water

1 tablespoon fresh lemon juice

1 tablespoon toasted sesame oil

2 tablespoons soy sauce

½ teaspoon sugar

12 ounces baked marinated tofu (see headnote), chopped or shredded

⅓ cup chopped unsalted roasted peanuts, for garnish

1. In a large bowl, combine the lettuce, carrot, green onions, and cilantro. Set aside.

2. In a blender or food processor, mince the garlic and ginger, then add the peanut butter, water, lemon juice, oil, soy sauce, and sugar. Blend until smooth. Pour the dressing over the lettuce mixture, add the tofu, and toss well to coat. Garnish with peanuts and serve.

# rice salad with cashews and dried papaya

makes 4 servings

*This hearty winter rice salad gets a taste of the tropics thanks to crunchy cashews and sweet bits of dried papaya.*

3½ cups cooked brown rice
½ cup chopped roasted cashews
½ cup thinly sliced dried papaya
4 green onions, chopped
3 tablespoons fresh lime juice
2 teaspoons agave nectar
1 teaspoon grated fresh ginger
⅓ cup grapeseed oil
Salt and freshly ground black pepper

1. In a large bowl, combine the rice, cashews, papaya, and green onions. Set aside.

2. In a small bowl, combine the lime juice, agave nectar, and ginger. Whisk in the oil and season with the salt and pepper to taste. Pour the dressing over the rice mixture, mix well, and serve.

# roasted cauliflower and rice salad with dijon vinaigrette

makes 4 servings

*This salad is so delicious it can make a cauliflower-lover out of almost anyone. The secret is roasting the cauliflower—a technique that brings out the best in many vegetables, but perhaps most remarkably so in cauliflower.*

3 cups small cauliflower florets
¼ cup plus 1 tablespoon olive oil
Salt and freshly ground black pepper
¼ cup white wine vinegar
2 teaspoons Dijon mustard

1 teaspoon sugar
1½ cups cooked or 1 (15.5-ounce) can navy beans or other white beans, rinsed and drained
3 cups cooked brown rice
1 fresh ripe tomato, chopped
½ cup minced red bell pepper
2 celery ribs, cut into ¼-inch slices
2 tablespoons green onions
2 tablespoons minced fresh parsley or dillweed

1. Preheat the oven to 425°F. Spread the cauliflower on a lightly oiled baking pan and drizzle with the 1 tablespoon of oil. Season with salt and black pepper and roast until tender and lightly browned, turning once, about 15 minutes. Set aside to cool.

2. While the cauliflower is roasting, combine the remaining ¼ cup oil, vinegar, mustard, sugar, ½ teaspoon salt, and black pepper to taste in a small bowl. Mix well and set aside.

3. In a large bowl, combine the rice, tomato, bell pepper, celery, green onions, and parsley. Pour on the reserved dressing, add the roasted cauliflower, and toss gently to combine.

# white and wild rice salad with walnuts, cranberries, and figs

makes 4 servings

*A combination of white and wild rice are used here for contrast, but a single rice (or other cooked grain) would work just as well. The next time you make rice, put some aside in the freezer for a salad such as this one.*

2 cups cooled cooked wild rice
3 cups cooled cooked basmati or other long-grain white rice
1 cup frozen baby peas, thawed
½ cup chopped toasted walnuts

½ cup sweetened dried cranberries

4 fresh ripe figs, finely chopped

2 green onions, finely minced

¼ cup cranberry juice

¼ cup olive oil

1½ tablespoons balsamic vinegar

½ teaspoon sugar

Salt and freshly ground black pepper

1. In a large bowl combine the wild rice, basmati rice, peas, walnuts, cranberries, figs, and green onions.

2. In a small bowl, combine the cranberry juice, olive oil, balsamic vinegar, and sugar, and pour over the rice mixture. Season with salt and pepper to taste and toss well to combine. Set aside for 30 minutes before serving or cover and refrigerate until ready to serve. Serve at room temperature.

# brown rice salad with black-eyed peas

makes 4 servings

*This Southern-style salad, made with black-eyed peas and rice, is a deliciously easy way to serve the traditional New Year's dish believed to bring good luck. Best of all, this dish can be made ahead of time and the recipe doubles easily if you're serving a crowd.*

3 cups cooked long-grain brown rice

1½ cups cooked or 1 (15.5-ounce) can black-eyed peas, rinsed and drained

½ cup minced red onion

2 celery ribs, cut into ¼-inch slices

¼ cup chopped toasted pecans

2 tablespoons minced fresh parsley

½ cup olive oil

3 tablespoons cider vinegar

½ teaspoon dried thyme

½ teaspoon salt

¼ teaspoon ground cayenne

1. In a large serving bowl, combine the rice, black-eyed peas, onion, celery, pecans, and parsley. Set aside.

2. In a small bowl, combine the oil, vinegar, thyme, salt, and cayenne. Mix well, then pour the dressing over the salad, toss to combine, and serve.

# eight treasure barley salad

makes 4 to 6 servings

*Barley, a delicious but underappreciated grain, will garner the attention it deserves in this delightful salad loaded with tasty treasures.*

1 cup pearl barley

1½ cups cooked or 1 (15.5-ounce) can navy beans, drained and rinsed

1 celery rib, finely chopped

1 medium carrot, shredded

3 green onions, minced

½ cup chopped pitted kalamata olives

½ cup dried cherries or sweetened dried cranberries

½ cup toasted pecans pieces, coarsely chopped

½ cup minced fresh parsley

1 garlic clove, pressed

3 tablespoons sherry vinegar

Salt and freshly ground black pepper

¼ cup grapeseed oil

1. In a large saucepan, bring 2½ cups salted water to boil over high heat. Add the barley and return to a boil. Reduce heat to low, cover, and simmer until the barley is tender, about 30 minutes. Transfer to a serving bowl.

2. Add the beans, celery, carrot, green onions, olives, cherries, pecans, and parsley. Set aside.

3. In a small bowl, combine the garlic, vinegar, and salt and pepper to taste. Whisk in the oil until well blended. Pour the dressing over the salad, toss to combine, and serve.

## pistachio-pear couscous salad

makes 4 servings

*Cooking the couscous in white grape juice adds a delightful sweetness that complements the pears in this elegant salad. It makes a lovely light lunch. For an attractive presentation, line salad plates with soft lettuce leaves and spoon the salad on top. If you don't have pistachios or ripe pears handy, swap them for apples and walnuts.*

2 cups white grape juice

1 cup water

1½ cups couscous

Salt

1 medium red bell pepper, cut into ¼-inch dice

½ cup chopped red onion

2 celery ribs, minced

2 ripe pears

3 tablespoons fresh lemon juice

⅓ cup olive oil

¼ teaspoon freshly ground black pepper

½ cup unsalted shelled pistachios

1. In a large saucepan, combine the grape juice and water and bring to a boil over high heat. Stir in the couscous and lightly salt the water. Cover, remove from heat, and set aside for 10 minutes.

2. In a large bowl, combine the bell pepper, onion, and celery. Peel and core the pears and cut them into chunks. Coarsely chop one of the pears and place it in the bowl with the vegetables. Add 1 tablespoon of the lemon juice and toss to combine.

3. In the blender or food processor, combine the remaining 1 pear, the remaining 2 tablespoons lemon juice, olive oil, salt to taste, and black pepper and process until smooth. Pour the dressing over the salad, add the cooked couscous and the pistachios, and toss to combine. Serve chilled or at room temperature.

## golden couscous salad

makes 4 servings

*Cooking the couscous with turmeric gives it a golden glow that complements the other golden-hued ingredients in this beautiful salad. Chopped cilantro adds a vivid color contrast, not to mention truly delicious flavor.*

¼ cup olive oil

1 medium shallot, minced

½ teaspoon ground coriander

½ teaspoon turmeric

¼ teaspoon ground cayenne

1 cup couscous

2 cups vegetable broth, homemade (page 141)
    or store-bought, or water

Salt

1 medium yellow bell pepper, chopped

1 medium carrot, shredded

½ cup chopped dried apricots

¼ cup golden raisins

¼ cup chopped unsalted roasted cashews

1½ cups cooked or 1 (15.5-ounce) can chickpeas,
    drained and rinsed

2 tablespoons minced fresh cilantro leaves

2 tablespoons fresh lemon juice

1 teaspoon sugar

1. In a large saucepan, heat 1 tablespoon of the oil over medium heat. Add the shallot, coriander, turmeric, cayenne, and couscous and stir until fragrant, about 2 minutes, being careful not to burn. Stir in the broth and salt to taste. Bring to a boil, then remove from the heat, cover, and let stand for 10 minutes.

2. Transfer the cooked couscous to a large bowl. Add the bell pepper, carrot, apricots, raisins, cashews, chickpeas, and cilantro. Toss gently to combine and set aside.

3. In a small bowl, combine the remaining 3 tablespoons of oil with the lemon juice and sugar, stirring to blend. Pour the dressing over the salad, toss gently to combine, and serve.

# classic tabbouleh

makes 4 servings

*This traditional Lebanese salad is made with bulgur, tomato, and lots of chopped parsley. Some fresh mint may be added, if desired.*

2 cups water

1 cup medium-grind bulgur

Salt

3 ripe plum tomatoes, finely chopped

½ cup minced red onion

½ cup chopped cucumber

¾ cup minced fresh parsley

¼ cup olive oil

2 tablespoons fresh lemon juice

Freshly ground black pepper

1. In a large saucepan, bring the water to boil over high heat. Stir in the bulgur and lightly salt the water. Cover, remove from heat, and set aside until the bulgur softens and the water is absorbed, about 20 minutes. If any water remains, drain it off, pressing out any remaining moisture.

2. Transfer the cooked bulgur to a large bowl and add the tomatoes, onion, cucumber, and parsley. Add the olive oil and lemon juice. Season with salt and pepper to taste and toss well to combine. Cover and set aside for at least 20 minutes before serving.

# garden variety couscous tabbouleh

makes 4 servings

*Couscous replaces the traditional bulgur for a lighter version of tabbouleh, which is especially welcome during hot summer months.*

2 cups water

1 cup couscous

Salt

1 ripe tomato, chopped

⅓ cup minced green onions

½ medium red bell pepper, chopped

½ medium English cucumber, peeled, seeded, and chopped

1½ cups cooked or 1 (15.5-ounce) can chickpeas, drained and rinsed

½ cup chopped fresh parsley

¼ cup olive oil

2 tablespoons fresh lemon juice

⅛ teaspoon ground cayenne

1. In a large saucepan, bring the water to boil over high heat. Stir in the couscous and lightly salt the water. Cover, remove from heat, and set aside until the water is absorbed, about 10 minutes.

2. In a large bowl, combine the tomato, green onions, bell pepper, cucumber, chickpeas, and parsley. Set aside.

3. In a small bowl, combine the olive oil, lemon juice, salt to taste, and cayenne. Pour the dressing over the salad, add the cooked couscous, and toss well to combine. Cover and refrigerate at least 30 minutes before serving.

# quinoa salad with black beans and tomatoes

makes 4 servings

*Protein-rich quinoa, the supergrain of the Incas, needs to be well rinsed before using to remove any remnants of saponin, a bitter white coating.*

3 cups water

1½ cups quinoa, well rinsed

Salt

1½ cups cooked or 1 (15.5-ounce) can
    black beans, drained and rinsed

4 ripe plum tomatoes, cut into ¼-inch dice

⅓ cup minced red onion

¼ cup chopped fresh parsley

¼ cup olive oil

2 tablespoons sherry vinegar

¼ teaspoon freshly ground black pepper

1. In a large saucepan, bring the water to boil over high heat. Add the quinoa, salt the water, and return to a boil. Reduce heat to low, cover, and simmer until the water is absorbed, about 20 minutes.

2. Transfer the cooked quinoa to a large bowl. Add the black beans, tomatoes, onion, and parsley.

3. In a small bowl, combine the olive oil, vinegar, salt to taste, and pepper. Pour the dressing over the salad and toss well to combine. Cover and set aside for 20 minutes before serving.

# southwestern quinoa salad with pinto beans and corn

makes 4 servings

*Quinoa, a delicious nutty-tasting grain, is considered a complete protein because it contains all eight essential amino acids.*

3 cups water

1½ cups quinoa, well rinsed

Salt

2 cups frozen corn kernels, thawed

1½ cups or 1 (15.5-ounce) can pinto beans,
    drained and rinsed

2 celery ribs, cut into ¼-inch slices

1 hot or mild chile, seeded and minced

2 tablespoons chopped fresh cilantro

1 garlic clove, minced

3 tablespoons fresh lemon juice

2 teaspoons agave nectar or 1 teaspoon sugar

¼ cup olive oil

¼ teaspoon freshly ground black pepper

1. In a large saucepan, bring the water to boil over high heat. Add the quinoa, salt the water, and return to a boil. Reduce heat to low, cover, and simmer until the water is absorbed, about 20 minutes.

2. Transfer the cooked quinoa to a large bowl, and add the corn, beans, celery, chile, and cilantro and set aside.

3. In a small bowl, combine the garlic, agave nectar, lemon juice, oil, salt to taste, and pepper. Mix well and pour onto the salad. Toss to combine and serve.

# mediterranean quinoa salad

makes 4 servings

*Quinoa provides a wholesome backdrop to the tasty array of ingredients in this recipe. This salad is also delicious made with brown rice or pasta.*

2 cups water

1 cup quinoa, well rinsed

Salt

1½ cups cooked or 1 (15.5-ounce) can chickpeas, drained and rinsed

1 cup ripe grape or cherry tomatoes, halved

2 green onions, minced

½ medium English cucumber, peeled and chopped

¼ cup pitted brine-cured black olives

2 tablespoons toasted pine nuts

¼ cup small fresh basil leaves

1 medium shallot, chopped

1 garlic clove, chopped

1 teaspoon Dijon mustard

2 tablespoons white wine vinegar

¼ cup olive oil

Freshly ground black pepper

1. In a large saucepan, bring the water to boil over high heat. Add the quinoa, salt the water, and return to a boil. Reduce heat to low, cover, and simmer until water is absorbed, about 20 minutes.

2. Transfer the cooked quinoa to a large bowl. Add the chickpeas, tomatoes, green onions, cucumber, olives, pine nuts, and basil. Set aside.

3. In a blender or food processor, combine the shallot, garlic, mustard, vinegar, oil, and salt and pepper to taste. Process until well blended. Pour the dressing over the salad, toss gently to combine, and serve.

# pasta salad with grilled summer vegetables

makes 4 servings

*Pasta salads are perfect for summer: the make-ahead convenience, great flavor and texture combinations, and the ability to serve it at room temperature for casual dining. This delicious salad combines all those elements with another summer love: grilled vegetables. Add chickpeas or diced baked tofu for a heartier dish. If a grill basket is unavailable, grill the vegetables whole or halved and cut them into bite-size pieces after they are cooked.*

8 ounces radiatore or other small pasta

½ cup plus 2 tablespoons olive oil

3 tablespoons cider vinegar

½ teaspoon sugar

¼ teaspoon dry mustard

½ teaspoon salt

⅛ teaspoon freshly ground black pepper

1 cup halved ripe cherry tomatoes

¼ cup minced fresh parsley

1 small zucchini, cut into ¼-inch slices

1 small yellow squash, cut into ¼-inch slices

1 medium red bell pepper, seeded and cut into ½-inch dice

1 medium red onion, cut into ½-inch dice

1 cup white mushrooms, lightly rinse, patted dry, and quartered

1. In a large pot of boiling salted water, cook the pasta, stirring occasionally, until al dente, about 10 minutes. Drain well and transfer to a large bowl.

2. Preheat the grill. In a small bowl, combine the ½ cup oil, vinegar, sugar, mustard, salt, and black pepper. Pour enough dressing onto the pasta to coat. Add the tomatoes and parsley and toss to combine. Set aside.

continues on next page

3. In a large bowl, combine the zucchini, yellow squash, bell pepper, onion, and mushrooms. Add the remaining 2 tablespoons oil and season with salt and black pepper to taste. Toss to coat. Transfer the vegetables to a lightly oiled grill basket. Place the basket on the hot grill, and cook until the vegetables are grilled on the outside and slightly tender on the inside, 12 to 15 minutes.

4. Add the grilled vegetables to the pasta mixture and toss to combine. Serve warm or at room temperature.

## winter pasta salad with creamy mustard vinaigrette 🅕

makes 4 servings

*The hearty character of the dressing and vegetables makes this an ideal choice for a winter salad and a good addition to a buffet table or potluck. The dressing is also perfect for a green salad, so you may want to double that part of the recipe to use again later.*

8 ounces ziti

2½ cups broccoli florets

1 small red onion, chopped

2 medium carrots, grated

1½ cups frozen peas, thawed

½ cup silken tofu, drained

3 tablespoons Dijon mustard

2 tablespoons cider vinegar

2 tablespoons olive oil

½ teaspoon salt

⅛ teaspoon freshly ground black pepper

1. In a large pot of boiling salted water, cook the ziti, stirring occasionally, until al dente,

about 10 minutes. About 2 minutes before the pasta is finished cooking, stir in the broccoli. Drain and rinse the pasta and broccoli under cold water. Transfer the pasta and broccoli to a large bowl and add the onion, carrots, and peas. Set aside.

2. In a blender or food processor, combine the tofu, mustard, vinegar, oil, salt, and pepper and blend until smooth. Taste, adjusting seasonings if necessary. Pour the dressing over the pasta salad and toss gently to combine. Serve chilled or at room temperature.

## tarragon pasta salad with red and green grapes 🅕

makes 4 servings

*The slightly licorice flavor of tarragon permeates this refreshing salad studded with juicy sweet grapes and crunchy toasted almond slivers.*

8 ounces penne

1½ cups red seedless grapes

1 cup green seedless grapes

¼ cup chopped red onion

1 celery rib, minced

¼ cup fresh lemon juice

½ teaspoon salt

¼ teaspoon freshly ground black pepper

⅓ cup olive oil

1 tablespoon minced fresh tarragon or 1 teaspoon dried

⅓ cup toasted slivered almonds

1. In a large pot of boiling salted water, cook the penne, stirring occasionally, until al dente, about 10 minutes. Drain well and rinse under cold water. Transfer the pasta to a large bowl and add the red and green grapes, onion, and celery. Set aside.

**2.** In a small bowl, combine the lemon juice, salt, and pepper. Whisk in the olive oil until blended, then pour dressing over pasta. Add the tarragon and almonds and toss gently to combine. Serve chilled or at room temperature.

# california pasta salad

makes 4 servings

*Three favorite California crops—avocados, walnuts, and Meyer lemons—are the inspiration for this tasty salad. If the delightfully fragrant Meyer lemons are unavailable, heave a sigh and move forward using regular lemons— you may need to add a pinch of sugar if the lemons are too tart.*

8 ounces penne

½ medium red bell pepper, cut into matchsticks

1 medium carrot, shredded

3 green onions, minced

¾ cup kalamata olives, pitted and halved

¾ cup coarsely chopped walnuts

⅓ cup olive oil

3 tablespoons Meyer lemon juice

Salt and freshly ground black pepper

2 ripe Hass avocados

¼ cup torn fresh basil leaves

**1.** In a pot of boiling salted water, cook the penne, stirring occasionally, until al dente, about 10 minutes. Drain well and transfer to a large bowl. Add the bell pepper, carrot, green onions, olives, and walnuts, and toss to combine. Set aside.

**2.** In a separate bowl, combine the oil, lemon juice, and salt and black pepper to taste. Pit, peel, and dice the avocado and add to the dressing, tossing to coat. Add the avocado mixture to the pasta mixture along with the basil leaves

and toss gently to combine. Taste, adjusting seasonings if necessary, and serve immediately.

# farfalle with crunchy crucifers and creamy poppy seed dressing

makes 4 servings

*The sweet-and-sour poppy seed dressing accents the flavor of the cauliflower and broccoli, two popular members of the crucifer family, known for their many health benefits.*

8 ounces farfalle

2 cups broccoli florets

2 cups cauliflower florets

4 ounces silken tofu, drained

1 tablespoon Dijon mustard

1 teaspoon pure maple syrup

1 tablespoon cider vinegar

2 teaspoons poppy seeds

2 tablespoons olive oil

½ teaspoon salt

¼ teaspoon freshly ground black pepper

**1.** In a large pot of boiling salted water, cook the farfalle, stirring occasionally, until al dente, about 10 minutes. During the last 5 minutes of cooking time, add the broccoli and cauliflower. Drain the pasta and vegetables and rinse under cold water. Transfer to a large bowl and set aside.

**2.** In a blender or food processor, combine the tofu, mustard, maple syrup, vinegar, poppy seeds, oil, salt, and pepper. Blend until smooth. Taste, adjusting seasonings if necessary. Pour the dressing over the pasta salad and toss gently to combine. Serve chilled or at room temperature.

# last-minute italian-style pasta salad 🅕

makes 4 to 6 servings

*While this salad is perfectly delicious made solely with pantry ingredients, feel free to add any fresh vegetables you may have on hand, such as green onions, red onions, cucumbers, or carrots.*

8 ounces penne, rotini, or other small pasta

1½ cups cooked or 1 (15.5-ounce) can chickpeas, drained and rinsed

½ cup pitted kalamata olives

½ cup minced oil-packed sun-dried tomatoes

1 (6-ounce) jar marinated artichoke hearts, drained

2 jarred roasted red peppers (or see page 10), chopped

½ cup frozen peas, thawed

1 tablespoon capers

2 teaspoons dried chives

½ cup olive oil

¼ cup white wine vinegar

½ teaspoon dried basil

1 garlic clove, minced

½ teaspoon sugar

Salt and freshly ground black pepper

1. In a pot of boiling salted water, cook the pasta, stirring occasionally, until al dente, about 10 minutes. Drain well and transfer to a large bowl. Add the chickpeas, olives, tomatoes, artichoke hearts, roasted peppers, peas, capers, and chives. Toss gently and set aside.

2. In a small bowl, combine the oil, vinegar, basil, garlic, sugar, and salt and black pepper to taste. Pour the dressing onto the pasta salad and toss to combine. Serve chilled or at room temperature.

# macaroni salad

makes 4 to 6 servings

*Vegan mayonnaise is used to make this creamy classic made with elbow macaroni, celery, and sweet pickle relish. The bell pepper and onion lend additional flavor and color, but you can omit these ingredients if you prefer a more basic version or are making it for children.*

12 ounces elbow macaroni

2 celery ribs, minced

¼ cup finely minced red bell pepper

3 tablespoons sweet pickle relish

2 tablespoons minced red onion

¾ cup vegan mayonnaise, homemade (page 573) or store-bought

1½ teaspoons Dijon mustard

3 tablespoons soy milk

3 tablespoons apple cider vinegar

2 teaspoons sugar

½ teaspoon salt

Paprika, for garnish

1. In a pot of boiling salted water, cook the macaroni, stirring occasionally, until al dente, about 8 minutes. Drain, rinse with cold water, and transfer to a large bowl. Add the celery, bell pepper, pickle relish, and onion, and set aside.

2. In a small bowl, combine the mayonnaise, mustard, soy milk, vinegar, sugar, and salt and blend well. Add the dressing to the macaroni mixture and stir gently to combine. Sprinkle with paprika, cover, and refrigerate to chill, about 2 hours, before serving.

# creamy curry pasta and vegetable salad

makes 4 to 6 servings

*Curry isn't usually the first thing that comes to mind when we think of pasta salads, but this combination is so flavorful, you may find yourself thinking about (and making) it more than once.*

8 ounces radiatore or other bite-size pasta

2 cups cauliflower, cut into 1-inch florets

1 small red bell pepper, cut into ¼-inch dice

½ cup minced red onion

1 cup ripe grape tomatoes, halved

½ medium English cucumber, peeled and cut into ¼-inch dice

2 tablespoons minced fresh cilantro

2 tablespoons fresh lemon juice

2 teaspoons Madras curry powder

½ teaspoon sugar

½ teaspoon salt

⅛ teaspoon ground cayenne

⅓ cup grapeseed oil

Chopped unsalted roasted cashews, for garnish

1. In a pot of boiling salted water, cook the pasta, stirring occasionally, until al dente, about 10 minutes. About halfway through the cooking time, add the cauliflower. Drain, rinse with cold water, and transfer to a large bowl. Add the bell pepper, onion, tomatoes, cucumber, and cilantro. Set aside.

2. In a small bowl, combine the lemon juice, curry powder, sugar, salt, and cayenne. Stir in the oil and blend well. Pour the dressing onto the salad and toss gently to combine. Sprinkle the salad with chopped cashews. Serve chilled or at room temperature.

# rotini remoulade

makes 4 servings

*This pasta salad pairs springy rotini with a lively remoulade, a mayonnaise-based sauce of French origin, popular in New Orleans. Similar to tartar sauce, but infinitely more flavorful, remoulade sauce includes capers, mustard, and chopped pickles, and often a healthy dash of hot sauce. The result is an intriguing and zesty variation on the old-fashioned macaroni salad.*

8 ounces rotini pasta

¼ cup grated red onion

1 celery rib, minced

¼ cup minced green bell pepper

¾ cup vegan mayonnaise, homemade (page 573) or store-bought

¼ cup soy milk

2 tablespoons sweet pickle relish

1 tablespoon minced capers

2 tablespoons minced fresh parsley

2 tablespoons fresh lemon juice

1 tablespoon tomato ketchup

1 teaspoon Creole mustard or other dark coarse mustard

Tabasco sauce, to taste

Salt

1. In a large pot of boiling salted water, cook the rotini, stirring occasionally, until al dente, about 10 minutes. Drain, rinse with cold water, and set aside in a large bowl. Add the onion, celery, and bell pepper and set aside.

2. In a small bowl, combine the mayonnaise, soy milk, relish, capers, parsley, lemon juice, ketchup, mustard, Tabasco, and salt to taste. Blend until smooth. Add the dressing to the pasta mixture and combine well. Taste, adjusting seasonings if necessary. Serve chilled or at room temperature.

# asian noodle salad with tempeh

makes 4 servings

*This salad combines chewy noodles and tempeh with crunchy vegetables and a creamy, spicy peanut dressing. It is hearty enough to make a satisfying side dish for four people or a one-dish meal for two.*

8 ounces tempeh

2 tablespoons grapeseed oil

3 tablespoons soy sauce

8 ounces linguine or thin rice noodles

1 tablespoon toasted sesame oil

½ cup creamy peanut butter

2 garlic cloves, minced

1 teaspoon Asian chili paste

1 teaspoon grated fresh ginger

1 teaspoon sugar

2 tablespoons rice wine vinegar

½ cup water

1 medium carrot, shredded

1 medium red bell pepper, cut into matchsticks

½ cup frozen baby peas, thawed

¼ cup minced green onions

1. In a medium saucepan of simmering water, cook the tempeh for 30 minutes. Drain and cool slightly, then cut into ½-inch dice. In a large skillet, heat the grapeseed oil over medium heat. Add the tempeh and cook until browned, about 8 minutes. Splash with 1 tablespoon of the soy sauce and set aside to cool.

2. In a large pot of boiling salted water, cook the linguine, stirring occasionally, until al dente, about 10 minutes. (If using rice noodles, cook according to package directions.) Drain, rinse under cold water, and transfer to a large bowl. Add the sesame oil and toss to coat the noodles.

3. In a small bowl, combine the peanut butter, garlic, chili paste, ginger, sugar, vinegar, water, and the remaining 2 tablespoons soy sauce, stirring well to blend. Add the dressing to the noodles along with the carrot, bell pepper, peas, green onions, and reserved tempeh. Toss gently to combine. Serve at room temperature.

# sesame udon salad with adzuki beans and baby spinach ⓕ

makes 4 servings

*The natural affinity of spinach and sesame are played out nicely against the backdrop of udon—thick and chewy Japanese wheat noodles. They are available in natural food stores and Asian markets, as are the adzuki beans, a small red protein-rich bean that can be found dried or canned.*

8 ounces udon noodles

¼ cup plus 1 teaspoon toasted sesame oil

3 cups fresh baby spinach, cut into ¼-inch strips

1½ cups cooked or 1 (15-ounce) can adzuki beans, drained and rinsed

¼ cup minced green onions

2 tablespoon rice vinegar

1 tablespoon soy sauce

1 teaspoon grated fresh ginger

1. Add the noodles to a pot of boiling water. Return the water to a gentle boil, then reduce the heat to a simmer. Cook, stirring occasionally, until the noodles are tender but not mushy, 6 to 8 minutes. Drain and rinse under cold water. Transfer the noodles to a large bowl and toss with the 1 teaspoon of the oil. Add the spinach, beans, and green onions and set aside.

2. In a small bowl, combine the vinegar, soy sauce, ginger, and remaining ¼ cup oil. Stir to

blend well. Pour the dressing over the salad, toss gently to combine, and serve.

## chilled glass noodles with snow peas and baked tofu

makes 4 servings

*Glass noodles, made from mung bean flour, are also called cellophane noodles, bean thread noodles, and* harusame. *Marinated baked tofu is available at well-stocked supermarkets and natural food stores. Look for one marinated with Thai or Asian flavors for best results.*

4 ounces glass noodles

1 (8-ounce) package marinated baked tofu, cut into ½-inch dice

1 ounce snow peas, trimmed and diagonally cut into 1-inch pieces

1 medium English cucumber, peeled, seeded, and cut into ¼-inch slices

1 medium carrot, grated

¼ cup minced green onions

2 tablespoons chopped fresh cilantro

½ cup unsalted roasted peanuts, crushed or chopped

2 tablespoons toasted sesame oil

2 tablespoons grapeseed oil

2 tablespoons rice vinegar

1 tablespoon soy sauce

1 garlic clove, minced

1. Soak the noodles in a heatproof bowl of boiling water until softened, 8 to 10 minutes. Drain well and rinse under cold water.

2. Cut the noodles into thirds and place them in a large bowl. Add the tofu, snow peas, cucumber, carrot, green onions, cilantro, and peanuts. Set aside.

3. In a small bowl, combine the oils, vinegar, soy sauce, and garlic, stirring to blend well. Add the dressing to the salad and toss gently to combine. Refrigerate for 30 minutes before serving.

## FRUIT SALADS

## mango-avocado salad with macadamias and pomegranate seeds (f)

makes 4 servings

*It has often been said that we first eat with our eyes and then with our mouths. Just taste this beautiful and delicious salad, and all your senses will be in for a treat! Substitute dried cranberries for color if pomegranate seeds are unavailable.*

1 firm ripe mango, peeled, pitted, and cut into ½-inch dice

2 ripe Hass avocados, pitted, peeled, and cut into ½-inch dice

2 tablespoons fresh lime juice

2 teaspoons agave nectar

¼ cup crushed macadamia nuts

1 tablespoon fresh pomegranate seeds

1 tablespoon fresh mint or cilantro leaves

1. In a large bowl, combine the mango and avocados.

2. Add the lime juice and agave nectar and toss gently to coat the fruit. Sprinkle with macadamias, pomegranate seeds, and mint leaves. Serve immediately.

# blazing sunset salad

makes 4 to 6 servings

*The fiery colors of a summer sunset were the inspiration for this fruit salad. Feel free to mix and match the ingredients with other similarly colored fruits such as nectarines, mango, cantaloupe, or apricots.*

2 tablespoons lemon juice

2 tablespoons agave nectar

1 Golden Delicious apple, unpeeled, cored, and cut into ½-inch dice

1 orange, peeled, sectioned, and cut into ½-inch dice

1 banana, cut into ¼-inch slices

1 peach or nectarine, halved, pitted, and cut into ½-inch dice

1 cup pitted fresh cherries

In a large bowl, combine the lemon juice and agave nectar, stirring to blend. Add the apple, orange, banana, peach, and cherries. Stir gently to combine and serve.

# fruit salad in winter

makes 4 servings

*Walnuts and walnut oil add a nutty richness to this flavorful fruit salad made with winter fruits. Thinly sliced star fruit adds a touch of whimsy.*

2 teaspoons walnut oil

2 tablespoons fresh lemon juice

1 tablespoon agave nectar

1 Fuji, Gala, or Red Delicious apple, cored and cut into ½-inch dice

1 large ripe pear, cored and cut into ½-inch dice

1 large orange, peeled and cut into ½-inch dice

1 cup seedless red grapes, halved

1 small star fruit (carambola), cut into ¼-inch slices

½ cup chopped walnuts

1. In a small bowl, combine the walnut oil, lemon juice, and agave nectar. Blend well and set aside.

2. In a large bowl, combine the apple, pear, orange, grapes, star fruit, and walnuts. Drizzle with dressing, toss to coat, and serve.

# summer berries with fresh mint

makes 4 to 6 servings

*This celebration of summer berries can be adapted, depending on availability. If one or more of the fruits are unavailable, double up on the others. You can serve the fruit without the sauce, but I think it truly adds a touch of elegance while also unifying the flavors.*

2 tablespoons fresh orange or pineapple juice

1 tablespoon fresh lime juice

1 tablespoon agave nectar

2 teaspoons minced fresh mint

2 cups pitted fresh cherries

1 cup fresh blueberries

1 cup fresh strawberries, hulled and halved

½ cup fresh blackberries or raspberries

1. In a small bowl, combine the orange juice, lime juice, agave nectar, and mint. Set aside.

2. In a large bowl, combine the cherries, blueberries, strawberries, and blackberries. Add the dressing and toss gently to combine. Serve immediately.

## curried fruit salad 🅕

makes 4 to 6 servings

*Serve this lovely salad as a refreshing accompaniment to a curry or other Indian-inspired meal.*

¾ cup vegan vanilla yogurt

¼ cup finely chopped mango chutney

1 tablespoon fresh lime juice

1 teaspoon mild curry powder

1 Fuji or Gala apple, cored and cut into ½-inch dice

2 ripe peaches, halved, pitted, and cut into ½-inch dice

4 ripe black plums, halved and cut into ¼-inch slices

1 ripe mango, peeled, pitted, and cut into ½-inch dice

1 cup red seedless grapes, halved

¼ cup unsweetened toasted shredded coconut

¼ cup toasted slivered almonds

1. In a small bowl, combine the yogurt, chutney, lime juice, and curry powder and stir until well blended. Set aside.

2. In a large bowl, combine the apple, peaches, plums, mango, grapes, coconut, and almonds. Add the dressing, toss gently to coat, and serve.

## "mixed grill" fruit platter 🅕

makes 4 to 6 servings

*Before grilling fruit, it is important that your grill is scrupulously clean.*

½ cup white grape juice

¼ cup sugar

1 pineapple, peeled, cored, and cut into ½-inch slices

2 ripe black or purple plums, halved and stoned

2 ripe peaches, halved and pitted

2 ripe bananas, halved lengthwise

1. Preheat the grill. In a small saucepan, heat the grape juice and sugar over medium heat, stirring, until the sugar dissolves. Remove from heat and set aside to cool.

2. Transfer the fruit to the hot grill and grill for 2 to 4 minutes, depending on the fruit. Arrange the grilled fruit on a serving platter and drizzle with the syrup. Serve at room temperature.

## fruit salad with a hint of heat 🅕

makes 4 servings

*A touch of cayenne enlivens this flavorful combination of fruit made especially appealing by the garnish of pumpkin seeds, dried cranberries, and fresh mint. If you don't like the idea of a slightly spicy fruit salad, leave out the cayenne.*

⅓ cup pineapple juice

2 tablespoons fresh lime juice

1 tablespoon agave nectar

Ground cayenne

1 navel orange, peeled and cut into 1-inch dice

1 ripe pear, cored and cut into 1-inch dice

1 ripe banana, cut into ¼-inch slices

1½ cups fresh or canned pineapple chunks

2 tablespoons sweetened dried cranberries

2 tablespoons shelled pumpkin seeds (pepitas)

1 tablespoon chopped fresh mint

1. In a large bowl, combine the pineapple juice, lime juice, agave nectar, and cayenne to taste, stirring to blend well.

2. Add the orange, pear, banana, and pineapple. Toss gently to combine, sprinkle with the cranberries, pumpkin seeds, and mint, and serve.

# orange and fig salad with walnuts and dried cherries 🅕

makes 4 servings

*In addition to serving this festive mélange as a salad or side, it makes a great winter dessert. If dried cherries are unavailable, substitute dried cranberries.*

3 oranges, peeled and chopped
½ cup coarsely chopped fresh or dried figs
½ cup chopped walnuts
3 tablespoons sweetened flaked coconut
1 tablespoon fresh lemon juice
1 teaspoon sugar
2 tablespoons sweetened dried cherries

In a bowl, combine the oranges, figs, and walnuts. Add the coconut, lemon juice, and sugar. Toss gently to combine. Sprinkle with the cherries and serve.

# strawberry, mango, and pineapple salad with banana-lime dressing 🅕

makes 4 servings

*When all or some of your fruit is past its peak, the sweet-tart dressing can improve the overall flavor. However, if your fruit is perfectly sweet and ripe, you may want to reserve the dressing for another day. The tangy dressing should enhance the flavors and textures of the fruit, not mask them.*

2 cups fresh or canned diced pineapple, juice reserved
1 mango, peeled, pitted, and cut into ½-inch dice
2 cups thinly sliced hulled fresh strawberries
1 ripe banana
¼ cup fresh orange juice
2 tablespoons fresh lime juice
1 tablespoon sugar

1. In a large bowl, combine the pineapple, mango, and strawberries. Set aside.

2. In a blender or food processor, puree the banana with the reserved pineapple juice, orange juice, lime juice, and sugar. Pour the dressing over the fruit, toss gently to combine, and serve.

# cherry berry watermelon salad 🅕

makes 4 to 6 servings

*The vivid colors of this salad are astonishingly beautiful. If your fruit is perfectly sweet, you may want to forgo making the sauce and just serve the fruit unadorned.*

⅓ cup fresh orange juice
1 tablespoon fresh lime juice
1 teaspoon pure vanilla extract
1 teaspoon sugar
4 cups seedless watermelon cubes or balls
2 cups pitted fresh cherries
1 cup fresh blueberries

In a large bowl, combine the orange juice, lime juice, vanilla, and sugar. Add the watermelon, cherries, and blueberries. Toss gently to combine and serve.

# SALAD DRESSINGS

## basic balsamic vinaigrette

makes about ¾ cup

*The rich, full-bodied flavor of balsamic vinegar has made it a favorite for dressing most any green salad. Try it tossed with mixed baby greens.*

1 tablespoon finely chopped shallots
½ teaspoon Dijon mustard
1 teaspoon sugar
½ teaspoon salt
¼ teaspoon freshly ground black pepper
2 tablespoons balsamic vinegar
½ cup olive oil

In a small bowl, combine the shallots, mustard, sugar, salt, and pepper. Stir in the vinegar. Add the oil, whisking constantly until blended. Store leftover dressing tightly covered in the refrigerator, where it will keep for 3 to 4 days.

## dijon vinaigrette

makes about 1¼ cups

*This tangy vinaigrette is best on a crisp crunchy lettuce such as romaine, perhaps in a mix with assertive greens like arugula or chicory.*

¼ cup white wine vinegar
2 tablespoons Dijon mustard
1 garlic clove
1 medium shallot

½ teaspoon dried basil or marjoram
1 tablespoon chopped fresh parsley
½ teaspoon salt
¼ teaspoon freshly ground black pepper
¾ cup olive oil

In a blender or food processor, puree the vinegar, mustard, garlic, shallot, basil, parsley, salt, and pepper. Stream in the oil and blend until smooth. Store leftover dressing tightly covered in the refrigerator, where it will keep for 3 to 4 days.

## oh-my-goddess dressing

makes about 1 cup

*A variety of herbs provides the lovely green color to this interpretation of green goddess dressing and tahini lends a creamy texture. Use it to dress the Greek Goddess Salad (page 54).*

2 garlic cloves, crushed
2 green onions, chopped
2 tablespoons chopped fresh parsley
1 tablespoon chopped fresh basil leaves
1 tablespoon chopped chives
¼ cup olive oil
¼ cup tahini (sesame paste)
2 tablespoons tarragon vinegar
1 tablespoon fresh lemon juice
½ teaspoon salt
¼ teaspoon freshly ground black pepper

Combine all the ingredients in a blender or food processor and process until well blended. Store leftover dressing tightly covered in the refrigerator, where it will keep for 2 to 3 days.

## tarragon-chive vinaigrette

makes about 1 cup

*This light, flavorful dressing is ideal for tossed green salads made with soft Bibb or butterhead lettuces. It's also good drizzled over steamed or roasted asparagus.*

3 tablespoons tarragon vinegar

2 tablespoons chopped fresh tarragon
or 2 teaspoons dried

1 tablespoon snipped fresh chives or
1 teaspoon dried

¼ teaspoon dry mustard

½ teaspoon sugar

½ teaspoon salt

⅛ teaspoon black pepper

½ cup olive oil

In a small bowl, whisk together the vinegar, tarragon, chives, mustard, sugar, salt, and pepper until blended. Whisk in the oil until smooth. Store leftover dressing tightly covered in the refrigerator, where it will keep for 2 to 3 days.

## carrot-ginger dressing

makes about 1 cup

*The fresh taste of carrot and ginger are the stars of this dressing that is great drizzled over a spinach salad or used as a slaw dressing with shredded cabbage.*

2 medium carrots, shredded

2 tablespoons chopped fresh ginger

3 tablespoons rice wine vinegar

3 tablespoons fresh orange juice

1 tablespoon soy sauce

1 tablespoon mirin

2 tablespoons grapeseed oil

In a blender or food processor, combine the carrots, ginger, and vinegar and blend until smooth. Add the orange juice, soy sauce, mirin, and oil and blend until smooth. Taste, adjusting seasonings if necessary, and add a splash more orange juice if a thinner dressing is desired. Store leftover dressing tightly covered in the refrigerator, where it will keep for 1 to 2 days.

## green olive herb dressing

makes ½ cup

*This boldly flavored dressing is well suited to a pairing with assertive greens such as arugula. It can also be used to dazzle baked tofu or roasted cauliflower.*

2 tablespoons green olive tapenade, homemade
(page 9) or store-bought

1 tablespoon fresh lemon juice

¼ cup olive oil

2 tablespoons chopped green onions

1 tablespoon chopped fresh parsley

1 teaspoon snipped fresh chives

½ teaspoon dried basil

¼ teaspoon dried marjoram

Pinch ground cayenne

In a small bowl, whisk together the tapenade, lemon juice, and olive oil until well blended. Stir in the green onions, parsley, chives, basil, marjoram, and cayenne. Mix until well blended. Store leftover dressing tightly covered in the refrigerator, where it will keep for 1 to 2 days.

# creamy cucumber dressing ⓕ

makes about 2 cups

*Drizzle this refreshing dressing over a simple salad of leaf lettuce and sliced tomatoes.*

1 medium English cucumber, peeled
¾ cup plain vegan yogurt
1½ tablespoons fresh lemon juice
¼ teaspoon salt
⅛ teaspoon ground cayenne
2 tablespoons minced fresh parsley

Finely chop ⅓ of the cucumber and set aside. Coarsely chop the remaining cucumber and transfer to a blender or food processor. Add the yogurt, lemon juice, salt, and cayenne and blend until smooth. Transfer to a bowl and stir in the parsley and reserved chopped cucumber. This dressing is best if used on the same day it is made.

# creamy artichoke dressing ⓕ

makes about 1½ cups

*Marinated artichoke hearts make this tart, tangy dressing quick and easy to prepare. It reminds me a little of a Caesar dressing, so I like to toss it with crisp romaine lettuce. It also makes a zesty dressing for a pasta salad or can be used to perk up steamed vegetables such as green beans or broccoli.*

1 (6-ounce) jar marinated artichoke hearts, undrained
2 garlic cloves, crushed
¼ cup olive oil
2 tablespoons fresh lemon juice
¼ teaspoon salt
⅛ teaspoon ground cayenne

Combine all the ingredients in a blender or food processor and process until smooth and creamy. Store leftover dressing tightly covered in the refrigerator, where it will keep for up to 2 days.

# sesame-orange dressing ⓕ

makes about 1 cup

*Tahini gives this dressing a creamy texture while sesame oil amps up the sesame flavor. It's great drizzled over a salad to accompany a sushi dinner.*

½ cup fresh orange juice
¼ cup tahini (sesame paste)
2 tablespoons soy sauce
1 tablespoon toasted sesame oil
2 tablespoons rice wine vinegar
⅛ teaspoon ground cayenne

In a small bowl, combine the orange juice and tahini and stir until well blended. Add the soy sauce, oil, vinegar, and cayenne. Stir until smooth. This dressing is best if used on the same day it is made.

# lemony white miso vinaigrette

makes about ½ cup

*This refreshing dressing, made with miso, soy sauce, and sesame oil, has a decidedly Asian flavor. In addition to being great on salads, it makes a good marinade for tofu.*

2 tablespoons white miso paste
1 tablespoon fresh lemon juice
1 tablespoon water
2 teaspoons soy sauce
1 teaspoon agave nectar
½ teaspoon Dijon mustard
¼ cup grapeseed oil
1 tablespoon toasted sesame oil

In a small bowl, combine the miso paste, lemon juice, water, soy sauce, agave nectar, and mustard, stirring until blended. Stir in the grapeseed oil and sesame oil and blend until smooth. Store leftover dressing tightly covered in the refrigerator, where it will keep for 2 to 3 days.

# creamy avocado dressing

makes about 1 cup

*If you prefer more of a Southwestern flavor, use lime juice instead of lemon juice and replace the parsley with cilantro. This creamy dressing is great on crunchy lettuces such as romaine or iceberg.*

2 garlic cloves, minced
1 ripe Hass avocado, pitted and peeled
¼ cup minced fresh parsley
1½ tablespoons fresh lemon juice
2 tablespoons water
½ teaspoon salt
⅛ teaspoon ground cayenne
¼ cup olive oil

In a blender or food processor, combine the garlic, avocado, parsley, lemon juice, water, salt, and cayenne and blend until smooth. Add the oil and process until smooth and creamy. This dressing is best if used on the same day it is made.

# creamy tahini dressing

makes about 1¼ cups

*In addition to using on green salads, this dressing is for noodle salads or can be drizzled on steamed chilled spinach.*

½ cup tahini (sesame paste)
¼ cup water
2 tablespoons fresh lemon juice
2 tablespoons soy sauce
1 tablespoon toasted sesame oil
2 tablespoons minced fresh parsley
Salt
Ground cayenne

In a small bowl, combine the tahini and water, stirring to blend. Add the lemon juice, soy sauce, sesame oil, and parsley and stir until well combined. Season with salt and cayenne to taste. Store leftover dressing tightly covered in the refrigerator, where it will keep for 2 to 3 days.

# lime-cilantro dressing

makes about 1 cup

*Serve this refreshing dressing on a salad made with crunchy romaine or iceberg lettuce to accompany a spicy Mexican meal. It also makes a good sauce for sandwich wraps.*

¾ cup plain vegan yogurt
¼ cup minced fresh cilantro
1 tablespoon fresh lime juice
½ teaspoon sugar
¼ teaspoon ground cumin
¼ teaspoon salt
⅛ teaspoon ground cayenne

Combine all the ingredients in a small bowl and whisk together until well blended. This dressing is best if used on the same day it is made.

# citrus vinaigrette

makes ½ cup

*This light and refreshing dressing is especially good on soft leaf salads such as Bibb, butterhead, or red leaf. It can also add sparkle to chilled steamed vegetables such as asparagus or broccoli.*

2 teaspoons agave nectar
½ teaspoon Dijon mustard
2 tablespoons fresh orange juice
½ tablespoon fresh lemon juice
½ tablespoon fresh lime juice
Salt
Ground cayenne
¼ cup olive oil

In a small bowl, whisk together the agave nectar, mustard, orange juice, lemon juice, and lime juice. Add salt and cayenne to taste. Whisk in the oil until well blended. This dressing is best if used on the same day it is made.

# ginger soy vinaigrette

makes about ½ cup

*A little of this dressing goes a long way, so drizzle—don't pour—onto your salad. It can also be used as a marinade for tofu or tempeh.*

2 teaspoons minced fresh ginger
1 large garlic clove, crushed
1 teaspoon sugar
3 tablespoons soy sauce
3 tablespoons rice wine vinegar
1 tablespoon toasted sesame oil

Combine all the ingredients in a small bowl. Whisk until well blended. Store leftover dressing tightly covered in the refrigerator, where it will keep for 3 to 4 days.

# SANDWICHES, PIZZA, AND MORE

❧ ❧ ❧ ❧ ❧

## SANDWICHES AND WRAPS

tempeh reuben sandwiches

portobello po'boys

tastes like tuna salad sandwiches

sloppy bulgur sandwiches

curried tofu "egg salad" pitas

garden patch sandwiches on multigrain bread

creamy, crunchy fruit-and-nut sandwiches

marinated mushroom wraps

peanutty tofu roll-ups

garden salad wraps

tempeh-walnut "chicken" salad wraps

avocado and tempeh bacon wraps

chickpea-tomato wraps

tofu waldorf salad wraps

teriyaki tofu wraps

tofu-tahini veggie wraps

deconstructed hummus pitas

muffaletta sandwiches

falafel sandwiches

vietnamese po'boys

## BURGERS

tempeh tantrum burgers

grilled portobello burgers

macadamia-cashew patties

pecan-lentil burgers

black bean burgers

some-kinda-nut burgers

golden veggie burgers

red lentil patties in pita

white bean and walnut patties

curried chickpea patties

pinto bean patties with chile-lime "mayo"

## Fajitas and Burritos

seared portobello fajitas

beer-marinated seitan fajitas

seitan tacos

refried bean and salsa quesadillas

spinach, mushroom, and black bean quesadillas

black bean and corn burritos

red bean burritos

## Pizzas, Calzones, Stromboli, and Turnovers

basic pizza dough

vegan margherita pizza

portobello and black olive pizza

ebap (everything but animal products) pizza

white pizza with potato, onion, and yellow tomatoes

spicy southwestern-style pizza

tapenade and tomato pizza

spicy mushroom and hot pepper calzones

roasted vegetable stromboli

spicy tempeh empanadas

quick pinto-potato empanadas

lentil walnut pasties

mushroom turnovers

indian-style pizza

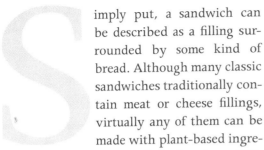

imply put, a sandwich can be described as a filling surrounded by some kind of bread. Although many classic sandwiches traditionally contain meat or cheese fillings, virtually any of them can be made with plant-based ingredients, such as the Tempeh Reuben (page 107), the Curried Tofu "Egg Salad" Pitas (page 110), and the Portobello Po'boys (page 107).

Other favorites in the sandwich family are burgers and wraps, and this chapter includes several made with tofu, tempeh, seitan, beans, nuts, and a variety of vegetables.

Of course, you can always make the reliable standby, a peanut butter and jelly sandwich, perhaps giving the classic PB&J your own creative spin by varying the flavor of jelly or jam, using a different nut butter, such as almond or cashew, or by slipping in a flavorful addition such as sliced bananas or some dried cranberries. For the ultimate PB&J, you can make your own nut butter, jam, and even bread.

Bread choices expand beyond white, wheat, or rye, and move into tortillas, pita, lavash, and baguettes. Portable and flavorful, sandwiches can be enjoyed in a brown-bag lunch or on a picnic, or served at home for lunch or a casual dinner accompanied by a soup, salad, or other sides.

Another casual mealtime favorite is pizza, America's most popular import. Given the prominence of a cheesy topping on today's average pizza, it's interesting to note that the original Italian pizzas were topped with no cheese at all, but with tomatoes, olive oil, garlic, and oregano—naturally and deliciously vegan. In addition to a master crust recipe, this chapter includes recipes for pizza with a variety of creative toppings as well as other dough-based delights such as calzones, stromboli, and empanadas.

# SANDWICHES AND WRAPS

## tempeh reuben sandwiches

makes 2 sandwiches

*Tempeh and sauerkraut have a natural affinity for one another, as you'll discover when you bite into this satisfying Reuben sandwich. It's perfectly delicious without the vegan cheese, but if you want to include it, lay some on. Garlicky deli-style pickles and coleslaw make good accompaniments.*

8 ounces tempeh

3 tablespoons vegan mayonnaise, homemade (page 573) or store-bought

1½ tablespoons ketchup

1 tablespoon sweet pickle relish

1 green onion, minced

2 tablespoons olive oil

Salt and freshly ground black pepper

1½ tablespoons vegan margarine

4 slices rye or pumpernickel bread

¾ cup sauerkraut, well drained

1. In a medium saucepan of simmering water, cook the tempeh for 30 minutes. Drain the tempeh and set aside to cool. Pat dry and cut into ¼-inch slices.

2. In a small bowl, combine the mayonnaise, ketchup, relish, and green onion. Season with salt and pepper to taste, blend well, and set aside.

3. In a medium skillet, heat the oil over medium heat. Add the tempeh and cook until golden brown on both sides, about 10 minutes

total. Season with salt and pepper to taste. Remove from the skillet and set aside.

4. Wipe out the skillet and set aside. Spread margarine on one side of each slice of bread. Place 2 slices of bread, margarine side down, in the skillet. Spread the dressing onto both slices of bread and layer with the fried tempeh and the sauerkraut.

5. Top each with the remaining 2 slices of bread, margarine side up. Transfer the sandwiches to the skillet and cook until lightly browned on both sides, turning once, about 2 minutes per side.

6. Remove the sandwiches from the skillet, cut in half, and serve immediately.

## portobello po'boys 🅕

makes 4 po'boys

*Juicy chunks of portobello mushrooms replace the traditional oysters in this flavorful interpretation of the Southern classic. Leave the Tabasco bottle on the table for anyone who wants an extra splash.*

3 tablespoons olive oil

4 portobello mushroom caps, lightly rinsed, patted dry, and cut into 1-inch pieces

1 teaspoon Cajun seasoning

Salt and freshly ground black pepper

¼ cup vegan mayonnaise, homemade (page 573) or store-bought

4 crusty sandwich rolls, halved horizontally

4 slices ripe tomato

1½ cups shredded romaine lettuce

Tabasco sauce

1. In a large skillet, heat the oil over medium heat. Add the mushrooms and cook until

continues on next page

browned and softened, about 8 minutes. Season with the Cajun seasoning and salt and pepper to taste. Set aside.

2. Spread mayonnaise onto the cut sides of each of the rolls. Place a tomato slice on the bottom of each roll, top with shredded lettuce. Arrange the mushroom pieces on top, sprinkle with Tabasco to taste, top with the other half of the roll, and serve.

# tastes like tuna salad sandwiches

makes 4 sandwiches

*Kelp powder, a nutrient-rich sea vegetable, gives this sandwich filling a delicate taste of the sea. Look for kelp powder at natural food stores. If unavailable, use a pair of kitchen scissors to finely snip some nori*

## shake up your sandwich routine

Whether we're packing a school lunch for the kids or brown bagging our own lunch for work, many of us get into a sandwich rut. After all, how can you improve on a good PB&J? It's fast, easy, and economical. But everyone likes a little variety now and then, and when you begin to think outside the lunchbox, the possibilities for variation become endless.

Much in the way the right accessories can make a great outfit, it's often the little touches that make a great sandwich. Here are some ways to shake up your sandwich routine:

1. **DO A BREAD SWAP:** If you normally ensconce your burger in a bun, try it in a wrap. If that hummus spread is always in a pita, try it on two slabs of pumpernickel.

2. **CHANGE YOUR CONDIMENTS:** Try a new spicy mustard or add some curry or wasabi to your vegan mayo. Use a chutney or relish instead of ketchup on your veggie burger. You'll be

amazed how the same old sandwich suddenly tastes brand-new.

3. **ADD A LAYER:** If it's a PB&J, add a layer of fresh or dried fruit, chopped nuts, or even minced celery or shredded carrot. Yum's the word. For a burger or other "meaty" sandwich like seitan or tempeh, add a layer of grilled or roasted veggies such as thinly sliced zucchini, bell pepper, mushroom, or onion.

4. **TURN OVER A NEW LEAF:** Still using iceberg on your sandwiches after all these years? Slide in a leaf of soft butter lettuce, crunchy romaine, or peppery arugula. Worried about wilting? Pack the lettuce separately in a zip-top bag and tuck it into your sandwich when it's time to eat.

5. **ON THE SIDE:** Even a sandwich deserves good company. Bring along a side of slaw, bean salad, potato salad, or fruit salad. And don't forget the pickles and chips.

*(about 2 teaspoons). Use whatever bread you like for these—toasted or not. The Basic White Bread (page 393) or Three-Grain Bread (page 394) would be good for these sandwiches.*

1½ cups cooked or 1 (15.5-ounce) can chickpeas, drained and rinsed

2 celery ribs, minced

¼ cup minced onion

1 teaspoon capers, drained and chopped

¾ cup vegan mayonnaise, homemade (page 573) or store-bought, divided

2 teaspoons fresh lemon juice

1 teaspoon Dijon mustard

1 teaspoon kelp powder

Salt and freshly ground black pepper

8 slices bread

4 lettuce leaves

4 slices ripe tomato

1. In a medium bowl, coarsely mash the chickpeas. Add the celery, onion, capers, ½ cup of the mayonnaise, lemon juice, mustard, and kelp powder. Season with salt and pepper to taste. Mix until well combined. Cover and refrigerate at least 30 minutes to allow flavors to blend.

2. When ready to serve, spread the remaining ¼ cup mayonnaise onto 1 side of each of the bread slices. Layer lettuce and tomato on 4 of the bread slices and evenly divide the chickpea mixture among them. Top each sandwich with the remaining slice of bread, mayonnaise side down, cut in half, and serve.

# sloppy bulgur sandwiches
makes 4 sandwiches

*A meatless sloppy Joe can be made with crumbled tempeh or tofu, lentils, ground seitan, or frozen veggie burger crumbles. All work well when simmered in the zesty tomato sauce we know and love. In this version, the use of bulgur, a tender, chewy grain, ensures that these sloppy sandwiches are not your average Joes.*

1¾ cups water

1 cup medium-grind bulgur

Salt

1 tablespoon olive oil

1 small red onion, minced

½ medium red bell pepper, minced

1 (14.5-ounce) can crushed tomatoes

1 tablespoon sugar

1 tablespoon yellow or spicy brown mustard

2 teaspoons soy sauce

1 teaspoon chili powder

Freshly ground black pepper

4 sandwich rolls, halved horizontally

1. In a large saucepan, bring the water to boil over high heat. Stir in the bulgur and lightly salt the water. Cover, remove from heat, and set aside until the bulgur softens and the water is absorbed, about 20 minutes.

2. Meanwhile, in a large skillet, heat the oil over medium heat. Add the onion and bell pepper, cover, and cook until soft, about 7 minutes. Stir in the tomatoes, sugar, mustard, soy sauce, chili powder, and salt and black pepper to taste. Simmer for 10 minutes, stirring frequently.

3. Spoon the bulgur mixture onto the bottom half of each of the rolls, top with the other half, and serve.

# curried tofu "egg salad" pitas

makes 4 sandwiches

*A lively curry dressing makes tofu terrific in this tofu egg salad—it's a good sandwich to serve someone who thinks tofu is bland. They're sure to eat their words. If pita bread isn't your favorite, use any bread you like: toasted wheat bread or even a bagel are good choices.*

1 pound extra-firm tofu, drained and patted dry
½ cup vegan mayonnaise, homemade (page 573) or store-bought
¼ cup chopped mango chutney, homemade (page 561) or store-bought
2 teaspoons Dijon mustard
1 tablespoon hot or mild curry powder
1 teaspoon salt
⅛ teaspoon ground cayenne
¾ cup shredded carrots
2 celery ribs, minced
¼ cup minced red onion
8 small Boston or other soft lettuce leaves
4 (7-inch) whole wheat pita breads, halved

1. Crumble the tofu and place it in a large bowl. Add the mayonnaise, chutney, mustard, curry powder, salt, and cayenne, and stir well until thoroughly mixed.

2. Add the carrots, celery, and onion and stir to combine. Refrigerate for 30 minutes to allow the flavors to blend.

3. Tuck a lettuce leaf inside each pita pocket, spoon some tofu mixture on top of the lettuce, and serve.

# garden patch sandwiches on multigrain bread 🅕

makes 4 sandwiches

*This could be considered a variation on the tofu egg salad, but the real stars of this sandwich filling are all the fresh veggies and the surprising crunch of sunflower seeds. Use your favorite lettuce and any fresh ripe slicing tomatoes. The Three-Grain Bread (page 394) is a good choice for these sandwiches.*

1 pound extra-firm tofu, drained and patted dry
1 medium red bell pepper, finely chopped
1 celery rib, finely chopped
3 green onions, minced
¼ cup shelled sunflower seeds
½ cup vegan mayonnaise, homemade (page 573) or store-bought
½ teaspoon salt
½ teaspoon celery salt
¼ teaspoon freshly ground black pepper
8 slices whole grain bread
4 (¼-inch) slices ripe tomato
4 lettuce leaves

1. Crumble the tofu and place it in a large bowl. Add the bell pepper, celery, green onions, and sunflower seeds. Stir in the mayonnaise, salt, celery salt, and pepper and mix until well combined.

2. Toast the bread, if desired. Spread the mixture evenly onto 4 slices of the bread. Top each with a tomato slice, lettuce leaf, and the remaining bread. Cut the sandwiches diagonally in half and serve.

# creamy, crunchy fruit-and-nut sandwiches ⓕ

makes 4 sandwiches

*This sandwich is a surefire favorite with kids. It was born out of the desire for a nutty and fruity sandwich beyond the confines of peanut butter and jelly. I chose almond butter because its mellow flavor allows the other ingredients to shine, but feel free to use peanut butter, cashew butter, or another nut butter of your choice. You can also experiment with the other ingredients, perhaps swapping pecans for walnuts and banana slices for the pear. The Three-Grain Bread (page 394) is a good choice for these sandwiches.*

⅔ cup almond butter
¼ cup agave nectar or pure maple syrup
¼ cup chopped walnuts or other nuts of choice
¼ cup sweetened dried cranberries
8 slices whole grain bread
2 ripe Bosc or Anjou pears, cored and thinly sliced

1. In a small bowl, combine the almond butter, agave nectar, walnuts, and cranberries, stirring until well mixed.

2. Divide the mixture among the bread slices and spread evenly. Top 4 slices of the bread with the pear slices, spread side up. Place the remaining slices of bread on top of the pear slices, spread side down. Slice the sandwiches diagonally and serve at once.

# marinated mushroom wraps

makes 2 wraps

*The juicy and flavorful mushrooms combined with the buttery avocado and crunchy vegetables create a delicious contrast of textures and flavors all rolled into one tasty wrap— well, two wraps, actually, if you make the entire recipe. To add color, flavor, and variety, try making these wraps with spinach or tomato tortillas.*

3 tablespoons soy sauce
3 tablespoons fresh lemon juice
1½ tablespoons toasted sesame oil
2 portobello mushroom caps, cut into ¼-inch strips
1 ripe Hass avocado, pitted and peeled
2 (10-inch) flour tortillas
2 cups fresh baby spinach leaves
1 medium red bell pepper, cut into ¼-inch strips
1 ripe tomato, chopped
Salt and freshly ground black pepper

1. In a medium bowl, combine the soy sauce, 2 tablespoons of the lemon juice, and the oil. Add the portobello strips, toss to combine, and marinate for 1 hour or overnight. Drain the mushrooms and set aside.

2. Mash the avocado with the remaining 1 tablespoon of lemon juice.

3. To assemble wraps, place 1 tortilla on a work surface and spread with some of the mashed avocado. Top with a layer of baby spinach leaves. In the lower third of each tortilla, arrange strips of the soaked mushrooms and some of the bell pepper strips. Sprinkle with the tomato and salt and black pepper to taste. Roll up tightly and cut in half diagonally. Repeat with the remaining ingredients and serve.

# peanutty tofu roll-ups

makes 4 wraps

*Combining tofu and peanut butter may sound unusual, but when mixed with ginger, lime, and garlic it makes a tasty protein-rich spread for these wrap sandwiches filled with crunchy vegetables.*

8 ounces extra-firm tofu, drained well and patted dry

⅔ cup creamy peanut butter

1 tablespoon soy sauce

1 tablespoon fresh lime juice

½ teaspoon grated fresh ginger

1 garlic clove, minced

¼ teaspoon ground cayenne

4 (10-inch) flour tortillas or lavash flatbread

2 cups shredded romaine lettuce

1 large carrot, grated

½ medium English cucumber, peeled and cut into ¼-inch slices

1. In a food processor, combine the tofu, peanut butter, and soy sauce and process until smooth. Add the lime juice, ginger, garlic, and cayenne and process until smooth. Set aside for 30 minutes at room temperature to allow flavors to blend.

2. To assemble wraps, place 1 tortilla on a work surface and spread with about ½ cup of the tofu mixture. Sprinkle with lettuce, carrot, and cucumber. Roll up tightly and cut in half diagonally. Repeat with the remaining ingredients and serve.

# garden salad wraps

makes 4 wraps

*These wraps are another great way to combine tofu and vegetables. Here, soy sauce–coated tofu strips get all wrapped up with a zesty vegetable salad, resulting in a tasty sandwich. The vegetables can be varied if you have others on hand that you'd like to add.*

6 tablespoons olive oil

1 pound extra-firm tofu, drained, patted dry, and cut into ½-inch strips

1 tablespoon soy sauce

¼ cup apple cider vinegar

1 teaspoon yellow or spicy brown mustard

½ teaspoon salt

¼ teaspoon freshly ground black pepper

3 cups shredded romaine lettuce

3 ripe Roma tomatoes, finely chopped

1 large carrot, shredded

1 medium English cucumber, peeled and chopped

⅓ cup minced red onion

¼ cup sliced pitted green olives

4 (10-inch) flour tortillas or lavash flatbread

1. In a large skillet, heat 2 tablespoons of the oil over medium heat. Add the tofu and cook until golden brown, about 10 minutes. Sprinkle with soy sauce and set aside to cool.

2. In a small bowl, combine the vinegar, mustard, salt, and pepper with the remaining 4 tablespoons oil, stirring to blend well. Set aside.

3. In a large bowl, combine the lettuce, tomatoes, carrot, cucumber, onion, and olives. Pour on the dressing and toss to coat.

4. To assemble wraps, place 1 tortilla on a work surface and spread with about one-quarter of

the salad. Place a few strips of tofu on the tortilla and roll up tightly. Slice in half diagonally. Repeat with remaining ingredients and serve.

# tempeh-walnut "chicken" salad wraps

makes 4 wraps

*This hearty, protein-rich sandwich filling is also terrific on toasted thickly sliced bread or on sesame-topped bagels.*

8 ounces tempeh

½ cup chopped walnuts

1 celery rib, chopped

¼ cup finely chopped green onions

¼ cup finely chopped red bell pepper

2 tablespoons minced fresh parsley

1 cup vegan mayonnaise, homemade (page 573) or store-bought, divided

1 tablespoon Dijon mustard

1 teaspoon fresh lemon juice

½ teaspoon salt

⅛ teaspoon freshly ground black pepper

4 (10-inch) tortillas or lavash flatbread

1 to 2 cups shredded romaine lettuce

1. In a medium saucepan of simmering water, cook the tempeh for 30 minutes. Remove tempeh from pan and set aside to cool.

2. Pat the tempeh dry, chop it finely, and place it in a bowl. Add the walnuts, celery, green onions, bell pepper, and parsley. Stir in ½ cup of the mayonnaise, the mustard, lemon juice, salt, and black pepper. Mix until thoroughly combined.

3. Cover and refrigerate at least 30 minutes to allow flavors to blend. Taste, adjusting seasonings if necessary.

4. To assemble wraps, place 1 tortilla on a work surface and spread with 1 tablespoon of the remaining mayonnaise. Top with about ⅔ cup of the tempeh mixture. Top with shredded lettuce and roll up tightly. Cut each tortilla in half diagonally. Repeat with remaining ingredients.

# avocado and tempeh bacon wraps 🅕

makes 4 wraps

*The creamy richness of the avocado is a perfect match for the smoky crispness of tempeh bacon. Add lettuce, tomato, and vegan mayo and it's a wrap!*

2 tablespoons olive oil

8 ounces tempeh bacon, homemade (page 525) or store-bought

4 (10-inch) soft flour tortillas or lavash flat bread

¼ cup vegan mayonnaise, homemade (page 573) or store-bought

4 large lettuce leaves

2 ripe Hass avocados, pitted, peeled, and cut into ¼-inch slices

1 large ripe tomato, cut into ¼-inch slices

1. In a large skillet, heat the oil over medium heat. Add the tempeh bacon and cook until browned on both sides, about 8 minutes. Remove from the heat and set aside.

2. Place 1 tortilla on a work surface. Spread with some of the mayonnaise and one-fourth of the lettuce and tomatoes.

3. Pit, peel, and thinly slice the avocado and place the slices on top of the tomato. Add the reserved tempeh bacon and roll up tightly. Repeat with remaining ingredients and serve.

# chickpea-tomato wraps 🅕

makes 4 wraps

*This is one of those tasty but sloppy fillings that would be a disaster between two slices of bread but is ideal for a wrap sandwich.*

1½ cups cooked or 1 (15.5-ounce) cans chickpeas, drained and rinsed

½ cup oil-packed sun-dried tomatoes, drained*

1 celery rib, minced

¼ cup minced red onion

3 tablespoons chopped fresh parsley

½ cup vegan mayonnaise, homemade (page 573) or store-bought

1 tablespoon spicy brown mustard

Salt and freshly ground black pepper

4 (10-inch) flour tortillas or lavash flatbread

4 lettuce leaves

1. Mash the chickpeas in a large bowl. Cut the tomatoes into ¼-inch pieces and add to the chickpeas along with the celery, onion, and parsley. Add the mayonnaise, mustard, and salt and pepper to taste, stirring to mix well.

2. To assemble wraps, place 1 tortilla on a work surface and spread about ½ cup of the chickpea mixture across the surface. Top with a lettuce leaf. Roll up tightly and cut in half diagonally. Repeat with the remaining ingredients and serve.

*To use dried sun-dried tomatoes, place them in a heatproof bowl and cover with boiling water. Set aside 10 minutes to reconstitute.*

# tofu waldorf salad wraps 🅕

makes 4 wraps

*Although it contains many of the same ingredients, this sweet and crunchy wrap bears little resemblance to the salad that inspired it. Created in the 1890s at New York's Waldorf-Astoria Hotel, the classic Waldorf salad consists of apples, celery, walnuts, and mayonnaise served on a lettuce leaf.*

1 pound extra-firm tofu, drained, patted dry, and cut in ½-inch dice

2 firm crisp apples, such as Gala or Fuji, cored and chopped

2 celery ribs, minced

⅓ minced red onion

⅓ cup chopped walnuts, toasted

2 tablespoons chopped fresh parsley

½ cup vegan mayonnaise, homemade (page 573) or store-bought

2 tablespoons fresh lemon juice

½ teaspoon sugar

½ teaspoon salt

¼ teaspoon freshly ground black pepper

4 (10-inch) flour tortillas or lavash flatbread

4 lettuce leaves

1. In a large bowl, combine the tofu, apples, celery, onion, walnuts, and parsley. Add the mayonnaise, lemon juice, sugar, salt, and pepper, stirring well to combine.

2. To assemble wraps, lay 1 tortilla on a work surface. Spread about ½ cup of the tofu mixture across the tortilla and top with a lettuce leaf. Roll up tightly and cut in half diagonally. Repeat with the remaining ingredients and serve.

# teriyaki tofu wraps 🅕

makes 4 wraps

*The sweetly pungent teriyaki sauce perme-
ates the tofu and imbues it with great flavor.
When you add the bell pepper strips, you can
toss in some green onions or other veggies as
well, for kind of a stir-fry wrap.*

3 tablespoons soy sauce

1 tablespoon fresh lemon juice

1 tablespoon sugar

1 garlic clove, minced

2 tablespoons toasted sesame oil

¼ teaspoon ground cayenne

1 pound extra-firm tofu, drained, patted dry,
    and cut into ½-inch strips

2 tablespoons olive oil

1 large red bell pepper, cut into ¼-inch strips

4 (10-inch) flour tortillas or lavash flatbread,
    warmed

1. In a small bowl, combine the soy sauce,
lemon juice, sugar, garlic, sesame oil, and cayenne and set aside.

2. Place the tofu in a shallow bowl. Pour the
teriyaki marinade over the tofu, turning gently to coat.

3. In a large skillet, heat the oil over medium
heat. Remove the tofu from the marinade,
reserving the marinade. Place the tofu in the
hot skillet along with the bell pepper and
cook until the tofu is browned and the peppers are tender, about 10 minutes. Pour the
reserved marinade over the tofu and peppers
and simmer, stirring gently to coat.

4. To assemble wraps, place 1 tortilla on a
work surface and place some of the tofu and

pepper strips across the lower third. Roll up
tightly. Repeat with remaining ingredients
and serve.

# tofu-tahini veggie wraps 🅕

makes 4 wraps

*The flavor of the tofu-tahini spread will
intensify if refrigerated for at least an hour
before serving. I also love this spread on a
toasted sesame bagel with sliced ripe tomato.*

8 ounces extra-firm tofu, drained and patted dry

½ cup tahini (sesame paste)

3 green onions, minced

2 celery ribs, minced

½ cup minced fresh parsley

2 tablespoons capers

2 tablespoons fresh lemon juice

1 tablespoon Dijon mustard

½ teaspoon salt

⅛ teaspoon ground cayenne

4 (10-inch) flour tortillas or lavash

1 medium carrot, shredded

4 lettuce leaves

1. In a food processor, combine the tofu,
tahini, green onions, celery, parsley, capers,
lemon juice, mustard, salt, and cayenne and
process until well combined.

2. To assemble wraps, place 1 tortilla on a
work surface and spread about ½ cup of the
tofu mixture across the tortilla. Sprinkle with
shredded carrot and top with a lettuce leaf.
Roll up tightly and cut in half diagonally.
Repeat with the remaining ingredients and
serve.

# deconstructed hummus pitas

makes 4 pitas

*This idea was a result of a desire for the taste of hummus but also the desire for texture—the solution was to leave the chickpeas mostly whole, mashing them just enough so they don't roll out of the sandwich.*

1 garlic clove, crushed

¾ cup tahini (sesame paste)

2 tablespoons fresh lemon juice

1 teaspoon salt

⅛ teaspoon ground cayenne

¼ cup water

1½ cups cooked or 1 (15.5-ounce) can chickpeas, rinsed and drained

2 medium carrots, grated (about 1 cup)

4 (7-inch) pita breads, preferably whole wheat, halved

1 large ripe tomato, cut into ¼-inch slices

2 cups fresh baby spinach

1. In a blender or food processor, mince the garlic. Add the tahini, lemon juice, salt, cayenne, and water. Process until smooth.

2. Place the chickpeas in a bowl and crush slightly with a fork. Add the carrots and the reserved tahini sauce and toss to combine. Set aside.

3. Spoon 2 or 3 tablespoons of the chickpea mixture into each pita half. Tuck a tomato slice and a few spinach leaves into each pocket and serve.

# muffaletta sandwiches

makes 4 sandwiches

*The muffaletta is a New Orleans classic that stars a piquant olive salad that plays nicely against the crusty bread. To me, the traditional inclusion of sliced ham and cheese are incidental to the flavorful filling, but sliced vegan ham and cheese can be added if desired.*

1 cup chopped pitted kalamata olives

1 cup chopped pimiento-stuffed green olives

½ cup chopped pepperoncini (pickled peppers)

½ cup jarred roasted red peppers (or see page 10), chopped

2 tablespoons capers

3 green onions, minced

3 plum tomatoes, chopped

2 tablespoons minced fresh parsley

½ teaspoon dried marjoram

½ teaspoon dried thyme

¼ cup olive oil

2 tablespoons white wine vinegar

Salt and freshly ground black pepper

4 individual kaiser rolls, boules, or other crusty sandwich rolls, halved horizontally

1. In a medium bowl, combine the kalamata olives, green olives, pepperoncini, red peppers, capers, green onions, tomatoes, parsley, marjoram, thyme, oil, vinegar, and salt and black pepper to taste. Set aside.

2. Pull out some of the inside of the sandwich rolls to make room for the filling. Spoon the filling mixture into the bottom half of the rolls, packing lightly. Top with remaining roll halves and serve.

# falafel sandwiches

makes 4 sandwiches

*Falafel is the fast-food burger of Middle Eastern cuisines. Made with chickpeas and fragrantly spiced, these sturdy patties are especially delicious stuffed into pitas and served with the Tahini-Lemon Sauce on page 558.*

1½ cups cooked or 1 (15.5-ounce) can chickpeas, drained and rinsed

3 garlic cloves, chopped

1 small yellow onion, chopped

3 tablespoons chopped fresh parsley

½ cup old-fashioned oats

1 teaspoon ground cumin

¾ teaspoon ground coriander

¾ teaspoon salt

¼ teaspoon freshly ground black pepper

Chickpea flour or all-purpose flour, for dredging

Olive oil, for frying

4 loaves pita bread, cut in half

Shredded romaine lettuce, to serve

1 ripe tomato, chopped

½ cup Tahini-Lemon Sauce (page 558)

1. In a food processor, combine the chickpeas, garlic, onion, parsley, oats, cumin, coriander, salt, and pepper and process to combine. Refrigerate for 20 to 30 minutes.

2. Form the mixture into small balls, about 2 inches in diameter. If the mixture is not firm enough, add up to ¼ cup of flour, a little at a time, until the desired consistency is reached. Flatten the balls into patties and dredge them in flour.

3. In a large skillet, heat a thin layer of oil over medium-high heat. Add the falafel and cook, turning once, until golden brown, about 8 minutes total.

4. Stuff the falafel patties into the pita pockets, along with lettuce, tomato, and tahini sauce. Serve immediately.

# vietnamese po'boys

makes 4 po'boys

*These extremely yummy and very filling sandwiches are inspired by the traditional Vietnamese* bahn mi *sandwich, with a nod to the po'boy of the American South. They are basically a hearty and delicious filling on a sub roll or baguette. I like to serve them with the Asian Slaw on page 74.*

1 tablespoon canola or grapeseed oil

1 recipe Soy-Tan Dream Cutlets (page 294)

2 tablespoons soy sauce

2 teaspoons Asian chili sauce (such as Sriracha)

3 tablespoons vegan mayonnaise, homemade (page 573) or store-bought

2 teaspoons fresh lime juice

4 (7-inch) baguettes, split lengthwise

½ small red onion, thinly sliced

1 medium carrot, shredded

½ medium English cucumber, cut into ¼-inch slices

½ cup fresh cilantro leaves

1 tablespoon minced jalapeño (optional)

1. In a skillet, heat the oil over medium heat. Add the soy-tan cutlets and cook until browned on both sides, turning once, about 8 minutes total.

2. About halfway through, sprinkle the cutlets with the soy sauce and 1 teaspoon of the chili sauce. Set aside to cool to room temperature.

3. In a small bowl, combine the remaining chili sauce with the mayonnaise and lime juice, stirring to blend well.

4. Spread the mayonnaise mixture onto the inside of the baguettes. Layer with the onion, carrot, cucumber, cilantro, and jalapeño, if using. Thinly slice the reserved soy-tan cutlets and arrange the slices on top. Serve immediately.

# BURGERS

## tempeh tantrum burgers

makes 4 burgers

*If commercially produced vegan burgers aren't your thing, but you want something substantial to eat on a bun, these tempeh burgers may be what you're looking for. I think they're especially good slathered with a bit of Dijon mustard, but you can use ketchup or relish if you prefer.*

8 ounces tempeh, cut into ½-inch dice

¾ cup chopped onion

2 garlic cloves, chopped

¾ cup chopped walnuts

½ cup old-fashioned or quick-cooking oats

1 tablespoon minced fresh parsley

½ teaspoon dried oregano

½ teaspoon dried thyme

½ teaspoon salt

¼ teaspoon freshly ground black pepper

3 tablespoons olive oil

Dijon mustard

4 whole grain burger rolls

Sliced red onion, tomato, lettuce, and avocado

1. In a medium saucepan of simmering water, cook the tempeh for 30 minutes. Drain and set aside to cool.

2. In a food processor, combine the onion and garlic and process until minced. Add the cooled tempeh, the walnuts, oats, parsley, oregano, thyme, salt, and pepper. Process until well blended. Shape the mixture into 4 equal patties.

3. In a large skillet, heat the oil over medium heat. Add the burgers and cook until cooked thoroughly and browned on both sides, about 7 minutes per side.

4. Spread desired amount of mustard onto each half of the rolls and layer each roll with lettuce, tomato, red onion, and avocado, as desired. Serve immediately.

## grilled portobello burgers ⓕ

makes 4 burgers

*This is my favorite way to enjoy portobello mushrooms—hot and juicy right off the grill. Served on a toasted roll, with fresh ripe tomato slices and a sprightly vinaigrette, these burgers are ideal for a backyard cookout.*

2 tablespoons olive oil

1 tablespoon balsamic vinegar

¼ teaspoon sugar

¼ teaspoon salt

⅛ teaspoon freshly ground black pepper

4 large portobello mushroom caps, lightly rinsed and patted dry

4 slices red onion

4 kaiser rolls, halved horizontally or other burger rolls

8 large fresh basil leaves

4 slices ripe tomato

1. Preheat the grill or broiler. In a small bowl, combine the oil, vinegar, sugar, salt, and pepper. Set aside.

2. Place the mushroom caps and onion slices on the hot grill and cook until grilled on both sides, turning once, about 10 minutes total.

3. Brush the tops of the mushrooms and onion with the vinaigrette and keep warm. Place the rolls cut side down on the grill and lightly toast, about 1 minute.

4. Layer an onion slice and mushroom onto the bottom half of each roll. Top each with two basil leaves and a tomato slice. Drizzle

with any remaining vinaigrette and cover each burger with the roll tops. Serve immediately.

# macadamia-cashew patties

makes 4 patties

*These exotic protein-rich nut patties are loaded with flavor and crunch. Serve on your favorite rolls with lettuce and a chutney or Ginger-Papaya Relish (page 570).*

¾ cup chopped macadamia nuts
¾ cup chopped cashews
1 medium carrot, grated
1 small onion, chopped
1 garlic clove, minced
1 jalapeño or other green chile, seeded and minced
¾ cup old-fashioned oats
¾ cup dry unseasoned bread crumbs
2 tablespoons minced fresh cilantro
½ teaspoon ground coriander
Salt and freshly ground black pepper
2 teaspoons fresh lime juice
Canola or grapeseed oil, for frying
4 sandwich rolls
Lettuce leaves and condiment of choice
   (see headnote)

1. In a food processor, combine the macadamia nuts, cashews, carrot, onion, garlic, chile, oats, bread crumbs, cilantro, coriander, and salt and pepper to taste. Process until well mixed. Add the lime juice and process until well blended. Taste, adjusting seasonings if necessary. Shape the mixture into 4 equal patties.

2. In a large skillet, heat a thin layer of oil over medium heat. Add the patties and cook until golden brown on both sides, turning once, about 10 minutes total. Serve on sandwich rolls with lettuce and condiments of choice.

# pecan-lentil burgers

makes 4 to 6 burgers

*The lentils and pecans combined with the other ingredients make a sturdy, healthful, and flavorful burger. A key to firm burgers is making sure your lentils are not wet. Usually a few minutes in a skillet over medium heat does the trick, although you can also spread them on a baking sheet and bake them for a few minutes to dry them out.*

1½ cups cooked brown lentils
½ cup ground pecans
½ cup old-fashioned oats
¼ cup dry unseasoned bread crumbs
¼ cup wheat gluten flour (vital wheat gluten)
½ cup minced onion
¼ cup minced fresh parsley
1 teaspoon Dijon mustard
½ teaspoon salt
⅛ teaspoon freshly ground pepper
2 tablespoons olive oil
4 to 6 burger rolls
Lettuce leaves, sliced tomato, sliced red onion,
   and condiments of choice

1. In a food processor, combine the lentils, pecans, oats, bread crumbs, flour, onion, parsley, mustard, salt, and pepper. Pulse to combine, leaving some texture. Shape the lentil mixture into 4 to 6 burgers.

2. In a large skillet, heat the oil over medium heat. Add the burgers and cook until golden brown, about 5 minutes per side.

3. Serve the burgers on the rolls with lettuce, tomato slices, onion, and condiments of choice.

# black bean burgers

makes 4 burgers

*Dense and meaty black beans transform easily into hearty tasty burgers that can be enjoyed with the usual condiments or tucked into a pita or wrap and topped with your sauce of choice.*

3 tablespoons olive oil

½ cup minced onion

1 garlic clove, minced

1½ cups cooked or 1 (15.5-ounce) can black beans, drained and rinsed

1 tablespoon minced fresh parsley

½ cup dry unseasoned bread crumbs

¼ cup wheat gluten flour (vital wheat gluten)

1 teaspoon smoked paprika

½ teaspoon dried thyme

Salt and freshly ground black pepper

4 burger rolls

4 lettuce leaves

1 ripe tomato, cut into ¼-inch slices

1. In a small skillet, heat 1 tablespoon of the oil over medium heat. Add the onion and garlic and cook until softened, about 5 minutes.

2. Transfer the onion mixture to a food processor. Add the beans, parsley, bread crumbs, flour, paprika, thyme, and salt and pepper to taste. Process until well combined, leaving some texture. Shape the mixture into 4 equal patties and refrigerate for 20 minutes.

3. In a large skillet, heat the remaining 2 tablespoons oil over medium heat. Add the burgers and cook until browned on both sides, turning once, about 5 minutes per side.

4. Serve the burgers on the rolls with lettuce and tomato slices.

# some-kinda-nut burgers

makes 4 burgers

*Nut lovers will go nuts over these hearty and protein-rich burgers. Mix and match your favorite nuts and nut butter at will. In addition to the usual burger condiments, these burgers are terrific topped with a little chutney or enjoyed "cutlet-style" as a main dish at dinner.*

2 tablespoons plus 1 teaspoon olive oil

1 small onion, chopped

1 medium carrot, grated

1 cup unsalted mixed nuts

¼ cup wheat gluten flour (vital wheat gluten), plus more if needed

½ cup old-fashioned oats, plus more if needed

2 tablespoons creamy peanut butter

2 tablespoons minced fresh parsley

½ teaspoon salt

¼ teaspoon freshly ground black pepper

4 burger rolls

4 lettuce leaves

1 ripe tomato, cut into ¼-inch slices

1. In a medium skillet, heat 1 teaspoon of the oil over medium heat. Add the onion and cook until soft, about 5 minutes. Stir in the carrot and set aside.

2. In a food processor, pulse the nuts until chopped. Add the onion-carrot mixture along with the flour, oats, peanut butter, parsley, salt, and pepper. Process until well blended. Shape the mixture into 4 equal patties, about 4 inches in diameter. If the mixture is too loose, add a little more flour or oats.

3. In a large skillet, heat the remaining 2 tablespoons oil over medium heat, add the burgers and cook until browned on both sides, about 5 minutes per side.

4. Serve the burgers on the rolls with lettuce and tomato slices.

# golden veggie burgers 🅕

makes 4 burgers

*Here's a great way to get your kids to eat more veggies—put them in burgers! These mellow yellow burgers fry up to a nice golden brown. The inclusion of wheat gluten flour (the main ingredient in seitan) assures a chewy burger that holds its shape. If you like monochrome, top them with sliced yellow tomatoes and a dab of mustard, although I prefer the stunning contrast of using a red tomato and ketchup. Instead of frying the burgers, you can bake them at 375°F on a lightly oiled baking sheet until firm, about 12 minutes.*

2 tablespoons olive oil

1 small yellow onion, chopped

½ small yellow bell pepper, chopped

1½ cups cooked or 1 (15.5-ounce) can chickpeas, drained and rinsed

¾ teaspoon salt

¼ teaspoon freshly ground black pepper

¼ cup wheat gluten flour (vital wheat gluten)

4 burger rolls

Condiments of choice

1. In a large skillet, heat 1 tablespoon of the oil over medium heat. Add the onion and pepper and cook until softened, about 5 minutes. Set aside to cool slightly.

2. Transfer the cooled onion mixture to a food processor. Add the chickpeas, salt, and black pepper and pulse to mix. Add the flour and process to combine.

3. Shape the mixture into 4 burgers, about 4 inches in diameter. If the mixture is too loose, add a little extra flour.

4. In a large skillet, heat the remaining 2 tablespoons of oil over medium heat. Add the burgers and cook until firm and browned on both sides, turning once, about 5 minutes per side.

5. Serve the burgers on the rolls with condiments of choice.

# red lentil patties in pita

makes 4 pitas

*The flavors of India permeate these fragrant little patties. If the mixture is too wet, add some bread crumbs or old-fashioned oats, if you like—just check for seasonings. I like tucking the patties into pita pockets and dousing them with mint and coconut chutney.*

½ cup red lentils, picked over, rinsed, and drained

2 tablespoons olive oil

½ cup minced onion

1 small potato, peeled and shredded

½ cup roasted cashews

¼ cup chickpea flour or wheat gluten flour

1 tablespoon minced fresh parsley

2 teaspoons hot or mild curry powder

½ teaspoon salt

⅛ teaspoon ground cayenne

4 (7-inch) pita breads, warmed and halved

Shredded romaine lettuce

Fresh Mint and Coconut Chutney (page 564)
    or your favorite chutney

1. Bring a small saucepan of salted water to boil over high heat. Add the lentils, return to a boil, then reduce heat to low. Cover and cook until tender, about 15 minutes. Drain well, then return to the saucepan and cook over low heat for 1 to 2 minutes, stirring, to evaporate any remaining moisture. Set aside.

2. In a large skillet, heat 1 tablespoon of the oil over medium heat. Add the onion and potato, cover, and cook until soft, about 5 minutes. Set aside.

3. In a food processor, process the cashews until finely ground. Add the cooked lentils and the onion-potato mixture and pulse to combine. Add the flour, parsley, curry powder, salt, and cayenne. Process until just mixed, leaving some texture. Shape the mixture into 8 small patties.

4. In a large skillet, heat the remaining 1 tablespoon of oil over medium heat. Add the patties and cook until browned on both sides, about 5 minutes per side.

5. Stuff a patty inside each pita half, along with some shredded lettuce and a spoonful of chutney. Serve immediately.

# white bean and walnut patties 🅕

makes 4 patties

*Instead of frying these sturdy and tasty patties, you can bake them on a lightly oiled baking sheet in a 375°F oven until browned on both sides, turning once, about 20 minutes total. In addition to enjoying them in a sandwich for lunch, they're also great topped with a sauce such as Roasted Yellow Tomato and Pepper Coulis (page 548) or Watercress Sauce (page 553) and served as a dinner entrée.*

¼ cup diced onion

1 garlic clove, crushed

¾ cup walnut pieces

¾ cup canned or cooked white beans, drained
    and rinsed

¾ cup wheat gluten flour (vital wheat gluten)

2 tablespoons minced fresh parsley

1 tablespoon soy sauce

1 teaspoon Dijon mustard, plus more to serve

½ teaspoon salt

½ teaspoon ground sage

½ teaspoon sweet paprika

¼ teaspoon turmeric

¼ teaspoon freshly ground black pepper

2 tablespoons olive oil

Bread or rolls of choice

Lettuce leaves and sliced tomatoes

1. In a food processor, combine the onion, garlic, and walnuts and process until finely ground.

2. Cook the beans in a small skillet over medium heat, stirring, for 1 to 2 minutes to evaporate any moisture. Add the beans to the food processor along with the flour, parsley, soy sauce, mustard, salt, sage, paprika, turmeric, and pepper. Process until well blended. Shape the mixture into 4 equal patties.

3. In a large skillet, heat the oil over medium heat. Add the patties and cook until browned on both sides, about 5 minutes per side.

4. Serve on your favorite sandwich bread with mustard, lettuce, and sliced tomatoes.

# curried chickpea patties

makes 4 patties

*Chickpeas are commonly used in Indian cooking, so it's no wonder that they taste so good in these patties spiced with curry powder. In addition to the curried mayo, you can dress these patties with your favorite chutney for added flavor.*

3 tablespoons olive oil

1 small onion, chopped

1½ teaspoons hot or mild curry powder

½ teaspoon salt

⅛ teaspoon ground cayenne

1 cup cooked chickpeas

1 tablespoon chopped fresh parsley

½ cup wheat gluten flour (vital wheat gluten)

⅓ cup dry unseasoned bread crumbs

¼ cup vegan mayonnaise, homemade (page 573) or store-bought

Bread or rolls of choice

Lettuce leaves

1 ripe tomato, cut into ¼-inch slices

1. In a large skillet, heat 1 tablespoon of the oil over medium heat. Add the onion, cover, and cook until softened, 5 minutes. Stir in 1 teaspoon of the curry powder, salt, and cayenne and remove from the heat. Set aside.

2. In a food processor, combine the chickpeas, parsley, wheat gluten flour, bread crumbs, and the cooked onion. Process to combine, leaving some texture.

3. Form the chickpea mixture into 4 equal patties and set aside.

4. In a large skillet, heat the remaining 2 tablespoons oil over medium heat. Add the patties, cover, and cook until golden brown on both sides, turning once, about 5 minutes per side.

5. In a small bowl, combine the remaining ½ teaspoon of curry powder with the mayonnaise, stirring to blend. Spread the curried mayonnaise on the bread. Top with the patties, lettuce, and tomato slices. Serve immediately.

# pinto bean patties with chile-lime "mayo"

makes 4 patties

*The zesty flavor of these crisply fried patties is enhanced by a lively lime-spiked dressing. In addition to being great in a sandwich, these patties can be enjoyed as a tasty dinner entrée.*

1½ cups cooked or 1 (15.5-ounce) can pinto beans, rinsed and drained

1 medium shallot, chopped

1 garlic clove, minced

2 tablespoons chopped fresh cilantro

1 teaspoon Creole seasoning

¼ cup wheat gluten flour (vital wheat gluten)

Salt and freshly ground black pepper

½ cup dry unseasoned bread crumbs

¾ cup vegan mayonnaise, homemade (page 573) or store-bought

2 teaspoons fresh lime juice

1 serrano chile, seeded and minced

2 tablespoons olive oil

Bread, flour tortillas, or sandwich rolls

Shredded lettuce

1 tomato, cut into ¼-inch slices

1. Blot the beans with paper towels to absorb excess moisture. In a food processor, combine the beans, shallot, garlic, cilantro, Creole seasoning, flour, and salt and pepper to taste. Process until well blended.

2. Shape the mixture into 4 equal patties, adding more flour if needed. Dredge the patties in the bread crumbs. Refrigerate for 20 minutes.

3. In a small bowl, combine the mayonnaise, lime juice, and serrano chile. Season with the salt and pepper to taste, mix well, and refrigerate until ready to serve.

4. In a large skillet, heat the oil over medium heat. Add the patties and cook until browned and crispy on both sides, about 5 minutes per side.

5. Spread the chile-lime mayo on the bread and top with the patties, lettuce, and tomato. Serve immediately.

## FAJITAS AND BURRITOS

## seared portobello fajitas 🅕

makes 4 fajitas

*This is an easy and tasty way to serve the infinitely versatile portobello mushroom. Its meaty texture makes it an ideal fajita filling along with a supporting cast of onion, spinach, and salsa. Serve with Green-Green Guacamole (page 9).*

2 tablespoons olive oil

3 large portobello mushroom caps, lightly rinsed, patted dry, and cut into ¼-inch strips

1 large red onion, halved and cut into ¼-inch slices

1 serrano or other hot chile, seeded and minced (optional)

3 cups fresh baby spinach

¼ teaspoon ground cumin

¼ teaspoon dried oregano

Salt and freshly ground black pepper

4 (10-inch) flour tortillas, warmed

1 cup tomato salsa, homemade (page 567) or store-bought

1. In a large skillet, heat the oil over medium high heat. Add the mushrooms, onion, and chile, if using, and cook until seared on the outside and slightly softened, stirring occasionally, about 5 minutes.

2. Add the spinach and cook until wilted, 1 to 2 minutes. Season with the cumin, oregano, and salt and pepper to taste.

3. To assemble the fajitas, place 1 tortilla on a work surface. Spread with one-quarter of the mushroom mixture. Spoon ¼ cup of the salsa on top and roll up tightly. Repeat with remaining ingredients. Serve immediately.

## beer-marinated seitan fajitas

makes 4 fajitas

*A robust beer-infused marinade gives these fajitas an added flavor dimension. For a refreshing variation, add some shredded lettuce when you assemble the fajitas.*

½ cup chopped red onion

1 garlic clove, minced

½ cup beer

2 teaspoons fresh lime juice

1 tablespoon chopped fresh cilantro

¼ teaspoon crushed red pepper

½ teaspoon salt

8 ounces seitan, homemade (page 305) or store-bought, cut into ¼-inch strips

2 tablespoons olive oil

1 ripe Hass avocado

4 (10-inch) flour tortillas, warmed

½ cup tomato salsa, homemade (page 567) or store-bought

1. In a shallow bowl, combine the onion, garlic, beer, lime juice, cilantro, crushed red pepper, and salt. Add the seitan and marinate for 4 hours or overnight in the refrigerator.

2. Remove the seitan from the marinade, reserving the marinade. In a large skillet, heat the oil over medium heat. Add the seitan and cook until browned on both sides, about 10 minutes. Add the reserved marinade and simmer until most of the liquid is evaporated.

3. Pit, peel, and cut the avocado into ½-inch slices. To assemble the fajitas, place 1 tortilla on a work surface and top with one-quarter of the seitan strips, salsa, and avocado slices. Roll up tightly and repeat with the remaining ingredients. Serve immediately.

# seitan tacos 🅕

makes 4 tacos

*Tacos are an all-time favorite, especially with kids and teens. You won't have to call anyone to the table twice on taco night! For an even quicker taco filling, use frozen vegan burger crumbles or thawed, finely chopped veggie burgers. The best part of tacos is building them yourself. Serve with Mexican hot sauce, lime-infused vegan sour cream, diced fresh tomato, and sliced black olives.*

2 tablespoons olive oil

12 ounces seitan, homemade (page 305) or store-bought, finely chopped

2 tablespoons soy sauce

1½ teaspoons chili powder

¼ teaspoon ground cumin

¼ teaspoon garlic powder

12 (6-inch) soft corn tortillas

1 ripe Hass avocado

Shredded romaine lettuce

1 cup tomato salsa, homemade (page 567) or store-bought

1. In a large skillet, heat the oil over medium heat. Add the seitan and cook until browned, about 10 minutes. Sprinkle with the soy sauce, chili powder, cumin, and garlic powder, stirring to coat. Remove from heat.

2. Preheat the oven to 225°F. In a medium skillet, warm the tortillas over medium heat and stack them on a heatproof plate. Cover with foil and place them in the oven to keep them soft and warm.

3. Pit and peel the avocado and cut into ¼-inch slices. Arrange the taco filling, avocado, and lettuce on a platter and serve along with the warmed tortillas, salsa, and any additional toppings.

# refried bean and salsa quesadillas

makes 4 quesadillas

*This zesty, protein-rich recipe is especially suited for those who prefer not to use vegan cheese products but still want to enjoy quesadillas. I like to offer a bowl of freshly made guacamole (page 9) on the side.*

1 tablespoon canola or grapeseed oil, plus more for frying

1½ cups cooked or 1 (15.5-ounce) can pinto beans, drained and mashed

1 teaspoon chili powder

4 (10-inch) flour tortillas

1 cup tomato salsa, homemade (page 567) or store-bought

½ cup minced red onion (optional)

1. In a medium saucepan, heat the oil over medium heat. Add the mashed beans and chili powder and cook, stirring, until hot, about 5 minutes. Set aside.

2. To assemble, place 1 tortilla on a work surface and spoon about ¼ cup of the beans across the bottom half. Top the beans with the salsa and onion, if using. Fold top half of the tortilla over the filling and press slightly.

3. In large skillet heat a thin layer of oil over medium heat. Place folded quesadillas, 1 or 2 at a time, into the hot skillet and heat until hot, turning once, about 1 minute per side.

4. Cut quesadillas into 3 or 4 wedges and arrange on plates. Serve immediately.

# spinach, mushroom, and black bean quesadillas  Ⓕ

makes 4 quesadillas

*Including tender fresh baby spinach in this flavorful quesadilla filling is a simple way to get kids to eat their greens. And if you still can't win them over, that means more quesadillas for you.*

1½ cups cooked or 1 (15.5 ounce) can black
    beans, drained and rinsed
1 tablespoon olive oil
½ cup minced red onion
2 garlic cloves, minced
2 cups sliced white mushrooms
4 cups fresh baby spinach
Salt and freshly ground black pepper
4 (10-inch) flour tortillas
Canola or grapeseed oil, for frying

1. Place the black beans in a medium bowl and coarsely mash them. Set aside.

2. In a small skillet, heat the olive oil over medium heat. Add the onion and garlic and cover and cook until softened, about 5 minutes. Stir in the mushrooms and cook, uncovered, until softened. Add the spinach, season with salt and pepper to taste, and cook, stirring, until the spinach is wilted, about 3 minutes.

3. Stir in the mashed black beans and continue cooking, stirring, until liquid is absorbed.

4. To assemble quesadillas, place 1 tortilla at a time on a work surface and spoon about one-quarter mixture onto the bottom half of the tortilla. Fold the top half of the tortillas over the filling and press lightly.

5. In a large skillet, heat a thin layer of oil over medium heat. Place the folded quesadillas, 1 or 2 at a time, into the hot skillet and heat over medium heat until hot, turning once, about 1 minute per side.

6. Cut the quesadillas into 3 or 4 wedges each and arrange on plates. Serve immediately.

# black bean and corn burritos  Ⓕ

makes 4 burritos

*These burritos are easy and quick to make. The great flavor is a result of the sweet burst of corn kernels playing against the zesty salsa and earthy beans. To warm tortillas, wrap them in foil and place them in a 275°F oven for a few minutes.*

1 tablespoon olive oil
½ cup chopped onion
1½ cups cooked or 1 (15.5-ounce) can
    black beans, drained and rinsed
½ cup fresh or thawed, frozen corn kernels
½ cup tomato salsa, homemade (page 567)
    or store-bought
4 (10-inch) flour tortillas, warmed

1. In a saucepan, heat the oil over medium heat. Add the onion, cover, and cook until softened, about 5 minutes. Add the beans and mash them until broken up.

2. Add the corn and salsa, stirring to combine. Simmer, stirring, until the bean mixture is hot about 5 minutes.

3. To assemble burritos, place 1 tortilla on a work surface and spoon about ½ cup of the filling mixture down the center. Roll up tightly, tucking in the sides. Repeat with the remaining ingredients. Serve seam side down.

# red bean burritos ⓕ

makes 4 burritos

*These easy and tasty burritos make a great weeknight meal when you're in a hurry but want something filling. It's a handy way to make a meal with a small amount of leftover rice and a can of kidney beans. These burritos can also be made with pinto beans or black beans. Serve with Green-Green Guacamole (page 9) or the basic guacamole also on page 9.*

1 tablespoon olive oil

1 medium onion, chopped

1 medium red bell pepper, chopped

1½ cups cooked or 1 (15.5-ounce) can dark red kidney beans, drained and rinsed

1 cup tomato salsa, homemade (page 567) or store-bought, plus extra if desired

4 (10-inch) flour tortillas, warmed

1 cup hot cooked rice

1 ripe Hass avocado, pitted, peeled, and cut into ¼-inch slices

1. In a medium saucepan, heat the oil over medium heat. Add the onion and bell pepper, cover, and cook until softened, about 5 minutes. Add the beans and salsa and cook, stirring to combine. Simmer, mashing the beans as you stir them, until hot.

2. To assemble burritos, place 1 tortillas on a work surface and spoon about ½ cup of the bean mixture down the center. Top with the rice, followed by slices of avocado and extra salsa, if desired. Roll up tightly, tucking in the sides. Repeat with the remaining ingredients. Serve seam-side down.

# PIZZA, CALZONE, STROMBOLI, AND TURNOVERS

## basic pizza dough

makes one 12-inch pizza

*This is a master recipe for a basic pizza dough. All the pizzas refer back to this recipe and begin with the dough already made and at rest. Variation: For a whole wheat crust, replace up to one half of the all-purpose flour with whole wheat flour.*

Olive oil

1 cup warm water

1 (¼ ounce) packet active dry yeast (2¼ teaspoons)

1¼ teaspoons salt

Pinch sugar

2½ cups all-purpose flour, plus more as needed

1. Lightly oil a medium bowl and set aside. In a separate medium bowl, combine the warm water and yeast. Stir until yeast is dissolved.

2. Add the salt, sugar, and flour, and mix just long enough to form a soft dough. Add small additional amounts of flour if the dough is too sticky. Do not overmix.

3. With well-floured hands, place the dough into the oiled bowl, turning the dough to coat with oil. Cover with plastic wrap or a clean kitchen towel. Let the dough rise in a warm spot until doubled in bulk, about 1 hour.

# vegan margherita pizza

makes 4 servings

*Pizza Margherita employs three flavorful Italian ingredients: tomatoes, basil, and cheese, to depict the colors of the Italian flag. Up until the late 1800s when Pizza Margherita was created, pizza toppings did not traditionally include cheese, and even to this day, pizza in Italy is not the cheese-sodden pie that you generally find in the United States. In this vegan version, seasoned tofu stands in for the cheese.*

1 recipe Basic Pizza Dough (page 128)
1 cup firm tofu, drained
1 tablespoon nutritional yeast
2 ripe plum tomatoes, sliced paper thin
1½ tablespoons olive oil
¼ cup vegan basil pesto, homemade (page 565) or store-bought, room temperature
Salt and freshly ground black pepper

1. Flatten the risen dough slightly, cover with plastic wrap or a clean towel, and set aside to relax for 10 minutes.

2. Place the oven rack on the lowest level of the oven. Preheat the oven to 450°F. Lightly oil a pizza pan or large baking sheet.

3. Turn the relaxed dough out onto a lightly floured surface and flatten with your hands, turning and flouring frequently, working it into a 12-inch round. Be careful not to overwork the middle or the center of the crust will be too thin. Transfer the dough to the prepared pizza pan or baking sheet.

4. In a food processor, combine the tofu and nutritional yeast and process until smooth. Add salt and pepper to taste and blend until smooth. Set aside.

5. Blot any excess liquid from the tomato slices with paper towels.

6. Spread ½ tablespoon of the olive oil onto the prepared pizza dough, using your fingertips to spread evenly. Top with the tofu mixture, spreading evenly to about ½ inch from the dough's edge.

7. Whisk the remaining 1 tablespoon of oil into the pesto and spread evenly over the tofu mixture to about ½ inch from the dough's edge. Arrange the tomato slices on the pizza and season with salt and pepper to taste.

8. Bake until the crust is golden brown, about 12 minutes. Cut the pizza into 8 wedges and serve hot.

# portobello and black olive pizza

makes 4 servings

*Mushrooms have long been an important pizza topping in my house, and we especially enjoy thin slices of meaty portobello mushrooms complemented by salty bits of good black olives.*

1 recipe Basic Pizza Dough (page 128)
2 tablespoons olive oil
2 portobello mushroom caps, lightly rinsed, patted dry, and cut into ¼-inch slices
1 tablespoon finely chopped fresh basil
¼ teaspoon dried oregano
Salt and freshly ground black pepper
½ cup pitted sliced kalamata olives
½ cup pizza sauce or marinara sauce (page 194)

1. Flatten the risen dough slightly, cover with plastic wrap or a clean dish towel, and set aside to relax for 10 minutes.

continues on next page

2. Place the oven rack on the lowest level of the oven. Preheat the oven to 450°F. Lightly oil a pizza pan or large baking sheet.

3. Turn the relaxed dough out onto a lightly floured work surface and flatten with your hands, turning and flouring frequently, working it into a 12-inch round. Be careful not to overwork the middle or the center of the crust will be too thin. Transfer the dough to the prepared pizza pan or baking sheet.

4. In a large skillet, heat 1 tablespoon of the oil over medium heat. Add the mushrooms and cook until softened, about 5 minutes. Remove from heat and add the basil, oregano, and salt and pepper to taste. Stir in the olives and set aside.

5. Spread the remaining 1 tablespoon oil onto the prepared pizza dough, using your fingertips to spread it evenly. Top with the pizza sauce, spreading evenly to about ¹/₂ inch from the dough's edge. Spread the vegetable mixture evenly over the sauce, to about ¹/₂ inch from the dough's edge.

6. Bake until the crust is golden brown, about 12 minutes. Cut the pizza into 8 wedges and serve hot.

# ebap (everything but animal products) pizza

makes 4 servings

*This is an "anything goes" kind of pizza where you can add as few or as many toppings as you like—as long as they're plant based. If you're making pizza for a crowd, it's fun to offer a variety of toppings and let everyone create his or her own section of the pies. Otherwise, you can customize it however you like.*

1 recipe Basic Pizza Dough (page 128)
2 tablespoons olive oil
½ cup thinly sliced red onion
¼ cup chopped red bell pepper
1 cup sliced white mushrooms
½ cup pizza sauce or marinara sauce, homemade (page 194) or store-bought
¼ teaspoon dried oregano
¼ teaspoon dried basil
Salt and freshly ground black pepper
2 tablespoons sliced pitted kalamata olives
Optional toppings: sautéed zucchini, sliced hot peppers, artichoke hearts, sun-dried tomatoes

1. Place the oven rack on the lowest level of the oven. Preheat the oven to 450°F. Lightly oil a pizza pan or large baking sheet.

2. Once the pizza dough has risen, flatten the dough slightly, cover with plastic wrap or a clean towel, and set aside to relax for 10 minutes.

3. Turn the dough out onto a floured surface and use your hands to flatten it, turning and flouring frequently, working it into a 12-inch round. Be careful not to overwork the middle or the center of the crust will be too thin. Transfer the dough to the prepared pizza pan or baking sheet.

4. In a large skillet, heat 1 tablespoon of the oil over medium heat. Add the onion, bell pepper, and mushrooms and cook until softened, about 5 minutes. Remove from heat and set aside.

5. Spread the remaining 1 tablespoon of oil onto the prepared pizza dough, using your

fingertips to spread it evenly. Top with the pizza sauce, spreading evenly to about $1/2$ inch from the dough's edge. Sprinkle with the oregano and basil.

6. Spread the vegetable mixture evenly over the sauce to within about $1/2$ inch from the dough's edge. Season with salt and black pepper to taste. Sprinkle with the olives and any desired toppings.

7. Bake until the crust is golden brown, about 12 minutes. Cut the pizza into 8 wedges and serve hot.

# white pizza with potato, onion, and yellow tomatoes

makes 4 servings

*Topping a pizza with crisp roasted Yukon Gold potato makes this pizza hearty and satisfying. Because the potato is thinly sliced, it really doesn't feel like carb overload, and when used in concert with sliced tomato and onion, the flavor is sublime.*

1 medium Yukon Gold potato, peeled and cut into ¼-inch slices

Salt and freshly ground black pepper

1 recipe Basic Pizza Dough (page 128)

2 tablespoons olive oil

1 medium Vidalia or other sweet onion, cut into ¼-inch slices

6 to 8 fresh basil leaves

2 ripe yellow tomatoes, cut into ¼-inch slices

1. Place the oven rack on the lowest level of the oven. Preheat the oven to 450°F. Arrange the potato slices on a lightly oiled baking sheet and season with salt and pepper to taste. Bake until soft and golden brown, about 10 minutes. Set aside. Lightly oil a pizza pan or large baking sheet.

2. Once the pizza dough has risen, flatten the dough slightly, cover with plastic wrap or a clean towel, and set aside to relax for 10 minutes.

3. Turn the relaxed dough out onto a lightly floured surface and flatten with your hands, turning and flouring frequently, working it into a 12-inch round. Be careful not to overwork the middle or the center of the crust will be too thin. Transfer the dough to the prepared pizza pan or baking sheet.

4. In a large skillet, heat 1 tablespoon of the oil over medium heat. Add the onion and cook until soft and caramelized, stirring frequently, about 30 minutes. Remove from heat, season with oregano and salt and pepper to taste, and set aside.

5. Spread the remaining 1 tablespoon of olive oil onto the prepared pizza dough, using your fingertips to spread it evenly. Top with the caramelized onion, spreading evenly to about $1/2$ inch from the dough's edge. Top with the basil leaves, then arrange the potato and tomato slices on top of the onions and basil.

6. Bake until the crust is golden brown, about 12 minutes. Cut the pizza into 8 wedges and serve hot.

## spicy southwestern-style pizza

makes 4 servings

*If your family can't agree on whether to have tacos or pizza for dinner, compromise by serving this pizza topped with the flavors of the Southwest and Mexico. The pizza dough is more substantial than tortillas, and when topped with pinto beans, this is one hearty meal. You can add a sprinkling of shredded vegan cheese, if you like.*

1 recipe Basic Pizza Dough (page 128)

1 tablespoon olive oil

1 teaspoon chili powder

1½ cups cooked or 1 (15.5-ounce) can pinto beans, drained

1 cup tomato salsa, homemade (page 567) or store-bought

2 tablespoons hot or mild canned minced green chiles

2 tablespoons sliced pitted kalamata olives

2 tablespoons minced fresh cilantro

1. Flatten the risen dough slightly, cover with plastic wrap or a clean dish towel, and set aside to relax for 10 minutes.

2. Place the oven rack on the lowest level of them oven. Preheat the oven to 450°F. Lightly oil a pizza pan or large baking sheet. Turn the relaxed dough out onto a lightly floured surface and flatten with your hands, turning and flouring frequently, working it into a 12-inch round. Be careful not to overwork the middle or the center of the crust will be too thin. Transfer the dough to the prepared pizza pan or baking sheet.

3. In a medium saucepan, heat the oil over medium heat. Stir in the chili powder, then add the beans, stirring to combine and warm the beans, about 5 minutes.

4. Remove from the heat and mash the beans well, adding a small amount of the salsa, if needed, to moisten the beans.

5. Spread the bean mixture evenly onto the prepared pizza dough to about ½ inch from the dough's edge. Spread the salsa evenly over the bean mixture and sprinkle with the chiles and olives.

6. Bake until the crust is golden brown, about 12 minutes. After removing the pizza from the oven, sprinkle with the cilantro, cut into 8 wedges, and serve hot.

## tapenade and tomato pizza

makes 4 servings

*The piquant flavor of tapenade, a zesty olive and caper-based spread, combined with additional olives and capers, makes this a supremely flavorful pizza. Sliced tomatoes replace the pizza sauce, making this more foccacia-like than your average pizza, since it doesn't have the usual pizza sauce and cheese topping.*

1 recipe Basic Pizza Dough (page 128)

3 ripe plum tomatoes, sliced paper thin

2 tablespoons olive oil

¼ cup black and green olive tapenade, homemade (page 9) or store-bought

½ cup sliced pitted black or green olives

2 teaspoons capers, drained and chopped if large

1. Flatten the risen dough slightly, cover with plastic wrap or a clean dish towel, and set aside to relax for 10 minutes.

2. Place the oven rack on the lowest level of the oven. Preheat the oven to 450°F. Lightly oil a pizza pan or large baking sheet. Turn the relaxed dough out onto a lightly floured work surface and flatten with your hands, turning and flouring frequently, working it into a 12-inch round. Be careful not to overwork the middle or the center of the crust will be too thin. Transfer the dough to the prepared pizza pan or baking sheet.

3. Blot any excess liquid from the tomatoes with paper towels. Spread 1 tablespoon of the oil onto the prepared pizza dough, using your fingertips to spread it evenly.

4. Whisk the remaining 1 tablespoon of oil into the tapenade and spread the tapenade onto the pizza dough. Arrange the tomato slices on the pizza and sprinkle with the olives and capers.

5. Bake until the crust is golden brown, about 12 minutes. Cut into 8 wedges and serve hot.

# spicy mushroom and hot pepper calzones

makes 4 calzones

*A calzone is basically a pizza folded in on itself to make a large savory turnover, although with a calzone, it's easier to enjoy all the flavors in every bite because the ingredients are enclosed and cooked together. Usually the stuffing is made with the same ingredients that you would use to top a pizza.*

1 recipe Basic Pizza Dough (page 128)

1 tablespoon olive oil

3 garlic cloves, minced

1 pound white mushrooms, lightly rinsed, patted, dry, and chopped

1 (12-ounce) jar cherry peppers, drained, stemmed, and seeded*

8 ounces extra-firm tofu, drained and crumbled

½ teaspoon dried oregano

1 teaspoon salt

¼ teaspoon freshly ground black pepper

1. Flatten the risen dough slightly, cover with plastic wrap or clean dish towel, and set aside to relax for 10 minutes.

2. Preheat the oven to 400°F. In a large skillet, heat the oil over medium heat. Add the garlic and cook until fragrant, about 30 seconds. Add the mushrooms and cook, stirring, until any liquid evaporates, about 5 minutes. Chop the cherry peppers and add to the mushrooms along with the tofu, oregano, salt, and pepper. Cook stirring to blend the flavors and evaporate any remaining liquid, about 5 minutes. Remove from the heat and set aside to cool.

3. Turn the relaxed dough out onto a lightly floured work surface and divide into 4 equal pieces. Use your hands to flatten each piece into 6-inch circles, turning and flouring as needed.

4. Divide the filling equally among the dough circles, leaving a ½-inch border. Fold each dough circle over the filling to meet the opposite edge of the dough.

5. With dampened fingers, press the edges of the dough together to seal the filling inside.

6. Transfer the calzones to the prepared pizza pan or baking sheet and bake until golden brown, about 20 minutes.

*If cherry peppers are unavailable, substitute another type of mild or hot jarred chile peppers or sauté one or two chopped fresh hot chiles with a chopped bell pepper.*

# roasted vegetable stromboli

makes 4 to 6 servings

*Like the calzone, a stromboli is a variant of the classic pizza—this time the pizza dough is topped and then rolled up before baking. Make the dough first and set it aside to rise while you make the filling. To serve, the baked stromboli is cut crosswise into slices. Variations: Instead of roasting the vegetables, you can also grill them whole and then cut them for the stromboli, or slice them first and grill them on a stovetop grill pan.*

1 recipe Basic Pizza Dough (page 128)

1 medium red onion, chopped

1 medium red or yellow bell pepper, chopped

1 medium zucchini, chopped

2 garlic cloves, minced

8 ounces white mushrooms, lightly rinsed, patted dry, and cut into ¼-inch slices

3 ripe plum tomatoes, chopped

1 tablespoon minced fresh basil

½ teaspoon dried oregano

¼ teaspoon crushed red pepper (optional)

Salt and freshly ground black pepper

2 tablespoons olive oil

½ cup pizza sauce or marinara sauce, homemade (page 192) or store-bought

2 tablespoons vegan Parmesan cheese or Parmasio (page 193; optional)

1. Make the dough. Preheat the oven to 450°F.

2. In a lightly oiled shallow baking pan, combine the onion, bell pepper, zucchini, garlic, mushrooms, tomatoes, basil, oregano, crushed red pepper, if using, and salt and black pepper to taste. Drizzle with the olive oil, stirring to coat the vegetables.

3. Place the baking pan in the oven and roast the vegetables until tender, stirring occasionally, 20 to 30 minutes. Remove from the oven and set aside to cool. Drain the vegetables and blot them dry.

4. Reduce the oven temperature to 375°F. Lightly oil a large baking sheet and set aside.

5. Punch down the dough down and divide it in half. Turn one of the dough pieces out onto a lightly floured surface and flatten with your hands, turning and flouring frequently, working it into a 9 × 12-inch rectangle.

6. Add the pizza sauce to the vegetable mixture, stirring to combine. Sprinkle with the Parmesan, if using.

7. Spread half of the cooled vegetable mixture across the dough leaving a 1-inch border on all sides.

8. Beginning at a long side, roll the stromboli into a cylinder, pinching the edges to seal in the filling.

9. Transfer the stromboli to the prepared baking sheet, seam side down. Repeat with the remaining ingredients.

10. Bake until the crust is golden brown, about 30 minutes. Remove from the oven and let stand 10 minutes. Use a serrated knife to cut into thick slices and serve.

# spicy tempeh empanadas

makes 6 empanadas

*From the Spanish for "to bake in pastry" these savory turnovers traditionally have a meat and vegetable filling. Here tempeh replaces the meat, but chopped seitan or black beans may be used instead. It's a long list of ingredients, but all are found at the supermarket.*

8 ounces tempeh

2 tablespoons olive oil

1 medium yellow onion, finely chopped

2 garlic cloves, minced

½ teaspoon dried oregano

½ teaspoon ground cumin

½ teaspoon crushed red pepper

1½ teaspoons salt

¼ teaspoon black pepper

½ cup ketchup

½ cup raisins

¼ cup fresh orange juice

1½ cups all-purpose flour

½ cup yellow or white cornmeal

1 teaspoon sugar

1 teaspoon baking powder

½ cup vegan margarine

⅓ cup plus 2 teaspoons soy milk

2 teaspoons Dijon mustard

1. In a medium saucepan of simmering water, cook the tempeh for 30 minutes. Drain well, chop, and set aside.

2. In a large skillet, heat the oil over medium heat, add onion and garlic, cover, and cook until softened, 5 minutes.

3. Stir in the chopped tempeh, oregano, cumin, crushed red pepper, the ½ teaspoon salt, and black pepper. Cook 5 minutes longer, then reduce the heat to low and stir in the ketchup, raisins, and orange juice. Simmer until flavors have blended and liquid has evaporated, about 15 minutes. Set aside to cool.

4. Preheat the oven to 400°F. In a food processor, combine the flour, cornmeal, sugar, the remaining 1 teaspoon salt, and baking powder. Pulse to blend. Add the margarine, soy milk, and mustard. Process until a soft dough forms.

5. Divide the dough into 6 equal pieces and roll them out into 7-inch circles on a lightly floured work surface.

6. Divide the filling mixture onto one half of each dough circle. Fold the other half of the dough over the filling and crimp the edges to seal the filling inside.

7. Bake until golden brown, 25 to 30 minutes. Serve hot.

# quick pinto-potato empanadas 🅕

makes 4 empanadas

*This is a great way to use up leftover baked potatoes. (I always toss an extra potato or two in the oven to have on hand for just such a recipe.) If you don't have any cooked potatoes, you can quickly "bake" one in the microwave, but be sure to pierce the skin first so it doesn't burst. Unlike the previous empanada recipe, this one uses ready-made puff pastry so it is great if you're short on time.*

1½ cups cooked or 1 (15.5-ounce) can pinto beans, drained and rinsed

1 small baked russet potato, peeled and coarsely chopped

½ cup tomato salsa, homemade (page 567) or store-bought

½ teaspoon chili powder

½ teaspoon salt

¼ teaspoon freshly ground black pepper

1 sheet frozen puff pastry, thawed

1. Preheat the oven to 400°F. In a medium bowl, mash the beans slightly with a fork. Add the potato, salsa, chili powder, salt, and pepper. Mash well and set aside.

2. Roll out the pastry on a lightly floured board and divide into quarters.

3. Spoon the bean mixture onto the four pieces of dough, dividing evenly. For each

continues on next page

empanada, fold one end of the dough over the filling to meet the opposite end of the dough. Use your fingers to seal and crimp the edges to enclose the filling. Use a fork to pierce the top of empanadas and place them on an ungreased baking sheet.

4. Bake until golden brown, about 20 minutes.

# lentil walnut pasties

makes 4 to 6 pasties

*These hearty pastry packages take a little extra time to prepare, but the delicious result is worth the effort. To save time, assemble them ahead and refrigerate for up to 1 day, covered. Then, just pop them in the oven. Serve these with a fruity relish or chutney.*

2 cups all-purpose flour

1½ teaspoons baking powder

1½ teaspoons salt

⅔ cup vegan margarine, softened

⅓ cup soy milk

1 tablespoon olive oil

1 small potato, peeled and shredded

1 medium carrot, finely chopped

½ cup minced onion

2 garlic cloves, minced

1 teaspoon soy sauce

½ teaspoon dried thyme

½ teaspoon dried savory

¼ teaspoon freshly ground black pepper

1 cup cooked brown lentils

½ cup finely chopped walnuts

1. In a large bowl, combine the flour, baking powder, and 1 teaspoon of the salt. Use a pastry blender or fork to cut in the margarine until the mixture resembles coarse crumbs. Slowly stir in the soy milk, adding just enough to form a dough.

2. Wrap the dough in plastic wrap and refrigerate for 20 minutes. Preheat the oven to 375°F. Grease a baking sheet and set aside.

3. In a large skillet, heat the oil over medium heat. Add the potato, carrot, onion, garlic, soy sauce, thyme, savory, pepper, and remaining ½ teaspoon salt. Cover and cook until the vegetables are soft, about 10 minutes. Stir in the cooked lentils and the walnuts and set aside.

4. Roll the chilled dough out on a lightly floured work surface until about ⅛ inch thick and use a 4-inch round cookie cutter (or the rim of a 4-inch bowl or glass) to cut the dough into four 4-inch circles.

5. Place about ¾ cup of the filling in the center of each dough circle. Overlap the dough and pinch the edges together to form a half circle. Roll up the ends to make a smooth edge.

6. Place the pasties on the prepared baking sheet. Brush with a little oil and bake until golden brown, about 20 minutes. Serve hot.

# mushroom turnovers

makes 4 turnovers

*Similar to an empanada and inspired by the Cornish pasty, a thyme-scented mushroom filling is the star of these savory turnovers. For added bulk, you can include some chopped cooked potato to the filling. The portability of these turnovers makes them ideal lunchbox fare, while at the same time they can look rather elegant plated on top of a brown sauce. Smaller versions would be tasty as an appetizer, too.*

1 tablespoon olive oil

1 small onion, minced

1 garlic clove, minced

3 cups sliced white mushrooms

½ teaspoon dried thyme

½ teaspoon dried savory

⅛ teaspoon ground cayenne

½ cup frozen peas, thawed

½ cup vegan sour cream, homemade (page 574) or store-bought, or pureed tofu

Salt and freshly ground black pepper

1 sheet frozen puff pastry, thawed

1 tablespoon soy milk

1. Preheat the oven to 425°F. In a large skillet, heat the oil over medium heat. Add the onion and garlic and cook until softened, about 5 minutes. Stir in the mushrooms, thyme, savory, and cayenne. Cover and cook until just tender, about 5 minutes.

2. Uncover and continue to cook until the liquid has evaporated. Remove from the heat and set aside to cool. Stir in the peas and sour cream and season to taste with salt and pepper. Set aside.

3. Roll out the pastry and divide into quarters. Spoon the mushroom mixture into the center of each piece of pastry, dividing evenly.

4. Fold the pastry in half over the filling to enclose the filling. Use your fingers to press the edges together to seal the filling inside.

5. Brush each turnover with soy milk and pierce the top with a fork. Bake until golden brown, 15 to 20 minutes. Serve warm.

# indian-style pizza

makes 2 servings

Uttappam, *the savory Southern Indian pancake, sometimes called "Indian pizza," is the inspiration for this delightful taste treat. Semolina flour, called* sooji, *is available in Indian markets and gourmet grocers. If unavailable, use half regular all-purpose flour and half chickpea flour. This recipe*

*makes two "personal pan"-size uttappam. I like to serve them with a vegetable sambar and coconut chutney.*

1 cup vegan plain yogurt

1 cup semolina flour

1 tablespoon cornstarch

⅓ cup plus 2 tablespoons water

1 medium carrot, grated

1 hot or mild green chile, seeded and finely minced

⅓ cup minced onion

¼ cup plus 1 tablespoon chopped fresh cilantro

¼ cup finely chopped unsalted cashews

¾ teaspoon ground coriander

½ teaspoon salt

2 tablespoons canola or grapeseed oil

1. Place the yogurt in a medium bowl and warm it in the microwave for 30 seconds. Stir in the flour and mix well to combine.

2. In a small bowl, combine the cornstarch with the 2 tablespoons of water. Blend well, then stir it into the flour mixture, adding the remaining ⅓ cup of water to form a thick batter.

3. Stir in the carrot, chile, onion, the ¼ cup of cilantro, cashews, coriander, and salt, blending well. Set aside for 20 minutes at room temperature. Preheat the oven to 250°F.

4. In a large skillet, heat the oil over medium heat. Pour half of the batter into the skillet. Cover and cook until the bottom is lightly browned and the batter is cooked through, about 5 minutes. Be careful not to burn.

5. Carefully slide the uttappam onto a baking sheet or heatproof platter and keep warm while you cook the second one with the remaining batter.

6. Invert each uttappam onto dinner plates, sprinkle with the remaining 1 tablespoon cilantro, and serve hot.

# SOUPS

## VEGETABLE BROTHS

light vegetable broth

roasted vegetable broth

root vegetable broth

mushroom vegetable broth

dashi

## CLEAR BROTH SOUPS

greens and beans soup

golden beet soup with a twist

chile-lime tortilla soup

hearty minestrone soup

broccoli noodle soup

potato and kale soup

shiitake mushroom soup
with sake

mushroom medley soup

golden harvest soup

versatile vegetable soup

summer vegetable soup

caramelized french onion soup

roasted tomato soup

vegan matzo ball soup

vietnamese-style noodle soup

miso soup

hot and sour soup

tom yum

## HEARTY SOUPS

ribollita

tuscan tomato and bread soup

moroccan vermicelli
vegetable soup

mulligatawny soup

southern-style beans-and-rice
soup with collards

chickpea and fennel soup

farro and white bean soup
with italian parsley

gumbo z'herbes

two-potato soup with
rainbow chard

sweet potato and peanut soup
with baby spinach

mexican fideo soup
with pinto beans

black bean soup with a splash

spicy black bean orzo soup

black bean and corn soup

three bean soup

spicy pinto bean soup

soba and green lentil soup

white and wild mushroom
barley soup

green and yellow split pea soup

rice and pea soup

lemony lentil and rice soup

moroccan lentil and
chickpea soup

corn and potato chowder

curried butternut and red lentil
soup with chard

tomato orzo soup

laksa come home

## CREAMY SOUPS

asparagus edamame bisque

golden potato soup

thai-inspired coconut soup

cream of broccoli soup

carrot soup with ginger

creamy tomato soup

butternut soup with a swirl
of cranberry

cream of fennel soup

squash soup with pecans
and ginger

root vegetable bisque

curried pumpkin soup

spinach, walnut, and
apple soup

spicy white bean
and tomato soup

peanutty two-potato soup

zucchini and butter bean
bisque

pumpkin soup with
chipotle puree

chestnut bisque with fresh pear

cream of artichoke soup

watercress–white bean soup
with toasted pine nuts

creamy mushroom soup

creamy potato-chard soup

almond soup with cardamom

roasted vegetable bisque

## COLD SOUPS

garden gazpacho

three-tomato gazpacho
with chipotle crème

gazpacho with ditalini
and chile aioli

black and gold gazpacho

senegalese soup

sweet potato vichyssoise

chilled avocado-tomato soup

cucumber cashew soup

chilled carrot soup

chilled beet soup

wild cherry soup

summer fruit soup

jewelbox fruit soup

f = fast

A steaming bowl of soup is both soothing and restorative. Because it is a simple and inexpensive way to get healthy and delicious food on the table, soup remains a favorite, even in today's convenience-oriented society. Innovative and versatile, soups can be enjoyed as a first course, main dish, or even dessert.

Soups often have very forgiving recipes. If it turns out too thick, add more water or broth; if too thin, cook uncovered to reduce liquid, add more solids, or puree some of the existing solids. To avoid overseasoning, add the herbs and spices judiciously and check the seasonings near the end of cooking time.

The foundation of most soups is a broth or stock, and this chapter includes several different broths: an all-purpose Light Vegetable Broth (page 141), as well as the richer Roasted Vegetable Broth (page 142), Root Vegetable Broth (page 142), and Mushroom Vegetable Broth (page 143), all of which can be used to add depth to heartier soups. A light Asian broth, called Dashi (page 143), can be used to enhance miso soup, hot and sour soup, and other Asian soups.

Since flavor intensity and saltiness of broths vary greatly, most of the soup recipes in this book list "salt to taste" rather than a prescribed amount. Be sure to taste your soup as it cooks, adding more salt and other seasonings as needed. Tightly covered, vegetable broth keeps well in the refrigerator for 3 to 4 days or in the freezer for up to three months. Homemade broths are easy and economical to prepare and freeze well. When freezing, it's a good idea to portion your broths into small containers so that you can use only what you need.

The soups in this chapter are organized by type, beginning with several "clear broth" soups, many of which are suitable for first courses or light lunches. Hearty soups featuring beans, grains, or noodles are also included. These can make satisfying meals in themselves. Rounding out the chapter is a selection of creamy soups that are made, of course, without dairy; the "creaminess" comes from pureed vegetables, beans, and other healthful ingredients. The chapter ends with several refreshing chilled soups, both savory and sweet.

# Vegetable Broths

## light vegetable broth

makes about 6 cups

*This basic broth recipe can be considered "all-purpose" and can be used in virtually any recipe in this book calling for vegetable broth. As with all broth recipes, use the ingredient list as a guide, adding more or less of the vegetables according to taste and availability.*

1 tablespoon olive oil
2 medium onions, quartered
2 medium carrots, chopped
1 celery rib, chopped
2 garlic cloves, unpeeled and crushed
8 cups water
2 teaspoons soy sauce
⅓ cup coarsely chopped fresh parsley
1 bay leaf
1 teaspoon salt
½ teaspoon black peppercorns

1. In a large stockpot, heat the oil over medium heat. Add the onions, carrots, celery, and garlic. Cover and cook until softened, about 10 minutes. Stir in the water, soy sauce, parsley, bay leaf, salt, and peppercorns. Bring to a boil and then reduce heat to low and simmer, uncovered, for 1½ hours.

2. Set aside to cool, then strain through a fine-mesh sieve into a large bowl or pot, pressing against the solids with the back of a spoon to release all the liquid. Discard solids. Cool broth completely, then portion into tightly covered containers and refrigerate for up to 4 days or freeze for up to 3 months.

## about vegetable broths

Vegetable broth can give extra flavor to soups along with added nutrients. If you are not inclined to prepare homemade broth, there are a number of commercial products that can be used instead. Vegetable broth is available in cans and aseptic or shelf-stable containers. Different brands produce broth of varying strengths, so try to be aware of how the flavor of a particular broth will affect your soup. As a general rule when using commercial broth, I recommend equal proportions of water to broth to dilute the broth a bit and minimize the potential for overpowering flavor; for example, use ½ cup of water for every ½ cup of broth. Another viable alternative is to use powdered vegetable base or vegetable bouillon cubes or paste to enrich your soup.

Perhaps the easiest way to begin preparing soup (and definitely most economical) is to use water instead of broth. I frequently use water (often with the addition of a little powdered vegetable soup base or a bouillon cube or two) instead of broth when making soups, especially hearty ones such as bean soups, since the ingredients impart loads of flavor on their own. When ingredients are simmered in water, the liquid transforms into a light broth—albeit lighter than if you had started with a broth, but in many cases, it is quite enough. For that reason, many of the soup recipes will call for broth or water. The choice is yours. Just be sure to adjust seasonings appropriately—a soup made with water as opposed to broth will need more salt to bring out the flavor of the other ingredients.

# roasted vegetable broth

makes about 6 cups

*Roast vegetables prior to adding them to your broth to give them a deeper flavor. The broth will, in turn, be richer-tasting and more full-bodied. You can use this broth in any recipe calling for vegetable broth where a rich vegetable flavor is desired.*

1 large onion, thickly sliced
2 large carrots, chopped
1 celery rib, chopped
1 large potato, unpeeled and chopped
3 garlic cloves, unpeeled and crushed
2 tablespoons olive oil
Salt and freshly ground black pepper
8 cups water
½ cup coarsely chopped fresh parsley
2 bay leaves
½ teaspoon black peppercorns
1 tablespoon soy sauce

1. Preheat the oven to 425°F. In a lightly oiled 9 × 13-inch baking pan, place the onion, carrots, celery, potato, and garlic. Drizzle with the oil and sprinkle with salt and pepper to taste. Roast the vegetables until they are slightly browned, turning once, about 30 minutes total. Set aside for 10 minutes to cool slightly.

2. Place the roasted vegetables in a large stockpot. Add the water, parsley, bay leaves, peppercorns, soy sauce, and salt to taste. Bring to a boil and then reduce heat to low and simmer, uncovered, until the broth has reduced slightly and is a deep golden color, about 1 hour.

3. Set aside to cool, then strain through a fine-mesh sieve into a large bowl or pot, pressing against the solids with the back of a spoon to release all the liquid. Discard solids. Cool broth completely, then portion into tightly covered containers and refrigerate for up to 4 days or freeze for up to 3 months.

# root vegetable broth

makes about 6 cups

*The sweetness of the root vegetables come through in this broth that works especially well when making hearty bean soups, such as the Three Bean Soup (page 161).*

1 tablespoon olive oil
1 large onion, coarsely chopped
2 medium carrots, coarsely chopped
2 medium parsnips, coarsely chopped
1 medium turnip, coarsely chopped
8 cups water
1 medium white potato, unpeeled and quartered
3 garlic cloves, unpeeled and crushed
¾ cup coarsely chopped fresh parsley
2 bay leaves
½ teaspoon black peppercorns
1 teaspoon salt

1. In a large stockpot, heat the oil over medium heat. Add the onion, carrots, parsnips, and turnip. Cover and cook until softened, about 8 minutes. Stir in the water. Add the potato, garlic, parsley, bay leaves, peppercorns, and salt. Bring to a boil and then reduce heat to low and simmer, uncovered, for 1½ hours.

2. Set aside to cool, then strain through a fine-mesh sieve into a large bowl or pot, pressing against the solids with the back of a spoon to release all the liquid. Discard solids. Cool broth completely, then portion into tightly covered containers and refrigerate for up to 4 days or freeze for up to 3 months.

# mushroom vegetable broth

makes about 6 cups

*While this broth can certainly add additional layers of mushroom flavor to a mushroom soup, I also like to freeze it in small amounts and use it to enrich sauces, gravies, and grains.*

1 tablespoon olive oil
1 medium onion, unpeeled and quartered
1 medium carrot, coarsely chopped
1 celery rib with leaves, coarsely chopped
8 ounces white mushrooms, lightly rinsed, patted dry, and coarsely chopped
5 dried shiitake or porcini mushrooms, soaked in 2 cups hot water, drained, soaking liquid strained and reserved
3 garlic cloves, unpeeled and crushed
½ cup coarsely chopped fresh parsley
2 bay leaves
½ teaspoon black peppercorns
1 teaspoon salt
5 cups water

1. In a large stockpot, heat the oil over medium heat. Add the onion, carrot, celery, and white mushrooms. Cover and cook until softened, about 7 minutes. Stir in the softened dried mushrooms and the reserved soaking liquid, along with the garlic, parsley, bay leaves, peppercorns, salt, and water. Bring to a boil and then reduce heat to low and simmer, uncovered, for 1½ hours.

2. Set aside to cool, then strain through a fine-mesh sieve into a large bowl or pot, pressing against the solids with the back of a spoon to release all the liquid. Discard solids. Cool broth completely, then portion into tightly covered containers and refrigerate for up to 4 days or freeze for up to 3 months.

# dashi

makes 4 cups

*Dashi is a delicate Japanese soup broth. Basic vegetarian dashi, called* kombu dashi, *is made with just two ingredients: kombu (dried kelp) and water. Look for kombu in natural food stores or Asian markets. For a little extra flavor dimension, add a dash of green onion and a little soy sauce.*

1 six-inch piece kombu (see headnote)
4 cups water
2 green onions, coarsely chopped
2 teaspoons soy sauce
Pinch salt

1. In a large saucepan, combine the kombu and water and let soak for 1 hour. Add green onions, soy sauce, and salt. Bring to a boil, then reduce heat to low and simmer, uncovered, for 20 minutes.

2. Set aside to cool to room temperature, then strain the broth into another saucepan or bowl, discarding the kombu and green onions. Cool broth completely, then portion into tightly covered containers and refrigerate for up to 4 days or freeze for up to 3 months.

## greens and beans soup

makes 4 servings

*This quick and easy soup contains the nutrient-rich goodness of dark leafy greens and the protein-packed richness of two kinds of beans. For a heartier dish, add cooked rice or pasta to the soup a few minutes before serving time. You can use just one kind of green or bean, if you prefer, or substitute different varieties for the ones given here.*

1 tablespoon olive oil

1 medium onion, chopped

3 large garlic cloves, minced

1½ cups cooked or 1 (15.5-ounce) can cannellini beans, drained and rinsed

1½ cups cooked or 1 (15.5-ounce) can dark red kidney beans, drained and rinsed

5 cups vegetable broth, homemade (page 141) or store-bought, or water

¼ teaspoon crushed red pepper

Salt and freshly ground black pepper

3 cups coarsely chopped stemmed Swiss chard

3 cups coarsely chopped stemmed kale

1. In a large soup pot, heat the oil over medium heat. Add the onion, cover, and cook until softened, about 5 minutes. Add the garlic and cook, uncovered, 1 minute.

2. Stir in the beans, broth, crushed red pepper, and salt and black pepper to taste and bring to a boil. Reduce heat to a simmer, uncovered, and stir in the greens. Continue to cook until the greens are tender, 15 to 20 minutes. Serve hot.

## golden beet soup with a twist

makes 6 servings

*This soup offers more than one twist on the borscht theme—using golden beets instead of red and adding a twist of lemon just before serving. If you prefer a smooth soup, puree it in a blender or food processor for a more creamy texture. This soup can be served hot or chilled.*

2 tablespoons olive oil

1 medium yellow onion, finely chopped

1 medium carrot, finely chopped

4 medium golden beets, peeled and diced

1 small yellow bell pepper, chopped

1 medium Yukon Gold potato, diced

5 cups vegetable broth, homemade (page 141) or store-bought, or water

2 teaspoons sugar

1 teaspoon dried thyme

Salt and freshly ground black pepper

1 tablespoon fresh lemon juice

2 tablespoons minced fresh dillweed or 1½ teaspoons dried, for garnish

1. In a large soup pot, heat the oil over medium heat. Add the onion and carrot. Cover and cook until softened, 5 minutes. Add the beets, bell pepper, and potato and cook, uncovered, stirring, for 1 minute. Stir in the broth, sugar, and thyme and season with salt and black pepper to taste. Cook until the vegetables are tender, about 45 minutes.

2. Serve hot or, alternately, set aside to cool, then refrigerate until chilled. Just before serving, stir in the lemon juice and garnish with the dill.

# chile-lime tortilla soup

makes 4 servings

*I like to use seitan in this zesty soup, but strips of lightly browned, extra-firm tofu will also work well. For an extra embellishment, add some cooked rice or corn kernels near serving time. For a less spicy soup, use only one chile.*

1 tablespoon olive oil

1 medium red onion, chopped

3 garlic cloves, minced

2 serrano chiles, seeded and cut into ¼-inch slices

6 cups vegetable broth, homemade (page 141) or store-bought, or water

8 ounces seitan, homemade (page 305) or store-bought, cut into ¼-inch strips

1 (14.5-ounce) can diced tomatoes, drained

1 (4-ounce) can mild chopped green chiles, drained

Salt and freshly ground black pepper

¼ cup chopped fresh cilantro

3 tablespoons fresh lime juice

3 to 4 (6-inch) corn tortillas, cut into strips

1 ripe Hass avocado

1. Preheat the oven to 350°F. In a large pot, heat the oil over medium heat. Add the onion, cover, and cook until softened, about 5 minutes. Add the garlic and serrano chiles, then stir in the broth, seitan, tomatoes, canned chiles, and salt and pepper to taste. Bring to a boil, then reduce heat to low and simmer, uncovered, for 20 minutes. Stir in the cilantro and lime juice and taste, adjusting seasonings if necessary.

2. While the soup simmers, spread the tortilla strips on a baking sheet and bake until crisp, about 8 minutes. Pit, peel, and dice the avocado. Ladle the soup into bowls and top with the tortilla strips and diced avocado and serve.

# hearty minestrone soup

makes 4 to 6 servings

*This classic Italian vegetable soup tastes better the day after it is made so plan to make it ahead of time. Feel free to vary the vegetables as desired. For example, you can substitute spinach for the cabbage or use white beans or chickpeas in place of the kidney beans. Instead of barley, small cooked soup pasta makes a good addition, but for best results, the pasta should be cooked separately and added when ready to serve.*

1 tablespoon olive oil

1 medium onion, minced

1 celery rib, chopped

1 medium large carrot, chopped

3 garlic cloves, minced

2 cups shredded cabbage

1 (14.5-ounce) can diced tomatoes with liquid

1½ cups cooked or 1 (15.5-ounce) can dark red kidney beans, drained and rinsed

¼ cup pearl barley

¼ cup split peas, picked over, rinsed, and drained

6 cups vegetable broth, homemade (page 141) or store-bought, or water

½ teaspoon dried oregano

½ teaspoon dried basil

Salt and freshly ground black pepper

3 tablespoons chopped fresh parsley

1. In a large soup pot, heat the oil over medium heat. Add the onion, celery, carrot, and garlic. Cover and cook until softened, about 5 minutes. Stir in the cabbage, tomatoes, beans, barley, and split peas. Add the broth, oregano, and basil, and salt and pepper to taste.

2. Bring to a boil, then reduce heat to low and simmer, partially covered, for 1 hour or longer, until the vegetables are tender. Taste, adjusting seasonings if necessary. Add a bit more broth if the liquid reduces too much. Stir in the parsley and serve.

# broccoli noodle soup

makes 4 servings

*The key to the success of this wholesome soup is to not overcook the broccoli or the noodles—the broccoli should be bright green and just tender and the noodles tender but firm. This recipe can be a pattern for numerous variations, using asparagus, zucchini, or another vegetable in place of the broccoli, or a small bite-size pasta (or even a grain) instead of the angel hair pasta.*

1 tablespoon olive oil

1 medium onion, chopped

2 medium carrots, cut into ¼-inch slices

3 garlic cloves, minced

6 cups vegetable broth, homemade (page 141) or store-bought, or water

Salt and freshly ground black pepper

3 cups small broccoli florets

2 ounces angel hair pasta, broken into thirds

1 tablespoon minced fresh parsley

1. In a large soup pot, heat the oil over medium heat. Add the onion, carrots, and garlic. Cover and cook until softened, about 5 minutes. Add the broth and season with salt and pepper to taste. Bring to a boil, then reduce heat to low and simmer, uncovered, until the vegetables are tender, about 30 minutes.

2. Add the broccoli and cook for 3 minutes, then bring to a boil and add the pasta. Cook until the pasta and broccoli are tender, about 5 minutes. Reduce heat to low, stir in the parsley, and simmer another minute or so to blend flavors before serving.

# potato and kale soup

makes 4 servings

*This rich brothy soup is satisfying enough to serve as a main dish for two or three when accompanied by warm crusty bread. For a more substantial soup, sauté slices of vegan sausage links until browned and add them when ready to serve.*

1 tablespoon olive oil

1 medium onion, chopped

2 garlic cloves, minced

6 cups vegetable broth, homemade (page 141) or store-bought, or water

2 large russet potatoes, peeled and cut into ½-inch dice

½ teaspoon dried oregano

¼ teaspoon crushed red pepper

1 bay leaf

Salt

4 cups chopped stemmed kale

1½ cups cooked or 1 (15.5-ounce) can Great Northern beans, drained and rinsed

1. In a large pot, heat the oil over medium heat. Add the onion and garlic, cover, and cook until softened, about 5 minutes. Add the broth, potatoes, oregano, crushed red pepper, bay leaf, and salt to taste, and bring to a boil. Reduce heat to low and simmer, uncovered, for 30 minutes.

2. Stir in the kale and the beans and cook until the vegetables are tender, 15 to 20 minutes longer. Remove, discard the bay leaf, and serve.

# shiitake mushroom soup with sake

makes 4 servings

*Consider serving this delicate soup as a starter to a Japanese meal of vegan sushi or donburi. You can make this soup using a light vegetable broth, dashi (page 143), or even water. However, the Mushroom Vegetable Broth (page 143) will offer the deepest mushroom flavor base. Substitute mirin in place of the sake, if you prefer.*

1 tablespoon canola or grapeseed oil

2 leeks, white parts only, well rinsed and chopped

2 celery ribs with leaves, chopped

8 ounces fresh shiitake mushrooms, lightly rinsed, patted dry, stemmed, and sliced

3 tablespoons sake

2 tablespoons soy sauce

6 cups vegetable broth, homemade (page 141) or store-bought, or water

Salt and freshly ground black pepper

2 tablespoons minced fresh parsley

1. In a large soup pot, heat the oil over medium heat. Add the leeks and celery. Cover and cook until softened, about 5 minutes.

2. Stir in the mushrooms, sake, soy sauce, and broth and season with salt and pepper to taste. Bring to a boil, then reduce heat to low and simmer, uncovered, until the mushrooms are tender, about 15 minutes. Stir in the parsley, taste, adjusting seasonings if necessary, and serve.

# mushroom medley soup

makes 4 to 6 servings

*For more contrast and depth of flavor, include some morels, porcini, or oyster mushrooms, if available. Cooked rice, barley, or orzo added near the end of cooking time thickens the soup. For more color, texture, and flavor, add ½ cup of frozen baby peas about 10 minutes prior to serving time.*

1 tablespoon olive oil

1 medium onion, chopped

1 large carrot, chopped

1 celery rib, chopped

8 ounces fresh shiitake mushrooms, lightly rinsed, patted dry, stemmed and cut into ¼-inch slices

8 ounces cremini mushrooms, lightly rinsed, patted dry, and quartered

8 ounces white mushrooms, lightly rinsed, patted dry, and quartered

6 cups vegetable broth, mushroom broth, homemade (pages 141, 143) or store-bought, or water

¼ cup chopped fresh parsley

1 teaspoon minced fresh thyme or ½ teaspoon dried

Salt and freshly ground black pepper

In a large pot, heat the oil over medium heat. Add the onion, carrot, and celery. Cover and cook until softened, about 10 minutes. Stir in all the mushrooms and broth, and bring to boil. Reduce heat to low, add the parsley and thyme, and season with salt and pepper to taste. Simmer, uncovered, until the vegetables are tender, about 30 minutes. Serve hot.

# golden harvest soup

makes 4 to 6 servings

*Turmeric is added to the pasta water to give it a golden hue to complement the yellow and orange vegetables in this vibrantly colored soup.*

2 tablespoons olive oil

1 medium yellow onion, finely chopped

2 medium carrots, chopped

1 medium sweet potato, peeled and chopped

1 medium yellow bell pepper, chopped

2 garlic cloves, minced

4 large ripe yellow tomatoes, chopped

6 cups vegetable broth, homemade (page 141) or store-bought, or water

1 bay leaf

1 teaspoon fresh savory or ½ teaspoon dried

Salt

Ground cayenne

1½ cups cooked or 1 (15.5-ounce) can chickpeas, drained and rinsed

⅓ cup ditalini or other small soup pasta

¼ teaspoon turmeric

1. In a large pot, heat the oil over medium heat. Add the onion, carrots, sweet potato, bell pepper, and garlic. Cover and cook until softened, about 10 minutes. Stir in the tomatoes, broth, bay leaf, savory, and salt and cayenne to taste. Bring to a boil, reduce heat, and simmer, uncovered, 30 minutes. Add the chickpeas and simmer another 15 minutes.

2. In a medium saucepan of boiling salted water, cook the ditalini and turmeric, stirring occasionally, until pasta is al dente, about 5 minutes. Drain well and stir into the soup. Remove and discard bay leaf before serving. Ladle soup into bowls and serve.

# versatile vegetable soup

makes 4 to 6 servings

*This basic vegetable soup recipe can be embellished at will, adding more or less of a particular ingredient in favor of another, depending on what's on hand or in season. For example, try chard or kale instead of the cabbage or white beans instead of the chickpeas, and so on.*

1 tablespoon olive oil

2 medium carrots, chopped

1 large onion, chopped

1 celery rib, chopped

2 garlic cloves, minced

2 cups chopped cabbage

½ medium red bell pepper, chopped

4 small red-skinned potatoes, unpeeled and quartered

6 cups vegetable broth, homemade (page 141) or store-bought, or water

1½ cups cooked or 1 (15.5-ounce) can chickpeas, drained and rinsed

Salt and freshly ground black pepper

½ cup fresh or frozen green peas, thawed

2 tablespoons chopped fresh parsley

1. In large soup pot, heat the oil over medium heat. Add the carrots, onion, celery, and garlic. Cover and cook until softened, about 5 minutes. Add the cabbage, bell pepper, potatoes, and broth. Bring to a boil, then reduce heat to low.

2. Add the chickpeas and salt and pepper to taste. Simmer, uncovered, until the vegetables are tender, about 45 minutes. About 5 minutes before serving, stir in the peas. Add the parsley, taste, adjusting seasonings if necessary, and serve.

# summer vegetable soup

makes 4 to 6 servings

*Garden fresh vegetables such as zucchini, corn, spinach, and tomatoes star in this flavorful soup, but other summer produce such as fennel, green beans, and chard are good choices as well. Although it calls for fresh basil, feel free to use a different herb such as chervil or tarragon to change up the flavor.*

2 tablespoons olive oil

2 medium leeks, white parts plus an inch of green, well rinsed and chopped

2 medium carrots, cut into ½-inch dice

2 garlic cloves, minced

3 small new potatoes, unpeeled and cut into ½-inch slices

1 medium zucchini, halved lengthwise and cut into ½-inch slices

1 medium yellow summer squash, halved lengthwise and cut into ½-inch slices

2 fresh ripe tomatoes, diced, or 1 (14.5-ounce) can diced tomatoes, drained

1½ cups fresh corn kernels

Salt and freshly ground black pepper

6 cups light vegetable broth, homemade (page 141) or store-bought, or water

2 cups chopped fresh spinach

¼ cup fresh basil leaves, chopped

1. In a large soup pot, heat the oil over medium heat. Add the leeks, carrots, and garlic. Cover and cook until softened, about 5 minutes. Add the potatoes, zucchini, yellow squash, tomatoes, corn, and salt and pepper to taste. Cook 5 minutes longer, then stir in the broth. Bring to a boil, reduce heat to low, and simmer, uncovered, until the vegetables are tender, about 30 minutes.

2. Stir in the spinach and the basil, then ladle into soup bowls, and serve.

# caramelized french onion soup

makes 4 servings

*Caramelizing the onions is what gives French onion soup its depth of flavor. Floating a thick slice of toasted bread in it to soak up that flavor is what makes it fun to eat. Use a mandoline or the slicing disc on your food processor to cut the onions as thin as possible.*

3 tablespoons olive oil

4 medium Vidalia or other sweet onions, thinly sliced

2 garlic cloves, minced

¼ cup calvados or brandy (optional)

½ cup apple cider or apple juice

5 cups vegetable broth, homemade (page 141) or store-bought, or water

½ teaspoon dried thyme

1 bay leaf

Salt and freshly ground black pepper

4 slices French baguette

Vegan Parmesan or Parmasio (page 193; optional)

1. In a large soup pot, heat the oil over medium heat. Add the onions and garlic. Cover and cook until softened. Uncover and continue to cook until the onions are very soft and begin to caramelize. Stir in the calvados, if using, then add the cider, broth, thyme, and bay leaf, and season with salt and pepper to taste. Bring to a boil, then reduce heat to low and simmer, uncovered, for 45 minutes to an hour to allow the flavors to mingle.

2. Preheat the broiler. When ready to serve, arrange the bread slices on a baking sheet and top each with a small amount of Parmesan, if using. Place under the broiler until toasted, about 1 minute. Remove and discard the bay leaf. Ladle the soup into 4 bowls, top with a toasted bread slice, and serve.

# roasted tomato soup

makes 4 servings

*This soup is best made in the summer during that short window of time when great-tasting tomatoes are plentiful. Roasting the tomatoes brings out their natural sweetness and provides a depth of flavor that is unmatched. The soup is equally delicious served warm or chilled.*

2 pounds ripe tomatoes, cored and halved

2 large garlic cloves, crushed

3 tablespoons olive oil

1 tablespoon balsamic vinegar

Salt and freshly ground black pepper

½ cup chopped red onion

2 cups light vegetable broth, homemade (page 141) or store-bought, or water

½ cup lightly packed fresh basil leaves

1. Preheat the oven to 450°F. In a large bowl, combine the tomatoes, garlic, 2 tablespoons of the oil, vinegar, and salt and pepper to taste. Spread the tomato mixture into a 9 × 13-inch baking pan and roast until the tomatoes begin to darken, about 30 minutes. Remove from the oven and set aside.

2. In a large soup pot, heat the remaining 1 tablespoon of oil over medium heat. Add the onion, cover, and cook until very soft, about 10 minutes, stirring occasionally. Add the roasted tomatoes and broth and bring to a boil. Reduce heat to low and simmer, uncovered, for 10 minutes. Remove from the heat, add the basil, and season with salt and pepper to taste. Puree the soup in the pot with an immersion blender or in a blender or food processor, in batches if necessary, and return to the pot. Reheat over medium heat, if necessary. To serve this soup chilled, refrigerate it for at least 1 hour before serving.

# vegan matzo ball soup

makes 4 servings

*Tofu stands in for eggs to make the matzo balls for this comforting soup. The recipe for matzo balls follows this recipe. If you don't have the time or inclination to make matzo balls, add some cooked noodles when ready to serve for an equally restorative pot of vegetable noodle soup.*

1 tablespoon olive oil

1 small onion, finely chopped

1 medium carrot, chopped

1 celery rib, chopped

3 green onions, chopped

6 cups vegetable broth, homemade (page 141) or store-bought, or water

2 tablespoons minced fresh parsley

1 teaspoon fresh or dried dillweed

½ teaspoon salt, or more if needed

¼ teaspoon freshly ground black pepper

Vegan Matzo Balls (recipe follows)

1. In a large soup pot, heat the oil over medium heat. Add the onion, carrot, and celery. Cover and cook until softened, about 5 minutes. Add the green onions and cook 3 minutes longer. Stir in the broth, parsley, dill, salt, and pepper. You may need to add additional salt, depending on the saltiness of your broth. Bring to a boil, then reduce heat to low and simmer, uncovered, until the vegetables are tender, about 30 minutes.

2. When ready to serve, place 3 of the matzo balls into each soup bowl and ladle the soup on top. Serve immediately.

## vegan matzo balls

makes about 12 matzo balls

*I like my matzo balls on the firm side, so I prefer baking them. For lighter, fluffier matzo balls, boil them instead by adding them to the broth and simmering, covered, for 30 minutes, then turn off the heat and set aside for 20 minutes.*

1 cup matzo meal

½ teaspoon onion powder

½ teaspoon salt

¼ teaspoon freshly ground black pepper

1 cup crumbled drained firm tofu

⅓ cup vegetable broth, homemade (page 141)
    or store-bought, or water

2 tablespoons fresh minced dillweed

2 tablespoons chopped fresh parsley

¼ cup olive oil

1. In a medium bowl, combine the matzo meal, onion powder, salt, and pepper. Set aside.

2. In a food processor, combine the tofu, broth, dill, parsley, and oil and puree. Stir the tofu mixture into the matzo mixture and blend well. Cover the bowl and refrigerate for 1 hour or overnight.

3. Preheat the oven to 375°F. Lightly oil a baking sheet and set aside. Divide the matzo mixture into 12 equal portions. Use your hands to form the mixture into tightly packed balls and arrange on the oiled baking sheet. Cover tightly with foil and bake for about 30 minutes. Set aside to cool. Serve warm.

## vietnamese-style noodle soup

makes 4 servings

*This flavorful soup is a variation of the Vietnamese noodle soup called pho, which is traditionally made with beef. Although some of the ingredients may sound exotic, they are all available in well-stocked supermarkets, natural food stores, and Asian markets. Accompany with the Sesame-Cilantro Scallion Pancakes (page 39).*

1 tablespoon canola or grapeseed oil

1 medium onion, coarsely chopped

1 serrano or other hot green chile, seeded
    and chopped

1 tablespoon coarsely chopped fresh ginger

3 tablespoons soy sauce

2 whole star anise

5 cups vegetable broth, homemade (page 141)
    or store-bought, or water

2 tablespoons barley miso paste

2 tablespoons hoisin sauce

1 tablespoon fresh lime juice

½ cup hot water

4 ounces dried rice noodles

6 ounces seitan, homemade (page 305)
    or store-bought, cut into strips

½ cup fresh bean sprouts, for garnish

3 green onions, chopped, for garnish

¼ cup chopped fresh cilantro, for garnish

1. In a large soup pot, heat the oil over medium heat. Add the onion, cover, and cook until softened, 5 minutes. Add the chile and ginger and cook until fragrant, about 1 minute. Stir in the soy sauce, anise, and broth. Simmer, uncovered, for 45 minutes to allow flavors to blend. Strain the soup and return it to the pot, discarding the solids.

continues on next page

**2.** In a small bowl, combine the miso, hoisin, lime juice, and water and add to the soup. Stir in the noodles and the seitan. Cook until the noodles are soft, about 10 minutes.

**3.** Ladle the soup into 4 bowls, garnish with bean sprouts, green onions, and cilantro, and serve.

## miso soup

makes 4 servings

*Miso is fermented soy bean paste, with a rich salty flavor, known for its restorative qualities, especially in Japan where it is eaten daily, even for breakfast. Quick and easy to prepare, traditional miso soup is usually little more than miso paste dissolved in dashi or water with a bit of green onion, sliced mushrooms, or diced tofu. Shredded daikon or carrot, as well as wakame or other sea vegetables, makes a good addition as well.*

5 cups water

2 tablespoons soy sauce, or to taste

4 white mushrooms, lightly rinsed, patted dry, and cut into ¼-inch slices

¼ cup chopped green onions

3 tablespoons mellow white miso paste

6 ounces extra-firm tofu, cut into small dice

**1.** In a large soup pot, bring the water and soy sauce to a boil. Add the mushrooms and green onions. Reduce the heat to low and simmer for 5 minutes to soften the vegetables.

**2.** Place ½ cup of the hot soup into a small bowl and add the miso paste, blending well. Stir the blended miso into the soup and simmer for 2 minutes. Do not boil. Add the tofu and adjust the seasonings, adding a little more miso paste or soy sauce if needed, and serve.

## hot and sour soup

makes 4 servings

*The amazing variety of texture and flavor elements may explain why this delicious and invigorating soup is a classic. Fresh shiitakes are preferred, but dried may be used in a pinch. Straw mushrooms make a good addition, as do reconstituted lily stems, available at Asian markets.*

1 cup fresh shiitake mushroom caps, lightly rinsed, patted dry, and cut into ¼-inch-thick strips

1 (6-ounce) can bamboo shoots, drained, rinsed, and cut into matchsticks

1 (6-ounce) can water chestnuts, drained, rinsed, and cut into ¼-inch dice

¼ cup minced green onions

2 garlic cloves, minced

3 tablespoons rice vinegar

3 tablespoons soy sauce

1 teaspoon minced fresh ginger

1 teaspoon Asian chili paste

6 cups light vegetable broth, homemade (page 141) or store-bought, or water

Salt and freshly ground black pepper

1 tablespoon cornstarch blended with 3 tablespoons water

6 ounces firm tofu, drained and cut into ½-inch dice

1 tablespoon toasted sesame oil

**1.** In a large soup pot, combine the mushrooms, bamboo shoots, water chestnuts, green onions, garlic, vinegar, soy sauce, ginger, and chili paste. Stir in the broth and season with salt and pepper to taste. Bring to a boil, then reduce heat to low and simmer for 30 minutes.

**2.** Return to a boil and stir in the cornstarch mixture, stirring until the soup thickens slightly. Add the tofu, then turn off the heat and drizzle with the sesame oil, and serve.

# tom yum

makes 4 servings

*This fragrant Thai soup is redolent of lemongrass, ginger, chile paste, and cilantro. At the first sign of a cold, a steaming bowl of this spicy and flavorful soup can be a soothing comfort, if not a surefire cure. If lemongrass is unavailable, substitute the zest of one lemon.*

1 medium onion, quartered and thinly sliced

1 tablespoon minced fresh lemongrass,
    white part only

2 teaspoons grated fresh ginger

1 teaspoon Asian chili paste

3 tablespoons soy sauce or Nothin' Fishy Nam Pla
    (page 560)

6 cups light vegetable broth, homemade (page 141)
    or store-bought, or water

8 ounces extra-firm tofu, drained and cut into
    ½-inch dice

4 green onions, chopped

2 small ripe tomatoes, cut into wedges

1 (14-ounce) can straw mushrooms, drained and
    rinsed

½ cup frozen baby peas

3 tablespoons chopped fresh cilantro

1 tablespoon fresh lime juice

½ teaspoon sugar

1. In a large soup pot, combine the onion, lemongrass, ginger, chile paste, and soy sauce. Stir in the broth and bring to a boil. Reduce heat to low and simmer for 20 minutes.

2. Strain the broth through a fine-mesh sieve into another pot, discarding the solids. To the strained broth, add the tofu, green onions, tomatoes, mushrooms, peas, cilantro, lime juice, and sugar and simmer 10 minutes longer. Taste, adjusting seasonings if necessary, and serve.

# HEARTY SOUPS

## ribollita

makes 4 servings

*Literally meaning "reboiled," ribollita is a Tuscan vegetable and bean soup, similar to a minestrone but made thick and hearty by the addition of Italian bread. This economical, stick-to-your-ribs soup has long been a favorite in my family.*

3 tablespoons olive oil

1 medium red onion, chopped

1 medium carrot, chopped

2 garlic cloves, minced

3 cups shredded cabbage

2 cups chopped stemmed kale

1 medium russet potato, peeled and cut into
    ½-inch dice

1 (14.5-ounce) can crushed tomatoes

3 cups cooked or 2 (15.5-ounce) cans Great Northern
    or other white beans, drained and rinsed

6 cups vegetable broth, homemade (page 141)
    or store-bought, or water

Salt and freshly ground black pepper

4 thick slices Italian bread, toasted and cut into
    ½-inch cubes

1. In a large soup pot, heat 2 tablespoons of the oil over medium heat. Add the onion, carrot, and garlic. Cover and cook until softened, about 5 minutes. Add cabbage, kale, potato, tomatoes, beans, broth, and salt and pepper to taste. Bring to a boil, then reduce heat to low and simmer, uncovered, until the vegetables are soft, about 1 hour.

2. Divide the bread among 4 soup bowls. Ladle the soup over the bread, drizzle with the remaining tablespoon oil, and serve.

# tuscan tomato and bread soup

makes 4 servings

*Like ribollita, this Tuscan soup is a rich thick bread soup. Here, tomatoes steal the show without competing with other vegetables. If fresh tomatoes aren't at their peak, substitute canned diced tomatoes.*

4 cups cubed Italian bread

¼ cup olive oil

4 garlic cloves, minced

1 (28-ounce) can crushed tomatoes

2 fresh ripe tomatoes, cut into ½-inch dice

4 cups vegetable broth, homemade (page 141)
    or store-bought, or water

2 tablespoons minced fresh parsley

Salt and freshly ground black pepper

Torn fresh basil leaves, for garnish

1. Preheat the oven to 400°F. Spread the bread cubes on a baking sheet and bake until lightly toasted, about 20 minutes, stirring once about halfway through.

2. In a large soup pot over medium heat, heat 2 tablespoons of the oil. Add the garlic and cook until softened, about 1 minute. Stir in the canned and fresh tomatoes, broth, parsley, and salt and pepper to taste. Bring to a boil, then reduce heat to low and simmer for 30 minutes.

3. Divide the toasted bread among 4 bowls and ladle the soup over the bread. The bread should absorb most of the liquid in the soup. Garnish with basil leaves, drizzle with the remaining 2 tablespoons oil, and serve.

# moroccan vermicelli vegetable soup

makes 4 to 6 servings

*Harissa is a zesty North African condiment available at specialty grocers. For a spicier soup, swirl in a small amount of harissa sauce at serving time, or pass a bowl of harissa at the table for everyone to add according to taste.*

1 tablespoon olive oil

1 small onion, chopped

1 large carrot, chopped

1 celery rib, chopped

3 small zucchini, cut into ¼-inch dice

1 (28-ounce) can diced tomatoes, drained

2 tablespoons tomato paste

1½ cups cooked or 1 (15.5-ounce) can chickpeas,
    drained and rinsed

2 teaspoons smoked paprika

1 teaspoon ground cumin

1 teaspoon za'atar spice (optional)

¼ teaspoon ground cayenne

6 cups vegetable broth, homemade (page 141)
    or store-bought, or water

Salt

4 ounces vermicelli

2 tablespoons minced fresh cilantro, for garnish

1. In a large soup pot, heat the oil over medium heat. Add the onion, carrot, and celery. Cover and cook until softened, about 5 minutes. Stir in the zucchini, tomatoes, tomato paste, chickpeas, paprika, cumin, za'atar, and cayenne. Add the broth and salt to taste. Bring to a boil, then reduce heat to low and simmer, uncovered, until the vegetables are tender, about 30 minutes.

2. Shortly before serving, stir in the vermicelli and cook until the noodles are tender, about 5 minutes. Ladle the soup into bowls, garnish with cilantro, and serve.

# mulligatawny soup

makes 4 to 6 servings

Mulligatawny *literally means "pepper water," from the Tamil words* molegoo *(pepper) and* tunes *(water). Originally a vegetarian Indian sauce, the British added meat and various other ingredients to create a soup. Rice and lentils combine with vegetables and spices to make this vegan version a warming and substantial soup.*

2 tablespoons olive oil

1 medium onion, chopped

1 medium carrot, chopped

1 celery rib, cut into ¼-inch slices

1 medium green bell pepper, chopped

1 garlic clove, minced

1 serrano or other hot green chile, seeded and minced

2 teaspoons grated fresh ginger

1 tablespoon hot or mild curry powder

5 cups vegetable broth, homemade (page 141) or store-bought, or water

½ cup red lentils, picked over, rinsed, and drained

Salt and freshly ground black pepper

⅓ cup brown basmati rice

1 (13.5-ounce) can unsweetened coconut milk

1 Granny Smith apple, finely chopped

1 tablespoon fresh lemon juice

¼ cup chopped fresh cilantro, for garnish

1. In a large soup pot, heat the oil over medium heat. Add the onion, carrot, celery, bell pepper, garlic, and chile. Cover and cook until softened, stirring occasionally, about 10 minutes. Stir in the ginger and curry powder and cook, uncovered, for 1 minute. Add the broth and lentils, and bring to a boil. Reduce heat and simmer, uncovered, for 30 minutes.

2. When the soup is done, season with the salt and black pepper to taste. Puree the soup in the pot with an immersion blender or in a blender or food processor, in batches if necessary, and return to the pot. Add the rice and cook over medium heat until tender, about 30 minutes.

3. Add the coconut milk, apple, and lemon juice. To serve, ladle the soup into bowls and sprinkle with cilantro.

# southern-style beans-and-rice soup with collards

makes 4 to 6 servings

*Beans, grains, and greens are a nutritious combination, and with so many varieties available, the combinations seem limitless. In this rich and flavorful soup, two strictly Southern ingredients—collards and black-eyed peas—are paired with nutritious and nutty brown rice. The collards are cooked separately before adding to the soup to remove bitterness. If collards are unavailable, other dark greens such as kale may be used.*

6 cups coarsely chopped stemmed collard greens

2 tablespoons olive oil

1 medium onion, chopped

2 garlic cloves, minced

3 cups cooked or 2 (15.5-ounce) cans black-eyed peas, drained and rinsed

5 cups vegetable broth, homemade (page 141) or store-bought, or water

Salt and freshly ground black pepper

½ cup long-grain brown rice

Tabasco sauce, for serving

1. In a pot of boiling salted water, cook the collards until tender, about 20 minutes. Drain and set aside.

2. In a large soup pot, heat the oil over medium heat. Add the onion and garlic, cover, and cook until softened, about 5 minutes. Stir in the black-eyed peas, broth, cooked collards, and salt and pepper to taste. Bring to a boil, then reduce heat to low, add the rice, and simmer, uncovered, until the rice is cooked, about 30 minutes. Serve with Tabasco sauce.

# chickpea and fennel soup

makes 4 servings

*In Sardinia they make a chickpea and fennel soup using a wild fennel that has no bulb, just fronds. This version uses bulb, fronds, and ground fennel seed to maximize the fennel flavor.*

2 tablespoons olive oil

1 small onion, chopped

3 garlic cloves, minced

1 medium fennel bulb with fronds, chopped

3 cups cooked or 2 (15.5-ounce) cans chickpeas, drained and rinsed

1 (14.5-ounce) can crushed tomatoes

5 cups vegetable broth, homemade (page 141) or store-bought, or water

1 teaspoon ground fennel seed

¼ teaspoon crushed red pepper

Salt and freshly ground black pepper

½ cup orzo or other soup pasta

1. In a large soup pot, heat the oil over medium heat. Add the onion, garlic, and the fennel bulb, reserving the fronds. Cover and cook until the vegetables are softened, about 5 minutes.

2. Add the chickpeas, tomatoes, broth, fennel seed, and crushed red pepper. Season with salt and black pepper to taste. Bring to a boil, then reduce heat to low and simmer, uncovered, for 30 minutes.

3. Stir in the orzo and ¼ cup of the reserved fennel fronds and continue cooking until the orzo is tender, about 10 minutes. Ladle into bowls, garnish with the reserved fennel fronds, and serve.

# farro and white bean soup with italian parsley

makes 6 servings

*Farro is an ancient grain popular in Tuscany, where I first enjoyed this soup in a restaurant in the charming town of Lucca. Farro is naturally high in fiber and contains significantly more protein than wheat. It is frequently confused with spelt or emmer wheat; though similar, it takes significantly longer to cook.*

3 tablespoons olive oil

2 celery ribs, chopped

2 medium carrots, chopped

3 medium shallots, chopped

3 garlic cloves, minced

1 cup farro

6 cups vegetable broth, homemade (page 141) or store-bought, or water

1 (14.5-ounce) can diced tomatoes, undrained

2 bay leaves

1 teaspoon salt

½ teaspoon freshly ground black pepper

3 cups cooked or 2 (15.5-ounce) cans cannellini or other white beans, drained and rinsed

¼ cup chopped flat-leaf parsley

1. In large soup pot, heat 2 tablespoons of the oil over medium heat. Add the celery, carrots, shallots, and garlic. Cover and cook, stirring occasionally, for 5 minutes.

2. Add the farro to the pot along with the broth, tomatoes, bay leaves, salt, and pepper. Bring to a boil, then reduce heat to low and cook, uncovered, until the vegetables and farro are tender, about 1 hour. Add the beans and parsley and simmer 20 minutes longer, adding more broth if the soup becomes too thick. Remove and discard bay leaves before serving.

3. Ladle into bowls, drizzle with the remaining 1 tablespoon oil, and serve.

# gumbo z'herbes

makes 6 servings

*There are many variations of gumbo, the Creole classic, but gumbo z'herbes is a natural addition to a vegan cookbook; it is a traditional meatless soup made with at least seven kinds of greens, such as collards, kale, chicory, and spinach. A wide variety of greens are now readily available in bulk, so use as many as you wish. Filé powder (ground sassafras leaves) is used to thicken and flavor the soup; if it is unavailable, simply omit it—you'll still have a delicious gumbo.*

¼ cup olive oil

1 medium onion, chopped

1 medium green bell pepper, chopped

1 celery rib, chopped

3 garlic cloves, minced

¼ cup all-purpose flour

1 (14.5-ounce) can diced tomatoes, drained

1 teaspoon dried marjoram

¼ teaspoon ground cayenne

7 cups vegetable broth, homemade (page 141) or store-bought, or water

4 cups chopped stemmed fresh spinach

4 cups chopped stemmed kale

2 medium bunches watercress, tough stems removed, chopped

1 medium bunch chicory

Salt and freshly ground black pepper

1½ cups cooked or 1 (15.5-ounce) can dark red kidney beans, drained and rinsed

½ cup chopped fresh parsley

1 teaspoon Tabasco sauce, or to taste

½ teaspoon gumbo filé powder (optional)

3 cups hot cooked long-grain white rice

1. In a large soup pot, heat the oil over medium heat. Add the onion, bell pepper, celery, and garlic. Cover and cook until softened, about 10 minutes.

2. Stir in the flour and cook, stirring constantly, until the flour darkens to a brownish color, about 10 minutes. Stir in the tomatoes, marjoram, cayenne, and broth and bring to a boil. Add the spinach, kale, watercress, and chicory. Reduce heat to low, season with salt and black pepper to taste, and simmer, stirring occasionally, until the vegetables are tender, about 20 minutes.

3. Add the beans, parsley, and Tabasco and cook 10 minutes longer. Stir in filé powder, if desired, and remove from heat.

4. Spoon ½ cup of rice into each shallow soup bowl, ladle gumbo over the rice, and serve.

# two-potato soup with rainbow chard

makes 6 servings

*In addition to vibrant rainbow chard, I use unpeeled red potatoes, sweet potatoes, and red onion to add color to this hearty soup. If rainbow chard is unavailable, regular Swiss chard or any dark green, such as spinach or kale, will do.*

2 tablespoons olive oil

1 medium red onion, chopped

1 medium leek, white part only, well rinsed and chopped

2 garlic cloves, minced

6 cups vegetable broth, homemade (page 141) or store-bought, or water

1 pound red potatoes, unpeeled and cut into ½-inch dice

1 pound sweet potatoes, peeled and cut into ½-inch dice

¼ teaspoon crushed red pepper

Salt and freshly ground black pepper

1 medium bunch rainbow chard, tough stems removed and coarsely chopped

1. In large soup pot, heat the oil over medium heat. Add the onion, leek, and garlic. Cover and cook until softened, about 5 minutes. Add the broth, potatoes, and crushed red pepper and bring to a boil. Reduce heat to low, season with salt and black pepper to taste, and simmer, uncovered, for 15 minutes.

2. Stir in the chard and cook until the vegetables are tender, about 15 minutes longer and serve.

# sweet potato and peanut soup with baby spinach

makes 4 servings

*A delectable merger of flavors and textures, this colorful soup combines bright chunks of sweet potato and strands of vivid green spinach in a silky broth enriched with peanut butter. Despite the rich, complex flavor, this delicious soup is extremely simple to make.*

1 tablespoon olive oil

1 medium onion, chopped

1½ pounds sweet potatoes, peeled and cut into ½-inch dice

6 cups vegetable broth, homemade (page 141) or store-bought, or water

⅓ cup creamy peanut butter

¼ teaspoon ground cayenne

⅛ teaspoon ground nutmeg

Salt and freshly ground black pepper

4 cups fresh baby spinach

1. In a large soup pot, heat the oil over medium heat. Add the onion, cover, and cook until softened, about 5 minutes. Add the sweet potatoes and broth and cook, uncovered, until the potatoes are tender, about 30 minutes.

2. Ladle about a cup of hot broth into a small bowl. Add the peanut butter and stir until smooth. Stir the peanut butter mixture into the soup along with the cayenne, nutmeg, and salt and pepper to taste.

3. About 10 minutes before ready to serve, stir in the spinach, and serve.

# mexican fideo soup
# with pinto beans

makes 4 servings

*Fideo is the Mexican word for a thin pasta
that is sold in coils. Before buying the noodles
check the package in case they are made with
eggs. Regular vermicelli or angel hair pasta
can be used instead.*

3 tablespoons olive oil

1 medium onion, chopped

3 garlic cloves, chopped

8 ounces fideo, vermicelli, or angel hair pasta,
   broken into 2-inch pieces

1 (14.5-ounce) can crushed tomatoes

1½ cups cooked or 1 (15.5-ounce) can pinto beans,
   rinsed and drained

1 (4-ounce) can chopped hot or mild green chiles

1 teaspoon ground cumin

½ teaspoon dried oregano

6 cups vegetable broth, homemade (page 141)
   or store-bought, or water

Salt and freshly ground black pepper

¼ cup chopped fresh cilantro, for garnish

1. In a large soup pot, heat 1 tablespoon of the
oil over medium heat. Add the onion, cover,
and cook until soft, about 10 minutes. Stir in
the garlic and cook 1 minute longer. Remove
the onion mixture with a slotted spoon and
set aside.

2. In the same pot, heat the remaining 2 tablespoons of oil over medium heat, add the noodles,
and cook until golden, stirring frequently, 5 to
7 minutes. Be careful not to burn the noodles.

3. Stir in the tomatoes, beans, chiles, cumin,
oregano, broth, and salt and pepper to taste.
Stir in the onion mixture and simmer until the
vegetables and noodles are tender, 10 to 15
minutes. Ladle into soup bowls, garnish with
cilantro, and serve.

# black bean soup
# with a splash

makes 4 to 6 servings

*Sherry makes a good addition to this creamy
smooth black bean soup, but since not everyone at your table may agree, serve the sherry
separately so they can add their own splash
at will. For a fun presentation, serve the
sherry in a cruet or shot glasses.*

1 tablespoon olive oil

1 medium onion, finely chopped

1 celery rib, finely chopped

2 medium carrots, finely chopped

1 small green bell pepper, finely chopped

2 garlic cloves, minced

4 cups vegetable broth, homemade (page 141)
   or store-bought, or water

4½ cups cooked or 3 (15.5-ounce) cans
   black beans, drained and rinsed

1 teaspoon dried thyme

1 teaspoon salt

¼ teaspoon ground cayenne

2 tablespoons minced fresh parsley, for garnish

⅓ cup dry sherry

1. In a large soup pot, heat the oil over
medium heat. Add the onion, celery, carrots,
bell pepper, and garlic. Cover and cook until
tender, stirring occasionally, about 10 minutes. Add the broth, beans, thyme, salt, and
cayenne. Bring to a boil, then reduce the heat
to low and simmer, uncovered, until the soup
has thickened, about 45 minutes.

2. Puree the soup in the pot with an immersion blender or in a blender or food processor,
in batches if necessary, and return to the pot.
Reheat if necessary.

3. Ladle the soup into bowls and garnish with
parsley. Serve accompanied by the sherry.

# spicy black bean orzo soup

makes 4 to 6 servings

*Orzo, the diminutive rice-shaped pasta, adds an interesting textural nuance to this hearty soup, while sun-dried tomatoes provide an added flavor dimension.*

2 tablespoons olive oil

3 garlic cloves, minced

1 tablespoon chili powder

1 teaspoon dried oregano

4½ cups cooked or 3 (15.5-ounce) cans black beans, drained and rinsed

1 small jalapeño, seeded and finely chopped (optional)

¼ cup minced oil-packed sun-dried tomatoes

4 cups vegetable broth, homemade (page 141) or store-bought, or water

1 cup water

Salt and freshly ground black pepper

½ cup orzo

2 tablespoons chopped fresh cilantro, for garnish

1. In a large soup pot, heat the oil over medium heat. Add the garlic and cook until fragrant, about 1 minute. Stir in the chili powder, oregano, beans, jalapeño, if using, tomatoes, broth, water, and salt and pepper to taste. Simmer for 30 minutes to blend flavors.

2. Puree the soup in the pot with an immersion blender or in a blender or food processor, in batches if necessary, and return to the pot. Cook the soup 15 minutes longer over medium heat. Taste, adjusting seasonings, and add more water if necessary.

3. While the soup is simmering, cook the orzo in a pot of boiling salted water, stirring occasionally, until al dente, about 5 minutes. Drain the orzo and divide it among the soup bowls. Ladle the soup into the bowls, garnish with cilantro, and serve.

# black bean and corn soup

makes 4 servings

*This soup is a favorite in my house, thanks to the way the corn kernels add a burst of sweetness, especially with a generous addition of hot sauce. Only a portion of the soup is pureed to add flavor and creaminess while still leaving lots of texture and color.*

2 tablespoons olive oil

1 medium red onion, chopped

1 medium red or yellow bell pepper, chopped

1 medium carrot, minced

4 garlic cloves, minced

1 teaspoon ground cumin

1 teaspoon dried oregano

1 (14.5-ounce) can diced tomatoes, drained

4 ½ cups cooked or 3 (15.5-ounce) cans black beans, rinsed and drained

6 cups vegetable broth, homemade (page 141) or store-bought, or water

2 cups fresh, frozen, or canned corn kernels

1 teaspoon fresh lemon juice

Salt and freshly ground black pepper

Tabasco sauce, to serve

1. In a large soup pot, heat the oil over medium heat. Add the onion, bell pepper, carrot, and garlic, cover, and cook until soft, about 10 minutes. Uncover and stir in the cumin and oregano, tomatoes, beans, and broth. Bring to a boil, then reduce heat to low and simmer, uncovered, for 30 minutes, stirring occasionally.

2. Puree about one-third of the soup in the pot with an immersion blender, or in a blender or food processor, then return to the pot. Add the corn, and simmer uncovered, for 10 minutes to heat through and blend flavors.

3. Just before serving, stir in the lemon juice and season with salt and pepper to taste. Ladle into bowls and serve with hot sauce on the side.

# three bean soup

makes 4 to 6 servings

*The colors of the beans play nicely against one another, making this a soup that is both satisfying and appealing. It's quick to assemble when you use canned beans, and it makes an economical and filling main dish.*

2 tablespoons olive oil

1 medium onion, chopped

1 medium carrot, chopped

1 cup chopped celery

2 garlic cloves, minced

1 (14.5-ounce) can diced tomatoes, drained

1½ cups cooked or 1 (15.5-ounce) can dark red kidney beans, drained and rinsed

1½ cups cooked or 1 (15.5-ounce) can black beans, drained and rinsed

1½ cups cooked or 1 (15.5-ounce) can navy or other white beans, drained and rinsed

4 cups vegetable broth, homemade (page 141) or store-bought, or water

1 tablespoon soy sauce

1 teaspoon dried thyme

1 bay leaf

Salt and freshly ground black pepper

2 tablespoons chopped fresh parsley

1. In a large soup pot, heat the oil over medium heat. Add the onion, carrot, celery, and garlic. Cover and cook until softened, about 7 minutes. Uncover, and stir in the tomatoes, all the beans, and the broth. Add the soy sauce, thyme, and bay leaf and season with salt and pepper to taste. Bring to a boil, then reduce heat to low and simmer until the vegetables are tender, about 45 minutes.

2. Remove the bay leaf and discard before serving. Add the parsley and serve.

# spicy pinto bean soup

makes 4 servings

*Flavors of the Southwest converge in this satisfying soup flavored with a smoky heat, courtesy of the chipotle chile. It's delicious with a few corn chips added to each bowl for a bit of crunch.*

4½ cups cooked or 3 (15.5-ounce) cans pinto beans, drained and rinsed

1 (14.5-ounce) can crushed tomatoes

1 teaspoon chipotle chile in adobo

2 tablespoons olive oil

1 medium onion, chopped

¼ cup chopped celery

2 garlic cloves, minced

½ teaspoon ground cumin

½ teaspoon dried oregano

4 cups vegetable broth, homemade (page 141) or store-bought, or water

Salt and freshly ground black pepper

2 tablespoons chopped fresh cilantro, for garnish

1. In a food processor, puree 1½ cups of the pinto beans with the tomatoes and chipotle. Set aside.

2. In a large soup pot, heat the oil over medium heat. Add the onion, celery, and garlic. Cover and cook until soft, stirring occasionally, about 10 minutes. Stir in the cumin, oregano, broth, pureed bean mixture, and the remaining 3 cups beans. Season with salt and pepper to taste.

3. Bring to a boil and reduce heat to low and simmer, uncovered, stirring occasionally, until the flavors are incorporated and the soup is hot, about 15 minutes. Ladle into bowls, garnish with cilantro, and serve.

# soba and green lentil soup

makes 4 to 6 servings

*Green lentils (also called French lentils) are tiny slate-green discs that hold their shape better than other lentils and complement the hearty flavor of buckwheat soba in this satisfying soup. Other lentils can be substituted, but keep in mind they may get mushy if overcooked. The addition of a few cups of dark greens, such as spinach or chard, during the last few minutes of cooking turns this into a great one-dish meal.*

2 tablespoons olive oil

1 medium onion, minced

1 medium carrot, halved lengthwise and sliced diagonally

2 garlic cloves, minced

1 (28-ounce) can crushed tomatoes

1 cup green (French) lentils, picked over, rinsed, and drained

1 teaspoon dried thyme

6 cups vegetable broth, homemade (page 141) or store-bought, or water

Salt and freshly ground black pepper

4 ounces soba noodles, broken into thirds

1. In a large soup pot over medium heat, heat the oil. Add the onion, carrot, and garlic. Cover and cook until softened, about 7 minutes. Uncover and stir in the tomatoes, lentils, thyme, and broth and bring to a boil. Reduce heat to medium, season with salt and pepper to taste, and cover and simmer until the lentils are just tender, about 45 minutes.

2. Stir in the noodles and cook until tender, about 10 minutes longer, and serve.

# white and wild mushroom barley soup

makes 4 to 6 servings

*A combination of both white and wild mushrooms gives this classic soup extra dimension. For even more mushroom flavor, use mushroom broth for at least a portion of the liquid. As with most soups and stews, the amount of salt you need to add depends on how much broth vs. water is used and the saltiness of the broth—it could mean the difference between using just one-half teaspoon of salt or closer to two teaspoons.*

1 tablespoon olive oil

1 medium onion, chopped

1 medium carrot, chopped

2 celery ribs, chopped

12 ounces white mushrooms, lightly rinsed, patted dry, and sliced

8 ounces cremini, shiitake, or other wild mushrooms, lightly rinsed, patted dry, and cut into ¼-inch slices

1 cup pearl barley

7 cups vegetable or mushroom broth, homemade (pages 141, 143) or store-bought, or water

1 teaspoon dried dillweed

Salt and freshly ground black pepper

2 tablespoons minced fresh parsley

1. In a large soup pot, heat the oil over medium heat. Add the onion, carrot, and celery. Cover and cook until soft, about 10 minutes. Uncover and stir in the mushrooms, barley, broth, dillweed, and salt and pepper to taste. Bring to a boil, then reduce heat to low and simmer, uncovered, until the barley and vegetables are tender, about 40 minutes.

2. Add the parsley, taste, adjust seasonings if necessary, and serve.

# green and yellow split pea soup

makes 4 to 6 servings

*This very creamy soup is a lovely shade of pale green, owing to the combined green and yellow split peas. You can also make the soup using all green or all yellow split peas, if you prefer. I use water rather than broth to make pea soup since the distinctive flavor doesn't really need help from broth. Naturally hearty and protein-rich, the soup doesn't require further embellishment, but the optional vegan kielbasa (Tofurky brand) is a tasty option.*

2 tablespoons olive oil

1 medium onion, chopped

1 medium carrot, chopped

1 celery rib, chopped

1 medium potato, peeled and cut into ¼-inch dice

8 ounces green split peas, picked over, rinsed, and drained

8 ounces yellow split peas, picked over, rinsed, and drained

7 cups water

1 bay leaf

1 teaspoon salt

¼ teaspoon freshly ground black pepper

8 ounces sliced vegan kielbasa (optional)

1. In a large soup pot, heat the oil over medium heat. Add the onion, carrot, and celery and cook until softened, about 5 minutes. Add the potato, green and yellow split peas, water, bay leaf, salt, and pepper and bring to a boil. Reduce heat to low, and simmer, stirring occasionally, until the peas are very soft and the soup is thick, about 1 hour.

2. Add vegan kielbasa, if using, and simmer another 15 to 20 minutes, adding more water if the soup becomes too thick. Remove and discard bay leaf before serving. Taste, adjusting seasonings if necessary, and serve.

# rice and pea soup

makes 4 servings

*Rice and peas are a popular combination in Venice and this comforting soup, known as risi e bisi, is a good example of why this is so. Arborio rice (used in risotto) is the choice here because its inherent creaminess adds a velvety texture to this soup.*

2 tablespoons olive oil

1 medium onion, minced

2 garlic cloves minced

1 cup Arborio rice

6 cups vegetable broth, homemade (page 141) or store-bought, or water

Salt and freshly ground black pepper

1 (16-ounce) bag frozen petite green peas

¼ cup chopped fresh flat-leaf parsley

1. In a large soup pot, heat the oil over medium heat. Add the onion and garlic, cover, and cook until softened about 5 minutes.

2. Uncover and add the rice, broth, and salt and pepper to taste. Bring to a boil, then reduce heat to low. Cover and simmer until the rice begins to soften, about 30 minutes.

3. Stir in the peas and cook, uncovered, for 15 to 20 minutes longer. Stir in the parsley and serve.

# lemony lentil and rice soup

makes 6 servings

*A small amount of lemon juice adds a clean refreshing taste to this hearty soup. Since this recipe calls for water, and both the lentils and rice need enough salt added to bring out their flavor, be sure to add enough salt—at least 1 teaspoon. This soup is very thick, so you may need to add extra liquid, especially if making it ahead and reheating later.*

2 tablespoons olive oil

1 medium onion, chopped

1 medium carrot, cut into ¼-inch dice

1 celery rib, cut into ¼-inch dice

1¼ cups brown lentils, picked over, rinsed, and drained

¾ cup long-grain brown rice

1 (14.5-ounce) can crushed tomatoes

2 cups tomato juice

2 bay leaves

½ teaspoon ground cumin

6 cups water

1 teaspoon salt

¼ teaspoon freshly ground black pepper

1 tablespoon fresh lemon juice

2 tablespoons minced fresh parsley

1. In a large soup pot, heat the oil over medium heat. Add the onion, carrot, and celery. Cover and cook until tender, about 10 minutes.

2. Add the lentils, rice, tomatoes, tomato juice, bay leaves, cumin, water, salt, and pepper. Bring to a boil, then reduce heat to medium low, and simmer, uncovered, until lentils and rice are tender, about 1 hour.

3. Just before serving, remove and discard the bay leaves, and stir in the lemon juice and parsley. Taste, adjusting seasonings if necessary, and serve.

# moroccan lentil and chickpea soup

makes 4 servings

*Lemon and ginger add refreshing notes and spicy harissa (a fiery North African sauce made with chiles, garlic, and spices) adds some heat to this satisfying soup inspired by the classic Moroccan soup, harira.*

1 tablespoon olive oil

1 medium onion, chopped

2 medium carrots, chopped

2 garlic cloves, chopped

2 teaspoons grated fresh ginger

½ teaspoon turmeric

½ teaspoon ground cumin

1 (14.5-ounce) can crushed tomatoes

1 cup dried brown lentils, picked over, rinsed, and drained

1½ cups cooked or 1 (15.5-ounce) can chickpeas, drained and rinsed

5 cups vegetable broth, homemade (page 141) or store-bought, or water

Salt and freshly ground black pepper

1 tablespoon fresh lemon juice

1 to 2 teaspoons Harissa Sauce (page 556)

1. In a large soup pot, heat the oil over medium heat. Add the onion, carrots, and garlic. Cover and cook until slightly softened, about 5 minutes. Stir in the ginger, turmeric, and cumin. Add the tomatoes, lentils, chickpeas, and broth. Season with salt and pepper to taste.

2. Bring to a boil, then reduce the heat to low and simmer, uncovered, until the lentils and vegetables are soft, about 1 hour.

3. About 10 minutes before serving, stir in the lemon juice and harissa. Taste, adjusting seasonings if necessary, and serve.

# corn and potato chowder

makes 4 to 6 servings

*Is this a corn chowder with potatoes or a potato chowder with corn? Once you taste this rich and flavorful soup, you'll realize there is no wrong answer.*

1 tablespoon olive oil

1 medium onion, chopped

1 celery rib, chopped

3 medium Yukon Gold potatoes, peeled and diced

4 cups vegetable broth, homemade (page 141) or store-bought, or water

Salt and freshly ground black pepper

3 cups fresh, frozen, or canned corn kernels

1 cup plain unsweetened soy milk

1 tablespoon minced green onions or chives, for garnish

1. In large soup pot, heat the oil over medium heat. Add the onion and celery. Cover and cook until the vegetables are softened, about 10 minutes.

2. Add the potatoes, broth, and salt and pepper to taste. Bring to a boil, then reduce heat to low and simmer, uncovered, until the potatoes begin to soften, about 30 minutes.

3. Add the corn and simmer 15 minutes longer. Puree about half the soup in the pot with an immersion blender or in a blender or food processor, and return to the pot. Stir in the soy milk and taste, adjusting seasonings if necessary.

4. Ladle the soup into bowls, garnish with green onions, and serve.

# curried butternut and red lentil soup with chard

makes 4 servings

*This beautiful soup has a rich complexity of flavor that tastes like it took hours to make. Serve it with warm roti, parantha, or other Indian bread.*

1 tablespoon olive oil

1 medium onion, chopped

1 medium butternut squash, peeled and diced

1 garlic clove, minced

1 tablespoon minced fresh ginger

1 tablespoon hot or mild curry powder

1 (14.5-ounce) can crushed tomatoes

1 cup red lentils, picked over, rinsed, and drained

5 cups vegetable broth, homemade (page 141) or store-bought, or water

Salt and freshly ground black pepper

3 cups chopped stemmed Swiss chard

1. In a large soup pot, heat the oil over medium heat. Add the onion, squash, and garlic. Cover and cook until softened, about 10 minutes.

2. Stir in the ginger and curry powder, then add the tomatoes, lentils, broth, and salt and pepper to taste. Bring to boil, then reduce heat to low and simmer, uncovered, until the lentils and vegetables are tender, stirring occasionally, about 45 minutes.

3. About 15 minutes before serving, stir in the chard. Taste, adjusting seasonings if necessary, and serve.

# tomato orzo soup

makes 4 servings

*Since great-tasting fresh tomatoes are often in short supply, this recipe calls for both canned and fresh tomatoes to maintain a good balance of flavor. Soy milk adds creaminess and orzo provides texture.*

1 tablespoon olive oil

1 medium onion, chopped

1 celery rib, minced

3 garlic cloves, minced

1 (28-ounce) can crushed tomatoes

3 cups chopped fresh ripe tomatoes

2 tablespoons tomato paste

3 cups vegetable broth, homemade (page 141)
    or store-bought, or water

Pinch sugar

2 bay leaves

Salt and freshly ground black pepper

1 cup plain unsweetened soy milk

1½ cups cooked orzo

2 tablespoons chopped fresh basil, for garnish

1. In large soup pot, heat the oil over medium heat. Add the onion, celery, and garlic. Cover and cook until softened, about 5 minutes. Stir in the canned and fresh tomatoes, tomato paste, broth, sugar, and bay leaves. Season with salt and pepper to taste and bring to a boil. Reduce the heat to low, cover, and simmer, uncovered, until the vegetables are tender, about 20 minutes.

2. Remove and discard bay leaves. Puree the soup in the pot with an immersion blender or in a blender or food processor, in batches if necessary, and return to the pot. Stir in the soy milk, taste, adjusting seasonings if necessary, and heat through.

3. Spoon about ⅓ cup of the orzo into the bottom of each bowl, ladle the hot soup on top, and serve sprinkled with the basil.

# laksa come home

makes 4 servings

*This spicy soup combines many elements of the hearty Singapore soup known as laksa; most traditional versions call for fresh laksa leaves, candlenuts, and other hard-to-find items. This version has been adapted for the home kitchen with readily available ingredients. Rice noodles may be used instead of the linguine, if you prefer.*

12 ounces linguine

1 cup chopped onion

5 dried red chiles, softened for 30 minutes in hot water

1 lemongrass stalk, white part only, crushed

2 teaspoons grated fresh ginger

½ teaspoon turmeric

2 teaspoons ground coriander

1 tablespoon hot or mild curry powder

¼ teaspoon ground cayenne

2 tablespoons canola or grapeseed oil

4 cups vegetable broth, homemade (page 141)
    or store-bought, or water

1 teaspoon salt

Freshly ground black pepper

1½ teaspoons sugar

8 ounces extra-firm tofu, drained and cut into
    ½-inch cubes

1 (13.5-ounce) can unsweetened coconut milk

1 tablespoon Asian chile paste

1 cup fresh bean sprouts, blanched

3 green onions, sliced

1 cup coarsely chopped pineapple (optional)

1 medium cucumber, peeled, seeded, and shredded

1 medium bunch cilantro, chopped

Lime wedges, for serving

1. In a pot of boiling salted water, cook the linguine until it is al dente, about 8 minutes. Drain and set aside.

2. In a food processor, combine the onion, chiles, lemongrass, and ginger, and process to a paste. Add the turmeric, coriander, curry powder, and cayenne, and process until blended.

3. In a large soup pot, heat the oil over medium heat. Add the onion mixture and cook, stirring for 3 minutes, stirring in a small amount of the broth to prevent burning. Add the remaining broth and bring to a boil. Reduce heat to medium and add the salt, pepper, and sugar. Simmer for 20 minutes, then strain and discard the solids.

4. Return the liquid to the pot. Stir in the tofu and heat until hot but do not boil. Add the cooked linguine, coconut milk, and chili paste; cover and simmer for another 10 minutes.

5. Divide the bean sprouts and green onions among 4 bowls and ladle the soup into the bowls. Garnish with the pineapple (if using), cucumber, and cilantro. Serve with lime wedges.

# CREAMY SOUPS

## asparagus edamame bisque

makes 4 servings

*For the creamiest texture, puree this elegant and delicious soup in a high-speed blender or, if using a food processor, strain through a fine-mesh sieve before serving. As an optional garnish, reserve some cooked edamame or asparagus tips.*

1 tablespoon olive oil

2 medium leeks, white parts only, well rinsed, and chopped

2 medium shallots, chopped

4 cups vegetable broth, homemade (page 141) or store-bought, or water

1½ cups fresh or frozen, edamame, thawed and shelled

Salt

1 pound asparagus, tough ends trimmed and cut into 1-inch lengths

Ground cayenne

Black sesame seeds or minced parsley, for garnish (optional)

1. In a large soup pot, heat the oil over medium heat. Add the leeks and shallots, cover, and cook until softened, about 5 minutes. Add the broth, edamame, and salt to taste. Bring to a boil, then reduce heat to low and simmer, uncovered, for 15 minutes. Add the asparagus and cayenne to taste. Return to a boil, then reduce heat to medium, cover, and cook until the vegetables are tender, about 12 minutes longer.

continues on next page

**2.** Puree the soup in a high-speed blender or food processor, in batches if necessary, and return to the pot. Taste, adjusting seasonings if necessary, adding more liquid if too thick. Reheat over low heat until hot.

**3.** Ladle the soup into bowls, and garnish with sesame seeds or parsley, if using.

# golden potato soup

makes 4 to 6 servings

*White and sweet potatoes join forces to create a lovely golden-colored soup with a velvety texture and delicious mellow flavor.*

1 tablespoon olive oil

3 medium shallots, chopped

4 cups vegetable broth, homemade (page 141) or store-bought, or water

3 medium russet potatoes, peeled and diced

2 medium sweet potatoes, peeled and diced

1 cup plain unsweetened soy milk

Salt and freshly ground black pepper

1 tablespoon minced chives, for garnish

**1.** In large saucepan, heat the oil over medium heat. Add the shallots, cover, and cook until softened, about 5 minutes. Add the broth and potatoes and bring to a boil. Reduce heat to low and simmer, uncovered, until the potatoes are soft, about 20 minutes.

**2.** Puree the potato mixture in the pot with an immersion blender or in a blender or food processor, in batches if necessary, and return to the pot. Stir in the soy milk and season with salt and pepper to taste. Simmer for 5 minutes to heat through and blend flavors.

**3.** Ladle the soup into bowls, sprinkle with chives, and serve.

# thai-inspired coconut soup

makes 4 servings

*Smooth, silky, and spicy, with all the complexity of flavor you'd expect from a Thai-inspired soup, but without all the fuss—or exotic ingredients. This soup is made with easy-to-find ingredients. Use ginger instead of galangal (a pungent rhizome similar to ginger) and lime juice instead of kaffir lime leaves. It makes a luscious beginning to a Thai meal such as the Thai-phoon Stir-Fry (page 288).*

1 tablespoon canola or grapeseed oil

1 medium onion, chopped

2 tablespoons minced fresh ginger

2 tablespoons soy sauce or Nothin' Fishy Nam Pla (page 560)

1 tablespoon light brown sugar

1 teaspoon Asian chili paste

2½ cups light vegetable broth, homemade (page 141) or store-bought, or water

8 ounces extra-firm tofu, drained and cut into ½-inch dice

2 (13.5-ounce) cans unsweetened coconut milk

1 tablespoon fresh lime juice

3 tablespoons chopped fresh cilantro, for garnish

**1.** In a large soup pot, heat the oil over medium heat. Add the onion and ginger and cook until softened, about 5 minutes. Stir in the soy sauce, sugar, and chile paste. Add the broth and bring to a boil. Reduce heat to medium and simmer for 15 minutes.

**2.** Strain the broth and discard solids. Return the broth to the pot over medium heat. Add the tofu and stir in the coconut milk and lime juice. Simmer 5 minutes longer to allow flavors to blend.

**3.** Ladle into bowls, sprinkle with cilantro, and serve.

# cream of broccoli soup

makes 4 to 6 servings

*You don't need cream to have a creamy soup—pureed vegetables and a touch of soy milk make a luxurious soup that, in this instance, is literally "cream of broccoli." The chopped black olive garnish adds a dramatic color contrast and tasty flavor.*

1 tablespoon olive oil

1 medium onion, chopped

2 medium russet or Yukon Gold potatoes, peeled and finely chopped or shredded

1 pound broccoli, trimmed and coarsely chopped

4 cups vegetable broth, homemade (page 141) or store-bought, or water

Salt and freshly ground black pepper

1 cup plain unsweetened soy milk

1 tablespoon chopped pitted kalamata olives, for garnish

1. In a large soup pot, heat the oil over medium heat. Add the onion and cover and cook until softened, about 5 minutes. Add the potatoes and broccoli and stir in the broth. Season with salt and pepper to taste. Bring to a boil, then reduce the heat to low and simmer, uncovered, until the vegetables are tender, about 20 minutes.

2. Puree the soup in the pot with an immersion blender or in a blender or food processor, in batches if necessary, and return to the pot. Stir in the soy milk, and taste, adjusting seasonings if necessary. Reheat the soup over low heat until hot.

3. Ladle soup into bowls, garnish with chopped olives, and serve.

# carrot soup with ginger

makes 4 to 6 servings

*Fresh ginger and a splash of lemon add vibrancy to the sweet flavor of carrots in a creamy and colorful soup loaded with beta-carotene and great taste. For a different flavor accent, use parsley, basil, dillweed, or other fresh herb to replace the chive garnish.*

2 tablespoons olive oil

1 medium yellow onion, chopped

1½ pounds carrots, coarsely chopped

1 medium Yukon Gold potato, peeled and chopped

1 tablespoon minced fresh ginger

Salt

5 cups vegetable broth, homemade (page 141) or store-bought, or water

Ground cayenne

1 teaspoon fresh lemon juice

2 tablespoons chopped fresh chives

1. In a large soup pot, heat the oil over medium heat. Add the onion, cover, and cook until softened, about 5 minutes. Stir in the carrots, potato, ginger, and salt to taste. Cover and cook for 5 minutes, stirring occasionally. Add the broth and cayenne to taste, and bring to a boil.

2. Reduce the heat to low and simmer, covered, until the vegetables are soft, 30 to 40 minutes.

3. Puree the soup mixture in the pot with an immersion blender or in a blender or food processor, in batches if necessary, adding additional broth to obtain the desired consistency.

4. Return the soup to a pot and reheat until hot. Stir in the lemon and taste, adjusting seasonings if necessary. Ladle into bowls, garnish with chives, and serve.

# creamy tomato soup

makes 4 servings

*If your last memory of tomato soup was the sodium-laced canned variety, then you're in for a pleasant surprise with this great-tasting version, made with fresh tomatoes and seasoned with ground fennel seeds and fresh basil.*

2 tablespoons olive oil

1 medium onion, chopped

1 medium carrot, chopped

1 garlic clove, minced

5 ripe plum tomatoes, cut into ½-inch dice

1 (14.5-ounce) can crushed tomatoes

3 cups vegetable broth, homemade (page 141) or store-bought, or water

½ teaspoon dried basil

¼ teaspoon ground fennel seeds

Salt and freshly ground black pepper

Fresh basil leaves, for garnish

1. In a large soup pot, heat the oil over medium heat. Add the onion, carrot, and garlic. Cover and cook until softened, about 5 minutes. Stir in the fresh and canned tomatoes, broth, dried basil, ground fennel seed, and salt and pepper to taste. Bring to a boil, then reduce heat to low and simmer, covered, until vegetables are tender, about 20 minutes.

2. Use an immersion blender to puree the soup in the pot or transfer in batches to a blender or food processor and puree. Return the soup to the pot and heat the soup until hot, adding additional broth, if necessary for desired consistency.

3. Ladle the soup into bowls, garnish with basil leaves, and serve.

# butternut soup with a swirl of cranberry

makes 4 to 6 servings

*Soups made with winter squashes are a fixture in my house from November through February. When I serve this for a holiday meal, I like to add a festive garnish, such as the swirl of cranberry in this recipe. The color contrast and flavor complement are extraordinary.*

2 tablespoons olive oil

1 medium onion, chopped

1 medium carrot, chopped

½ teaspoon ground allspice

¼ teaspoon ground ginger

1 medium russet potato, peeled and chopped

3 pounds butternut squash, peeled, seeded, and cut into 1-inch pieces

4 cups vegetable broth, homemade (page 141) or store-bought, or water

Salt

½ cup whole berry cranberry sauce, homemade (Triple Cranberry Relish, page 571) or canned

2 tablespoons fresh orange juice

1. In a large soup pot, heat the oil over medium heat. Add the onion and carrot, cover, and cook, stirring occasionally, until softened, about 5 minutes. Stir in the allspice, ginger, potato, squash, broth, and salt to taste. Simmer, uncovered, until the vegetables are very soft, about 30 minutes.

2. While the soup is cooking, puree the cranberry sauce and orange juice in a blender or food processor. Run the pureed cranberry sauce through a strainer and discard solids. Set aside.

3. When the soup is done cooking, puree it in the pot with an immersion blender or in a blender or food processor, in batches if necessary, and return to the pot. Reheat the soup and taste, adjusting seasonings if necessary.

Ladle into bowls, swirl a tablespoon or so of the reserved cranberry puree into the center of each bowl, and serve.

## cream of fennel soup

makes 4 servings

*The delicate, slightly anise flavor of cooked fennel makes this an ideal first-course soup for a special dinner. The green peas enhance the pale green color, and the potato adds thickness.*

1 tablespoon olive oil

1 medium onion, chopped

1 large bulb fennel with fronds, chopped

1 large russet or Yukon Gold potato, peeled and cut into ½-inch dice

3 cups vegetable broth, homemade (page 141) or store-bought, or water

½ cup frozen peas

½ teaspoon dried tarragon

1 teaspoon fresh lemon juice

Salt and freshly ground black pepper

1 cup plain unsweetened soy milk

1. In large soup pot, heat the oil over medium heat. Add the onion, fennel, and potato. Cover and cook until the vegetables begin to soften, about 5 minutes. Add the broth and bring to a boil. Reduce heat to low and simmer, uncovered, until the vegetables are tender, about 30 minutes. Stir in the peas and tarragon and cook 5 minutes longer.

2. Puree the soup in the pot with an immersion blender or in a blender or food processor, in batches if necessary, and return to the pot.

3. Reheat the soup over medium heat. Stir in the lemon juice and season with salt and pepper to taste. Stir in the soy milk and heat to a simmer.

4. Ladle the soup into bowls, sprinkle each bowl with a small amount of minced fennel fronds, and serve.

## squash soup with pecans and ginger

makes 4 servings

*The sweet rich flavor and deep orange-colored flesh of the kabocha squash make it by far my favorite of the winter squashes. The pecans and crystallized ginger garnish further enhances the natural sweetness of the squash. If kabocha squash is unavailable, substitute buttercup squash, which is similar in appearance, with its dark green skin and squat round shape.*

⅓ cup toasted pecans

2 tablespoons chopped crystallized ginger

1 tablespoon canola or grapeseed oil

1 medium onion, chopped

1 celery rib, chopped

1 teaspoon grated fresh ginger

5 cups vegetable broth, homemade (page 141) or store-bought, or water

1 kabocha squash, peeled, seeded, and cut into ½-inch dice

¼ cup pure maple syrup

2 tablespoons soy sauce

¼ teaspoon ground allspice

Salt and freshly ground black pepper

1 cup plain unsweetened soy milk

1. In a food processor, combine the pecans and crystallized ginger and pulse until coarsely chopped. Set aside.

2. In a large soup pot, heat the oil over medium heat. Add the onion, celery, and fresh ginger. Cover and cook until softened, about 5 minutes. Stir in the broth and squash, cover, and bring to a boil. Reduce the heat to low and simmer, covered, stirring occasionally, until the squash is tender, about 30 minutes.

3. Stir in the maple syrup, soy sauce, allspice, and salt and pepper to taste. Puree in the pot

continues on next page

with an immersion blender or in a blender or food processor, in batches if necessary, and return to the pot.

4. Stir in the soy milk and heat over low heat until hot. Ladle the soup into bowls and sprinkle with the pecan and ginger mixture, and serve.

# root vegetable bisque
makes 4 to 6 servings

*You may vary the type and quantity of the vegetables according to your personal preference. For example, a turnip or small rutabaga may be used to replace the parsnips. For a more intense root vegetable flavor, use the Root Vegetable Broth on page 142.*

1 tablespoon olive oil
3 large shallots, chopped
2 large carrots, shredded
2 medium parsnips, shredded
1 medium potato, peeled and chopped
2 garlic cloves, minced
½ teaspoon dried thyme
¼ teaspoon dried marjoram
4 cups vegetable broth, homemade (page 141) or store-bought, or water
1 cup plain unsweetened soy milk
Salt and freshly ground black pepper
1 tablespoon minced fresh parsley, garnish

1. In a large soup pot, heat the oil over medium heat. Add the shallots, carrots, parsnips, potato, and garlic. Cover and cook until softened, about 5 minutes. Add the thyme, marjoram, and broth and bring to a boil. Reduce heat to low and simmer, uncovered, until the vegetables are tender, about 30 minutes.

2. Puree the soup in the pot with an immersion blender or in a blender or food processor in batches if necessary, then return to the pot.

Stir in the soy milk and taste, adjusting seasonings if necessary. Heat the soup over low heat until hot. Ladle into bowls, sprinkle with parsley, and serve.

# curried pumpkin soup
makes 4 to 6 servings

*The flavors of pumpkin, coconut milk, and curry merge harmoniously in this creamy soup. For added texture and flavor, use both of the optional garnishes, chutney and cashews.*

1 tablespoon olive oil
1 medium onion, chopped
1 garlic clove, minced
1 teaspoon grated fresh ginger
1 tablespoon hot or mild curry powder
1 tablespoon sugar
1 (16-ounce) can pumpkin puree or 2 cups cooked fresh pumpkin
3 cups vegetable broth, homemade (page 141) or store-bought, or water
Salt
1 (13.5-ounce) can unsweetened coconut milk
1 tablespoon minced fresh parsley, for garnish
Mango chutney, for garnish (optional)
Chopped roasted cashews, for garnish (optional)

1. In a large soup pot, heat the oil over medium heat. Add the onion and garlic and cover and cook until softened, about 7 minutes. Stir in the ginger, curry powder, and sugar and cook for 30 seconds over low heat, stirring constantly. Stir in the pumpkin, broth, and salt to taste and bring to a boil. Reduce heat to low, cover, and simmer, uncovered, until the flavors are blended, about 15 minutes.

2. Use an immersion blender to puree the soup in the pot or transfer in batches to a blender or food processor, puree, then return to the pot, and season with salt and pepper to taste. Add coconut milk and heat until hot.

3. Ladle into soup bowls, sprinkle with parsley and a spoonful of chutney sprinkled with chopped cashews, if using, and serve.

## spinach, walnut, and apple soup

makes 4 servings

*This light and luscious soup makes a refreshing first-course soup for a dinner. It's also great paired with a sandwich for lunch. The crisp apple and crunchy walnut garnish provides textural contrast.*

1 tablespoon olive oil

1 small onion, chopped

3 cups vegetable broth, homemade (page 141) or store-bought, or water

2 Fuji or other flavorful apples

1 cup apple juice

4 cups fresh spinach

¾ cup ground walnuts

1 teaspoon minced fresh sage or ½ teaspoon dried

¼ teaspoon ground allspice

Salt and freshly ground black pepper

1 cup soy milk

¼ cup toasted walnut pieces

1. In a large soup pot, heat the oil over medium heat. Add the onion, cover, and cook until softened, 5 minutes. Add about 1 cup of the vegetable broth, cover, and cook until the onion is very soft, about 5 minutes longer.

2. Peel, core, and chop one of the apples and add it to the pot with the onion and broth. Add the apple juice, spinach, ground walnuts, sage, allspice, the remaining 2 cups broth, and salt and pepper to taste. Bring to a boil, then reduce heat to low and simmer for 10 minutes.

3. Puree the soup in the pot with an immersion blender or in a blender or food processor, in batches if necessary, and return to the pot.

Stir in the soy milk and reheat over medium heat until hot.

4. Chop the remaining apple. Ladle the soup into bowls, garnish each bowl with some of the chopped apple, sprinkle with the walnut pieces, and serve.

## spicy white bean and tomato soup

makes 4 to 6 servings

*The surprising peanut butter here adds a mellow richness to this spicy soup. If you don't like the heat, use mild green chiles instead of hot ones—the soup will still be immensely flavorful.*

2 tablespoons olive oil

1 medium onion, chopped

1 (28-ounce) can crushed tomatoes

1 (4-ounce) can diced hot green chiles, drained

3 cups cooked or 2 (15.5-ounce) cans white beans, drained and rinsed

2 tablespoons creamy peanut butter

3 cups vegetable broth, homemade (page 141) or store-bought, or water

Salt

1 tablespoon fresh lime juice

Minced fresh parsley or cilantro, for garnish

1. In a large soup pot, heat the oil over medium heat. Add the onion, cover, and cook until soft, about 10 minutes. Add the tomatoes, chiles, and beans. Simmer, covered, for 15 minutes.

2. Stir in peanut butter, broth, and salt to taste, and simmer, uncovered, 15 minutes longer.

3. Puree the soup in the pot with an immersion blender or in a blender or food processor, in batches if necessary and return to the pot.

4. Stir in the lime juice and simmer over medium, stirring, until hot. Ladle into bowls, garnish with parsley, and serve.

# peanutty two-potato soup

makes 4 to 6 servings

*Sweet and white potatoes blend harmoniously with peanut butter in this creamy and wholesome soup that is easy to prepare and a delight to eat. I usually garnish it with chopped peanuts to mirror the flavor of the peanut butter and add a bit of crunch, but you can also add chopped fresh parsley, chives, or other herb of your choosing for a bit of color contrast. An easy way to crush peanuts is to place them in a zip-top bag on a flat surface and roll over them firmly and repeatedly with a rolling pin or a can turned on its side. You can chop peanuts in a food processor, but not too much or you'll end up with peanut butter.*

1 tablespoon olive oil

1 medium onion, chopped

1 celery rib, chopped

1 large sweet potato, peeled and chopped

1 large russet potato, peeled and chopped

4 cups vegetable broth, homemade (page 141) or store-bought, or water

½ cup plus 2 teaspoons creamy peanut butter

Salt

Ground cayenne

3 tablespoons chopped or crushed unsalted roasted peanuts, for garnish

1. In a large soup pot, heat the oil over medium heat. Add the onion and celery, cover, and cook until softened, about 5 minutes. Add the potatoes and broth and bring to a boil. Reduce heat to low and simmer, uncovered, until the vegetables are tender, about 30 minutes.

2. Puree the soup in the pot with an immersion blender or in a blender or food processor, in batches if necessary, and return to the pot. Ladle about 1 cup of the soup into a small bowl and stir in the peanut butter until blended. Stir the peanut butter mixture into the soup and season with salt and cayenne to taste. Reheat the soup over medium heat until hot.

3. Ladle the soup into bowls, sprinkle with the peanuts, and serve.

# zucchini and butter bean bisque

makes 4 to 6 servings

*Fresh butter beans, a type of lima bean, are one of the delights of summer in the southern United States, where you can find them in the pod or already shelled. Terrific on their own or in succotash, butter beans also pair well with zucchini, another summer crop. If butter beans are unavailable, use lima beans instead.*

2 tablespoons olive oil

1 medium onion, chopped

1 garlic clove, minced

2 cups fresh or frozen butter beans or lima beans

4 cups vegetable broth, homemade (page 141) or store-bought, or water

3 medium zucchini, cut into ¼-inch slices

½ teaspoon dried marjoram

Salt and freshly ground black pepper

½ cup plain unsweetened soy milk

2 tablespoons minced jarred pimiento

1. In a large soup pot, heat the oil over medium heat. Add the onion and garlic, cover, and cook until softened, about 5 minutes. Add the butter beans and the broth. Cover and cook for 20 minutes. Add the zucchini,

marjoram, and salt and pepper to taste. Bring to a boil, then reduce heat to low and simmer, covered, until the vegetables are soft, about 20 minutes.

2. Puree the soup in the pot with an immersion blender or in a blender or food processor, in batches if necessary, and return to the pot. Stir in the soy milk and taste, adjusting seasonings if necessary. Reheat over low heat until hot. Ladle into bowls, garnish with the pimiento, and serve.

# pumpkin soup with chipotle puree

makes 4 servings

*Smoky hot chipotle chiles enliven the flavor in this creamy pumpkin soup while adding a dramatic swath of color. Best of all, everyone can add as much or as little as they like, since the chipotle puree gets swirled into each bowl at serving time. Note: leftover canned chipotles can be portioned and frozen for later use.*

2 to 3 teaspoons chipotle chiles in adobo
1 tablespoon water
2 tablespoons olive oil
1 medium onion, chopped
2 celery ribs, chopped
1 (16-ounce) can pumpkin puree or 2 cups pureed
    cooked fresh pumpkin
1 teaspoon ground cumin
1 bay leaf
4 cups vegetable broth, homemade (page 141)
    or store-bought, or water
Salt
Freshly ground black pepper
1 cup plain unsweetened soy milk

1. In a blender or food processor, combine the chipotle and water and puree. Set aside.

2. In a large soup pot, heat the oil over medium heat. Add the onion and celery. Cover and cook until soft, about 10 minutes. Stir in the pumpkin, cumin, bay leaf, broth, and salt and pepper to taste. Bring to a boil, then reduce the heat to low and simmer, uncovered, for 20 minutes, stirring occasionally.

3. Remove the bay leaf and discard. Puree the soup in the pot with an immersion blender or in a blender or food processor, in batches if necessary, and return to the pot. Stir in the soy milk and taste, adjusting seasonings if necessary. Cook over low heat for 5 minutes.

4. Ladle the soup into bowls, garnish with a swirl of the chipotle puree, and serve.

# chestnut bisque with fresh pear

makes 4 to 6 servings

*Definitely not an everyday soup, this elegant flavorful bisque is a wonderful first course for a special autumn or winter meal. Since fresh chestnuts can be difficult to find and time-consuming to prepare, I stock up on frozen or jarred chestnuts whenever I find them on sale.*

1 tablespoon olive oil
1 medium onion, chopped
2 celery ribs, chopped
2 ripe Bosc pears
12 ounces fresh, frozen, or jarred cooked and peeled chestnuts
4 cups roasted vegetable broth, homemade (page 142) or store-bought, or other vegetable broth
¼ teaspoon ground allspice
¼ teaspoon ground ginger
⅛ teaspoon ground cayenne
1 bay leaf
Salt
½ cup plain unsweetened soy milk

1. In a large saucepan, heat the oil over medium heat. Add the onion and celery. Cover and cook until the vegetables are softened, about 10 minutes.

2. Peel, core, and dice one of the pears and add to the pot along with the chestnuts, broth, allspice, ginger, cayenne, bay leaf, and salt to taste. Bring to a boil, then reduce heat to low and simmer, covered, for 30 minutes.

3. Remove the bay leaf and discard. Puree the soup in the pot with an immersion blender or in a blender or food processor, in batches if necessary, and return to the pot. Stir in the soy milk and taste, adjusting seasonings if necessary. Reheat over medium heat until hot.

4. Peel, core, and chop the remaining pear. When the soup is hot, ladle it into bowls, garnish with chopped pear, and serve.

# cream of artichoke soup

makes 4 servings

*Almond butter adds a subtle nutty undertone to this luscious and lovely soup. Frozen artichoke hearts are used because they are superior in flavor to canned and don't have the expense or labor of fresh ones. However, if frozen artichoke hearts are unavailable, substitute two 15-ounce cans (not marinated) and proceed with the recipe after the frozen artichoke cooking instructions.*

1 tablespoon olive oil
2 medium shallots, chopped
2 (10-ounce) packages frozen artichoke hearts, thawed
3 cups vegetable broth, homemade (page 141) or store-bought, or water
1 teaspoon fresh lemon juice
Salt
⅓ cup almond butter
⅛ teaspoon ground cayenne
1 cup plain unsweetened soy milk
1 tablespoon snipped fresh chives, for garnish
2 tablespoons sliced toasted almonds, for garnish

1. In a large soup pot, heat the oil over medium heat. Add the shallots, cover, and cook until softened. Uncover and stir in the artichoke hearts, broth, lemon juice, and salt to taste. Bring to a boil, then reduce heat to low and simmer, uncovered, until the artichokes are tender, about 20 minutes.

2. Add the almond butter and cayenne to the artichoke mixture. Puree in a high-speed blender or food processor, in batches if necessary, and return to the pot. Stir in the soy milk and taste, adjusting seasonings if necessary. Simmer the soup over medium heat until hot, about 5 minutes.

3. Ladle into bowls, sprinkle with chives and almonds, and serve.

## watercress–white bean soup with toasted pine nuts

makes 4 servings

*This is one of those soups that looks and tastes great whether it is pureed or not. I like to puree the soup because it gives it a more elegant appearance and the various flavors merge into one. Unpureed, the soup offers the distinct flavors and texture of the various ingredients. Why not try it both ways and decide for yourself?*

1 tablespoon olive oil

2 medium shallots, chopped

2 medium bunches watercress, thick stems removed and chopped

1½ cups cooked or 1 (15.5-ounce) can Great Northern or other white beans, drained and rinsed

4 cups vegetable broth, homemade (page 141) or store-bought, or water

Salt and freshly ground black pepper

1 cup plain unsweetened soy milk

¼ cup toasted pine nuts, for garnish

1. In a large soup pot, heat the oil over medium heat. Add the shallots, cover, and cook until softened, about 5 minutes. Add the watercress and cook until wilted, about 3 minutes. Stir in the beans and broth and season with salt and pepper to taste. Bring to a boil, then reduce heat to low and simmer, uncovered, for 20 minutes.

2. Puree the soup in the pot with an immersion blender or in a blender or food processor, in batches if necessary, and return to the pot. Stir in the soy milk, and taste, adjusting seasonings if necessary. Reheat over low heat until hot.

3. Ladle into bowls, sprinkle with pine nuts, and serve.

## creamy mushroom soup

makes 4 servings

*To maximize the mushroom flavor, use mushroom broth for all or part of the liquid and include some wild mushrooms in with the regular white ones.*

1 tablespoon plus 1 teaspoon olive oil

1 medium onion, chopped

½ cup chopped celery

1 medium russet potato, peeled and chopped

2 garlic cloves, minced

16 ounces white mushrooms, lightly rinsed, patted dry, and sliced

½ teaspoon minced fresh thyme or ⅛ teaspoon dried

3 cups vegetable broth, homemade (page 141) or store-bought, or water

Salt and freshly ground black pepper

1 cup plain unsweetened soy milk

2 teaspoons soy sauce

1 tablespoon minced fresh parsley, for garnish

1. In a large pot, heat 1 tablespoon of the oil over medium heat. Add the onion, celery, potato, and garlic. Cover and cook until softened, about 10 minutes. Add all but 1 cup of the mushrooms, thyme, broth, and salt and pepper to taste. Bring to a boil, then reduce heat to low and simmer, uncovered, until the vegetables are tender, about 30 minutes.

2. Puree the soup in the pot with an immersion blender or in a blender or food processor, and return to the pot. Stir in the soy milk, and taste, adjusting seasonings if necessary. Heat the soup over low heat until hot.

3. In a small skillet, heat the remaining 1 teaspoon of oil over medium-high heat. Add the remaining 1 cup of mushrooms and sauté until golden brown and softened. Splash with the soy sauce, tossing to coat. Set aside.

4. Ladle the soup into bowls and spoon some of the cooked mushrooms into each bowl. Sprinkle with parsley and serve.

# creamy potato-chard soup

makes 4 to 6 servings

*Swiss chard, with its dark green leaves and pale green stalks, is almost too pretty to puree, but once you taste this delicious soup, you'll be glad you did. Yukon Golds add a buttery richness to the soup, although another variety of potato may be used successfully.*

1 tablespoon olive oil

1 medium onion, chopped

1 celery rib, chopped

2 garlic cloves, chopped

2 pounds Yukon Gold potatoes, peeled and cut into ½-inch dice

4 cups vegetable broth, homemade (page 141) or store-bought, or water

½ teaspoon ground fennel seed

⅛ teaspoon ground nutmeg

Salt and freshly ground black pepper

3 cups chopped Swiss chard

1. In a large soup pot, heat the oil over medium heat. Add the onion, celery, and garlic. Cover, and cook until softened, about 5 minutes. Add the potatoes and stir in the broth, fennel seed, nutmeg, and salt and pepper to taste. Bring to a boil, then reduce heat to low and simmer, uncovered, until the vegetables are soft, about 30 minutes. Stir in the chard and cook until tender, about 15 minutes.

2. Puree the soup in the pot with an immersion blender or in a blender or food processor, in batches if necessary, and return to the pot. Taste, adjusting seasonings if necessary. Reheat the soup over medium heat, stirring, until hot and serve.

# almond soup with cardamom

makes 4 servings

*This unusual soup makes an elegant start to an Indian meal. It's very rich, so plan to serve it in small bowls. Cardamom belongs to the ginger family and is used in Indian cooking. Because of its aromatic but strong spicy-sweet flavor, it should be used judiciously so the flavor doesn't overpower the soup. If you're not a fan of cardamom, you can leave it out altogether or add a touch of allspice or ground coriander instead.*

1 tablespoon olive oil

1 medium onion, chopped

1 medium russet potato, chopped

1 medium red bell pepper, chopped

4 cups vegetable broth, homemade (page 141) or store-bought, or water

½ teaspoon ground cardamom

Salt and freshly ground black pepper

½ cup almond butter

¼ cup sliced toasted almonds, for garnish

1. In a large soup pot, heat the oil over medium heat. Add the onion, potato, and bell pepper. Cover and cook until softened, about 5 minutes. Add the broth, cardamom, and salt and pepper to taste. Bring to a boil, then reduce heat to low and simmer, uncovered, until the vegetables are tender, about 30 minutes.

2. Add the almond butter and puree in the pot with an immersion blender or in a blender or food processor, in batches if necessary, and return to the pot. Reheat over medium heat until hot. Taste, adjusting seasonings if necessary, and add more broth or some soy milk if needed for desired consistency.

3. Ladle the soup into bowls, sprinkle with toasted sliced almonds, and serve.

# roasted vegetable bisque

makes 6 servings

*Roasting vegetables brings out their natural sweetness, resulting in an intensely flavorful soup, and gives further dimension if you use roasted vegetable broth as your liquid of choice.*

1 large onion, coarsely chopped

2 medium carrots, coarsely chopped

1 large russet potato, peeled and cut into ½-inch dice

1 medium zucchini, thinly sliced

1 large ripe tomato, quartered

2 garlic cloves, crushed

2 tablespoons olive oil

½ teaspoon dried savory

½ teaspoon dried thyme

Salt and freshly ground black pepper

4 cups vegetable broth, homemade (page 141) or store-bought, or water

1 tablespoon minced fresh parsley, for garnish

1. Preheat the oven to 400°F. In a lightly oiled 9 × 13-inch baking pan, place the onion, carrots, potato, zucchini, tomato, and garlic. Drizzle with the oil and season with savory, thyme, and salt and pepper to taste. Cover tightly with foil and bake until softened, about 30 minutes. Uncover and bake, stirring once, until vegetables are lightly browned, about 30 minutes more.

2. Transfer the roasted vegetables to a large soup pot, add the broth, and bring to a boil. Reduce the heat to low and simmer, uncovered, for 15 minutes.

3. Puree the soup in the pot with an immersion blender or in a blender or food processor, in batches if necessary, and return to the pot. Heat over medium heat until hot. Taste, adjusting seasonings if necessary.

4. Ladle into bowls, sprinkle with parsley, and serve.

# COLD SOUPS

# garden gazpacho

makes 4 servings

*Brimming with garden-fresh veggies and always refreshing, this is an ideal soup to prepare when summer produce is plentiful.*

6 ripe plum tomatoes, chopped

1 medium red onion, chopped

1 medium cucumber, peeled, seeded, and chopped

1 medium red bell pepper, chopped

4 green onions, minced

1 garlic clove, minced

1 celery rib, minced

3 tablespoons sherry vinegar

2 tablespoons olive oil

1 teaspoon sugar

Salt

Tabasco sauce

2 cups blended vegetable juice

¼ cup chopped fresh parsley

¼ cup sliced pitted kalamata olives

1. In a blender or food processor, combine all but ¼ cup each of the tomatoes, onion, cucumber, and bell pepper. Add half of the green onions and all of the garlic and celery and process until smooth. Add the vinegar, oil, and sugar and season with salt and Tabasco to taste. Process until well blended.

2. Transfer the soup to a large nonmetallic bowl and stir in the vegetable juice. Cover and refrigerate until chilled, at least 3 hours.

3. When ready to serve, add the remaining tomatoes, onion, cucumber, bell pepper, and green onions. Ladle the soup into bowls, garnish with parsley and black olives, and serve.

# three-tomato gazpacho with chipotle crème

makes 4 servings

*Fresh, canned, and sun-dried tomatoes provide layers of tomato flavor in this delicious interpretation of the Spanish classic. The addition of chipotle crème adds heat and richness to the soup.*

1 tablespoon olive oil

1½ teaspoons chipotle chile in adobo

¼ cup vegan sour cream, homemade (page 574) or store-bought

1 medium red onion, chopped

1 medium red bell pepper, chopped

1 medium cucumber, peeled, seeded, and chopped

2 garlic cloves, minced

¼ cup minced oil-packed sun-dried tomatoes

1 (14.5-ounce) can crushed tomatoes

3 cups blended vegetable juice

1 pound ripe plum tomatoes, chopped

Salt

¼ cup minced green onions, for garnish

1. In a blender or food processor, combine the oil, chipotle, and sour cream and process until smooth. Set aside.

2. In a blender or food processor, combine the onion, bell pepper, half the cucumber, garlic, sun-dried tomatoes, and crushed tomatoes. Process until smooth. Transfer to a large bowl and stir in the vegetable juice, fresh tomatoes, remaining cucumber, and salt to taste. Cover and refrigerate until well chilled, at least 3 hours.

3. When chilled, taste, adjusting seasonings if necessary. Ladle into bowls and swirl in a spoonful of the chipotle crème into each bowl. Garnish with minced green onions and serve.

# gazpacho with ditalini and chile aioli

makes 4 to 6 servings

*The addition of cooked pasta to the famous "salad soup" makes this gazpacho a "pasta salad" soup. The chile aioli provides heat and amplifies the flavor of the soup.*

AIOLI

1 small hot chile, seeded

3 garlic cloves

½ teaspoon salt

1 teaspoon red wine vinegar

½ cup olive oil

GAZPACHO

4 large ripe tomatoes, peeled, seeded, and chopped

2 large cucumbers, peeled, seeded, and chopped

1 medium yellow bell pepper, chopped

½ cup minced green onions

1 tablespoon minced garlic

3 cups tomato juice

Salt

½ cup ditalini or other soup pasta

1 tablespoon olive oil

1. Make the aioli: In a blender or food processor, combine the chile, garlic, and salt and puree until smooth. Add the vinegar and process to blend. With the machine running, stream in the oil, until blended. Do not overprocess. Transfer to a bowl and set aside at room temperature until serving time.

2. Make the gazpacho: In a blender or food processor, combine half the tomatoes, half the cucumbers, half the bell pepper, half the green onions, and all of the garlic. Process to blend, then transfer to a large nonmetallic bowl and stir in the tomato juice and remaining tomato, cucumber, bell pepper, and green onion. Season with salt to taste. Cover and refrigerate until well chilled, at least 2 hours.

3. While the soup is chilling, cook the pasta in a pot of boiling salted water, stirring occasionally, until al dente, 6 to 8 minutes. Drain and rinse the pasta, then toss it with the olive oil and set aside.

4. When ready to serve, add the pasta to the soup and taste, adjusting seasonings if necessary. Ladle into bowls and swirl a spoonful of the aioli into each bowl. Serve with additional aioli on the side.

# black and gold gazpacho

makes 4 servings

*Yellow bell pepper and yellow tomatoes create a golden background for black beans in this unusual and dramatic-looking gazpacho variation.*

1½ pounds ripe yellow tomatoes, chopped
1 large cucumber, peeled, seeded, and chopped
1 large yellow bell pepper, seeded, and chopped
4 green onions, white part only
2 garlic cloves, minced
2 tablespoons olive oil
2 tablespoons white wine vinegar
Salt
Ground cayenne
1½ cups cooked or 1 (15.5-ounce) can black beans, drained and rinsed
2 tablespoons minced fresh parsley
1 cup toasted croutons (optional)

1. In a blender or food processor, combine half the tomatoes with the cucumber, bell pepper, green onions, and garlic. Process until smooth. Add the oil and vinegar, season with salt and cayenne to taste, and process until blended.

2. Transfer the soup to a large nonmetallic bowl and stir in the black beans and remaining tomatoes. Cover the bowl and refrigerate for 1 to 2 hours. Taste, adjusting seasonings if necessary.

3. Ladle the soup into bowls, garnish with parsley and croutons, if using, and serve.

# senegalese soup

makes 4 servings

*In addition to a garnish of chutney, this cold curried soup may be further enhanced with garnish of chopped nuts or thinly sliced apples.*

1 tablespoon canola or grapeseed oil
1 medium onion, chopped
1 medium carrot, chopped
1 garlic clove, minced
3 Granny Smith apples, peeled, cored, and chopped
2 tablespoons hot or mild curry powder
2 teaspoons tomato paste
3 cups light vegetable broth, homemade (page 141) or store-bought, or water
Salt
1 cup plain unsweetened soy milk
4 teaspoons mango chutney, homemade (page 561) or store-bought, for garnish

1. In a large soup pot, heat the oil over medium heat. Add the onion, carrot, and garlic. Cover and cook until softened, about 10 minutes. Add the apples and continue to cook, uncovered, stirring occasionally, until the apples begin to soften, about 5 minutes. Add the curry powder and cook, stirring, 1 minute. Stir in the tomato paste, broth, and salt to taste. Simmer, uncovered, for 30 minutes.

2. Puree the soup in the pot with an immersion blender or in a blender or food processor, in batches if necessary. Pour the soup into a large container, stir in the soy milk, cover, and refrigerate until chilled, about 3 hours.

3. Ladle the soup into bowls, garnish each with a teaspoonful of chutney, and serve.

# sweet potato vichyssoise

makes 4 servings

*This update on the classic vichyssoise uses sweet potatoes instead of white potatoes for a luxuriously rich soup with a lovely blush of color. If you prefer traditional vichyssoise, simply substitute white potatoes for the sweet potatoes. This tastes great heated, as well.*

1 tablespoon olive oil

2 medium leeks, white parts only, well rinsed and chopped

3 large sweet potatoes, peeled and chopped

3 cups vegetable broth, homemade (page 141) or store-bought, or water

Salt

Pinch ground cayenne

1 cup plain unsweetened soy milk, or more as needed

Snipped fresh chives, for garnish

1. In a large soup pot, heat the oil over medium heat. Add the leeks and cook until soft, about 5 minutes. Add the sweet potatoes, broth, and salt and cayenne to taste. Bring to a boil, then reduce heat to low and simmer, uncovered, until the potatoes are soft, about 30 minutes.

2. Puree the soup in the pot with an immersion blender or in a blender or food processor, in batches if necessary. Transfer to a large container and stir in the soy milk. Cover and refrigerate until chilled, at least 3 hours. Taste, adjusting seasonings if necessary, and adding a bit more soy milk if the soup is too thick.

3. Ladle into bowls, sprinkle with chives, and serve.

# chilled avocado-tomato soup

makes 4 servings

*Tomatoes and avocados have a natural affinity and this simple chilled soup makes the most of that relationship. Flavorful ripe tomatoes are often at a premium, so both canned and fresh tomatoes are used. If you have a bumper crop of fresh tomatoes, omit the canned and add a few more fresh ones to the soup. To change the flavor, use lime juice and cilantro in place of the lemon juice and basil.*

2 garlic cloves, crushed

Salt

2 ripe Hass avocados

2 teaspoons lemon juice

2 pounds ripe plum tomatoes, coarsely chopped

1 (14.5-ounce) can crushed tomatoes

1 cup tomato juice

Freshly ground black pepper

8 fresh basil leaves, for garnish

1. In a blender or food processor, combine the garlic and ½ teaspoon of salt and process to a paste. Pit and peel one of the avocados and add it to the food processor along with the lemon juice. Process until smooth. Add the fresh and canned tomatoes, tomato juice, and salt and pepper to taste. Process until smooth.

2. Transfer the soup to a large container, cover, and refrigerate until chilled, 2 to 3 hours.

3. Taste, adjusting seasonings if necessary. Pit and peel the remaining avocado and cut it into a small dice. Slice the basil leaves into thin strips. Ladle the soup into bowls, add the diced avocado, garnish with basil, and serve.

# cucumber cashew soup

makes 4 servings

*Raw cashews ground to a paste provide a creamy richness to this flavorful soup. Be sure the cashews are ground to a powder and then blended until smooth or the soup may have a gritty consistency.*

¾ cup raw unsalted cashews

1 garlic clove, crushed

½ teaspoon salt

1 cup plain unsweetened soy milk

2 medium English cucumbers, peeled and chopped

2 tablespoons chopped green onions

1 tablespoon fresh lemon juice

1 tablespoon minced fresh parsley

2 teaspoons minced fresh dillweed or ½ teaspoon dried

1 tablespoon snipped fresh chives, for garnish

1. In a blender or food processor, grind the cashews to a fine powder. Add the garlic and salt, blending until to form a thick paste. Add ¼ cup of the soy milk and blend until smooth and creamy. Add the cucumbers, green onions, lemon juice, parsley, and dillweed and process until smooth. Add the remaining ¾ cup soy milk and process until well blended.

2. Transfer the mixture to a large container, cover, and refrigerate until well chilled and flavors are blended, 2 to 3 hours. Taste, adjusting seasonings if necessary.

3. Ladle the soup into bowls, garnish with chives, and serve.

# chilled carrot soup

makes 4 to 6 servings

*Ginger, coconut milk, and lime juice give this flavorful soup a decidedly Asian accent.*

1 tablespoon canola or grapeseed oil

1 small onion, chopped

1 pound carrots, shredded

3 ripe plum tomatoes, chopped

1 teaspoon grated fresh ginger

1 teaspoon sugar

½ teaspoon salt

⅛ teaspoon ground cayenne

3 cups vegetable broth, homemade (page 141) or store-bought, or water

1 (13.5-ounce) can unsweetened coconut milk

1 teaspoon fresh lime juice

1 tablespoon minced fresh basil or cilantro

1. In a large soup pot, heat the oil over medium heat. Add the onion, cover, and cook until softened, 5 minutes. Stir in the carrots, cover, and cook 5 minutes longer. Add the tomatoes, ginger, sugar, salt, cayenne, and broth. Bring to a boil, then reduce heat to low and simmer, uncovered, until the vegetables are soft, about 30 minutes.

2. Puree the soup in the pot with an immersion blender or in a blender or food processor, in batches if necessary. Pour the soup into a large bowl, stir in the coconut milk and lime juice, and refrigerate until chilled, at least 3 hours.

3. Taste, adjusting seasonings if necessary, and ladle into bowls. Garnish with basil and serve.

# chilled beet soup

makes 4 to 6 servings

*Beets combine with balsamic vinegar and a variety of vegetables for a beguiling soup that is beyond your basic borscht.*

1½ pounds red beets
2 tablespoons olive oil
1 small red onion, chopped
1 garlic clove, minced
1 teaspoon sugar
3 tablespoons balsamic vinegar
1 (14.5-ounce) can crushed tomatoes
1 medium russet potato, peeled and chopped
1 medium carrot, chopped
4 cups vegetable broth, homemade (page 141)
    or store-bought, or water
1 cup apple juice
Salt and freshly ground black pepper
Vegan sour cream, homemade (page 574)
    or store-bought, for garnish
Chopped fresh dillweed, for garnish

1. In a large saucepan of boiling water, cook the beets just long enough to loosen the skins so they remove easily, 15 to 20 minutes. Drain and allow to cool, then slip off the skins and discard. Coarsely chop the beets and set aside.

2. In a large soup pot, heat the oil over medium heat. Add the onion, cover, and cook until softened, about 5 minutes. Stir in the garlic, sugar, and vinegar and cook, uncovered, until the vinegar evaporates, about 1 minute. Add the tomatoes, chopped beets, potato, and carrot. Stir in the broth and apple juice. Season with salt and pepper to taste. Bring to a boil, then reduce to low and simmer, uncovered, until the vegetables are tender, about 30 minutes. Remove from heat and let cool slightly.

3. Puree the soup in a blender or food processor, in batches if necessary. Transfer the soup to a large container, cover, and refrigerate until chilled, at least 3 hours.

4. Ladle into bowls, garnish with the sour cream and dillweed, and serve.

# wild cherry soup

makes 4 servings

*This sweet dessert soup makes a lovely ending to a spicy meal. Note: If cherry liqueur is unavailable, substitute framboise, kirsch, or for a nonalcoholic version, use cherry juice, cherry nectar, or cherry preserves. Frozen cherries may be used if fresh are unavailable.*

1½ pounds ripe cherries, pitted
2 cups white grape juice or cranberry juice
⅓ cup sugar
1 tablespoon fresh lemon juice
1 cup vegan vanilla ice cream, softened
2 tablespoons cherry liqueur (see headnote)

1. Chop 8 of the cherries and set aside. Place the remaining cherries in a blender or food processor and process until smooth. Add the grape juice, sugar, lemon juice, and ½ cup of the ice cream and process until smooth. Pour the soup into a nonmetallic bowl. Cover and refrigerate until chilled, about 3 hours.

2. In a small bowl, combine the remaining ½ cup ice cream and the cherry liqueur, stirring to blend well. Set aside.

3. Ladle the chilled soup into bowls, garnish with a spoonful of the ice cream mixture and chopped cherries, and serve.

# summer fruit soup

makes 4 servings

*An alluring assortment of fruit joins forces in this creamy soup that tastes as sweet and fresh as summertime.*

2 cups chopped cantaloupe or honeydew melon

1 cup chopped fresh pineapple

1 ripe mango or 2 peaches, peeled, pitted, and chopped

1 ripe banana, chopped

1 tablespoon fresh lemon juice

1 cup fresh orange juice

1 cup apple or pineapple juice

½ cup plain unsweetened soy milk

⅓ cup vegan plain yogurt or vegan sour cream, homemade (page 574) or store-bought

2 tablespoons agave nectar

½ cup hulled sliced strawberries, for garnish

Fresh mint sprigs, for garnish

1. In a food processor, combine the cantaloupe, pineapple, mango, and banana and process until smooth. Add the lemon juice, orange juice, apple juice, and soy milk and process until well blended. Pour the soup into a large container. Cover and refrigerate until well chilled, at least 3 hours.

2. In a small bowl, combine the yogurt and agave nectar in a small bowl and blend until smooth. Ladle the chilled soup into bowls, garnish with a spoonful of the yogurt mixture, a few strawberry slices, and fresh mint sprigs, and serve.

# jewelbox fruit soup

makes 4 servings

*The bright fruit nestled in a light and creamy fruit broth reminds me of a jewel box filled with precious gems.*

2 cups white grape juice

2 cups pear nectar

1 ripe banana, chopped

1 tablespoon fresh lemon juice

Pinch salt

½ cup unsweetened coconut milk (optional)

1 cup blueberries

1 ripe mango, peeled, pitted, and cut into ¼-inch dice

1 cup diced pineapple

1 cup diced strawberries

Fresh mint leaves, for garnish

1. In a food processor, combine the grape juice, pear nectar, banana, lemon juice, and salt. Process until smooth, then pour into a large bowl. Stir in the coconut milk, if using. Cover and refrigerate until well chilled, for 3 hours or overnight.

2. Ladle the chilled soup into bowls and spoon ¼ cup each of the blueberries, mango, pineapple, and strawberries into each bowl. Garnish with mint leaves and serve.

# PASTA AND NOODLES

## PASTA AND NOODLES

egg-free pasta dough

orecchiette

parmasio

marinara sauce

## PASTA WITH TOMATOES

spaghetti and t-balls

pasta arrabbiata

linguine puttanesca

radiatore with aurora sauce

sicilian penne with tomatoes and eggplant

penne with vodka-spiked tomato sauce

perciatelli with slow-roasted tomato sauce

fettuccine with chard and red lentil tomato sauce

tagliatelle with porcini bolognese sauce

ziti with abruzzese vegetable ragù

## PASTA WITH PESTO

linguine with ligurian pesto

orzo, white beans, and tomatoes with lemony spinach pesto

fettuccine with puttanesca pesto

tricolor rotini with pesto bianco

penne with peanut pesto

rotini and almond-mint pesto with orange zest

campanelle and zucchini with squash blossoms and sunflower pesto

gemelli with green beans, potatoes, and basil pesto

radiatore with walnut-parsley pesto

## PASTA WITH VEGETABLES AND MORE

pasta primavera

orecchiette with rapini

penne with creamy asparagus sauce

fusilli with fennel and sun-dried tomatoes

ziti with red pepper–walnut sauce

carbonara-style spaghetti

paglia e fieno with peas

lemon-kissed linguine with garlicky white bean sauce

farfalle with white beans
and roasted asparagus

penne with chickpeas
and rosemary

fettuccine with fresh figs
and walnuts

angel hair pasta with olive oil
and garlic

penne with white beans,
red chard, and grape tomatoes

inspired by spaghetti
with white clam sauce

ziti with catalan vegetables

austrian noodles and cabbage

persian noodles and lentils

## LASAGNA EIGHT WAYS

classic tofu lasagna

red chard and baby spinach
lasagna

roasted vegetable lasagna

lasagna with radicchio
and cremini mushrooms

lasagna primavera

tex-mex lasagna

black bean and pumpkin
lasagna

lasagna pinwheels

## BAKED AND BEYOND

penne baked with
eggplant-tomato sauce

creamy cashew fettuccine
with mushrooms and peas

baked mac and cheeze

mac and chard

baked pasta shells and broccoli

wild west pasta bake

cheezy tomato macaroni

pastitsio

pasta gratin with
provençal vegetables

buckwheat noodles with
cabbage and potatoes

## STUFFED PASTA AND DUMPLINGS

chard-stuffed manicotti
with creamy cashew sauce

spinach manicotti
with white walnut sauce

spicy eggplant and
tempeh-stuffed pasta shells

pumpkin ravioli with peas
and caramelized shallots

artichoke-walnut ravioli
with sage and walnut sauce

tortellini with orange-scented
tomato cream sauce

gnocchi with red wine–
tomato sauce

pierogi with fried onions

## ASIAN NOODLES

vegetable lo mein with tofu

sesame soba noodles

pad thai

springtime rice noodles
with coconut crème

bok choy and ginger-sesame
udon noodles

szechuan sesame noodles
with asparagus

chinese noodles and broccoli
with spicy black bean sauce

spicy sesame noodles
with green beans

drunken spaghetti with tofu

singapore noodles with tempeh

korean noodle stir-fry

noodles with spicy peanut
sauce

indian double chickpea noodles

Easy to prepare, infinitely versatile, and always delicious, pasta is a convenient and economical way to enjoy a satisfying and nutritious one-dish vegan meal. When prepared with beans, vegetables, or nuts, or served with a salad, a pasta meal can provide vegans with a good balance of carbohydrates, fiber, protein, vitamins, and minerals. Best of all, many traditional Italian pasta dishes are naturally vegan.

These flavorful recipes call for particular pasta types and shapes for variety, but feel free to mix and match according to availability and your personal preferences. In some cases, however, the shape or texture helps to pick up more sauce with every bite, so it's usually best to use a similar shape to the pasta called for in the recipe. I also recommend that you try any available protein-enriched or whole-grain pastas, as these provide better nutrition than the standard bleached-flour variety.

# common pasta names

Attempting to list all the pasta shapes would be daunting (estimates range between 300 and 750). However, below is a list of the most common ones, many of which are used in this chapter.

## LONG STRANDS

**cappellini**—literally "fine hairs"; very thin noodles

**fettuccine**—literally "small ribbons"; thin, flat noodles about ¼ inch wide

**lasagna**—long, broad noodles with straight or rippled edges

**linguine**—literally "little tongues"; very narrow, ⅛-inch-wide ribbons

**pappardelle**—long, wide ribbons with rippled edges

**perciatelli**—long, thin, hollow noodles

**spaghetti**—literally "little strings"; long thin, round strands

**spaghettini**—thin spaghetti

**tagliatelle**—long thin noodles, about ¼ inch wide

**vermicelli**—literally "little worms"; very thin spaghetti

## HOLLOW SHAPES

**cannelloni**—literally "large reeds"; large round tubes for stuffing

**lumache**—literally "snails"; large shells for stuffing

**manicotti**—literally "small muffs"; very large tubes for stuffing

**mostaccioli**—literally "small mustaches"; 2-inch-long ridged or smooth tubes

**penne**—literally "quill pens"; diagonally cut smooth tubes

**rigatoni**—large grooved tubes

**ziti**—literally "bridegrooms"; thin 2-inch tubes

## CURVED SHAPES

**campanelle**—literally "bell flower; small rolled pasta

**cavatappi**—literally "corkscrews"; short thin spirals

**conchiglie**—literally "conch shells"; ridged shell-shaped pasta

**farfalle**—literally "butterflies"; bow-tie shaped pasta

**fusilli**—literally "little springs"; spiraled spaghetti that can be long or cut into 2-inch lengths

**gemelli**—literally "twins"; short twisted strands

**orecchiette**— literally "little ears"; tiny disk-shaped pasta

**radiatore**—literally "little radiators"; short chunky pasta with rippled edges

**rotini**—short spirals

**ruote**—literally "wagon wheels"; small wheel-shaped pasta

**strozzapreti**—literally "priest stranglers": long hand-rolled pasta

## SMALL SHAPES (SOUP PASTA)

**acini di pepe**—literally "peppercorns"; tiny, rice-shaped pasta

**anelli**— literally "little rings"; tiny ring-shaped pasta

**ditalini**— literally "little thimbles"; very small short tubes

**orzo**—literally "barley"; small rice-shaped pasta

**stelline**— literally "little stars"; tiny star-shaped pasta

**tubetti**—literally "little tubes"; tiny, hollow tubes

**tubettini**—smaller tubetti

# PASTA AND NOODLES

## egg-free pasta dough
makes about 1 pound

*This is an all-purpose pasta dough that can be used to make the ravioli and tortellini recipes on pages 230–232, or other handmade pasta shapes such as farfalle and papardelle. You can also crank this dough through a pasta maker to make your own linguine and fettuccine. The olive oil gives the dough a rich texture and flavor.*

2 cups all-purpose flour
1 teaspoon salt
2 tablespoons olive oil
½ to ¾ cup hot water

1. In a large mixing bowl, combine the flour and salt. Make a well in the center and add the olive oil. Pour in ½ cup of the water and, stirring with a fork, gradually incorporate the flour into the liquid. Add additional water if needed to make a stiff dough.

2. When the dough is pliable, and not sticky, knead it on a lightly floured work surface until smooth, 2 to 3 minutes. If the dough is sticky, sprinkle it with a small amount of flour. Shape the dough into a disk and wrap it in plastic wrap and let it rest unrefrigerated for 15 minutes. The dough is now ready to roll out and cut per recipe instructions.

food processor variation: To save time, you can make this dough in the food processor instead of by hand. Place the flour and salt in the food processor and pulse to distribute evenly. With machine running, add the oil and then the water in a slow steady stream until incorporated. The dough should form into a ball. If the dough is too sticky, add more flour a tablespoon at a time and pulse until dough holds together. Remove dough from machine, knead for about 5 minutes, then cover and rest unrefrigerated for 15 minutes before rolling out.

## fresh pasta shapes

The Egg-Free Pasta Dough (see left) can be used to make the tortellini and ravioli recipes in this book. It can also be used to make a variety of other fresh pasta shapes, even without benefit of an extrusion machine or other equipment. Some examples of hand-crafted fresh pasta include:

fusilli—Shape fusilli by winding cut pasta strips around a floured thin wooden dowel or knitting needle—just slide them off the stick and let them dry.

maltagliati—Even if you think you're all thumbs, you can make pasta: maltagliati, which means "badly cut," is made by cutting uneven and lopsided triangles from the rolled-out dough.

farfalle—Known as butterflies or bow-ties, farfalle are surprisingly simple to shape: cut pasta into 1¼ × 2½-inch rectangles, then pinch together in middle and let dry.

fazzoletti—To make these elegant herb-pressed pasta squares ("handkerchiefs"), simply lay leaves of soft herbs between two very thin strips of rolled-out fresh pasta dough and then roll out again to sandwich the herbs between the pasta sheets.

# making fresh pasta

One of my earliest memories is helping my mother make homemade pasta, a weekly ritual in my Italian household. When Mom cooked, she never referred to a recipe and she used her cupped hands or a small glass instead of measuring spoons or cups. The pasta always turned out perfectly. My mother's pasta dough contained eggs, so when I went vegan, it was important to me to develop a recipe for a good egg-free fresh pasta dough.

Because most fresh pasta is made with eggs, vegans are usually limited to using the dried pasta varieties. However, certain regions of Italy are famous for their delicious egg-free pasta dough recipes, including the one used to make orecchiette (little ears) in the Puglia region and the soft Ligurian dough enhanced with white wine that is used to make thin pasta squares called fazzoletti ("handkerchiefs"). A versatile egg-free pasta dough recipe is provided on page 191. It is easy and can be made in advance. Just keep the dough tightly wrapped in plastic wrap in the refrigerator overnight or frozen for up to two weeks. Before rolling it out, bring the dough to room temperature.

Use this dough to make your own ravioli, tortellini, and other stuffed pasta recipes in this book, as well as other handcrafted pastas such as *papardelle, trofie, trenette,* and *crozetti.* If you have a pasta machine, you can crank out your own linguine and fettuccine as well. Also in this chapter is a recipe for homemade orecchiette, although dried orecchiette is generally available in supermarkets, if you don't want to take the time to make it from scratch.

Uncooked homemade stuffed pastas such as tortellini and ravioli can be refrigerated overnight if not using right away or frozen for up to two weeks. To freeze, arrange the individual pieces in a single layer on baking sheets (spaced so they do not touch) and place them in the freezer. Once frozen, carefully remove the pieces from the baking sheets and place them in freezer bags until needed. To prevent the pasta pieces from sticking together, lightly dust them with flour. When ready to use, do not thaw the frozen pasta shapes—they are best when cooked frozen and not defrosted.

# orecchiette

makes about 1 pound

*A specialty of the Puglia region of Italy, orecchiette, or "little ears," are a small disk-shaped pasta traditionally made with a combination of semolina and all-purpose flour—and no eggs. When finished shaping orecchiette, cook them right away or air-dry them for up to 24 hours. If the center is still damp, leave them out. You will know they are dry when they are too hard to cut with a knife. Dried orecchiette will keep at room temperature in an airtight container for several months. If preparing fresh, they will cook in about 7 minutes, whereas dried may take up to 15 minutes to cook.*

1 cup semolina flour
1½ cups all-purpose flour
1 cup warm water

1. On a lightly floured work surface, combine both flours and shape into a mound. Make a well in the center and pour in ½ cup of the water. With a fork, stir the flour into the water to form a paste. Continue adding the rest of the water as you stir in the flour, to make a soft but not sticky dough.

2. Once a dough ball has been formed, knead it for 5 to 7 minutes. Divide the dough into four pieces, reserve three, and cover them with a clean dish towel or plastic wrap. Take the remaining piece of dough and roll it into ½-inch cylindrical shape, then cut into ⅛-inch disks.

3. One at a time, place a disk in the palm of your hand, and press an indentation into the center of the disk with the thumb of your other hand, moving your thumb to thin out center of disk and stretch it to about 1 inch wide. Place on clean dish towel. Repeat process with remaining disks, flouring your thumb if it sticks to the dough. When finished, sprinkle flour over the pasta and repeat with remaining three pieces of dough.

## introducing parmasio

Believe it or not, Americans use way more cheese on their pasta and pizza than Italians do, so vegans who simply skip the cheese on these dishes are often eating a more authentic preparation. But if you have a taste for Parmesan on your pasta, then you may want to investigate the various vegan Parmesan cheese alternatives on the market. Or simply make your own, using the recipe below.

### parmasio

makes about 1 cup

*I call this topping "Parmasio" because it is basically gomasio, a wonderful Japanese sesame seed and salt condiment, with nutritional yeast added for its salty-cheesy flavor. Use this whenever vegan Parmesan is called for in recipes.*

½ cup sesame seeds
½ cup nutritional yeast
½ teaspoon salt

1. In a dry skillet, toast the sesame seeds over medium heat, stirring, until golden brown, 4 to 5 minutes. Immediately remove from the pan to cool so they don't burn.

2. In a food processor, combine the toasted sesame seeds, nutritional yeast, and salt and pulse until finely ground. Store in the refrigerator in a dry container with a tight-fitting lid.

# marinara sauce

makes about 3½ cups

*Despite its seaworthy name, "mariner's style" sauce does not contain seafood. The simple tomato sauce with few ingredients was supposedly favored by Italian sailors who had limited ingredients at hand. This basic all-purpose tomato sauce isn't just for spaghetti; it's great on other pasta shapes too. It can also can be used in any recipe where an Italian tomato sauce is desired, such as polenta (page 276), Spicy Eggplant and Tempeh-Stuffed Pasta Shells (page 229), or lightly breaded and sautéed seitan or tofu.*

1 tablespoon olive oil

3 garlic cloves, crushed

1 (28-ounce) can crushed tomatoes

1 tablespoon minced fresh basil or 1 teaspoon dried

¾ teaspoon minced fresh oregano or ½ teaspoon dried

½ teaspoon salt

¼ teaspoon freshly ground black pepper

Pinch sugar

2 bay leaves

1. In a large saucepan, heat the oil over medium heat. Add the garlic and cook until fragrant, about 30 seconds. Add the tomatoes, basil, oregano, salt, pepper, sugar, and bay leaves.

2. Reduce heat to low and simmer for 15 minutes, stirring occasionally. Remove and discard the garlic cloves and bay leaves before serving.

variations: Add any of the following to this basic tomato sauce, alone or in combination: 2 or 3 tablespoons dry red wine, ½ teaspoon ground fennel seeds, ½ teaspoon crushed red pepper, 1 cup sautéed sliced mushrooms.

## PASTA WITH TOMATOES

# spaghetti and t-balls

makes 4 servings

*Everyone's favorite Italian pasta dish, spaghetti and meatballs, goes vegan with these delicious little "T-Balls" made with tempeh.*

1 pound tempeh

2 or 3 garlic cloves, finely minced

3 tablespoons finely minced fresh parsley

3 tablespoons soy sauce

1 tablespoon olive oil, plus more for cooking

¾ cup fresh bread crumbs

⅓ cup wheat gluten flour (vital wheat gluten)

3 tablespoons nutritional yeast

½ teaspoon dried oregano

½ teaspoon salt

¼ teaspoon freshly ground black pepper

1 pound spaghetti

3 cups marinara sauce, homemade (see left) or store-bought

1. In a medium saucepan of simmering water, cook the tempeh for 30 minutes. Drain well and cut into chunks.

2. Place the cooked tempeh in a food processor, add the garlic and parsley, and pulse until coarsely ground. Add the soy sauce, olive oil, bread crumbs, gluten flour, yeast, oregano, salt, and black pepper, and pulse to combine, leaving some texture. Scrape the tempeh mixture into a bowl and use your hands to knead the mixture until well blended, 1 to 2 minutes. Use your hands to roll the mixture into small balls, no larger than 1½ inches in diameter. Repeat with the remaining tempeh mixture.

3. In a lightly oiled large skillet, heat a thin layer of oil over medium heat. Add the T-balls, in batches if necessary, and cook until browned, moving them in the pan as needed for even browning, 15 to 20 minutes. Alternatively, you can arrange the T-balls on an oiled baking sheet and bake at 350°F for 25 to 30 minutes, turning once about halfway through.

4. In a large pot of boiling salted water, cook the spaghetti over medium-high heat, stirring occasionally, until al dente, about 10 minutes.

5. While the spaghetti is cooking, heat the marinara sauce in a medium saucepan over medium heat until hot.

6. When the pasta is cooked, drain well and divide among 4 dinner plates or shallow pasta bowls. Top each serving with a few of the T-balls. Spoon the sauce over the T-Balls and spaghetti and serve hot. Combine any remaining T-balls and sauce in a serving bowl and serve.

# pasta arrabbiata

makes 4 servings

*The name of this popular Roman pasta dish means "angry" or "enraged" because of the hot nature of the sauce. If you prefer the sauce more or less "enraged," adjust the amount of crushed red pepper accordingly. Gemelli ("twins") is a short twisted pasta that resembles two strands of spaghetti twisted together. I like its chewy texture and the way it holds the sauce in this recipe, although another bite-size pasta shape such as penne or* radiatore *may be used instead.*

2 tablespoons olive oil

3 garlic cloves, minced

1 teaspoon crushed red pepper

1 (28-ounce) can diced tomatoes, drained

3 tablespoons tomato paste

3 tablespoons dry red wine

Salt and freshly ground black pepper

1 pound gemelli, or other bite-size pasta shape

1. In a large skillet, heat the oil over medium heat. Add the garlic and crushed red pepper and cook until fragrant, about 30 seconds. Add the tomatoes, tomato paste, and wine and season with salt and pepper to taste. Cook, stirring, for 10 to 15 minutes, or until the tomatoes have broken down and the flavors are well combined. Keep warm, partially covered, over low heat while you cook the pasta.

2. In a large pot of boiling salted water, cook the pasta over medium-high heat, stirring occasionally, until al dente, about 10 minutes. Drain well and transfer to a shallow serving bowl. Add the sauce and toss gently to combine. Serve immediately.

# linguine puttanesca 🅕

makes 4 servings

*The lusty richness of olives and capers combines with fragrant garlic, herbs, and tomatoes to make one of the most captivating sauces ever created for pasta. It is said that this "streetwalker-style" pasta got its name because it was a quick meal that the ladies of the evening could easily prepare from pantry ingredients after a hard night's work. You can omit or cut back on the crushed red pepper for a milder sauce.*

2 tablespoons olive oil

3 garlic cloves, minced

½ teaspoon crushed red pepper

1 (14.5-ounce) can crushed tomatoes

1 (14.5-ounce) can diced tomatoes, drained

½ teaspoon dried oregano

½ teaspoon dried basil

Salt and freshly ground black pepper

¾ cup kalamata or Moroccan olives, pitted and halved

¼ cup Manzanilla or other green olives, pitted and halved

3 tablespoons capers

2 tablespoons minced fresh parsley

1 pound linguine

1. In a large a saucepan, heat the oil over medium heat. Add the garlic and crushed red pepper and cook until fragrant, about 30 seconds. Stir in the crushed tomatoes, diced tomatoes, oregano, and basil. Season with salt and black pepper to taste. Bring the sauce to a boil, then reduce heat to low and simmer for 15 minutes, stirring occasionally. Stir in the black olives, green olives, capers, and parsley, cover, and keep warm.

2. In a large pot of boiling salted water, cook the linguine over medium-high heat, stirring occasionally, until al dente, about 10 minutes. Drain well and transfer to a shallow serving bowl. Add the sauce and toss gently to combine. Serve immediately.

# radiatore with aurora sauce

makes 4 servings

*"Aurora" is the name given to a tomato sauce that has been lightened with cream to a pink blush. Here, tofu cream cheese both lightens and enriches the sauce, adding protein and a creamy texture. Be sure to use good-quality imported Italian tomatoes for the best flavor. Radiatore ("little radiators") are small square pasta with rippled edges that look like, well, little radiators. Their shape allows the sauce to adhere to its nooks and crannies, but another pasta shape of your choice may be used instead.*

1 tablespoon olive oil

3 garlic cloves, minced

3 green onions, minced

1 (28-ounce) can crushed tomatoes

1 teaspoon dried basil

½ teaspoon dried marjoram

1 teaspoon salt

¼ teaspoon freshly ground black pepper

⅓ cup vegan cream cheese or drained soft tofu

1 pound radiatore or other small, shaped pasta

2 tablespoons minced fresh parsley, for garnish

1. In a large saucepan, heat the oil over medium heat. Add the garlic and green onions and cook until fragrant, 1 minute. Stir in the tomatoes, basil, marjoram, salt, and pepper. Bring the sauce to a boil, then reduce heat to low and simmer for 15 minutes, stirring occasionally.

2. In food processor, blend the cream cheese until smooth. Add 2 cups of the tomato sauce and blend until smooth. Scrape the tofu-tomato mixture back into the saucepan with the tomato sauce, stirring to blend. Taste, adjusting seasonings if necessary. Keep warm over low heat.

3. In a large pot of boiling salted water, cook the pasta over medium-high heat, stirring occasionally, until al dente, about 10 minutes. Drain well and transfer to a large serving bowl. Add the sauce and toss gently to combine. Sprinkle with parsley and serve immediately.

# sicilian penne with tomatoes and eggplant

makes 4 servings

*In Sicily, pasta dishes made with eggplant are called "ala Norma." It is believed this name honors the Bellini opera of the same name, though some food writers note that the word "norma" in the Sicilian dialect means "normal." Thus, it can be inferred that pasta with eggplant is simply pasta in the "normal" way, since eggplant figures prominently in Sicilian cuisine.*

2 tablespoons olive oil
1 medium onion, chopped
2 garlic cloves, minced
1 medium eggplant, peeled and chopped
2 tablespoons tomato paste
1 (28-ounce) can crushed tomatoes
½ cup dry red wine
Salt and freshly ground black pepper
1 pound penne
2 tablespoons minced fresh basil

1. In a large saucepan, heat the oil over medium heat. Add the onion and garlic, cover, and cook until softened, about 5 minutes. Add the eggplant, and cook, covered, 7 or 8 minutes longer. Stir in the tomato paste, then add the tomatoes, wine, and salt and pepper to taste; reduce heat to low and simmer, uncovered, until the vegetables are soft and the sauce thickens, about 15 minutes. Keep warm over low heat while you cook the pasta.

2. In a large pot of boiling salted water, cook the penne over medium-high heat, stirring occasionally, until al dente, about 8 to 10 minutes. Drain well and transfer to a shallow serving bowl. Add the sauce and toss gently to combine. Sprinkle with basil and serve immediately.

# penne with vodka-spiked tomato sauce

makes 4 servings

*Anyone who enjoys Bloody Marys will tell you tomatoes and vodka make a great pair. The combination extends to a popular pasta sauce as well. Here, white beans and soy milk replace the traditional heavy cream, while cayenne adds just the right bite.*

1 tablespoon olive oil

1 medium yellow onion, chopped

¼ cup vodka

1 (28-ounce) can crushed tomatoes

1 tablespoon minced fresh marjoram
    or 1 teaspoon dried

½ teaspoon salt

½ cup cooked or canned white beans, drained
    and rinsed

½ cup plain unsweetened soy milk

1 pound penne

1. In a large saucepan, heat the oil over medium heat. Add the onion, cover, and cook until soft, about 7 minutes. Add the vodka and simmer for a minute to let the alcohol burn off. Stir in the tomatoes, marjoram, and salt and simmer over low heat for 10 minutes.

2. Puree the beans and soy milk in a blender or food processor until smooth. Add 1 cup of the tomato sauce and blend until smooth and creamy. Add the bean mixture to the tomato sauce in the saucepan, and stir to blend. Taste, adjusting seasonings if necessary, and keep warm over low heat while you cook the pasta.

3. In a large pot of boiling salted water, cook the penne over medium-high heat, stirring occasionally, until al dente, about 10 minutes. Drain well and transfer to a large serving bowl. Add the sauce, toss gently to combine, and serve immediately.

# perciatelli with slow-roasted tomato sauce

makes 4 servings

*The intense flavor of this versatile sauce comes from the caramelization of natural sugars achieved by roasting the tomatoes. Perciatelli are long hollow pasta strands about double the thickness of spaghetti. If they are unavailable, use your favorite pasta shape. In this recipe, I combine fresh and canned tomatoes, but you could use all fresh tomatoes if they are plentiful. This recipe can be easily tweaked to suit your own tastes; for example, you can add more garlic if desired or, near the end of cooking time, add some crushed red pepper or pitted chopped kalamata olives.*

¼ cup plus 2 tablespoons olive oil

2 pounds ripe plum tomatoes or cherry tomatoes,
    halved lengthwise

1 (28-ounce) can whole plum tomatoes,
    drained and halved lengthwise

1 small red onion, chopped

2 garlic cloves, finely chopped

1 teaspoon dried oregano

½ teaspoon dried basil

½ teaspoon salt

Freshly ground black pepper

⅓ cup dry red wine

1 pound perciatelli

1. Preheat the oven to 375°F. Lightly oil a 9 × 13-inch baking dish with the 2 tablespoons of oil. Arrange the fresh and canned tomatoes cut side up in the dish. Sprinkle with the onion, garlic, oregano, basil, salt, and pepper to taste. Drizzle with the remaining ¼ cup oil. Bake until the tomatoes are soft and just starting to brown, about 90 minutes. Remove from oven and allow to cool slightly.

2. Press the roasted tomato mixture through a fine-mesh sieve or run through a food mill set over a large saucepan. Discard the solids. Add the wine and bring to a boil, reduce heat to low, and simmer for 15 minutes. Remove from heat and taste, adjusting seasonings if necessary. Keep warm while you cook the pasta.

3. In a large pot of boiling salted water, cook the perciatelli over medium-high heat, stirring occasionally, until al dente, about 12 minutes. Drain well and transfer to a large serving bowl. Add the sauce and toss gently to combine. Serve immediately.

# fettuccine with chard and red lentil tomato sauce

makes 4 servings

*You'd expect to find red lentils in an Indian dish, not paired with linguine in an Italian tomato sauce, but just one taste will convince you it's a great idea. Softly cooked lentils blend effortlessly into the sauce, adding substance and protein. The chard adds texture and flavor, making this a nutritious one-dish meal that is also extremely tasty.*

½ cup red lentils, picked over, rinsed, and drained
1 medium bunch Swiss chard, tough stems removed and cut into ½-inch pieces
2 tablespoons olive oil
2 garlic cloves, sliced
½ teaspoon crushed red pepper
1 (28-ounce) can crushed tomatoes
Salt and freshly ground black pepper
1 pound linguine

1. Bring a small saucepan of salted water to boil over high heat. Add the lentils, return to a boil, then reduce heat to low. Cover and cook until softened, about 30 minutes. Drain and set aside.

2. In a large saucepan of boiling water, cook the chard until just tender, about 3 minutes. Drain and set aside.

3. In a large skillet, heat the oil over medium heat. Add the garlic and cook until fragrant, about 30 seconds. Add the crushed red pepper, tomatoes, the cooked lentils, and the cooked chard. Reduce the heat to low, season with salt and pepper to taste, and simmer for 10 minutes to incorporate the flavors.

4. In a large pot of boiling salted water, cook the linguine over medium-high heat, stirring occasionally, until al dente, about 10 minutes. Drain well and transfer to a large serving bowl. Add the sauce and toss gently to combine. Serve immediately.

# tagliatelle with porcini bolognese sauce

makes 4 servings

*This rich Bolognese sauce relies on hearty porcini mushrooms to add texture and flavor instead of the traditional ground meat. Tagliatelle are long flat pasta ribbons and are virtually interchangeable with fettuccine.*

2 tablespoons olive oil

1 medium onion, minced

1 medium carrot, minced

1 celery rib, minced

3 garlic cloves, minced

12 ounces fresh porcini mushrooms, lightly rinsed, patted dry, and chopped

½ cup dry white wine

1 (28-ounce) can crushed tomatoes

Salt and freshly ground black pepper

½ cup plain unsweetened soy milk or soy creamer

1 pound tagliatelle or fettuccine

2 tablespoons minced fresh flat-leaf parsley, for garnish

1. In a large saucepan, heat the oil over medium heat. Add the onion, carrot, celery, and garlic. Cover and cook until tender, about 10 minutes. Stir in the mushrooms and the wine and simmer for 5 minutes. Add the tomatoes and season with salt and pepper to taste. Simmer, uncovered, for 15 minutes, then reduce heat to low and stir in the soy milk. Remove from heat and keep warm while you cook the pasta.

2. In a large pot of boiling salted water, cook the pasta over medium-high heat, stirring occasionally, until al dente, about 10 minutes. Drain well and transfer to a large serving bowl. Add the sauce and toss gently to combine. Sprinkle with parsley and serve immediately.

# ziti with abruzzese vegetable ragù

makes 4 servings

*This rich, full-bodied sauce is typical of the Abruzzi region of Italy, as is the use of yellow bell peppers. To add Abruzzese authenticity to the dish, use "guitar" macaroni (maccheroni alla chitarra) instead of the ziti called for in this recipe. Maccheroni alla chitarra is named for the guitar string–like cutter on which the square-shaped pasta strands are cut.*

1 tablespoon olive oil

1 medium onion, chopped

1 medium carrot, finely chopped

1 medium yellow bell pepper, chopped

3 garlic cloves, minced

2 tablespoons tomato paste

½ cup dry red wine

½ teaspoon dried oregano

1 (28-ounce) can diced tomatoes, drained

¼ teaspoon crushed red pepper

Salt and freshly ground black pepper

1 pound ziti

¼ cup minced fresh parsley, for garnish

1. In a large skillet, heat the oil over medium heat. Add the onion, carrot, bell pepper, and garlic. Cover and cook until soft, about 10 minutes. Uncover and stir in the tomato paste, wine, and oregano. Add the tomatoes, crushed red pepper, and salt and black pepper to taste. Simmer for 20 minutes, uncovered, stirring occasionally.

2. In a large pot of boiling salted water, cook the ziti over medium-high heat, stirring occasionally, until al dente, about 10 minutes. Drain well and transfer to a large serving bowl. Add the sauce and toss gently to combine. Sprinkle with parsley and serve immediately.

# Pasta with Pesto

## linguine with ligurian pesto 🅕

makes 4 servings

*Pesto, the famous basil sauce, originated in Liguria, where it is more mellow than most of the pesto made in America. This is because the Ligurian basil is much milder and more tender that the large basil grown in America. The Ligurian olive oil is lighter and fruitier and the garlic smaller and milder. Enjoy this aromatic fresh-tasting pasta dish during the hot summer months when fresh basil is at its peak and a lighter meal is especially welcome.*

3 garlic cloves

⅓ cup pine nuts

½ teaspoon salt

2½ cups fresh basil leaves

½ cup olive oil (Ligurian, if available)

¼ cup vegan Parmesan or Parmasio (page 193; optional)

1 pound linguine

1. In a food processor, combine the garlic, pine nuts, and salt and process until ground to a paste. Add the basil and process until well blended. With the machine running, slowly stream in the oil. Transfer to a small bowl and stir in the Parmesan, if using.

2. In a large pot of boiling salted water, cook the linguine over medium-high heat, stirring occasionally, until al dente, about 10 minutes. Drain well, reserving about ½ cup of the pasta water. Transfer the pasta to a large serving bowl. Add the reserved pasta water to about 1 cup of the pesto, stirring to make a smooth sauce. Add the pesto to the pasta and toss gently to combine. Serve immediately.

## orzo, white beans, and tomatoes with lemony spinach pesto 🅕

makes 4 servings

*Orzo, the tiny rice-shaped pasta, is what gives this colorful and sprightly dish a more risotto-like quality. If you prefer a heartier dish, use penne or another large pasta variety.*

2 cups fresh baby spinach

2 garlic cloves

⅓ cup pine nuts

½ teaspoon salt

2 teaspoons fresh minced marjoram or 1 teaspoon dried

¼ cup coarsely chopped fresh parsley

Freshly ground black pepper

¼ cup olive oil

1½ cups orzo

1½ cups cooked or 1 (15.5-ounce) can cannellini beans, drained and rinsed if canned

Juice of 1 lemon

1½ cups ripe grape tomatoes, halved

1. Microwave the spinach in a microwave-safe bowl until wilted, about 1 minute. Set aside. In a food processor, combine the garlic, pine nuts, and salt and process to a paste. Add the spinach, marjoram, parsley, and pepper to taste and process to combine. With the machine running, stream in the oil. Transfer the pesto to a small bowl and set aside.

2. In a large pot of boiling salted water, cook the orzo over medium-high heat, stirring occasionally, until al dente, about 5 minutes. Drain well and return to the pot over low heat. Add the white beans and lemon juice and stir to heat the beans, about 5 minutes. Add the tomatoes and pesto and toss gently to combine. Transfer to a serving bowl. Serve immediately.

# fettuccine with puttanesca pesto ⑥

makes 4 servings

*My all-time favorite pasta sauce is puttan-esca, that incomparable fusion of tomatoes, olives, capers, and garlic. But, I also love pesto and was up to my eyeballs in fresh basil from the garden. The only logical solu-tion was to bring the two together to create a delicious, flavorful sauce that pairs perfectly with long pasta ribbons like fettuccine.*

3 garlic cloves

¼ cup pine nuts or slivered almonds

¼ teaspoon salt

2 cups fresh basil leaves (small tender leaves, if available)

2 ripe plum tomatoes, chopped

⅓ cup pitted Manzanilla or other green olives, chopped

1 tablespoon capers

Freshly ground black pepper

⅓ cup olive oil

1 pound fettuccine

1. In a food processor, combine the garlic, pine nuts, and salt and process to a paste. Add the basil, tomatoes, olives, capers, and pepper to taste and process until well blended. With the machine running, slowly stream in the oil. Transfer to a small bowl and set aside.

2. In a large pot of boiling salted water, cook the fettuccine over medium-high heat, stir-ring occasionally, until al dente, about 10 min-utes. Drain well, reserving ⅓ cup of the pasta water. Transfer the pasta to a large serving bowl. Add the reserved pasta water to the pesto, stirring to make a smooth sauce. Add the pesto to the pasta and toss gently to combine. Serve immediately.

# tricolor rotini with pesto bianco ⑥

makes 4 servings

*Creamy and flavorful, this pesto bianco, or "white pesto," is made with pine nuts, cashews, and artichoke hearts. It lightly cloaks the colorful short spiral rotini pasta, although you can substitute another pasta shape if you prefer. Sprinkle with parsley, basil, green peas, or chopped black olives for added color and flavor. Do not use marinated artichoke hearts because the flavor is too strong. Use frozen artichoke hearts instead of canned, but you'll need to cook them first according to package directions.*

2 or 3 garlic cloves

⅓ cup pine nuts

⅓ cup unsalted raw cashews

1 teaspoon salt

1 cup coarsely chopped canned artichoke hearts, drained and rinsed

½ cup plain unsweetened soy milk

¼ cup olive oil

1 pound tricolor rotini

1. In a food processor, combine the garlic, pine nuts, cashews, and salt and process to a paste. Add the artichokes and process until smooth. Add the soy milk and process until well blended. With the machine running, slowly stream in the oil. Transfer to a small bowl and set aside. Alternatively, you can warm the sauce in a saucepan over very low heat but, like most pestos, tossing it with the hot cooked pasta is usually enough to warm it up.

2. In a large pot of boiling salted water, cook the rotini over medium-high heat, stirring occasionally, until al dente, about 10 minutes.

Drain the pasta and transfer to a large serving bowl. Add the pesto and toss gently to combine. Serve immediately.

# penne with peanut pesto 🅕

makes 4 servings

*Asian flavors permeate this garlicky-peanutty pesto. I serve it with penne just for the fun of alliteration, but an Asian rice noodle would also be a great match.*

3 garlic cloves, minced
½ cup unsalted roasted peanuts
1 teaspoon sugar
¼ cup soy sauce
1 tablespoon fresh lime juice
½ teaspoon Asian chili paste
¼ cup creamy peanut butter
2 tablespoons toasted sesame oil
1 pound penne
¼ cup chopped fresh cilantro, for garnish
2 tablespoons chopped green onions, for garnish

1. In a food processor, combine the garlic, peanuts, and sugar and process to a paste. Add the soy sauce, lime juice, and chili paste and process until well blended. Add the peanut butter and sesame oil and process until smooth. Transfer to a small bowl and set aside.

2. In a large pot of boiling salted water, cook the penne over medium-high heat, stirring occasionally, until al dente, about 10 minutes. Drain well, reserving ⅓ cup of the pasta water. Transfer the pasta to a large serving bowl. Add the reserved pasta water to the pesto, stirring to make a smooth sauce. Add the sauce and toss gently to combine. Garnish with cilantro and green onions and serve immediately.

# rotini and almond-mint pesto with orange zest 🅕

makes 4 servings

*Almonds, mint, and orange are a traditional Sicilian flavor combination in savory dishes. The faintly sweet taste of mint and almond are a great complement to the bite of the orange zest.*

2 garlic cloves
½ cup slivered almonds
¾ teaspoon salt
2 cups fresh mint leaves
½ cup olive oil
2 teaspoons orange zest
1 pound rotini

1. In a food processor, combine the garlic, almonds, and salt and process until finely chopped. Add the mint and process until ground to a paste. With the machine running, stream in the oil. Transfer to a small bowl and stir in the orange zest.

2. In large pot of boiling salted water, cook the rotini over medium-high heat, stirring occasionally, until al dente, about 10 minutes. Drain well, reserving about ½ cup of the pasta water. Transfer pasta to a large serving bowl. Add the reserved pasta water to the pesto, stirring to make a smooth sauce. Add the pesto to the pasta and toss gently to combine. Serve immediately.

# campanelle and zucchini with squash blossoms and sunflower pesto 🅕

makes 4 servings

*This summertime recipe has an underlying "flower" theme: the campanelle means "bell flowers," for the shape of the pasta. In this recipe, they are tossed with sunflower pesto and zucchini flowers. Zucchini flowers or blossoms are delicious fried in olive oil and seasoned with nothing more than salt and pepper. They make a lovely addition to this pasta dish. Look for them at your local supermarket or farmer's market (or in your own vegetable garden) during the summer months, when zucchini is at its peak. If zucchini flowers are unavailable, you can omit them and the dish will still be delicious. Campanelle pasta is sometimes hard to find, so feel free to substitute another variety of pasta.*

2 cups fresh parsley leaves

½ cup shelled unsalted sunflower seeds

2 garlic cloves

Salt

Freshly ground black pepper

⅓ cup plus 3 tablespoons olive oil

1 pound campanelle

2 small zucchini, cut into ¼-inch slices

4 zucchini flowers, washed and dried

1. In a food processor, combine the parsley, sunflower seeds, garlic, ½ teaspoon salt, and a pinch of pepper and pulse until coarsely ground. With the machine running, stream in the ⅓ cup of oil until well blended. Set aside.

2. In large pot of boiling salted water, cook the campanelle over medium-high heat, stirring occasionally, until al dente, about 10 minutes.

3. While the pasta is cooking, heat 2 tablespoons of the oil in a large skillet over medium heat. Add the zucchini, cover, and cook until tender, about 7 minutes. Add salt and pepper to taste, cover, and keep warm over very low heat.

4. In a small nonstick skillet, heat the remaining 1 tablespoon oil over medium heat. Add the zucchini flowers and cook until softened, turning once, about 5 minutes. Season with salt and pepper to taste and keep warm over very low heat.

5. Drain the cooked pasta well and transfer to a large serving bowl. Add the pesto and cooked zucchini and toss gently to combine. Top with the cooked zucchini flowers and serve immediately with plenty of freshly ground black pepper.

# gemelli with green beans, potatoes, and basil pesto 🅕

makes 4 servings

*When tossed with linguine, this pesto dish, made with green beans and potatoes, is called "pesto Genovese" because it is a popular combination in Genoa, where pesto is prevalent. While the dish is certainly wonderful with linguine, I prefer gemelli for its size (about 1½ inches long) and chewy texture. The name gemelli means "twins," for the way the pasta looks like two twisted strands of spaghetti. If you don't have pine nuts, you can substitute walnut pieces or slivered almonds.*

3 garlic cloves

⅓ cup pine nuts

2 cups fresh basil leaves

Salt

Freshly ground black pepper

½ cup olive oil

8 ounces new potatoes, unpeeled and cut into ¼-inch slices

4 ounces green beans, trimmed and cut into 1-inch pieces

1 pound gemelli

1. In a food processor, combine the garlic and pine nuts and process to a paste. Add the basil, about 1 teaspoon of salt, pepper to taste, and oil. Process, scraping down the sides as necessary, until the pesto is smooth. Set aside.

2. Steam the potatoes over boiling water until just tender, 10 to 12 minutes, then transfer to a large bowl. When the potatoes are finished steaming, steam the green beans until tender, 7 to 8 minutes.

3. In a large pot of boiling salted water, cook the gemelli over medium-high heat, stirring occasionally, until al dente, about 10 minutes. Drain well, reserving ⅓ cup of the pasta water. Transfer the pasta to a large serving bowl.

4. Add the pesto to the steamed potatoes and green beans, along with the reserved pasta water. Season with salt and pepper to taste. Add the vegetable-pesto mixture to the cooked pasta and toss gently to combine. Serve immediately.

# radiatore with walnut-parsley pesto  🅕

makes 4 servings

*Walnuts are a common ingredient in Ligurian cooking, and they add iron, magnesium, and other essential nutrients to this flavorful pesto. Spicy food lovers may want to add the optional crushed red pepper to the pesto for a little heat, but it is perfectly delicious without it.*

2 garlic cloves

½ teaspoon salt

½ cup lightly toasted walnut pieces

½ cup chopped fresh parsley

½ teaspoon crushed red pepper (optional)

⅓ cup olive oil

1 pound radiatore

1 tablespoon walnut oil (optional)

1. In a food processor, combine the garlic and salt and process until garlic is minced. Add the walnuts, parsley, and crushed red pepper, if using, and process until ground to a paste. With the machine running, stream in the oil and process until well blended. Set aside.

2. In a large pot of boiling salted water, cook the radiatore over medium-high heat, stirring occasionally, until al dente, about 10 minutes. Drain well, reserving ⅓ cup of the pasta water. Transfer the pasta to a large serving bowl. Add the reserved pasta water to the pesto and blend to make a smooth sauce. Add the pesto to the pasta and toss gently to combine. Drizzle with the walnut oil, if using, and serve immediately.

# PASTA WITH VEGETABLES AND MORE

## pasta primavera

makes 4 servings

*The name* pasta primavera *means "springtime pasta." Countless versions of the famous dish exist, including one made with olive oil and others made with cream. What they have in common is a variety of fresh vegetables and, to be true to the name, the vegetables should be the first of the springtime crop. Tricolor rotini are used to play up the colorful spring theme. The dish is said to be an American invention created at New York's Le Cirque restaurant, but the pairing of pasta with spring vegetables is actually quite common in Italy.*

1 pound tricolor rotini

2 tablespoons olive oil

1 medium red or yellow bell pepper, cut into ½-inch strips

2 garlic cloves, minced

1 small zucchini, halved lengthwise and cut into ¼-inch slices

8 thin asparagus spears, tough ends trimmed and cut into 2-inch lengths

1 small bunch green onions, chopped

Salt and freshly ground black pepper

2 tablespoons minced fresh basil

2 tablespoons minced fresh flat-leaf parsley

1. In a large pot of boiling salted water, cook the rotini over medium-high heat, stirring occasionally, until al dente, about 10 minutes.

2. In a large skillet, heat the oil over medium heat, add the bell pepper and garlic, and cook 4 minutes, until slightly softened. Add the zucchini, asparagus, and green onions and cook until tender, about 7 minutes longer. Season with salt and pepper to taste and keep warm.

3. Drain the pasta well and transfer it to a large serving bowl. Add the cooked vegetables, along with the basil, and parsley. Toss gently and serve immediately.

## orecchiette with rapini

makes 4 servings

*Orecchiette come from the Puglia region of southeastern Italy, where it is traditionally served with broccoli rabe (rapini) or other green vegetable such as arugula. A different pasta shape can be used, if desired.*

¼ cup olive oil

3 garlic cloves, minced

9 ounces broccoli rabe (rapini), thick stems removed and chopped

¼ teaspoon crushed red pepper

Salt and freshly ground black pepper

1 tablespoon dry white wine (optional)

1 pound orecchiette, homemade (page 193) or store-bought

1. In a medium saucepan, heat 2 tablespoons of the oil over medium heat. Add the garlic and cook until fragrant, about 30 seconds Add the rapini, crushed red pepper, and salt and black pepper to taste. Cook, stirring frequently, until the rapini is tender, about 5 minutes. Stir in the wine, if using, and keep warm over very low heat.

2. In a large pot of boiling salted water, cook the orecchiette over medium-high heat, stirring occasionally, until it is tender. Drain well and transfer to a large serving bowl. Add the remaining 2 tablespoons oil and the rapini mixture

and season with salt and pepper to taste. Toss gently to combine and serve immediately.

# penne with creamy asparagus sauce 🅕

makes 4 servings

*Asparagus lovers will enjoy this luxurious pasta dish—the creamy sauce contains pureed asparagus and is also thick with pieces of the luscious green vegetable.*

1 pound asparagus, tough ends trimmed and cut into 2-inch pieces
1 tablespoon olive oil
½ cup chopped yellow onion
3 garlic cloves, minced
¼ cup dry white wine or vegetable broth
1 teaspoon dried basil
½ teaspoon salt
⅛ teaspoon ground cayenne
1 cup cooked or canned Great Northern beans, drained and rinsed
Plain unsweetened soy milk, as needed
1 pound penne

1. Steam the asparagus until just tender, about 5 minutes. Rinse under cold water and set aside. In a large skillet, heat the oil over medium heat. Add the onion, cover, and cook until soft, about 5 minutes. Add the garlic and cook until softened, 1 minute. Stir in the wine, basil, salt, and cayenne and simmer, uncovered, for 2 minutes. Add half of the steamed asparagus along with the beans and stir to combine.

2. Transfer the asparagus and bean mixture to a food processor and puree until smooth, adding a little soy milk if too thick. Transfer the sauce to a large saucepan and add the reserved steamed asparagus. Cook, stirring, over medium heat until hot. Taste, adjusting

seasonings if necessary. Keep the sauce warm over very low heat.

3. In a pot of boiling salted water, cook the penne over medium-high heat, stirring occasionally, until al dente, about 10 minutes. Drain well and transfer to a large serving bowl. Add the sauce and toss gently to combine. Serve immediately.

# fusilli with fennel and sun-dried tomatoes

makes 4 servings

*Both fennel and sun-dried tomatoes are popular ingredients in Calabrian cooking. Fusilli is a spiral-shaped spaghetti, often sold cut as small 2-inch pieces. In Calabria, homemade fusilli is made by wrapping the pasta dough around knitting needles to dry. If fusilli is unavailable, use your favorite pasta shape.*

2 tablespoons olive oil
2 medium fennel bulbs, cut into ¼-inch slices
3 medium shallots, minced
1 large garlic clove, minced
1 (14.5-ounce) can diced tomatoes, undrained
1 (14.5-ounce) can crushed tomatoes
½ cup oil-packed sun-dried tomatoes, drained and finely chopped
Salt and freshly ground black pepper
2 tablespoons chopped fresh basil
1 pound fusilli

1. In a large saucepan, heat the oil over medium heat. Add the fennel, shallots, and garlic. Cover and cook, stirring occasionally, until softened, about 7 minutes. Stir in the diced tomatoes and their juice, crushed tomatoes, and sun-dried tomatoes and bring to a boil. Reduce heat to low, season with salt and pepper to taste, and

continues on next page

simmer, uncovered, for about 25 minutes or until the sauce thickens. Stir in the fresh basil and taste, adjusting seasonings if necessary. Keep warm over very low heat.

2. In a large pot of boiling salted water, cook the fusilli over medium-high heat, stirring occasionally, until al dente, about 10 minutes. Drain well and transfer to a large serving bowl. Add the sauce and toss gently to combine. Serve immediately.

# ziti with red pepper– walnut sauce ⓕ

makes 4 servings

*Finely ground walnuts are sprinkled over the pasta and sauce, much as you would do with grated Parmesan cheese. The protein-rich walnuts add a rich flavor note as well as nutrition since they contain iron and magnesium, as well as vitamins A, B, and E. Using bottled roasted red peppers makes this recipe especially quick, but fresh roasted may be used as well.*

2 tablespoons olive oil

1 medium onion, chopped

3 garlic cloves

1 teaspoon dried basil

½ teaspoon dried oregano

2 jarred roasted red peppers (or see page 10), chopped

1 (14.5-ounce) can crushed tomatoes

2 tablespoons chopped fresh flat-leaf parsley

½ teaspoon salt

¼ teaspoon freshly ground black pepper

1 pound ziti

½ cup lightly toasted walnut pieces, ground or finely minced

1. In a skillet, heat the oil over medium heat. Add the onion and garlic, cover, and cook until softened, 5 minutes. Stir in the basil and oregano. Remove from heat and set aside.

2. In a blender or food processor, process the bell peppers until smooth. Add the onion and garlic mixture and process until smooth. Add the tomatoes, parsley, salt, and black pepper and process until well blended. Set aside.

3. In a large pot of boiling salted water, cook the penne over medium-high heat, stirring occasionally, until al dente, about 10 minutes. Drain well and transfer to a large serving bowl. Add the sauce and toss gently to combine. Sprinkle with walnuts and serve immediately.

# carbonara-style spaghetti ⓕ

makes 4 servings

*Inspired by the "bacon and eggs" Italian classic, this delicious vegan version is made with heart-healthy soy. Toss in ½ cup of thawed green peas when adding the parsley for additional color, if desired.*

2 tablespoons olive oil

3 medium shallots, minced

4 ounces tempeh bacon, homemade (page 525) or store-bought, chopped

1 cup plain unsweetened soy milk

½ cup soft or silken tofu, drained

¼ cup nutritional yeast

Salt and freshly ground black pepper

½ cup vegan Parmesan or Parmasio (page 193)

1 pound spaghetti

3 tablespoons minced fresh parsley

1. In a large skillet, heat the oil over medium heat. Add the shallots and cook until tender, about 5 minutes. Add the tempeh bacon and cook, stirring frequently, until lightly browned, about 5 minutes. Set aside.

**2.** In a blender, combine the soy milk, tofu, nutritional yeast, and salt and pepper to taste. Blend until smooth. Set aside.

**3.** In a large pot of boiling salted water, cook the spaghetti over medium-high heat, stirring occasionally, until al dente, about 10 minutes. Drain well and transfer to a large serving bowl. Add the tofu mixture, ¼ cup of the Parmesan, and all but 2 tablespoons of the tempeh bacon mixture. Toss gently to combine and taste, adjusting seasonings if necessary, adding a little more soy milk if too dry. Top with several grindings of pepper, the remaining tempeh bacon, the remaining Parmesan, and parsley. Serve immediately.

## paglia e fieno with peas ⓕ
makes 4 servings

*The name of this dish translates to "straw and hay"—named for the green and yellow colors of the noodles. Since fresh peas are not always available, this recipe calls for frozen baby peas, which are much sweeter and more tender than the larger frozen ones.*

⅓ cup plus 1 tablespoon olive oil

2 medium shallots, finely minced

¼ cup chopped tempeh bacon, homemade (page 525) or store-bought (optional)

1½ cups sliced white mushrooms

Salt and freshly ground black pepper

2½ cups frozen baby peas

8 ounces regular or whole wheat linguine

8 ounces spinach linguine

Vegan Parmesan or Parmasio (page 193)

**1.** In a large skillet, heat the 1 tablespoon of oil over medium heat. Add the shallots and cook until tender, about 5 minutes. Add the tempeh bacon, if using, and cook until nicely browned. Stir in the mushrooms and cook

until softened, about 5 minutes. Season with salt and pepper to taste. Stir in the peas and the remaining ⅓ cup oil. Cover and keep warm over very low heat.

**2.** In a large pot of boiling salted water, cook the linguine over medium-high heat, stirring occasionally, until al dente, about 10 minutes. Drain well and transfer to a large serving bowl.

**3.** Add the sauce, season with salt and pepper to taste, and sprinkle with Parmesan. Toss gently to combine and serve immediately.

## lemon-kissed linguine with garlicky white bean sauce ⓕ
makes 4 servings

*Creamy white cannellini beans, or white kidney beans, make this a satisfying and nutritious dish with a light sparkle of lemon.*

3 tablespoons olive oil

4 garlic cloves, minced

1½ cups cooked or 1 (15.5-ounce) can cannellini beans, drained and rinsed

2 tablespoons fresh lemon juice

½ teaspoon dried oregano

½ teaspoon dried basil

Salt and freshly ground black pepper

1 pound linguine

3 tablespoons minced fresh parsley

**1.** In large skillet, heat the oil over medium heat. Add the garlic and cook until fragrant, about 30 seconds. Add the beans, lemon juice, oregano, basil, and salt and pepper to taste and cook until heated through, about 5 minutes. Keep warm over low heat.

continues on next page

**2.** In a large pot of boiling salted water, cook the linguine over medium-high heat, stirring occasionally, until al dente, about 10 minutes. Drain well, reserving $\frac{1}{3}$ cup of the pasta water. Transfer pasta to a large serving bowl.

**3.** Mix the reserved pasta water into the bean mixture to make a smooth sauce. Add the bean mixture to the pasta along with the parsley and toss gently to combine. Serve immediately.

## farfalle with white beans and roasted asparagus ⓕ

makes 4 servings

*The delectable flavor of roasted asparagus is enhanced by the garlicky white beans and chewy pasta for a truly delicious one-dish meal.*

8 ounces thin asparagus, tough ends trimmed and cut into 1-inch pieces

¼ cup olive oil

Salt and freshly ground black pepper

3 garlic cloves, minced

1½ cups cooked or 1 (15.5-ounce) can cannellini beans, drained and rinsed

1 pound farfalle or other small pasta

10 fresh basil leaves, cut into thin strips

**1.** Preheat the oven to 425°F. Toss the asparagus pieces with 1 tablespoon of the oil and spread them on a lightly oiled baking sheet. Season with salt and pepper to taste and roast until the asparagus is tender, about 8 minutes. Set aside.

**2.** In large skillet, heat the remaining 3 tablespoons of oil over medium heat. Add the garlic and cook until fragrant, about 30 seconds. Stir in the beans and cook until heated through, about 5 minutes. Add the asparagus and keep warm over very low heat.

**3.** In a large pot of boiling salted water, cook the pasta over medium-high heat, stirring occasionally, until al dente, about 10 minutes. Drain the pasta and transfer to a large serving bowl. Add the bean and asparagus mixture, basil, and lots of freshly ground black pepper and toss gently to combine. Serve immediately.

## penne with chickpeas and rosemary ⓕ

makes 4 servings

*This is a quick and easy dish made with pantry ingredients. If you're not a fan of the distinctively fragrant rosemary, feel free to use a different herb, such as basil or parsley.*

2 tablespoons olive oil

3 garlic cloves, minced

2 teaspoons chopped fresh rosemary leaves or 1 teaspoon dried

1 (28-ounce) can diced tomatoes, drained

1½ cups cooked or 1 (15.5-ounce) can chickpeas, drained and rinsed

Salt and freshly ground black pepper

1 pound penne

**1.** In a large saucepan, heat the oil over medium heat. Add the garlic and rosemary and cook until fragrant, about 1 minute. Stir in the tomatoes, chickpeas, and salt and pepper to taste. Cook, stirring occasionally, for 15 minutes to allow the flavors to blend. Keep warm over very low heat.

**2.** In a large pot of boiling salted water, cook the rotini over medium-high heat, stirring occasionally, until al dente, about 10 minutes. Drain well and transfer to a large serving bowl. Add the sauce and toss gently to combine. Serve immediately.

# fettuccine with fresh figs and walnuts 🅕

makes 4 servings

*My mother always served homemade pasta and tomato sauce sprinkled with a fig, walnut, and bread crumb topping as part of my family's traditional Christmas Eve supper. I prefer to use a white sauce instead, so it doesn't compete with the tasty topping.*

¼ cup olive oil

⅓ cup dry bread crumbs

¼ cup minced fresh parsley

Salt and freshly ground black pepper

1 pound fettuccine

3 garlic cloves, finely minced

1 cup chopped fresh figs

¾ cup chopped toasted walnut pieces

2 cups Creamy Cashew Sauce (page 551)

1. In a medium skillet, heat 1 tablespoon of the oil over medium heat. Add the bread crumbs and stir until lightly browned, about 5 minutes. Transfer to a small bowl, mix in the parsley and salt and pepper to taste, and set aside.

2. In a large pot of boiling salted water, cook the fettuccine over medium-high heat, stirring occasionally, until al dente, about 10 minutes.

3. While the pasta is cooking, heat the remaining 3 tablespoons oil in a skillet over medium heat. Add the garlic and cook until soft and fragrant, about 1 minute. Do not brown. Stir in the figs and walnuts and keep warm over very low heat.

4. Drain the pasta well and transfer to a large serving bowl. Add the cashew sauce and the fig mixture and toss gently to combine. Top with the bread crumb mixture and salt and pepper to taste. Serve immediately.

# angel hair pasta with olive oil and garlic 🅕

makes 4 servings

*A good olive oil with lots of garlic and fresh ground black pepper are all you need for this classic dish, pasta* aglio-olio, *making it a perfect choice for when you're in a hurry. Use a quick-cooking pasta such as angel hair or cappellini, so dinner can be on the table in minutes. It is important not to let the oil get too hot, since you don't want the garlic to turn brown or it will taste bitter. This simple recipe can serve as the basis for infinite variations, from the minimal addition of minced parsley or crushed red pepper to more substantial options such as cooked beans or vegetables.*

½ cup olive oil

4 garlic cloves, finely minced

Salt and freshly ground black pepper

1 pound angel hair pasta

1. Put a large pot of salted water on to boil for the pasta. In a medium skillet, heat the oil over low heat. Add the garlic and about ½ teaspoon of salt and cook, stirring frequently, until the garlic is fragrant and softened, about 2 minutes. Be careful not brown the garlic. Add 1 cup of the hot pasta water and simmer over medium heat until the liquid reduces a bit. Keep warm over very low heat.

2. Add the pasta to the boiling salted water and cook over medium-high heat, stirring occasionally, until al dente, 3 to 4 minutes. Drain well and transfer to a large serving bowl. Add the sauce, season with salt to taste, and several grindings of fresh black pepper. Toss gently to combine and serve immediately.

## penne with white beans, red chard, and grape tomatoes 🅕

makes 4 servings

*Infused with the flavor of garlic and basil, this fresh-tasting dish is also pretty to look at, thanks to the tender chard leaves and sweet grape tomatoes. Creamy white beans add protein and substance for a satisfying one-dish meal.*

2 tablespoons olive oil

2 garlic cloves, finely chopped

1 medium bunch red chard, tough stems removed and coarsely chopped

Salt and freshly ground black pepper

1½ cups cooked or 1 (15.5-ounce) can white beans, drained and rinsed

1½ cups ripe grape tomatoes, halved lengthwise

1 pound penne

2 tablespoons finely chopped fresh basil, for garnish

1. In a large saucepan, heat the oil over medium heat. Add the garlic and cook until fragrant, about 30 seconds. Add the chard and season with salt and pepper to taste. Cook, stirring, until wilted, about 3 minutes. Add the beans and tomatoes, reduce heat to low, and simmer for 10 minutes, stirring occasionally. Taste, adjusting seasonings if necessary.

2. In a large pot of boiling salted water, cook the penne over medium-high heat, stirring occasionally, until al dente, about 10 minutes. Drain well and transfer to a large serving bowl. Add the sauce and toss gently to combine. Sprinkle with basil and serve immediately.

## inspired by spaghetti with white clam sauce 🅕

makes 4 servings

*Spaghetti with white clam sauce was one of my husband Jon's favorite meals before going vegan. Since I didn't want to be married to a "bivalve-mollusk-vegetarian," I came up with this vegan alternative to appease his craving for the dish. Cannellini beans and a touch of kelp powder are used in place of clams in the garlicky sauce and white miso paste adds saltiness. Kelp powder and miso are available at natural food stores, but if unavailable, use a scissors to finely snip a 3-inch square piece of nori and sprinkle it on the finished dish.*

¼ cup olive oil

4 or 5 garlic cloves, minced

1½ cups cooked or 1 (15.5-ounce) can cannellini beans, drained and rinsed

¼ cup dry white wine

1 cup vegetable broth, homemade (page 141) or store-bought

½ teaspoon dried basil

¼ teaspoon dried oregano

Salt and freshly ground black pepper

2 teaspoons white miso paste dissolved in ¼ cup hot water

½ teaspoon kelp powder

¼ teaspoon crushed red pepper

4 tablespoons minced fresh flat-leaf parsley

1 pound spaghetti

1. In a large saucepan, heat the oil over medium heat. Add the garlic and cook until fragrant, about 1 minute. Stir in the beans, wine, broth, basil, oregano, and salt and black pepper to taste and simmer for about 5 minutes. Stir in the miso paste, kelp powder,

crushed red pepper, and 2 tablespoons of the parsley and keep warm over very low heat.

2. In a large pot of boiling salted water, cook the spaghetti over medium-high heat, until al dente, about 10 minutes. Drain well and transfer to a large serving bowl. Add the sauce and toss gently to combine. Sprinkle with the remaining 2 tablespoons parsley and serve immediately.

# ziti with catalan vegetables

makes 4 servings

*Inspired by the Catalan vegetable dish* escalivada, *this dish pairs sturdy ziti with a rousing medley of grilled vegetables laced with capers, lemon juice, and crushed red pepper.*

1 medium eggplant
1 medium red bell pepper
1 medium yellow pepper
¼ cup olive oil
1 medium red onion, chopped
2 garlic cloves, minced
1 (14.5-ounce) can diced tomatoes, drained
1 tablespoon capers
1 tablespoon fresh lemon juice
Salt and freshly ground black pepper
1 pound ziti
2 tablespoons minced fresh parsley,
    for garnish

1. Preheat a grill or broiler. Grill the eggplant and bell peppers, turning so that they are evenly charred, 10 to 15 minutes. Place the charred vegetables in a bowl, cover, and set aside to cool. When cool enough to handle, remove and discard the charred skins from the vegetables. Dice the vegetables and set them aside.

2. In a large saucepan, heat 1 tablespoon of the oil. Add the onion and garlic, cover, and cook until softened, 7 minutes. Add the grilled eggplant and bell peppers, along with the tomatoes, capers, lemon juice, and remaining 3 tablespoons oil. Season with salt and black pepper to taste. Mix gently to combine. Simmer over low heat for 20 minutes to blend the flavors.

3. In a large pot of boiling salted water, cook the ziti, stirring occasionally, until al dente, about 10 minutes. Drain well and transfer to a large serving bowl. Spoon the sauce over the pasta, sprinkle with parsley, and serve immediately.

# austrian noodles and cabbage

makes 4 servings

*The popular Eastern European pairing of noodles and cabbage is known as* krautfleckerln *in Austria. It makes a tasty and satisfying meal that is especially good on a cold winter night, served with a side of cinnamon-laced applesauce and baked tempeh. To save the time of shredding savoy cabbage, use a bag of shredded cabbage (sold for coleslaw) instead.*

2 tablespoons olive oil
1 medium yellow onion, chopped
3 cups shredded savoy cabbage
Salt and freshly ground black pepper
12 ounces linguine, broken into thirds
2 tablespoons vegan margarine
1 teaspoon sugar
1 teaspoon caraway seeds

1. In a large skillet, heat the oil over medium heat. Add the onion, cover, and cook until soft

continues on next page

and golden brown, about 10 minutes. Add the cabbage and salt and pepper to taste. Cook, uncovered, stirring occasionally, until the cabbage begins to brown slightly, about 10 minutes. Cover, reduce heat to low, and continue cooking until cabbage is soft, about 10 minutes longer.

2. In a large pot of boiling salted water, cook the linguine, stirring occasionally, until al dente, about 10 minutes. Drain well and transfer to a large serving bowl. Add the cabbage mixture, margarine, sugar, and caraway seeds and toss gently to combine. Serve immediately.

# persian noodles and lentils

makes 4 servings

*Sweet and savory noodle dishes are found throughout the regions of the Mediterranean. This Middle Eastern dish is sometimes called* rishta, *for the thin noodles that are traditionally used to make it. You can easily substitute vermicelli or other thin pasta in its place. Fragrant spices such as coriander, cumin, and allspice, combined with lentils and tomatoes, are tossed with the noodles for a satisfying and flavorful meal.*

¾ cup brown lentils, picked over, rinsed, and drained
3 tablespoons olive oil
1 medium yellow onion, chopped
2 garlic cloves, minced
½ cup walnut pieces
½ cup pitted dates, halved
1 teaspoon ground coriander
½ teaspoon ground cumin
¼ teaspoon ground allspice
¼ teaspoon ground cayenne
1 (14.5-ounce) can diced tomatoes, drained
8 ounces vermicelli or other thin pasta, broken into thirds
Salt and freshly ground black pepper

1. In a saucepan of boiling salted water, cook the lentils until tender, about 45 minutes.

2. In a large skillet, heat the oil over medium heat. Add the onion and garlic, cover, and cook until soft, about 10 minutes. Stir in the walnuts, dates, coriander, cumin, allspice, and cayenne. Cook, stirring, for 2 minutes to bring out the flavors of the spices. Stir in the tomatoes and cook, stirring, until hot, about 5 minutes.

3. When the lentils are cooked, drain them and return to the pot. Stir in the tomato mixture and keep warm over very low heat. In a pot of boiling salted water, cook the pasta over medium-high heat, stirring occasionally until al dente, 5 to 7 minutes. Drain well and transfer to a large serving bowl. Add the lentil mixture and toss gently to combine. Season with salt and pepper to taste. Serve immediately.

# LASAGNA EIGHT WAYS

## classic tofu lasagna

makes 6 servings

*This recipe relies on tofu and vegan Parmesan to create a traditional-style lasagna. Served with a crisp green salad, this is a great way to feed a crowd.*

12 ounces lasagna noodles

1 pound firm tofu, drained and crumbled

1 pound soft tofu, drained and crumbled

2 tablespoons nutritional yeast

1 teaspoon fresh lemon juice

1 teaspoon salt

¼ teaspoon freshly ground black pepper

3 tablespoons minced fresh parsley

½ cup vegan Parmesan or Parmasio (page 193)

4 cups marinara sauce, homemade (page 194)
   or store-bought

1. In a pot of boiling salted water, cook the noodles over medium-high heat, stirring occasionally until just al dente, about 7 minutes. Preheat the oven to 350°F. In a large bowl, combine the firm and soft tofus. Add the nutritional yeast, lemon juice, salt, pepper, parsley, and ¼ cup of the Parmesan. Mix until well combined.

2. Spoon a layer of the tomato sauce into the bottom of 9 × 13-inch baking dish. Top with a layer of the cooked noodles. Spread half of the tofu mixture evenly over the noodles. Repeat with another layer of noodles followed by a layer of sauce. Spread the remaining tofu mixture on top of the sauce and finish with a final layer of noodles and sauce. Sprinkle with the remaining ¼ cup Parmesan. If any sauce remains, save it and serve it hot in a bowl alongside the lasagna.

3. Cover with foil and bake for 45 minutes. Remove cover and bake 10 minutes longer. Let stand for 10 minutes before serving.

## red chard and baby spinach lasagna

makes 6 servings

*Fresh red chard and baby spinach add color and nutrients to this family favorite recipe. Plus it's a great way to serve more greens to those who might otherwise not choose to eat them. If red chard is unavailable, substitute another variety of chard or use all spinach if you prefer.*

12 ounces lasagna noodles

1 tablespoon olive oil

2 garlic cloves, minced

8 ounces fresh red chard, tough stems removed
   and coarsely chopped

9 ounces fresh baby spinach, coarsely chopped

1 pound firm tofu, drained and crumbled

1 pound soft tofu, drained and crumbled

2 tablespoons nutritional yeast

1 teaspoon fresh lemon juice

2 tablespoons minced fresh flat-leaf parsley

1 teaspoon salt

¼ teaspoon freshly ground black pepper

3½ cups marinara sauce, homemade (page 194)
   or store-bought

¼ cup vegan Parmesan or Parmasio (page 193)

1. In a pot of boiling salted water, cook the noodles over medium-high heat, stirring occasionally until just al dente, about 7 minutes. Preheat the oven to 350°F.

continues on next page

2. In a large saucepan, heat the oil over medium heat. Add the garlic and cook until fragrant. Add the chard and cook, stirring until wilted, about 5 minutes. Add the spinach and continue to cook, stirring until wilted, about 5 minutes more. Cover and cook until soft, about 3 minutes. Uncover and set aside to cool. When cool enough to handle, drain any remaining moisture from the greens, pressing against them with a large spoon to squeeze out any excess liquid. Place the greens in a large bowl. Add tofus, the nutritional yeast, lemon juice, parsley, salt, and pepper. Mix until well combined.

3. Spoon a layer of the tomato sauce into the bottom of 9 × 13-inch baking dish. Top with a layer of the noodles. Spread half of the tofu mixture evenly over the noodles. Repeat with another layer of noodles and a layer of sauce. Spread the remaining tofu mixture on top of the sauce and finish with a final layer of noodles, sauce, and top with the Parmesan.

4. Cover with foil and bake for 45 minutes. Remove cover and bake 10 minutes longer. Let stand for 10 minutes before serving.

## roasted vegetable lasagna

makes 6 servings

*Thin layers of roasted vegetables lend their rich flavors to the lasagna, melding with the tofu filling and noodles. I like to use zucchini, eggplant, and red bell pepper in this lasagna because, not only are they the quintessential Italian vegetables, but also their flavors are especially enhanced when roasted. For added flavor, roast some chopped onion or garlic as well.*

1 medium zucchini, cut into ¼-inch slices
1 medium eggplant, cut into ¼-inch slices
1 medium red bell pepper, diced
2 tablespoons olive oil
Salt and freshly ground black pepper
8 ounces lasagna noodles
1 pound firm tofu, drained, patted dry, and crumbled
1 pound soft tofu, drained, patted dry, and crumbled
2 tablespoons nutritional yeast
2 tablespoons minced fresh flat-leaf parsley
3½ cups marinara sauce, homemade (page 194) or store-bought
¼ cup vegan Parmesan or Parmasio (page 193)

1. Preheat the oven to 425°F. Spread the zucchini, eggplant, and bell pepper on a lightly oiled 9 × 13-inch baking pan. Drizzle with the oil and season with salt and black pepper to taste. Roast the vegetables until soft and lightly browned, about 20 minutes. Remove from the oven and set aside to cool. Lower the oven temperature to 350°F.

2. In a pot of boiling salted water, cook the noodles over medium-high heat, stirring occasionally until just al dente, about 7 minutes. Drain and set aside. In a large bowl, combine the tofu with the nutritional yeast, parsley, and salt and pepper to taste. Mix well.

3. To assemble, spread a layer of tomato sauce in bottom of a 9 × 13-inch baking dish. Top the sauce with a layer of noodles. Top the noodles with half of the roasted vegetables, then spread half the tofu mixture over the vegetables. Repeat with another layer of noodles, and top with more sauce. Repeat layering process with remaining vegetables and tofu mixture, ending with a layer of noodles and sauce. Sprinkle Parmesan on top.

4. Cover and bake for 45 minutes. Remove cover and bake another 10 minutes. Remove from oven and let stand for 10 minutes before cutting.

**variation:** Instead of the zucchini and eggplant, use sliced and roasted portobello mushrooms and butternut squash along with the bell pepper.

# lasagna with radicchio and cremini mushrooms

makes 6 servings

*This sophisticated lasagna is made with woodsy cremini mushrooms and the slightly bitter Italian chicory known as radicchio. If cremini mushrooms are unavailable, substitute another type of fresh mushroom. Although it is made with a red sauce here, it is also good when paired with the Vegan White Sauce (page 551).*

1 tablespoon olive oil

2 garlic cloves, minced

1 small head radicchio, shredded

8 ounces cremini mushrooms, lightly rinsed, patted dry, and thinly sliced

Salt and freshly ground black pepper

8 ounces lasagna noodles

1 pound firm tofu, drained, patted dry, and crumbled

1 pound soft tofu, drained, patted dry, and crumbled

3 tablespoons nutritional yeast

2 tablespoons minced fresh parsley

3 cups marinara sauce, homemade (page 194) or store-bought

½ cup ground walnut pieces

1. In a large skillet, heat the oil over medium heat. Add the garlic, radicchio, and mushrooms. Cover and cook, stirring occasionally, until tender, about 10 minutes. Season with salt and pepper to taste and set aside.

2. In a pot of boiling salted water, cook the noodles over medium-high heat, stirring occasionally until just al dente, about 7 minutes. Drain and set aside. Preheat oven to 350°F.

3. In a large bowl, combine the firm and soft tofu. Add the nutritional yeast and parsley and mix until well combined. Mix in the radicchio and mushroom mixture and season with salt and pepper to taste.

4. Spoon a layer of the tomato sauce into the bottom of 9 × 13-inch baking dish. Top with a layer of the noodles. Spread half of the tofu mixture evenly over the noodles. Repeat with another layer of noodles followed by a layer of sauce. Spread the remaining tofu mixture on top and finish with a final layer of noodles and sauce. Sprinkle the top with ground walnuts.

5. Cover with foil and bake for 45 minutes. Remove cover and bake 10 minutes longer. Let stand for 10 minutes before serving.

# lasagna primavera

makes 6 to 8 servings

*In typical "primavera" style, this lasagna includes lots of veggies. The vegetables you use are not cast in stone—feel free to swap any of the set for others you may prefer, such as escarole, mushrooms, peas, fennel, or asparagus. I think the vegetables look best in this dish when cut into fairly small pieces, no more than ¼ inch in size.*

8 ounces lasagna noodles

2 tablespoons olive oil

1 small yellow onion, chopped

3 garlic cloves, minced

6 ounces silken tofu, drained

3 cups plain unsweetened soy milk

3 tablespoons nutritional yeast

⅛ teaspoon ground nutmeg

Salt and freshly ground black pepper

2 cups chopped broccoli florets

2 medium carrots, minced

1 small zucchini, halved or quartered lengthwise and cut into ¼-inch slices

1 medium red bell pepper, chopped

2 pounds firm tofu, drained and patted dry

2 tablespoons minced fresh flat-leaf parsley

½ cup vegan Parmesan or Parmasio (page 193)

½ cup ground almonds or pine nuts

1. Preheat the oven to 350°F. In a pot of boiling salted water, cook the noodles over medium-high heat, stirring occasionally until just al dente, about 7 minutes. Drain and set aside.

2. In a small skillet, heat the oil over medium heat. Add the onion and garlic, cover, and cook until soft, about 5 minutes. Transfer the onion mixture to a blender. Add the silken tofu, soy milk, nutritional yeast, nutmeg, and salt and pepper to taste. Blend until smooth and set aside.

3. Steam the broccoli, carrots, zucchini, and bell pepper until tender. Remove from heat. Crumble the firm tofu into a large bowl. Add the parsley and ¼ cup of the Parmesan and season with salt and pepper to taste. Mix until well combined. Stir in the steamed vegetables and mix well, adding more salt and pepper, if needed.

4. Spoon a layer of the white sauce into the bottom of lightly oiled 9 × 13-inch baking dish. Top with a layer of the noodles. Spread half of the tofu and vegetable mixture evenly over the noodles. Repeat with another layer of noodles, followed by a layer of sauce. Spread the remaining tofu mixture on top and finish with a final layer of noodles and sauce, ending with the remaining ¼ cup Parmesan.

5. Cover with foil and bake for 45 minutes. Remove cover, sprinkle with almonds, and bake 10 minutes longer. Let stand for 10 minutes before serving.

# tex-mex lasagna

makes 6 to 8 servings

*The zesty flavors of Tex-Mex cuisine are layered among chewy noodles for a hearty and substantial lasagna that will feed a hungry crowd. If you like vegan Cheddar cheese, sprinkle some on top of the lasagna when it is done baking and bake another few minutes to melt the cheese. Or top with some of Mylie's Secret Queso Dip (page 13).*

12 lasagna noodles

3 cups cooked or 2 (15.5-ounce) cans pinto beans, drained and rinsed

1 teaspoon dried oregano

1 teaspoon chili powder

½ teaspoon ground cumin

1 pound firm tofu, drained

1 (4-ounce) can chopped mild green chiles, drained

½ cup chopped green onions

¼ cup sliced pitted black olives

2 tablespoons minced fresh cilantro

Salt and freshly ground black pepper

4 cups tomato salsa, homemade (page 567) or store-bought

1. In a pot of boiling salted water, cook the noodles over medium-high heat, stirring occasionally until just al dente, about 7 minutes. Drain and set aside. Preheat the oven to 375°F.

2. In a large bowl, combine the pinto beans, oregano, chili powder, and cumin. Mash the beans well and incorporate the spices. Set aside. In a separate large bowl, combine the tofu, chiles, green onions, olives, cilantro, and salt and pepper to taste. Mix well and set aside.

3. Spread ½ cup of the salsa in the bottom of a 9 × 13-inch baking dish. Arrange 4 of the noodles on top of the salsa. Spread half of the bean mixture over the noodles, followed by another ½ cup of the salsa. Top with 4 noodles followed by the tofu mixture, spreading evenly. Top with 1 cup of the salsa, followed by the remaining bean mixture and top with the remaining noodles. Spread the remaining salsa on top.

4. Cover with foil and bake until hot and bubbly, 45 to 50 minutes. Uncover and let stand 10 minutes before serving.

# black bean and pumpkin lasagna

makes 6 to 8 servings

*This combination of ingredients may seem unusual for lasagna, but the result is a tasty merger of colors, textures, and flavors that is especially fun to serve around Halloween.*

12 lasagna noodles

1 tablespoon olive oil

1 medium yellow onion, chopped

1 medium red bell pepper, chopped

2 garlic cloves, minced

1½ cups cooked or 1 (15.5-ounce) can black beans, drained and rinsed

1 (14.5-ounce) can crushed tomatoes

2 teaspoons chili powder

Salt and freshly ground black pepper

1 pound firm tofu, well drained

3 tablespoons minced fresh parsley or cilantro

1 (16-ounce) can pumpkin puree

3 cups tomato salsa, homemade (page 567) or store-bought

½ cup coarsely ground pumpkin seeds (pepitas)

1. In a pot of boiling salted water, cook the noodles over medium-high heat, stirring occasionally until just al dente, about 7 minutes. Drain and set aside. Preheat the oven to 375°F.

2. In a large skillet, heat the oil over medium heat. Add the onion, cover, and cook until softened. Add the bell pepper and garlic and cook until softened, 5 minutes longer. Stir in the beans, tomatoes, 1 teaspoon of the chili powder, and salt and black pepper to taste. Mix well and set aside.

3. In a large bowl, combine the tofu, parsley, the remaining 1 teaspoon chili powder, and salt and black pepper to taste. Set aside. In a

continues on next page

medium bowl, combine the pumpkin with the salsa and stir to blend well. Season with salt and pepper to taste.

4. Spread about ¾ cup of the pumpkin mixture in the bottom of a 9 × 13-inch baking dish. Top with 4 of the noodles. Top with half of the bean mixture, followed by half of the tofu mixture. Top with four of the noodles, followed by a layer of the pumpkin mixture, then the remaining bean mixture, topped with the remaining noodles. Spread the remaining tofu mixture over the noodles, followed by the remaining pumpkin mixture, spreading it to the edges of the pan.

5. Cover with foil and bake until hot and bubbly, about 50 minutes. Uncover, sprinkle with pumpkin seeds, and let stand 10 minutes before serving.

# lasagna pinwheels

makes 4 servings

*If you love the taste of lasagna but dislike the struggle of getting it out of the pan, then this pretty and elegant-looking alternative will definitely appeal to you. The pinwheels look a bit like flowers, especially when arranged on a pool of sauce in groups of three per person.*

12 lasagna noodles

4 cups lightly packed fresh spinach

1 cup cooked or canned white beans, drained and rinsed

1 pound firm tofu, drained and patted dry

½ teaspoon salt

¼ teaspoon freshly ground black pepper

⅛ teaspoon ground nutmeg

3 cups marinara sauce, homemade (page 194) or store-bought

1. Preheat the oven to 350°F. In a pot of boiling salted water, cook the noodles over medium-high heat, stirring occasionally, until just al dente, about 7 minutes.

2. Place the spinach in a microwavable dish with 1 tablespoon of water. Cover and microwave for 1 minute until wilted. Remove from bowl, squeeze out any remaining liquid. Transfer the spinach to a food processor and pulse to chop. Add the beans, tofu, salt, and pepper and process until well combined. Set aside.

3. To assemble the pinwheels, lay the noodles out on a flat work surface. Spread about 3 tablespoons of tofu-spinach mixture onto the surface of each noodle and roll up. Repeat with remaining ingredients. Spread a layer of the tomato sauce in the bottom of a shallow casserole dish. Place the rolls upright on top of the sauce and spoon some of the remaining sauce onto each pinwheel. Cover with foil and bake for 30 minutes. Serve immediately.

# BAKED AND BEYOND

## penne baked with eggplant-tomato sauce

makes 6 servings

*The size of the eggplant you use, as well as how large or small you dice it, will depend on how much you want the eggplant to dominate the dish. Along the same lines, the decision to peel the eggplant or not is a personal one— peel it if you want the eggplant to "melt" into the dish or leave the skin on if you find the contrast in texture and color appealing. For convenience, this dish can be assembled ahead of time and refrigerated. Bring to room temperature before baking.*

12 ounces penne

1 tablespoon olive oil

1 medium yellow onion, chopped

1 medium eggplant, finely chopped

1 (28-ounce) can crushed tomatoes

¼ cup dry red wine

¼ cup chopped fresh flat-leaf parsley

1 teaspoon minced fresh marjoram
    or ½ teaspoon dried

Salt and freshly ground black pepper

½ cup vegan Parmesan or Parmasio (page 193)

¼ cup dry unseasoned bread crumbs

1. Preheat the oven to 375°F. In a large pot of boiling salted water, cook the penne over medium-high heat, stirring occasionally, until al dente, about 10 minutes. Drain well and set aside.

2. In a large skillet, heat the oil over medium-high heat. Add the onion, cover, and cook until softened, about 5 minutes. Add the eggplant, cover, and cook until soft, 12 to 14 minutes. Stir in the tomatoes, wine, parsley, marjoram, and salt and pepper to taste. Simmer, uncovered, until the liquid reduces, about 15 minutes.

3. In a large bowl, combine the cooked penne with the eggplant-tomato mixture and spoon it into a lightly oiled 3-quart casserole. In a small bowl, combine the Parmesan with the bread crumbs and sprinkle on top.

4. Cover with foil and bake for 30 minutes. Uncover and bake until lightly browned on top, about 10 minutes longer. Serve immediately.

## creamy cashew fettuccine with mushrooms and peas

makes 6 servings

*From the shallots and mushrooms sautéed in sherry to the rich and creamy sauce, this flavorful pasta dish is luxurious enough to serve guests, yet it's easy and economical to make. Best of all, it can be assembled ahead of time so there's no need for a messy kitchen when company arrives.*

1 tablespoon olive oil

4 medium shallots, minced

12 ounces white mushrooms, lightly rinsed,
    patted dry, and cut into ¼-inch slices

¼ cup dry sherry

1 cup frozen baby peas, thawed

Salt and freshly ground black pepper

12 ounces fettuccine, broken into thirds

3 cups Creamy Cashew Sauce (page 551)

½ cup finely chopped roasted unsalted cashews

¼ cup dry unseasoned bread crumbs

2 tablespoons minced fresh parsley, for garnish

1. In a large skillet, heat the oil over medium heat. Add the shallots and cook until soft,

continues on next page

about 5 minutes. Add the mushrooms and cook until softened, about 4 minutes. Add the sherry and cook, stirring, for 1 minute to cook off alcohol. Remove from the heat, stir in the peas, season with salt and pepper to taste, and set aside. Preheat oven to 375°F. Lightly oil a 9 × 13-inch baking dish and set aside.

2. In a large pot of boiling salted water, cook the fettuccine over medium-high heat, stirring occasionally, until al dente, about 10 minutes. Drain well and return it to the pot. Add the mushroom and pea mixture along with the cashew sauce. Mix gently to combine, then transfer to the prepared baking dish. Sprinkle the top with cashews and bread crumbs.

3. Cover with foil and bake for 30 minutes. Uncover and bake 10 until lightly browned on top, about 10 minutes more. Sprinkle with parsley and serve immediately.

# baked mac and cheeze

makes 4 to 6 servings

*This is the latest entry in my quest for a vegan mac and cheeze, the ultimate kid-friendly recipe, that comes close in flavor and texture to my mom's dairy-filled version. To make this a one-dish meal, add some chopped cooked spinach or another vegetable to the pasta mixture before baking.*

12 ounces elbow macaroni

3 tablespoons olive oil

½ cup minced onion

¼ cup all-purpose flour

¾ cup nutritional yeast

2½ cups plain unsweetened soy milk

1 tablespoon soy sauce

2 teaspoons white miso paste

1 teaspoon yellow mustard

1 teaspoon sweet paprika

½ teaspoon turmeric

½ teaspoon salt

⅛ teaspoon ground cayenne

3 tablespoons cornstarch

1 cup vegetable broth, homemade (page 141) or store-bought

½ cup dry unseasoned bread crumbs

1. In a pot of boiling salted water, cook the macaroni over medium-high heat until al dente, about 8 minutes. Drain and set aside. Preheat the oven to 375°F. Lightly oil a 3-quart casserole and set aside.

2. In a medium saucepan, heat 2 tablespoons of the oil over medium heat. Add the onion, cover, and cook 5 minutes, or until soft. Stir in the flour and the nutritional yeast and cook, uncovered, stirring, for 1 minute. Reduce heat to low, and slowly whisk in the soy milk. Continue to cook, stirring, until the mixture thickens. Stir in the soy sauce, miso, mustard, ½ teaspoon of the paprika, turmeric, salt, and cayenne.

3. In a small bowl, combine the cornstarch with the vegetable broth, stirring to blend. Stir the cornstarch mixture into the sauce and cook, stirring, until the sauce thickens. Taste, adjusting seasonings if necessary.

4. Combine the sauce and the cooked macaroni in the prepared casserole dish. Top with the bread crumbs and the remaining ½ teaspoon of paprika and drizzle with the remaining 1 tablespoon of oil. Bake until the mixture is hot and the crumbs are browned, about 30 minutes. Serve immediately.

# mac and chard

makes 4 to 6 servings

*If you're not a fan of nutritional yeast or soy, try this yeast-free, soy-free (and cheese-free) version of macaroni and cheese, with the lovely and healthful addition of chopped rainbow chard. (If unavailable, use another variety of chard or substitute spinach.) To make the sauce silky smooth, it is best to use a high-speed blender such as a Vita-Mix to help truly grind the cashews to a powder; otherwise the sauce may be a bit grainy, but tasty nonetheless. Like the preceding Baked Mac and Cheeze recipe (page 222), this one also makes a kid-friendly meal.*

12 ounces elbow macaroni

1 medium bunch rainbow chard, tough stems removed and chopped

3 tablespoons olive oil

½ cup chopped yellow onion

1 garlic clove, chopped

1 medium Yukon Gold potato, peeled and cut into ¼-inch slices

Salt and freshly ground black pepper

2 cups vegetable broth, homemade (page 141) or store-bought

½ teaspoon turmeric

¾ teaspoon sweet paprika

½ cup unsalted roasted cashews

1 tablespoon fresh lemon juice

1 teaspoon Dijon mustard

½ cup dry bread crumbs

1. In a pot of boiling salted water, cook the macaroni over medium-high heat until al dente, about 8 minutes. Drain well and set aside.

2. Steam the chard until tender, about 5 minutes. Set aside to cool. When cool enough to handle, squeeze any remaining moisture from the chard and set chard aside. Lightly oil a 9 × 13-inch baking dish and set aside. Preheat the oven to 350°F.

3. In a large saucepan, heat 2 tablespoons of the oil over medium heat. Add the onion, garlic, and potato. Season with salt and pepper to taste, cover, and cook until the vegetables are softened, about 10 minutes. Add 1 cup of the broth, the turmeric, and ½ teaspoon of the paprika and continue cooking, uncovered, until the vegetables are very soft. Remove from the heat and set aside.

4. Grind the cashews in a high-speed blender until ground to a fine powder. Add the onion and potato mixture, the remaining broth, lemon juice, mustard, and salt and pepper to taste and blend until smooth. Taste, adjusting seasonings if necessary.

5. Combine the sauce with the cooked macaroni and steamed chard and transfer to the prepared casserole. Sprinkle with the bread crumbs and remaining ¼ teaspoon paprika and drizzle with the remaining 1 tablespoon of oil. Bake until hot and golden brown on top, about 30 minutes. Serve immediately.

# baked pasta shells and broccoli

makes 6 servings

*Broccoli is believed to have originated in Rome, so pairing it with pasta seems like a natural fit in this homey casserole. Broccoli is a tremendous source of calcium and vitamin C— a half cup of broccoli contains about 40 milligrams of calcium and as much vitamin C as an orange. If you have trouble getting your kids to eat broccoli, this dish may do the trick.*

1 medium bunch broccoli, trimmed and cut into small florets
8 ounces small shell pasta
3 cups Mornay-Style Cheeze Sauce (page 552)
Salt and freshly ground black pepper
½ cup dry unseasoned bread crumbs
1 teaspoon sweet paprika

1. Steam the broccoli until just tender, about 5 minutes. Run under cold water to stop the cooking process and set aside. Preheat the oven to 375°F. Lightly oil a 9 × 13-inch baking dish and set aside.

2. In a pot of boiling salted water, cook the pasta over medium-high heat until al dente, about 8 minutes. Drain well and return to the pot. Add the steamed broccoli, the Mornay sauce, and salt and pepper to taste. Mix gently to combine, then spoon the mixture into the prepared baking dish and top with the bread crumbs and paprika.

3. Cover with foil and bake for 30 minutes. Uncover and bake until the top is lightly browned, about 10 minutes longer. Serve immediately.

# wild west pasta bake

makes 6 servings

*Picante sauce, pinto beans, and "wagon wheel" pasta team up for a zesty "wild west" version of macaroni and cheese. Use a mild picante sauce to make it child-friendly.*

1 tablespoon olive oil
2 garlic cloves, minced
3 cups cooked or 2 (15.5-ounce) cans pinto beans, drained and rinsed
1 tablespoon chili powder
½ teaspoon dried oregano
1½ cups bottled picante sauce
1 (14.5-ounce) crushed tomatoes
Salt and freshly ground black pepper
½ cup plain unsweetened soy milk
1 pound roulle or other small pasta
½ cup coarsely chopped roasted pumpkin seeds (pepitas)

1. In large skillet, heat the oil over low heat, add the garlic, and cook until fragrant, about 30 seconds. Add the beans, chili powder, and oregano. Stir in the picante sauce and tomatoes and mix well. Reduce heat to low and simmer for 10 minutes. Season with salt and pepper to taste and set aside. In a food processor, combine half of the bean mixture with the soy milk and process until well blended. Taste, adjusting seasonings if necessary. Preheat oven to 350°F. Lightly oil a 9 × 13-inch baking dish and set aside.

2. In a pot of boiling salted water, cook the pasta over medium-high heat, stirring occasionally, until al dente, about 10 minutes. Drain well and return to the pot. Add the remaining bean-tomato mixture and transfer to the

prepared baking dish. Top with the reserved pureed pinto bean mixture and sprinkle with the pumpkin seeds.

3. Cover with foil and bake for 30 minutes. Uncover and continue baking 10 minutes longer. Serve immediately.

# cheezy tomato macaroni

makes 4 to 6 servings

*Both fresh and canned tomatoes are used in this simple and tasty casserole made with the vegan Mornay-Style Cheeze Sauce on page 552. Like the other mac-and-cheese-style recipes in this chapter, this is a good one to make for children.*

1 tablespoon olive oil

½ cup finely chopped onion

2 garlic cloves, minced

1 (14.5-ounce) can crushed tomatoes

½ teaspoon dried oregano

½ teaspoon dried basil

Salt and freshly ground black pepper

8 ounces elbow macaroni

2½ cups Mornay-Style Cheeze Sauce (page 552)

1 ripe tomato, cut into ¼-inch slices

2 tablespoons vegan Parmesan or Parmasio
    (page 193)

1. In large skillet, heat the oil over medium heat. Add the onion and garlic, cover, and cook until soft, about 10 minutes. Stir in the tomatoes, oregano, and salt and pepper to taste. Reduce heat to low and simmer, uncovered, for 10 minutes. Set aside. Preheat the oven to 350°F. Lightly oil a 9 × 13-inch baking dish and set aside.

2. In a pot of boiling salted water, cook the macaroni over medium-high heat, stirring occasionally, until al dente, about 8 minutes. Drain well and return to the pot. Add the tomato mixture and the Mornay sauce and mix well. Transfer the mixture to the prepared baking dish. Top with the sliced tomato, fanning the slices around the perimeter of the casserole. Sprinkle with Parmesan.

3. Cover with foil and bake for 30 minutes. Uncover and continue baking until top is lightly browned, about 10 minutes longer. Serve immediately.

# pastitsio

makes 6 servings

*The classic Greek pasta dish is called* pastitsio *because it is a "pastiche" of several ingredients that are cooked separately and then combined to create one dish. This vegan version remains true to the "pastiche" idea, but it is made with chickpeas and spinach instead of the traditional ground meat.*

3 cups cooked or 2 (15.5-ounce) cans chickpeas, drained and rinsed

12 ounces elbow macaroni

1 tablespoon olive oil

1 medium yellow onion, chopped

2 garlic cloves, chopped

1 (10-ounce) package frozen chopped spinach, thawed

½ teaspoon dried oregano

½ teaspoon ground cinnamon

½ teaspoon dried mint

¼ cup dry white wine

2 cups marinara sauce, homemade (page 194) or store-bought

2 tablespoons chopped fresh flat-leaf parsley

Salt and freshly ground black pepper

2 cups Vegan White Sauce (page 551)

½ cup chopped pine nuts

1. In a food processor, pulse the chickpeas until coarsely chopped and set aside.

2. In a pot of boiling salted water, cook the macaroni over medium-high heat, stirring occasionally, until al dente, about 8 minutes. Drain well and set aside. Preheat the oven to 375°F. Lightly oil a 9 × 13-inch baking dish and set aside.

3. In a large skillet, heat the oil over medium heat. Add the onion and garlic, cover, and cook until softened, about 5 minutes. Stir in the spinach, chopped chickpeas, oregano, cinnamon, mint, and wine and simmer, uncovered, for 3 minutes. Stir in the tomato sauce, parsley, and salt and pepper to taste. Cook over low heat for 10 minutes to blend flavors.

4. Spread half of the cooked pasta in the prepared baking dish and spread the tomato-chickpea sauce on top. Spread the remaining pasta on top of the tomato-chickpea sauce and top the pasta with the white sauce. Sprinkle with pine nuts.

5. Cover with foil and bake for 30 minutes. Uncover and bake 10 minutes longer. Let stand at room temperature for 10 minutes before serving.

# pasta gratin with provençal vegetables

makes 4 to 6 servings

*Inspired by the vegetables for which the southern region of France is known, this light and delicious gratin mingles bite-size penne pasta with a tantalizing sauce studded with zucchini, bell peppers, artichokes, and tomatoes.*

2 tablespoons olive oil

3 medium shallots, minced

2 garlic cloves, minced

1 medium red bell pepper, chopped

1 medium zucchini, chopped

1 (28-ounce) can crushed tomatoes

½ teaspoon dried thyme

1 tablespoon minced fresh flat-leaf parsley

Salt and freshly ground black pepper

12 ounces penne or other small pasta

1 cup canned artichoke hearts, drained and rinsed

½ cup dry unseasoned bread crumbs

1. In a large skillet, heat the oil over medium heat. Add the shallots and garlic and cook until softened, about 3 minutes. Add the bell pepper and zucchini and cook until tender, about 10 minutes. Stir in the tomatoes, thyme, parsley, and salt and black pepper to taste. Finely chop the artichokes and add to the skillet. Reduce heat to low and simmer 10 minutes to blend the flavors. Preheat the oven to 350°F. Lightly oil a 2-quart gratin dish or casserole and set aside.

2. In a pot of boiling salted water, cook the penne, stirring occasionally, until al dente, about 10 minutes. Drain and return to the pot. Add the vegetable mixture to the pasta, mix well to combine, then transfer to the prepared dish.

3. Top with the bread crumbs, cover with foil, and bake until hot, about 30 minutes. Uncover and bake 10 minutes longer to brown the crumbs. Serve immediately.

# buckwheat noodles with cabbage and potatoes

makes 4 to 6 servings

*This robust dish, known as* pizzoccheri, *is made with buckwheat or whole wheat pasta, potatoes, and cabbage. It comes from the Lombardy region of northern Italy near the Swiss border. The addition of cashew sauce gives it extra richness. Savoy cabbage remains green when cooked and has a more subtle fragrance than regular green cabbage, allowing the other ingredients to really shine through. It's also delicious made with Swiss chard.*

2 tablespoons olive oil

2 large Yukon Gold potatoes, peeled and cut in ¼-inch slices

Salt and freshly ground black pepper

8 ounces savoy cabbage, shredded

2 garlic cloves, minced

4 fresh or dried sage leaves, chopped or crumbled

8 ounces buckwheat noodles or whole wheat fettuccine, broken into thirds

2 cups Creamy Cashew Sauce (page 551)

¼ cup vegan Parmesan or Parmasio (page 193)

1. In large skillet, heat the oil over medium heat. Add the potatoes and season with salt and pepper to taste. Cover and cook, stirring occasionally, until the potatoes begin to soften, about 10 minutes. Stir in the cabbage, garlic, sage, and salt and pepper to taste. Cover and cook until the cabbage and potatoes are soft, about 10 minutes. Set aside. Preheat the oven to 350°F. Lightly oil a 9 × 13-inch baking dish and set aside.

2. In a large pot of boiling salted water, cook the pasta over medium-high heat, stirring occasionally, until al dente, about 10 minutes. Drain well, reserving ⅓ cup of the pasta water. Return the pasta to the pot. Add the vegetable mixture to the pasta. Stir in the cashew sauce and the reserved pasta water and simmer over low heat for about 1 minute, stirring gently to blend the flavors. Taste, adjusting seasonings if necessary.

3. Transfer to the prepared baking dish and sprinkled with Parmesan. Cover with foil and bake until hot, about 20 minutes. Serve immediately.

## chard-stuffed manicotti with creamy cashew sauce

makes 4 servings

*This is a great dish to serve company because it can be assembled in advance and it has an opulent sophisticated quality to it, thanks to the rich cashew sauce and the tasty filling studded with bits of Swiss chard.*

12 manicotti

3 tablespoons olive oil

1 small onion, minced

1 medium bunch Swiss chard, tough stems trimmed and chopped

1 pound firm tofu, drained and crumbled

Salt and freshly ground black pepper

1 cup raw cashews

3 cups plain unsweetened soy milk

1/8 teaspoon ground nutmeg

1/8 teaspoon ground cayenne

1 cup dry unseasoned bread crumbs

1. Preheat the oven to 350°F. Lightly oil a 9 × 13-inch baking dish and set aside.

2. In a pot of boiling salted water, cook the manicotti over medium-high heat, stirring occasionally, until al dente, about 8 minutes. Drain well and run under cold water. Set aside.

3. In a large skillet, heat 1 tablespoon of the oil over medium heat. Add the onion, cover, and cook until softened about 5 minutes. Add the chard, cover, and cook until the chard is tender, stirring occasionally, about 10 minutes. Remove from the heat and add the tofu, stirring to mix well. Season well with salt and pepper to taste and set aside.

4. In a blender or food processor, grind the cashews to a powder. Add 1 1/2 cups of the soy milk, the nutmeg, the cayenne, and salt to taste. Blend until smooth. Add the remaining 1 1/2 cups soy milk and blend until creamy. Taste, adjusting seasonings if necessary.

5. Spread a layer of the sauce on the bottom of the prepared baking dish. Pack about 1/3 cup of the chard stuffing into the manicotti. Arrange the stuffed manicotti in single layer in the baking dish. Spoon the remaining sauce over the manicotti.

6. In a small bowl, combine the bread crumbs and the remaining 2 tablespoons oil and sprinkle over the manicotti. Cover with foil and bake until hot and bubbly, about 30 minutes. Serve immediately.

## spinach manicotti with white walnut sauce

makes 4 servings

*I've always loved pairing spinach with walnuts, whether in a salad, a sauté, or a pesto, so it didn't take me long to realize how great they would taste together in a manicotti dish. Here the spinach is part of the stuffing, while the walnuts are finely ground to become the basis for the rich-tasting sauce. I usually serve three stuffed manicotti per person, but you could stretch it further depending on what else you are serving.*

12 manicotti

1 tablespoon olive oil

2 medium shallots, chopped

2 (10-ounce) packages frozen chopped spinach, thawed

1 pound extra-firm tofu, drained and crumbled

¼ teaspoon ground nutmeg

Salt and freshly ground black pepper

1 cup toasted walnut pieces

1 cup soft tofu, drained and crumbled

¼ cup nutritional yeast

2 cups plain unsweetened soy milk

1 cup dry bread crumbs

1. Preheat the oven to 350°F. Lightly oil a 9 × 13-inch baking dish. In a pot of boiling salted water, cook the manicotti over medium-high heat, stirring occasionally, until al dente, about 10 minutes. Drain well and run under cold water. Set aside.

2. In a large skillet, heat the oil over medium heat. Add the shallots and cook until softened, about 5 minutes. Squeeze spinach to remove as much liquid as possible and add to the shallots. Season with nutmeg and salt and pepper to taste, and cook 5 minutes, stirring to blend flavors. Add the extra-firm tofu and stir to blend well. Set aside.

3. In a food processor, process the walnuts until finely ground. Add the soft tofu, nutritional yeast, soy milk, and salt and pepper to taste. Process until smooth.

4. Spread a layer of the walnut sauce on the bottom of the prepared baking dish. Fill the manicotti with the stuffing. Arrange the stuffed manicotti in single layer in the baking dish. Spoon the remaining sauce on top. Cover with foil and bake until hot, about 30 minutes. Uncover, sprinkle with bread crumbs, and bake 10 more minutes to lightly brown the top. Serve immediately.

# spicy eggplant and tempeh-stuffed pasta shells

makes 4 servings

*Large pasta shells are easier to fill than manicotti, and I think they look adorable nestled on dinner plates in groups of three. For variety, stuff the shells with one of the manicotti stuffings instead, such as the spinach stuffing in the previous recipe.*

8 ounces tempeh

1 medium eggplant

12 large pasta shells

1 garlic clove, mashed

¼ teaspoon ground cayenne

Salt and freshly ground black pepper

Dry unseasoned bread crumbs

3 cups marinara sauce, homemade (page 194) or store-bought

¼ cup vegan Parmesan or Parmasio (page 193)

1. In a medium saucepan of simmering water, cook the tempeh for 30 minutes. Drain and set aside to cool.

2. Preheat the oven to 450°F. Pierce the eggplant with a fork and bake on a lightly oiled baking sheet until soft, about 45 minutes.

3. While eggplant is baking, cook the pasta shells in a pot of boiling salted water, stirring occasionally, until al dente, about 7 minutes. Drain and run under cold water. Set aside.

4. Remove the eggplant from oven, halve lengthwise, and drain off any liquid. Reduce the oven temperature to 350°F. Lightly oil a 9 × 13-inch baking pan. In a food processor, process the garlic until finely ground. Add

continues on next page

the tempeh and pulse until coarsely ground. Scrape the eggplant pulp from its shell and add to the food processor with the tempeh and garlic. Add the cayenne, season with salt and pepper to taste, and pulse to combine. If the filling is loose, add some bread crumbs.

5. Spread a layer of the tomato sauce on the bottom the prepared baking dish. Stuff the filling into the shells until well packed.

6. Arrange shells on top of the sauce and pour the remaining sauce over and around shells. Cover with foil and bake until hot, about 30 minutes. Uncover, sprinkle with the Parmesan, and bake 10 minutes longer. Serve immediately.

## pumpkin ravioli with peas and caramelized shallots

makes 4 servings

*Ravioli made with a savory pumpkin filling is a classic dish in Lombardy. Accented with golden brown shallots and green peas, this makes a lovely late autumn meal. Because making ravioli is time-consuming, I prefer to prepare them in advance, then freeze them. To store, place the assembled uncooked ravioli on a lightly floured baking sheet in a single layer and freeze for one to two hours. When frozen, remove from the baking sheet and store in a tightly sealed freezer bag for up to two weeks.*

1 cup canned pumpkin puree
½ cup extra-firm tofu, well drained and crumbled
¼ cup nutritional yeast
2 tablespoons minced fresh parsley
Pinch ground nutmeg

Salt and freshly ground black pepper
1 recipe Egg-Free Pasta Dough (page 191)
¼ cup olive oil
2 or 3 medium shallots, halved longwise and cut into ¼-inch slices
1 cup frozen baby peas, thawed

1. Use a paper towel to blot excess liquid from the pumpkin and the tofu, then combine in a food processor with the nutritional yeast, parsley, nutmeg, and salt and pepper to taste. Set aside.

2. To make the ravioli, roll out the pasta dough thinly on a lightly floured surface. Cut the dough into 2-inch-wide strips. Place 1 heaping teaspoonful of stuffing onto 1 pasta strip, about 1 inch from the top. Place another teaspoonful of filling on the pasta strip, about an inch below the first spoonful of filling. Repeat along the entire length of the dough strip. Lightly wet the edges of the dough with water and place a second strip of pasta on top of first one, covering the filling. Press the two layers of dough together between the portions of filling. Use a knife to trim the sides of the dough to make it straight, then cut across the dough in between each mound of filling to make square ravioli. Be sure to press out air pockets around filling before sealing. Use the tines of a fork to press along the edges of the dough to seal the ravioli. Transfer the ravioli to a floured plate and repeat with remaining dough and sauce. Set aside.

3. In a large skillet, heat the oil over medium heat. Add the shallots and cook, stirring occasionally, until the shallots are a deep golden brown but not burned, about 15 minutes. Stir in the peas and season with salt and pepper to taste. Keep warm over very low heat.

**4.** In a large pot of boiling salted water, cook the ravioli until they float to the top, about 5 minutes. Drain well and transfer to the pan with the shallots and peas. Cook for a minute or two to mingle the flavors, then transfer to a large serving bowl. Season with lots of pepper and serve immediately.

# artichoke-walnut ravioli with sage and walnut sauce

makes 4 servings

*Walnuts in the filling and walnuts in the sauce add a double helping of rich nutty flavor as well as providing an excellent source of omega-3 essential fatty acids and other nutrients, including antioxidants. If that weren't enough of a reason to make these delectable dough pillows, the transcendent fragrance of sage makes it a shoo-in. Because the dough needs to rest, make it first before preparing the filling. If frozen artichoke hearts are unavailable, substitute canned ones (not marinated).*

⅓ cup plus 2 tablespoons olive oil

3 garlic cloves, minced

1 (10-ounce) package frozen spinach, thawed and squeezed dry

1 cup frozen artichoke hearts, thawed and chopped

⅓ cup firm tofu, drained and crumbled

1 cup toasted walnut pieces

¼ cup tightly packed fresh parsley

Salt and freshly ground black pepper

1 recipe Egg-Free Pasta Dough (page 191)

12 fresh sage leaves

**1.** In a large skillet, heat 2 tablespoons of the oil over medium heat. Add the garlic, spinach, and artichoke hearts. Cover and cook until the garlic is soft and the liquid is absorbed, about 3 minutes, stirring occasionally. Transfer the mixture to a food processor. Add the tofu, ¼ cup of the walnuts, the parsley, and salt and pepper to taste. Process until minced and thoroughly mixed. Set aside to cool.

**2.** To make the ravioli, roll out the dough very thinly (about ⅛ inch) on a lightly floured surface and cut it into 2-inch-wide strips. Place 1 heaping teaspoonful of stuffing onto a pasta strip, about 1 inch from the top. Place another teaspoonful of filling on the pasta strip, about 1 inch below the first spoonful of filling. Repeat along the entire length of the dough strip. Lightly wet the edges of the dough with water and place a second strip of pasta on top of first one, covering the filling. Press the two layers of dough together between the portions of filling. Use a knife to trim the sides of the dough to make it straight, then cut across the dough in between each mound of filling to make square ravioli. Use the tines of a fork to press along the edges of the dough to seal the ravioli. Transfer the ravioli to a floured plate and repeat with remaining dough and filling.

**3.** Cook the ravioli in a large pot of boiling salted water until they float to the top, about 7 minutes. Drain well and set aside. In a large skillet, heat the remaining ⅓ cup oil over medium heat. Add the sage and the remaining ¾ cup walnuts and cook until the sage becomes crisp and the walnuts become fragrant. Add the cooked ravioli and cook, stirring gently, to coat with the sauce and heat through. Serve immediately.

# tortellini with orange-scented tomato cream sauce

makes 4 servings

*Tortellini can be tricky to make, but if you have searched in vain to find vegan tortellini and simply crave the little stuffed dough rings, then getting your hands in the flour may be the only solution. You can also serve them with regular marinara sauce, but as long as you're going through the trouble of making them, you might as well make a special sauce, too.*

1 tablespoon olive oil

3 garlic cloves, finely minced

1 cup firm tofu, drained and crumbled

¾ cup chopped fresh parsley

¼ cup vegan Parmesan or Parmasio (page 193)

Salt and freshly ground black pepper

1 recipe Egg-Free Pasta Dough (page 191)

2½ cups marinara sauce, homemade (page 194) or store-bought

Zest of 1 orange

½ teaspoon crushed red pepper

½ cup soy creamer or plain unsweetened soy milk

1. In a large skillet, heat the oil over medium heat. Add the garlic and cook until soft, about 1 minute. Stir in the tofu, parsley, Parmesan, and salt and black pepper to taste. Mix until well blended. Set aside to cool.

2. To make the tortellini, roll out the dough thinly (about ⅛ inch) and cut into 2½-inch squares. Place 1 teaspoon of stuffing just off center and fold one corner of the pasta square over the stuffing to form a triangle. Press edges together to seal, then wrap triangle, center point down, around your index finger, pressing the ends together so they stick. Fold down the point of the triangle and slide off your finger. Set aside on a lightly floured plate and continue with the rest of the dough and filling.

3. In a large saucepan, combine the marinara sauce, orange zest, and crushed red pepper. Heat until hot, then stir in the soy creamer and keep warm over very low heat.

4. In a pot of boiling salted water, cook the tortellini until they float to the top, about 5 minutes. Drain well and transfer to a large serving bowl. Add the sauce and toss gently to combine. Serve immediately.

# gnocchi with red wine–tomato sauce

makes 4 servings

*Made with potatoes and flour, gnocchi are tasty little dumplings that take some extra time to make, but since they freeze well, you can make them ahead of when you need them. Freeze gnocchi by arranging them in rows on lightly floured baking sheets and place in the freezer for several hours or overnight. Once frozen, you can transfer them to freezer bags. They will keep for several weeks in the freezer.*

2 medium russet potatoes

1 tablespoon olive oil

3 garlic cloves, minced

1 (28-ounce) can crushed tomatoes

⅓ cup dry red wine

1½ teaspoons dried basil

1 teaspoon dried oregano

2 tablespoons minced fresh parsley

Salt

Freshly ground black pepper

1 cup all-purpose flour, plus more if needed

Fresh basil, for garnish (optional)

1. Preheat the oven to 450°F. Place the potatoes in the oven and bake until soft when pierced with a fork, about 1 hour.

2. In a large saucepan, heat the oil over medium heat. Add the garlic and cook until fragrant, about 1 minute. Do not burn. Stir in the tomatoes, wine, basil, oregano, 1 tablespoon of the parsley, and salt and pepper to taste. Reduce the heat to low and simmer for 20 minutes. Keep warm over low heat.

3. To make the gnocchi, combine the flour and 1 teaspoon of salt in a large bowl. Set aside. While the baked potatoes are still hot, carefully cut them in half, scrape the insides into a separate large bowl, and run them through a potato ricer or food mill to make them fluffy. Place the riced potatoes in the center of the flour along with the remaining 1 tablespoon parsley. Season well with salt and pepper to taste.

4. Gradually mix the flour into the potatoes to make a dough, adding more flour as needed. Knead the dough until smooth, about 4 minutes. Do not overwork the dough. Divide the dough into 4 pieces. On a lightly floured surface, using the palm of your hands, roll each dough section into a 1/2-inch-thick roll. Cut each dough roll into 3/4-inch pieces.

5. In a large pot of boiling salted water, cook the gnocchi until they float to the top, about 3 minutes. Retrieve the cooked gnocchi with a slotted spoon and place in colander to drain well. Transfer to a large serving bowl and add the tomato sauce, tossing gently to combine. Garnish with fresh basil, if using, and serve immediately.

# pierogi with fried onions
makes 6 servings

*Pierogi are like ravioli with a potato filling. I sometimes add some shredded cabbage when frying the onions and cook until soft and golden brown. It's important to cool the filling before assembly; otherwise the pierogi will fall apart. If not cooking right away, freeze the pierogi on baking sheets for 1 hour, then dust the frozen pierogi with a little flour, transfer to freezer bags, and keep frozen until needed.*

1 pound russet potatoes, peeled and cut into chunks
1 teaspoon salt
1/4 teaspoon freshly ground black pepper
2 tablespoons plus 1 teaspoon olive oil
1 medium yellow onion, minced
1 recipe Egg-Free Pasta Dough (page 191)

1. In a large pot of salted water, cook the potatoes until tender, about 20 minutes. Drain and return to the pot. Add the salt and pepper, mash the potatoes, and set aside. In a skillet, heat the 2 tablespoons oil over medium heat. Add the onion, cover, and cook until soft, about 7 minutes. Stir the cooked onion into the mashed potatoes. Mix well and taste, adjusting seasonings if necessary. Set aside to cool completely.

2. Divide the dough into 2 equal portions and roll out, one piece at a time, on a lightly floured surface until very thin, about 1/8 inch thick. Cut the dough into 3-inch-wide strips, and then cut across the strips to create 3-inch squares. Put 1 heaping teaspoonful of filling onto one half of each dough square. Moisten

continues on next page

the edge of each square with water and fold into triangles, folding one corner of the dough over the filling to press against the opposite corner. Using your finger, press all the edges together to seal well. Repeat with the remaining dough and filling. If there is filling left over, reserve it for another use. Press the tines of a fork along the edge of the pierogi to seal. Set aside on a lightly floured plate.

3. In a large pot of boiling salted water, cook the pierogi until they float to the top, about 3 minutes. Drain well. Brown the pierogi lightly in a large skillet with the remaining 1 teaspoon oil. Season with salt and plenty of pepper. Serve immediately.

# ASIAN NOODLES

## vegetable lo mein with tofu 🅕

makes 4 servings

*Since lo mein is traditionally made with Chinese-style egg noodles, I use linguine to make a vegan version. You could also use Shanghai noodles, if you can find them at an Asian market, which are made with wheat and water and contain no egg.*

12 ounces linguine

1 tablespoon toasted sesame oil

3 tablespoons soy sauce

2 tablespoons dry sherry, (optional; if not using, add an extra tablespoon of soy sauce and a pinch of salt)

1 tablespoon water

Pinch sugar

1 tablespoon cornstarch

2 tablespoons canola or grapeseed oil

1 pound extra-firm tofu, drained and diced

1 medium onion, halved and thinly sliced

3 cups small broccoli florets

1 medium carrot, cut into ¼-inch slices

1 cup sliced fresh shiitake or white mushrooms

2 garlic cloves, minced

2 teaspoons grated fresh ginger

2 green onions, chopped

1. In a large pot of boiling salted water, cook the linguine, stirring occasionally, until tender, about 10 minutes. Drain well and transfer to a bowl. Add 1 teaspoon of the sesame oil and toss to coat. Set aside.

2. In a small bowl, combine the soy sauce, sherry, water, sugar, and the remaining 2 teaspoons sesame oil. Add the cornstarch and stir to dissolve. Set aside.

3. In a large skillet or wok, heat 1 tablespoon of the canola over medium-high heat. Add the tofu and cook until golden brown, about 10 minutes. Remove from the skillet and set aside.

4. Reheat the remaining canola oil in the same skillet. Add the onion, broccoli, and carrot and stir-fry until just tender, about 7 minutes. Add the mushrooms, garlic, ginger, and green onions and stir-fry for 2 minutes. Stir in the sauce and the cooked linguine and toss to mix well. Cook until heated through. Taste, adjusting seasonings and adding more soy sauce if needed. Serve immediately.

# about asian noodles

Long before the first Italian twirled strands of spaghetti onto a fork, people throughout Asia were eating a variety of noodles made from rice, wheat, mung bean, and other flours. Although Asians don't create fanciful pasta shapes as do the Italians, they do enjoy a wide variety of thin and thick noodles, including rice sticks, buckwheat soba, udon, and somen.

Among the differences between Italian pasta and Asian noodles is the fact that Asian noodles are cooked until soft rather than al dente. In fact, many Asian noodles such as bean thread noodles and rice noodles do not require cooking, but can, instead, be soaked in water until tender. Unlike for their Italian counterparts, the cooking water for Asian noodles is not salted. Once cooked, the noodles are merely rinsed under the tap.

Noodles have an ancient history in Asia, where they are said to represent longevity for those who eat them. Perhaps it is for that reason that Asian noodles, with the exception of wontons and other dumplings, are long strands.

Here are some of the more common types of Asian noodles:

**bean thread noodles**—also known as "cellophane noodles," "mung bean noodles," and "glass noodles." Used throughout Asia, they are made from mung bean starch and are thin, colorless, and virtually flavorless, but they absorb surrounding flavors well. Usually sold dried.

**ramen**—instant noodles pressed into blocks. Usually sold with seasoning packets and combined with hot water to make a quick noodle soup.

**rice sticks**—a little thinner than fettuccine, usually flat but can be round. Difficult to break or separate when raw. Common in China, Thailand, Indonesia, and Vietnam. White when dry, they lighten in color as they cook becoming nearly transparent.

**rice vermicelli**—thin rice noodles used cold in salads or hot in soups and stir-fries. Sometimes fried in a large clump where they expand and turn crunchy.

**soba**—a nutritious noodle made from buckwheat flour and a delicacy of Japan. They come in long strands, like spaghetti, and are served hot in broth and cold with dipping sauce. Appealing flavor with a nutty brown color.

**somen**—thin, fine, and fragile Japanese wheat noodles made with a small amount of oil in the dough. Frequently used in cold dishes like salads or served cold with a dipping sauce.

**udon**—a Japanese wheat noodle with a firm, chewy texture. Usually the same width and thickness (can be round or square), available dried, fresh, and frozen. In Japan, udon is often served hot in broth in the winter and chilled with dipping sauce in summer.

# sesame soba noodles

makes 4 servings

*Soba are thin buckwheat noodles that are popular in Japan, traditionally served in a hot broth or cold with a dipping sauce. Stir-fry some diced extra-firm tofu and add it to the noodles and vegetables to make the dish more substantial and satisfying.*

12 ounces soba noodles

1 tablespoon toasted sesame oil

2 tablespoons canola or grapeseed oil

3 cups shredded napa cabbage or bok choy

1 medium yellow onion, halved and thinly sliced

2 medium carrots, thinly sliced

1½ cups snow peas, trimmed

2 teaspoons grated fresh ginger

3 tablespoons soy sauce

2 tablespoons toasted sesame seeds, for garnish

1. In a large pot of boiling water, cook the soba until tender, stirring occasionally, about 5 minutes. Drain well and transfer to a large bowl. Add the sesame oil and toss to coat. Set aside.

2. In a large skillet or wok, heat the canola oil over medium-high heat. Add the cabbage, onion, carrot, and snow peas and stir-fry until softened, about 5 minutes. Add the ginger and soy sauce and stir-fry 2 minutes longer. Add the cooked soba and stir-fry to combine and heat through. Sprinkle with sesame seeds and serve.

# pad thai 🅕

makes 4 servings

*Now you can make everyone's favorite Thai noodle dish in your own kitchen. While I never think homemade pad thai tastes exactly like the kind you can find in Thai restaurants, this is certainly close enough to satisfy those Thai noodle cravings when you want to make dinner at home. To make this a one-dish meal, add a few cups of lightly steamed broccoli florets to the stir-fry. Tamarind paste is available at Asian markets or online. If you can't find it, substitute 1 teaspoon molasses or brown sugar combined with 1 teaspoon lime juice.*

12 ounces dried rice noodles

⅓ cup soy sauce

2 tablespoons fresh lime juice

2 tablespoons light brown sugar

1 tablespoon tamarind paste (see headnote)

1 tablespoon tomato paste

3 tablespoons water

½ teaspoon crushed red pepper

3 tablespoons canola or grapeseed oil

1 pound extra-firm tofu, drained, pressed (page xiv), and cut into ½-inch dice

1 small red onion, quartered and cut into ¼-inch slices

4 green onions, minced

2 garlic cloves, minced

⅓ cup coarsely chopped dry-roasted unsalted peanuts

¼ cup chopped fresh cilantro

1 cup bean sprouts, for garnish

1 lime, cut into wedges, for garnish

1. Soak the noodles in a large bowl of hot water until softened, 5 to 15 minutes, depending on the thickness of the noodles. Drain well and rinse under cold water. Transfer the drained noodles to a large bowl and set aside.

2. In a small bowl, combine the soy sauce, lime juice, sugar, tamarind paste, tomato paste, water, and crushed red pepper. Stir to mix well and set aside.

3. In a large skillet or wok, heat 2 tablespoons of the oil over medium heat. Add the tofu and stir-fry until golden brown, about 5 minutes. Transfer to a platter and set aside.

4. In the same skillet or wok, heat the remaining 1 tablespoon oil over medium heat. Add the onion and stir-fry for 1 minute. Add the green onions and garlic, stir-fry for 30 seconds, then add the cooked tofu and cook about 5 minutes, tossing occasionally, until golden brown. Add the cooked noodles and toss to combine and heat through.

5. Stir in the sauce and cook, tossing to coat, adding a splash or two of additional water, if needed, to prevent sticking. When the noodles are hot and tender, mound them on a serving platter and sprinkle with peanuts and cilantro. Garnish with bean sprouts and lime wedges on the side of the platter. Serve hot.

# springtime rice noodles with coconut crème 🅕

makes 4 servings

*With its colorful vegetables and creamy sauce, this dish is like an Asian pasta primavera.*

*Any size rice noodles can be used, from thin rice vermicelli to flat rice stick noodles.*

12 ounces rice noodles
2 tablespoons canola or grapeseed oil
1 small red bell pepper, finely chopped
2 medium shallots, minced
2 teaspoons grated fresh ginger
¼ teaspoon crushed red pepper
1 (13-ounce) can unsweetened coconut milk
3 tablespoons soy sauce
2 teaspoons light brown sugar
1 cup cooked shelled edamame
4 green onions, coarsely chopped
1 medium carrot, shredded
1 cup frozen green peas, thawed
Salt and freshly ground black pepper
¼ cup chopped fresh cilantro, for garnish

1. Soak the rice noodles in a large bowl of hot water until softened, 5 to 15 minutes, depending on the thickness of the noodles. Drain well and rinse under cold water, and set aside.

2. In a medium saucepan, heat 1 tablespoon of oil over medium heat. Add the bell pepper and shallots and cook until softened, about 3 minutes. Add the ginger and crushed red pepper. Stir in the coconut milk, soy sauce, and sugar. Add the cooked edamame and keep warm over low heat.

3. In a large skillet or wok, heat the remaining 1 tablespoon oil over medium high heat. Add the green onions, carrot, and peas and cook 2 minutes. Season with salt and pepper to taste. Add the cooked noodles and sauce to the skillet and toss gently to combine and heat through. Serve sprinkled with cilantro.

# bok choy and ginger-sesame udon noodles 🅯

makes 4 servings

*For a flavorful variation, add some sliced shiitake mushrooms when you add the shallots and ginger.*

1 large head bok choy, cut crosswise into ¼-inch slices

12 ounces udon noodles

1 tablespoon toasted sesame oil

2 tablespoons tahini (sesame paste)

3 tablespoons soy sauce

2 tablespoons water

1 tablespoon mirin

2 tablespoons canola or grapeseed oil

½ cup thinly sliced shallots

1 tablespoon grated fresh ginger

¼ teaspoon crushed red pepper

1 tablespoon toasted sesame seeds

1. Lightly steam the bok choy until just tender, about 3 minutes. Set aside.

2. Cook the udon in a pot of boiling water until tender, stirring occasionally, 6 to 7 minutes. Drain, rinse under cold water, and place in a bowl. Toss with sesame oil and set aside.

3. In a small bowl, combine the tahini, soy sauce, water, and mirin, stirring to blend well. Set aside.

4. Heat 1 tablespoon of the canola oil in skillet or wok over medium-high heat. Add the shallots, ginger, and crushed red pepper and stir for 1 minute. Add the reserved bok choy, noodles, and sauce. Cook, stirring, until hot, 5 to 7 minutes. Serve at once sprinkled with sesame seeds.

# szechuan sesame noodles with asparagus 🅯

makes 4 servings

*Instead of linguine, make this dish with fettuccine, spaghetti, or an Asian noodle of your choice—virtually any noodle tastes great coated with this sweet and spicy sesame sauce. Chinese sesame paste has a more intense flavor than tahini because it is made from toasted ground sesame seeds. Tahini, however, is made from the untoasted seeds. Chinese black vinegar is an intensely flavorful vinegar made from glutinous rice. Look for Chinese sesame paste and black vinegar in Asian markets. For a flavor variation, use creamy peanut butter instead of sesame paste.*

12 ounces linguine or other noodles

12 ounces asparagus, tough ends trimmed and cut diagonally into 2-inch pieces

1 tablespoon toasted sesame oil

¼ cup Chinese sesame paste (see headnote)

2 teaspoons Asian chili paste

3 tablespoons soy sauce

1 tablespoon Chinese black vinegar (see headnote)

1 teaspoon light brown sugar, or more to taste

3 tablespoons water

2 tablespoons canola or grapeseed oil

3 green onions, chopped

1 teaspoon grated fresh ginger

1 tablespoon toasted sesame seeds, for garnish

1. Cook the linguine in a pot of boiling salted water until al dente, about 10 minutes. (If using another type of noodle, cook according to package directions.) During the last few minutes of cooking time, add the asparagus

to lightly cook. Drain well, rinse, and transfer the noodles and asparagus to a large bowl. Toss with the sesame oil and set aside.

2. In a small bowl, combine the sesame paste, chili paste, soy sauce, vinegar, sugar, and water and mix until well blended. Set aside.

3. In a large skillet or wok, heat the canola oil over medium-high heat. Add the green onions and ginger and cook until fragrant, about 30 seconds. Add the reserved noodles and asparagus. Stir in the reserved sauce and toss gently to combine until hot. Transfer to a large serving bowl and sprinkle with sesame seeds. Serve immediately.

# chinese noodles and broccoli with spicy black bean sauce ⓕ

makes 4 servings

*This recipe is fast, easy, and delicious. Kim Hammond, who tested this recipe for me, said, "Even my six-year-old (who usually hates everything except peanut butter) ate it and said it was delicious…that's high praise!" You can vary this recipe by adding additional veggies: edamame or sliced carrots are good choices. Chinese noodles are often made with egg, but some (usually called Chinese wheat noodles) are not. If egg-free Chinese noodles are unavailable, use linguine or spaghetti. Look for Chinese black bean sauce in Asian markets and well-stocked supermarkets.*

12 ounces egg-free Chinese noodles or linguine
3 cups broccoli florets
1 teaspoon toasted sesame oil
1 tablespoon canola or grapeseed oil
1 medium red onion, thinly sliced
1 garlic clove, minced
1 teaspoon grated fresh ginger
3 tablespoons black bean sauce (see headnote)
3 tablespoons soy sauce
1 teaspoon Asian chili paste
½ cup water
1 tablespoon cornstarch dissolved in
    2 tablespoons water
¼ cup chopped cashews, for garnish

1. Cook the noodles in a pot of boiling water until tender. (Dried Chinese noodles take about 5 minutes to cook; linguine takes about 10 minutes.) During the last few minutes of cooking time, add the broccoli florets to lightly cook. Drain well, rinse with cold water, and transfer the noodles and broccoli to a large bowl. Toss with the sesame oil and set aside.

2. In a large skillet or wok, heat the canola oil over medium-high heat. Add the onion and stir-fry until soft, about 5 minutes. Add the garlic and ginger and stir-fry until fragrant, about 30 seconds. Stir in the black bean paste, soy sauce, chili paste, and water. Simmer 30 seconds to blend flavors. Add the cornstarch mixture and stir to thicken. Add the cooked noodles and broccoli and toss to coat with sauce and heat through.

3. Transfer to a large serving bowl and sprinkle with cashews. Serve immediately.

# spicy sesame noodles with green beans 🅕

makes 4 servings

*Soba noodles are a good choice for this dish, but rice noodles or even linguine work great as well. You can also add extra veggies to this versatile stir-fry, instead of or in addition to the green beans.*

2 tablespoons tahini (sesame paste)

1 tablespoon sugar

3 tablespoons rice wine vinegar

¼ teaspoon crushed red pepper

¼ cup soy sauce

2 tablespoons water

8 ounces green beans, trimmed and cut into 1-inch pieces

12 ounces noodles of choice (see headnote)

2 tablespoons toasted sesame oil

1 tablespoon canola or grapeseed oil

1 medium red bell pepper, thinly sliced

2 garlic cloves, minced

2 teaspoons grated fresh ginger

1 tablespoon sesame seeds, for garnish

1. In a small bowl, combine the tahini, sugar, rice wine vinegar, and crushed red pepper until well blended. Stir in the soy sauce and water until blended. Set aside.

2. Steam the green beans until just tender, about 5 minutes. Remove and rinse under cold water. Drain well and set aside. Cook the noodles according to package directions. Drain well, rinse, toss with the sesame oil, and set aside.

3. In a large skillet or wok, heat the canola oil over medium heat. Add the bell pepper, garlic, and ginger and stir-fry until softened, about 1 minute. Add the steamed green beans, cooked noodles, and sauce and toss to combine; heat through.

4. Transfer to a large serving bowl and sprinkle with sesame seeds. Serve immediately.

# drunken spaghetti with tofu 🅕

makes 4 servings

*This spicy noodle dish is traditionally made with flat rice stick noodles, but I've been hooked on making it with spaghetti ever since my favorite Thai restaurant served it as a lunch special that way. If you can't find vegetarian oyster sauce, use an extra tablespoon of soy sauce and an extra pinch of sugar. If Thai basil is unavailable, substitute regular basil or cilantro. In either case, the dish will still turn out well, just not quite as "intoxicating," although the story I heard as to why these noodles are called "drunken" has to do with the spiciness of the dish, since hot chiles are said to be a hangover remedy.*

12 ounces spaghetti

3 tablespoons soy sauce

1 tablespoon vegetarian oyster sauce (optional)

1 teaspoon light brown sugar

8 ounces extra-firm tofu, drained and pressed (page xiv)

2 tablespoons canola or grapeseed oil

1 medium red onion, thinly sliced

1 medium red bell pepper, thinly sliced

1 cup snow peas, trimmed

2 garlic cloves, minced

½ teaspoon crushed red pepper

1 cup fresh Thai basil leaves

1. In a pot of boiling salted water, cook the spaghetti over medium-high heat, stirring

occasionally, until al dente, about 8 minutes. Drain well and transfer to a large bowl. In a small bowl, combine the soy sauce, oyster sauce, if using, and sugar. Mix well, then pour onto the reserved spaghetti, tossing to coat. Set aside.

2. Cut the tofu into ½-inch strips. In a large skillet or wok, heat 1 tablespoon of the oil over medium-high heat. Add the tofu and cook until golden, about 5 minutes. Remove from the skillet and set aside.

3. Return the skillet to the heat and add the remaining 1 tablespoon canola oil. Add the onion, bell pepper, snow peas, garlic, and crushed red pepper. Stir-fry until the vegetables are just tender, about 5 minutes. Add the cooked spaghetti and sauce mixture, the cooked tofu, and the basil and stir-fry until hot, about 4 minutes.

# singapore noodles with tempeh

makes 4 servings

*This popular Indonesian dish is also known as* bami goreng *or* mee goreng, *a counterpart to the rice dish* nasi goreng. *Tofu or seitan may be used instead of tempeh, if you prefer.*

8 ounces tempeh, cut into ½-inch dice

8 ounces rice vermicelli

1 tablespoon toasted sesame oil

2 tablespoons canola or grapeseed oil

4 tablespoons soy sauce

⅓ cup creamy peanut butter

½ cup unsweetened coconut milk

½ cup water

1 tablespoon fresh lemon juice

1 teaspoon light brown sugar

½ teaspoon ground cayenne

1 medium red bell pepper, chopped

3 cups shredded cabbage

3 garlic cloves

1 cup chopped green onions

2 teaspoons grated fresh ginger

1 cup frozen peas, thawed

Salt

¼ cup chopped unsalted roasted peanuts, for garnish

2 tablespoons minced fresh cilantro, for garnish

1. In a medium saucepan of simmering water, cook the tempeh for 30 minutes. Drain and blot dry. Soak the rice vermicelli in a large bowl of hot water until softened, about 5 minutes. Drain well, rinse, and transfer to a large bowl. Toss with the sesame oil and set aside.

2. In a large skillet, heat 1 tablespoon of the canola oil over medium-high heat. Add cooked tempeh and cook until browned on all sides, adding 1 tablespoon of the soy sauce to add color and flavor. Remove the tempeh from the skillet and set aside.

3. In a blender or food processor, combine the peanut butter, coconut milk, water, lemon juice, sugar, cayenne, and the remaining 3 tablespoons soy sauce. Process until smooth and set aside.

4. In a large skillet, heat the remaining 1 tablespoon canola oil over medium-high heat. Add the bell pepper, cabbage, garlic, green onions, and ginger and cook, stirring occasionally until softened, about 10 minutes. Reduce heat to low; stir in the peas, the browned tempeh, and the softened noodles. Stir in the sauce, add salt to taste, and simmer until hot.

5. Transfer to a large serving bowl, garnish with chopped peanuts and cilantro, and serve.

# korean noodle stir-fry

makes 4 servings

*Seitan takes the place of beef in this Korean noodle stir-fry called* chap chae. *It is traditionally made with Korean potato starch noodles called* dang myun, *which can be found in Asian markets. If unavailable, Chinese bean thread noodles will work well. For more heat, drizzle with a small amount of Asian chili oil when ready to serve.*

8 ounces dang myun (see headnote)
    or bean thread noodles

⅓ cup soy sauce

2 tablespoons toasted sesame oil

1 tablespoon sugar

¼ teaspoon salt

¼ teaspoon ground cayenne

2 tablespoons canola or grapeseed oil

8 ounces seitan, homemade (page 305)
    or store-bought, cut into ¼-inch strips

1 medium onion, halved lengthwise and
    thinly sliced

1 medium carrot, cut into thin matchsticks

6 ounces fresh shiitake mushrooms, stemmed
    and thinly sliced

3 cups finely sliced bok choy or other Asian
    cabbage

3 green onions, chopped

3 garlic cloves, finely minced

1 cup bean sprouts

2 tablespoons sesame seeds, for garnish

1. Soak the noodles in hot water for 15 minutes. Drain and rinse under cold water. Set aside.

2. In a small bowl, combine the soy sauce, sesame oil, sugar, salt, and cayenne and set aside.

3. In a large skillet, heat 1 tablespoon of the oil over medium-high heat. Add the seitan and stir-fry until browned, about 2 minutes. Remove from the skillet and set aside.

4. Add the remaining 1 tablespoon canola oil to the same skillet and heat over medium-high heat. Add the onion and carrot and stir-fry until softened, about 3 minutes. Add the mushrooms, bok choy, green onions, and garlic and stir-fry until softened, about 3 minutes.

5. Add the bean sprouts and stir-fry 30 seconds, then add the cooked noodles, browned seitan, and soy sauce mixture and stir to coat. Continue to cook, stirring occasionally, until the ingredients are hot and well combined, 3 to 5 minutes. Transfer to a large serving dish, sprinkle with sesame seeds, and serve immediately.

# noodles with spicy peanut sauce

makes 4 servings

*A lightly steamed green vegetable, such as broccoli, green beans, or snow peas, would make a good addition to toss in with the noodles for extra color and crunch, as well as nutrition.*

1 pound flat rice noodles or linguine

3 tablespoons toasted sesame oil

2 tablespoons canola or grapeseed oil

2 green onions, minced

2 garlic cloves, minced

1 teaspoon grated fresh ginger

2 teaspoons sugar

½ cup creamy peanut butter

3 tablespoons soy sauce

1 tablespoon rice vinegar

½ teaspoon Asian chili paste

⅓ cup hot water

1 small red onion, cut into ¼-inch slices

1 small red bell pepper, cut into ¼-inch slices

2 tablespoons minced fresh cilantro

2 tablespoons chopped unsalted roasted peanuts

1. If using rice noodles, soak them in hot water until softened, 15 to 20 minutes. If using linguine, cook them in a pot of boiling salted water until tender, about 10 minutes. Drain well, rinse with cold water, toss with the sesame oil, and set aside.

2. In a large saucepan, heat 1 tablespoon of the canola oil over medium heat. Add the green onions, garlic, and ginger and cook, stirring, for 1 minute. Add the sugar, peanut butter, soy sauce, rice vinegar, chili paste, and water. Stir until the sugar is dissolved and the mixture is smooth. Remove from the heat. Add additional hot water, if necessary, to achieve the desired consistency.

3. Heat the remaining 1 tablespoon canola oil over medium heat in the same pot in which you cooked the noodles. Add the onion and bell pepper and cook, stirring until softened, about 5 minutes. Add the cooked noodles and peanut sauce and toss to coat. Transfer to a large serving bowl, sprinkle with cilantro and peanuts, and serve immediately.

# indian double chickpea noodles 🅕

makes 4 servings

*Look for crispy chickpea noodles in Indian grocery stores. Called* sev, *these fried noodles are made from chickpea flour using a special noodle press. Cooked chickpeas are added to give this dish a double helping of chickpeas. Note: if* sev *are unavailable, this dish tastes great made with cooked angel hair pasta.*

1 tablespoon canola or grapeseed oil

2 garlic cloves, chopped

1 serrano or other hot green chile, minced

1 teaspoon grated fresh ginger

1½ teaspoons ground coriander

1 teaspoon ground cumin

½ teaspoon turmeric

1 (14.5-ounce) can crushed tomatoes

1½ cups cooked or 1 (15.5-ounce) can chickpeas, drained and rinsed

1 cup vegetable broth, homemade (page 141) or store-bought, or water

½ teaspoon salt

Freshly ground black pepper

3 cups crispy chickpea noodles, plus more for garnish (see headnote)

¼ cup chopped fresh cilantro, for garnish

1. In a large skillet, heat the oil over medium heat. Add the garlic, chile, and ginger and cook, stirring until fragrant, about 1 minute. Stir in coriander, cumin, and turmeric. Add the tomatoes, chickpeas, and broth. Bring to a boil, then reduce heat to low and simmer for 5 minutes, stirring occasionally. Season with salt and pepper to taste.

2. Add the noodles, gently stirring to mix them in. Cook just long enough to heat the noodles and barely soften them, about 1 minute. Transfer to a large serving bowl, sprinkle with noodles and cilantro, and serve immediately.

# MAIN DISHES

## BEANS

three-bean chili

four-alarm chili

chinese black bean chili

new world chili

jerk-spiced red bean chili

red bean and bulgur chili

red bean jambalaya

jamaican red bean stew

beans bourguignon

argentinean bean
and vegetable stew

african-inspired red bean stew

brazilian black bean stew

black beans and wild rice

black beans with serrano "aioli"

tuscan white beans
and broccoli rabe

three-bean cassoulet

maple baked beans

chickpea, tomato,
and eggplant stew

chickpea and vegetable curry

coconut-peanut chickpeas
and vegetables

tamarind chickpea stew

pomegranate-infused lentil
and chickpea stew

autumn medley stew

moroccan-spiced chickpea
and sweet potato stew

edamame donburi

yellow dal with spinach

three lentil dal

black bean and bulgur loaf

chickpea and vegetable loaf

millet-topped lentil
shepherd's pie

piccata-style cashew chickpea
medallions

black bean and walnut
croquettes

## GRAINS

vegetable fried rice

caribbean rice, squash,
and peas

wild rice and millet croquettes

green tea rice with lemon
snow peas and tofu

brown rice and lentil pilaf

savory beans and rice

mexican green rice and beans

italian rice with seitan
and mushrooms

creole rice and red beans

spanish rice and beans

brown rice with artichokes,
chickpeas, and tomatoes

coconut jasmine rice
and edamame

italian truck-stop
artichoke risotto

roasted winter squash risotto

barley risotto with asparagus
and mushrooms

barley and winter
vegetable stew

barley pilaf with carrots,
walnuts, and golden raisins

basic polenta

polenta with spicy tomato ragu

fried double-corn grits

couscous pilaf

couscous-chickpea loaf

quinoa and summer
squash pilaf

quinoa and chickpea pilaf
with orange and pistachios

quinoa and mixed
vegetable sauté

kasha with roasted sweet
potatoes and peas

herbed millet and pecan loaf

millet, chard, and white bean
casserole

millet and amaranth loaf

savory amaranth patties

## TOFU AND TEMPEH

soy-glazed tofu

cajun-style tofu

crispy tofu with sizzling
caper sauce

country-fried tofu with
golden gravy

orange-glazed tofu
and asparagus

tofu pizzaiola

"ka-pow" tofu

sicilian-style tofu

thai-phoon stir-fry

chipotle-painted baked tofu

grilled tofu with tamarind glaze

tofu stuffed with watercress
and tomatoes

tofu with pistachio-
pomegranate sauce

spice island tofu

ginger tofu with citrus-hoisin
sauce

tofu with lemongrass
and snow peas

double-sesame tofu
with tahini sauce

tofu and edamame stew

soy-tan dream cutlets

my kinda meat loaf

tempeh and vegetable stir-fry

teriyaki tempeh

barbecued tempeh

orange-bourbon tempeh

pineapple-glazed tempeh
and sweet potatoes

creole tempeh

tempeh with lemon
and capers

tempeh with maple, mustard,
and balsamic glaze

tempting tempeh chili

ginger-peanut tempeh

tempeh cacciatore

indonesian tempeh
in coconut gravy

tempeh with potatoes
and cabbage

southern succotash stew

baked jambalaya casserole

tempeh and sweet potato
shepherd's pie

## SEITAN

basic simmered seitan

stuffed baked seitan roast

seitan pot roast

almost one-dish thanksgiving
dinner

seitan milanese with panko
and lemon

seitan with dried plums,
olives, and capers

sesame-crusted seitan

pan-seared seitan
with artichokes and olives

seitan with ancho-chipotle
sauce

seitan piccata

three-seed seitan

fajitas without borders

seitan with green apple relish

seitan and broccoli-shiitake
stir-fry

seitan brochettes
with peaches and herbs

grilled seitan and
vegetable kabobs

seitan en croute

seitan and potato torta

seitan noodle casserole

rustic cottage pie

seitan with spinach
and sun-dried tomatoes

seitan and scalloped potatoes
casserole

seitan and chickpea stew

## VEGETABLES

sesame-baked vegetables

ratatouille

vegetable paella

three-green tian

eggplant paprikash

chard and new potato gratin
with herbes de provence

sesame spinach noodle pie

broccoli and white beans
with potatoes and walnuts

eggplant with pomegranate
walnut sauce

garden vegetable stew

mediterranean vegetable stew

potato and artichoke gratin
with spinach and pine nuts

artichoke-walnut tart

mushroom goulash

green bean and mushroom
stroganoff

tamarind eggplant with
bell peppers and mango

stir-fried curried vegetables

spinach soufflé

roasted cauliflower and shallots
with millet

artichoke and chickpea loaf

grilled vegetable skewers
with mop sauce

pastry-wrapped portobellos

spinach, white bean,
and pine nut strudel

roasted vegetable strudel

indonesian vegetable stew

moroccan vegetable stew

## STUFFED VEGETABLES

bell peppers stuffed
with white beans, mushrooms,
and walnuts

quinoa and pinto bean–stuffed
peppers

millet-stuffed bell peppers
with watercress and orange

cabbage rolls stuffed
with bulgur and chickpeas

sweet-and-sour kasha
cabbage rolls

stuffed eggplant rolls

orzo-and-spinach–stuffed
eggplant

couscous-stuffed eggplant

potato-and-artichoke–stuffed
portobello mushrooms

peruvian-inspired stuffed
potatoes

potatoes stuffed
with fennel and peas

great stuffed pumpkin

buttercup squash stuffed
with pistachio-apricot rice

fruit-studded millet-stuffed
acorn squash

black bean, rice, and
mango-stuffed squash

sesame-stuffed spaghetti
squash

three sisters stuffed squash

winter squash with forbidden
rice stuffing

walnut-and-cranberry–stuffed
sweet potatoes

sicilian stuffed tomatoes

spaghetti-stuffed tomatoes

quinoa-stuffed zucchini

pesto-and-ditalini–stuffed
zucchini

This chapter will give you enough main dish ideas to feed you and your family and friends for months without any repeats. Included are satisfying recipes for hearty stews and chilis such as Brazilian Black Bean Stew (page 255) and Four-Alarm Chili (page 249), numerous gratins and casseroles such as Chard and New Potato Gratin with Herbes de Provence (page 322) and Three-Green Tian (page 320), lightning quick sautés and stir-fries such as Seitan Piccata (page 310) and Thai-Phoon Stir-Fry (page 288), as well as dishes that are stuffed, baked, and grilled, including Artichoke and Chickpea Loaf (page 330), Grilled Vegetable Skewers with Mop Sauce (page 330), and Winter Squash with Forbidden Rice Stuffing (page 346).

These satisfying recipes feature a variety of grains and beans, as well as delicious protein-rich meat alternatives such as tofu, tempeh, and seitan. As explained in the Introduction (page xiv), tofu, tempeh, and seitan are three of the most nutritious sources of protein. They are also among the most popular because they lend themselves to a number of recipes, including ones that traditionally use meat, thus making it possible to enjoy familiar favorite dishes with plant-based ingredients. This trio of ingredients can be sautéed, stir-fried, grilled, baked, and braised. Seitan can even be stuffed and made into a roast. All three can be chopped or ground and used in chilis, soups, salads, and stews. Enjoying meals prepared with tofu, tempeh, and seitan, along with beans, whole grains, and produce, ensures a well-balanced diet rich in protein and other nutrients.

This chapter is organized by the main dish's primary protein source. While there are other main dish recipes in other chapters in this book that are organized by type, such as the Soups or Pasta and Noodles chapters, in this chapter you will find recipes organized by ingredient, such as beans, grains, tofu, tempeh, seitan, or vegetables. This can be helpful if, for example, you have some tofu or tempeh in the refrigerator and are looking for an interesting way to prepare it or if you've never tried seitan and want to see the many ways it can be used in recipes.

# BEANS

## three-bean chili

makes 4 servings

*I love the color contrast of the red, black, and white beans in this robust chili. Serve over rice or noodles and top with corn kernels, diced avocado, or your favorite topping. Accompany with a salad to complete the meal.*

1 tablespoon olive oil
1 medium yellow onion, chopped
3 garlic cloves, minced
1 (28-ounce) can crushed tomatoes
1 (4-ounce) can chopped mild green chiles, drained
1 cup water
3 tablespoons chili powder
1 canned chipotle chile in adobo, minced
1 teaspoon ground cumin
½ teaspoon dried marjoram
½ teaspoon sugar
1½ cups cooked or 1 (15.5-ounce) can black beans, drained and rinsed
1½ cups cooked or 1 (15.5-ounce) can Great Northern or other white beans, drained and rinsed
1½ cups cooked or 1 (15.5-ounce) can dark red kidney beans, drained and rinsed
Salt and freshly ground black pepper

1. In a large saucepan, heat the oil over medium heat. Add the onion and garlic, cover, and cook until softened, about 7 minutes.

2. Add the tomatoes, green chiles, water, chili powder, chipotle, cumin, marjoram, and sugar. Stir in the black beans, Great Northern beans, and kidney beans and season with salt and pepper to taste. Bring to a boil, then reduce the heat to low and simmer, uncovered, stirring occasionally, for 45 minutes.

3. Uncover, and cook an additional 10 minutes to allow flavors to develop and the chili to thicken. Serve immediately.

## four-alarm chili

makes 4 servings

*Depending on your heat tolerance, you can make this chili more or less alarming. If you like it really hot, use two chiles and a hot chili powder; to tone it down, omit the chiles, use a medium chili powder, and add the cayenne at your own discretion.*

1 tablespoon olive oil
1 medium yellow onion, chopped
1 or 2 serrano chiles, seeded and minced
3 garlic cloves, minced
1 (28-ounce) can crushed tomatoes
1 cup water
3 tablespoons chili powder
½ teaspoon dried marjoram
¼ teaspoon ground cayenne
Salt and freshly ground black pepper
1½ cups cooked or 1 (15.5-ounce) can pinto beans, drained and rinsed
3 cups cooked or 2 (15.5-ounce) cans dark red kidney beans, drained and rinsed

1. In a large saucepan, heat the oil over medium heat. Add the onion, chiles, and garlic and cook, covered, until softened, about 10 minutes.

2. Add tomatoes, water, chili powder, marjoram, cayenne, and salt and pepper to taste. Bring to a boil, then reduce the heat to low, add the pinto beans and kidney beans, and simmer, covered, stirring occasionally, for 30 minutes.

3. Taste, adjusting seasonings if necessary, and simmer, uncovered, about 15 minutes longer. Serve immediately.

# chinese black bean chili

makes 4 servings

*Garlicky Chinese black bean sauce is a salty intense seasoning that adds a rich layer of flavor to this satisfying and unusual chili. Look for it in Asian markets or gourmet grocers. This chili is good served over freshly cooked long-grain rice to complement this Asian-style dish.*

1 tablespoon olive oil

1 medium yellow onion, finely chopped

2 medium carrots, finely chopped

1 teaspoon grated fresh ginger

2 tablespoons chili powder

1 teaspoon sugar

1 (28-ounce) can diced tomatoes, undrained

½ cup Chinese black bean sauce

¾ cup water

4½ cups cooked or 3 (15.5-ounce) cans black beans, drained and rinsed

Salt and freshly ground black pepper

2 tablespoons minced green onion, for garnish

1. In a large pot, heat the oil over medium heat. Add the onion and carrot. Cover and cook, until softened, about 10 minutes.

2. Stir in the ginger, chili powder, and sugar. Add the tomatoes, black bean sauce, and water. Stir in the black beans and season with salt and pepper to taste.

3. Bring to a boil, then reduce the heat to medium and simmer, covered, until the vegetables are tender, about 30 minutes. Simmer, uncovered, 10 to 15 minutes longer. Serve immediately, garnished with the green onion.

# new world chili

makes 4 servings

*This chili incorporates ingredients that early explorers discovered in the New World from pinto beans and squash to corn, tomatoes, and lima beans. The chipotle chile adds a smoky heat. Portion and freeze remaining chipotle in adobo sauce for future use. Sprinkle with diced avocado and chopped red onion for a flavorful garnish.*

1 small butternut squash, peeled, halved, and seeded

1 tablespoon olive oil

1 medium onion, chopped

3 cups mild tomato salsa, homemade (page 567) or store-bought

3 cups cooked or 2 (15.5-ounce) cans pinto beans, drained and rinsed

1 cup frozen lima beans

1 cup fresh or frozen corn kernels

1 canned chipotle chile in adobo, minced

1 cup water

3 tablespoons chili powder

½ teaspoon ground allspice

½ teaspoon sugar

Salt and freshly ground black pepper

1. Cut the squash into ¼-inch dice and set aside. In a large saucepan, heat the oil over medium heat. Add the onion and squash, cover, and cook, until softened, about 10 minutes.

2. Add the salsa, pinto beans, lima beans, corn, and chipotle chile. Stir in the water, chili powder, allspice, sugar, and salt and black pepper to taste. Bring to a boil, then reduce the heat to medium and simmer, covered, until the vegetables are tender, about 45 minutes.

3. Uncover and simmer about 10 minutes longer. Serve immediately.

# jerk-spiced red bean chili

makes 4 servings

*Spices found in jerk seasoning blends combine with barbecue sauce to give a spicy-sweet flavor to this hearty chili. Make it hot or mild according to your preference by adjusting the amount of cayenne and choosing mild or hot green chiles.*

1 tablespoon olive oil

1 medium onion, chopped

8 ounces seitan, homemade (page 305) or store-bought, chopped

3 cups cooked or 2 (15.5-ounce) cans dark red kidney beans, drained and rinsed

1 (14.5-ounce) can crushed tomatoes

1 (14.5-ounce) can diced tomatoes, drained

1 (4-ounce) can chopped mild or hot green chiles, drained

½ cup barbecue sauce, homemade (page 549) or store-bought

1 cup water

1 tablespoon soy sauce

1 tablespoon chili powder

1 teaspoon ground cumin

1 teaspoon ground allspice

1 teaspoon sugar

½ teaspoon ground oregano

¼ teaspoon ground cayenne

½ teaspoon salt

¼ teaspoon freshly ground black pepper

1. In a large pot, heat the oil over medium heat. Add the onion and seitan. Cover and cook, until the onion is softened, about 10 minutes.

2. Stir in the kidney beans, crushed tomatoes, diced tomatoes, and chiles. Stir in the barbecue sauce, water, soy sauce, chili powder, cumin, allspice, sugar, oregano, cayenne, salt, and black pepper.

3. Bring to a boil, then reduce the heat to medium and simmer, covered, until the vegetables are tender, about 45 minutes. Uncover and simmer about 10 minutes longer. Serve immediately.

# red bean and bulgur chili

makes 4 servings

*This chili combines dark red kidney beans with bulgur, a sturdy grain that gives the chili a delicious flavor and pleasing texture.*

2 tablespoons olive oil

1 medium red onion, chopped

1 medium red bell pepper, chopped

3 garlic cloves, minced

3 tablespoons chili powder

½ teaspoon dried oregano

1 (14.5-ounce) can diced tomatoes, drained

2 cups tomato salsa, homemade (page 567) or store-bought

3 cups cooked or 2 (15.5-ounce) cans dark red kidney beans, rinsed and drained

1 cup water

1 cup bulgur

1 (4-ounce) can chopped mild green chiles, drained

½ teaspoon salt

1. In a large saucepan, heat the oil over medium heat. Add the onion and bell pepper, cover, and cook until softened, about 7 minutes.

2. Stir in the garlic, chili powder, and oregano, and cook, uncovered, until fragrant, 1 minute. Add the tomatoes, salsa, beans, water, bulgur, chiles, and salt.

3. Cover and simmer, stirring occasionally, until the bulgur is tender and the chili is thick and flavorful, about 45 minutes. Serve immediately.

# red bean jambalaya

makes 4 servings

*Red beans are a popular Creole ingredient, so I think they are the natural alternative to meat in this vegan jambalaya, the quintessential Creole dish that combines rice with a spicy tomato-based stew. For a hearty addition, sauté some diced seitan or sliced vegan sausage links, and add to the jambalaya during the last few minutes of cooking.*

1 tablespoon olive oil

1 medium yellow onion, chopped

2 celery ribs, chopped

1 medium green bell pepper, chopped

3 garlic cloves, minced

1 cup long-grain rice

3 cups cooked or 2 (15.5-ounce) cans dark red kidney beans, drained and rinsed

1 (14.5-ounce) can diced tomatoes, drained

1 (14.5-ounce) can crushed tomatoes

1 (4-ounce) can mild green chiles, drained

1 teaspoon dried thyme

½ teaspoon dried marjoram

1 teaspoon salt

Freshly ground black pepper

2½ cups vegetable broth, homemade (page 141) or store-bought, or water

1 tablespoon chopped fresh parsley, for garnish

Tabasco sauce (optional)

1. In a large saucepan, heat the oil over medium heat. Add the onion, celery, bell pepper, and garlic. Cover and cook until softened, about 7 minutes.

2. Stir in the rice, beans, diced tomatoes, crushed tomatoes, chiles, thyme, marjoram, salt, and black pepper to taste. Add the broth, cover, and simmer until the vegetables are soft and the rice is tender, about 45 minutes.

3. Sprinkle with parsley and a splash of Tabasco, if using, and serve.

# jamaican red bean stew

makes 4 servings

*This hearty stew will fill your home with the fragrant scent of the flavors of Jamaica. It is especially good served over rice or couscous, since the luscious sauce in the stew will be absorbed by the grain.*

1 tablespoon olive oil

1 medium yellow onion, chopped

2 large carrots, cut into ¼-inch slices

2 garlic cloves, minced

1 large sweet potato, peeled and cut into ¼-inch dice

¼ teaspoon crushed red pepper

3 cups cooked or 2 (15.5-ounce) cans dark red kidney beans, drained and rinsed

1 (14.5-ounce) can diced tomatoes, drained

1 teaspoon hot or mild curry powder

1 teaspoon dried thyme

¼ teaspoon ground allspice

½ teaspoon salt

¼ teaspoon freshly ground black pepper

½ cup water

1 (13.5-ounce) can unsweetened coconut milk

1. In a large saucepan, heat the oil over medium heat. Add the onion and carrots, cover, and cook until softened, 5 minutes.

2. Add the garlic, sweet potato, and crushed red pepper. Stir in the kidney beans, tomatoes, curry powder, thyme, allspice, salt, and black pepper.

3. Stir in the water, cover, and simmer until the vegetables are tender, about 30 minutes. Stir in the coconut milk and simmer, uncovered, for 10 minutes to blend flavors and thicken the sauce. If a thicker sauce is desired, puree some of the vegetables with an immersion blender. Serve immediately.

# beans bourguignon

makes 4 servings

*The common kidney bean gets star treatment in this oh-so-French stew traditionally made with lots of red wine and thickened with a vegan* beurre manie, *a French term meaning "kneaded butter." In this version it's vegan margarine that gets kneaded with the flour. The stew is, of course, best served with crusty French bread and dry red wine, preferably from the Burgundy region of France, since* Bourguignon *means "as prepared in Burgundy."*

2 tablespoons vegan margarine

2 tablespoons all-purpose flour

1 tablespoon olive oil

3 medium shallots, cut into ½-inch dice

4 medium carrots, cut diagonally into ¼-inch slices

2 garlic cloves, minced

12 ounces white mushrooms, lightly rinsed, patted dry, and quartered

1 teaspoon dried thyme

1 bay leaf

1 cup canned crushed tomatoes

½ cup vegetable broth, homemade (page 141) or store-bought, or water

1 cup dry red wine

3 cups cooked or 2 (15.5-ounce) cans dark red kidney beans, drained and rinsed

Salt and freshly ground black pepper

1. In a small bowl, combine the margarine and flour and knead until incorporated. Refrigerate until needed.

2. In a large saucepan, heat the oil over medium heat. Add the shallots, carrots, and garlic. Cover and cook until softened, about 5 minutes. Add the mushrooms and cook, uncovered, 5 minutes longer.

3. Stir in the thyme, bay leaf, tomatoes, broth, and ½ cup of the wine. Bring to a boil, then reduce heat to low, cover, and simmer until vegetables are cooked, about 30 minutes. Add the remaining wine, beans, and salt and pepper to taste.

4. Return to a boil, then reduce the heat to low and simmer, uncovered, for about 10 minutes. While the stew is simmering, pinch off pieces of the beurre manie and add it to the stew, stirring after each addition to thicken. Remove and discard the bay leaf before serving. Serve immediately.

# argentinean bean and vegetable stew

makes 6 servings

*My former neighbor was from Argentina, where she learned to make a wonderful stew thick with a variety of vegetables and laced with bits of orange. Her original recipe included beef, which I've substituted with dark red kidney beans to add another color to an already vibrant stew. This would also be good made with chunks of seitan. Serve it over freshly cooked quinoa, a protein-rich grain from South America.*

2 tablespoons olive oil

1 medium red onion, chopped

4 garlic cloves, minced

1 medium red bell pepper, chopped

1 medium butternut squash, peeled, halved, and seeded

1 (14.5-ounce) can diced tomatoes, undrained

1 (4-ounce) can chopped mild green chiles, drained

1½ cups vegetable broth, homemade (page 141) or store-bought

2 tablespoons sugar

½ teaspoon crushed red pepper

½ teaspoon dried oregano

¼ teaspoon freshly ground black pepper

3 cups cooked or 2 (15.5-ounce) cans kidney beans, drained and rinsed if canned

1 cup fresh or frozen corn kernels

1 teaspoon salt

1 seedless orange, peeled and chopped

2 tablespoons minced fresh parsley or cilantro, for garnish

1. In a large saucepan, heat the oil over medium heat. Add the onion, garlic, bell pepper, and squash. Cover and cook, stirring occasionally, until the vegetables begin to soften, about 10 minutes.

2. Add tomatoes, chiles, broth, sugar, crushed red pepper, oregano, and black pepper and bring to a boil. Reduce heat and simmer, uncovered, until the vegetables are tender, about 20 minutes. Add the kidney beans, corn, and salt. Simmer, uncovered, and taste, adjusting seasonings if necessary.

3. Add the orange and stir to heat through. Serve immediately, sprinkled with parsley.

# african-inspired red bean stew

makes 4 servings

*Peanut butter is used to thicken and enrich this delectable stew studded with mahogany-colored kidney beans. Spoon it over a bed of rice, quinoa, or couscous.*

1 tablespoon olive oil

1 medium yellow onion, chopped

2 medium carrots, cut into ¼-inch slices

3 garlic cloves, minced

1 teaspoon grated fresh ginger

½ teaspoon ground cumin

⅛ teaspoon ground cayenne

2 large Yukon Gold or russet potatoes, peeled and cut into ½-inch dice

3 cups cooked dark red kidney beans or 2 (15.5-ounce) cans, drained and rinsed

1 (14.5-ounce) can crushed tomatoes

1 (4-ounce) can diced mild green chiles, drained

1½ cups vegetable broth, homemade (page 141) or store-bought, or water

Salt and freshly ground black pepper

¼ cup creamy peanut butter

3 cups fresh baby spinach

⅓ cup chopped unsalted roasted peanuts

1. In a large saucepan, heat the oil over medium heat. Add the onion and carrots. Cover and cook until softened, about 10 minutes. Stir in

the garlic and ginger. Cook, uncovered, until fragrant, about 1 minute.

2. Add the cumin, cayenne, potatoes, beans, tomatoes, chiles, and 1 cup of the broth. Season with salt and pepper to taste. Cover and bring to a boil, then reduce heat to low and simmer until the vegetables are soft, about 30 minutes.

3. In a small bowl, combine the peanut butter and the remaining $1/2$ cup of broth, stirring until blended, then add it to the stew. Add the spinach and cook, stirring, until wilted, about 3 minutes. Taste, adjusting seasonings if necessary. Sprinkle with peanuts and serve immediately.

# brazilian black bean stew

makes 4 servings

*This tantalizing recipe was shared with me by my friend Francis Janes, a talented vegan chef and former owner of Café Ambrosia in Seattle, Washington. Not only is this gorgeous stew visually appealing, but also the flavor is truly sublime. Serve it over freshly cooked quinoa or rice.*

1 tablespoon olive oil

1 large red onion, chopped

2 garlic cloves, minced

2 medium sweet potatoes, peeled and cut into ½-inch dice

1 medium red bell pepper, cut into ½-inch dice

1 small jalapeño, seeded and minced

1 (14.5-ounce) can diced tomatoes, drained

½ cup vegetable broth, homemade (page 141) or store-bought

3 cups cooked or 2 (15.5-ounce) cans black beans, drained and rinsed if canned

1 ripe mango, peeled, pitted, and cut into ½-inch dice

1 firm ripe banana, cut into ½-inch slices

½ teaspoon salt

½ cup chopped fresh cilantro

1. In a large saucepan, heat the oil over medium heat. Add the onion, cover, and cook until softened, about 7 minutes. Stir in garlic and cook, uncovered, another 2 minutes.

2. Stir in the sweet potatoes, bell pepper, tomatoes, jalapeño, and broth. Bring to a boil. Reduce heat to low, cover, and simmer until the sweet potatoes are tender but still firm, about 20 minutes.

3. Stir in the beans and simmer gently, uncovered, until heated through, about 5 minutes. Stir in the mango, banana, and salt and cook until heated through, about 1 minute. Stir in the cilantro and serve immediately.

# black beans and wild rice

makes 4 servings

*Chewy, dark brown wild rice combines with black beans for a wholesome and dramatically appealing dish punctuated by bits of tomato and strands of spinach. For a study in contrast, serve over white basmati rice and garnish with a sprinkling of chopped avocado.*

¾ cup wild rice

3 cups cooked or 2 (15.5-ounce) cans black beans, drained and rinsed

1 (14.5-ounce) can diced tomatoes, undrained

1 teaspoon dried marjoram

½ teaspoon salt

¼ teaspoon freshly ground black pepper

3 cups fresh baby spinach

1. Combine the wild rice in a large saucepan with 3 cups of salted water. Bring to a boil, then reduce heat to low, cover, and simmer for 40 minutes or until tender. Add the beans, tomatoes, marjoram, salt, and pepper.

2. Cover and cook over low heat, stirring occasionally, until the flavors are well combined,

continues on next page

about 15 minutes, adding a splash of water if too dry.

3. Stir in the spinach and cook until the spinach is wilted and the flavors have blended, about 5 minutes. Taste, adjusting seasonings if necessary. Serve immediately.

# black beans with serrano "aioli" 🅕

makes 4 servings

*In this recipe, a spicy "aioli" adds a creamy heat to black beans and tomatoes that is also good with the addition of cooked rice, quinoa, or other grain. If you prefer not to add a grain to the dish, you can serve it on a bed of freshly cooked grain to help mellow the heat from the aioli. Otherwise, if you prefer a less spicy version, you can simply cut back on the amount of chile in the aioli.*

1 or 2 serrano chiles, seeded and coarsely chopped

1 garlic clove, crushed

2 tablespoons fresh lemon juice

½ cup vegan mayonnaise, homemade (page 573) or store-bought

¼ teaspoon sugar

¼ cup olive oil

Salt and freshly ground black pepper

3 cups or 2 (15.5-ounce) cans black beans, drained and rinsed

2 large ripe tomatoes, chopped or 1 (14.5) ounce can diced tomatoes, drained

¼ cup chopped fresh cilantro, for garnish

1. In a food processor, combine the chiles and garlic and process until finely minced. Add the lemon juice, mayonnaise, and sugar. With the machine running, slowly add the oil in a thin stream until the mixture is thin and smooth. Season with salt and pepper to taste. Scrape the aioli into a small bowl. Cover and set aside until needed. If not using right away, refrigerate until ready to use. Properly stored, the aioli will keep for up to 2 days.

2. In a large saucepan, combine the beans and tomatoes and cook over medium heat until hot, stirring occasionally. Season with salt and pepper to taste. Transfer the bean and tomato mixture to a shallow bowl. Drizzle with the aioli and garnish with the cilantro. Serve immediately.

# tuscan white beans and broccoli rabe 🅕

makes 4 servings

*Pair this hearty Tuscan dish with grilled focaccia or toasted garlic bread, or toss it with some cooked pasta and a little additional olive oil, for a healthful yet scrumptious meal.*

1 medium bunch broccoli rabe (rapini), tough stems removed

2 tablespoons olive oil

2 garlic cloves, minced

3 cups cooked or 2 (15.5-ounce) cans cannellini beans or other white beans, drained and rinsed

1 teaspoon minced fresh rosemary

Salt and freshly ground black pepper

1. In a saucepan of boiling salted water, cook the broccoli rabe until tender, about 5 minutes. Drain and run under cold water, then coarsely chop. Set aside.

2. In a large skillet, heat the oil over medium heat. Add the garlic and cook for 30 seconds. Stir in the beans and the rosemary, then add the cooked broccoli rabe and season with salt and pepper to taste.

3. Cook, stirring, until the flavors are well blended and the mixture is hot, about 10 minutes. Serve immediately.

# three-bean cassoulet

makes 4 to 6 servings

*Since cassoulet, the classic stew from the south of France, is all about white beans, I use three different kinds in this recipe. The size difference and subtle taste variance add interest. For a hearty addition, cut veggie sausage links into ½-inch slices, sauté in a little oil, and then add them to the cassoulet with the beans.*

1 tablespoon olive oil

1 medium onion, chopped

2 medium carrots, chopped

1 celery rib, chopped

3 garlic cloves, minced

1½ cups cooked or 1 (15.5-ounce) cans Navy beans, drained and rinsed

1½ cups cooked or 1 (15.5-ounce) cans Great Northern beans, drained and rinsed

1½ cups cooked or 1 (15.5-ounce) cans cannellini beans, drained and rinsed

1 (14.5-ounce) can crushed tomatoes

1 cup vegetable broth, homemade (page 141) or store-bought, or water

1 tablespoon minced fresh parsley

1 teaspoon dried savory

1 teaspoon dried thyme

1 teaspoon salt

¼ teaspoon freshly ground black pepper

½ cup dry unseasoned bread crumbs

1. Preheat the oven to 375°F. Lightly oil a 3-quart casserole and set aside.

2. In a large skillet, heat the oil over medium heat. Add the onion, carrots, celery, and garlic. Cover and cook until softened, about 10 minutes.

3. Transfer the vegetable mixture to the prepared casserole. Stir in the beans, tomatoes, broth, parsley, savory, thyme, salt, and pepper. Cover tightly and bake until the vegetables are tender and the flavors are blended, about 45 minutes.

4. Remove the cassoulet from the oven, uncover, and top with the bread crumbs. Return to the oven and bake, uncovered, 10 minutes longer to lightly brown the crumbs. Serve immediately.

# maple baked beans

makes 4 servings

*Sure you can take the easy way out and heat a can of vegetarian baked beans. But why not make your own from scratch? That way you can tweak the luscious sauce to your liking. If you begin with canned beans instead of dried, you'll have this dish in the oven in no time.*

1 tablespoon olive oil

1 medium yellow onion, minced

3 garlic cloves, minced

1 (14.5-ounce) can crushed tomatoes

½ cup pure maple syrup

2 tablespoons blackstrap molasses

1 tablespoon soy sauce

1½ teaspoons dry mustard

¼ teaspoon ground cayenne

Salt and freshly ground black pepper

3 cups cooked or 2 (15.5-ounce) cans Great Northern beans, drained and rinsed

1. Preheat the oven to 350°F. Lightly oil a 2-quart casserole and set aside.

continues on next page

2. In a large saucepan, heat the oil over medium heat. Add the onion and garlic. Cover and cook until softened, about 5 minutes.

3. Stir in the tomatoes, maple syrup, molasses, soy sauce, mustard, and cayenne and bring to a boil. Reduce heat to low and simmer, uncovered, until slightly reduced, about 10 minutes. Season with salt and pepper to taste.

4. Place the beans in the prepared casserole. Add the sauce, stirring to combine and coat the beans. Cover and bake until hot and bubbly, about 30 minutes. Serve immediately.

# chickpea, tomato, and eggplant stew

makes 4 servings

*This stew is easy to bring together, since everything goes into the same pot nearly at the same time and then simmers until done. It's also quite versatile: for example, if you don't like chickpeas, use white beans such as cannellini beans; if you're not a fan of eggplant, you can use zucchini instead (or use some of both, if you want to add extra veggies). I make this stew year-round; in the winter, I use canned tomatoes and veggies from the supermarket. When I make this in the summer, I use fresh tomatoes from the garden, where I also get my herbs, eggplant, and zucchini.*

1 tablespoon olive oil
1 large onion, chopped
1 medium eggplant, peeled and cut into ½-inch dice

2 medium carrots, cut into ¼-inch slices
1 large Yukon Gold potato, peeled and cut into
    ½-inch dice
1 medium red bell pepper, cut into 1-inch dice
3 garlic cloves, minced
2 cups cooked or 1 (15.5-ounce) cans chickpeas,
    drained and rinsed if canned
1 (28-ounce) can diced tomatoes, undrained
1 tablespoon minced fresh parsley
½ teaspoon dried oregano
½ teaspoon dried basil
1 tablespoon soy sauce
½ cup vegetable broth, homemade (page 141)
    or store-bought, or water
Salt and freshly ground black pepper

1. In a large saucepan, heat the oil over medium heat. Add the onion, eggplant, and carrots, cover, and cook until vegetables begin to soften, about 5 minutes.

2. Reduce heat to low. Add the potato, bell pepper, and garlic and cook, stirring, uncovered, for 5 minutes. Stir in the chickpeas, tomatoes, parsley, oregano, basil, soy sauce, and broth. Season with salt and black pepper to taste. Cover and cook until vegetables are tender, about 45 minutes. Serve immediately.

# chickpea and vegetable curry

makes 4 servings

*This exotically spiced dish is simply wonderful served over freshly cooked rice paired with your favorite chutney and some warm Chapati (page 417).*

1 tablespoon canola or grapeseed oil

1 medium onion, chopped

2 medium carrots, chopped

1 large potato, peeled and cut into ½-inch dice

2 garlic cloves, minced

1 teaspoon grated fresh ginger

1 tablespoon hot or mild curry powder

½ teaspoon ground cumin

½ teaspoon ground coriander

1 cup water

3 cups cooked or 2 (15.5-ounce) cans chickpeas, drained and rinsed if canned

1 cup frozen peas, thawed

1 (4-ounce) can chopped mild or hot green chiles, drained

1 (13.5-ounce) can unsweetened coconut milk

½ cup raisins

1 teaspoon sugar

Salt and freshly ground black pepper

1. In a large saucepan, heat the oil over medium heat. Add the onion, carrots, potato, and garlic. Cover and cook until softened, about 5 minutes.

2. Stir in the ginger, curry powder, cumin, and coriander and cook, uncovered, 1 minute longer. Add the water and simmer, covered, until the vegetables are soft, about 20 minutes.

3. Add the chickpeas, peas, chiles, coconut milk, raisins, sugar, and salt and pepper to taste. Simmer, uncovered, for about 20 minutes longer to allow flavors to intensify and reduce the liquid. If a thicker sauce is desired, puree a small amount of the solids with an immersion blender or blend 1 teaspoon of cornstarch in 1 tablespoon of water and add to the saucepan, stirring to thicken. Serve immediately.

# coconut-peanut chickpeas and vegetables 🅕

makes 4 servings

*Rich coconut milk and peanut butter combine beautifully with garlic and curry powder to create a flavorful backdrop for chickpeas and vegetables. Serve this dish over basmati rice to catch every drop of the yummy sauce.*

1 tablespoon olive oil

1 medium onion, chopped

1 medium red bell pepper, chopped

3 garlic cloves, minced

1 tablespoon hot or mild curry powder

2 tablespoons creamy peanut butter

1 (13.5-ounce) can unsweetened coconut milk

3 cups cooked or 2 (15.5-ounce) cans chickpeas, drained and rinsed

1 (14.5-ounce) can diced tomatoes, drained

3 cups fresh baby spinach

Salt and freshly ground black pepper

Crushed unsalted roasted peanuts, for garnish

1. In a large saucepan, heat the oil over medium heat. Add the onion and bell pepper, cover, and cook until soft, about 10 minutes. Add the garlic and curry powder, stirring until fragrant, about 30 seconds.

2. Add the peanut butter and gradually stir in the coconut milk until well blended. Add the chickpeas, tomatoes, and spinach, stirring to wilt the spinach, about 5 minutes. Season with salt and pepper to taste.

3. Simmer until hot and the flavors are well blended, about 7 minutes. Serve immediately, sprinkled with the peanuts.

# tamarind chickpea stew

makes 4 servings

*The uniquely delicious tang of tamarind permeates this luscious stew thick with meaty chickpeas, vegetables, and fragrant spices. Tamarind is one of those ingredients you may not find in your supermarket, but it's available in Indian, Asian, or Middle Eastern markets, gourmet grocers, and online. The easiest way to buy it is in a jar labeled "tamarind concentrate" or "tamarind paste." For a homemade substitute, blend 1 tablespoon of lemon or lime juice with 1 teaspoon brown sugar or molasses; add it near the end of cooking time.*

1 tablespoon olive oil

1 large onion, chopped

2 medium Yukon Gold potatoes, peeled and cut into ¼-inch dice

3 cups cooked chickpeas or 2 (15.5-ounce) cans chickpeas, drained and rinsed

1 (28-ounce) can crushed tomatoes

1 (4-ounce) can mild chopped green chiles, drained

2 tablespoons tamarind paste

¼ cup pure maple syrup

1 cup vegetable broth, homemade (page 141) or store-bought, or water

2 tablespoons chili powder

1 teaspoon ground coriander

½ teaspoon ground cumin

Salt and freshly ground black pepper

1 cup frozen baby peas, thawed

1. In a large saucepan, heat the oil over medium heat. Add the onion, cover, and cook until softened, about 5 minutes. Add the potatoes, chickpeas, tomatoes, and chiles and simmer, uncovered, for 5 minutes.

2. In a small bowl, combine the tamarind paste, maple syrup, and broth and blend until smooth. Stir the tamarind mixture into the vegetables, along with the chili powder, coriander, cumin, and salt and pepper to taste. Bring to a boil, then reduce the heat to medium and simmer, covered, until the potatoes are tender, about 40 minutes.

3. Taste, adjusting seasonings if necessary, and stir in the peas. Simmer, uncovered, about 10 minutes longer. Serve immediately.

# pomegranate-infused lentil and chickpea stew

makes 4 servings

*Pomegranate juice seems to be everywhere these days, which is a good thing considering its antioxidant properties and other health benefits. As if having a great-tasting juice and beautiful ruby-red seeds weren't enough, enter pomegranate molasses, a sweet-sour syrup used to flavor many Middle Eastern dishes. You can find it bottled in specialty markets or make your own using the recipe following this one.*

¾ cup brown lentils, picked over, rinsed, and drained

2 tablespoons olive oil

½ cup chopped green onions

2 teaspoons minced fresh ginger

¾ cup long-grain brown rice

½ cup dried apricots, quartered

¼ cup golden raisins

¼ teaspoon ground allspice

¼ teaspoon ground cumin

¼ teaspoon ground cayenne

1 teaspoon turmeric

Salt and freshly ground black pepper

⅓ cup pomegranate molasses, homemade (recipe follows) or store-bought

3 cups water

1½ cups cooked or 1 (15.5-ounce) can chickpeas, drained and rinsed

¼ cup minced fresh cilantro or parsley

1. Soak the lentils in a medium bowl of hot water for 45 minutes. Drain and set aside.

2. In a large saucepan, heat the oil over medium heat. Add the green onions, ginger, soaked lentils, rice, apricots, raisins, allspice, cumin, cayenne, turmeric, and salt and pepper to taste. Cook, stirring, for 1 minute.

3. Add the pomegranate molasses and water and bring to a boil. Reduce heat to low. Cover and simmer until the lentils and rice are tender, about 40 minutes.

4. Stir in the chickpeas and cilantro. Simmer, uncovered, for 15 minutes, to heat through and allow the flavors to blend. Serve immediately.

## pomegranate molasses

makes about ¾ cup

2 cups pomegranate juice

⅓ cup sugar

2 tablespoons fresh lemon juice

1. In a large saucepan, combine the pomegranate juice and sugar and cook over medium-high heat. Cook, stirring until the sugar dissolves. Reduce heat to low and simmer over medium-high heat until the sugar has dissolved, about 5 minutes.

2. Reduce heat just enough to maintain a simmer and cook until the juice thickens and reduces to less than a cup.

3. Stir in the lemon juice and pour into a container or jar with a tight-fitting lid. Let cool, uncovered, then store tightly covered in the refrigerator where it will keep for several days.

# autumn medley stew

makes 4 to 6 servings

*Chickpeas and seitan combine with a harvest of autumn vegetables for a satisfying stew that is an especially welcome meal when the weather turns cold.*

2 tablespoons olive oil

8 ounces seitan, homemade (page 305) or store-bought, cut in 1-inch cubes

Salt and freshly ground black pepper

1 large yellow onion, chopped

2 garlic cloves, minced

1 large russet potato, peeled and cut into ½-inch dice

1 medium carrot, cut into ¼-inch dice

1 medium parsnip, cut into ¼-inch dice chopped

1 small butternut squash, peeled, halved, seeded, and cut into ½-inch dice

1 small head savoy cabbage, chopped

1 (14.5-ounce) can diced tomatoes, drained

1½ cups cooked or 1 (15.5-ounce) can chickpeas, drained and rinsed

2 cups vegetable broth, homemade (page 141) or store-bought, or water

½ cup dry white wine

½ teaspoon dried marjoram

½ teaspoon dried thyme

½ cup crumbled angel hair pasta

1. In a large skillet, heat 1 tablespoon of the oil over medium-high heat. Add the seitan and cook until browned on all sides, about 5 minutes. Season with salt and pepper to taste and set aside.

2. In a large saucepan, heat the remaining 1 tablespoon oil over medium heat. Add the onion and garlic. Cover and cook for until softened, about 5 minutes. Add the potato, carrot, parsnip, and squash. Cover and cook until softened, about 10 minutes.

continues on next page

3. Stir in the cabbage, tomatoes, chickpeas, broth, wine, marjoram, thyme, and salt and pepper to taste. Bring to a boil, then reduce heat to low. Cover and cook, stirring occasionally, until the vegetables are tender, about 45 minutes.

4. Add the cooked seitan and the pasta and simmer until the pasta is tender and the flavors are blended, about 10 minutes longer. Serve immediately.

variation: Leave out the pasta and serve with some warm crusty bread.

# moroccan-spiced chickpea and sweet potato stew

makes 4 to 6 servings

*Dazzling colors and exotic spices punctuate this mouthwatering stew thick with colorful vegetables, sweet potatoes, and chickpeas. It's delicious when served over couscous for added texture and flavor.*

1 tablespoon olive oil
1 large yellow onion, chopped
2 medium carrots, cut into ¼-inch dice
1 celery rib, cut into ¼-inch dice
2 garlic cloves, minced
1 teaspoon grated fresh ginger
1 teaspoon ground coriander
1 teaspoon ground cumin
½ teaspoon turmeric
¼ teaspoon ground cinnamon
¼ teaspoon ground nutmeg
½ teaspoon sugar
2 medium sweet potatoes, peeled and cut into ½-inch dice

8 ounces green beans, trimmed and cut into 1-inch lengths
1½ cups cooked or 1 (15.5-ounce) can chickpeas, drained and rinsed
1 (14.5-ounce) can diced tomatoes, undrained
1½ cups vegetable broth, homemade (page 141) or store-bought, or water
Salt and freshly ground black pepper
2 tablespoons minced fresh parsley or cilantro
1 teaspoon fresh lemon juice

1. In a large saucepan, heat the oil over medium heat. Add the onion, carrots, celery, garlic, and ginger. Cover and cook until softened, about 10 minutes.

2. Stir in the coriander, cumin, turmeric, cinnamon, nutmeg, and sugar. Add the sweet potatoes, green beans, chickpeas, and tomatoes with their juice. Stir in the broth and bring to a boil. Reduce heat to low and season with salt and pepper to taste.

3. Cover and simmer until the vegetables are tender, about 40 minutes. Stir in the parsley and lemon juice and cook 10 minutes longer. Taste, adjusting seasonings if necessary, and serve immediately.

# edamame donburi

makes 4 servings

*A "fast food" of Japan, donburi is typically a bowl of soft rice topped with meat, vegetables, and/or eggs for a complete meal on the go. This vegan version includes two favorite Japanese ingredients, edamame and tofu, for the protein-rich topping and is seasoned with ginger, green onions, soy sauce, and sesame. For extra authenticity, add some strips of aburage (fried tofu found in Asian markets) sautéed in a bit of mirin and soy sauce.*

1 cup fresh or frozen shelled edamame

1 tablespoon canola or grapeseed oil

1 medium yellow onion, minced

5 shiitake mushroom caps, lightly rinsed, patted dry, and cut into ¼-inch strips

1 teaspoon grated fresh ginger

3 green onions, minced

8 ounces firm tofu, drained and crumbled

2 tablespoons soy sauce

3 cups hot cooked white or brown rice

1 tablespoon toasted sesame oil

1 tablespoon toasted sesame seeds, for garnish

1. In a small saucepan of boiling salted water, cook the edamame until tender, about 10 minutes. Drain and set aside.

2. In a large skillet, heat the canola oil over medium heat. Add the onion, cover, and cook until softened, about 5 minutes. Add the mushrooms and cook, uncovered, 5 minutes longer. Stir in the ginger and green onions. Add the tofu and soy sauce and cook until heated through, stirring to combine well, about 5 minutes. Stir in the cooked edamame and cook until heated through, about 5 minutes.

3. Divide the hot rice among 4 bowls, top each with the edamame and tofu mixture, and drizzle on the sesame oil. Sprinkle with sesame seeds and serve immediately.

# yellow dal with spinach

makes 4 servings

*Dal is a Hindi word for both the many varieties of beans, peas, and lentils, and the dish made from them. The baby spinach and chopped tomato add lively streaks of green and red to the savory yellow puree.*

1¼ cups yellow split peas, picked over, rinsed, and drained

3½ cups water

1 teaspoon salt

3 cups fresh baby spinach

2 ripe plum tomatoes, finely chopped

¼ cup chopped fresh cilantro

1 tablespoon canola or grapeseed oil

2 garlic cloves, minced

1 tablespoon finely chopped fresh ginger

1 serrano or other hot green chile, seeded and minced

1 teaspoon ground cumin

½ teaspoon ground coriander

½ teaspoon turmeric

2 teaspoons fresh lemon juice

1. Soak the split peas in a medium bowl of hot water for 45 minutes. Drain and transfer to a large saucepan. Add the water and bring to a boil. Add the salt, reduce heat to medium, and cook until split peas are tender and thickened, about 40 minutes.

2. Add the spinach, tomatoes, and cilantro, stirring to wilt the spinach. Keep warm over very low heat.

3. In a small skillet, heat the oil over medium heat. Add the garlic, ginger, and chile. Heat until fragrant, about 1 minute.

4. Remove from the heat and add the cumin, coriander, turmeric, and lemon juice, stirring to mix well. Add the mixture to the dal, stirring to combine. Serve immediately.

# three lentil dal

makes 6 servings

*Since the different varieties of lentils have subtle variations in taste and texture, here's an interesting blend of three in one dal.*

½ cup green lentils, picked over, rinsed, and drained

½ cup brown lentils, picked over, rinsed, and drained

3 cups water

Salt

½ cup red lentils, picked over, rinsed, and drained

2 tablespoons canola or grapeseed oil

1 medium yellow onion, minced

2 garlic cloves, minced

2 teaspoons grated fresh ginger

1 tablespoon hot or mild curry powder

½ teaspoon ground cumin

½ teaspoon ground coriander

¼ teaspoon ground cayenne

1 (14.5-ounce) can crushed tomatoes

1. Soak the green lentils and brown lentils in separate medium bowls of hot water for 45 minutes. Drain the green lentils and place them in a large saucepan with the water. Bring to a boil. Reduce heat to low and simmer for 10 minutes.

2. Drain the brown lentils and add to the green lentils with salt to taste. Simmer, partially covered, for 20 minutes, stirring occasionally. Add the red lentils and simmer, uncovered, until the sauce thickens and the beans are very soft, 20 to 25 minutes longer.

3. In a large skillet, heat the oil over medium heat. Add the onion, cover, and cook until softened about 10 minutes. Add the garlic and ginger and cook until fragrant, about 30 seconds.

4. Add the curry powder, cumin, coriander, cayenne, and tomatoes, stirring constantly for about 1 minute. Add the tomato mixture to the cooked lentils and stir to mix well. Cook another 10 minutes until the flavors are blended. Taste, adjusting seasonings if necessary. Serve immediately.

# black bean and bulgur loaf

makes 4 to 6 servings

*Be sure to remove any moisture from the bulgur and beans for a firmer loaf. If the mixture seems too sticky, toss some additional oats into the mix before shaping into a loaf. Top the loaf with a bit of Basic Brown Sauce (page 545).*

1 tablespoon olive oil

1 medium yellow onion, minced

1 cup medium-grind bulgur

2 cups water

Salt

3 cups cooked or 2 (15.5-ounce) cans black beans, drained, rinsed, and mashed

½ cup quick-cooking oats

⅓ cup wheat gluten flour (vital wheat gluten)

2 tablespoons nutritional yeast

1½ teaspoons dried thyme

1½ teaspoons dried savory

½ teaspoon dried oregano

¼ teaspoon freshly ground black pepper

**1.** In a large saucepan, heat the oil over medium heat. Add the onion, cover, and cook until softened, 5 minutes. Add the bulgur and water and bring to a boil. Salt the water, reduce heat to low, cover, and simmer until bulgur is tender and water is absorbed, 15 to 20 minutes. If any water remains, drain well in a fine-mesh sieve, pressing any excess liquid from the bulgur.

**2.** Preheat the oven to 350°F. Lightly oil a 9-inch loaf pan and set aside. Transfer the bulgur mixture to a large bowl. Add the mashed beans to the bulgur. Stir in the oats, flour, yeast, thyme, savory, oregano, and salt and pepper to taste. Mix well until thoroughly combined.

**3.** Spoon the mixture into the prepared loaf pan, pressing with your hands to make a smooth loaf. Bake until firm, about 40 minutes. Remove from the oven and set aside to cool for 10 minutes before slicing.

# chickpea and vegetable loaf

makes 4 servings

*If you shred the potato and carrot in the food processor, it will save time and there's no need to rinse out the bowl, since you need it to make the loaf mixture anyway. Serve topped with Golden Mushroom Gravy (page 547).*

1 small white potato, peeled and shredded

1 medium carrot, shredded

1 small yellow onion, chopped

2 garlic cloves, minced

1½ cups cooked or 1 (15.5-ounce) can chickpeas, drained and rinsed

¾ cup wheat gluten flour or chickpea flour, or more if needed

¾ cup quick-cooking oats

½ cup dry unseasoned bread crumbs

¼ cup minced fresh parsley

1 tablespoon soy sauce

1 teaspoon dried savory

½ teaspoon dried sage

1 teaspoon salt

¼ teaspoon freshly ground black pepper

**1.** Preheat the oven to 350°F. Lightly oil a 9-inch loaf pan and set aside. Squeeze the excess liquid from the shredded potato and place it in a food processor, along with the carrot, onion, and garlic. Add the chickpeas and pulse to blend the ingredients while retaining some texture. Add the flour, oats, bread crumbs, parsley, soy sauce, savory, sage, salt, and black pepper. Pulse just until blended.

**2.** Scrape the mixture onto a lightly floured work surface. Use your hands to form the mixture into a loaf, adding more flour or oats if the mixture is too loose. Place the loaf in the prepared pan, smoothing the top. Bake until firm and golden, about 1 hour. Remove from oven and let stand for 10 minutes before slicing.

# millet-topped lentil shepherd's pie

makes 4 servings

*Millet is a super-nutritious and versatile grain that is a staple in much of the world. Rich in protein and mild in flavor, millet can be boiled and enjoyed plain as a side dish or used in a pilaf or loaf. I especially like the way millet smooths over the top of the casserole to mimic the classic mashed potato topping of a shepherd's pie.*

2 cups water

Salt

1 cup millet

1 tablespoon nutritional yeast

1 tablespoon vegan margarine

1 tablespoon olive oil

1 medium yellow onion, chopped

2 garlic cloves, minced

1 medium red bell pepper, chopped

2 medium carrots, chopped

1 (14.5-ounce) can diced tomatoes, drained and finely chopped

½ cup brown lentils, picked over, rinsed, and drained

1 cup chopped white mushrooms

1 cup fresh or frozen corn kernels

1 cup frozen peas

1 cup vegetable broth, homemade (page 141) or store-bought

1 teaspoon dried thyme

1 teaspoon dried marjoram

Freshly ground black pepper

½ teaspoon sweet or smoked paprika

1. Preheat the oven to 350°F. Lightly a 3-quart casserole and set aside. In a large saucepan, bring the water to boil. Salt the water, add the millet, cover, and reduce heat to low. Simmer until the millet is cooked, about 30 minutes. Stir in the nutritional yeast and margarine and set aside.

2. In a separate large saucepan, heat the oil over medium heat. Add the onion, garlic, bell pepper, and carrots. Cover and cook until softened, about 10 minutes. Add the tomatoes, lentils, mushrooms, corn, peas, broth, thyme, marjoram, and salt and black pepper to taste. Cover and simmer until the lentils are soft and the mixture has thickened, about 40 minutes, adding a little water if the mixture becomes too thick.

3. Place the lentil mixture into the prepared casserole, spoon the cooked millet on top, and spread it evenly over the lentil mixture. Sprinkle with paprika. Bake until hot, about 30 minutes. Serve immediately.

# piccata-style cashew chickpea medallions 🅕

makes 4 servings

*This easy recipe transforms a cup of chickpeas and a handful of cashews into a sophisticated main dish. I like to serve these lemony medallions with roasted asparagus and potatoes or a rice pilaf.*

1 large garlic clove, crushed

¾ cup unsalted roasted cashews

1 cup cooked or canned chickpeas, drained, rinsed, and blotted dry

¾ cup wheat gluten flour (vital wheat gluten)

2 tablespoons soy sauce

½ teaspoon sweet or smoked paprika

¼ teaspoon turmeric

Salt

2 tablespoons olive oil

¼ cup dry white wine

2 tablespoons fresh lemon juice

1 tablespoon capers

2 tablespoons minced fresh parsley

Freshly ground black pepper

1 tablespoon vegan margarine

1. Preheat the oven to 275° F. In a food processor, combine the garlic and cashews and process until finely ground. Add the chickpeas and pulse until chopped. Add the flour, soy sauce, paprika, turmeric, and salt to taste and pulse until well mixed.

2. Turn the mixture out onto a work surface and mix with your hands for a minute or two to fully incorporate. Divide the mixture into eight pieces and shape into ¼-inch-thick medallions.

3. In a large skillet, heat the oil over medium heat. Add the medallions, cover, and cook until nicely browned, about 5 minutes per side. Transfer the medallions to a baking sheet and keep warm in the oven while you make the sauce.

4. To the same skillet, add the wine, lemon juice, capers, and parsley. Season with salt and pepper to taste. Simmer until the liquid is reduced by a third. Swirl in the margarine, stirring until melted. Transfer the medallions to dinner plates and drizzle with the sauce. Serve immediately.

# black bean and walnut croquettes

makes 4 servings

*The earthly flavors of walnuts and black beans combine to make these versatile and delicious croquettes. For a lovely dinner entrée, serve them topped with Hollandaze Sauce (page 552) or Roasted Yellow Tomato and Pepper Coulis (page 548). For a more casual meal, tuck them into sandwiches with lettuce, tomato, and a blend of coarse brown mustard and vegan mayo.*

¾ cup walnut pieces

3 green onions, chopped

3 tablespoons fresh parsley, coarsely chopped

1 cup cooked or canned black beans, drained, rinsed, and patted dry

1 tablespoon soy sauce

½ cup wheat gluten flour (vital wheat gluten)

1 teaspoon dried savory

Salt and freshly ground black pepper

½ cup dry unseasoned bread crumbs

2 tablespoons olive oil

1. In a food processor, combine the walnuts, green onions, and parsley and process until finely ground. Add the black beans, soy sauce, flour, savory, and salt and pepper to taste. Process until smooth and well combined.

2. Use your hands to shape the mixture into 8 small patties. Place the bread crumbs in a shallow bowl. Dredge the croquettes in the crumbs until coated and arrange on a plate. Refrigerate to firm up, about 20 minutes.

3. In a large skillet, heat the oil over medium heat. Add the croquettes and cook until browned on both sides, about 5 minutes per side. Serve immediately.

# GRAINS

## vegetable fried rice 🅕

makes 4 servings

*For best results, use cold cooked long-grain
rice so it remains fluffy and separated when
fried with the veggies. Fried rice is a delicious reason to plan ahead and make extra
rice to store for later. Rice actually freezes
quite well, so keep a container in the freezer.
The optional turmeric will turn the rice a
pretty yellow color.*

2 tablespoons canola or grapeseed oil
1 medium yellow onion, finely chopped
1 large carrot, finely chopped
1 medium zucchini, finely chopped
2 garlic cloves, minced
2 teaspoons grated fresh ginger
3 green onions, minced
½ teaspoon turmeric (optional)
3½ cups cold cooked long-grain rice
1 cup frozen peas, thawed
3 tablespoons soy sauce
2 teaspoons mirin or dry white wine
1 tablespoon toasted sesame oil

1. In a large skillet, heat the canola oil over
medium-high heat. Add the onion, carrot,
and zucchini and stir-fry until softened, about
5 minutes. Add the garlic, ginger, and green
onions and stir-fry until softened, about
3 minutes.

2. Stir in the turmeric, if using. Add the rice,
peas, soy sauce, and mirin and stir-fry until
hot, about 5 minutes. Drizzle with the sesame
oil, toss to combine, and taste, adjusting seasonings and adding more soy sauce if necessary. Serve immediately.

## caribbean rice, squash, and peas

makes 4 servings

*Pigeon peas are traditional in Caribbean
cooking, but black-eyed peas are easier to
find, especially if using canned. For a spicy
version, add a seeded and minced hot chile
when you add the squash and garlic.*

2 tablespoons olive oil
1 small yellow onion, chopped
2 cups peeled, seeded, and diced butternut
    or other winter squash
3 garlic cloves, minced
1 teaspoon dried thyme
½ teaspoon ground cumin
1½ cups cooked or 1 (15.5-ounce) can
    black-eyed peas, drained and rinsed
1 cup long-grain rice
2½ cups hot water
2 tablespoons chopped fresh cilantro

1. In a large saucepan, heat the oil over medium
heat. Add the onion, cover, and cook until
softened, about 5 minutes. Add the squash,
garlic, thyme, and cumin. Cover and cook until
the squash is softened, about 10 minutes. Stir
in the peas, rice, and water.

2. Bring to a boil, then reduce heat to low.
Cover and simmer until the rice is cooked,
about 30 minutes. Fluff with a fork and sprinkle with cilantro. Serve immediately.

# wild rice and millet croquettes

makes 4 to 6 servings

*Spiky black wild rice and soft white millet may be the odd couple of grains, but the contrasts of color and texture add up to great-tasting and appealing croquettes that make an attractive main dish. They look especially pretty nestled on a shallow pool of Roasted Yellow Tomato and Pepper Coulis (page 548). You can make the croquette mixture ahead of when you need it so it has time to chill.*

¾ cup cooked millet

½ cup cooked wild rice

3 tablespoons olive oil

¼ cup minced onion

1 celery rib, finely minced

¼ cup finely shredded carrot

⅓ cup all-purpose flour

¼ cup chopped fresh parsley

2 teaspoons dried dillweed

Salt and freshly ground black pepper

1. Place the cooked millet and wild rice in a large bowl and set aside.

2. In a medium skillet, heat 1 tablespoon of the oil over medium heat. Add the onion, celery, and carrot. Cover and cook until softened, 5 minutes. Add the vegetables to the cooked grains. Stir in the flour, parsley, dillweed, and salt and pepper to taste. Mix until well combined. Refrigerate until chilled, about 20 minutes.

3. Use your hands to shape the mixture into small patties and set aside. In a large skillet, heat the remaining 2 tablespoons oil over medium heat. Add the croquettes and cook until golden brown, turning once, about 8 minutes total. Serve immediately.

# green tea rice with lemon snow peas and tofu

makes 4 servings

*This light and lovely rice dish is flavored with green tea and lemon for a sophisticated taste. Crunchy snow peas and golden fried tofu complete the meal.*

3 cups water

4 green tea bags

1½ cups white sushi rice

2 tablespoons canola or grapeseed oil

8 ounces extra-firm tofu, drained and cut into
    ¼-inch dice

3 green onions, minced

2 cups snow peas, trimmed and cut diagonally
    into 1-inch pieces

1 tablespoon fresh lemon juice

1 teaspoon grated lemon zest

Salt and freshly ground black pepper

1. In a large saucepan, bring the water to a boil. Add the tea bags and remove from the heat. Let stand for 7 minutes and remove and discard the tea bags. Rinse the rice under running water until the water runs clear, then add to the brewed tea. Cover and cook over medium heat until tender, about 25 minutes. Remove from heat and set aside.

2. In a large skillet, heat the oil over medium heat. Add the tofu and cook until golden brown, 5 minutes. Add the green onions and snow peas and cook until softened, 3 minutes. Stir in the lemon juice and zest.

3. In a large bowl, combine the cooked rice with the tofu and snow pea mixture. Season with salt and pepper to taste, and serve immediately.

# brown rice and lentil pilaf

makes 4 to 6 servings

*The hearty combination of lentils and brown rice is spiced with ground coriander. The use of cilantro as a garnish mirrors the ground coriander, since coriander seeds and cilantro leaves are from the same plant.*

¾ cup brown lentils, picked over, rinsed, and drained
1 tablespoon olive oil
1 large yellow onion, minced
1 medium carrot, chopped
2 garlic cloves, minced
1 cup long-grain brown rice
1½ teaspoons ground coriander
½ teaspoon ground cumin
3 cups water
Salt
3 tablespoons minced fresh cilantro
Freshly ground black pepper

1. Bring a saucepan of salted water to a boil over high heat. Add the lentils, return to a boil, then reduce heat to medium and cook for 15 minutes. Drain and set aside. In a large saucepan, heat the oil over medium heat. Add the onion, carrot, and garlic, cover, and cook until tender, 10 minutes.

2. Add the lentils to the vegetable mixture. Add the rice, coriander, and cumin. Stir in the water and bring to a boil. Reduce heat to low, salt the water, and cook, covered, until the lentils and rice are tender, about 30 minutes. Remove from heat and set aside for 10 minutes.

3. Transfer to a large bowl, fluff with a fork, and sprinkle with the cilantro and freshly ground black pepper. Serve immediately.

# savory beans and rice

makes 4 servings

*This hearty dish includes the herb savory among its ingredients. Interestingly, the German word for savory is* bohnenkraut, *which means "bean herb," making this dish doubly "savory."*

1 tablespoon olive oil
3 green onions, chopped
1 teaspoon grated fresh ginger
1 cup brown basmati rice
2 cups water
1 tablespoon soy sauce
Salt
1½ cups cooked or 1 (15.5-ounce) can Great Northern white beans, drained and rinsed
1 tablespoon nutritional yeast
1 tablespoon minced fresh savory or 1½ teaspoons dried

1. In a large saucepan, heat the oil over medium heat. Add the green onions and ginger and cook until fragrant, about 1 minute. Add the rice, water, soy sauce, and salt to taste. Cover and bring to a boil.

2. Reduce heat to low and simmer, covered, until the rice is tender, about 30 minutes. Stir in the beans, nutritional yeast, and savory. Cook, uncovered, stirring, until heated through and the liquid is absorbed, about 10 minutes. Serve immediately.

# mexican green rice and beans

makes 4 servings

*This green rice, or arroz verde, is hearty enough to serve as a main dish thanks to the addition of dark red kidney beans, which also give it a pretty color accent. For a mild* version, omit the chiles and add an extra green bell pepper.

1 large green bell pepper

2 or 3 small fresh jalapeño or other hot green chiles

2½ cups vegetable broth, homemade (page 141) or store-bought

½ cup coarsely chopped fresh parsley

1 small yellow onion, chopped

2 garlic cloves, chopped

¼ teaspoon freshly ground black pepper

1 teaspoon sugar

½ teaspoon dried oregano

¼ teaspoon ground cumin

3 tablespoons canola or grapeseed oil

1 cup long-grain white rice

Salt

1½ cups cooked or 1 (15.5-ounce) can dark red kidney beans, drained and rinsed

2 tablespoons minced fresh cilantro, garnish

1. Roast the bell pepper and chiles over a gas flame or under a broiler until the skin blisters, turning on all sides. Place in a paper bag for 5 minutes. Use a damp towel to rub off scorched bits of skin. Stem, seed, and chop the bell pepper and chiles and place them in a food processor. Add 1 cup of the broth, parsley, onion, garlic, pepper, sugar, oregano, and cumin and process until smooth. Set aside.

2. In a large skillet, heat the oil over medium heat. Add the rice and stir constantly for a few minutes to coat the rice with the oil. Add the pureed vegetables and simmer, stirring occasionally, for 5 minutes. Add the remaining 1½ cups broth and bring to a boil. Reduce the heat to medium, add salt to taste, cover, and cook until the liquid is absorbed, about 30 minutes. About 10 minutes before ready to serve, stir in the kidney beans. Garnish with cilantro and serve immediately.

# italian rice with seitan and mushrooms

makes 4 servings

*Seasoned with fragrant basil and fennel seed, and spiced with crushed red pepper, this tasty dish is like an Italian version of dirty rice. Instead of seitan, you can make this with chopped vegetarian sausage links. If you have cold cooked rice on hand, you can use it to make this recipe in just a few minutes.*

2 cups water

1 cup long-grain brown or white rice

2 tablespoons olive oil

1 medium yellow onion, chopped

2 garlic cloves, minced

8 ounces seitan, homemade (page 305) or store-bought, chopped

8 ounces white mushrooms, chopped

1 teaspoon dried basil

½ teaspoon ground fennel seed

¼ teaspoon crushed red pepper

Salt and freshly ground black pepper

1. In a large saucepan, bring the water to boil over high heat. Add the rice, reduce the heat to low, cover, and cook until tender, about 30 minutes.

2. In a large skillet, heat the oil over medium heat. Add the onion, cover, and cook until softened, about 5 minutes. Add the seitan and cook uncovered until browned. Stir in the mushrooms and cook until tender, about 5 minutes longer. Stir in the basil, fennel, crushed red pepper, and salt and black pepper to taste.

3. Transfer the cooked rice to large serving bowl. Stir in the seitan mixture and mix thoroughly. Add a generous amount of black pepper and serve immediately.

# creole rice and red beans

makes 4 servings

*As economical as it is delicious and filling, red beans and rice is the quintessential Creole dish, made with the onion, bell pepper, and celery and flavored with chiles, garlic, thyme, and cumin. If you prefer a milder version, omit the hot chile. If you like it spicier, serve it with a bottle of Tabasco or other hot sauce on the table. Filé powder is ground sassafras leaves and is available in specialty food shops or the gourmet section of well-stocked supermarkets.*

1 tablespoon olive oil

1 medium sweet yellow onion, finely chopped

1 small green bell pepper, finely chopped

1 celery rib, minced

2 garlic cloves, minced

1 jalapeño or serrano chile, seeded and minced

1 (28-ounce) can diced tomatoes, drained

3 cups cooked or 2 (15.5-ounce) cans dark kidney beans, drained

1½ cups long-grain white rice

3 cups vegetable broth, homemade (page 141) or store-bought

1 teaspoon Tabasco sauce, or to taste

1 teaspoon dried thyme

½ teaspoon ground cumin

¼ teaspoon filé powder (see headnote; optional)

Salt

Ground cayenne

1. In a large saucepan, heat the oil over medium heat. Add the onion, bell pepper, celery, and garlic. Cover and cook until softened, about 10 minutes.

2. Stir in the jalapeño, tomatoes, beans, rice, broth, Tabasco sauce, thyme, cumin, filé powder, salt, and cayenne. Cover and simmer until the rice is tender and liquid is absorbed, about 30 minutes. Taste, adjusting seasonings if necessary. Serve immediately.

# spanish rice and beans

makes 4 servings

*Spanish rice is typically a side dish made with white rice and tomatoes, but when you use brown rice and add beans, it becomes a satisfying and nutritious main dish. Pungent capers and spicy crushed red pepper add extra flavor.*

1 tablespoon olive oil

1 medium yellow onion, chopped

1 medium green bell pepper, chopped

2 garlic cloves, minced

1 (14.5-ounce) can diced tomatoes, undrained

1 tablespoon capers, chopped if large

¼ teaspoon crushed red pepper

1½ cups long-grain brown rice

3 cups vegetable broth, homemade (page 141) or store-bought, or water

Salt

1½ cups cooked or 1 (15.5-ounce) can dark red kidney beans, drained and rinsed

¼ cup sliced pitted kalamata olives

2 tablespoons minced fresh parsley

1. In a large saucepan, heat the oil over medium heat. Add the onion, bell pepper, and garlic. Cover and cook until softened, about 5 minutes. Add the tomatoes and their juice, the capers, and the crushed red pepper. Stir to combine and simmer for 5 minutes to blend the flavors.

**2.** Add the rice and broth and bring to a boil, then reduce heat to low. Add salt to taste. Cover and cook until the rice is tender and the liquid is evaporated, 30 to 40 minutes. Remove from heat and stir in the beans, olives, and parsley. Cover and set aside for 10 minutes before serving. Serve immediately.

# brown rice with artichokes, chickpeas, and tomatoes

makes 4 servings

*This is an extremely versatile dish that can be adapted to use different beans and vegetables (or grains, for that matter), depending on your mood or what's on hand.*

2 tablespoons olive oil

3 garlic cloves, minced

1 cup frozen artichokes hearts, thawed and chopped

1 teaspoon dried basil

½ teaspoon dried marjoram

1½ cups cooked or 1 (15.5-ounce) can chickpeas, drained and rinsed

1½ cups long-grain brown rice

3 cups vegetable broth, homemade (page 141) or store-bought, or hot water

Salt and freshly ground black pepper

1 cup ripe grape tomatoes, quartered

2 tablespoons minced fresh parsley

**1.** In a large saucepan, heat the oil over medium heat. Add the garlic and cook until softened, about 1 minute. Add the artichokes, basil, marjoram, and chickpeas. Stir in the rice and broth. Season with salt and pepper to taste.

**2.** Cover tightly and reduce heat to low. Simmer until the rice is cooked, about 30 minutes. Transfer to a serving bowl, add the tomatoes and parsley, taste, adjusting seasonings if necessary, and fluff with a fork. Serve immediately.

# coconut jasmine rice and edamame

makes 4 servings

*When you start with delectable ingredients like fragrant jasmine rice, creamy coconut milk, and flavorful edamame, you suspect you may be in for a great meal. When you add a flourish of fresh cilantro and crunchy cashews, there's no room for doubt.*

1½ cups shelled fresh or frozen edamame

1½ cups jasmine rice

2 (13.5-ounce) cans unsweetened coconut milk

1 cup water

Salt

½ cup minced fresh cilantro

½ cup chopped roasted cashews

**1.** Bring a large saucepan of salted water to a boil over high heat. Add the edamame and cook until tender, about 10 minutes. Drain and set aside. In a large saucepan, combine the rice, coconut milk, and water and bring to a boil, stirring occasionally. Reduce heat to low, add salt to taste, cover, and simmer until the rice is tender, about 20 minutes.

**2.** Stir in the cooked edamame, cover, and remove from heat. Set aside for 10 minutes. Transfer to a serving bowl and stir in the cilantro and cashews. Serve immediately.

# italian truck-stop artichoke risotto

makes 4 servings

*This recipe is inspired by the best risotto my husband ever had—at a truck-stop diner in the middle of Tuscany. Since fresh artichokes are prohibitively expensive for most of us to chop up for a recipe, the frozen variety works just fine. If frozen artichoke hearts are unavailable, substitute a 15-ounce can (not marinated) and proceed with the recipe after the frozen-artichoke cooking instructions.*

2 tablespoons olive oil

1½ cups frozen artichoke hearts, thawed and chopped

2 garlic cloves, minced

1½ cups Arborio rice

½ cup dry white wine

4½ cups hot vegetable broth, homemade (page 141) or store-bought

Salt and freshly ground black pepper

¼ cup chopped fresh basil

1. In a large saucepan, heat the oil over medium heat. Add the artichoke hearts and garlic. Cover and cook until softened, for 5 minutes. Add the rice and stir to coat with oil. Add the wine and stir gently until liquid is absorbed.

2. Add the broth 1 cup at a time, stirring until liquid is absorbed before each addition. Add salt and pepper to taste. Simmer until the rice is soft and the consistency is creamy. Add the basil and taste, adjusting seasonings if necessary. Serve immediately.

# roasted winter squash risotto

makes 4 servings

*Studded with lovely orange pieces of winter squash and redolent of sage, this creamy risotto makes a soothing cold-weather meal. My favorite squash is the sweet and flavorful kabocha variety. If unavailable, use butter-cup or butternut squash.*

1 small winter squash, peeled, halved, and seeded

2 tablespoons olive oil

3 garlic cloves, minced

¾ teaspoon ground sage

½ cup dry white wine

1½ cups Arborio rice

5 cups hot vegetable broth, homemade (page 141) or store-bought

Salt and freshly ground black pepper

Fresh sage leaves, for garnish (optional)

1. Preheat the oven to 425°F. Lightly oil a 9 × 13-inch baking pan. Cut the squash into ½-inch dice and arrange in a single layer in the prepared baking pan. Roast until tender, about 25 minutes, turning once.

2. In a large saucepan, heat the oil over medium heat. Add the garlic and cook 1 minute. Stir in the ground sage, wine, and rice, stirring until the liquid is absorbed.

3. Add the broth 1 cup at a time, stirring until liquid is absorbed before each addition. Season with salt and pepper to taste and continue to simmer, stirring, until the rice is soft and creamy.

4. When the risotto is nearly ready, stir in 2 cups of the roasted squash. Spoon the risotto into 4 shallow bowls and garnish each serving with a spoonful of the remaining squash and the sage leaves, if using. Serve immediately.

# barley risotto with asparagus and mushrooms

makes 4 servings

*Although Arborio rice is traditional in risotto, barley cooks up thick and creamy, resulting in a dish that is very risotto-like in appearance and texture, with the unique wholesome flavor of barley.*

2 tablespoons olive oil

½ pound thin asparagus, tough ends trimmed and cut diagonally into 1-inch pieces

8 ounces white mushrooms, lightly rinsed, patted dry, and cut into ¼-inch slices

3 garlic cloves, minced

1 cup pearl barley

1 teaspoon minced fresh thyme or ¼ teaspoon dried

½ cup dry white wine

3 cups hot vegetable broth, homemade (page 141) or store-bought, or more if needed

Salt and freshly ground black pepper

1. In a large saucepan, heat the oil over medium heat. Add the asparagus, mushrooms, and garlic. Cover and cook for 5 minutes. Add the barley and stir to coat with oil. Add the thyme and wine and stir gently until the liquid is absorbed.

2. Add the broth, 1 cup at a time, stirring until liquid is absorbed before each addition. Add salt and pepper to taste. Simmer, stirring frequently, until creamy. Serve immediately.

# barley and winter vegetable stew

makes 4 servings

*This substantial and satisfying stew is just the thing to take the chill off on a cold winter evening. As with most soups and stews, this one tastes better the day after it is made, so plan ahead and make it in advance. You'll be rewarded the next day, when you just have to heat and serve. If you use water or a very light broth, you'll probably want to add an extra splash of soy sauce to boost the flavor.*

1 tablespoon olive oil

2 medium carrots, chopped

1 medium yellow onion, chopped

1 celery rib, chopped

2 garlic cloves, minced

¾ cup pearl barley

3 cups shredded cabbage

1 medium russet potato, peeled and cut into ½-inch dice

1 cup sliced cremini or white mushrooms

1 tablespoon soy sauce

1 teaspoon dried thyme

2 teaspoons dried dillweed

Salt and freshly ground black pepper

3 cups vegetable broth, homemade (page 141) or store-bought, or water

1½ cups cooked or 1 (15.5-ounce) can white beans, drained and rinsed

1. In a large saucepan, heat the oil over medium heat. Add the carrots, onion, and celery. Cover and cook until softened, about 10 minutes. Add the garlic and cook until fragrant, 1 minute. Add the barley, cabbage, potato, mushrooms, soy sauce, thyme, dillweed, and salt and pepper to taste. Stir in the broth and bring to a boil.

2. Reduce heat to low, add the beans, and simmer, uncovered, until the barley is cooked and the vegetables are tender, about 45 minutes. Taste, adjusting seasonings if necessary, depending on the saltiness of your broth. Serve immediately.

# barley pilaf with carrots, walnuts, and golden raisins

makes 4 servings

*Carrots and golden raisins add color and walnuts add crunch to this tasty pilaf made with hearty and wholesome barley. It makes a nice change of pace from the usual pilafs made with rice.*

2 tablespoons olive oil
1 medium yellow onion, finely chopped
1 medium carrot, finely chopped
½ cup chopped walnuts
2 cups vegetable broth, homemade (page 141)
    or store-bought
1 cup pearl barley
⅓ cup golden raisins
1 tablespoon minced fresh dillweed or 1 teaspoon
    dried

1. In a large skillet, heat the oil over medium heat. Add the onion and carrot, cover, and cook until softened, about 5 minutes. Stir in the walnuts and cook, uncovered, 5 minutes longer.

2. Add the broth and barley and bring to a boil. Reduce heat to low, cover, and simmer until the barley and vegetables are tender, stirring occasionally about 30 minutes. About 5 minutes before ready to serve, stir in the raisins and dillweed. Serve immediately.

# basic polenta

makes 4 servings

*Polenta is a versatile and economical Italian dish made from cornmeal. Enjoy it sprinkled with Parmasio (page 193) and drizzled with a little good olive oil or try one of the variations below. After the polenta is cooked, it can be spread into a loaf pan and cooled until firm, then sliced and pan-fried. Unlike the finely ground cornmeal used to make cornbread, the cornmeal used for polenta is medium or coarsely ground.*

3 cups vegetable broth, homemade (page 141)
    or store-bought, or water
Salt
1 cup polenta cornmeal
1 tablespoon olive oil
Freshly ground black pepper

1. Bring the broth to a boil in a large saucepan. Salt the water, then slowly stream in the polenta, whisking constantly. Reduce the heat to low and continue whisking until the polenta thickens and pulls away from the sides of the saucepan, about 15 minutes. Stir in the olive oil.

2. Serve as is, seasoned with salt and pepper to taste and with your sauce or topping of choice, or smooth into a loaf pan and chill for at least 2 hours, then slice and fry.

variations: Once the polenta is cooked, stir in any of the following:

- sautéed shallots, red chard or spinach, and porcini mushrooms
- chopped cooked artichoke hearts
- thawed frozen peas
- canned chopped mild or hot green chiles
- chopped sautéed Tempeh Bacon (page 525)
- fresh or thawed frozen corn kernels
- finely minced canned chipotle chiles in adobo
- chopped fresh cilantro or parsley

# polenta with spicy tomato ragù 🅕

makes 4 servings

*Creamy polenta topped with a spicy tomato sauce made a regular appearance on the menu when I was growing up. Today, it remains my favorite way to enjoy polenta. For a quicker version, use precooked polenta, available in the produce section of well-stocked supermarkets. Cut it into slices and sauté in a skillet in a small amount of olive oil, then top with the sauce.*

1 tablespoon olive oil

1 medium yellow onion, chopped

3 garlic cloves, chopped

8 ounces white mushrooms, lightly rinsed, patted dry, and chopped

3 cups marinara sauce, homemade (page 194) or store-bought

1 teaspoon ground fennel seed

½ teaspoon crushed red pepper

¼ teaspoon dried oregano

1 recipe Basic Polenta (page 276), warm

1. In a large saucepan, heat the oil over medium heat. Add the onion, cover, and cook until softened, 5 minutes. Add the garlic and mushrooms and cook until softened, uncovered, about 3 minutes.

2. Stir in the marinara sauce, fennel seed, crushed red pepper, and oregano. Reduce the heat to low and simmer for 10 minutes. Spoon the warm polenta into 4 shallow bowls, top with sauce, and serve.

# fried double-corn grits

makes 4 servings

*Grits, the polenta of the South, are made from ground dried corn kernels from which the hull of the corn has been removed. Since fried foods are also a specialty of Southern cooking, it's a natural fit to fry these tasty grits. Serve with black-eyed peas and the Slow-Simmered Collard Greens (page 365).*

4 cups water

1 cup stone-ground grits

Salt

1 cup fresh or frozen corn kernels, thawed

2 or 3 green onions, minced

Freshly ground black pepper

½ cup all-purpose flour

Canola or grapeseed oil, for frying

1. In a large saucepan, bring the water to a boil over high heat. Stir in the grits, salt the water, and reduce the heat to medium. Simmer, stirring constantly, until the grits are cooked and thickened, about 20 minutes. Stir in the corn and green onions. Season with salt and pepper to taste.

2. Pour the hot grits into a lightly oiled baking dish or loaf pan and smooth the top. Set aside to cool, then cover and refrigerate to chill thoroughly, 2 hours. When the grits are firm, cut into ½-inch slices. Dredge the grits slices in the flour, shaking off the excess.

3. In a large nonstick skillet, heat a thin layer of oil. Add the grit slices and cook until golden brown on both sides, about 8 minutes total. Transfer to a plate lined with paper towels to absorb any excess oil. Season with salt and pepper to taste and serve immediately.

# couscous pilaf ⓕ

makes 4 servings

*From the crunchy toasted almonds and chewy sweet dried apricots and cranberries, this colorful pilaf is a delight for the senses. Delicious either hot or cold, it makes a great addition to a potluck.*

2 tablespoons olive oil

1 medium red onion, chopped

1 medium carrot, shredded

1 cup frozen baby peas, thawed

¼ cup chopped dried apricots

¼ cup sweetened dried cranberries

1 cup couscous

2 cups water

Salt and freshly ground black pepper

2 tablespoons minced fresh parsley

½ cup toasted slivered almonds

1. In a large skillet, heat the oil over medium heat. Add the onion, cover, and cook until softened, 5 minutes. Add the carrot and cook, uncovered, 3 minutes longer. Stir in the peas, apricots, cranberries, couscous, and water. Season with salt and pepper to taste. Bring to a boil, then remove from the heat and cover with a lid. Set aside for 10 minutes.

2. Transfer pilaf to a serving bowl, stir in the parsley and almonds and serve immediately.

# couscous-chickpea loaf

makes 6 servings

*Quick-cooking couscous combines with chickpeas, tomatoes, and Mediterranean spices in this wholesome and flavorful loaf.*

2 cups vegetable broth, homemade (page 141) or store-bought

1 cup couscous

Salt

1 tablespoon olive oil

3 garlic cloves, minced

1½ cups cooked or 1 (15.5-ounce) can chickpeas, drained and rinsed

1 (14.5-ounce) can diced tomatoes, drained

¼ cup minced oil-packed sun-dried tomatoes

1 tablespoon chopped capers

1 teaspoon dried basil

½ teaspoon dried oregano

Freshly ground black pepper

8 ounces firm tofu, drained and patted dry

1. In a large saucepan, bring the broth to a boil over high heat. Add the couscous and salt to taste. Turn off the heat, cover, and let sit for 10 minutes.

2. Preheat the oven to 350°F. Lightly oil a 9-inch loaf pan and set aside. In a large skillet, heat the oil over medium heat. Add the garlic and cook until softened, about 30 seconds. Add the chickpeas, tomatoes, sun-dried tomatoes, capers, basil, oregano, and salt and pepper to taste. Stir to mix well, then reduce heat to low and simmer until the liquid evaporates, about 5 minutes. Set aside.

3. In a blender or food processor, combine the tofu, 1 cup of the chickpea mixture, and salt and pepper to taste. Process until smooth and stir back into the chickpea mixture.

4. In a large bowl, combine the cooked couscous with the chickpea and tofu mixture and transfer to the prepared loaf pan. Cover and bake for 25 minutes. Uncover and continue baking until the top is lightly browned, about 10 minutes longer. Allow to sit at room temperature for 15 minutes and then slice and serve.

# quinoa and summer squash pilaf

makes 4 servings

*It always amazes me that this tiny "super-grain of the Incas" can be so densely packed with nutrients and is, in fact, a complete protein. That's something to ponder while enjoying this light and lovely summertime pilaf.*

1 tablespoon olive oil

1 medium red onion, minced

2 medium yellow summer squash or zucchini, chopped

Salt and freshly ground black pepper

1½ cups quinoa, well rinsed

3 cups vegetable broth, homemade (page 141) or store-bought, or water

1 cup ripe grape or cherry tomatoes, quartered

¼ cup chopped fresh basil

1. In a large saucepan, heat the oil over medium heat. Add the onion, cover, and cook until tender, 10 minutes. Add the squash and season with salt and pepper to taste. Cook, uncovered, until softened, 5 minutes.

2. Stir in the quinoa, then add the broth and bring to a boil. Reduce heat to low, add salt to taste, cover, and simmer until the quinoa has absorbed all the liquid, 20 to 30 minutes. When ready to serve, transfer to a serving bowl and stir in the tomatoes and basil. Serve immediately.

# quinoa and chickpea pilaf with orange and pistachios

makes 4 servings

*"Easy" and "elegant" are the keywords for this flavorful pilaf enlivened by the sweet tang of orange and the gentle crunch of pistachios. To turn it into a fabulous one-dish meal, stir in some thawed frozen peas or add a few cups of baby spinach and cook until wilted.*

1 tablespoon olive oil

1 medium red onion, minced

1½ cups quinoa, well rinsed

3 cups vegetable broth, homemade (page 141) or store-bought, or water

Salt

3 cups or 2 (15.5-ounce) cans chickpeas, drained and rinsed

¼ teaspoon ground cayenne

1 tablespoon minced fresh chives

1 orange, peeled, segmented, and chopped

½ cup shelled pistachios

1. In a large saucepan, heat the oil over medium heat. Add the onion, cover, and cook until tender, 10 minutes. Stir in the quinoa, add the broth, and bring to a boil.

2. Reduce heat to low, add salt to taste, cover, and simmer until the quinoa has absorbed all the liquid, 20 to 30 minutes. Remove from heat and set aside for 5 minutes, then stir in the chickpeas, cayenne, chives, orange, and pistachios. Taste, adjusting seasonings if necessary. Serve immediately.

# quinoa and mixed vegetable sauté

makes 4 servings

*This colorful grain and vegetable mélange is as versatile as the vegetables in your refrigerator. For example, you can substitute green onions for the red onion, yellow squash or carrots for the zucchini, or cilantro or basil for the parsley. It's terrific on its own or served with the Chipotle-Painted Baked Tofu (page 288).*

3 cups water

Salt

1½ cups quinoa, well rinsed

1 tablespoon olive oil

1 small red onion, chopped

1 medium red bell pepper, chopped

1 medium zucchini, chopped

2 cups cooked shelled edamame

2 cups frozen corn kernels, thawed

2 ripe Roma tomatoes, chopped

Freshly ground black pepper

3 tablespoons chopped fresh parsley

1. In a large saucepan, bring the water to a boil over high heat. Salt the water and add the quinoa. Reduce the heat to medium and cook 20 to 30 minutes. Remove from the heat and set aside.

2. In a large skillet, heat the oil over medium heat. Add the onion and bell pepper, cover, and cook until softened, 5 minutes. Add the zucchini and cook, uncovered, until softened, about 7 minutes, stirring occasionally. Stir in the edamame, corn, tomatoes, and salt and black pepper to taste. Cook 5 minutes, stirring occasionally, until heated through.

3. Add the cooked quinoa and parsley and stir gently to combine. Serve immediately.

# kasha with roasted sweet potatoes and peas

makes 4 servings

*When the weather turns cold, visions of kasha dance in my head. Also known as buckwheat groats, kasha is a hearty grain that combines beautifully with nutritious and colorful sweet potatoes and peas for a warming winter meal.*

2 large sweet potatoes, peeled and cut into ½-inch dice

2 tablespoons olive oil

Salt and freshly ground black pepper

1 large yellow onion, finely chopped

1 cup coarse kasha (buckwheat groats)

2 cups vegetable broth, homemade (page 141) or store-bought, or water

1 cup frozen peas

1. Preheat the oven to 425°F. Spread the sweet potatoes on a lightly oiled baking pan and drizzle with 1 tablespoon of the oil. Season with salt and pepper to taste and roast until tender, about 25 minutes, stirring once about halfway through. Set aside.

2. In a large skillet, heat the remaining 1 tablespoon oil over medium heat. Add the onion, cover, and cook, stirring occasionally, until browned, about 10 minutes. Stir in the kasha. Add the broth and bring to a boil. Reduce the heat to low, cover, and simmer until the kasha is cooked, about 15 minutes.

3. Add the peas and roasted sweet potatoes and season with salt and pepper to taste. Stir gently to combine. Serve immediately.

# herbed millet and pecan loaf

makes 4 to 6 servings

*The recipe for this delectable loaf was shared with me by Francis Janes, former chef-owner of Café Ambrosia in Seattle. It is so moist and flavorful, it doesn't really need a sauce, but if you'd like one, consider the Mushroom Sauce on page 546.*

½ cup millet

1½ cups vegetable broth, homemade (page 141) or store-bought

1 tablespoon olive oil

1 medium yellow onion, finely chopped

1 celery rib, minced

4 garlic cloves, minced

1 medium carrot, finely shredded

2 cups pecan pieces

6 green onions, minced

1 cup fresh parsley, finely chopped

½ cup fresh basil, finely chopped

2 tablespoons soy sauce

¼ teaspoon freshly ground black pepper

1. In a medium saucepan, bring the millet and broth to a boil. Reduce heat to low, cover, and cook until water is absorbed, 35 to 40 minutes.

2. Preheat the oven to 350°F. Lightly oil a 9-inch loaf pan and set aside. In a large skillet, heat the oil over medium heat. Add the onion, celery, and garlic. Cover and cook until softened, about 5 minutes. Stir in the carrot and transfer to a large bowl. Set aside.

3. In a food processor, combine the pecans, green onions, parsley, and basil. Pulse until the pecans are finely ground. Add to the celery mixture and stir to combine. Add the cooked millet along with the soy sauce and pepper. Stir well to mix.

4. Transfer the mixture to the prepared loaf pan and smooth the top. Bake until firm, about 30 minutes. Let stand at room temperature for 15 minutes before slicing.

# millet, chard, and white bean casserole

makes 4 to 6 servings

*The creamy white color and mild flavor of millet and white beans create a perfect backdrop to the vibrant red bell pepper, chard, and tomatoes. This satisfying comfort-food casserole can be assembled in advance of when you need it and then popped in the oven.*

2¾ cups water

1 cup millet

Salt

1 tablespoon olive oil

1 medium yellow onion, chopped

1 medium red bell pepper, chopped

2 garlic cloves, minced

3 cups chopped stemmed Swiss chard

Salt and freshly ground black pepper

1½ cups cooked or 1 (15.5-ounce) can Great Northern beans, drained and rinsed

1 cup ripe cherry tomatoes, quartered

2 tablespoons fresh lemon juice

¼ cup nutritional yeast (optional)

2 tablespoons minced fresh dillweed

2 tablespoons minced fresh parsley

⅓ cup dry unseasoned bread crumbs

1. In a large saucepan, bring the water to a boil over high heat. Add the millet and ½ teaspoon of salt and return to a boil. Reduce the heat to low, cover, and simmer until tender, 30 to 40 minutes. Set aside.

continues on next page

2. Preheat the oven to 350°F. Lightly oil a 2-quart casserole and set aside. In a large skillet, heat the oil over medium heat. Add the onion and bell pepper, cover, and cook until softened, 7 minutes. Add the garlic and chard and season with salt and black pepper to taste. Cover and cook, stirring occasionally, until the chard is wilted, about 5 minutes. Stir the chard mixture into the cooked millet, along with the beans, tomatoes, lemon juice, yeast, dillweed, and parsley.

3. Transfer the mixture to the prepared casserole and sprinkle evenly with the bread crumbs. Bake, uncovered, until golden brown on top, 20 to 25 minutes. Serve immediately.

# millet and amaranth loaf

makes 4 servings

*Millet is a nutritious, nonglutinous grain with a mild, nutlike flavor. Rich in protein, fiber, and B-complex vitamins, it is also high in iron, magnesium, and potassium. Similarly, amaranth has a slightly sweet, nutty flavor and is full of amazing nutritional benefits, being extremely high in protein, iron, calcium, and fiber. Both millet and amaranth are gluten-free, making this is an especially good recipe to serve to those who are gluten-sensitive.*

3 cups vegetable broth, homemade (page 141) or store-bought, or water

¾ cup millet

¼ cup amaranth

Salt

1 medium yellow onion, finely chopped

2 garlic cloves, minced

1 medium zucchini, finely chopped

½ cup frozen peas

¼ cup minced fresh parsley

1 teaspoon dried thyme

Freshly ground black pepper

1. In a large saucepan, bring the broth to a boil over high heat. Add the millet, amaranth, and salt to taste. Cook until the grains are soft and the water is absorbed, about 25 minutes.

2. Preheat the oven to 350°F. Lightly oil a 9-inch loaf pan and set aside. In a large skillet, heat the oil over medium heat. Add the onion, cover, and cook until soft, about 8 minutes. Add the garlic, zucchini, and peas and cook until the vegetables are softened. Add the parsley, thyme, and salt and pepper to taste.

3. Stir in the cooked millet and amaranth, then transfer the mixture to the prepared loaf pan. Bake until golden brown on top, about 20 minutes. Serve immediately.

# savory amaranth patties

makes 4 patties

*The nutty flavor of amaranth combines with walnuts to make these hearty, protein-rich patties. Serve them with Chipotle Mayonnaise (page 574) or Tahini-Lemon Sauce (page 558) or enjoy them in a sandwich with lettuce, tomato, and your favorite condiment. Although amaranth is often thought of as a grain, it is actually a small super-nutritious seed. A small serving of amaranth provides nearly 30 percent of the daily requirement of protein. In fact, amaranth contains higher essential amino acids than any other grain, making it one of the best sources of vegetable protein on the planet.*

1 cup water

½ cup amaranth

Salt

3 tablespoons olive oil

½ cup minced onion

½ cup shredded carrot

½ cup ground walnuts

1 teaspoon soy sauce

2 tablespoons wheat gluten flour (vital wheat gluten)

2 tablespoons minced fresh parsley or cilantro

Freshly ground black pepper

1. In a small saucepan, bring the water to a boil over high heat. Add the amaranth and salt to taste and reduce the heat to low. Cover and simmer until the amaranth is cooked, about 15 to 20 minutes. Set aside.

2. In a large skillet, heat 1 tablespoon of the oil over medium heat. Add the onion and carrot. Cover and cook until soft, 5 minutes. Stir in the walnuts and cook, uncovered, 2 minutes longer. Transfer the mixture to a large bowl. Add the soy sauce, flour, parsley, and salt and pepper to taste. Add the cooked amaranth and stir to mix well.

3. Form the mixture into 4 patties. Heat the remaining 2 tablespoons oil in a large nonstick skillet. Add the patties and cook until browned on both sides, turning once, about 10 minutes total. Serve immediately.

# TOFU AND TEMPEH

## soy-glazed tofu

makes 4 servings

*Now you can make baked marinated tofu at home for a fraction of the cost of the packaged variety. This easy and versatile tofu can be served hot as a main dish or cooled to room temperature and refrigerated to use in salads and sandwiches. Instead of baking it in slices, you can cut the tofu into strips or cubes, if you prefer.*

1 pound extra-firm tofu, drained, cut into ½-inch slices, and pressed (page xiv)

⅓ cup soy sauce

¼ cup toasted sesame oil

¼ cup rice vinegar

2 teaspoons sugar

1. Blot the tofu dry and arrange in a 9 × 13-inch baking dish and set aside.

2. In a small saucepan, combine the soy sauce, oil, vinegar, and sugar and bring to a boil. Pour the hot marinade onto the tofu and set aside to marinate 30 minutes, turning once.

3. Preheat the oven to 350°F. Bake the tofu for 30 minutes, turning once about halfway through. Serve immediately or allow to cool to room temperature, then cover and refrigerate until needed.

# cajun-style tofu

makes 4 servings

*A crisp outer coating of Cajun spices and a spicy hot tomato sauce dispels any rumors that tofu has no flavor. One of tofu's greatest qualities is its ability to absorb the flavor of its surrounding ingredients, so if you like it hot and spicy, this tofu is for you. Use more or less of the spice blend according to taste.*

1 pound extra-firm tofu, drained and patted dry
Salt
1 tablespoon plus 1 teaspoon Cajun seasoning
2 tablespoons olive oil
¼ cup minced green bell pepper
1 tablespoon minced celery
2 tablespoons minced green onion
2 garlic cloves, minced
1 (14.5-ounce) can diced tomatoes, drained
1 tablespoon soy sauce
1 tablespoon minced fresh parsley

1. Cut the tofu into ½-inch thick slices and sprinkle both sides with salt and the 1 tablespoon Cajun seasoning. Set aside.

2. In a small saucepan, heat 1 tablespoon of the oil over medium heat. Add the bell pepper and celery. Cover and cook for 5 minutes. Add the green onion and garlic and cook, uncovered, 1 minute longer. Stir in the tomatoes, soy sauce, parsley, the remaining 1 teaspoon Cajun spice blend, and salt to taste. Simmer for 10 minutes to blend the flavors and set aside.

3. In a large skillet, heat the remaining 1 tablespoon oil over medium-high heat. Add the tofu and cook until browned on both sides, about 10 minutes. Add the sauce and simmer 5 minutes. Serve immediately.

# crispy tofu with sizzling caper sauce 🅕

makes 4 servings

*The piquant sparkle of the caper sauce is the perfect complement to the crisp slices of tofu. Rice pilaf and roasted asparagus make good accompaniments.*

1 pound extra-firm tofu, drained, cut into ¼-inch slices, and pressed (page xiv)
Salt and freshly ground black pepper
½ cup cornstarch
3 tablespoons olive oil, plus more if needed
1 medium shallot, minced
3 tablespoons capers
3 tablespoons minced fresh parsley
2 tablespoons vegan margarine
Juice of 1 lemon

1. Preheat the oven to 275°F. Pat the tofu dry and season with salt and pepper to taste. Place the cornstarch in a shallow bowl. Dredge the tofu in the cornstarch, coating all sides.

2. In a large skillet, heat 2 tablespoons of the oil over medium heat. Add the tofu, in batches if necessary, and cook until golden brown on both sides, about 4 minutes per side. Transfer the fried tofu to a heatproof platter and keep warm in the oven.

3. In the same skillet, heat the remaining 1 tablespoon of the oil over medium heat. Add the shallot and cook until softened, about 3 minutes. Add the capers and parsley and cook for 30 seconds, then stir in the margarine, lemon juice, and salt and pepper to taste, stirring to melt and incorporate the margarine. Top the tofu with caper sauce and serve immediately.

# country-fried tofu with golden gravy 🅕

makes 4 servings

*The rich golden gravy is made with pureed chickpeas for a wholesome and satisfying sauce to cloak the crisply fried tofu.*

1 pound extra-firm tofu, drained, cut into
 ½-inch slices, and pressed (page xiv)
Salt and freshly ground black pepper
⅓ cup cornstarch
3 tablespoons olive oil
1 medium sweet yellow onion, chopped
2 tablespoons all-purpose flour
1 teaspoon dried thyme
⅛ teaspoon turmeric
1 cup vegetable broth, homemade (page 141)
 or store-bought
½ cup plain unsweetened soy milk
1 tablespoon soy sauce
¾ cup cooked or canned chickpeas,
 drained and rinsed
2 tablespoons minced fresh parsley, for garnish

1. Blot the tofu dry and season with salt and pepper to taste. Place the cornstarch in a shallow bowl. Dredge the tofu in the cornstarch, coating all sides. Preheat the oven to 250°F.

2. In a large skillet, heat 2 tablespoons of the oil over medium heat. Add the tofu, in batches if necessary, and cook until golden brown on both sides, about 10 minutes. Transfer the fried tofu to a heatproof platter and keep warm in the oven.

3. In the same skillet, heat the remaining 1 tablespoon of the oil over medium heat. Add the onion, cover, and cook until softened, 5 minutes. Uncover and reduce heat to low. Stir in the flour, thyme, and turmeric and cook for 1 minute, stirring constantly. Slowly whisk in the broth, then the soy milk and soy sauce.

Add the chickpeas and season with salt and pepper to taste. Continue to cook, stir frequently, for 2 minutes. Transfer to a blender and process until smooth and creamy. Return to the saucepan and heat until hot, adding a little more broth if the sauce is too thick. Spoon the sauce over the tofu and sprinkle with the parsley. Serve immediately.

# orange-glazed tofu and asparagus

makes 4 servings

*This is an elegant and extremely tasty way to serve tofu. I especially enjoy it served over a fragrant rice, such as basmati or jasmine. If you have a little extra time and don't mind dirtying another pan, consider roasting the asparagus separately on an oiled baking sheet (425°F for 8 to 10 minutes)—you can actually roast it while the tofu is marinating and then add it to the skillet just long enough to heat through. Although asparagus is perfectly fine prepared other ways, I roast it every chance I get because I think the flavor is incomparable.*

2 tablespoons mirin
1 tablespoon cornstarch
1 (16-ounce) package extra-firm tofu, drained and
 cut into ¼-inch strips
⅓ cup fresh orange juice
2 tablespoons soy sauce
1 teaspoon toasted sesame oil
1 teaspoon sugar
¼ teaspoon Asian chili paste
2 tablespoons canola or grapeseed oil
1 garlic clove, minced
½ teaspoon minced fresh ginger
8 ounces thin asparagus, tough ends trimmed
 and cut into 1½-inch pieces

continues on next page

1. In a shallow bowl, combine the mirin and cornstarch and blend well. Add the tofu and toss gently to coat. Set aside to marinate for 30 minutes.

2. In a small bowl, combine the orange juice, soy sauce, sesame oil, sugar, and chili paste. Set aside.

3. In a large skillet or wok, heat the canola oil over medium heat. Add the garlic and ginger and stir-fry until fragrant, about 30 seconds. Add the marinated tofu and the asparagus and stir-fry until the tofu is golden brown and the asparagus is just tender, about 5 minutes. Stir in the sauce and cook for about 2 minutes more. Serve immediately.

## tofu pizzaiola

makes 4 servings

*Although the term* pizzaiola *indicates a sauce made with tomatoes, garlic, and oregano only, I've included some olives and capers for extra flavor.*

2 tablespoons olive oil

1 (16-ounce) package extra-firm tofu, drained, cut into ½-inch slices, and pressed (page xiv)

Salt

4 garlic cloves, minced

1 (14.5-ounce) can diced tomatoes, drained

¼ cup oil-packed sun-dried tomatoes, cut into ¼-inch strips

¼ cup pitted kalamata olives, halved

1 tablespoon capers

1 teaspoon dried oregano

½ teaspoon sugar

Freshly ground black pepper

2 tablespoons minced fresh parsley, for garnish

1. Preheat the oven to 275°F. In a large skillet, heat 1 tablespoon of the oil over medium heat. Add the tofu and cook until golden brown on both sides, turning once, about 5 minutes per side. Sprinkle the tofu with salt to taste. Transfer the fried tofu to a heatproof platter and keep warm in the oven.

2. In the same skillet, heat the remaining 1 tablespoon oil over medium heat. Add the garlic and cook until softened, about 1 minute. Do not brown. Stir in the diced tomatoes, sun-dried tomatoes, olives, and capers. Add the oregano, sugar, and salt and pepper to taste. Simmer until the sauce is hot and the flavors are well combined, about 10 minutes. Top the fried tofu slices with the sauce and sprinkle with the parsley. Serve immediately.

## "ka-pow" tofu

makes 4 servings

*I order tofu kaprao in my favorite Thai restaurant, knowing it will contain the wonderfully fragrant Thai basil called kaprao. I also know it will pack a spicy punch, so I've come to call it "ka-pow." Serve over jasmine rice. If the sublime Thai basil is unavailable, there's no exact substitute, though you could use regular basil or cilantro and still have a tasty meal. Vegetarian oyster sauce is available at Asian markets or online. If you can't find it, leave it out and add a little extra soy sauce.*

1 pound extra-firm tofu, drained, patted dry,
    and cut into 1-inch cubes

Salt

2 tablespoons cornstarch

3 tablespoons soy sauce

1 tablespoon vegetarian oyster sauce

2 teaspoons Nothin' Fishy Nam Pla (page 560)
    or 1 teaspoon rice vinegar

1 teaspoon light brown sugar

½ teaspoon crushed red pepper

2 tablespoons canola or grapeseed oil

1 medium sweet yellow onion, halved and cut into
    ½-inch slices

1 medium red bell pepper, cut into ¼-inch slices

3 green onions, chopped

½ cup Thai basil leaves

1. In a medium bowl, combine the tofu, salt to taste, and cornstarch. Toss to coat and set aside.

2. In a small bowl, combine the soy sauce, oyster sauce, nam pla, sugar, and crushed red pepper. Stir well to combine and set aside.

3. In a large skillet, heat 1 tablespoon of the oil over medium-high heat. Add the tofu and cook until golden brown, about 8 minutes. Remove from the skillet and set aside.

4. In the same skillet, heat the remaining 1 tablespoon oil over medium heat. Add the onion and bell pepper and stir-fry until softened, about 5 minutes. Add the green onions and cook 1 minute longer. Stir in the fried tofu, the sauce, and the basil and stir-fry until hot, about 3 minutes. Serve immediately.

# sicilian-style tofu

makes 4 servings

*The zesty tomato sauce on the crisply fried tofu is also great over pasta. In fact, if you cut the tofu into bite-size pieces before cooking, the entire dish can be served over your favorite noodles.*

2 tablespoons olive oil

1 pound extra-firm tofu, drained, cut into
    ¼-inch slices, and pressed (page xiv)

Salt and freshly ground black pepper

1 small yellow onion, chopped

2 garlic cloves, minced

1 (28-ounce) can diced tomatoes, drained

¼ cup dry white wine

¼ teaspoon crushed red pepper

⅓ cup pitted kalamata olives

1½ tablespoons capers

2 tablespoons chopped fresh basil or 1 teaspoon
    dried (optional)

1. Preheat the oven to 250°F. In a large skillet, heat 1 tablespoon of the oil over medium heat. Add the tofu, in batches if necessary, and cook until golden brown on both sides, 5 minutes per sides. Season with salt and black pepper to taste. Transfer the cooked tofu to a heatproof platter and keep warm in the oven while you prepare the sauce.

2. In the same skillet, heat the remaining 1 tablespoon oil over medium heat. Add the onion and garlic, cover, and cook until the onion is softened, 10 minutes. Add the tomatoes, wine, and crushed red pepper. Bring to a boil, then reduce heat to low and simmer, uncovered, for 15 minutes. Stir in the olives and capers. Cook for 2 minutes more.

3. Arrange the tofu on a platter or individual plates. Spoon the sauce on top. Sprinkle with fresh basil, if using. Serve immediately.

# thai-phoon stir-fry

makes 4 servings

*I call this spicy-sweet tofu and vegetable stir-fry a "Thai-phoon" because the tasty garnishes are scattered on top as if by a strong wind. Serve over freshly cooked rice or your favorite noodles.*

1 pound extra-firm tofu, drained and patted dry

2 tablespoons canola or grapeseed oil

3 medium shallots, halved lengthwise and cut into ⅛-inch slices

2 garlic cloves, minced

2 teaspoons grated fresh ginger

8 ounces white mushroom caps, lightly rinsed, patted dry, and cut into ½-inch slices

1 tablespoon creamy peanut butter

2 teaspoons light brown sugar

1 teaspoon Asian chili paste

3 tablespoons soy sauce

1 tablespoon mirin

1 (13.5-ounce) can unsweetened coconut milk

6 ounces chopped fresh spinach

1 tablespoon toasted sesame oil

Freshly cooked rice or noodles, to serve

¼ cup unsweetened shredded coconut

2 tablespoons finely chopped fresh Thai basil or cilantro

2 tablespoons crushed unsalted roasted peanuts

2 teaspoons minced crystallized ginger (optional)

1. Cut the tofu into ½-inch dice and set aside. In a large skillet, heat 1 tablespoon of the oil over medium-high heat. Add the tofu and stir-fry until golden brown, about 7 minutes. Remove the tofu from the skillet and set aside.

2. In the same skillet, heat the remaining 1 tablespoon oil over medium heat. Add shallots, garlic, ginger, and mushrooms and stir-fry until softened, about 4 minutes.

3. Stir in the peanut butter, sugar, chili paste, soy sauce, and mirin. Stir in the coconut milk and mix until well blended. Add the fried tofu and the spinach and bring to a simmer. Reduce the heat to medium-low and simmer, stirring occasionally, until the spinach is wilted and the flavors are well blended, 5 to 7 minutes. Stir in the sesame oil and simmer for another minute. To serve, spoon the tofu mixture onto your choice of rice or noodles and top with coconut, basil, peanuts, and crystallized ginger, if using. Serve immediately.

# chipotle-painted baked tofu 🅕

makes 4 servings

*If you like the smoky heat of chipotle chiles, then you'll love what it does for tofu. A little chipotle goes a long way, but there's no need to waste the rest when opening a can for just a small amount. Simply measure out what you need and then freeze the rest in small measured amounts for use in future recipes.*

3 tablespoons soy sauce

2 canned chipotle chiles in adobo

1 tablespoon olive oil

1 pound extra-firm tofu, drained, cut into ½-inch thick slices, and pressed (page xiv)

1. Preheat the oven to 375°F. Lightly oil a 9 × 13-inch baking pan and set aside.

2. In a food processor, combine the soy sauce, chipotles, and oil and process until blended. Scrape the chipotle mixture into a small bowl.

3. Brush the chipotle mixture onto both sides of the tofu slices and arrange them in a single layer in the prepared pan. Bake until hot, about 20 minutes. Serve immediately.

# grilled tofu with tamarind glaze

makes 4 servings

*Vegan chef Tal Ronnen is a first-class soy-meister. Here's my version of his grilled tamarind tofu. Serve over freshly cooked rice so none of the scrumptious sauce goes to waste.*

1 pound extra-firm tofu, drained and patted dry
Salt and freshly ground black pepper
2 tablespoons olive oil
2 medium shallots, minced
2 garlic cloves, minced
2 ripe tomatoes, coarsely chopped
3 tablespoons ketchup
¼ cup water
2 tablespoons Dijon mustard
1 tablespoon dark brown sugar
2 tablespoons agave nectar
2 tablespoons tamarind concentrate
1 tablespoon dark molasses
½ teaspoon ground cayenne
1 tablespoon smoked paprika
1 tablespoon soy sauce

1. Cut the tofu into 1-inch slices, season with salt and pepper to taste, and set aside in a shallow baking pan.

2. In a large saucepan, heat the oil over medium heat. Add the shallots and garlic and sauté for 2 minutes. Add all the remaining ingredients, except for the tofu. Reduce the heat to low and simmer for 15 minutes. Transfer the mixture to a blender or food processor and blend until smooth. Return to the saucepan and cook 15 minutes longer, then set aside to cool. Pour the sauce over the tofu and refrigerate for at least 2 hours. Preheat a grill or broiler.

3. Grill the marinated tofu, turning once, to heat through and brown nicely on both sides. While the tofu is grilling, reheat the marinade in a saucepan. Remove the tofu from the grill, brush each side with the tamarind sauce, and serve immediately.

variation: Instead of grilling, the tofu can be sautéed in a skillet or baked in a moderate oven for 20 to 30 minutes.

# tofu stuffed with watercress and tomatoes 🄵

makes 4 servings

*This light, fresh-tasting way to serve tofu is like stuffing your salad into your main course. Just be careful when you cut and stuff the fragile tofu, as it can tear easily.*

1 pound extra-firm tofu, drained, cut into
    ¾-inch slices, and pressed (page xiv)
Salt and freshly ground black pepper
1 small bunch watercress, tough stems removed
    and chopped
2 ripe plum tomatoes, chopped
½ cup minced green onions
2 tablespoons minced fresh parsley
2 tablespoons minced fresh basil
1 teaspoon minced garlic
4 tablespoons olive oil
1 tablespoon balsamic vinegar
Pinch sugar
½ cup all-purpose flour
½ cup water
1½ cups dry unseasoned bread crumbs

1. Cut a long deep pocket in side of each slice of tofu and place the tofu on a baking sheet. Season with salt and pepper to taste and set aside.

continues on next page

2. In a large bowl, combine the watercress, tomatoes, green onions, parsley, basil, garlic, 2 tablespoons of the oil, vinegar, sugar, and salt and pepper to taste. Mix until well combined, then carefully stuff the mixture into the tofu pockets.

3. Place the flour in a shallow bowl. Pour the water into a separate shallow bowl. Place the bread crumbs on a large plate. Dredge the tofu in the flour, then carefully dip it in the water, and then dredge it in the bread crumbs, coating thoroughly.

4. In a large skillet, heat the remaining 2 tablespoons oil over medium heat. Add the stuffed tofu to the skillet and cook until golden brown, turning once, 4 to 5 minutes per side. Serve immediately.

# tofu with pistachio-pistachio-pomegranate sauce

makes 4 servings

*This is a lovely, simple recipe, but the beautiful mahogany-red sauce studded with pale green pistachios has such a delicious, complex flavor that it turns everyday tofu into gourmet fare. This recipe can also be made with seitan or tempeh, if you prefer.*

1 pound extra-firm tofu, drained, cut into
    ¼-inch slices, and pressed (page xiv)
Salt and freshly ground black pepper
2 tablespoons olive oil
½ cup pomegranate juice
1 tablespoon balsamic vinegar
1 tablespoon light brown sugar
3 green onions, minced
½ cup unsalted shelled pistachios, coarsely chopped

1. Season the tofu with salt and pepper to taste.

2. In a large skillet, heat the oil over medium heat. Add the tofu slices, in batches if necessary, and cook until lightly browned, about 4 minutes per side. Remove from skillet and set aside.

3. In the same skillet, add the pomegranate juice, vinegar, sugar, and green onions and simmer over medium heat, for 5 minutes. Add half of the pistachios and cook until sauce is slightly thickened, about 5 minutes.

4. Return the fried tofu to the skillet and cook until hot, about 5 minutes, spooning the sauce over the tofu as it simmers. Serve immediately, sprinkled with the remaining pistachios.

# spice island tofu

makes 4 servings

*Tofu gets a double dose of flavor in this recipe—first, from the crisp coating of herbs and spices and second, from the zesty sauce that includes bits of pineapple for a touch of the tropics. Serve on a bed of freshly cooked rice or couscous. Seitan or tempeh may be used instead of the tofu.*

½ cup cornstarch
½ teaspoon minced fresh thyme or ¼ teaspoon dried
½ teaspoon minced fresh marjoram or ¼ teaspoon
    dried
½ teaspoon salt
¼ teaspoon ground cayenne
¼ teaspoon sweet or smoked paprika
¼ teaspoon light brown sugar
⅛ teaspoon ground allspice
1 pound extra-firm tofu, drained and cut into
    ½-inch strips
3 tablespoons canola or grapeseed oil
1 medium red bell pepper, cut into ¼-inch strips
3 green onions, chopped
1 garlic cloves, minced

1 jalapeño, seeded and minced

2 ripe plum tomatoes, seeded and chopped

1 cup chopped fresh or canned pineapple

2 tablespoons soy sauce

¼ cup water

2 teaspoons fresh lime juice

1 tablespoon minced fresh parsley, for garnish

1. In a shallow bowl, combine the cornstarch, thyme, marjoram, salt, cayenne, paprika, sugar, and allspice. Mix well. Dredge the tofu in the spice mixture, coating on all sides. Preheat the oven to 250°F.

2. In a large skillet, heat 2 tablespoons of the oil over medium heat. Add the dredged tofu, in batches if necessary and cook until golden brown, about 4 minutes per side. Transfer the fried tofu to a heatproof platter and keep warm in the oven.

3. In the same skillet, heat the remaining 1 tablespoon oil over medium heat. Add the bell pepper, green onions, garlic, and jalapeño. Cover and cook, stirring occasionally, until tender, about 10 minutes. Add the tomatoes, pineapple, soy sauce, water, and lime juice and simmer until the mixture is hot and the flavors have combined, about 5 minutes. Spoon the vegetable mixture over the fried tofu. Sprinkle with minced parsley and serve immediately.

# ginger tofu with citrus-hoisin sauce  f

makes 4 servings

*Serve this luscious sweet and pungent tofu over freshly cooked rice. Add some steamed broccoli florets when heating the tofu in the sauce for a colorful and nutritious accent. For a variation, omit the lemon and lime juices and use all orange juice in the sauce.*

1 pound extra-firm tofu, drained, patted dry, and cut into ½-inch cubes

2 tablespoons soy sauce

2 tablespoons plus 1 teaspoon cornstarch

1 tablespoon plus 1 teaspoon canola or grapeseed oil

1 teaspoon toasted sesame oil

2 teaspoons grated fresh ginger

3 green onions, minced

⅓ cup hoisin sauce

½ cup vegetable broth, homemade (page 141) or store-bought

¼ cup fresh orange juice

1½ tablespoons fresh lime juice

1½ tablespoons fresh lemon juice

Salt and freshly ground black pepper

1. Place the tofu in a shallow bowl. Add the soy sauce and toss to coat, then sprinkle with 2 tablespoons of cornstarch and toss to coat.

2. In a large skillet, heat 1 tablespoon of the canola oil over medium heat. Add the tofu and cook until golden brown, turning occasionally, about 10 minutes. Remove the tofu from the pan and set aside.

3. In the same skillet, heat the remaining 1 teaspoon canola oil and the sesame oil over medium heat. Add the ginger and green onions and cook until fragrant, about 1 minute. Stir in the hoisin sauce, broth, and orange juice and bring to a simmer. Cook until the liquid is reduced slightly and the flavors have a chance to meld, about 3 minutes. In a small bowl, combine the remaining 1 teaspoon cornstarch with the lime juice and lemon juice and add to the sauce, stirring to thicken slightly. Season with salt and pepper to taste.

4. Return the fried tofu to the skillet and cook until coated with the sauce and heated through. Serve immediately.

# tofu with lemongrass and snow peas ⓕ

makes 4 servings

*The vibrant green snow peas are a lovely contrast to the tofu, which seems at home with the distinctive Southeast Asian flavor of lemongrass. To mince the lemongrass, remove the hard outer layers of the stalk and discard, then peel off the medium layers and discard. The remaining soft inner part is what you mince for this recipe.*

3 tablespoons canola or grapeseed oil

1 medium red onion, halved and thinly sliced

2 garlic cloves, minced

1 teaspoon grated fresh ginger

1 pound extra-firm tofu, drained and cut into ½-inch dice

3 tablespoons soy sauce

1 tablespoon mirin or sake

1 teaspoon sugar

½ teaspoon crushed red pepper

8 ounces snow peas, trimmed

1 tablespoon minced lemongrass or zest of 1 lemon

2 tablespoons coarsely ground unsalted roasted peanuts, for garnish

1. In a large skillet or wok, heat the oil over medium-high heat. Add the onion, garlic, and ginger and stir-fry for 2 minutes. Add the tofu and cook until golden brown, about 7 minutes.

2. Stir in the soy sauce, mirin, sugar, and crushed red pepper. Add the snow peas and lemongrass and stir-fry until the snow peas are crisp-tender and the flavors are well blended, about 3 minutes. Garnish with peanuts and serve immediately.

# double-sesame tofu with tahini sauce ⓕ

makes 4 servings

*Sesame and tofu are both rich in calcium and high in protein, making this luscious dish as healthful as it is attractive. For an even bigger calcium wallop, serve with steamed broccoli.*

½ cup tahini (sesame paste)

2 tablespoons fresh lemon juice

2 tablespoons soy sauce

2 tablespoons water

¼ cup white sesame seeds

¼ cup black sesame seeds

½ cup cornstarch

1 pound extra-firm tofu, drained, patted dry, and cut into ½-inch strips

Salt and freshly ground black pepper

2 tablespoons canola or grapeseed oil

1. In a small bowl, combine the tahini, lemon juice, soy sauce, and water, stirring to blend well. Set aside.

2. In a shallow bowl, combine the white and black sesame seeds and cornstarch, stirring to blend. Season the tofu with salt and pepper to taste. Set aside.

3. In a large skillet, heat the oil over medium heat. Dredge the tofu in the sesame seed mixture until well coated, then add to the hot skillet and cook until browned and crispy all over, turning as needed, 3 to 4 minutes per side. Be careful not to burn the seeds. Drizzle with tahini sauce and serve immediately.

# tofu and edamame stew

makes 4 servings

*The health benefits of soy are well known, and this comforting stew serves it up two ways: chunks of tofu, sautéed to a golden brown and edamame, the popular fresh soybean, available in supermarkets already shelled and sold fresh and frozen. With the lovely color of the edamame, green is the dominant hue of this mellow stew. You can continue the theme by adding some baby spinach at the last minute, or if you prefer to add colors, you can include some carrot or red bell pepper when you sauté the onion and celery.*

2 tablespoons olive oil

1 medium yellow onion, chopped

½ cup chopped celery

2 garlic cloves, minced

2 medium Yukon Gold potatoes, peeled and cut into ½-inch dice

1 cup shelled fresh or frozen edamame

2 cups peeled and diced zucchini

½ cup frozen baby peas

1 teaspoon dried savory

½ teaspoon crumbled dried sage

⅛ teaspoon ground cayenne

1½ cups vegetable broth, homemade (page 141) or store-bought

Salt and freshly ground black pepper

1 pound extra-firm tofu, drained, patted dry, and cut into ½-inch dice

2 tablespoons minced fresh parsley

1. In a large saucepan, heat 1 tablespoon of the oil over medium heat. Add the onion, celery, and garlic. Cover and cook until softened, about 10 minutes. Stir in the potatoes, edamame, zucchini, peas, savory, sage, and cayenne. Add the broth and bring to a boil. Reduce heat to low and season with salt and pepper to taste. Cover and simmer until the vegetables are tender and the flavors are blended, about 40 minutes.

2. In a large skillet, heat the remaining 1 tablespoon oil over medium-high heat. Add the tofu and cook until golden brown, about 7 minutes. Season with salt and pepper to taste and set aside. About 10 minutes before the stew is finished cooking, add the fried tofu and parsley. Taste, adjusting seasonings if necessary, and serve immediately.

# soy-tan dream cutlets

makes 6 servings

*I love to sauté both seitan and extra-firm tofu but sometimes the texture isn't always ideal—the tofu may not be firm enough or the seitan may be too chewy. My dream has long been to create a vegan cutlet with a texture that was "just right." This is it. These cutlets can be used in virtually any sauté or stir-fry recipe calling for seitan, tempeh, or extra-firm tofu. Try them in the Vietnamese Po'Boy sandwiches (page 117) or serve as is, topped with your favorite sauce.*

6 ounces firm tofu, drained and crumbled

3 tablespoons soy sauce

¼ teaspoon sweet paprika

¼ teaspoon onion powder

¼ teaspoon garlic powder

¼ teaspoon freshly ground black pepper

¾ cup wheat gluten flour (vital wheat gluten)

2 tablespoons olive oil

1. In a food processor, combine the tofu, soy sauce, paprika, onion powder, garlic powder, pepper, and flour. Process until well mixed. Transfer the mixture to a flat work surface and shape into a cylinder. Divide the mixture into 6 equal pieces and flatten them into very thin cutlets, no more than ¼-inch thick. (To do this, place each cutlet between two pieces of waxed paper, film wrap, or parchment paper and roll flat with a rolling pin.)

2. In a large skillet, heat the oil over medium heat. Add the cutlets, in batches if necessary, cover, and cook until nicely browned on both sides, 5 to 6 minutes per side. The cutlets are now ready to use in recipes or serve immediately, topped with a sauce.

# my kinda meat loaf

makes 4 to 6 servings

*This wholesome loaf combines tofu, oats, and wheat gluten flour with walnuts and tahini for a nutritious protein-packed vegan "meat-loaf" that is great with oven-roasted potatoes and vegetables for a nostalgic comfort-food meal. It looks remarkably like a meat loaf and is especially good topped with the Mushroom Sauce (page 546). Instead of baking in a loaf pan, it can be shaped into a loaf and baked in an oiled baking dish.*

2 tablespoons olive oil

⅔ cup minced onion

2 garlic cloves, minced

1 pound extra-firm tofu, drained and patted dry

3 tablespoons ketchup

2 tablespoons tahini (sesame paste) or creamy peanut butter

2 tablespoons soy sauce

½ cup ground walnuts

¾ cup old-fashioned oats

¾ cup wheat gluten flour (vital wheat gluten)

2 tablespoons minced fresh parsley

½ teaspoon salt

½ teaspoon sweet paprika

¼ teaspoon freshly ground black pepper

1. Preheat the oven to 375°F. Lightly oil a 9-inch loaf pan and set aside. In a large skillet, heat 1 tablespoon of the oil over medium heat. Add the onion and garlic, cover, and cook until softened, 5 minutes.

2. In a food processor, combine the tofu, ketchup, tahini, and soy sauce and process until smooth. Add the reserved onion mixture and all the remaining ingredients. Pulse until well combined, but with some texture remaining.

**3.** Scrape the mixture into the prepared pan. Press the mixture firmly into the pan, smoothing the top. Bake until firm and golden brown, about 1 hour. Let stand for 10 minutes before slicing.

# tempeh and vegetable stir-fry

makes 4 servings

*Broccoli, red bell pepper, and tempeh are a dynamic team, not just because they're immensely nutritious ingredients but also because they look and taste great when combined in this spicy stir-fry.*

8 ounces tempeh

Salt and freshly ground black pepper

2 teaspoons cornstarch

3 cups small broccoli florets

2 tablespoons canola or grapeseed oil

3 tablespoons soy sauce

2 tablespoons water

1 tablespoon mirin

½ teaspoon crushed red pepper

2 teaspoons toasted sesame oil

1 medium red bell pepper, cut into ½-inch slices

8 ounces white mushrooms, lightly rinsed, patted dry, and cut into ½-inch slices

2 garlic cloves, minced

3 tablespoons minced green onions

1 teaspoon grated fresh ginger

**1.** In a medium saucepan of simmering water, cook the tempeh for 30 minutes. Drain, pat dry, and set aside to cool. Cut the tempeh into ½-inch cubes and place in a shallow bowl. Season with salt and black pepper to taste, sprinkle with the cornstarch, and toss to coat. Set aside.

**2.** Lightly steam the broccoli until almost tender, about 5 minutes. Run under cold water to stop the cooking process and retain the bright green color. Set aside.

**3.** In a large skillet or wok, heat 1 tablespoon of the canola oil over medium-high heat. Add the tempeh and stir-fry until golden brown, about 5 minutes. Remove from the skillet and set aside.

**4.** In a small bowl, combine the soy sauce, water, mirin, crushed red pepper, and sesame oil. Set aside.

**5.** Reheat the same skillet over medium-high heat. Add the remaining 1 tablespoon of canola oil. Add the bell pepper and mushrooms and stir-fry until softened, about 3 minutes. Add the garlic, green onions, and ginger and stir-fry 1 minute. Add the steamed broccoli and fried tempeh and stir-fry for 1 minute. Stir in the soy sauce mixture and stir-fry until the tempeh and vegetables are hot and well coated with the sauce. Serve immediately.

# teriyaki tempeh

makes 4 servings

*Tempeh and teriyaki were made for each other. After simmering the tempeh to mellow its flavor, it is placed in the marinade to absorb the flavors of the teriyaki mixture. It is then cooked in the same liquid, which thickens and coats the tempeh with a mahogany glaze. You can accompany it with your favorite stir-fried vegetables or simply add some steamed broccoli or green beans to the tempeh to coat them with the teriyaki sauce. Serve over freshly cooked rice.*

1 pound tempeh, cut into ¼-inch slices

¼ cup soy sauce

¼ cup fresh lemon juice

1 teaspoon minced garlic

2 tablespoons minced green onions

2 teaspoons grated fresh ginger

2 tablespoons sugar

2 tablespoons toasted sesame oil

1 tablespoon cornstarch

2 tablespoons water

2 tablespoons canola or grapeseed oil

1. In a medium saucepan of simmering water, cook the tempeh for 30 minutes. Drain and place in a large shallow dish. In a small bowl, combine the soy sauce, lemon juice, garlic, green onions, ginger, sugar, sesame oil, cornstarch, and water. Blend well, then pour the marinade over the cooked tempeh, turning to coat. Marinate the tempeh for 1 hour.

2. In large skillet, heat the canola oil over medium heat. Remove the tempeh from the marinade, reserving the marinade. Add the tempeh to the hot skillet and cook until golden brown on both sides, about 4 minutes per side. Add the reserved marinade and simmer until the liquid thickens, about 8 minutes. Serve immediately.

# barbecued tempeh

makes 4 servings

*Barbecue sauce seems to be the great equalizer when it comes to finicky family members who might otherwise not be tempted to try tempeh. This luscious sauce is also terrific paired with tofu or seitan.*

1 pound tempeh, cut into 2-inch bars

2 tablespoons olive oil

1 medium onion, minced

1 medium red bell pepper, minced

3 garlic cloves, minced

1 (14.5-ounce) can crushed tomatoes

3 tablespoons dark molasses

2 tablespoons apple cider vinegar

1 tablespoon soy sauce

2 teaspoons spicy brown mustard

1 tablespoon sugar

½ teaspoon salt

¼ teaspoon ground allspice

¼ teaspoon ground cayenne

1. In a medium saucepan of simmering water, cook the tempeh for 30 minutes. Drain and set aside.

2. In a large saucepan, heat 1 tablespoon of the oil over medium heat. Add the onion, bell pepper, and garlic. Cover and cook until softened, about 5 minutes. Stir in the tomatoes, molasses, vinegar, soy sauce, mustard, sugar, salt, allspice, and cayenne and bring to a boil. Reduce heat to low and simmer, uncovered, for 20 minutes.

3. In a large skillet, heat the remaining 1 tablespoon oil over medium heat. Add the tempeh and cook until golden brown, turning once, about 10 minutes. Add enough of the sauce to

generously coat the tempeh. Cover and simmer to blend the flavors, about 15 minutes. Serve immediately.

## orange-bourbon tempeh

makes 4 to 6 servings

*I adapted this recipe from one shared with me by my friend and vegan chef Tal Ronnen. Even people who think they don't like tempeh may change their minds when they taste this dish.*

2 cups water

½ cup soy sauce

6 thin slices fresh ginger

2 garlic cloves, sliced

Zest of ½ an orange

1 pound tempeh, cut into thin slices

Salt and freshly ground black pepper

½ cup all-purpose flour

¼ cup canola or grapeseed oil

1 tablespoon light brown sugar

⅛ teaspoon ground allspice

⅓ cup fresh orange juice

¼ cup bourbon

4 or 5 orange slices, halved

1 tablespoon cornstarch mixed with
    2 tablespoons water

1. In a large saucepan, combine the water, soy sauce, ginger, garlic, and orange zest. Place the tempeh in the marinade and bring to a boil. Reduce heat to low and simmer for 30 minutes. Remove the tempeh from the marinade, reserving the marinade. Sprinkle the tempeh with salt and pepper to taste. Place the flour in a shallow bowl. Dredge the cooked tempeh in the flour and set aside.

2. In a large skillet, heat the oil over medium heat. Add the tempeh, in batches if necessary, and cook until browned on both sides, about 4 minutes per side. Gradually stir in the reserved

marinade. Add the sugar, allspice, orange juice, and bourbon. Top the tempeh with the orange slices. Cover and simmer until the sauce is syrupy and the flavors are melded, about 20 minutes.

3. Use a slotted spoon or spatula to remove the tempeh from the pan and transfer it to a serving platter. Keep warm. Add the cornstarch mixture to the sauce and cook, stirring, to thicken. Reduce the heat to low and simmer, uncovered, stirring constantly, until the sauce is thickened. Spoon the sauce over the tempeh and serve immediately.

## pineapple-glazed tempeh and sweet potatoes

makes 4 servings

*The sturdy texture and distinctive flavor of tempeh provide the perfect backdrop for the dazzling array of bold ingredients in this recipe.*

1 pound tempeh

3 tablespoons soy sauce

1 teaspoon ground coriander

½ teaspoon turmeric

3 tablespoons olive oil

3 large shallots, chopped

1 or 2 medium sweet potatoes, peeled and
    cut into ½-inch dice

2 teaspoons grated fresh ginger

1 cup pineapple juice

2 teaspoons light brown sugar

Juice of 1 lime

1. In a medium saucepan of simmering water, cook the tempeh for 30 minutes. Transfer it to a shallow bowl. Add 2 tablespoons of the

continues on next page

soy sauce, coriander, and turmeric, tossing to coat. Set aside.

2. In a large skillet, heat 1 tablespoon of the oil over medium heat. Add the tempeh and cook until browned on both sides, about 4 minutes per side. Remove from the skillet and set aside.

3. In the same skillet, heat the remaining 2 tablespoons oil over medium heat. Add the shallots and sweet potatoes. Cover and cook until slightly softened and lightly browned, about 10 minutes. Stir in the ginger, pineapple juice, the remaining 1 tablespoon soy sauce, and sugar, stirring to combine. Reduce heat to low, add the cooked tempeh, cover, and cook until the potatoes are soft, about 10 minutes. Transfer the tempeh and sweet potatoes to a serving dish and keep warm. Stir the lime juice into the sauce and simmer for 1 minute to blend the flavors. Drizzle the sauce over the tempeh and serve immediately.

# creole tempeh

makes 4 to 6 servings

*Firm slices of tempeh stand up well to the lively Creole seasoning. Serve over freshly cooked rice and celebrate Mardi Gras.*

1 pound tempeh, cut into ¼-inch slices

¼ cup soy sauce

3 tablespoons Creole seasoning

½ cup all-purpose flour

2 tablespoons olive oil

1 medium sweet yellow onion, chopped

2 celery ribs, chopped

1 medium green bell pepper, chopped

3 garlic cloves, chopped

1 (14.5-ounce) can diced tomatoes, drained

1 teaspoon dried thyme

½ cup dry white wine

Salt and freshly ground black pepper

1. Place the tempeh in a large saucepan with enough water to cover. Add the soy sauce and 1 tablespoon of the Creole seasoning. Cover and simmer for 30 minutes. Remove the tempeh from the liquid and set aside, reserving the liquid.

2. In a shallow bowl, combine the flour with the remaining 2 tablespoons Creole seasoning and mix well. Dredge the tempeh in the flour mixture, coating well. In a large skillet, heat 1 tablespoon of the oil over medium heat. Add the dredged tempeh and cook until browned on both sides, about 4 minutes per side. Remove the tempeh from the skillet and set aside.

3. In the same skillet, heat the remaining 1 tablespoon oil over medium heat. Add the onion, celery, bell pepper, and garlic. Cover and cook until the vegetables are softened, about 10 minutes. Stir in the tomatoes, then add the tempeh back to the pan along with the thyme, wine, and 1 cup of the reserved simmering liquid. Season with salt and pepper to taste. Bring to a simmer, and cook, uncovered, for about 30 minutes to reduce the liquid and blend the flavors. Serve immediately.

# tempeh with lemon and capers

makes 4 to 6 servings

*Tempeh is usually at its best in recipes that require longer cooking times and bold flavors to help mellow its distinctive flavor. Here, the relatively short cooking time is augmented not only by the requisite pre-recipe simmer-*

*ing (with the addition of soy sauce), but also by the thin slices, allowing the flavors of the sauce to soak in more readily for a delicious finish.*

1 pound tempeh, cut horizontally into ¼-inch slices

½ cup soy sauce

½ cup all-purpose flour

Salt and freshly ground black pepper

3 tablespoons olive oil

2 medium shallots, minced

2 garlic cloves, minced

2 tablespoons capers

½ cup dry white wine

½ cup vegetable broth, homemade (page 141) or store-bought

2 tablespoons vegan margarine

Juice of 1 lemon

2 tablespoons minced fresh parsley

1. Place the tempeh in a large saucepan with enough water to cover. Add the soy sauce and simmer for 30 minutes. Remove the tempeh from the pot and set aside to cool. In a shallow bowl, combine the flour and salt and pepper to taste. Dredge the tempeh in the flour mixture, coating both sides. Set aside.

2. In a large skillet, heat 2 tablespoons of the oil over medium heat. Add the tempeh, in batches if necessary, and cook until browned on both sides, about 8 minutes total. Remove the tempeh from the skillet and set aside.

3. In the same skillet, heat the remaining 1 tablespoon oil over medium heat. Add the shallots and cook about 2 minutes. Add the garlic, then stir in the capers, wine, and broth. Return the tempeh to the skillet and simmer for 6 to 8 minutes. Stir in the margarine, lemon juice, and parsley, stirring to melt the margarine. Serve immediately.

# tempeh with maple, mustard, and balsamic glaze

makes 4 servings

*The bold flavors of balsamic vinegar, mustard, and maple syrup combine in a robust and delicious glaze that complements the distinctive flavor of tempeh. It makes a wonderful cold-weather meal when paired with garlicky greens and the Corn Fritters on page 366.*

1 pound tempeh, cut into 2-inch bars

3 tablespoons balsamic vinegar

3 tablespoons pure maple syrup

1½ tablespoons spicy brown mustard

1 teaspoon Tabasco sauce

1 tablespoon olive oil

2 garlic cloves, minced

½ cup vegetable broth, homemade (page 141) or store-bought

Salt and freshly ground black pepper

1. In a medium saucepan of simmering water, cook the tempeh for 30 minutes. Drain and pat dry.

2. In a small bowl, combine the vinegar, maple syrup, mustard, and Tabasco. Set aside.

3. In a large skillet, heat the oil over medium heat. Add the tempeh and cook until browned on both sides, turning once, about 4 minutes per side. Add the garlic and cook 30 seconds longer.

4. Stir in the broth and salt and pepper to taste. Increase the heat to medium-high and cook, uncovered, for about 3 minutes, or until the liquid is nearly evaporated.

5. Add the reserved mustard mixture and cook for 1 to 2 minutes, turning the tempeh to coat with the sauce and glaze nicely. Be careful not to burn. Serve immediately.

# tempting tempeh chili

makes 4 to 6 servings

*Tempeh provides an ideal texture for chili and absorbs the flavors of the spices as it simmers. It's especially good served with warm cornbread.*

1 pound tempeh
1 tablespoon olive oil
1 medium yellow onion, chopped
1 medium green bell pepper, chopped
2 garlic cloves, minced
3 tablespoons chili powder
1 teaspoon dried oregano
1 teaspoon ground cumin
1 (28-ounce) can crushed tomatoes
½ cup water, plus more if needed
1½ cups cooked or 1 (15.5-ounce) can pinto beans, drained and rinsed
1 (4-ounce) can chopped mild green chiles, drained
Salt and freshly ground black pepper
2 tablespoons minced fresh cilantro

1. In a medium saucepan of simmering water, cook the tempeh for 30 minutes. Drain and allow to cool, then finely chop and set aside.

2. In a large saucepan, heat the oil. Add the onion, bell pepper, and garlic, cover, and cook until softened, about 5 minutes. Add the tempeh and cook, uncovered, until golden, about 5 minutes. Add the chili powder, oregano, and cumin. Stir in the tomatoes, water, beans, and chiles. Season with salt and black pepper to taste. Mix well to combine.

3. Bring to a boil, then reduce the heat to low, cover and simmer for 45 minutes, stirring occasionally, adding a little more water if needed.

4. Sprinkle with cilantro and serve immediately.

# tempeh cacciatore

makes 4 to 6 servings

*Despite its decidedly non-vegan name, this Italian "hunter-style" stew is deliciously animal friendly when made with tempeh. Serve over hot cooked noodles.*

1 pound tempeh, cut thinly sliced
2 tablespoons canola or grapeseed oil
1 medium red onion, cut into ½-inch dice
1 medium red bell pepper, cut into ½-inch dice
1 medium carrot, cut into ¼-inch slices
2 garlic cloves, minced
1 (28-ounce) can diced tomatoes, drained
¼ cup dry white wine
1 teaspoon dried oregano
1 teaspoon dried basil
Salt and freshly ground black pepper

1. In a medium saucepan of simmering water, cook the tempeh for 30 minutes. Drain and pat dry.

2. In a large skillet, heat 1 tablespoon of the oil over medium heat. Add the tempeh and cook until browned on both sides, 8 to 10 minutes total. Remove from the skillet and set aside.

3. In the same skillet, heat the remaining 1 tablespoon oil over medium heat. Add the onion, bell pepper, carrot, and garlic. Cover, and cook until softened, about 5 minutes. Add the tomatoes, wine, oregano, basil, and salt and black pepper to taste and bring to a boil. Reduce heat to low, add the reserved tempeh, and simmer, uncovered, until the vegetables are soft and the flavors are well combined, about 30 minutes. Serve immediately.

# indonesian tempeh in coconut gravy

makes 4 to 6 servings

*Tempeh is a traditional ingredient in Indonesia where it is often prepared with coconut milk. If spicy food isn't your thing, then omit the chiles for a mild version of the creamy and flavorful sauce. Be sure you use the unsweetened coconut milk and not the sweetened coconut milk that is used in cocktails. Serve over rice.*

1 pound tempeh, cut into ¼-inch slices

2 tablespoons canola or grapeseed oil

1 medium yellow onion, chopped

3 garlic cloves, minced

1 medium red bell pepper, chopped

1 medium green bell pepper, chopped

1 or 2 small serrano or other fresh hot chiles, seeded and minced

1 (14.5-ounce) can diced tomatoes, drained

1 (13.5-ounce) can unsweetened coconut milk

Salt and freshly ground black pepper

½ cup unsalted roasted peanuts, ground or crushed, for garnish

2 tablespoons minced fresh cilantro, for garnish

1. In a medium saucepan of simmering water, cook the tempeh for 30 minutes. Drain and pat dry.

2. In a large skillet, heat 1 tablespoon of the oil over medium heat. Add the tempeh and cook until golden brown on both sides, about 10 minutes. Remove from the skillet and set aside.

3. In the same skillet, heat the remaining 1 tablespoon oil over medium heat. Add the onion, garlic, red and green bell peppers, and chiles. Cover and cook until softened, about 5 minutes. Stir in tomatoes and coconut milk. Reduce heat to low, add the reserved tempeh, season with salt and pepper to taste and simmer, uncovered, until the sauce is slightly reduced, about 30 minutes. Sprinkle with peanuts and cilantro and serve immediately.

# ginger-peanut tempeh

makes 4 servings

*The bold flavor of ginger stands out in this fragrant tempeh stir-fry strewn with crunchy peanuts. To crush peanuts, place them in a zip-top plastic bag on a flat work surface and firmly roll over them a few times with a rolling pin.*

1 pound tempeh, cut into ½-inch dice

2 tablespoons canola or grapeseed oil

1 medium red bell pepper, cut into ½-inch dice

1 garlic clove, minced

1 small bunch green onions, chopped

1 tablespoon grated fresh ginger

3 tablespoons soy sauce

1 tablespoon sugar

¼ teaspoon crushed red pepper

1 tablespoon cornstarch

¾ cup water

¾ cup crushed unsalted roasted peanuts

3 tablespoons minced fresh cilantro

1. In a medium saucepan of simmering water, cook the tempeh for 30 minutes. Drain and pat dry. In a large skillet or wok, heat the oil over medium heat. Add the tempeh and cook until lightly browned, about 8 minutes. Add the bell pepper and stir-fry until softened, about 5 minutes. Add the garlic, green onions, and ginger and stir-fry until fragrant, 1 minute.

2. In a small bowl, combine the soy sauce, sugar, crushed red pepper, cornstarch, and water. Mix well, then pour into the skillet. Cook, stirring, for 5 minutes, until slightly thickened. Stir in the peanuts and cilantro. Serve immediately.

# tempeh with potatoes and cabbage

makes 4 servings

*This stick-to-your-ribs cold-weather comfort food can be made with sauerkraut instead of fresh cabbage if you prefer. The addition of the optional vegan sour cream will make it reminiscent of goulash.*

1 pound tempeh, cut into ½-inch dice

2 tablespoons canola or grapeseed oil

1 medium yellow onion, chopped

1 medium carrot, chopped

1½ tablespoons sweet Hungarian paprika

2 medium russet potatoes, peeled and cut into ½-inch dice

3 cups shredded cabbage

1 (14.5-ounce) can diced tomatoes, drained

¼ cup dry white wine

1 cup vegetable broth, homemade (page 141) or store-bought

Salt and freshly ground black pepper

½ cup vegan sour cream, homemade (page 574) or store-bought (optional)

1. In a medium saucepan of simmering water, cook the tempeh for 30 minutes. Drain and pat dry.

2. In a large skillet, heat 1 tablespoon of the oil over medium heat. Add the tempeh and cook until golden brown on both sides, about 10 minutes. Remove tempeh and set aside.

3. In the same skillet, heat the remaining 1 tablespoon oil over medium heat. Add the onion and carrot, cover, and cook until softened, about 10 minutes. Stir in the paprika, potatoes, cabbage, tomatoes, wine, and broth and bring to a boil. Season with salt and pepper to taste.

4. Reduce the heat to medium, add the tempeh, and simmer, uncovered, for 30 minutes, or until the vegetables are tender and the flavors are blended. Whisk in the sour cream, if using, and serve immediately.

# southern succotash stew

makes 4 servings

*This savory Southern stew is a frequent menu item at my house during the winter months. The smoky flavor in the stew comes from liquid smoke, which is a hickory flavoring available at well-stocked supermarkets. Instead of, or in addition to, the tempeh, you could add sliced Tofurky brand vegan sausage links or a can of kidney beans.*

8 ounces tempeh

2 tablespoons olive oil

1 large sweet yellow onion, finely chopped

2 medium russet potatoes, peeled and cut into ½-inch dice

2 carrots, cut into ¼-inch slices

1 (14.5-ounce) can diced tomatoes, drained

1 (16-ounce) package frozen succotash

2 cups vegetable broth, homemade (page 141) or store-bought, or water

2 tablespoons soy sauce

1 teaspoon dry mustard

1 teaspoon sugar

½ teaspoon dried thyme

½ teaspoon ground allspice

¼ teaspoon ground cayenne

Salt and freshly ground black pepper

½ teaspoon liquid smoke

1. In a medium saucepan of simmering water, cook the tempeh for 30 minutes. Drain, pat dry, and cut into 1-inch dice.

2. In a large skillet, heat 1 tablespoon of the oil over medium heat. Add the tempeh and cook until browned on both sides, about 10 minutes. Set aside.

3. In a large saucepan, heat the remaining 1 tablespoon oil over medium heat. Add the onion and cook until softened, 5 minutes. Add the potatoes, carrots, tomatoes, succotash, broth, soy sauce, mustard, sugar, thyme, allspice, and cayenne. Season with salt and pepper to taste. Bring to a boil, then reduce heat to low and add the tempeh. Simmer, covered, until the vegetables are tender, stirring occasionally, about 45 minutes.

4. About 10 minutes before the stew is finished cooking, stir in the liquid smoke. Taste, adjusting seasonings if necessary. Serve immediately.

# baked jambalaya casserole

makes 4 servings

*All the flavor of jambalaya without a pot to watch. Once you put it together, just pop it in the oven and let it bake. This is a great way to make jambalaya for company, since you can assemble it ahead of time and then bake and serve it in the same dish. If you like vegan sausage links, you can use them instead of or in addition to the tempeh or kidney beans.*

8 ounces tempeh

2 tablespoons olive oil

1 medium yellow onion, chopped

1 medium green bell pepper, chopped

2 garlic cloves, minced

1 (28-ounce) can diced tomatoes, undrained

½ cup white rice

1½ cups vegetable broth, homemade (page 141) or store-bought, or water

1½ cups cooked or 1 (15.5-ounce) can dark red kidney beans, drained and rinsed

1 tablespoon chopped fresh parsley

1½ teaspoons Cajun seasoning

1 teaspoon dried thyme

½ teaspoon salt

¼ teaspoon freshly ground black pepper

1. In a medium saucepan of simmering water, cook the tempeh for 30 minutes. Drain and pat dry. Cut into $1/2$-inch dice. Preheat the oven to 350°F.

2. In a large skillet, heat 1 tablespoon of the oil over medium heat. Add the tempeh and cook until browned on both sides, about 8 minutes. Transfer the tempeh to a 9 × 13-inch baking dish and set aside.

3. In the same skillet, heat the remaining 1 tablespoon oil over medium heat. Add the onion, bell pepper, and garlic. Cover and cook until the vegetables are softened, about 7 minutes.

4. Add the vegetable mixture to the baking dish with the tempeh. Stir in the tomatoes with their liquid, the rice, broth, kidney beans, parsley, Cajun seasoning, thyme, salt, and black pepper. Mix well, then cover tightly and bake until the rice is tender, about 1 hour. Serve immediately.

# tempeh and sweet potato shepherd's pie

makes 4 servings

*This is satisfying comfort food that is ideal fare for a casual company dinner on a cold autumn or winter evening. Assemble it ahead of time so there's no messy clean-up at dinnertime. Instead of making this with tempeh, you could use chopped seitan or veggie burgers or frozen vegetarian burger crumbles.*

8 ounces tempeh

3 medium sweet potatoes, peeled and cut into ½-inch dice

2 tablespoons vegan margarine

¼ cup plain unsweetened soy milk

Salt and freshly ground black pepper

2 tablespoons olive oil

1 medium yellow onion, finely chopped

2 medium carrots, chopped

1 cup frozen peas, thawed

1 cup frozen corn kernels, thawed

1½ cups Mushroom Sauce (page 546)

½ teaspoon dried thyme

1. In a medium saucepan of simmering water, cook the tempeh for 30 minutes. Drain and pat dry. Finely chop the tempeh and set it aside.

2. Steam the sweet potatoes until tender, about 20 minutes. Preheat the oven to 350°F. Mash the sweet potatoes with the margarine, soy milk, and salt and pepper to taste. Set aside.

3. In a large skillet, heat 1 tablespoon of the oil over medium heat. Add the onion and carrots, cover, and cook until soft, about 10 minutes. Transfer to a 10-inch baking pan.

4. In the same skillet, heat the remaining 1 tablespoon oil over medium heat. Add the tempeh and cook until browned on both sides, 8 to 10 minutes. Add the tempeh to the baking pan with the onion and carrots. Stir in the peas, corn, and mushroom sauce. Add the thyme and salt and pepper to taste. Stir to combine.

5. Spread the mashed sweet potatoes on top, using a spatula to spread evenly to the edges of the pan. Bake until the potatoes are lightly browned and the filling is hot, about 40 minutes. Serve immediately.

# SEITAN

## basic simmered seitan

makes about 2 pounds

*Traditional seitan made entirely from scratch is a messy and time-consuming process that involves repeated rinsing of whole wheat flour to separate the starch and bran from the gluten. By using vital wheat gluten, or gluten flour, the starch and bran are already removed, which provides a way to make a delicious and economical homemade seitan in a fraction of the time and without all the fuss. This recipe makes about two pounds of seitan—I like to make a double batch and refrigerate or freeze half so I have some on hand when I need it.*

SEITAN

1¾ cups wheat gluten flour (vital wheat gluten)

¼ cup nutritional yeast

½ teaspoon salt

½ teaspoon onion powder

¼ teaspoon sweet paprika

1 tablespoon olive oil

3 tablespoons soy sauce

1⅔ cups cold water

SIMMERING LIQUID

2 quarts water

½ cup soy sauce

2 garlic cloves, crushed

1. Make the seitan: In a food processor, combine the wheat gluten flour, nutritional yeast, salt, onion powder, and paprika. Pulse to blend. Add the oil, soy sauce, and water and process for a minute to form a dough. Turn the mixture out onto a lightly floured work surface and knead until smooth and elastic, about 2 minutes.

2. Make the simmering liquid: In a large saucepan, combine the water, soy sauce, and garlic.

3. Divide the seitan dough into 4 equal pieces and place in the simmering liquid. Bring just to a boil over medium-high heat, then reduce heat to medium-low, cover, and simmer gently, turning occasionally, for 1 hour. Turn off the heat and allow the seitan to cool in the liquid. Once cool, the seitan can be used in recipes or refrigerated in the liquid in a tightly sealed container for up to a week or frozen for up to 3 months.

## seitan in recipes

Seitan is a popular and versatile meat alternative made from the protein part of wheat: the gluten. It is available in natural food stores, usually in refrigerated tubs. It is simple to make at home totally from scratch (using whole wheat flour that must undergo a lengthy kneading and rinsing process) or almost from scratch with wheat gluten flour, also called "vital wheat gluten," a flour that already has the bran and starch removed, so there is no tedious rinsing required.

The recipe for Basic Simmered Seitan, left, makes about two pounds. Almost all of the recipes calling for seitan in this book can be made with this seitan as well as store-bought seitan. Any exceptions are noted in that particular recipe.

# stuffed baked seitan roast

makes 6 servings

*This stuffed and rolled seitan roast has become my traditional main dish for holiday meals and other special occasions. The recipe begins with the Basic Simmered Seitan, but instead of simmering on top of the stove, the seitan is rolled out, stuffed, and baked. Serve with the Basic Brown Sauce (page 545) or Mushroom Sauce (page 546).*

1 recipe Basic Simmered Seitan (page 305), uncooked

1 tablespoon olive oil

1 small yellow onion, minced

1 celery rib, minced

1/2 teaspoon dried thyme

1/2 teaspoon dried sage

1/2 cup water, or more if needed

Salt and freshly ground black pepper

4 cups fresh bread cubes

1/4 cup minced fresh parsley

1. Place the raw seitan on a lightly floured work surface and stretch it out with lightly floured hands until it is flat and about 1/2 inch thick. Place the flattened seitan between two sheets of plastic wrap or parchment paper. Use a rolling pin to flatten it as much as you can (it will be elastic and resistant). Top with a baking sheet weighed down with a gallon of water or canned goods and let it rest while you make the stuffing.

2. In a large skillet, heat the oil over medium heat. Add the onion and celery. Cover and cook until soft, 10 minutes. Stir in the thyme, sage, water, and salt and pepper to taste. Remove from heat and set aside. Place the bread and parsley in a large mixing bowl. Add the onion mixture and blend well, adding a little more water if the stuffing is too dry. Taste, adjusting seasonings if necessary. if necessary. Set aside.

3. Preheat the oven to 350°F. Lightly oil a 9 × 13-inch baking pan and set aside. Roll out the flattened seitan with a rolling pin until it is about 1/4 inch thick. Spread the stuffing across the surface of the seitan and roll it up carefully and evenly. Place the roast seam side down in the prepared baking pan. Rub a little oil on the top and sides of the roast and bake, covered for 45 minutes, then uncover and bake until firm and glossy brown, about 15 minutes longer.

4. Remove from the oven and set aside for 10 minutes before slicing. Use a serrated knife to cut it into 1/2-inch slices. Note: For easiest slicing, make the roast ahead and cool completely before slicing. Slice all or part of the roast and then reheat in the oven, tightly covered, for 15 to 20 minutes, before serving.

# seitan pot roast

makes 4 servings

*This is simple comfort food at its finest that can be adjusted to serve up to eight people simply by adding a few additional vegetables and using the entire recipe of Basic Simmered Seitan (page 305).*

1 recipe Basic Simmered Seitan (page 305)

2 tablespoons olive oil

3 to 4 medium shallots, halved lengthwise

3 medium carrots, cut into 1/4-inch slices

1 pound Yukon Gold potatoes, peeled and cut into 2-inch chunks

1/2 teaspoon dried thyme

1/2 teaspoon dried savory

1/4 teaspoon ground sage

Salt and freshly ground black pepper

1/2 teaspoon sweet paprika

Horseradish, to serve

1. Follow the directions for making Basic Simmered Seitan, but divide the seitan dough into 2 pieces instead of 4 before simmering. After the seitan has cooled in its broth for 30 minutes, remove it from the saucepan and set aside. Reserve the cooking liquid, discarding any solids. Reserve 1 piece of the seitan (about 1 pound) for future use by placing it in a bowl and covering it with some of the reserved cooking liquid. Cover and refrigerate until needed. If not using within 3 days, cool the seitan completely, wrap tightly, and freeze.

2. In a large saucepan, heat 1 tablespoon of the oil over medium heat. Add the shallots and carrots. Cover and cook for 5 minutes. Add the potatoes, thyme, savory, sage, and salt and pepper to taste. Add 1½ cups of reserved cooking liquid and bring to a boil. Reduce heat to low and cook, covered, for 20 minutes.

3. Rub the reserved seitan with the remaining 1 tablespoon oil and the paprika. Place the seitan on top of the simmering vegetables. Cover and continue cooking until the vegetables are tender, about 20 minutes more. Cut the seitan into thin slices and arrange on a large serving platter surrounded by the cooked vegetables. Serve immediately, with horseradish on the side.

# almost one-dish thanksgiving dinner

makes 6 servings

*Why almost one dish? Because I thought that it might be over the top to add a layer of green bean casserole to this amazing recipe— but everything else is there, including "white and dark meat" (tofu and seitan), stuffing, mashed potatoes, and gravy. There's even a*

*golden brown crust that fills in nicely for hot rolls. Add a green vegetable side dish and round up the Pilgrims for dinner.*

2 tablespoons olive oil
1 cup finely chopped onion
2 celery ribs, finely chopped
2 cups sliced white mushrooms
½ teaspoon dried thyme
½ teaspoon dried savory
½ teaspoon ground sage
Pinch ground nutmeg
Salt and freshly ground black pepper
4 cups fresh bread cubes
2½ cups vegetable broth, homemade (page 141) or store-bought
½ cup chopped walnuts
⅓ cup sweetened dried cranberries
8 ounces extra-firm tofu, drained and cut into ¼-inch slices
8 ounces seitan, homemade (page 305) or store-bought, very thinly sliced
1½ cups Basic Brown Sauce (page 545)
2½ cups Basic Mashed Potatoes (page 373)
1 sheet frozen puff pastry, thawed

1. Preheat the oven to 400°F. Lightly oil a 10-inch square baking dish. In a large skillet, heat the oil over medium heat. Add the onion and celery. Cover and cook until softened, about 5 minutes. Stir in the mushrooms, thyme, savory, sage, nutmeg, and salt and pepper to taste. Cook, uncovered, until the mushrooms are tender, about 3 minutes longer. Set aside.

2. In a large bowl, combine the bread cubes with as much of the broth as needed to moisten (about 1½ cups). Add the cooked vegetable mixture, walnuts, and cranberries. Stir to mix well and set aside.

3. In the same skillet, bring the remaining 1 cup broth to a boil, reduce heat to medium,

continues on next page

add the tofu, and simmer, uncovered, until the broth is absorbed, about 10 minutes. Set aside.

4. Spread half of the prepared stuffing in the bottom of the prepared baking dish, followed by half of the seitan, half of the tofu, and half of the brown sauce. Repeat layering with the remaining stuffing, seitan, tofu, and sauce. Spread the mashed potatoes evenly over top. Roll out the sheet of pastry and place on top of the potatoes. Pinch down the edges of the pastry to seal in the filling. Use a sharp knife to make a few slits in the top. Bake until the crust is golden brown, about 45 minutes. Serve immediately.

## seitan milanese with panko and lemon ⓕ

makes 4 servings

*This simple and basic seitan preparation is one of my favorites. I prefer to serve the lemon wedges on the side for people to squeeze on at will. If panko crumbs are unavailable, regular bread crumbs can be used instead.*

2 cups panko
¼ cup minced fresh parsley
½ teaspoon salt
¼ teaspoon freshly ground black pepper
1 pound seitan, homemade (page 305) or store-bought, cut ¼-inch slices
2 tablespoons olive oil
1 lemon, cut into wedges

1. Preheat the oven to 250°F. In a large bowl, combine the panko, parsley, salt, and pepper. Moisten the seitan with a little water and dredge it in the panko mixture.

2. In a large skillet, heat the oil over medium-high heat. Add the seitan and cook, turning once, until golden brown, working in batches,

if necessary. Transfer the cooked seitan to a baking sheet and keep warm in the oven while you cook the rest. Serve immediately, with lemon wedges.

## seitan with dried plums, olives, and capers ⓕ

makes 4 servings

*This sweet and savory dish with the flavors of Morocco was inspired by a popular chicken recipe that made the rounds in the early 1980s. This is a fun dish to serve to guests if their tastes lean to the exotic. It's great served over rice, millet, or couscous accompanied with a salad or sautéed greens.*

3 tablespoons olive oil
1 pound seitan, homemade (page 305) or store-bought, cut into ¼-inch slices
Yellow cornmeal, for dredging
Salt and freshly ground black pepper
2 garlic cloves, minced
½ cup dry white wine
½ cup vegetable broth, homemade (page 141) or store-bought
2 tablespoons red wine vinegar
2 tablespoons sugar
1 teaspoon chopped fresh oregano or ½ teaspoon dried
¼ teaspoon crushed red pepper
¾ cup pitted dried plums (prunes)
½ cup pitted green olives
⅓ cup dried apricots, halved
¼ cup capers
2 tablespoons chopped fresh parsley

1. Preheat the oven to 250°F. In a large skillet, heat 2 tablespoons of the oil over medium heat. Dredge the seitan slices in cornmeal and add to the skillet, in batches if necessary. Season with salt and black pepper to taste and cook until browned on both sides, 3 to 4 minutes per

side. Transfer the cooked seitan to a heatproof platter and keep warm in the oven.

2. In the same skillet, heat the remaining 1 tablespoon oil over medium heat. Add the garlic and cook until fragrant, about 30 seconds. Stir in the white wine, broth, vinegar, sugar, oregano, and crushed red pepper. Bring to a boil, stirring to dissolve the sugar. Reduce heat to low and simmer until the liquid reduces slightly. Stir in the dried plums, olives, apricots, and capers, and cook until heated through, about 5 minutes. Spoon the sauce over the browned seitan and sprinkle with the parsley. Serve immediately.

## sesame-crusted seitan

makes 4 servings

*The flavor of toasted sesame seeds exalts this seitan dish to new flavor heights and makes a sauce unnecessary. For an unusual presentation and a delicious mirror of the sesame flavor, serve on a bed of Crunchy Sesame Slaw (page 74).*

⅓ cup sesame seeds
⅓ cup all-purpose flour
½ teaspoon salt
¼ teaspoon freshly ground black pepper
½ cup plain unsweetened soy milk
1 pound seitan, homemade (page 305) or
      store-bought seitan, cut into ¼-inch slices
2 tablespoons olive oil

1. Place the sesame seeds in a dry skillet over medium heat and toast until light golden, stirring constantly, 3 to 4 minutes. Set aside to cool, then grind them in a food processor or spice grinder.

2. Place the ground sesame seeds in a shallow bowl and add the flour, salt, and pepper, and mix well. Place the soy milk in a shallow bowl. Dip the seitan in the soy milk, then dredge it in the sesame mixture.

3. In a large skillet, heat the oil over medium heat. Add the seitan, in batches if necessary, and cook until crisp and golden brown on both sides, about 10 minutes. Serve immediately.

## pan-seared seitan with artichokes and olives

makes 4 servings

*Pungently redolent of olives, capers, and artichoke hearts, this full-flavored dish is terrific over freshly cooked rice or pasta.*

2 tablespoons olive oil
1 pound seitan, homemade (page 305)
      or store-bought, cut into ¼-inch slices
2 garlic cloves, minced
1 (14.5-ounce) can diced tomatoes, drained
1½ cups canned or frozen (cooked) artichoke
      hearts, cut into ¼-inch slices
⅓ cup oil-cured black olives, pitted and halved
1 tablespoon capers
3 tablespoons chopped fresh parsley
Salt and freshly ground black pepper
1 cup Tofu Feta (page 358; optional)

1. Preheat oven to 250°F. In a large skillet, heat 1 tablespoon of the oil over medium-high heat. Add the seitan and brown on both sides, about 5 minutes. Transfer the seitan to a heatproof platter and keep warm in the oven.

2. In same skillet, heat the remaining 1 tablespoon oil over medium heat. Add the garlic and cook until fragrant, about 30 seconds. Add the tomatoes, artichoke hearts, olives, capers, and parsley. Season with salt and pepper to taste and cook until hot, about 5 minutes. Set aside.

3. Place the seitan on a serving platter, top with the vegetable mixture, and sprinkle with tofu feta, if using. Serve immediately.

# seitan with ancho-chipotle sauce

makes 4 servings

*I enjoyed a dish similar to this at the home of my friend, Chef Tal Ronnen, which he made with tempeh. Inspired by the smoky heat of the sauce, I've reinterpreted his dish and use seitan instead of tempeh. Fire-roasted tomatoes add complexity to the sauce. If unavailable, however, the sauce will still be good using regular crushed tomatoes. For a milder sauce, omit the chipotle chile and use two anchos instead.*

3 tablespoons olive oil
1 medium onion, chopped
2 medium carrots, chopped
2 garlic cloves, minced
1 (28-ounce) can crushed fire-roasted tomatoes
½ cup vegetable broth, homemade (page 141)
    or store-bought
2 dried ancho chiles
1 dried chipotle chile
½ cup yellow cornmeal
½ teaspoon salt
¼ teaspoon freshly ground black pepper
1 pound seitan, homemade (page 305)
    or store-bought, cut into ¼-inch slices

1. In a large saucepan, heat 1 tablespoon of the oil over medium heat. Add the onion and carrots, cover, and cook for 7 minutes. Add the garlic and cook 1 minute. Stir in the tomatoes, broth, and the ancho and chipotle chiles. Simmer, uncovered, for 45 minutes, then pour the sauce into a blender and blend until smooth. Return to the saucepan and keep warm over very low heat.

2. In a shallow bowl, combine the cornmeal with the salt and pepper. Dredge the seitan in the cornmeal mixture, coating evenly.

3. In a large skillet, heat the 2 remaining tablespoons oil over medium heat. Add the seitan and cook until browned on both sides, about 8 minutes total. Serve immediately with the chile sauce.

# seitan piccata

makes 4 servings

*This may seem like a special-occasion dish, but it's so easy to prepare that you could make it anytime. The lemon and capers add a lively flavor to the seitan. Potatoes or a rice pilaf are equally good with this dish. Add your favorite green vegetable and you're all set to enjoy a great meal.*

1 pound seitan, homemade (page 305)
    or store-bought, cut into ¼-inch slices
Salt and freshly ground black pepper
½ cup all-purpose flour
3 tablespoons olive oil
1 medium shallot, minced
2 garlic cloves, minced
2 tablespoons capers
⅓ cup white wine
⅓ cup vegetable broth, homemade (page 141)
    or store-bought
2 tablespoons fresh lemon juice
2 tablespoons vegan margarine
2 tablespoons minced fresh parsley

1. Preheat the oven to 275°F. Season the seitan with salt and pepper to taste and dredge in the flour.

2. In a large skillet, heat 2 tablespoons of the oil over medium heat. Add the dredged seitan and cook until lightly browned on both sides, about 10 minutes. Transfer the seitan to a heatproof platter and keep warm in the oven.

3. In the same skillet, heat the remaining 1 tablespoon oil over medium heat. Add the shallot and garlic, cook for 2 minutes, then stir in the capers, wine, and broth. Simmer for a minute or two to reduce slightly, then add the lemon juice, margarine, and parsley, stirring until the margarine is blended into the sauce. Pour the sauce over the browned seitan and serve immediately.

## three-seed seitan

makes 4 servings

*Crisp, crunchy, and loaded with flavor, these seitan nuggets will disappear as quickly as you make them. They're quite flavorful on their own, but a dipping sauce is always fun, depending on what else you're serving. I think they're especially good served with Vegan Aioli (page 556) accompanied by roasted sweet potato sticks. If you can't find smoked paprika, use regular paprika instead.*

¼ cup unsalted shelled sunflower seeds

¼ cup unsalted shelled pumpkin seeds (pepitas)

¼ cup sesame seeds

¾ cup all-purpose flour

1 teaspoon ground coriander

1 teaspoon smoked paprika

½ teaspoon salt

¼ teaspoon freshly ground black pepper

1 pound seitan, homemade (page 305) or store-bought, cut into bite-size pieces

2 tablespoons olive oil

1. In a food processor, combine the sunflower seeds, pumpkin seeds, and sesame seeds and grind to a powder. Transfer to a shallow bowl, add the flour, coriander, paprika, salt, and pepper, and stir to combine.

2. Moisten the seitan pieces with water, then dredge in the seed mixture to coat completely.

3. In a large skillet, heat the oil over medium heat. Add the seitan and cook until lightly browned and crispy on both sides. Serve immediately.

## fajitas without borders

makes 4 servings

*This is a great dish to make with leftover baked sweet potatoes, especially on a busy night when you're too tired to even roll a fajita—just put everything in bowls! If you don't have leftover sweet potatoes on hand, you can "bake" some quickly in a microwave oven.*

1 tablespoon olive oil

1 small red onion, chopped

8 ounces seitan, homemade (page 305) or store-bought, cut into ½-inch strips

2 medium baked sweet potatoes, peeled and cut into ¼-inch strips

¼ cup canned hot or mild minced green chiles

½ teaspoon dried oregano

Salt and freshly ground black pepper

4 (10-inch) soft flour tortillas

2 cups tomato salsa, homemade (page 567) or store-bought

¼ cup sliced pitted kalamata olives (optional)

1. In a large skillet, heat the oil over medium heat. Add the onion, cover, and cook until softened, about 7 minutes. Add the seitan and cook, uncovered, for 5 minutes.

2. Add the sweet potatoes, chiles, oregano, and salt and pepper to taste, stirring to mix well. Continue to cook until the mixture is hot and

continues on next page

the flavors are well combined, stirring occasionally, about 7 minutes.

3. Warm the tortillas in a dry skillet. Place each tortilla in a shallow bowl. Spoon the seitan and sweet potato mixture into the tortillas, then top each with about ⅓ cup of the salsa. Sprinkle each bowl with 1 tablespoon of the olives, if using. Serve immediately, with any remaining salsa served on the side.

variations: Instead of seitan, you can substitute tempeh, extra-firm tofu, or your favorite beans. Instead of sweet potatoes, use baked white potatoes or put some cooked rice on the bottom of the tortilla. You can also add toppings such as guacamole, shredded lettuce, or vegan sour cream.

## seitan with green apple relish 🄵

makes 4 servings

*The brisk sweet-tart apple relish makes a zesty, fresh-tasting condiment for seitan in this recipe adapted from one shared with me by vegan chef Tal Ronnen.*

2 Granny Smith apples, coarsely chopped

½ cup finely chopped red onion

½ jalapeño chile, seeded and minced

1½ teaspoons grated fresh ginger

3 tablespoons fresh lime juice

2 teaspoons agave nectar

Salt and freshly ground black pepper

2 tablespoons olive oil

1 pound seitan, homemade (page 305) or store-bought, cut into ½-inch slices

¼ cup apple juice

1. In a medium bowl, combine the apples, onion, chile, ginger, lime juice, agave nectar, and salt and pepper to taste. Set aside.

2. Heat the oil in a skillet over medium heat. Add the seitan and cook until browned on both sides, turning once, about 4 minutes per side. Season with salt and pepper to taste. Add the apple juice and cook for a minute until it reduces. Serve immediately with the apple relish.

## seitan and broccoli-shiitake stir-fry 🄵

makes 4 servings

*The woodsy flavor and chewy texture of the shiitakes are a good match for the seitan in this flavorful stir-fry. A bed of freshly cooked rice is a natural accompaniment.*

2 tablespoons canola or grapeseed oil

8 ounces seitan, homemade (page 305) or store-bought, cut into ¼-inch slices

8 ounces shiitake mushrooms, lightly rinsed, patted dry, stemmed, and cut into ¼-inch slices

3 garlic cloves, minced

2 teaspoons grated fresh ginger

3 green onions, minced

1 medium bunch broccoli, cut into 1-inch florets

½ cup water

3 tablespoons soy sauce

2 tablespoons dry sherry

1 teaspoon toasted sesame oil

1 tablespoon toasted sesame seeds

1. In a large skillet, heat 1 tablespoon of the oil over medium-high heat. Add the seitan and cook, stirring occasionally until lightly browned, about 3 minutes. Transfer the seitan to a bowl and set aside.

**2.** In the same skillet, heat the remaining 1 tablespoon of oil over medium-high heat. Add the mushrooms and cook, stirring frequently, until browned, about 3 minutes. Stir in the garlic, ginger, and green onions and cook 30 seconds longer. Add the mushroom mixture to the cooked seitan and set aside.

**3.** Add the broccoli and water to the same skillet. Cover and cook until the broccoli begins to turn bright green, about 3 minutes. Uncover and cook, stirring frequently, until the liquid evaporates and the broccoli is crisp-tender, about 3 minutes longer.

**4.** Return the seitan and mushroom mixture to the skillet. Add the soy sauce and sherry and stir-fry until the seitan and vegetables are hot, about 3 minutes. Sprinkle with the sesame oil and sesame seeds and serve immediately.

# seitan brochettes with peaches and herbs

makes 4 servings

*This lovely summer entrée takes full advantage of fresh herbs, ripe peaches—and the grill. If you have a rosemary bush, cut off eight branches to use as skewers for added flavor and flair of presentation, although you may need to pierce the ingredients with a metal skewer first since the rosemary branches may be too fragile. If using wooden skewers, be sure to soak them for 30 minutes before using. And for those of you old enough to remember the duo who sang "Love Is Strange," I hope this recipe title made you smile.*

⅓ cup balsamic vinegar
3 tablespoons dry red wine
3 tablespoons light brown sugar
¼ cup chopped fresh basil
¼ cup chopped fresh marjoram
2 tablespoons minced garlic
3 tablespoons olive oil
1 pound seitan, homemade (page 305)
    or store-bought, cut into 1-inch chunks
4 shallots, halved lengthwise and blanched
Salt and freshly ground black pepper
2 ripe peaches, pitted and cut into 1-inch chunks

**1.** Combine the vinegar, wine, and sugar in a small saucepan and bring to a boil. Reduce heat to medium and simmer, stirring, until reduced by half, about 15 minutes. Remove from the heat.

**2.** In a large bowl, combine the basil, marjoram, garlic, and olive oil. Add the seitan, shallots, and peaches, and toss to coat. Season with salt and pepper to taste.

**3.** Preheat the grill.* Thread the seitan, shallots, and peaches onto the skewers and brush with the balsamic mixture.

**4.** Place the brochettes on the grill and cook until the seitan and peaches are grilled, about 3 minutes per side. Brush with the remaining balsamic mixture and serve immediately.

*\*Instead of grilling, you can put these brochettes under the broiler. Broil 4 to 5 inches from the heat until hot and lightly browned around the edges, about 10 minutes, turning once halfway through.*

# grilled seitan and vegetable kabobs

makes 4 servings

*Summer hasn't officially arrived until I make kabobs on the grill. Because the kabobs are assembled ahead of time to marinate, this is an especially good dish to serve guests. When served on a bed of freshly cooked rice or other grain, they make a lovely presentation. Remember, if you're using wooden skewers, soak them in water at least 30 minutes before using.*

1/3 cup balsamic vinegar

2 tablespoons olive oil

1 tablespoon minced fresh oregano or 1 teaspoon dried

1 teaspoon minced fresh thyme or 1/2 teaspoon dried

2 garlic cloves, minced

1/2 teaspoon salt

1/4 teaspoon freshly ground black pepper

1 pound seitan, homemade (page 305) or store-bought, cut into 1-inch cubes

8 ounces small white mushrooms, lightly rinsed and patted dry

2 small zucchini, cut into 1-inch chunks

1 medium yellow bell pepper, cut into 1-inch squares

12 ripe cherry tomatoes

1. In a medium bowl, combine the vinegar, oil, oregano, thyme, garlic, salt, and black pepper. Add the seitan, mushrooms, zucchini, bell pepper, and tomatoes, turning to coat. Marinate at room temperature for 30 minutes, turning occasionally. Drain the seitan and vegetables, reserving the marinade.

2. Preheat the grill.* Thread the seitan, mushrooms, and tomatoes onto skewers.

3. Place the skewers on the hot grill and cook, turning kabobs once halfway through grilling, about 10 minutes total. Drizzle with a small amount of the reserved marinade and serve immediately.

*Instead of grilling, you can put these skewers under the broiler. Broil 4 to 5 inches from the heat until hot and lightly browned around the edges, about 10 minutes, turning once halfway through broiling.*

# seitan en croute

makes 4 servings

*Serve these classy little numbers to special guests for a holiday meal or to non-vegan relatives who ask: "What do vegans eat?" One taste is worth a thousand words. Inspired by the classic beef Wellington, here seitan slices and a flavorful mushroom stuffing are wrapped in pastry as individual parcels and baked to a golden brown. For the most effective (and show-stopping) presentation, place each baked pastry-wrapped seitan on a dinner plate nestled in a mound of fresh mashed potatoes and surrounded by a few spoonfuls of Madeira Sauce (page 546). Criss-cross spears of roasted asparagus and carrot strips in front of each plated pastry-wrapped seitan package and serve hot.*

1 tablespoon olive oil

2 medium shallots, minced

8 ounces white mushrooms, minced

1/4 cup Madeira

1 tablespoon minced fresh parsley

1/2 teaspoon dried thyme

1/2 teaspoon dried savory

2 cups finely chopped dry bread cubes

Salt and freshly ground black pepper

1 frozen puff pastry sheet, thawed

8 (1/4-inch-thick) seitan slices (page 305), about 3 × 4-inch ovals or rectangles, patted dry

1. In a large skillet, heat the oil over medium heat. Add the shallots and cook until softened, about 3 minutes. Add the mushrooms and cook, stirring occasionally, until the mushrooms are softened, about 5 minutes. Add the Madiera, parsley, thyme, and savory and cook until the liquid is nearly evaporated. Stir in the bread cubes and season with salt and pepper to taste. Set aside to cool.

2. Lay the puff pastry sheet on a large piece of plastic film wrap on a flat work surface. Top with another piece of plastic wrap and use a rolling pin to roll out the pastry slightly to smooth out. Cut the pastry into quarters. Place 1 slice of seitan in the center of each piece of pastry. Divide the stuffing among them, spreading it to cover the seitan. Top each with the remaining seitan slices. Fold up the pastry to enclose the filling, crimping the edges with your fingers to seal.

3. Place the pastry packages, seam side down, on a large ungreased baking sheet and refrigerate for 30 minutes. Preheat the oven to 400°F. Bake until the crust is golden brown, about 20 minutes. Serve immediately.

# seitan and potato torta

makes 6 servings

*I like to make this delicious torta when company's coming. I usually bake it part-way just before guests arrive and then put it back into the oven for the final 15 minutes. A mandoline slicer can be used—the thinner the potato slices, the less time this will take to bake. Bread crumbs can be sprinkled with the final sprinkling of vegan Parmesan, if desired.*

2 tablespoons olive oil

1 medium yellow onion, minced

4 cups chopped fresh baby spinach or stemmed chard

8 ounces seitan, homemade (page 305) or store-bought, finely chopped

1 teaspoon minced fresh marjoram

½ teaspoon ground fennel seed

¼ to ½ teaspoon crushed red pepper

Salt and freshly ground black pepper

1 ripe tomato, cut into ¼-inch slices

2 pounds Yukon Gold potatoes, peeled and cut into ¼-inch slices

½ cup vegan Parmesan or Parmasio (page 193)

1. Preheat the oven to 400°F. Lightly oil a 3-quart casserole or 9 × 13-inch baking pan and set aside.

2. In a large skillet, heat the 1 tablespoon of the oil over medium heat. Add the onion, cover, and cook until softened, about 7 minutes. Add the spinach and cook, uncovered, until wilted, about 3 minutes. Stir in the seitan, marjoram, fennel seed, and crushed red pepper, and cook until well combined. Season with salt and pepper to taste. Set aside.

3. Spread the tomato slices in the bottom of the prepared pan. Top with a layer of slightly overlapping potato slices. Brush the potato layer with some of the remaining 1 tablespoon oil and season with salt and pepper to taste. Spread about half of the seitan and spinach mixture over the potatoes. Top with another layer of potatoes, followed by the remaining seitan and spinach mixture. Top with a final layer of potatoes, drizzle with the remaining oil and salt and pepper to taste. Sprinkle with the Parmesan. Cover and bake until the potatoes are tender, 45 minutes to 1 hour. Uncover and continue baking to brown the top, 10 to 15 minutes. Serve immediately.

# seitan noodle casserole

makes 4 servings

*This satisfying casserole is a cinch to put together and may be assembled in advance for easy clean-up. You can also make it with tofu or tempeh instead of seitan if you prefer. The sherry imparts a wonderful flavor, but you can leave it out for a child-friendly version.*

8 ounces fettuccine, broken into thirds

1 tablespoon olive oil

8 ounces white mushrooms, lightly rinsed, patted dry, and cut into ¼-inch slices

8 ounces seitan, homemade (page 305) or store-bought, chopped

1 cup frozen baby peas, thawed

¼ cup vegan margarine

¼ cup all-purpose flour

2 cups vegetable broth, homemade (page 141) or store-bought

2 tablespoons minced fresh parsley

¾ teaspoon dried thyme

¼ cup dry sherry

Salt and freshly ground black pepper

¼ cup vegan Parmesan or Parmasio (page 193)

Sweet paprika, for garnish

1. Lightly oil a 10-inch baking dish and set aside. Cook the noodles in a saucepan of boiling salted water until al dente, about 10 minutes. Drain and set aside.

2. Preheat the oven to 350°F. In a large skillet, heat the oil over medium heat. Add the mushrooms and cook until softened, about 5 minutes. Stir in the seitan and peas and set aside.

3. In a medium saucepan, melt the margarine and stir in the flour. Slowly add the broth, then add the parsley, thyme, and sherry and season with salt and pepper to taste. Cook, stirring, until thickened.

4. Transfer the noodles, sauce, and seitan mixture to the prepared baking pan, mixing to evenly coat the noodles with sauce. Sprinkle with the Parmesan and paprika. Cover and bake for 30 minutes. Uncover and bake, until browned, about 10 minutes longer. Serve immediately.

# rustic cottage pie

makes 4 to 6 servings

*Coarsely mashed skin-on potatoes serve as the tasty topping for this savory baked dish. In the vegan world, a cottage pie is virtually the same as a shepherd's pie, just made with different kinds of meat.*

4 Yukon Gold potatoes, peeled and cut into 1-inch dice

2 tablespoons vegan margarine

¼ cup plain unsweetened soy milk

Salt and freshly ground black pepper

1 tablespoon olive oil

1 medium yellow onion, finely chopped

1 medium carrot, finely chopped

1 celery rib, finely chopped

12 ounces seitan, homemade (page 305) or store-bought, finely chopped

1½ cups Mushroom Sauce (page 546)

1 cup frozen peas

1 cup frozen corn kernels

1 teaspoon dried savory

½ teaspoon dried thyme

1. In a saucepan of boiling salted water, cook the potatoes until tender, 15 to 20 minutes. Drain well and return to the pot. Add the margarine, soy milk, and salt and pepper to taste. Coarsely mash with a potato masher and set aside. Preheat the oven to 350°F.

2. In a large skillet, heat the oil over medium heat. Add the onion, carrot, and celery. Cover and cook until tender, about 10 minutes. Transfer the vegetables to a 9 × 13-inch baking pan. Stir in the seitan, mushroom sauce, peas, corn, savory, and thyme. Season with salt and pepper to taste and spread the mixture evenly in the baking pan.

3. Top with the mashed potatoes, spreading to the edges of the baking pan. Bake until the potatoes are browned and the filling is bubbly, about 45 minutes. Serve immediately.

# seitan with spinach and sun-dried tomatoes 

makes 4 servings

*This satisfying seitan dish is imbued with the lusty flavors of the Mediterranean, so I like to serve it over freshly cooked pasta tossed with a bit of good olive oil. You can substitute chard for the spinach or add fresh basil or oregano. Give it a squeeze of lemon when ready to serve.*

2 tablespoons olive oil

1 pound seitan, homemade (page 305) or store-bought, cut into ¼-inch strips

Salt and freshly ground black pepper

3 garlic cloves, minced

3 cups fresh baby spinach

4 oil-packed sun-dried tomatoes, cut into ¼-inch strips

½ cup pitted kalamata olives, halved

1 tablespoon capers

¼ teaspoon crushed red pepper

1. In a large skillet, heat the oil over medium heat. Add the seitan, season with salt and black pepper to taste, and cook until browned, about 5 minutes per side.

2. Add the garlic and cook for 1 minute to soften. Add the spinach and cook until it is wilted, about 3 minutes. Stir in the tomatoes, olives, capers, and crushed red pepper. Season with salt and black pepper to taste. Cook, stirring, until the flavors have blended, about 5 minutes. Serve immediately.

# seitan and scalloped potatoes casserole

makes 4 servings

*Serve this hearty casserole to the skeptical "meat and potatoes" person in your family and watch it disappear. It's also a good dish to serve children. If you'd like to add a little color to the dish (beyond the final sprinkle of parsley, add 1 cup of thawed frozen peas to the mixture before baking.*

2 tablespoons olive oil

1 small yellow onion, minced

¼ cup minced green bell pepper

3 large Yukon Gold potatoes, peeled and cut into ¼-inch slices

½ teaspoon salt

¼ teaspoon freshly ground black pepper

8 ounces seitan, homemade (page 305) or store-bought, chopped

1½ cups Basic Brown Sauce (page 545)

½ cup plain unsweetened soy milk

1 tablespoon vegan margarine

2 tablespoons minced fresh parsley, as garnish

1. Preheat the oven to 350°F. Lightly oil a 10-inch square baking pan and set aside.

continues on next page

2. In a skillet, heat the oil over medium heat. Add the onion and bell pepper and cook until tender, about 7 minutes. Set aside.

3. In the prepared baking pan, layer half of the potatoes and sprinkle with salt and black pepper to taste. Sprinkle the onion and bell pepper mixture and the chopped seitan on top of the potatoes. Top with the remaining potato slices and season with salt and black pepper to taste.

4. In a medium bowl, combine the brown sauce and soy milk until well blended. Pour over the potatoes. Dot the top layer with margarine and cover tightly with foil. Bake for 1 hour. Remove the foil and bake for an additional 20 minutes or until the top is golden brown. Serve immediately sprinkled with the parsley.

# seitan and chickpea stew

makes 6 servings

*This is one of those fortifying winter stews that tastes even better the day after it is made. Make it in advance of when you need it and you'll be rewarded with a hot and satisfying meal. Serve with warm crusty bread and a crisp green salad.*

2 tablespoons olive oil
1 pound seitan, homemade (page 305) or store-bought, cut into 1-inch cubes
Salt and freshly ground black pepper
1 large yellow onion, chopped
2 medium carrots, cut into ½-inch slices
1 celery rib, cut into ¼-inch slices
1 pound small new potatoes, unpeeled and quartered
3 cups chopped savoy cabbage
1 (14.5-ounce) can diced tomatoes, drained
1½ cups cooked or 1 (15.5-ounce) can chickpeas, drained and rinsed
½ cup dry white wine
1 teaspoon dried thyme
½ teaspoon dried marjoram
2 cups vegetable broth, homemade (page 141) or store-bought, or water

1. In a large saucepan, heat 1 tablespoon of the oil over medium-high heat. Add the seitan and cook until browned on all sides, about 5 minutes. Season with salt and pepper to taste, remove from the saucepan, and set aside.

2. In the same saucepan, heat the remaining 1 tablespoon oil over medium heat. Add the onion, carrots, and celery. Cover and cook until softened, about 5 minutes. Add the potatoes and cabbage. Stir in the tomatoes, chickpeas, wine, thyme, marjoram, and broth. Season with salt and pepper to taste and bring to a boil. Reduce the heat to low and simmer, uncovered, for 45 minutes.

3. Add the reserved seitan and simmer the stew to blend flavors, about 15 more minutes longer. Serve immediately.

# VEGETABLES

## sesame-baked vegetables

makes 4 servings

*A creamy sesame sauce and flaky crust make these vegetables deceptively rich. Sesame seeds, sprinkled on both the filling and the crust, further enhance the sesame flavor.*

4 cups broccoli florets
1 tablespoon olive oil
1 medium yellow onion, minced
2 medium carrots, minced
1 (14.5-ounce) can diced tomatoes, undrained
¼ cup tahini (sesame paste)
2 to 3 tablespoons soy sauce
¼ cup sesame seeds
1 sheet frozen puff pastry, thawed

1. Preheat the oven to 400°F. Steam the broccoli until just tender, about 5 minutes, then coarsely chop and set aside.

2. In a large skillet, heat the oil over medium heat. Add the onion and carrots, cover, and cook until tender, about 10 minutes. Stir in the tomatoes with their juice, tahini, and soy sauce and cook, uncovered, stirring until well mixed, about 5 minutes. Remove from the heat and stir in the steamed broccoli. Taste, adjusting seasonings, adding a little more soy sauce if necessary.

3. Spread the mixture evenly into a 9- or 10-inch square baking pan and sprinkle with half the sesame seeds. Set aside.

4. Roll out the pastry on a flat work surface so that it will fit on top of the baking dish, then place it on top of the filling and crimp the edges. Brush the crust with a little water or soy milk and sprinkle with the remaining sesame seeds. Bake until golden brown, about 45 minutes. Serve immediately.

## ratatouille

makes 4 to 6 servings

*This classic Provencale vegetable stew is too hearty to relegate to the realm of side dish. The addition of white beans makes it a main dish that is especially good served with warm crusty bread.*

2 tablespoons olive oil
1 medium yellow onion, chopped
3 garlic cloves, minced
1 medium eggplant, peeled and chopped
1 medium red bell pepper, chopped
1 medium yellow bell pepper, chopped
2 medium zucchini, chopped
1 (14.5-ounce) can diced tomatoes, undrained
1½ cups cooked or 1 (15.5-ounce) can white
   beans, drained and rinsed
½ teaspoon salt
¼ teaspoon freshly ground black pepper
½ cup vegetable broth, homemade (page 141)
   or store-bought, or water
1 teaspoon dried marjoram
1 teaspoon dried thyme
2 tablespoons minced fresh parsley

1. In a large saucepan, heat the oil over medium heat. Add the onion, cover, and cook until softened, about 5 minutes. Add the garlic and cook 30 seconds. Stir in the eggplant, red and yellow bell peppers, zucchini, tomatoes, and beans. Add the salt and pepper and cook, uncovered, stirring, for 5 minutes.

2. Add the broth, marjoram, and thyme. Cover, reduce heat to low, and simmer until the vegetables are tender but not mushy, about 30 minutes. Stir in the parsley and taste, adjusting seasonings if necessary. Serve immediately.

# vegetable paella

makes 4 servings

*I like to serve this vegan paella with a robust Rioja and round out the meal with a green salad and toasted garlic bread. For a more substantial dish, add some sautéed seitan, tempeh, or sliced vegan sausage links.*

2 tablespoons olive oil

2 medium carrots, cut into ¼-inch slices

1 celery rib, cut into ¼-inch slices

1 medium yellow onion, chopped

1 medium red bell pepper, cut into ½-inch dice

3 garlic cloves, chopped

8 ounces green beans, trimmed and cut into
    1-inch pieces

1½ cups cooked or 1 (15.5-ounce) can dark red
    kidney beans, drained and rinsed

1 (14.5-ounce) can diced tomatoes, drained

2½ cups vegetable broth, homemade (page 141)
    or store-bought

Salt

½ teaspoon dried marjoram

½ teaspoon crushed red pepper

½ teaspoon ground fennel seed

¼ teaspoon saffron or turmeric

¾ cup long-grain rice

2 cups oyster mushrooms, lightly rinsed
    and patted dry

1 (14-ounce) can artichoke hearts, drained
    and quartered

1. In a large saucepan, heat the oil over medium heat. Add the carrots, celery, onion, bell pepper, and garlic. Cover and cook for 10 minutes.

2. Add the green beans, kidney beans, tomatoes, broth, salt, oregano, crushed red pepper, fennel seed, saffron, and rice. Cover and simmer for 30 minutes.

3. Stir in the mushrooms and artichoke hearts. Taste, adjusting seasonings, adding more salt if necessary. Cover and simmer 15 minutes longer. Serve immediately.

# three-green tian

makes 4 to 6 servings

*The word* tian *refers both to the earthenware gratin dish and the food cooked in the dish. A tian is a lighter gratin, from the south of France, that is often made with olive oil or a tomato coulis. If all three greens are not available, you can use just one or two of the greens with good results. Crusty bread and a crisp green salad make good accompaniments.*

2 medium baking potatoes, cut into ¼-inch slices

3 medium zucchini, cut into ¼-inch slices on the
    diagonal

¾ cup olive oil

Salt and freshly ground black pepper

1 medium yellow onion, chopped

3 garlic cloves, minced

3 cups packed fresh spinach leaves, tough stems
    removed and coarsely chopped

2 cups packed stemmed and chopped kale

2 cups stemmed and chopped Swiss chard

1 cup loosely packed fresh basil leaves

5 to 6 ripe plum tomatoes, cut into ¼-inch slices

¾ cup fresh bread crumbs

3 tablespoons vegan Parmesan or Parmasio
    (page 193)

1. Preheat the oven to 400°F. Lightly oil a 9 × 13-inch baking pan and set aside. Lightly oil two large baking sheets and arrange the potato slices on one of them, overlapping as needed. Arrange the zucchini slices on the

other, overlapping as needed. Drizzle with 1 or 2 tablespoons of the oil and season with salt and pepper to taste. Bake the zucchini slices until softened, about 10 minutes, and the potato slices until softened, about 20 minutes. Remove from the oven and set aside.

2. In a large skillet, heat 1 tablespoon of the oil over medium heat. Add the onion and garlic. Cover and cook until softened, about 5 minutes. Stir in the spinach, kale, and chard and season with salt and pepper to taste. Cover and cook until the greens are wilted, about 7 minutes.

3. Transfer the greens mixture to a blender or food processor and process with the basil and 3 tablespoons of the remaining oil until smooth. Season with salt and pepper to taste.

4. Line the bottom of the prepared pan with a half of the cooked potato slices, overlapping as needed. Spoon a very thin layer of the pureed greens evenly over the potatoes. Arrange a layer of half of the cooked zucchini slices on top, overlapping as needed, followed by more of the pureed greens. Arrange a layer of tomato slices on top, followed by more of the greens. Repeat using the remaining potato, zucchini, and tomato slices and the remaining pureed greens, seasoning each layer with salt and pepper to taste.

5. Cover tightly with foil and bake until the vegetables are tender, about 45 minutes. Remove from the oven and sprinkle the tian with the bread crumbs and Parmesan and drizzle with the remaining olive oil. Return to the oven and bake uncovered for 10 minutes to brown the topping. Serve immediately.

# eggplant paprikash
makes 4 servings

*The hearty Hungarian paprikash dish is traditionally made with chicken, sour cream, and bacon drippings. In this version, paprikash goes vegan with meaty chunks of eggplant, vegan sour cream, and a touch of liquid smoke. If eggplant isn't your thing, you can use tempeh or seitan instead.*

2 tablespoons olive oil

1 medium yellow onion, chopped

3 garlic cloves, minced

3 tablespoons sweet Hungarian paprika

2 medium eggplants, peeled and cut into ½-inch dice

1 medium green bell pepper, chopped

1 (14.5-ounce) can diced tomatoes, undrained

1 cup vegetable broth, homemade (page 141) or store-bought

½ teaspoon salt

½ cup vegan sour cream, homemade (page 574) or store-bought

½ teaspoon liquid smoke

1. In a large saucepan, heat the oil over medium heat. Add the onion, cover, and cook until softened, about 8 minutes. Add the garlic and paprika. Cook, stirring, for 1 minute.

2. Add the eggplants, bell pepper, tomatoes, broth, and salt. Cover and simmer until the eggplant is tender, 20 to 30 minutes.

3. Stir in the sour cream and liquid smoke and cook until the sauce is blended and heated through, about 1 minute. Taste, adjusting seasonings if necessary, and serve immediately.

# chard and new potato gratin with herbes de provence

makes 4 servings

*Gratins tend to turn out best when the ingredients used in them are precooked. This translates to shorter cooking times and ensures that vegetables won't release too much liquid into the gratin. The skin of new potatoes is tender and nutritious, so leave it on—just be sure to scrub your potatoes well. A mandoline works best for slicing the potatoes very thin, but use a sharp knife if you don't have one.*

3 tablespoons olive oil

1 medium yellow onion, minced

3 garlic cloves, minced

1 medium bunch Swiss chard, tough stems removed and coarsely chopped

Salt and freshly ground black pepper

2 pounds new potatoes, unpeeled and cut into ¼-inch slices

1 teaspoon herbes de Provence

2 tablespoons vegan Parmesan or Parmasio (page 193)

1. Preheat the oven to 350°F. Lightly oil a 9- or 10-inch square baking pan or large gratin dish. Heat 1 tablespoon of the oil in a large skillet over medium heat. Add the onion and garlic, cover, and cook to soften, about 5 minutes. Add the Swiss chard and cook, uncovered, turning it until it is wilted. Season with salt and pepper and set aside.

2. Layer half of the potatoes in the bottom of the prepared pan, overlapping as necessary. Season with some of the herbes de Provence and salt and pepper to taste. Drizzle with 1 tablespoon of the olive oil. Add the chard and onion mixture in a layer across the potatoes. Season with salt and herbes de Provence and top with the remaining potatoes. Drizzle with the remaining tablespoon of the oil and season with salt and pepper.

3. Cover tightly with aluminum foil and bake until the vegetables are tender, about 1 hour. Sprinkle with vegan Parmesan and bake 10 minutes longer. Serve hot directly from the gratin dish.

# sesame spinach noodle pie

makes 4 servings

*Linguine and spinach are bathed in a creamy tahini sauce in this Asian version of mac and cheese. If you don't have a large deep-dish pie plate, a shallow baking dish works just as well.*

¾ cup tahini (sesame paste)

3 garlic cloves, coarsely chopped

3 tablespoons mellow white miso paste

3 tablespoons fresh lemon juice

¼ teaspoon ground cayenne

1 cup water

8 ounces linguine, broken into thirds

9 ounces fresh baby spinach

1 tablespoon toasted sesame oil

2 tablespoons sesame seeds

1. Preheat the oven to 350°F. In a food processor, combine the tahini, garlic, miso, lemon juice, cayenne, and water and process until smooth. Set aside.

2. Cook the linguine in a large saucepan of boiling salted water, stirring occasionally, until al dente, about 10 minutes. Add the spinach, stirring until wilted, about 1 minute. Drain well, then return to the pot. Add the oil and the tahini sauce and toss to mix well.

**3.** Transfer the mixture to a 9-inch deep-dish pie plate or round baking pan. Sprinkle with sesame seeds and bake until hot, about 20 minutes. Serve immediately.

# broccoli and white beans with potatoes and walnuts

*makes 4 servings*

*Sometimes it's the simplest dishes that are the best because they let the flavors of the ingredients shine through. That is certainly the case with this one, which pairs creamy fingerling potatoes and white beans with tender broccoli and crunchy walnuts for satisfying textural contrast. The luscious flavor is heightened by garlic, lemon juice, and a touch of heat.*

1½ pounds fingerling potatoes

4 cups broccoli florets

3 tablespoons olive oil

3 garlic cloves, minced

¾ cup chopped walnut pieces

¼ teaspoon crushed red pepper

1½ cups or 1 (15.5-ounce) can white beans, drained and rinsed

1 teaspoon dried savory

Salt and freshly ground black pepper

1 tablespoon fresh lemon juice

**1.** Steam the potatoes until tender, about 20 minutes. Set aside.

**2.** Steam the broccoli until crisp-tender, about 7 minutes. Set aside.

**3.** In a large skillet, heat 2 tablespoons of the oil over medium heat. Add the garlic, walnuts, and crushed red pepper. Cook until the garlic is softened, about 1 minute.

**4.** Stir in the steamed potatoes and broccoli. Add the beans and savory and season with salt and black pepper to taste. Cook until

heated through, about 5 minutes. Sprinkle with lemon juice and drizzle with the remaining 1 tablespoon olive oil. Serve immediately.

# eggplant with pomegranate walnut sauce

*makes 4 servings*

*This recipe was inspired by fesanjun, a Middle Eastern dish usually made with chicken. If pomegranate molasses is unavailable, make your own using the recipe on page 261. Serve over basmati rice.*

1 large or 2 small eggplants

2 tablespoons olive oil

Salt and freshly ground black pepper

1 medium yellow onion, finely chopped

¾ cup ground walnut pieces

1 cup vegetable broth, homemade (page 141) or store-bought

⅓ cup pomegranate molasses

1 tablespoon sugar

1 tablespoon fresh lemon juice

¼ teaspoon ground cinnamon

1 tablespoon chopped fresh parsley, for garnish

**1.** Preheat the oven to 250°F. Peel the eggplants, halve lengthwise, and cut crosswise into ½-inch-thick slices. In a large skillet, heat 1 tablespoon of the oil over medium heat. Add the eggplant slices in a single layer, in batches if necessary, and cook until tender and browned on both sides, about 5 minutes per side. Season with salt and pepper to taste. Transfer the eggplant to a heatproof platter and keep warm in the oven.

**2.** In the same skillet, heat the remaining 1 tablespoon oil over medium heat. Add the onion, cover, and cook until soft, about

continues on next page

10 minutes. Stir in the walnuts and broth. Stir in the pomegranate molasses, sugar, lemon juice, cinnamon, and salt and pepper to taste. Bring to a boil, then reduce heat to low, and simmer, uncovered, until the sauce is slightly thickened, about 20 minutes.

3. Spoon the sauce over the eggplant and sprinkle with parsley. Serve immediately.

## garden vegetable stew

makes 4 servings

*This light and colorful vegetable stew has no rules except that the vegetables are garden-fresh, even if not from your own garden, perhaps made after a trip to the farmer's market. Mix and match veggies according to your "harvest."*

2 tablespoons olive oil

1 medium red onion, chopped

1 medium carrot, cut into ¼-inch slices

½ cup dry white wine

3 medium new potatoes, unpeeled and cut into 1-inch pieces

1 medium red bell pepper, cut into ½-inch dice

1½ cups vegetable broth, homemade (page 141) or store-bought

2 medium zucchini, trimmed, halved lengthwise, and cut into ½-inch slices

1 medium yellow summer squash, trimmed, halved lengthwise, and cut into ½-inch slices

1 pound ripe plum tomatoes, chopped

Salt and freshly ground black pepper

2 cups fresh corn kernels

1 cup fresh peas

¼ cup fresh basil

¼ cup chopped fresh parsley

1 tablespoon minced fresh savory or 1 teaspoon dried

1. In a large saucepan, heat the oil over medium heat. Add the onion and carrot, cover, and cook until softened, 7 minutes. Add the wine and cook, uncovered, for 5 minutes. Stir in the potatoes, bell pepper, and broth and bring to a boil. Reduce the heat to medium and simmer for 15 minutes.

2. Add the zucchini, yellow squash, and tomatoes. Season with salt and black pepper to taste, cover, and simmer until the vegetables are tender, 20 to 30 minutes. Stir in the corn, peas, basil, parsley, and savory. Taste, adjusting seasonings if necessary. Simmer to blend flavors, about 10 minutes more. Serve immediately.

## mediterranean vegetable stew

makes 4 servings

*If you have fresh herbs, by all means use them in this stew to add fresher flavor. Serve over pasta or polenta, or simply accompany with good crusty bread.*

1 tablespoon olive oil

1 medium yellow onion, chopped

1 medium carrot, chopped

3 garlic cloves, minced

1 medium red bell pepper, cut into ½-inch dice

1 medium fennel bulb, quartered and cut into ¼-inch slices

1 medium zucchini, chopped

1 (14.5-ounce) can diced tomatoes, undrained

1 cup vegetable broth, homemade (page 141) or store-bought

Salt

Freshly ground black pepper

8 ounces white or porcini mushrooms, lightly rinsed, patted dry, and sliced

3 cups fresh baby spinach

1½ cups cooked or 1 (15.5-ounce) can cannellini beans, drained and rinsed

½ teaspoon dried basil

½ teaspoon dried marjoram

2 tablespoons minced fresh parsley

1. In a large saucepan, heat the oil over medium heat. Add the onion, carrot, garlic, and bell pepper. Cover and cook until softened, 7 minutes.

2. Add the fennel, zucchini, tomatoes, and broth. Bring to a boil, then reduce heat to low. Season with salt and black pepper to taste, cover, and simmer until the vegetables are tender, about 30 minutes.

3. Stir in the mushrooms, spinach, beans, basil, marjoram, and parsley. Taste, adjusting seasonings if necessary. Simmer 10 minutes more. Serve immediately.

# potato and artichoke gratin with spinach and pine nuts

makes 4 servings

*This savory gratin, adorned with chopped pine nuts, makes a satisfying main dish when served with hot grilled garlic bread and a crisp salad. If frozen artichoke hearts are unavailable, substitute a 15-ounce can (not marinated) and proceed with the recipe after the frozen-artichoke cooking instructions.*

1 (10-ounce) package frozen artichoke hearts

2 tablespoons olive oil

2 garlic cloves, minced

5 cups fresh baby spinach

Salt and freshly ground black pepper

1 teaspoon dried basil

½ teaspoon dried thyme

2 large russet potatoes, peeled and cut into ¼-inch slices

½ cup vegetable broth, homemade (page 141) or store-bought

2 tablespoons nutritional yeast

½ cup coarsely ground pine nuts

1. Preheat the oven to 375°F. Lightly oil a 2-quart gratin dish or casserole. If using frozen artichoke hearts, cook them in a small saucepan of boiling salted water until tender, about 12 minutes. Drain well. Cut the artichoke hearts into thin slices and set aside.

2. In a large skillet, heat 1 tablespoon of the oil over medium heat. Add the garlic, spinach, and salt and pepper to taste. Cover and cook until the spinach is wilted, stirring occasionally, about 2 minutes. Stir in the basil, thyme, and salt and pepper to taste. Set aside.

3. Layer half of the potato slices in the prepared gratin dish. Season with salt and pepper to taste. Top with the sliced artichokes, followed by the spinach mixture. Top with a layer of the remaining potatoes.

4. In a small bowl, combine the broth and nutritional yeast and stir until blended. Pour over the gratin. Sprinkle ground pine nuts on top of the gratin and drizzle with the 1 tablespoon remaining oil. Cover with foil and bake until the potatoes are tender, about 40 minutes. Uncover and bake until the top is golden brown, about 10 minutes longer. Serve immediately.

# artichoke-walnut tart

makes 4 servings

*The convenience of packaged puff pastry and frozen artichoke hearts makes this elegant and flavorful tart so easy to prepare that you won't need to wait for a special occasion to serve it. If frozen artichoke hearts are unavailable, substitute a (drained) 15-ounce can (not marinated) and proceed with the recipe after the frozen-artichoke cooking instructions.*

1 (10-ounce) package frozen artichoke hearts

1 frozen puff pastry sheet, thawed

½ cup toasted walnut pieces

8 ounces extra-firm tofu, drained and crumbled

3 green onions, minced

2 teaspoons fresh lemon juice

2 tablespoons minced fresh parsley

1 tablespoon minced fresh marjoram,
      or 1 teaspoon dried

Salt and freshly ground black pepper

2 ripe plum tomatoes, sliced paper thin

1. Preheat the oven to 400°F. Cook the artichoke hearts in a small saucepan of boiling salted water until tender, about 12 minutes. Drain and set aside.

2. On a lightly floured work surface, roll out the pastry, then press it into the bottom and up the sides of a 9-inch tart pan or pie plate. Trim and crimp the edges. Partially bake the crust for 10 minutes. Remove from the oven and set aside.

3. Coarsely chop 2 of the artichoke hearts and set aside. In a food processor, combine the remaining artichoke hearts, ³/₄ cup of the walnuts, tofu, and green onions and process until finely chopped. Add the lemon juice, parsley,

marjoram, and salt and pepper to taste and process until well blended. Spoon the mixture into a bowl and add the remaining ¹/₄ cup walnuts and reserved artichokes. Stir to blend.

4. Spread the artichoke-walnut mixture evenly over the partially baked pastry. Arrange the tomato slices on top, overlapping slightly. Season with salt and pepper to taste. Bake until the crust is golden brown and the filling is hot, about 25 minutes. Cool 10 to 15 minutes before serving.

# mushroom goulash

makes 4 servings

*Although the hearty Hungarian stew called goulash is typically made with beef, chunks of juicy portobello mushrooms fill the role deliciously, especially because mushrooms are a prominent ingredient in Eastern European cooking. Serve over freshly cooked wide noodles such as fettuccine, which have been broken into thirds, or egg-free noodles.*

1 tablespoon olive oil

1 large yellow onion, chopped

3 garlic cloves, minced

1 large russet potato, cut into ½-inch dice

4 large portobello mushrooms, lightly rinsed,
      patted dry, and cut into 1-inch chunks

1 tablespoon tomato paste

½ cup dry white wine

1½ tablespoons sweet Hungarian paprika

1 teaspoon caraway seeds

1½ cups fresh or canned sauerkraut, drained

1½ cups vegetable broth, homemade (page 141)
      or store-bought, or water

Salt and freshly ground black pepper

½ cup vegan sour cream, homemade (page 574)
      or store-bought

1. In large saucepan, heat the oil over medium heat. Add the onion, garlic, and potato. Cover and cook until softened, about 10 minutes. Add the mushrooms and cook, uncovered, 3 minutes longer. Stir in the tomato paste, wine, paprika, caraway seeds, and sauerkraut. Add the broth and bring to a boil, then reduce heat to low and season with salt and pepper to taste. Cover and simmer until the vegetables are soft and the flavor is developed, about 30 minutes.

2. Spoon about 1 cup of liquid into a small bowl. Add the sour cream, stirring to blend. Stir the sour cream mixture back into the saucepan and taste, adjusting seasonings if necessary. Serve immediately.

# green bean and mushroom stroganoff

makes 4 servings

*While using seitan instead of green beans would certainly make this more similar to the classic dish, I like the texture and flavor of the green beans in the creamy sauce studded with slices of juicy mushrooms. Serve over rice pilaf or noodles.*

1 pound green beans, trimmed and cut into
    1-inch lengths
2 tablespoons olive oil
1 large yellow onion, chopped
12 ounces white mushrooms, lightly rinsed,
    patted dry, and cut into ¼-inch slices
1 tablespoon sweet Hungarian paprika
2 tablespoons all-purpose flour
1 tablespoon tomato paste
½ cup dry white wine
2 cups vegetable broth, homemade (page 141)
    or store-bought, or water

Salt and freshly ground black pepper
½ cup vegan sour cream, homemade (page 574)
    or store-bought

1. Lightly steam the green beans until just tender, 5 to 7 minutes. Set aside.

2. In a large saucepan, heat the oil over medium heat. Add the onion, cover, and cook until soft, about 10 minutes. Add the mushrooms and cook, uncovered, until mushrooms release their juices, about 3 minutes more. Stir in the paprika and the flour, and cook, stirring for 1 minute. Add the tomato paste and wine, stirring until smooth.

3. Add the steamed green beans and broth and bring to a boil. Reduce heat to low, season with salt and pepper to taste, and simmer until the vegetables are tender and the sauce thickens slightly, about 20 minutes.

4. Spoon about 1 cup of the broth into a small bowl. Add the sour cream, stirring to blend. Stir the sour cream mixture back into the saucepan. Serve immediately.

# tamarind eggplant with bell peppers and mango

makes 4 servings

*If you think eggplant is boring, then you just haven't allowed it to realize its full potential. Like tofu, eggplant readily absorbs its surrounding flavors, so when mingled with lively ingredients such as tamarind, chile, mango, and cilantro, the result is anything but bland. Serve over rice or quinoa. Tamarind paste can be found in Asian or Indian markets or online. If unavailable, use 1 tablespoon lime juice blended with 1 teaspoon sugar or molasses, and add near the end of cooking time. The slender Asian eggplants are used in this dish because they are more tender and have fewer seeds than the large globe eggplant, although a large eggplant can be substituted if necessary.*

2 tablespoons olive oil

1 medium yellow onion, cut into ½-inch dice

3 small Asian eggplants, peeled and cut into 1-inch chunks

1 medium red pepper, cut into ½-inch dice

1 medium yellow bell pepper, cut into ½-inch dice

3 garlic cloves, minced

1 serrano or other small hot chile, seeded and minced

2 tablespoons tamarind paste

½ cup fresh orange juice

2 teaspoons light brown sugar

Salt and freshly ground black pepper

1 ripe mango, peeled, pitted, and cut into ½-inch dice

½ cup finely chopped fresh cilantro

1. In a large skillet, heat the oil over medium heat. Add the onion, cover, and cook until softened, 5 minutes. Add the eggplants, red and yellow bell peppers, garlic, and chile. Cook, covered, until softened, 10 minutes.

2. Add the tamarind paste, orange juice, sugar, and salt and black pepper to taste. Bring to a boil, then reduce heat to low and simmer, uncovered, until the vegetables are soft and the liquid thickens and reduces by half, about 20 minutes.

3. Stir in the mango and cilantro and serve immediately.

# stir-fried curried vegetables 🅕

makes 4 servings

*The speed of a stir-fry combines with the flavors of India for this curry in a hurry. Strips of seitan or extra-firm tofu may be added for a more substantial dish. Serve over freshly cooked brown basmati rice.*

2 tablespoons canola or grapeseed oil

2 garlic cloves, minced

2 teaspoons grated fresh ginger

1 medium carrot, sliced diagonally

1 medium red pepper, cut into ¼-inch strips

2 cups broccoli florets

2 tablespoons water

Salt and freshly ground black pepper

1 cup sliced white mushrooms

½ cup snow peas, trimmed

1 ripe tomato, chopped

1½ tablespoons hot or mild curry paste or powder

1 cup unsweetened coconut milk

1. In a large skillet or wok, heat the oil over medium heat. Add the garlic and ginger and cook until fragrant, 30 seconds. Add the carrot, bell pepper, broccoli, water, and salt and black pepper to taste. Cover and cook for 2 minutes. Uncover, and stir-fry 2 minutes longer. Add the mushrooms, snow peas, and tomato. Stir-fry until the vegetables have softened, about 3 to 5 minutes.

**2.** In a small bowl, combine the curry paste with the coconut milk, stirring until smooth. Pour the sauce over the vegetables and stir-fry until the vegetables are coated with the sauce, then simmer to thicken the sauce, about 2 minutes more. Serve immediately.

## spinach soufflé

makes 4 servings

*If you thought your soufflé days were over when you went vegan, try this light and flavorful egg-free version made with tofu. Baking powder is used to get a rise out of it and while perhaps not as fluffy as an egg-based soufflé, it still provides a delicious soufflé-like experience.*

4 tablespoons olive oil

1 medium yellow onion, minced

4 cups fresh baby spinach

Salt and freshly ground black pepper

1 pound firm tofu, drained

1 cup all-purpose flour

1 teaspoon baking powder

¾ cup vegetable broth, homemade (page 141) or store-bought, or water

2 tablespoons soy sauce

**1.** Preheat the oven to 350°F. Lightly oil a 3 quart-casserole or round baking dish and set aside. In a large skillet, heat 1 tablespoon oil over medium heat. Add the onion, cover, and cook until soft, about 10 minutes. Stir in the spinach and season with salt and pepper to taste. Cover and cook until the spinach is wilted, about 3 minutes. Set aside.

**2.** In a food processor, combine the tofu and the onion and spinach mixture and process until blended. Add the flour, baking powder, broth, soy sauce, and remaining 3 tablespoons oil and process until smooth.

**3.** Scrape the mixture into the prepared casserole and bake until firm, about 60 minutes. Serve immediately.

## roasted cauliflower and shallots with millet

makes 4 servings

*The process of roasting heightens the flavor of the cauliflower and shallots, making them exceptionally sweet and flavorful. When combined with creamy millet and green peas, you get a uniquely delicious medley of textures and flavors.*

1 cup millet

3 cups vegetable broth, homemade (page 141) or store-bought

½ cup frozen baby peas

3 cups small cauliflower florets

3 medium shallots, quartered

2 tablespoons olive oil

Salt and freshly ground black pepper

**1.** In a medium saucepan, bring the millet and broth to a boil. Cover with a tight-fitting lid and cook until the broth is absorbed, about 40 minutes. Stir in the peas and set aside, covered, and keep warm. Preheat the oven to 425°F. Lightly oil a 9 × 13-inch baking pan and set aside.

**2.** Spread the cauliflower and shallots in the prepared baking pan and drizzle with the oil. Season with salt and pepper to taste and roast until tender and lightly browned, turning once, about 20 minutes.

**3.** In a large serving bowl, combine the roasted cauliflower and shallots with the cooked millet and peas. Toss gently to combine. Serve immediately.

# artichoke and chickpea loaf

makes 6 to 8 servings

*This mellow yet flavorful loaf is equally delicious served hot, cold, or at room temperature. In addition to serving as an entrée with a sauce (try it with the Hollandaze on page 552), it can be served with crackers much like a country pâté. While chickpea flour is preferable for its distinct color and flavor, you can use another type of flour such as spelt or oat flour, if it is unavailable. The resulting loaf will still be delicious, and only slightly less complex in flavor. Note: if serving it whole as an appetizer pâté, you might want to dress it up a bit by sprinkling the top with minced parsley topped with a few thin strips of oil-packed sun-dried tomatoes. If frozen artichoke hearts are unavailable, substitute a 15-ounce can (not marinated) and proceed with the recipe after the frozen-artichoke cooking instructions.*

1 large russet potato, peeled and cut into
    ½-inch dice

1 (10-ounce) package frozen artichoke hearts

¼ cup olive oil

1 large yellow onion, chopped

1½ cups or 1 (15.5-ounce) can chickpeas,
    drained and rinsed

¼ cup vegetable broth, homemade (page 141)
    or store-bought

2 tablespoons tahini

1½ tablespoons soy sauce

1½ tablespoons fresh lemon juice

⅔ cup wheat gluten flour (vital wheat gluten)

⅔ cup chickpea flour

½ cup nutritional yeast

1 teaspoon dried marjoram

1 teaspoon dried thyme

1 teaspoon salt

¼ teaspoon freshly ground black pepper

½ cup chopped oil-packed sun-dried tomatoes

¼ cup minced fresh parsley

1. Preheat the oven to 375°F. Lightly oil a 9-inch loaf pan or square baking pan. Steam the potato and artichoke hearts (if using frozen) until tender, about 15 minutes. Blot off any excess moisture and set aside, reserving 2 of the artichoke hearts. Chop the reserved artichoke hearts and set aside.

2. In a large skillet, heat the oil over medium heat. Add the onion, cover, and cook until tender, about 10 minutes. Stir in the steamed potatoes and artichoke hearts.

3. Spoon the potato and artichoke mixture into a food processor. Add the chickpeas, broth, tahini, soy sauce, and lemon juice, and blend until smooth.

4. In a large bowl, combine both kinds of flour, the nutritional yeast, marjoram, thyme, salt, and pepper and stir to combine well.

5. Add the wet ingredients to the dry ingredients. Add the sun-dried tomatoes, parsley, and reserved chopped artichoke hearts and mix until well combined. Scrape the mixture into the prepared. Bake until firm and golden brown, about 1 hour. Let sit at room temperature for 15 minutes before slicing.

# grilled vegetable skewers with mop sauce

makes 4 servings

*A mop sauce is a thin sauce used for grilled and barbecued foods. Like most marinades and barbecue sauces, mop sauces can contain a variety of ingredients and range from mild to spicy. If using wooden skewers, soak them in water for at least 1 hour before use to prevent burning.*

½ cup strong black coffee

¼ cup soy sauce

½ cup ketchup

2 tablespoons olive oil

1 teaspoon hot sauce

1 teaspoon sugar

¼ teaspoon salt

¼ teaspoon freshly ground black pepper

1 large red or yellow bell pepper, cut into
   1½-inch pieces

2 small zucchini, cut into 1-inch chunks

8 ounces fresh small white mushrooms,
   lightly rinsed and patted dry

6 medium shallots, halved lengthwise

12 ripe cherry tomatoes

1. In a small saucepan, combine the coffee, soy sauce, ketchup, oil, hot sauce, sugar, salt, and black pepper. Simmer for 20 minutes, then keep warm over very low heat.

2. Thread the bell pepper, zucchini, mushrooms, shallots, and cherry tomatoes onto skewers and arrange them in a shallow baking dish. Pour about half of the mop sauce over the skewered vegetables and marinate at room temperature for 20 minutes. Preheat the grill.

3. Remove the skewered vegetables from the pan, reserving the marinade. Place the skewers on the grill directly over the heat source. Grill until the vegetables are browned and tender, turning once halfway through, about 10 minutes total. Transfer to a platter and spoon the remaining sauce over all. Serve immediately.

broiled vegetable skewers: Place the skewered vegetables on a broiler pan and place under the broiler, about 4 inches from the heat. Broil until tender and nicely browned, about 8 minutes total, turning once halfway through.

# pastry-wrapped portobellos
makes 4 servings

*Mushrooms are a good source of fiber, B vitamins, potassium, iron, zinc, and other minerals. It's important that the mushrooms and stuffing are completely cool and blotted dry before wrapping in pastry, otherwise the pastry will become soggy. These pastry-wrapped mushrooms make an attractive and delicious entrée served with Madeira Sauce (page 546) or Basic Brown Sauce (page 545). If you want to bulk up the stuffing a bit, add some chopped seitan to the stuffing mixture.*

5 large portobello mushrooms, lightly rinsed
   and patted dry

2 tablespoons olive oil

1 medium bunch green onions, chopped

½ cup finely chopped walnuts

1 tablespoon soy sauce

½ cup dry unseasoned bread crumbs

½ teaspoon dried thyme

Salt and freshly ground black pepper

1 sheet frozen puff pastry, thawed

1. Stem the mushrooms and reserve. Carefully scrape the gills out of the mushrooms and set 4 of the mushroom caps aside. Chop the fifth mushroom and the reserved stems and set aside.

2. In a large skillet, heat 1 tablespoon of the oil over medium heat. Add the chopped mushrooms, green onions, and walnuts, and cook, stirring for 5 minutes. Transfer to a large bowl and set aside to cool.

3. In the same skillet, heat the remaining 1 tablespoon of oil. Add the reserved mushroom caps and cook until they soften slightly.

continues on next page

Sprinkle with soy sauce and cook until the liquid evaporates. Set aside on paper towels to cool and drain any liquid.

4. Add the bread crumbs, thyme, and salt and pepper to taste to the cooked mushroom mixture. Mix well, then set aside until completely cool. Preheat the oven to 425°F.

5. Unfold the puff pastry sheet on a lightly floured work surface and quarter. Roll out each piece of pastry slightly to make a 5-inch square. Center each mushroom cap on a pastry square, gill side up. Press one-fourth of the stuffing mixture into each mushroom cap. Fold the pastry over each mushroom to enclose, overlapping slightly. Press the edges together to seal. Set the bundles, seam side down, on a baking sheet. Use a small knife to cut a few small steam vents in the tops of the pastry. Bake until the pastry is golden brown, about 12 minutes. Serve immediately.

# spinach, white bean, and pine nut strudel

makes 4 to 6 servings

*Tender baby spinach is delicious, good for you, and easy to use. It combines well with creamy white beans and crunchy pine nuts in flaky pastry for a strudel vaguely reminiscent of spanakopita. Since pine nuts can be a bit pricey, use walnuts instead for a more economical alternative.*

2 tablespoons olive oil
3 medium shallots, minced
2 garlic cloves, minced
9 ounces fresh baby spinach, chopped
1½ cups or 1 (15.5-ounce) can white beans, drained, rinsed, and mashed
1 tablespoon fresh lemon juice
½ teaspoon dried oregano
¾ teaspoon salt
¼ teaspoon freshly ground black pepper
1 sheet frozen puff pastry, thawed
½ cup chopped pine nuts

1. In a saucepan, heat the oil over medium heat. Add the shallots and garlic, cover, and cook until softened, 3 minutes. Add the spinach, and cook, uncovered, stirring until the spinach is wilted and any liquid is evaporated, 3 to 5 minutes and transfer to a large bowl.

2. Add the beans to the spinach mixture. Add the lemon juice, oregano, salt, and pepper, stirring to mix well. Refrigerate to cool completely.

3. Preheat the oven to 425°F. Cover a baking sheet with parchment paper and set aside. Roll out the puff pastry on a flat work surface and sprinkle with about ⅓ of the pine nuts. Spread the cooled spinach mixture evenly across the dough and sprinkle with about ⅓ more of the pine nuts. Fold the sides in and then roll up. Place the strudel on the prepared baking sheet, seam side down. Sprinkle the top with the remaining pine nuts, pressing gently with your hand so they stick to the pastry. Bake until golden brown, 20 to 25 minutes. Serve immediately.

# roasted vegetable strudel

makes 4 to 6 servings

*Roasting the vegetables gives them a deep rich flavor that combines with white beans and thyme to make a tantalizing filling for the flaky pastry in this delicious strudel. Serve it as a light and lovely dinner entrée on its own or with a drizzle of Hollandaze Sauce (page 552).*

1 medium red onion, halved and thinly sliced

1 medium red or yellow bell pepper, cut into ½-inch strips

12 asparagus spears, tough ends trimmed

1 small zucchini, cut into 3-inch-long strips

8 ounces white mushrooms, lightly rinsed, patted dry, and chopped

2 medium carrots, cut into ¼-inch slices

3 tablespoons olive oil

Salt and freshly ground black pepper

3 ripe plum tomatoes, halved lengthwise and cut into strips

2 cups fresh spinach leaves, stemmed and coarsely chopped

1 teaspoon dried thyme

1½ cups cooked or 1 (15.5-ounce) can white beans, drained, rinsed, and mashed

6 sheets frozen phyllo dough, thawed*

¼ cup vegan margarine, melted

1. Preheat the oven to 400°F. In a large bowl, combine the onion, bell pepper, asparagus, zucchini, mushrooms, carrots, and olive oil, tossing to coat. Sprinkle the vegetables with salt and black pepper to taste, then transfer to a 9 × 13-inch baking pan and roast until tender, about 30 minutes.

2. Transfer the roasted vegetables to a large bowl. Add the tomatoes, spinach leaves, and thyme, and stir to mix well.

3. Blot off any moisture from the beans and add them to the vegetables. Mix well and set aside to cool, draining off any liquid that may remain in the vegetables.

4. When the vegetables are completely cool, place 1 sheet of phyllo dough on a flat work surface. Brush with some of the melted margarine. Top with a second piece of phyllo and brush with melted margarine. Repeat with the remaining phyllo sheets and melted margarine. Spoon the vegetable mixture lengthwise down the center of the phyllo, spreading it to within 1 inch of the edge. Fold in the short edges about 1 inch, then tuck in the sides and roll up. Place the roll, seam side down, on a large baking sheet. Brush the strudel with the remaining melted margarine. Bake until golden brown, about 20 minutes. Let stand for 5 minutes before slicing.

*If you don't have time to fuss with phyllo pastry, you can make this strudel using thawed frozen puff pastry instead.*

# indonesian vegetable stew

makes 4 to 6 servings

*Tamarind, coconut milk, and chiles combine with herbs and spices to transform everyday vegetables into a rich and exotic-tasting stew.*

2 tablespoons canola or grapeseed oil

1 yellow onion, chopped

3 garlic cloves, minced

1 or 2 fresh hot chiles, seeded and minced

1 tablespoon grated fresh ginger

1 large russet potato, cut into ½-inch dice

1 medium eggplant, peeled and cut into ½-inch dice

8 ounces green beans, cut into 1-inch pieces

2 cups small cauliflower florets

continues on next page

1½ cups vegetable broth, homemade (page 141) or store-bought

1 (14.5-ounce) can crushed tomatoes

2 tablespoons soy sauce

½ teaspoon ground turmeric

1 (13.5-ounce) can unsweetened coconut milk

1 tablespoon tamarind paste

1 tablespoon light brown sugar

Salt and freshly ground black pepper

2 tablespoons fresh lime juice

3 tablespoons minced fresh cilantro

2 tablespoons minced scallions, for garnish

1. Heat the oil in a large pot over medium heat. Add the onion, garlic, chile, and ginger. Cover and cook until softened, about 7 minutes.

2. Add the potato, eggplant, green beans, cauliflower, broth, tomatoes, soy sauce, and turmeric. Cover and cook until the vegetables are tender, stirring occasionally, about 45 minutes.

3. Uncover, reduce heat to low, and add the coconut milk, tamarind paste, sugar, and salt and pepper to taste. The amount of salt needed depends on the saltiness of your broth. Simmer uncovered, until the sauce thickens, stirring occasionally, about 10 minutes. Stir in the lime juice. Serve hot, sprinkled with cilantro and scallions, if using.

# moroccan vegetable stew

makes 4 servings

*Despite the long list of ingredients, this recipe comes together easily. In order to give the complex flavors time to blend together, this is best made a day ahead of when you plan to serve it. The flavors will then have a chance to meld, for wonderful sweet and savory flavor layers.*

1 tablespoon olive oil

2 medium yellow onions, chopped

2 medium carrots, cut into ½-inch dice

½ teaspoon ground cumin

½ teaspoon ground cinnamon or allspice

½ teaspoon ground ginger

½ teaspoon sweet or smoked paprika

½ teaspoon saffron or turmeric

1 (14.5-ounce) can diced tomatoes, undrained

8 ounces green beans, trimmed and cut into 1-inch pieces

2 cups peeled, seeded, and diced winter squash

1 large russet or other baking potato, peeled and cut into ½-inch dice

1½ cups vegetable broth, homemade (page 141) or store-bought, or water

1½ cups cooked or 1 (15.5-ounce) can chickpeas, drained and rinsed

¾ cup frozen peas

½ cup pitted dried plums (prunes)

1 teaspoon lemon zest

Salt and freshly ground black pepper

½ cup pitted green olives

1 tablespoon minced fresh cilantro or parsley, for garnish

½ cup toasted slivered almonds, for garnish

1. In a large saucepan, heat the oil over medium heat. Add the onions and carrots, cover, and cook for 5 minutes. Stir in the cumin, cinnamon, ginger, paprika, and saffron. Cook, uncovered, stirring, for 30 seconds. Add the tomatoes, green beans, squash, potato, and broth and bring to a boil. Reduce heat to low, cover, and simmer until the vegetables are tender, about 20 minutes.

2. Add the chickpeas, peas, dried plums, and lemon zest. Season with salt and pepper to taste. Stir in the olives and simmer, uncovered, until the flavors are blended, about 10 minutes. Sprinkle with cilantro and almonds and serve immediately.

# STUFFED VEGETABLES

## bell peppers stuffed with white beans, mushrooms, and walnuts

makes 4 servings

*The mellow flavor of the stuffing complements the natural sweetness of the peppers. Use all of one color bell pepper or two of each, as desired. If you use dillweed instead of parsley, the stuffing will have a decidedly Eastern European flavor that would be supported by the addition of some cooked barley if you have it on hand.*

2 large or 4 small red or yellow bell peppers

2 tablespoons olive oil

1 small yellow onion, minced

2 garlic cloves, minced

12 ounces white mushrooms, lightly rinsed, patted dry, and chopped

3 cups cooked or 2 (15.5-ounce) cans white beans, drained, rinsed, and mashed

1 cup finely chopped walnuts

2 tablespoons minced fresh parsley or dillweed

½ cup dry unseasoned bread crumbs

Salt and freshly ground black pepper

1. Cut the bell peppers in half lengthwise and remove the seeds and membranes. Cook the peppers in a pot of boiling water to soften slightly, 3 to 4 minutes. Drain and set aside. Preheat the oven to 375°F. Lightly oil a 9 × 13-inch baking pan and set aside.

2. In a large skillet, heat the oil over medium heat. Add the onion, cover, and cook until softened, about 5 minutes. Add the garlic and mushrooms and cook, uncovered, 5 minutes longer. Add the beans, walnuts, parsley, and ¼ cup of the bread crumbs to the mushroom mixture. Season with salt and black pepper to taste and mix well.

3. Stuff the softened pepper halves with the enough of the stuffing mixture to fill the peppers (½ to 1 cup, depending on the size of the pepper) and arrange stuffing side up in the prepared baking pan. Cover with foil and bake for 20 minutes. Uncover, sprinkle with the remaining bread crumbs, and continue baking until the peppers are hot and the crumbs are golden brown, about 10 minutes longer. Serve immediately.

# quinoa and pinto bean–stuffed peppers

makes 4 servings

*Bell peppers come in all sorts of colors, from orange to black. I generally prefer red or yellow because I think they have the sweetest flavor and they are usually as readily available as the common green bell pepper, which tends to be more on the bitter side.*

2½ cups water

1 cup quinoa, well rinsed

Salt

4 large red or yellow bell peppers

2 tablespoons olive oil

½ cup minced red onion

1 garlic clove, minced

1½ cups cooked or 1 (15.5-ounce) can pinto beans, drained, rinsed, and mashed

3 tablespoons minced fresh cilantro or parsley

Freshly ground black pepper

1. In a medium saucepan, bring 2 cups of the water to a boil over high heat. Stir in the quinoa, salt the water, reduce the heat to low, cover, and simmer for 25 minutes. Remove from heat and set aside. Preheat the oven to 350°F. Lightly oil a 9 × 13-inch baking pan and set aside.

2. Slice off the tops of the peppers and remove the seeds and membranes. Chop the pepper tops and reserve. Cook the peppers in a pot of boiling water until slightly softened, 3 to 4 minutes. Drain and set aside, cut side down.

3. In a large skillet, heat the oil over medium heat. Add the onion and reserved pepper tops. Cover and cook until tender, about 5 minutes. Stir in the garlic and cook until fragrant,

about 30 seconds. Add the cooked quinoa, beans, cilantro, and salt and black pepper to taste. Mix well.

4. Fill the peppers with the quinoa mixture, packing well (½ to 1 cup of stuffing each, depending on the size of the pepper), and place upright in the prepared baking pan. Add the remaining ½ cup water to the baking pan, cover tightly with foil, and bake until the peppers are tender and the stuffing is hot, about 45 minutes. Serve immediately.

# millet-stuffed bell peppers with watercress and orange

makes 4 servings

*Millet makes a great stuffing because it compresses nicely into the peppers. In this stuffing, the mild yet flavorful grain is augmented by the peppery bite of watercress and the sweetness of orange.*

3 cups water

1 cup millet

Salt

4 medium red or yellow bell peppers

1 tablespoon olive oil

1 medium red onion, minced

2 cups coarsely chopped stemmed watercress

½ teaspoon ground coriander

Freshly ground black pepper

1 sweet seedless orange, peeled and chopped

1 cup fresh orange juice

1. In a large saucepan, bring 2 cups of water to a boil over high heat. Stir in the millet and salt the water. Cover, reduce heat to low, and

simmer until tender, about 35 minutes. Set aside. Preheat the oven to 375°F. Lightly oil a 9 × 13-inch baking pan and set aside.

2. Cut the bell peppers in half lengthwise and remove the seeds and membranes. Cook the peppers in a pot of boiling water for 3 to 4 minutes to soften slightly. Drain and set aside.

3. In a large skillet, heat the oil over medium heat. Add the onion, cover, and cook until softened, about 5 minutes. Add the watercress and cook until wilted, about 3 minutes. Stir in the coriander and season with salt and black pepper to taste. Set aside.

4. Add the cooked millet and the orange pieces to the watercress mixture and stir to combine well. Taste, adjusting seasonings if necessary.

5. Tightly pack the peppers with the stuffing (about $1/2$ to 1 cup each, depending on the size of the pepper) and place them in the prepared baking pan. Pour the orange juice into the bottom of the baking dish and cover with foil. Bake until the peppers are tender, about 30 minutes. Serve immediately.

# cabbage rolls stuffed with bulgur and chickpeas

makes 4 to 6 servings

*Stuffed cabbage rolls are great cold weather fare and can be assembled in advance to heat and serve for a one-dish meal on a busy weeknight. Allow two or three rolls per person, depending on what else you're serving.*

1 large head green cabbage, cored
1 tablespoon olive oil
1 medium yellow onion, minced
1 cup medium-grind bulgur
2 cups water
Salt
$1\frac{1}{2}$ cups cooked or 1 (15.5-ounce) can chickpeas, drained, rinsed, and mashed
2 tablespoons minced fresh dillweed or 1 tablespoon dried
Freshly ground black pepper
2 cups tomato juice

1. Carefully remove 12 large leaves from the cabbage, reserving the remaining cabbage for another use. Steam the cabbage leaves until softened, 8 to 10 minutes. Set aside to cool.

2. In a large saucepan, heat the oil over medium heat. Add the onion and cook, covered, until softened, about 5 minutes. Stir in the bulgur, water, and $1/2$ teaspoon of salt. Bring to a boil. Cover, reduce heat to low, and simmer until the bulgur has absorbed the water, about 15 minutes. Transfer to a large bowl. Add the beans to the bulgur mixture along with the dillweed and salt and pepper to taste. Mix well.

3. Place the cabbage leaves, one a time, on a flat work surface, rib side down. Place about $1/3$ cup of the stuffing mixture at the stem end of each leaf. Beginning at the stem end, roll up the leaf around the stuffing, tucking in the sides of the leaf as you roll it up. Repeat the process with the remaining leaves and stuffing.

4. Pour 1 cup of the tomato juice into a large deep skillet with a lid. Arrange the stuffed cabbage rolls in the pot, seam side down. Pour the remaining 1 cup tomato juice over the cabbage rolls. Cover and cook over low heat until tender, 20 to 30 minutes. Serve immediately.

# sweet-and-sour kasha cabbage rolls

makes 4 to 6 servings

*These hearty cabbage rolls, bathed in a tangy sweet and sour sauce, are stuffed with tasty mixture of walnuts, raisins, and kasha, also known as buckwheat groats. Variation: use rice in place of the kasha, increasing the cooking time to about 30 minutes or until the rice is tender.*

1 large head green cabbage, cored

1 tablespoon olive oil

1 medium yellow onion, minced

1 medium carrot, grated

1 cup kasha (buckwheat groats)

2 cups water

Salt

½ cup chopped walnuts

⅓ cup golden raisins

¼ cup minced fresh parsley

Freshly ground black pepper

1½ cups tomato juice

¼ cup light brown sugar

2 tablespoons cider vinegar

1. Carefully remove 12 large leaves from the cabbage, reserving the remaining cabbage for another use. Steam the cabbage leaves until softened, 8 to 10 minutes. Set aside to cool.

2. In a large saucepan, heat the oil over medium heat. Add the onion and cook, covered, until softened, about 5 minutes. Stir in the carrot, kasha, water, and ½ teaspoon of salt. Bring to a boil. Cover, reduce heat to low, and simmer until the kasha has absorbed the water, about 15 minutes. Stir in the walnuts, raisins, parsley, and salt and pepper to taste. Mix well, cover, and set aside for 10 minutes.

3. Place the cabbage leaves, one a time, on a flat work surface, rib side down. Place about ⅓ cup of the stuffing mixture at the stem end of each leaf. Beginning at the stem end, roll up the leaf around the stuffing, tucking in the sides of the leaf as you roll it up. Repeat the process with remaining leaves and stuffing.

4. In a medium bowl, combine the tomato juice, sugar, and vinegar and stir to blend. Pour half of the juice mixture into a large deep skillet with a lid. Arrange the filled cabbage rolls in the pot, seam side down. Pour the remaining juice mixture over the cabbage rolls. Cover and cook over low heat until tender, 20 to 30 minutes. Serve immediately.

# stuffed eggplant rolls

makes 4 servings

*Instead of the usual stuffed eggplant dishes, this one involves rolling up individual slices of eggplant that have been spread with a zesty mixture of raisins, garlic, pine nuts, and sun-dried tomatoes. The rolled bundles are then topped with a rich marinara sauce and baked until tender.*

1 large or 2 medium eggplants

Salt and freshly ground black pepper

1 tablespoon olive oil

2 garlic cloves, minced

2 green onions, chopped

¼ cup ground pine nuts

2 tablespoons finely chopped oil-packed sun-dried tomatoes

3 tablespoons golden raisins

3 tablespoons vegan Parmesan or Parmasio (page 193)

1 tablespoon minced fresh parsley

2 cups marinara sauce, homemade (page 194) or store-bought

1. Preheat the oven to 375°F. Lightly oil a large baking sheet and a 9 × 13-inch baking pan and set side. Cut the eggplants lengthwise into ¼-inch-thick slices and arrange them on the prepared baking sheet. Bake until partially softened, about 15 minutes. Remove from the oven, sprinkle with salt and pepper to taste, and set aside to cool.

2. In a large skillet, heat the oil over medium heat. Add the garlic, green onions, and pine nuts and cook, stirring for 1 minute. Stir in the tomatoes, raisins, Parmesan, parsley, and salt and pepper to taste. Mix well. Taste, adjusting seasonings if necessary.

3. Spread about 2 tablespoons of the stuffing mixture onto each of the softened eggplant slices and roll up the eggplant. Arrange the eggplant bundles, seam side down, in the prepared baking pan. Top with the marinara sauce, cover tightly with foil, and bake until tender and hot, about 30 minutes. Serve immediately.

# orzo-and-spinach–stuffed eggplant

makes 4 servings

*To complement this Greek-inspired dish, top with a sprinkling of Tofu Feta (page 358) and serve with a Greek Goddess Salad (page 54).*

2 medium eggplants, halved lengthwise

½ cup orzo

2 tablespoons olive oil

2 garlic cloves, minced

½ teaspoon dried oregano

Salt and freshly ground black pepper

3 cups fresh baby spinach

½ cup toasted pine nuts

1. Use a small sharp knife to cut a ¼-inch-thick perimeter inside each eggplant half, then scoop out the flesh, leaving the shell intact. Chop the flesh and set aside. Steam the eggplant shells until softened, about 7 minutes. Set aside to cool.

2. In a pot of salted boiling water, cook the orzo until just tender, about 5 minutes. Drain and set aside. Preheat the oven to 375°F. Lightly oil a 9 × 13-inch baking pan and set aside.

3. In a large skillet, heat the oil over medium heat. Add the garlic, chopped eggplant, oregano, and salt and pepper to taste. Cover and cook until the eggplant is tender, about 10 minutes. Stir in the spinach and cover and cook until the spinach is wilted, about 5 minutes. Remove from the heat and stir in the cooked orzo and the pine nuts. Taste, adjusting seasonings if necessary.

4. Divide the stuffing mixture among the eggplant shells and transfer to the prepared baking pan, stuffing side up. Cover with foil and bake until hot and tender, about 30 minutes. Serve immediately.

# couscous-stuffed eggplant

makes 4 servings

*The couscous stuffing is embellished with sweet golden raisins, crunchy walnuts, and red bell pepper, making it as colorful as it is delicious.*

2 medium eggplants, halved lengthwise

2 cups water

1 cup couscous

2 cups water

2 tablespoons olive oil

1 medium yellow onion, chopped

1 medium red bell pepper, chopped

Salt and freshly ground black pepper

½ cup chopped walnuts

½ cup golden raisins

½ teaspoon ground coriander

2 tablespoons minced fresh parsley or cilantro, for garnish

1. Use a small sharp knife to cut a ¼-inch-thick perimeter inside each eggplant half, then scoop out the flesh, leaving the shell intact. Chop the eggplant flesh and set aside. Steam the eggplant shells until softened, 7 to 8 minutes. Set aside to cool.

2. In a large saucepan, bring the water to a boil. Add the couscous, cover, and remove from heat. Preheat the oven to 375°F. Lightly oil a 9 × 13-inch baking pan and set aside.

3. In a large skillet, heat the oil over medium heat. Add the onion, cover, and cook for 5 minutes. Stir in the bell pepper and chopped eggplant and season with salt and black pepper to taste. Cover and cook until the eggplant is tender, about 10 minutes. Remove from the heat and stir in the cooked couscous, walnuts, raisins, coriander, and salt and black pepper to taste. Mix well, then taste, adjusting seasonings if necessary.

4. Divide the stuffing among the eggplant shells and transfer them to the prepared baking pan, stuffing side up. Cover with foil and bake until hot, about 30 minutes. Sprinkle with parsley and serve immediately.

# potato-and-artichoke–stuffed portobello mushrooms

makes 4 servings

*When you use the large meaty portobello mushrooms, stuffed mushroom caps suddenly become a hearty main dish, and nutritious as well, thanks to a savory stuffing of potatoes and artichokes. The bold flavor of artichokes (and its natural affinity to mushrooms) makes a sauce unnecessary, although a drizzle of Hollandaze (page 552) or Basic Brown Sauce (page 545) can make a good thing even better.*

1 pound Yukon Gold potatoes, peeled and cut into ½-inch dice

1 tablespoon vegan margarine

2 tablespoons nutritional yeast

Salt and freshly ground black pepper

1½ cups canned or cooked frozen artichoke hearts

2 tablespoons olive oil

½ cup minced onion

3 garlic cloves, minced

1 teaspoon minced fresh thyme or ½ teaspoon dried

4 large portobello mushroom caps, lightly rinsed and patted dry

¼ teaspoon sweet paprika

1. Steam the potatoes until tender, about 15 minutes. Transfer the steamed potatoes to a large bowl. Add the margarine, nutritional yeast, and salt and pepper to taste. Mash well. Finely chop the cooked or canned artichoke hearts and add them to the potatoes. Stir to combine and set aside.

2. Preheat the oven to 375°F. Lightly oil a 9 × 13-inch baking pan and set aside. In a large skillet, heat 1 tablespoon of the oil over medium heat. Add the onion, cover, and cook until softened, about 5 minutes. Add the garlic and cook, uncovered, 1 minute longer. Add the thyme and salt and pepper to taste. Cook for 5 minutes to blend the flavors. Stir the onion mixture into the potato mixture and mix until well blended.

3. Use the edge of a teaspoon to scrape out and discard the brown gills from the undersides of the mushroom caps. Carefully spoon the stuffing mixture into the mushroom caps, packing them tightly and smoothing the tops.

4. Transfer the stuffed mushrooms to the prepared baking pan and drizzle with the remaining 1 tablespoon oil. Sprinkle with paprika, cover tightly with foil, and bake until the mushrooms have softened and the stuffing is hot, about 20 minutes. Uncover and cook until the stuffing is lightly browned, about 10 minutes longer. Serve immediately.

# peruvian-inspired stuffed potatoes

makes 4 servings

*If you're tired of the same old baked potatoes, this stuffing made with black olives and raisins is sure to wake up your taste buds. The addition of protein-rich tofu elevates these tasty spuds to main-dish status.*

4 large baking potatoes, unpeeled
2 tablespoons plus 1 teaspoon olive oil
1 medium onion, minced
2 garlic cloves, minced
8 ounces soft tofu, drained and mashed
⅓ cup raisins
⅓ cup brine-cured black olives, pitted and chopped
2 tablespoons minced fresh parsley
½ teaspoon dried oregano
Salt and freshly ground black pepper
Plain unsweetened soy milk, as needed

1. Preheat the oven to 425°F. Pierce the potatoes with a fork and bake until soft, about 1 hour. When cool enough to handle, cut the potatoes in half lengthwise and, leaving the shells intact, scoop out the flesh and transfer to a large bowl. Mash well and set aside. Reduce the oven temperature to 375°F. Lightly oil a 9 × 13-inch baking pan and set aside.

2. In large skillet, heat the 2 tablespoons oil over medium heat. Add the onion and cover and cook until tender, about 10 minutes. Add the garlic and cook, uncovered, 1 minute longer. Stir in the tofu, raisins, olives, parsley, and oregano. Season with salt and pepper to taste and cook for 5 minutes to blend flavors. Add the mixture to the mashed potatoes and mix well to combine. Taste, adjusting seasonings if necessary. If the stuffing seems too dry, add a little soy milk to moisten.

3. Fill the potato shells evenly with the stuffing and arrange in the prepared pan. Drizzle each potato with the remaining 1 teaspoon oil. Bake until the tops brown lightly and the potatoes are heated through, 15 to 20 minutes. Serve immediately.

## potatoes stuffed with fennel and peas

makes 4 servings

*The addition of tarragon amplifies the faintly licorice flavor of the fennel in these lovely stuffed potatoes studded with shades of green from the fennel, peas, green onions, and herbs.*

4 large baking potatoes, unpeeled

2 tablespoons olive oil, plus more to drizzle on top

1 small yellow onion, chopped

1 medium fennel bulb, minced

4 green onions, minced

½ cup frozen baby peas

1 teaspoon minced fresh tarragon or ½ teaspoon dried

Salt and freshly ground black pepper

2 tablespoons minced fresh parsley

Unsweetened soy milk, as needed

1. Preheat the oven to 425°F. Pierce the potatoes with a fork and bake until soft, about 1 hour. When cool enough to handle, cut the potatoes in half lengthwise and, leaving the shells intact, scoop out the flesh and transfer to a large bowl. Mash well and set aside. Reduce the oven temperature to 375°F. Lightly oil a 9 × 13-inch baking pan.

2. In a large skillet, heat the oil over medium heat. Add the onion and fennel. Cover and cook until tender, stirring occasionally, about 10 minutes. Stir in the green onions, peas, tarragon, and salt and pepper to taste. Cook for 2 minutes to blend the flavors.

3. Add the fennel mixture to the mashed potatoes and add the parsley; mix well to combine. Taste, adjusting seasonings if necessary.

If the filling seems too dry, add a little soy milk to moisten.

4. Fill the potato shells evenly with the filling and arrange in the prepared baking pan. Drizzle each potato with a little olive oil. Bake until the tops brown lightly and potatoes are heated through, about 15 minutes. Serve immediately.

## great stuffed pumpkin

makes 6 servings

*One of my recipe testers, Kim Hammond, created this recipe for a pumpkin cooking contest at her church last year. She said it was fun to show the kids a whole cooked pumpkin rather than just out of a can. Best of all, she won the contest. Try this prize-winning recipe to let your kitchen fill with the aroma of baked pumpkin. If you're not a fan of rosemary, substitute thyme, sage, or a combination of fresh or dried herbs.*

2 small pie pumpkins

2 tablespoons olive oil

2 medium yellow onions, minced

3 celery ribs, minced

3 medium carrots, minced

½ cup vegetable broth, homemade (page 141) or store-bought, or water

1 teaspoon salt

3 cups cooked brown rice

2 teaspoons fresh rosemary or 1 teaspoon dried

2 teaspoons fresh minced sage or 1 teaspoon dried

1 teaspoon fresh minced thyme or ½ teaspoon dried

¼ teaspoon freshly ground black pepper

½ cup unsalted roasted pumpkin seeds (pepitas)*

1. Preheat the oven to 350°F. Lightly oil a 9 × 13-inch baking pan and set aside. Cut the tops off the pumpkins and scoop out seeds and membranes and discard. (If you want to roast the seeds, see note below.)

2. In a large skillet, heat the oil over medium heat. Add the onions, cover, and cook until softened, about 5 minutes. Add the celery and carrots. Cover and cook until softened, about 5 minutes. Stir in the broth and salt and simmer for 10 minutes. Add the cooked rice, rosemary, sage, thyme, pepper, and pumpkin seeds.

3. Divide the rice mixture between the two hollowed-out pumpkins. Place the pumpkins in the prepared pan and cover tightly with foil. Bake until the pumpkins are soft, but not collapsing, about 1½ hours. Serve immediately.

*If roasted pumpkin seeds are unavailable, you can make your own using the seeds from the pumpkins. Remove any pulp adhering to the seeds and rinse the seeds in a colander. Pat dry. Spread the seeds evenly in a single layer on a lightly oiled baking sheet. Bake at 350°F until lightly brown, about 10 minutes.

# buttercup squash stuffed with pistachio-apricot rice

makes 4 servings

*Buttercup squash is my go-to squash for stuffing. Not only is the deep orange flesh characteristically sweet, but it also has a nice large cavity, ideal for stuffing and is slightly squat, providing a reasonably flat bottom and top for standing up in the baking dish. If buttercup squash is unavailable, substitute another sweet winter squash. To make cutting the squash easier, microwave it for a few minutes to slightly soften the hard outer skin. Note: If your dried apricots are difficult to mince, soak them in hot water for 10 minutes to soften them.*

1 large buttercup squash, halved crosswise and seeded
2 tablespoons olive oil
1 large yellow onion, chopped
1 cup brown basmati rice
Salt
2 cups water
½ cup dried apricots, minced
½ cup chopped unsalted shelled pistachios
3 tablespoons minced fresh cilantro
1 teaspoon ground coriander
Freshly ground black pepper

1. Preheat the oven to 375°F. Lightly oil a 9 × 13-inch baking pan and set aside. Place the squash halves, cut side down, in the prepared baking pan. Add ¼ inch of water, cover tightly, and bake until almost tender, about 30 minutes.

2. In a large saucepan, heat the oil over medium heat. Add the onion, cover, and cook until tender, about 5 minutes. Add the rice, salt to taste, and water and bring to a boil. Cover, reduce heat to low, and simmer until the rice is cooked, about 30 minutes. Remove from the heat and set aside.

3. Remove the squash halves from the oven and carefully turn them over, cut side up.

4. Fluff the rice with a fork and add the apricots, pistachios, cilantro, and coriander. Season with salt and pepper to taste. Divide the stuffing between the squash halves, packing tightly. Cover with foil and bake until hot, 20 to 30 minutes. Serve immediately.

# fruit-studded millet-stuffed acorn squash

makes 4 servings

*A sweet and savory millet stuffing dotted with the colors of autumn turns acorn squash into a tasty main course.*

4 small acorn squash

Salt

2 tablespoons olive oil

5 green onions, minced

1 medium carrot, grated

2 teaspoons grated fresh ginger

1 cup millet

2 cups vegetable broth, homemade (page 141) or store-bought, or water

1 (8-ounce) can crushed pineapple, well drained

2 tablespoons golden raisins

½ teaspoon dried marjoram

Freshly ground black pepper

1. Cut a small slice off the bottom of each squash so they stand upright. Cut the top off each squash, reserving the tops to use as lids. Scoop out and discard the seeds and pulp. Season the squash cavities with salt and set aside.

2. Preheat the oven to 350°F. Lightly oil a 10-inch square baking pan and set aside. In a large saucepan, heat the oil over medium heat. Add the green onions, carrot, and ginger and cook until fragrant, about 1 minute. Add the millet, the broth, and about ½ teaspoon of salt. Reduce heat to low, cover, and simmer until the millet is tender, about 30 minutes.

3. Add the pineapple, raisins, marjoram, and salt and pepper to taste to the cooked millet, stirring to mix well. Spoon the millet mixture into the squash cavities, packing tightly. Set the tops back on the squashes and arrange them in the prepared pan. Pour about ½ inch of hot water into the pan. Cover tightly with foil. Bake until the squashes are tender but not collapsing, about 45 minutes. Serve immediately.

# black bean, rice, and mango-stuffed squash

makes 4 servings

*The vivid color contrasts and delectable flavors set this stuffed squash apart. If you can find the super-sweet brilliantly orange-fleshed kabocha squash, please buy it—it's the best-tasting squash on the planet. If you can't find a squash with a large cavity, use two smaller squashes.*

1 large sweet winter squash, halved and seeded

Salt

1 tablespoon olive oil

6 green onions, minced

1 tablespoon grated fresh ginger

1 small hot or mild chile, seeded and minced

2 cups cooked brown rice

1½ cups cooked or 1 (15.5-ounce) can black beans, drained and rinsed

2 teaspoons fresh lemon juice

2 teaspoons sugar

¼ cup minced fresh parsley

Freshly ground black pepper

1 ripe mango, peeled, pitted, and chopped

1. Preheat the oven to 375°F. Lightly oil a 9 × 13-inch baking pan and set aside. Season the squash halves with salt and place them in the prepared pan, cut side down. Add ¼ inch of water to the pan and cover tightly. Bake until slightly softened, about 20 minutes.

2. In a large skillet, heat the oil over medium heat. Add the green onions, ginger, and chile and cook until softened, about 3 minutes.

Transfer to a large bowl. Add the cooked rice, beans, lemon juice, sugar, and parsley and season with salt and pepper to taste. Mix thoroughly to combine well, then taste, adjusting seasonings if necessary.

3. Turn the roasted squash halves over, cut side up, and fill the cavities with the stuffing, packing tightly. Cover with foil and bake until the stuffing is hot and the squash is tender, 35 to 45 minutes. Serve immediately.

# sesame-stuffed spaghetti squash

makes 4 servings

*Spaghetti squash is just plain fun—what's not to like about a squash that combs out to look like spaghetti? It can be a dieter's dream when bathed in marinara sauce, but it's also terrific cloaked in a tantalizing sesame sauce and returned to its shell for a quick bake. Black sesame seeds provide a contrasting garnish, but regular sesame seeds can be used instead if black ones are unavailable.*

1 large spaghetti squash

1 tablespoon canola or grapeseed oil

½ cup chopped onion

1 medium red bell pepper, chopped

1 garlic clove, minced

1 teaspoon grated fresh ginger

1 medium carrot, shredded

½ cup frozen peas, thawed

3 tablespoons minced fresh cilantro

⅓ cup tahini (sesame paste)

3 tablespoons soy sauce

1 tablespoon toasted sesame oil

½ cup water

2 tablespoons black sesame seeds, for garnish

1. Preheat the oven to 400°F. Pierce the squash with a fork and place it on ungreased baking sheet. Bake until just tender, about 45 minutes. Remove from the oven and set aside to cool. Lower the oven temperature to 350°F. Lightly oil a 9 × 13-inch baking pan and set aside.

2. When the squash is cool enough to handle, cut it in half lengthwise and remove and discard the seeds. Use a fork to scoop out the "spaghetti" strands and reserve along with the shells.

3. In a large skillet, heat the oil over medium heat. Add the onion, bell pepper, and garlic. Cover and cook until tender, about 5 minutes. Stir in the ginger, carrot, and peas and cook, uncovered, 1 minute longer. Add the reserved squash pulp and cilantro and set aside. In a small bowl, combine the tahini, soy sauce, sesame oil, and water, stirring until well blended. Add more water if necessary to make a smooth and creamy sauce. Stir as much of the sauce into the stuffing mixture as needed to moisten. Toss gently to combine.

4. Spoon the mixture into the squash shells and arrange them in the prepared pan. Cover tightly with foil and bake until hot, about 20 minutes. Drizzle with any remaining sauce and garnish with black sesame seeds. Serve immediately.

# three sisters stuffed squash

makes 4 servings

*This is a great way to assemble a reunion of the "three sisters" of Iroquois lore: squash, corn, and beans. Not surprisingly, the flavors of these three complementary ingredients merge deliciously in this autumnal main dish.*

1 tablespoon olive oil

1 medium yellow onion, minced

2 garlic cloves, minced

1 hot or mild chile, seeded and minced

1½ cups cooked or 1 (15.5-ounce) can pinto beans, drained, rinsed, and mashed

1 cup fresh or frozen corn kernels

2 tablespoons minced fresh cilantro or parsley

Salt and freshly ground black pepper

1 large buttercup or other winter squash, halved and seeded

1 cup hot water

1. Preheat the oven to 350°F. Lightly oil a 9 × 13-inch baking pan and set aside. In a large skillet, heat the oil over medium heat. Add the onion, cover, and cook until softened, about 5 minutes. Add the garlic and chile and cook, uncovered, until fragrant, about 1 minute.

2. Add the beans, corn, cilantro, and salt and pepper to taste to the skillet. Mix well, then spoon the stuffing mixture into the squash cavities, packing tightly.

3. Place the stuffed squash halves in the prepared pan. Pour the water into the bottom of the baking dish and cover tightly with foil. Bake until the squash is tender, about 1½ hours. Serve immediately.

# winter squash with forbidden rice stuffing

makes 4 servings

*The sophisticated appeal of black forbidden rice adds more than drama to this dish—it also has a wonderful nutty flavor vaguely reminiscent of popcorn. Look for it in natural food stores and Asian markets.*

1 large kabocha squash or other large winter squash, halved and seeded

Salt

1 tablespoon canola or grapeseed oil

6 green onions, minced

2 garlic cloves, minced

½ cup slivered almonds

2 teaspoons grated fresh ginger

2 cups cooked black forbidden rice

¼ cup minced fresh parsley or cilantro

Freshly ground black pepper

1 teaspoon toasted sesame oil

1. Preheat the oven to 350°F. Lightly oil a 9 × 13-inch baking pan and set aside. Season the squash halves with salt and place them in the prepared pan, cut side down. Add ¼ inch of water to the pan and cover tightly with foil. Bake until slightly softened, about 20 minutes.

2. In a large skillet, heat the oil over medium heat; add the green onions, garlic, almonds, and ginger, and cook until the almonds are slightly toasted, about 5 minutes. Transfer to a large bowl. Add the rice, parsley, and salt and pepper to taste. Mix thoroughly to combine well, then taste, adjusting seasonings if necessary.

3. Turn the roasted squash halves over, cut side up, and fill the squash cavities with the stuffing, packing tightly. Cover and bake until the stuffing is hot and the squash is tender, about 45 minutes. Drizzle with toasted sesame oil before serving. Serve immediately.

# walnut-and-cranberry–stuffed sweet potatoes

makes 4 servings

*I think it's time that sweet potatoes regain some respect at the Thanksgiving dinner table. Baked and stuffed with a delectable walnut and cranberry stuffing, these beauties will make you forget about that marshmallow-topped glop that dominated holidays past.*

4 large sweet potatoes, unpeeled
1 tablespoon olive oil
½ cup minced red onion
½ cup chopped walnuts
½ cup sweetened dried cranberries
1 tablespoon vegan margarine
1 tablespoon pure maple syrup
Salt
¼ teaspoon freshly ground black pepper
2 teaspoons walnut oil (optional)

1. Preheat the oven to 425°F. Lightly oil a baking sheet and set aside. Pierce the potatoes with a fork and bake until soft, about 1 hour. When cool enough to handle, cut the potatoes in half lengthwise and, leaving the shells and ¼-inch-wide perimeter of the flesh intact, scoop out the middle of the potatoes and place them in a bowl. Mash well and set aside.

2. In a large skillet, heat the oil over medium heat. Add the onion, cover, and cook until softened, about 5 minutes. Stir in the walnuts, cranberries, and margarine. Add the mixture to the mashed sweet potatoes. Add the maple syrup and season with salt and pepper to taste. Mix well to combine.

3. Fill the potato shells with the filling and arrange on a baking sheet. Bake until the potatoes are heated through, about 15 minutes. Drizzle each potato with a little walnut oil, if using. Serve immediately.

# sicilian stuffed tomatoes

makes 4 servings

*Sicilian cuisine, with its sweet and savory flavor combinations, varies greatly from that of the mainland. These luscious stuffed tomatoes are typically Sicilian, right down to the use of couscous, raisins, and orange zest.*

2 cups water
1 cup couscous
Salt
3 green onions, minced
⅓ cup golden raisins
1 teaspoon finely grated orange zest
4 large ripe tomatoes
⅓ cup toasted pine nuts
¼ cup minced fresh parsley
Freshly ground black pepper
2 teaspoons olive oil

1. Preheat the oven to 375°F. Lightly oil a 9 × 13-inch baking pan and set aside. In a large saucepan, bring the water to a boil over high heat. Stir in the couscous and salt to taste and remove from the heat. Stir in the green onions, raisins, and orange zest. Cover and set aside for 5 minutes.

2. Cut a ½-inch-thick slice off the top of each of the tomatoes. Scoop out the pulp, keeping the tomato shells intact. Chop the pulp and place it in a large bowl. Add the couscous mixture along with the pine nuts, parsley, and salt and pepper to taste. Mix well.

3. Fill the tomatoes with the mixture and place them in the prepared pan. Drizzle the tomatoes with the oil, cover with foil, and bake until hot, about 20 minutes. Serve immediately.

# spaghetti-stuffed tomatoes

makes 4 servings

*If any spaghetti is remaining after you've stuffed the tomatoes, reheat it when ready to serve and arrange it on plates to serve as nests for the baked tomatoes. To save time, you could use jarred marinara sauce instead of making your own tomato sauce. This is a fun dish to serve children because they get to eat their spaghetti out of their own little tomato bowl.*

2 tablespoons olive oil

3 garlic cloves, minced

1 (15.5-ounce) can crushed tomatoes

2 tablespoons oil-packed sun-dried tomatoes, minced

2 tablespoons minced fresh parsley

½ teaspoon dried basil

¼ teaspoon dried oregano

½ teaspoon salt

¼ teaspoon freshly ground black pepper

6 ounces spaghetti

4 large ripe tomatoes

½ cup coarsely ground walnuts

1. In a large skillet, heat 1 tablespoon of the oil over medium heat. Add the garlic and cook until fragrant, 1 minute. Stir in the crushed tomatoes, sun-dried tomatoes, parsley, basil, oregano, salt, and pepper. Simmer, stirring occasionally, to blend flavors, 15 to 20 minutes.

2. While the sauce is simmering, cook the spaghetti in a pot of boiling salted water, stirring occasionally, until al dente, about 10 minutes. Drain well and set aside.

3. Preheat the oven to 350°F. Lightly oil a 9 × 13-inch baking dish and set aside.

4. In a large bowl, combine the cooked pasta with the tomato sauce and mix well.

5. Slice the tops off the tomatoes and gently remove the seeds. Carefully stuff the tomatoes with the pasta mixture, then sprinkle with the walnuts and drizzle with the remaining 1 tablespoon oil. Arrange the stuffed tomatoes in the prepared pan and cover with foil. Bake until the filling is hot and the tomatoes are tender, but not collapsing, 15 to 20 minutes. Uncover and bake 5 to 10 minutes longer to toast the walnuts. Serve immediately.

# quinoa-stuffed zucchini

makes 4 servings

*Much in the way restaurants have their "soup of the day," our vegetable garden's prolific zucchini yield inspired me to prepare "zucchini of the day"—taking on the challenge to prepare it a different way each day. This quinoa-stuffed zucchini—aka "zuc-quinoa"—is one such meal.*

2 cups water

1 cup quinoa, well rinsed

4 medium zucchini, halved lengthwise, ends trimmed

2 tablespoons olive oil

1 small yellow onion, minced

1 garlic clove, minced

Salt and freshly ground black pepper

⅓ cup chopped pitted black olives

⅓ cup minced oil-packed sun-dried tomatoes

2 tablespoons minced fresh parsley

½ cup dry bread crumbs

1. Lightly oil a 9 × 13-inch baking pan and set aside. In a large saucepan, bring the water to a boil over high heat. Add the quinoa, salt the water, and return to a boil. Reduce heat to

low, cover, and simmer until tender, about 20 minutes.

2. Scoop out the zucchini flesh, leaving shells intact. Chop the flesh and set aside. Steam the zucchini shells until slightly softened, about 5 minutes. Set aside to cool.

3. In a large skillet, heat the 1 tablespoon of the oil over medium heat and add the onion, garlic, chopped zucchini, and salt and pepper to taste. Cover and cook until the vegetables are tender, about 10 minutes.

4. Preheat the oven to 350°F. In a large bowl, combine the cooked quinoa with the onion and zucchini mixture. Add the olives, tomatoes, parsley, and salt and pepper to taste. Mix well to combine.

5. Stuff the zucchini shells with the quinoa mixture, then sprinkle with the breadcrumbs and arrange in the prepared pan. Add $1/4$ inch of water to bottom of the pan. Cover tightly with foil and bake until the filling is hot and the zucchini are tender but not collapsing, 20 to 30 minutes. Uncover and bake 10 minutes longer to lightly brown the topping. Serve immediately.

# pesto-and-ditalini–stuffed zucchini

makes 4 servings

*The only thing my garden has more of than zucchini is basil, so it seemed like a good fit to combine the two in the same recipe. If ditalini (small pasta tubes) is unavailable, use any tiny soup pasta; such as rice-shaped orzo, pastina, or acini di pepe.*

6 ounces ditalini

4 medium zucchini, halved lengthwise, ends trimmed

2 tablespoons olive oil

1 small yellow onion, minced

1 garlic clove, minced

Salt and freshly ground black pepper

½ cup Presto Pesto (page 565)

2 tablespoons minced fresh flat-leaf parsley

½ cup dry bread crumbs

1. Cook the pasta in a pot of boiling salted water, stirring occasionally, until al dente, about 7 minutes. Drain well and set aside.

2. Scoop out the zucchini flesh, leaving the shells intact. Chop the flesh and set aside. Steam the zucchini shells over until slightly softened, about 5 minutes. Set aside to cool.

3. Preheat the oven to 350°F. In a large skillet, heat 1 tablespoon of the oil over medium heat and add the onion, garlic, chopped zucchini, and salt and pepper to taste. Cover and cook until the vegetables are tender, about 10 minutes.

4. In a large bowl, combine the cooked ditalini with the onion and zucchini mixture. Add the pesto, parsley, and salt and pepper to taste. Mix well to combine.

5. Stuff the zucchini shells with the mixture, then sprinkle with the bread crumbs. Arrange in the prepared pan. Add $1/4$ inch of water to the bottom of the dish. Cover tightly with foil and bake until the filling is hot and the zucchini are tender but not collapsing, 20 to 30 minutes. Uncover and bake 10 minutes longer to lightly brown the topping. Serve immediately.

# VEGETABLE SIDE DISHES

basic vegetable fritters

mediterranean artichoke sauté

ted's artichoke and
green bean bake

asparagus dijon

orange-dressed asparagus

stir-fried sesame asparagus

roasted lemon asparagus
with pine nuts

beets with greens
and slivered apricots

sherry-braised baby bok choy

broccoli sauté with tofu feta

broccoli with black beans
and walnuts

broccoli with almonds

spicy sautéed broccoli rabe

roasted brussels sprouts

brussels sprouts
with shallots and dillweed

braised cabbage and apples

lemon-glazed baby carrots
with cranberries

marsala carrots

carrots and parsnips
with diced apple

cardamom carrots with orange

tzimmes

spicy indian cauliflower

roasted cauliflower
with lemon and capers

creamy cauliflower

braised celery with black olives

rainbow chard with goji berries
and pistachios

slow-simmered collard greens

corn fritters

spicy coconut creamed corn

ginger-tamari braised eggplant

indian eggplant fritters

escarole with garlic and capers

fennel with olives and
sun-dried tomatoes

lemon braised fennel

green beans niçoise

green beans and
grape tomatoes

green bean casserole redux

green bean bake
with crispy leeks

kale and sweet potatoes

thai kale with coconut milk

madeira mushroom sauté

shiitake snow pea stir-fry

spicy sautéed pea vines

basic mashed potatoes

mashed potatoes and greens

rosemary-scented mashed potatoes with limas

fennel and garlic mashed potatoes

spiced oven-roasted potato sticks

rosemary fingerling potatoes with caramelized shallots

roasted baby potatoes with spinach, olives, and grape tomatoes

potato and root vegetable paillasson

potato pancakes with green onions

sweet potato pancakes

rum-spiked sweet potatoes with pomegranate pecans

spiced sweet potatoes with dried cherries

sweet potato and apple gratin

thyme-scented sweet potatoes with black olives and garlic

roasted ratatouille gratin

caramelized root vegetables

winter salad sauté

sesame spinach

indian-spiced spinach (saag)

baby spinach with lemon and garlic

spaghetti squash with tomatoes and basil

orange-and-maple–baked acorn squash

bourbon-baked squash

yellow squash with corn, edamame, and dill

roasted rosemary yellow squash and chayote

zucchini sauté with sun-dried tomatoes, olives, and peppers

zucchini walnut fritters

roasted zucchini and tomatoes

cornmeal-crusted fried green tomatoes

panko-fried green tomatoes with peanut sauce

curry roasted vegetables

versatile roasted vegetables

balsamic braised vegetables

grilled vegetable skewers with charmoula sauce

chimichurri grilled vegetables

The term "side dish" generally implies that the vegetable dish plays a second-class role to the main dish, or the meat in a non-vegan meal. The fact is, when vegetables are given the respect they deserve and are prepared with care, they can be the best-tasting and often the most nutritious foods on the dinner table. Often, different types of vegetables are combined with grains, beans, or other ingredients to create "one-dish" meals—no side dishes required. That said, there are, of course, times when vegan entrées such as tempeh or seitan cutlets need some company at mealtime. And so I have assembled a selection of many of my favorite vegetable "side" dishes.

While some of the recipes in this chapter are substantial enough to claim main-dish status, there are others that take quite well to being on the sidelines. Better yet, make a few side dishes and let them share the spotlight. If you're looking for "main dish" vegetable dishes, you can find them in the "Main Dishes" chapter (pages 244 to 349). The primary difference between vegetable side dishes and main dishes is portion size, certainly, but there is also a different heartiness and balance of ingredients. For example, most of us probably wouldn't feel satisfied getting up from the dinner table if we were served only a portion of Lemon Braised Fennel (page 368), whereas we probably would if we had just enjoyed some Vegetable Paella (page 320).

Since many vegan meals are grain- and bean-centered, I generally consider those ingredients as part of main dishes rather than sides (although you can certainly use them as sides, too, if you wish). However, you will find most of the bean and grain recipes, including pilafs, gratins, risottos, and numerous stuffed vegetables, included in the "Main Dishes" chapter.

The recipes in this chapter are organized in alphabetical order by the primary vegetable so you can quickly find your favorites, but I also note when different vegetables can be used in similar preparations.

# basic vegetable fritters

makes 4 to 6 servings

*Use your choice of grated raw vegetables or chopped cooked vegetables. If raw, be sure to squeeze out excess liquid. Herbs and spices can be added to give the fritters a different flavor profile. The amount of soy milk will depend on the moistness of your vegetables.*

2 cups raw, grated, or cooked mashed vegetables

¼ cup grated onion or minced green onions

1 cup all-purpose flour or dry bread crumbs

1 teaspoon baking powder

½ teaspoon salt

⅛ teaspoon freshly ground black pepper

Unsweetened soy milk, as needed

Canola or grapeseed oil, for frying

1. Preheat the oven to 250° F. In a large bowl, combine the vegetables with the onion. Add the flour, baking powder, salt, and pepper. Mix well. Add a little soy milk, if needed.

2. In a large nonstick skillet or griddle, heat a thin layer of oil over medium heat. Drop the fritter batter by the heaping tablespoonful onto the hot skillet. Cook, turning once, until browned on both sides, about 12 minutes. Transfer the cooked fritters to a heatproof platter and keep warm in the oven while you fry the rest. Serve immediately.

## all about fritters

"Fritter" is a broad term that can be used to describe both sweet and savory fried cakes. Fritters can be either a combination of chopped or grated ingredients in a thick batter, such as corn or zucchini fritters, or large pieces of food dipped in batter, such as apple fritters. Sometimes fritters go by other names, as in the case of potato cakes or potato pancakes. Italian batter-dipped vegetables are called "*fritto misto*" and Japanese batter-fried vegetables are known as "tempura." Korean-style vegetable pancakes are called "*pa-jun*."

Both raw and cooked vegetables can be used to make fritters. While large pieces of batter-dipped vegetables are usually deep fried in a large amount of oil, the flatter pancake-like fritters can be fried in a skillet in a thin layer of oil. Fritters are fun to make and a great way to stretch a small amount of vegetables—potato pancakes and corn fritters, for example, are often made with leftovers.

Vegetables for fritters can be used alone or in combination. They can be raw/grated or cooked/minced or mashed. Among the vegetables that make good fritters are corn, potatoes, sweet potatoes, zucchini, yellow summer squash, winter squash, carrots, spinach, eggplant, mushrooms, cauliflower, and artichoke hearts.

A variety of vegetable fritters can be found in this chapter, using both cooked and raw vegetables: Corn Fritters (page 366); Indian Eggplant Fritters (page 367); Potato Pancakes with Green Onions (page 377); Sweet Potato Pancakes (page 378); and Zucchini Walnut Fritters (page 385).

You can experiment with your own combinations using the basic fritter recipe above. Prior to cooking, the texture should be like a thick pancake batter. Simply substitute your favorite ingredients, and you'll be frying fritters in no time.

# mediterranean artichoke sauté 🅕

makes 4 servings

*Fresh artichokes can be expensive, but fro-zen artichoke hearts can be quite flavorful, especially when combined with a retinue of Mediterranean ingredients. This dish makes a lovely accompaniment to a meal of sautéed Seitan Milanese (page 308) and roasted pota-toes. It can also be transformed into a zesty pasta sauce with the addition of 2 cups diced fresh or canned tomatoes. If frozen artichoke hearts are unavailable, substitute a 15-ounce can (not marinated) and proceed with the recipe after the frozen-artichoke cooking instructions.*

1 tablespoon olive oil

2 medium shallots, chopped

2 garlic cloves, minced

1 medium red bell pepper, cut into matchsticks

1 (10-ounce) bag frozen artichoke hearts, thawed and quartered

2 tablespoons dry white wine

2 tablespoons water

Salt and freshly ground black pepper

3 ripe plum tomatoes, cut into ½-inch dice

¼ cup kalamata olives, pitted and halved

1 tablespoon capers

2 tablespoons torn fresh basil leaves

1. In a large skillet, heat the oil over medium heat. Add the shallots, cover, and cook for 3 minutes. Stir in the garlic and cook, uncov-ered, for 1 minute. Add the red bell pepper and the artichoke hearts. Add the white wine and water and season with salt and black pep-per to taste. Cover and simmer until the veg-etables are tender, about 10 minutes.

2. Stir in the tomatoes, olives, and capers and cook, uncovered, until the vegetables are hot

and the liquid is absorbed, about 5 minutes. Add the basil and toss to combine. Serve hot.

# ted's artichoke and green bean bake

makes 6 servings

*Recipe tester Robin Dempsey's father, Ted Faulkner, was a creative cook who was writ-ing a cookbook when he died in 1998. Robin had planned to one day complete her dad's rec-ipe collection and publish it in his honor. When hurricane Katrina destroyed Robin's home, it also took most of her father's recipes and her hope of getting them into print. I'm happy to include a veganized adaptation of one of Ted's surviving (and delicious) recipes here.*

1 pound fresh green beans, trimmed and cut into 1-inch pieces

2 tablespoons olive oil

½ cup finely chopped onion

½ cup finely chopped celery

½ cup finely chopped red bell pepper

4 garlic cloves, minced

8 ounces white mushrooms, lightly rinsed, patted dry, and thinly sliced

½ teaspoon dried basil

½ teaspoon dried oregano

3 tablespoons all-purpose flour

2 cups vegetable broth, homemade (page 141) or store-bought

Salt

¼ teaspoon freshly ground black pepper

1 (15-ounce) can artichoke hearts, drained and thinly sliced

½ cup vegan Parmesan or Parmasio (page 193)

⅓ cup dry bread crumbs

1. Preheat the oven to 350°F. Lightly oil a 2-quart casserole. Steam the green beans until

tender, about 8 minutes. Transfer to a large bowl and set aside.

2. In a large skillet, heat the oil over medium heat. Add the onion, celery, and bell pepper. Cover and cook until softened, about 5 minutes. Add the garlic, mushrooms, basil, and oregano and continue to cook, uncovered, for another 3 minutes.

3. Stir in the flour and cook 1 more minute. Add the vegetable broth and cook, stirring, until thickened. Reduce heat to low and simmer an additional 5 minutes. Stir in the salt to taste and black pepper and set aside.

4. Add the artichoke hearts to the steamed green beans. Add the mushroom mixture and all but 1 tablespoon of the Parmesan and stir to combine. Spread the mixture evenly in the prepared casserole.

5. Sprinkle with the bread crumbs and the remaining 1 tablespoon of Parmesan. Bake until heated through, about 20 minutes. Serve immediately.

## asparagus dijon

makes 4 servings

*Since this dish is terrific served either hot or chilled, it makes a good addition to a buffet table or make-ahead meal. The bold Dijon vinaigrette is also a great dressing for cauliflower or broccoli.*

1 tablespoon Dijon mustard
1 tablespoon minced shallots
1 tablespoon sherry vinegar
1 tablespoon soy sauce
3 tablespoons olive oil
1 pound asparagus, tough ends trimmed

1. In a small bowl, combine the mustard, shallots, vinegar, and soy sauce. Whisk in the oil and set aside.

2. Steam the asparagus until just tender, about 5 minutes. If serving hot, transfer to a serving platter, drizzle with the vinaigrette, and serve at once.

3. If serving chilled, run the asparagus under cold water to stop the cooking process and retain the color. Drain on paper towels, then cover and refrigerate until chilled, about 1 hour. Arrange the asparagus on a serving platter, drizzle with the dressing, and serve.

## orange-dressed asparagus

makes 4 servings

*Asparagus and orange have a natural affinity and this delicious make-ahead side dish is a great way to showcase their flavors. While the components can be made in advance, don't dress the asparagus until serving time or the citrus will dull the bright green spears. This recipe can be served either hot or chilled.*

1 medium shallot, minced
2 teaspoons orange zest
⅓ cup fresh orange juice
1 tablespoon fresh lemon juice
Pinch sugar
2 tablespoons olive oil
Salt and freshly ground black pepper
1 pound asparagus, tough ends trimmed

1. In a small bowl, combine the shallot, orange zest, orange juice, lemon juice, sugar, and oil. Add salt and pepper to taste and mix well. Set aside to allow flavors to blend, for 5 to 10 minutes.

continues on next page

**2.** Steam the asparagus until just tender, 4 to 5 minutes. If serving hot, arrange on a serving platter and drizzle the dressing over the asparagus. Serve at once.

**3.** If serving chilled, run the asparagus under cold water to stop the cooking process and retain the color. Drain on paper towels, then cover and refrigerate until chilled, about 1 hour. To serve, arrange the asparagus on a serving platter and drizzle with the dressing.

# stir-fried sesame asparagus 🅕

makes 4 servings

*The toasted nutty flavor of sesame combines with ginger and soy sauce in this simple and fragrant stir-fry. In addition to being a delicious side dish, it can also transition to a one-dish meal with the addition of tofu and by serving it over rice or tossing it with noodles.*

1 tablespoon canola or grapeseed oil
1 pound asparagus, tough ends trimmed and cut diagonally into 1-inch pieces
1 garlic clove, minced
1 teaspoon minced fresh ginger
2 tablespoons soy sauce
1 tablespoon toasted sesame oil
1 tablespoon sesame seeds

**1.** In a large skillet, heat the canola oil over medium heat. Add the asparagus and stir-fry for 2 minutes. Add the garlic and ginger and stir-fry for 1 minute longer.

**2.** Add the soy sauce and sesame oil. Cover and cook until the asparagus is tender, about 3 minutes. Add the sesame seeds, stirring to coat. Serve immediately.

# roasted lemon asparagus with pine nuts 🅕

makes 4 servings

*Roasting produces the absolute best-tasting asparagus on earth, bringing out its natural flavor and at the same time, adding a bit of crispness to the tips. The lemon and pine nuts contribute balanced tartness and richness, making a great dish even better.*

1 pound thin asparagus, tough ends trimmed
2 tablespoons olive oil
Salt and freshly ground black pepper
1 garlic clove, minced
¼ cup pine nuts
1 tablespoon fresh lemon juice

**1.** Preheat the oven to 425°F. Lightly oil a baking sheet.

**2.** Arrange the asparagus in a single layer on the prepared baking sheet. Drizzle with the oil and season with salt and pepper to taste. Sprinkle with garlic and pine nuts and roast until the asparagus is tender, about 10 minutes. Transfer to a serving platter and sprinkle with lemon juice. Serve immediately.

# beets with greens and slivered apricots

makes 4 servings

*Beets served with their greens are lovely to behold and packed with nutrients. Roasting beets intensifies their sweet, rich flavor, which is amplified by the apricot sauce. The tender greens cook up quickly and taste similar to Swiss chard.*

1 medium bunch beets with greens
⅓ cup fresh lemon juice
2 tablespoons light brown sugar
½ cup dried apricots
Salt and freshly ground black pepper

1. Preheat the oven to 400°F. Remove the greens from the beets and wash them well, then cut them crosswise into ¹/₂-inch-wide strips. Set aside. Scrub the beets well.

2. Wrap the beets tightly in aluminum foil and bake until tender, about 1 hour.

3. While the beets are roasting, place the apricots in a small heatproof bowl and cover with boiling water to soften, about 10 minutes. Drain and cut into thin slivers and set aside.

4. When the beets are roasted, unwrap them and set them aside to cool. When cool enough to handle, peel the beets and cut them into ¹/₄-inch-thick slices and set aside.

5. In a small saucepan, combine the lemon juice, sugar, and sliced apricots and bring to a boil. Reduce heat to low and simmer for 5 minutes. Set aside.

6. Place the reserved greens in a skillet with 2 tablespoons of water. Cover and bring to a boil, then reduce the heat to medium and cook until the greens are wilted and the liquid is evaporated, about 2 minutes. Stir the apricot-lemon mixture into the greens and season with salt and pepper to taste. Add the beet slices and cook until they are heated through, about 3 minutes. Serve immediately.

# sherry-braised baby bok choy

makes 4 servings

*Tender baby bok choy is imbued with the mellow richness of sherry in this delicious side dish that matches well with the Soy-Glazed Tofu (page 283) or the Ginger-Peanut Tempeh (page 301). In addition to having wonderful flavor, baby bok choy looks great on a plate when served whole or halved lengthwise as it is in this recipe. Note: If the bok choy are exceptionally small, leave them whole, if desired, and prepare four heads instead of two.*

2 tablespoons canola or grapeseed oil
2 garlic cloves, minced
1 teaspoon grated fresh ginger
2 medium heads baby bok choy, trimmed
    and halved lengthwise
¼ cup dry sherry
2 tablespoons tamari soy sauce
⅓ cup water

1. In a large skillet, heat the oil over medium heat. Add the garlic and ginger and cook until softened, about 30 seconds.

2. Arrange the bok choy halves in the skillet in a single layer. Add the sherry, soy sauce, and water. Cover and simmer until the bok choy is tender, 15 to 20 minutes, turning once about halfway through, and adding a bit more water if needed so the vegetables do not burn. Serve immediately.

# broccoli sauté with tofu feta

makes 4 servings

*This lively vegetable sauté features Mediterranean flavors including a zesty vegan feta. Since the tofu feta needs some time to marinate, make it first so it can sit while you prepare the vegetables.*

4 cups broccoli florets
2 tablespoons olive oil
1 medium red bell pepper, coarsely chopped
2 garlic cloves, thinly sliced
2 green onions, minced
2 tablespoons capers
2 tablespoons coarsely chopped fresh flat-leaf
    parsley
2 teaspoons finely chopped fresh marjoram
    or 1 teaspoon dried
1 tablespoon fresh lemon juice
Salt and freshly ground black pepper
Tofu Feta (recipe follows)

1. Steam the broccoli until bright green, about 5 minutes. In a large skillet, heat the oil over medium heat. Add the broccoli and cook, stirring, until just tender, about 5 minutes. Add the bell pepper, garlic, and green onion, and cook, stirring, until just tender, about 3 minutes.

2. Add the capers, parsley, marjoram, lemon juice, and salt and black pepper to taste. Cook, stirring, to heat through.

3. Transfer to a shallow serving bowl and sprinkle with the tofu feta. Serve immediately.

## tofu feta

8 ounces extra-firm tofu, drained and patted dry
⅓ cup olive oil
⅓ cup fresh lemon juice
¾ teaspoon salt

Cut the tofu into ½-inch dice and place in a shallow bowl. Add the oil, lemon juice, and salt, and toss to combine. Set aside for 20 minutes to marinate, turning once about halfway through.

# broccoli with black beans and walnuts 🅕

makes 4 servings

*One might think it's enough that this side dish is colorful and loaded with flavor. But it doesn't stop there—it's also rich in vitamin C, calcium, iron, and other important nutrients. Protein-packed with black beans and walnuts, this is hearty enough to enjoy as a main dish for two when served over rice or quinoa. To amplify the walnut flavor, drizzle a little walnut oil on top when ready to serve.*

4 cups small broccoli florets
2 tablespoons olive oil
2 garlic cloves, minced
2 green onions, chopped
1 cup cooked or canned black beans, drained and
    rinsed
⅓ cup chopped walnuts
2 tablespoons chopped fresh parsley
Salt and freshly ground black pepper

1. Lightly steam the broccoli until bright green, about 5 minutes.

2. In a large skillet, heat the oil over medium heat. Add the broccoli and cook, stirring, until just tender, 5 to 7 minutes.

3. Stir in the garlic and green onions and cook 1 to 2 minutes longer. Add the black beans, walnuts, parsley, and salt and pepper to taste. Cook, stirring, for another minute or two or until hot. Serve immediately.

# broccoli with almonds

makes 4 servings

*Simmering broccoli with mushrooms, garlic, and wine adds sophistication and flavor to this calcium-rich crucifer. For a quicker version, simply steam the broccoli until just tender and then sauté for a few minutes with the almonds in olive oil or margarine.*

1 pound broccoli, cut into small florets
2 tablespoons olive oil
3 garlic cloves, minced
1 cup thinly sliced white mushrooms
¼ cup dry white wine
2 tablespoons minced fresh parsley
Salt and freshly ground black pepper
½ cup slivered toasted almonds

1. Steam the broccoli until just tender, about 5 minutes. Run under cold water and set aside.

2. In a large skillet, heat 1 tablespoon of the oil over medium heat. Add the garlic and mushrooms and cook until soft, about 5 minutes. Add the wine and cook 1 minute longer. Add the steamed broccoli and parsley and season with salt and pepper to taste. Cook until the liquid is evaporated and the broccoli is hot, about 3 minutes.

3. Transfer to a serving bowl, drizzle with the remaining 1 tablespoon oil and the almonds, and toss to coat. Serve immediately.

# spicy sautéed broccoli rabe

makes 4 servings

*Popular in Italy, this bitter green vegetable, also known as* rapini, *is now common in the United States. If broccoli rabe is unavailable, use spinach, chard, or escarole.*

1 medium bunch broccoli rabe (rapini), tough stems removed
2 tablespoons olive oil
2 garlic cloves, minced
½ teaspoon crushed red pepper
Salt and freshly ground black pepper

1. In a saucepan of boiling salted water, cook the broccoli rabe until just tender, about 5 minutes. Drain and run under cold water, then coarsely chop. Set aside.

2. In a large skillet, heat the oil over medium heat. Add the garlic and cook for 30 seconds. Stir in the rabe and the crushed red pepper. Season with salt and black pepper to taste and cook, stirring, until heated through, about 3 minutes. Serve immediately.

# roasted brussels sprouts

makes 4 servings

*I used to like Brussels sprouts, until I started roasting them—now I love them! A splash of lemon adds sparkle.*

1 pound Brussels sprouts, halved lengthwise
2 tablespoons olive oil
Salt and freshly ground black pepper
1 tablespoon fresh lemon juice

1. Preheat the oven to 425°F. Lightly oil a baking sheet and set aside.

2. Steam the Brussels sprouts until just tender, about 5 minutes, then spread them in a single layer on the prepared baking sheet. Drizzle with oil and season with salt and pepper to taste.

3. Roast the Brussels sprouts until slightly browned, about 8 minutes. Transfer to a serving bowl, add the lemon juice, and toss gently to combine. Serve immediately.

# brussels sprouts with shallots and dillweed

makes 4 servings

*The key to great-tasting Brussels sprouts is to not overcook or undercook them. I like coaxing a little extra flavor out of them by sautéing them in olive oil with shallots. Fresh dillweed adds a complementary flavor, but try other herbs, if you like.*

1 pound Brussels sprouts, trimmed and halved
    lengthwise
2 tablespoons olive oil
3 or 4 small shallots, quartered lengthwise
Salt and freshly ground black pepper
2 teaspoons chopped fresh dillweed or
    1 teaspoon dried

1. Steam the Brussels sprouts until just tender, about 7 minutes. Set aside.

2. In a large skillet, heat the oil over medium heat. Add the shallots and cook until softened, 5 minutes.

3. Add the Brussels sprouts and season with salt and pepper to taste. Cook until the shallots and Brussels sprouts become lightly browned, about 5 minutes. Add the dillweed and stir to combine. Serve immediately.

# braised cabbage and apples

makes 6 servings

*While you can certainly use either red or green cabbage and apples, I like the color variation of using both. If you can't find very small heads of cabbage, you can use half a head of each kind or simply pick your favorite and use either green or red. To help you decide: one pound of cabbage equals about 4 cups shredded, which results in about 2 cups cooked.*

2 tablespoons olive oil
1 small head red cabbage, shredded
1 small head savoy cabbage, shredded
1 Granny Smith apple
1 red cooking apple, such as Rome or Gala
2 tablespoons sugar
1 cup water
¼ cup cider vinegar
Salt and freshly ground black pepper

1. In a large saucepan, heat the oil over medium heat. Add the shredded red and savoy cabbage, cover, and cook until slightly wilted, 5 minutes.

2. Core the apples and cut them into ¼-inch dice. Add the apples to the cabbage, along with the sugar, water, vinegar, and salt and pepper to taste. Reduce heat to low, cover, and simmer until the cabbage and apples are tender, stirring frequently, about 20 minutes. Serve immediately.

# lemon-glazed baby carrots with cranberries

makes 4 servings

*Those baby carrots sold in the supermarket may be cute as the dickens, but sometimes they're lacking in flavor. This sweet-tart glaze helps the flavor as do the cranberries, which also make the dish especially pretty.*

1 pound baby carrots
½ cup water, plus more if needed
1 teaspoon sugar
Salt and freshly ground black pepper
1 tablespoon vegan margarine
1 tablespoon fresh lemon juice
½ cup sweetened dried cranberries

1. In a large skillet, combine the carrots, water, and sugar and cook over medium heat. Season with salt and pepper to taste. Cover and cook, stirring occasionally, until the carrots are just tender, 10 to 15 minutes. If the water evaporates before the carrots are done, add a little more water so the carrots don't burn.

2. When the carrots are tender, add the margarine, lemon juice, and cranberries. Cook, uncovered, stirring frequently, until the liquid is absorbed and the carrots are glazed. Serve immediately.

## marsala carrots 🅕

makes 4 servings

*This sophisticated dish is great anytime you want to dress up your carrots in something different and delicious. It's also good to keep in mind when you find yourself with a bunch of carrots that are less than flavorful and need a little help.*

2 tablespoons vegan margarine
1 pound carrots, cut diagonally into ¼-inch slices
1 tablespoon sugar
Salt and freshly ground black pepper
½ cup Marsala
¼ cup water
¼ cup chopped fresh parsley, for garnish

1. In a large skillet, melt the margarine over medium heat. Add the carrots and toss well to coat evenly with the margarine. Cover and cook, stirring occasionally, for 5 minutes.

2. Sprinkle the sugar over the carrots and season with salt and pepper to taste, tossing to coat. Add the Marsala and water. Reduce heat to low, cover, and simmer until the carrots are tender, about 15 minutes.

3. Uncover and cook over medium-high heat until the liquid is reduced into a syrupy sauce, stirring to prevent burning.

4. Transfer to a serving bowl and sprinkle with parsley. Serve immediately.

## carrots and parsnips with diced apple 🅕

makes 4 servings

*This homey mélange features parsnips, a wonderfully flavorful vegetable that resembles pale carrots, but with a more starchy, potatolike texture. Since parsnips cook somewhat faster than carrots, I slice them a bit thicker so I can cook them at the same time. The addition of apple and a touch of maple syrup makes this a kid-friendly recipe.*

1 pound carrots, cut diagonally into ¼-inch slices
1 pound parsnips, cut diagonally into ½-inch slices
1 tablespoon olive oil
1 Granny Smith apple, peeled, cored, and cut into ½-inch dice
1 teaspoon pure maple syrup
1 tablespoon fresh lemon juice
⅛ teaspoon ground nutmeg
Salt and freshly ground black pepper

1. Steam the carrots and parsnips until just tender, about 5 minutes. Set aside.

2. In a large skillet, heat the oil over medium heat. Add the apple, maple syrup, lemon juice, and nutmeg. Cover and cook until the apple is softened, about 4 minutes.

3. Add the steamed carrots and parsnips and season with salt and pepper to taste. Stir gently to mix well and heat through. Serve immediately.

# cardamom carrots with orange

makes 4 servings

*The flavor combination of carrots and car-
damom was inspired by a lovely cardamom-
laced carrot pudding I had for dessert at an
Indian restaurant. Cardamom is one of those
spices you either love or hate. Since it's so
expensive, it's a good idea to make sure you
love it before investing in a whole jar. Look
for a market that sells bulk spices so you can
buy a small amount.*

1 pound carrots, cut into ¼-inch slices
2 tablespoons vegan margarine
1 tablespoon finely grated orange zest
½ teaspoon ground cardamom
Salt
Ground cayenne

1. Steam the carrots until tender, about 7 minutes. Set aside.

2. In a large skillet, melt the margarine over
medium heat. Add the carrots, orange zest,
and cardamom and season with salt and cayenne to taste. Cook, stirring occasionally, until
flavors are blended, about 2 minutes. Serve
immediately.

# tzimmes

makes 4 to 6 servings

*Carrots are the star of this traditional Jewish
dish that has numerous variations. This one
includes sweet potatoes and pineapple and is
baked in the oven. If you prefer to cook it on
top of the stove, simply combine all the ingredients in a large saucepan, cover, and cook
until tender.*

1 tablespoon canola or grapeseed oil
1 pound carrots, shredded
1 medium sweet potato, peeled and shredded
2 tablespoons sugar
½ teaspoon salt
¼ cup fresh orange juice
1 cup finely chopped drained canned
    or fresh pineapple
½ cup golden raisins
¾ teaspoon ground cinnamon

1. Preheat the oven to 350°F. Lightly oil a
9-inch square baking pan and set aside.

2. In a large saucepan, heat the oil over low
heat. Add the carrots, sweet potato, sugar, and
salt. Cover and cook, stirring occasionally, for
10 minutes.

3. Spoon the mixture into the prepared pan.
Stir in the orange juice, pineapple, raisins, and
cinnamon and mix well. Cover tightly with
foil and bake until tender, about 45 minutes.
Serve immediately.

# spicy indian cauliflower 🅕

makes 4 servings

*Ever since my first taste in an Indian restaurant, I've found this dish completely addictive, so I had to start making it at home. If you love spicy food, but aren't sure if you like cauliflower, give this dish a try.*

1 medium head cauliflower, cut into small flowerets

2 tablespoons canola or grapeseed oil

½ cup shredded onion

1 teaspoon grated fresh ginger

1 teaspoon minced garlic

½ cup pureed tomatoes

1 tablespoon ground coriander

2 teaspoons ground cumin

½ teaspoon ground cayenne

1 teaspoon sugar

1 teaspoon salt

1 tablespoon chopped fresh cilantro

1. Steam the cauliflower until just tender, about 5 minutes. Set aside.

2. In a large skillet, heat the oil over medium heat. Add the onion, ginger, and garlic and cook, stirring until softened, about 5 minutes. Do not burn.

3. Stir in the tomatoes, coriander, cumin, cayenne, sugar, and salt.

4. Add the steamed cauliflower and cook, stirring until the cauliflower is coated with the spice mixture. Add a small amount of water if the mixture is too dry. Reduce the heat to low, cover, and cook until the cauliflower is tender, about 5 minutes. Garnish with cilantro and serve immediately.

# roasted cauliflower with lemon and capers 🅕

makes 4 servings

*The best flavor comes from cooking the cauliflower long enough so that it is tender and sweet inside and crisp and browned outside. The lemon and capers are a flavor bonus, though it's actually quite good unadorned, as well.*

1 medium head cauliflower

2 tablespoons olive oil

Salt and freshly ground black pepper

2 tablespoons fresh lemon juice

2 tablespoons capers

1. Preheat the oven to 425°F. Lightly oil a baking sheet and set aside. Remove the core and leaves from the cauliflower, then use a large serrated knife to cut the head lengthwise into ½-inch slices.

2. Arrange the sliced cauliflower in a single layer on the prepared baking sheet. Drizzle with olive oil and season with salt and pepper to taste.

3. Roast the cauliflower until it is tender and slightly browned, turning once, about 15 minutes. During the last 5 minutes of cooking time, sprinkle with lemon juice and capers. Serve immediately.

# creamy cauliflower

makes 4 servings

*If you're counting your carbs, this cauliflower casserole is a great alternative to mashed potatoes. (One cup of boiled cauliflower contains about 2.5 grams of carbohydrates, while the same amount of boiled potato is around 15 grams.) Smoked paprika adds a touch of extra flavor and color, but you can substitute regular paprika if you wish. For a spicy variation, add 1 teaspoon of pureed canned chipotle chile in adobo to the cauliflower mixture before baking.*

1 medium head cauliflower, cut into florets

¼ cup plain unsweetened soy milk

2 tablespoons vegan margarine

¾ teaspoon salt

¼ teaspoon ground cayenne

⅛ teaspoon ground nutmeg

2 tablespoons minced fresh chives or green onions

¼ teaspoon smoked paprika

1. Preheat the oven to 350°F. Lightly oil a 2-quart casserole and set aside.

2. Steam the cauliflower until tender, 12 to 15 minutes. Rinse the cauliflower under cold water and drain well.

3. Transfer the steamed cauliflower to a food processor. Add the soy milk and margarine and process until smooth. Add the salt, cayenne, nutmeg, and chives and puree until blended.

4. Transfer the mixture to the prepared casserole and sprinkle with paprika. Bake until hot, about 20 minutes. Serve immediately.

# braised celery with black olives

makes 4 servings

*Celery is like the Cinderella of the vegetable kingdom, always working in the background, but never the star of the show. This wine-braised dish, complemented by briny black olives, is an easy and elegant way to give celery the royal treatment. For extra flavor, sprinkle with a minced fresh herb such as tarragon, basil, or parsley when you add the olives.*

1 pound celery

2 tablespoons olive oil

⅓ cup dry white wine

⅓ cup vegetable broth, homemade (page 141) or store-bought

Salt and freshly ground black pepper

½ cup pitted kalamata olives, halved

1. Trim and remove the strings from the celery ribs. Cut each celery rib into uniform pieces, about ½ inch wide by 2 inches long.

2. In a large skillet, heat the oil over medium heat. Add the celery and cook, turning once, until golden brown, about 5 minutes.

3. Add the wine and broth and season with salt and pepper to taste. Cover and cook on low until the celery is tender but not mushy, 10 to 12 minutes. Spoon the celery into a serving bowl and sprinkle with olives. Serve immediately.

# rainbow chard with goji berries and pistachios

makes 4 servings

*Inspired by the Sicilian tradition of adding raisins and nuts to sautéed greens, I took the combination to another level by focusing on color. In this recipe, the brilliant hues of rainbow chard are amplified by the addition of pistachios and goji berries, which also provide interesting flavor and textural counterpoints. Super-rich in antioxidants, goji berries are sold dried and look like red raisins, but have a tangy sweet-and-sour flavor. Available in natural food stores, goji berries are expensive, so use one of the variations below if you find them cost prohibitive. If rainbow chard is unavailable, use regular Swiss chard or another leafy green.*

2 tablespoons olive oil

1 small red onion, minced

2 garlic cloves, minced

1 medium bunch rainbow chard, tough stems removed and finely chopped

Salt and freshly ground black pepper

⅓ cup goji berries*

⅓ cup unsalted shelled pistachios*

1. In a large skillet, heat the oil over medium heat. Add the onion, cover, and cook until softened, about 5 minutes. Add the garlic and cook, stirring, to soften. for 30 seconds.

2. Add the chard and cook, stirring until wilted, 3 to 4 minutes. Season with salt and pepper to taste and cook, uncovered, stirring occasionally, until tender, about 5 to 7 minutes.

3. Add the goji berries and pistachios and toss to combine. Serve immediately.

*Instead of goji berries, try raisins, dried cranberries, or bits of another dried fruit. You can also replace the pistachios with almonds, walnuts, or cashews.

# slow-simmered collard greens

makes 4 servings

*To give this great Southern institution a little zing, add the optional chipotle chile. It lends spicy smokiness to the greens and their cooking liquid, known as "pot liquor," which is great sopped up with cornbread.*

2 tablespoons olive oil

1 large sweet yellow onion, chopped

2 garlic cloves, minced

1 large bunch collard greens, tough stems removed and coarsely chopped

1 cup vegetable broth, homemade (page 141) or store-bought

1 canned chipotle chile in adobo, minced (optional)

Salt

1. In a large saucepan, heat the oil over medium heat. Add the onion, cover, and cook until soft, about 10 minutes. Add the garlic and cook 1 minute longer. Reduce heat to low.

2. Stir in the collards, broth, and chipotle, if using. Season with salt to taste. Cover and cook until tender, about 30 minutes, stirring occasionally. Serve immediately.

# corn fritters 🅕

makes 4 servings

*Corn fritters make a fun and versatile side dish that can also be enjoyed as a snack. Serve with a drizzle of maple syrup for the ultimate in kid-friendly vegetable dishes. This basic down-home version is my favorite, bursting with the flavor of corn, but you can add various herbs and spices to change it if you like. For a Southeast Asian variation, add some minced hot chile and cilantro and serve with a squeeze of lime juice.*

½ cup all-purpose flour
½ cup yellow cornmeal
1 teaspoon baking powder
¼ teaspoon salt
Pinch sugar
½ cup plain soy milk
2 cups fresh or thawed frozen corn kernels
Canola or grapeseed oil, for frying

1. Preheat the oven to 250°F. In a large mixing bowl, combine the flour, cornmeal, baking powder, salt, and sugar. Stir in the soy milk, then add the corn kernels and stir to combine.

2. In a large skillet, heat a thin layer of oil over medium heat. Drop the batter by the tablespoonful into the skillet and fry until golden brown, turning once, 2 to 3 minutes per side. Transfer cooked fritters to a heat-proof platter and keep warm in the oven while you cook the rest. Serve immediately.

# spicy coconut creamed corn 🅕

makes 4 servings

*My inspiration for this flavorful side dish was a bowl of coconut and corn soup I had in a Thai restaurant. This is definitely not your mother's creamed corn. For a creamier texture, use an immersion blender to puree a portion of the corn before serving.*

1 tablespoon olive oil
1 small red bell pepper, minced
2 garlic cloves, minced
3 green onions, minced
3 cups fresh or thawed frozen corn kernels
1 cup unsweetened coconut milk
2 tablespoons canned minced hot or mild green chiles
2 teaspoons soy sauce
Ground cayenne
Salt and freshly ground black pepper

1. In a large saucepan, heat the oil over medium heat. Add the bell pepper, garlic, and green onions and cook until softened, about 5 minutes.

2. Stir in the corn, coconut milk, chiles, soy sauce, and a pinch of cayenne. Season with salt and black pepper to taste. Bring to a simmer, then reduce heat to low and cook, stirring occasionally, until the liquid reduces and thickens, about 10 minutes. Taste, adjusting seasonings if necessary. Serve immediately.

# ginger-tamari braised eggplant 🅕

makes 4 servings

*The long slender Chinese eggplant has pale purple skin and is mild in flavor. It is ideally suited to absorbing the luscious flavors of the braising liquid. If unavailable, any kind of Asian eggplant can be used.*

2 garlic cloves, minced

2 teaspoons grated fresh ginger

2 tablespoons tamari soy sauce

1 tablespoon dry sherry

1 teaspoon toasted sesame oil

½ teaspoon sugar

1 tablespoon canola or grapeseed oil

2 medium Asian eggplants, unpeeled and cut into 1-inch thick slices

¼ cup water

2 green onions, minced

1. In a small bowl, combine the garlic, ginger, tamari, sherry, sesame oil, and sugar. Mix well and set aside.

2. In a large skillet, heat the canola oil over medium heat. Add the eggplant slices and cook until slightly softened, turning once, about 8 minutes.

3. Pour the ginger-tamari sauce over the eggplant. Add the water, cover, and simmer until the eggplant is tender, about 10 minutes. Remove the lid and cook until liquid is reduced by half, about 5 minutes.

4. Transfer the eggplant to a serving platter and garnish with the green onions. Serve immediately.

# indian eggplant fritters

makes 4 servings

*Eggplant is a versatile vegetable that is featured in a wide variety of cuisines, including Italian, Indian, Middle Eastern, Japanese, and Thai. It has an amazing ability to take on the flavors surrounding it, and these fritters can be seasoned differently to complement the rest of your meal. For example, omit the coriander and cumin and add basil and oregano for a Mediterranean flavor. And leave out the chile if you don't like the heat. Serve with plain vegan yogurt.*

1 small eggplant, peeled and cut into a ½-inch dice

½ cup water

1 tablespoon fresh lemon juice

2 tablespoons minced green onions

1 garlic clove, minced

1 serrano or other fresh hot green chile, seeded and minced (optional)

1 tablespoon minced fresh parsley

½ cup all-purpose flour

1½ teaspoons ground coriander

¾ teaspoon ground cumin

½ teaspoon baking powder

½ teaspoon salt

Canola or grapeseed oil, for frying

1. Preheat the oven to 250°F. In a large saucepan, combine the eggplant, water, and lemon juice. Cover and bring to a boil, then reduce heat to low, and cook until the eggplant is very soft, about 10 minutes.

2. Drain the eggplant, pressing out any excess liquid, then place in a small bowl. Add the green onions, garlic, and chile, if using, and mix well.

3. In a separate small bowl, combine the flour, coriander, cumin, baking powder, and salt. Add the flour mixture to the eggplant mixture and toss to combine.

4. In a large skillet, heat a thin layer of oil over medium-high heat. Add the eggplant mixture, a tablespoonful at a time, adding as many fritters as you can without crowding. Fry the fritters, turning as needed, until golden brown all over, 2 to 3 minutes per side.

5. Transfer the cooked fritters to a heat-proof platter and keep warm in the oven while you cook the rest. Serve immediately.

# escarole with garlic and capers

makes 4 servings

*Since escarole made regular appearances at the dinner table when I was a child, I've long had an appreciation for this flavorful, slightly bitter green. It can be added to a salad or sautéed from the raw state, but I think it tastes best when boiled for a few minutes to soften and then sautéed in olive oil to add flavor. Be sure the escarole is well washed because it tends to retain bits of dirt.*

1 medium head escarole, leaves separated
2 tablespoons olive oil
2 garlic cloves, minced
1 tablespoon capers
Salt and freshly ground black pepper

1. In a saucepan of boiling salted water, cook the escarole leaves until tender, for 5 minutes. Drain and run under cold water. Coarsely chop and set aside.

2. In a large skillet, heat the oil over medium heat. Add the garlic and cook for 30 seconds. Stir in the capers, then add the chopped escarole and season with salt and pepper to taste. Cook, stirring, until the flavors are well blended and the mixture is hot, about 5 minutes. Serve immediately.

# fennel with olives and sun-dried tomatoes

makes 4 servings

*Fennel can be enjoyed raw in salads or cooked in soups, stews, or on the grill. I also like it this way—sautéed until crisp-tender with olives and sun-dried tomatoes boldly punctuating the subtle taste of the fennel. Fragrant basil plays up the fennel's faintly licorice flavor.*

1 tablespoon olive oil
1 small red onion, halved lengthwise and cut into ¼-inch slices
2 small fennel bulbs, halved lengthwise and cut into ¼-inch slices
Salt and freshly ground black pepper
⅓ cup kalamata olives, pitted and halved
¼ cup oil-packed sun-dried tomatoes, cut into ¼-inch slices
¼ cup fresh basil leaves, shredded

1. In a large skillet, heat the oil over medium heat. Add the onion, cover, and cook until tender, about 7 minutes. Add the fennel and season with salt and pepper to taste. Cover and cook until the fennel is tender, about 10 minutes.

2. Add the olives and tomatoes and cook, uncovered, for 2 or 3 minutes, stirring, to blend flavors. Stir in the basil and serve immediately.

# lemon braised fennel

makes 4 servings

*A gentle lemony braise is used to cook the mild-tasting fennel bulbs. If you want to bring out the licorice flavor, garnish with chopped tarragon instead of parsley.*

2 tablespoons olive oil
2 medium shallots, minced
2 small fennel bulbs, quartered lengthwise
2 tablespoons fresh lemon juice
2 tablespoons water
Salt and freshly ground black pepper
2 tablespoons minced fresh parsley or tarragon, for garnish

1. In a large skillet, heat the oil over medium heat. Add the shallots and fennel and cook for 5 minutes.

2. Stir in the lemon juice, water, and salt and pepper to taste. Cover and cook until tender, stirring occasionally, 15 to 18 minutes. Sprinkle with parsley and serve immediately.

## green beans niçoise

makes 4 servings

*This recipe is inspired by the classic* salade niçoise, *the differences being that it is served hot rather than cold and without the lettuce, potatoes, and, of course, the tuna. To make this mélange more like the classic, simply add diced cooked potatoes to the green bean mixture and allow to come to room temperature, then serve over lettuce that has been tossed in a light vinaigrette.*

1 pound green beans, trimmed
2 tablespoons olive oil
2 garlic cloves, minced
3 or 4 ripe plum tomatoes, cut into a ½-inch dice
⅓ cup niçoise or other black olives, pitted and
    halved
1 tablespoon capers
2 tablespoons chopped fresh parsley
Salt and freshly ground black pepper

1. Steam the green beans until just tender, about 7 minutes. Run the beans under cold water and set aside.

2. In a large skillet, heat the oil over medium heat. Add the garlic and cook for 30 seconds. Add the steamed green beans, tomatoes, olives,

capers, and parsley. Cook for 5 minutes to heat through and blend the flavors. Season with salt and pepper to taste. Serve immediately.

## green beans and grape tomatoes

makes 4 servings

*This recipe is another result of using what's fresh and available from my vegetable garden—in this case, bumper crops of both green beans and grape tomatoes. Though they really need no embellishment, the ground fennel seed and fresh basil add lively flavor notes.*

1 pound green beans, trimmed
2 tablespoons olive oil
2 medium shallots, minced
2 garlic cloves, minced
1 cup ripe grape tomatoes, halved lengthwise
½ teaspoon ground fennel seed
2 tablespoons torn fresh basil leaves
Salt and freshly ground black pepper

1. Steam the green beans until just tender, about 7 minutes. Rinse under cold water and set aside.

2. In a large skillet, heat the oil over medium heat. Add the shallots and garlic, cover, and cook for 1 minute. Add the steamed green beans and cook, stirring occasionally, for 2 minutes. Add the tomatoes, fennel seed, basil, and salt and pepper to taste. Cook until the heated through, about 2 minutes longer. Serve immediately.

# green bean casserole redux

makes 4 to 6 servings

*If ever a recipe needed an extreme makeover, that gloppy 1950s casserole is it. Based on the canned-soup casserole using frozen (or worse, canned) green beans, this version uses fresh beans and mushrooms. The only holdout from the original is the fried onion rings, but you can omit them and use slivered almonds instead. Note: It's important to use unsweet-ened soy milk (or other dairy-free milk) in this and other savory recipes, since many brands contain added sweeteners, which will affect the flavor of the finished dish.*

1 pound green beans, trimmed and cut into
    1-inch pieces
1 tablespoon olive oil
1 small yellow onion, finely chopped
1½ cups chopped white mushrooms
2 garlic cloves, minced
2 cups plain unsweetened soy milk
½ teaspoon dried savory or thyme (optional)
½ teaspoon celery salt
¼ teaspoon salt
¼ teaspoon freshly ground black pepper
1 tablespoon cornstarch blended with
    2 tablespoons water
1 (8-ounce) can fried onion rings

1. Preheat the oven to 375°F. Lightly oil a 9 × 13-inch baking pan and set aside. Steam the green beans until just tender, about 7 minutes. Set aside.

2. In a large skillet, heat 1 tablespoon of the oil over medium heat. Add the onion, cover, and cook until softened, about 5 minutes. Add the mushrooms and garlic and cook, uncovered, until softened, 3 to 4 minutes. Continue to cook until any liquid evaporates. Stir in the soy milk, savory, if using, celery salt, salt, and pepper and bring to a boil. Reduce heat to low, stir in the cornstarch mixture, and continue stirring until thick-ened. Remove from the heat and set aside.

3. In the prepared pan, combine the green beans and the sauce mixture until well blended. Stir in half of the fried onions. Cover with foil and bake until hot, about 20 minutes. Uncover, top with the remaining fried onions, and bake 15 minutes longer, until hot and bubbly. Serve immediately.

# green bean bake with crispy leeks

makes 4 to 6 servings

*This sophisticated dish is another take on the infamous green bean casserole with crispy leeks standing in for the fried onion rings. Leeks are notoriously sandy, so be sure to wash very well under running water. These crisp-fried strands of leeks make a welcome addition to a variety of dishes, from roasted vegetables to mashed potatoes, to sautéed seitan.*

GREEN BEAN BAKE

1 pound fresh green beans, trimmed and halved
2 tablespoons olive oil
2 medium shallots, finely chopped
2 garlic cloves, minced
12 ounces white mushrooms, lightly rinsed,
    patted dry, and cut into ¼-inch slices
¾ teaspoon salt
½ teaspoon freshly ground black pepper
½ teaspoon dried thyme
½ teaspoon dried sage

¼ teaspoon ground nutmeg

3 tablespoons all-purpose flour

¼ cup dry sherry

1 cup vegetable broth, homemade (page 141) or store-bought

1 cup soy creamer or plain unsweetened soy milk

CRISPY LEEKS

½ cup all-purpose flour

½ teaspoon salt

¼ teaspoon freshly ground black pepper

1 leek, well rinsed, trimmed, and halved lengthwise

½ cup canola or grapeseed oil

1. Make the green bean bake: In a saucepan of boiling salted water, cook the green beans for 7 minutes. Drain and set aside. Preheat the oven to 350°F. Lightly oil a 10-inch square baking pan and set aside.

2. In a large skillet, heat the olive oil over medium heat. Add the shallots and garlic and cook for 2 minutes. Add the mushrooms, salt, pepper, thyme, sage, and nutmeg and cook, stirring occasionally, until the mushrooms release their liquid, about 5 minutes. Stir in the flour and cook 3 more minutes. Add the sherry and stir until smooth.

3. Stir in the vegetable broth and simmer an additional 5 minutes. Reduce the heat to low and stir in the soy creamer. Cook until the mixture thickens, stirring occasionally, about 5 minutes.

4. Remove from the heat and stir in the cooked green beans. Transfer the mixture to the prepared baking pan.

5. Make the leek: Combine the flour, salt, and pepper in a shallow bowl. Set aside. Cut leek in half lengthwise into long, thin strips. Set aside.

6. In a large skillet, heat the canola oil until hot but not smoking. Dredge the leek strips in the flour mixture, then add to the hot oil. Fry the leek until crisp and golden, 1 to 2 minutes. Remove from the oil and drain on paper towels and keep warm.

7. Cover the green beans with foil and bake until bubbly, about 20 minutes. Remove from the oven, uncover, and top with the fried leeks. Return to the oven and bake 10 minutes longer. Serve immediately.

# kale and sweet potatoes
makes 4 servings

*This is a great autumn or winter dish—so hearty and flavorful. For a satisfying one-dish meal, add sautéed sliced seitan or cooked red or white kidney beans.*

1 tablespoon olive oil

1 small red onion, minced

1 pound kale, thick stems removed and chopped

1 pound sweet potatoes, peeled and cut into ½-inch dice

1½ cups vegetable broth, homemade (page 141) or store-bought

Salt and freshly ground black pepper

1. In a large saucepan, heat the oil over medium heat. Add the onion, cover, and cook until softened. Add the kale, sweet potatoes, and broth. Season with salt and pepper to taste.

2. Cover and bring to a boil, then reduce heat to medium and cook, partially covered, stirring occasionally, until the vegetables are tender and the liquid has evaporated, about 20 minutes. Serve immediately.

# thai kale with coconut milk

makes 4 servings

*Shallots and coconut milk turn this everyday green into an exotic treat. For a spicy version, add crushed red pepper to taste.*

1 tablespoon canola or grapeseed oil
2 or 3 medium shallots, cut into ¼-inch slices
Crushed red pepper (optional)
1 medium bunch kale, thick stems removed and coarsely chopped
1 (13.5-ounce) can unsweetened coconut milk
1 teaspoon light brown sugar
Salt

1. In a large saucepan, heat the oil over medium heat. Add the shallots, cover, and cook until softened, 3 minutes. Stir in crushed red pepper to taste, if using. Add the kale, stirring to coat.

2. Pour in the coconut milk and sugar and bring to a boil. Reduce heat to low and simmer, uncovered, stirring occasionally, until tender, about 8 minutes. Season with salt to taste. Cook for 5 more minutes to blend flavors. Serve immediately.

# madeira mushroom sauté

makes 4 servings

*Dried porcini add an extra layer of flavor to the white mushrooms sautéed with Madeira, although you could use virtually any combination of your favorite fresh and dried mushrooms with good results. I like to serve these fragrant mushrooms over sautéed seitan slices, but they are also good over cooked rice, quinoa, or other grains.*

1 ounce dried porcini mushrooms
1 tablespoon olive oil
2 medium shallots, minced
1 pound white mushrooms, lightly rinsed, patted dry, and quartered
½ cup Madeira
1 (14.5-ounce) can diced tomatoes, drained
½ teaspoon dried thyme
Salt and freshly ground black pepper
1 tablespoon minced fresh parsley, for garnish

1. Soak the porcini mushrooms in hot water for 1 hour. Drain and cut into ¼-inch strips. Set aside.

2. In a large skillet, heat the oil over medium heat. Add the shallots and cook until softened, about 2 minutes. Add the white mushrooms and cook until slightly softened, about 2 minutes.

3. Add the Madeira, tomatoes, thyme, and rehydrated porcini mushrooms. Season with salt and pepper to taste. Cook until the mushrooms have softened and the mixture has thickened slightly, about 5 minutes. Sprinkle with parsley and serve immediately.

# shiitake snow pea stir-fry

makes 4 servings

*This colorful and delicious vegetable stir-fry makes a great accompaniment to the Soy Glazed Tofu on page 283.*

2 tablespoons soy sauce
1 tablespoon toasted sesame oil
1 teaspoon sugar
1 teaspoon cornstarch
1 tablespoon canola or grapeseed oil
1 garlic clove, minced
2 teaspoons grated fresh ginger
6 shiitake mushroom caps, lightly rinsed, patted dry, and cut into ¼-inch strips

1 red bell pepper, cut into ¼-inch slices
8 ounces snow peas, trimmed
½ teaspoon crushed red pepper
1 tablespoon toasted sesame seeds, garnish

1. In a small bowl, combine the soy sauce, sesame oil, sugar, and cornstarch and set aside.

2. In large skillet, heat the canola oil over medium heat. Add the garlic, ginger, mushrooms, bell pepper, snow peas, and crushed red pepper and stir-fry 2 to 3 minutes.

3. Add the sauce and cook until hot, 2 to 3 minutes longer. Garnish with sesame seeds and serve.

## spicy sautéed pea vines ⓕ
makes 4 servings

*I tasted my first pea vines (the tender greens from snow pea plants) at a Chinese restaurant in Washington, D.C., and have been making them at home ever since. You can find fresh pea vines at Asian markets. If unavailable, try this simple sauté with spinach, watercress, or chard.*

2 tablespoons olive oil
2 garlic cloves, chopped
½ teaspoon crushed red pepper
1 pound pea vines (see headnote)
Salt and freshly ground black pepper

1. In a large skillet, heat the oil over medium heat. Add the garlic and crushed red pepper and cook until fragrant, 1 minute.

2. Add the pea vines, tossing to coat with the oil. Cover and cook until wilted, stirring occasionally, about 5 minutes. Reduce heat to low, season with salt and black pepper, cover, and cook until tender, about 10 minutes longer. Serve immediately.

## basic mashed potatoes
makes 4 to 6 servings

*Mashed potatoes are one of the all-time greatest comfort foods. For best results, use a potato masher to mash the potatoes—never try to mash potatoes in a food processor or you will have a gluey mass. For a more rustic version, leave the skins on the potatoes—just be sure to scrub them extra well. Mashed potatoes can be quite versatile: the simple addition of different spices or herbs can transform the flavor dramatically. For example, add a spoonful of pesto or a small amount of wasabi and you get two completely different flavor experiences. Leftover mashed potatoes can be used to make potato pancakes, croquettes, bread or muffins or to top a shepherd's pie.*

2 pounds Yukon Gold potatoes
½ cup plain unsweetened soy milk
4 tablespoons vegan margarine
Salt

1. Peel the potatoes, if desired, and cut them into uniform chunks.

2. Transfer the potatoes to a large pot with enough salted water to cover. Bring to a boil, then reduce heat to medium-low, cover, and simmer until they are soft when pierced, 20 to 25 minutes.

3. In a small saucepan, heat the soy milk and margarine over medium heat until hot and the margarine is melted.

4. Drain the potatoes well, then return to the pot. Mash with a potato masher or ricer.

5. Stir in the hot soy milk mixture. Season with salt to taste. Serve immediately.

# mashed potatoes and greens

makes 4 to 6 servings

*Reminiscent of the Irish potato and kale dish known as* colcannon, *this version has a decidedly non-Irish twist with the added splash of healthful flaxseed oil and umeboshi vinegar.* Umeboshi *vinegar is the tart, salty liquid drained from pickled umeboshi plums, a traditional Japanese food and is available in natural food stores and Asian markets. If unavailable, use brown rice vinegar instead.*

2 pounds Yukon Gold potatoes, peeled and
    cut into 1-inch chunks

4 cups finely shredded, stemmed kale
    or Swiss chard

1 tablespoon flaxseed oil

1 teaspoon umeboshi vinegar (see headnote)

½ cup warm plain unsweetened soy milk

2 tablespoons vegan margarine

1 small bunch green onions, green part only,
    finely minced

1 teaspoon salt

Freshly ground black pepper

1. In a large pot of boiling salted water, cook the potatoes until tender, about 20 minutes.

2. In a large saucepan of boiling water, cook the kale until tender, 3 to 4 minutes. Drain well and transfer to large bowl. Add the oil and vinegar and toss to combine.

3. Drain the potatoes and mash well with the warm soy milk and margarine. Blend in the cooked kale, green onions, salt, and pepper to taste. Serve immediately.

# rosemary-scented mashed potatoes with limas

makes 4 to 6 servings

*The lima beans remain somewhat chunky in this simple rustic recipe. If you prefer a smoother version, puree the cooked limas in a food processor and then incorporate them into the mashed potatoes. This recipe can also be made with chickpeas or fava beans.*

1 cup frozen lima beans

2 pounds Yukon Gold potatoes, peeled and
    cut into 1-inch chunks

1 teaspoon minced fresh rosemary

3 tablespoons vegan margarine

Salt and freshly ground black pepper

1. In a pot of boiling salted water, cook the lima beans until tender, about 10 minutes. Drain and transfer to a medium bowl. Use a potato masher or ricer to coarsely mash the beans and set aside.

2. In a pot of boiling salted water, cook the potatoes and rosemary until potatoes are tender, about 20 minutes. Drain well and transfer to a large mixing bowl.

3. Add the margarine and use a potato masher or ricer to mash the potatoes. Add the mashed lima beans and season with salt and pepper to taste. Continue mashing the potato and lima bean mixture until the desired consistency is reached. Serve immediately.

# fennel and garlic mashed potatoes

makes 4 servings to 6

*Garlic and fennel transform everyday mashed potatoes into super-luscious spuds. Fragrant ground fennel seed amplifies the mild licorice flavor of the fennel bulb. These potatoes pair nicely with the Tempeh with Lemon and Capers (page 298) or the Pan-Seared Seitan with Artichoke and Olives (page 309).*

2 pounds Yukon Gold potatoes, peeled and cut into 1-inch chunks
4 garlic cloves, peeled
2 tablespoons olive oil
1 fennel bulb, finely chopped, fronds reserved
1 teaspoon ground fennel seed
Salt and freshly ground black pepper
2 tablespoons vegan margarine
½ cup plain unsweetened soy milk

1. In a large saucepan of boiling salted water, add the potatoes and garlic. Cook until tender, about 20 minutes.

2. In a large skillet, heat the oil over medium heat. Add the fennel bulb and cook until softened, stirring occasionally. Add the fennel seed and salt and pepper to taste. Cover and cook until tender, about 10 minutes. Stir in the margarine and soy milk and keep warm over low heat.

3. Drain the potatoes and garlic and return to the saucepan.

4. Mash the potatoes with a potato masher or ricer, then stir in the fennel mixture and mix well to incorporate all the ingredients. Taste, adjusting seasonings if necessary, and serve immediately.

# spiced oven-roasted potato sticks

makes 4 servings

*The healthy alternative to French fries gets even healthier by using a combination of sweet and white potatoes. In addition to contributing lots of vitamin A, the sweet potatoes provide a lovely flavor and color contrast. The optional sprinkling of Old Bay Seasoning adds extra flavor. For variety, you can substitute different herbs or spices for the Old Bay, such as Cajun seasoning, a sprinkling of herbes de Provence, or jerk spices.*

¾ pound russet potatoes, peeled or well scrubbed
¾ pound sweet potatoes, peeled
1 teaspoon Old Bay Seasoning (optional)
Salt and freshly ground black pepper
2 tablespoons olive oil

1. Preheat the oven to 425°F. Lightly oil a baking sheet and set aside.

2. Cut the white and sweet potatoes in half lengthwise, then cut each half into ½-inch slices. Cut each slice in half lengthwise and place them in a bowl. Sprinkle with the Old Bay Seasoning, if using, and salt and pepper to taste. Drizzle with olive oil and toss to coat.

3. Arrange the potatoes on the prepared baking sheet in a single layer. Bake for 20 minutes, turn once, and bake until crisp and brown, about 15 minutes longer. Serve immediately.

# rosemary fingerling potatoes with caramelized shallots

makes 4 servings

*Serving these sweet, buttery fingerling pota-*
*toes (named for their fingerlike shape) and*
*shallots can make any meal special, espe-*
*cially when seasoned with fragrant rosemary*
*and a touch of sugar.*

1½ pound fingerling potatoes, unpeeled
2 tablespoons vegan margarine
5 small shallots, halved lengthwise
1 teaspoon sugar
Sweet paprika
Salt and freshly ground black pepper
1 teaspoon chopped fresh rosemary

1. In a saucepan of boiling salted water, cook the potatoes until almost tender, about 12 minute. Drain, pat dry, and set aside.

2. In a large skillet, melt the margarine over medium heat. Add the shallots, sprinkle with the sugar, and cook until softened and slightly caramelized, about 7 minutes. Add the potatoes and season with paprika and salt and pepper to taste. Sprinkle with the rosemary and continue cooking until the potatoes are coated and tender, 5 to 7 minutes. Serve immediately.

# roasted baby potatoes with spinach, olives, and grape tomatoes

makes 4 servings

*This recipe has everything you want in a side*
*dish—ease of preparation, depth of flavor,*
*and, if you're like me, potatoes! Once the*
*potatoes are roasted, the spinach, olives,*
*and tomatoes are stirred in and put back in*
*the oven just long enough to heat the final*
*ingredients. There are a number of ways to*
*transform this dish with a simple change of*
*seasonings. For example, omit the savory and*
*add dried basil or oregano for an Italian fla-*
*vor, perhaps adding a few shakes of crushed*
*red pepper and some minced garlic as well.*
*You can also add some chopped fresh herbs*
*at the end to mirror the dried herbs or to*
*complement them.*

1½ pounds baby red potatoes, unpeeled,
    halved or quartered, depending on size
3 tablespoons olive oil
1½ teaspoons dried savory
Salt and freshly ground black pepper
2 cups fresh baby spinach
1 cup ripe grape tomatoes, halved lengthwise
⅓ cup black olives, pitted and halved

1. Preheat the oven to 425°F. Lightly oil a 9 × 13-inch baking pan and set aside.

2. Arrange the potatoes in a single layer in the prepared pan. Drizzle with the olive oil and season with the savory and salt and pepper to taste. Roast until tender and golden brown, about 30 minutes.

3. About 5 minutes before the potatoes are ready to serve, remove from the oven and add the spinach, tomatoes, and olives. Toss gently to combine and season with salt and pepper to taste. Return the pan to the oven to wilt the spinach and heat the tomatoes, about 5 to 7 minutes. Serve immediately.

# potato and root vegetable paillasson

makes 4 to 6 servings

*This dish is named for the French word for a*
*woven straw doormat because of the "straw*

mat" appearance of the vegetables when cooked. Ultimately, it's just a fancy way to make hash brown potatoes. You can add different herbs or spices to change up the flavor, if you like.

2 medium russet potatoes, peeled and shredded (about 2 cups when shredded)

2 medium carrots, shredded (about 1 cup when shredded)

2 medium parsnips, shredded (about 1 cup when shredded

2 medium shallots, minced

2 green onions, minced

1 teaspoon salt

¼ teaspoon freshly ground black pepper

¼ cup olive oil

1. Squeeze out as much liquid as possible from the potatoes and transfer them to a large bowl. Add the carrots, parsnips, shallots, green onions, salt, and pepper. Toss to combine.

2. In a large skillet, heat 2 tablespoons of the oil over medium heat. Spread the vegetable mixture in the skillet. Press the vegetables flat with a spatula. Cover and cook until golden brown on the bottom, about 15 minutes. Use a spatula to loosen the edges and give the pan a shake to help loosen it from the bottom of the pan. Use a spatula to help slide the paillasson out of the pan and onto a large plate.

3. In the same skillet, heat the remaining 2 tablespoons oil over medium heat. Invert the paillasson onto another plate and then slide it back into skillet, browned side up. Cook, uncovered, until the bottom is golden brown, 12 to 15 minutes. To serve, slide onto a cutting board and cut into wedges. Serve immediately.

# potato pancakes with green onions

makes 4 servings

*Green onions and parsley add flecks of green to these crisp fried potato pancakes. Recipe tester Edie Fidler served these to her German mother, who thought these were just as good as her own. Serve them hot with cinnamon-laced applesauce or vegan sour cream. A shredded small yellow onion can be used to replace the green onions, if you prefer.*

1½ pounds russet potatoes

1 medium bunch green onions, minced

1 tablespoon minced fresh parsley

¼ cup all-purpose flour

½ teaspoon baking powder

1 teaspoon salt

¼ teaspoon freshly ground black pepper

Canola or grapeseed oil, for frying

1. Peel and grate the potatoes, place them in a colander, and set it over a large bowl. Use your hands to squeeze the liquid from the potatoes. Pour off the liquid and discard. Transfer the squeezed potatoes to the bowl. Add the green onions, parsley, flour, baking powder, salt, and pepper and mix well.

2. Preheat the oven to 275°F. In a large skillet, heat a thin layer of oil over medium heat. Press a heaping tablespoon of the potato mixture flat, then gently place in the hot oil. Repeat this process to make 3 or 4 more potato pancakes and add them to the pan. Do not crowd. Fry until golden brown on both sides, turning once, 7 to 8 minutes total. Remove the cooked pancakes to paper towels to drain, then transfer to a heat-proof platter and keep warm in the oven while you cook the rest. Serve immediately.

# sweet potato pancakes

makes 4 servings

*A nice change from regular potato pancakes, these are made with sweet potatoes and a touch of creamy peanut butter for flavor and to help hold them together—it's also a great selling point for finicky children. Variations include using almond butter instead of peanut butter or cilantro instead of parsley. If you want to add a touch of heat, add some minced hot chile or a few shakes of cayenne.*

1½ pounds sweet potatoes, peeled and shredded
1 small yellow onion, shredded
2 tablespoons chopped fresh parsley
1 tablespoon creamy peanut butter
¼ cup all-purpose flour
½ teaspoon baking powder
1½ teaspoons salt
½ teaspoon freshly ground black pepper
Canola or grapeseed oil, for frying

1. In a large bowl, combine the sweet potatoes, onion, parsley, peanut butter, flour, baking powder, salt, and pepper and mix well.

2. Preheat the oven to 275°F. In a large skillet, heat a thin layer of oil over medium heat. Press a heaping tablespoon of the potato mixture flat between your hands, then gently place it in the hot oil. Make 3 or 4 more pancakes in the same way and add to the pan. Do not crowd. Fry the pancakes until the edges become golden brown and crisp, turning once, about 4 minutes per side. Remove the cooked pancakes to paper towels to drain, then transfer to a heat-proof platter and keep warm in the oven while you cook the rest. Serve immediately.

# rum-spiked sweet potatoes with pomegranate pecans

makes 4 servings

*These sweet potatoes, fragrant with rum and crunchy pecans, will steal the show at your next Thanksgiving dinner. If you can't find bottled pomegranate molasses (available at Indian and Middle Eastern markets or gourmet grocers), make your own using the recipe on page 261.*

2 pounds sweet potatoes, peeled and cut into ½-inch slices
Salt
½ cup coarsely chopped pecans
2 tablespoons pomegranate molasses, homemade (page 261) or store-bought
2 tablespoons olive oil
2 tablespoons dark rum
1 tablespoon sugar
Freshly ground black pepper

1. Place the sweet potatoes in a saucepan with water to cover and bring to a boil. Reduce heat to low, salt the water, cover, and simmer until just tender, 8 to 10 minutes. Drain and set aside.

2. Toast the pecans in a dry skillet over medium-high heat for 3 minutes, stirring frequently so they don't burn. Stir in the pomegranate molasses and cook until the pecans are coated and begin to caramelized, about 3 minutes.

3. Remove from the heat and set aside on waxed paper or other nonstick surface, keeping them separated so they don't harden together.

4. Heat the oil in a large skillet over medium heat. Add the reserved sweet potatoes and

cook until the edges begin to crisp, about 5 minutes. Stir in the rum and sugar and season with salt and pepper to taste. Cook until the potatoes are coated. To serve, transfer the sweet potatoes to a serving bowl and top with the reserved pecans. Serve immediately.

## spiced sweet potatoes with dried cherries

makes 4 servings

*Vibrantly colored and exceptionally flavorful, these potatoes are as spicy as they are sweet. Dried cherries add an unexpected nuance, but if they are unavailable, sweetened dried cranberries fill in quite well.*

2 tablespoons olive oil

1 small red onion, minced

1½ pounds sweet potatoes, peeled and cut into ½-inch dice

¼ cup water

1 tablespoon pure maple syrup or agave nectar

1 tablespoon fresh lemon juice

½ teaspoon chili powder

½ teaspoon ground allspice

⅛ teaspoon ground cayenne

Salt

½ cup sweetened dried cherries

1. In a large skillet, heat the oil over medium heat. Add the onion, cover, and cook for 5 minutes. Add the sweet potatoes, cover, and cook, stirring occasionally, for 10 minutes.

2. Add the water, maple syrup, lemon juice, chili powder, allspice, cayenne, and salt to taste. Cook, stirring frequently, until the potatoes are tender, about 10 minutes longer. About 2 minutes before ready to serve, stir in the cherries. Serve immediately.

## sweet potato and apple gratin

makes 4 to 6 servings

*This tasty autumn dish combines the natural sweetness of apples and sweet potatoes with fragrant "apple pie" spices, giving it a good balance of savory and sweet flavors. It's also very kid-friendly and makes a terrific addition to a Thanksgiving dinner menu.*

1 cup water

3 tablespoons vegan margarine

2 pounds sweet potatoes, peeled and shredded

1 large Granny Smith apple, peeled, cored, and shredded

1½ tablespoons light brown sugar

1 teaspoon ground allspice

1 teaspoon ground cinnamon

½ teaspoon salt

¼ teaspoon freshly ground black pepper

2 tablespoons coarsely ground pecans or other nuts

1. Preheat the oven to 375°F. Lightly oil a large gratin dish or 10-inch square baking pan and set aside.

2. In a large saucepan, bring the water to a boil over high heat. Add 2 tablespoons of the margarine, stirring to melt. Add the sweet potatoes, apple, sugar, allspice, cinnamon, salt, and pepper. Mix thoroughly, then spoon the mixture into the prepared gratin dish.

3. Dot with the remaining 1 tablespoon margarine. Bake until firm and crisp around the edges, 50 to 60 minutes. During the last 10 minute of baking, sprinkle with the pecans. Serve immediately.

# thyme-scented sweet potatoes with black olives and garlic

makes 4 servings

*If those awful candied sweet potatoes in a can have left you avoiding sweet potatoes at every turn, you need to try them fresh and prepared in a savory rather than sweet way. This recipe, redolent of garlic and thyme and studded with black olives, should change your mind about sweet potatoes once and for all.*

1½ pounds sweet potatoes
2 tablespoons olive oil, plus more if desired
3 garlic cloves, crushed
1 teaspoon dried thyme
Salt and freshly ground black pepper
⅓ cup pitted oil-cured black olives

1. Peel the sweet potatoes, cut in half lengthwise, then cut into ¼-inch slices.

2. In a large skillet, heat the oil over medium heat. Add the sliced sweet potatoes and garlic. Sprinkle with the thyme and season with salt and pepper to taste. Cook for 1 minute, stirring to coat. Reduce the heat to low, cover, and cook, stirring occasionally, until the potatoes are tender, about 20 minutes.

3. A few minutes before it is done cooking, add the olives and taste, adjusting seasonings if necessary. Drizzle with a little additional olive oil, if desired. Serve immediately.

# roasted ratatouille gratin

makes 4 to 6 servings

*Ratatouille is a classic vegetable mélange from Provence usually made up of eggplant, bell peppers, tomatoes, onions, and herbs, although the ingredients and proportions vary from cook to cook. Traditionally simmered on top of the stove, this oven-baked variation is a delicious change, and you can cook and serve it in the same baking dish. Ratatouille can also be served at room temperature and spooned onto toasted bread as an appetizer. Or add white beans to this gratin and serve it over rice or another grain, for a hearty main dish.*

1 medium red onion, chopped
1 medium eggplant, peeled and cut into ¼-inch slices
1 medium red bell pepper, chopped
1 medium zucchini, cut into ¼-inch slices
1 (28-ounce) can diced tomatoes, drained
3 garlic cloves, crushed and coarsely chopped
3 tablespoons olive oil
1 tablespoon minced fresh parsley
1½ teaspoons dried thyme
½ teaspoon salt
¼ teaspoon freshly ground black pepper
¼ cup dry unseasoned bread crumbs
2 tablespoons vegan Parmesan or Parmasio (page 193; optional)

1. Preheat the oven to 400°F. Lightly oil a large gratin dish or 9 × 13-inch baking pan and set aside.

2. In a large bowl, combine the onion, eggplant, bell pepper, zucchini, tomatoes, and garlic. Drizzle with 2 tablespoons of the oil and season with the parsley, 1 teaspoon of the thyme, salt, and black pepper. Toss to combine.

3. Spread the vegetable mixture in the prepared gratin dish. Cover tightly with foil and bake until the vegetables are tender, about 45 minutes.

4. Uncover and sprinkle with the bread crumbs, remaining ½ teaspoon thyme, and Parmesan, if using. Drizzle with the remaining 1 tablespoon of oil. Bake, uncovered until crumbs are lightly browned, about 15 minutes longer. Serve hot directly from the gratin dish.

## caramelized root vegetables

makes 4 servings

*A sweet and sour flavor balance of sherry vinegar and sugar creates a luscious flavor harmony with braised root vegetables.*

2 tablespoons olive oil
2 garlic cloves, minced
4 medium shallots, halved or quartered
3 large carrots, cut into 1-inch chunks
3 large parsnips, cut into 1-inch chunks
2 small turnips, cut into 1-inch dice
½ cup light brown sugar
¼ cup water
¼ cup sherry vinegar
Salt and freshly ground black pepper

1. In a large skillet, heat the oil over medium heat. Add the garlic and shallots and cook for 1 minute to soften. Add the carrots, parsnips, and turnips and cook, stirring, until lightly brown and softened, about 5 minutes.

2. Stir in the sugar and 2 tablespoons of the water and cook, stirring until the sugar dissolves, about 5 minutes.

3. Stir in the remaining 2 tablespoons water and the vinegar and simmer for 2 to 3 minutes to blend the flavors. Season with salt and pepper to taste. Cover and cook on low until the vegetables are soft, about 25 minutes, stirring occasionally. Serve immediately.

## winter salad sauté

makes 4 servings

*This is a fun way to turn the table on the crisp green salad. The best time to serve this is during winter's deep freeze, when you want warm food to help take the chill off.*

1 tablespoon olive oil
1 small red onion, halved and cut into ¼-inch slices
2 medium English cucumbers, peeled, halved lengthwise, and cut into ¼-inch slices
5 leaves red leaf lettuce, cut into ½-inch strips
Salt and freshly ground black pepper
6 ripe cherry tomatoes, halved lengthwise
1 tablespoon minced fresh parsley

1. In a large skillet, heat the oil over medium heat. Add the onion and cook until tender, 5 minutes. Add the cucumber and cook until slightly softened, 2 minutes.

2. Add the lettuce and season with salt and pepper to taste. Cook 1 minute. Add the tomatoes and parsley and cook 1 minute longer. Serve immediately.

## sesame spinach

makes 4 servings

*This recipe is inspired by the Japanese salad called* gomai, *made with chilled spinach and a tahini dressing. Instead of a salad, it's presented here as a hot side dish.*

¼ cup tahini (sesame paste)
2 tablespoons fresh lemon juice
1 garlic clove, minced
¼ cup toasted sesame oil
Salt and freshly ground black pepper
9 ounces fresh baby spinach
1 tablespoon black sesame seeds, for garnish

continues on next page

1. In a blender or food processor, combine the tahini, lemon juice, garlic, oil, and salt and pepper to taste. Blend until smooth and set aside.

2. Place the spinach in a large pot with 2 tablespoons of water over medium heat. Cover and cook until the spinach is wilted and the water is evaporated, stirring occasionally, 3 to 4 minutes. Season with salt and pepper to taste.

3. Transfer the spinach to a bowl and drizzle with the tahini sauce. Sprinkle with sesame seeds and serve immediately.

## indian-spiced spinach (saag) 🅕

makes 4 servings

*Since fresh spinach can be expensive, I prefer to save it for recipes where its flavor is the star. That's why I use frozen spinach when I make saag, since the fragrant Indian spices are deliciously dominant, and the spinach flavor is in the background. That said, you can certainly use fresh spinach to make this, if you prefer.*

1 tablespoon canola or grapeseed oil
1 small yellow onion, chopped
2 garlic cloves, minced
1 teaspoon grated fresh ginger
1 teaspoon ground cumin
1 teaspoon ground coriander
1 teaspoon garam masala
1 ripe tomato, chopped
1 (10-ounce) package frozen chopped spinach, thawed
¼ cup water
Salt

1. In a large skillet, heat the oil over medium heat. Add the onion, cover, and cook until softened, 5 minutes. Add the garlic and ginger and cook until fragrant, 30 seconds. Stir in the cumin, coriander, and garam masala.

2. Add the tomato, spinach, and water. Season with salt to taste. Simmer, uncovered, until the spinach is cooked and the flavors are blended, about 15 minutes.

3. Transfer the spinach mixture to a blender or food processor and puree. Return the pureed spinach to the saucepan and heat until hot. Serve immediately.

## baby spinach with lemon and garlic 🅕

makes 4 servings

*Be sure to add the lemon juice just as you're ready to serve so it doesn't have time to discolor the spinach. For added richness, swirl in a tablespoon of vegan margarine just before you add the lemon juice.*

2 tablespoons olive oil
2 garlic cloves, minced
9 ounces fresh baby spinach
Salt and freshly ground black pepper
1 tablespoon fresh lemon juice

1. In a skillet, heat the oil over medium heat. Add the garlic and spinach and season with salt and pepper to taste. Cook, stirring, until the spinach is wilted, about 5 minutes.

2. Sprinkle with lemon juice and serve immediately.

# spaghetti squash with tomatoes and basil

makes 4 servings

*Spaghetti squash is a darling of the carb-counting set because it contains a fraction of the carbohydrates found in actual spaghetti. But it's also just plain fun to make and eat. While you certainly could just serve it straight from its shell, I like to sauté it in a bit of olive oil and garlic for added flavor. Fresh grape tomatoes and basil add color and texture.*

1 large spaghetti squash
2 tablespoons olive oil
3 garlic cloves, minced
1½ cups ripe grape tomatoes, halved lengthwise
¼ cup shredded fresh basil leaves
Salt and freshly ground black pepper

1. In a large pot of boiling water, cook the squash until it is soft when pierced with a fork, 30 to 40 minutes.

2. Halve the squash lengthwise, scoop out the seeds, and discard. Use a fork to scrape out the strands of squash and transfer them to a bowl. Discard the shell.

3. In a large skillet, heat the oil over medium heat. Add the garlic and cook until fragrant, 30 seconds. Add the cooked squash, tomatoes, basil, and salt and pepper to taste. Cook, stirring, until hot, about 5 minutes. Serve immediately.

# orange-and-maple–baked acorn squash

makes 4 servings

*This is an easy and pretty way to prepare acorn squash. The orange juice and maple syrup give it a sweet flavor boost.*

1 medium acorn squash
½ cup fresh orange juice
3 tablespoons pure maple syrup
½ teaspoon ground cinnamon
Salt and freshly ground black pepper

1. Preheat the oven to 350°F. Lightly oil a 9 × 13-inch baking pan and set aside.

2. Cut the squash crosswise into half-inch rings and remove seeds. Arrange the squash rings in the prepared baking pan and sprinkle with orange juice, maple syrup, cinnamon, and salt and pepper to taste. Cover tightly with foil and bake until tender, about 45 minutes. Serve immediately

# bourbon-baked squash

makes 4 servings

*Just a small amount of bourbon is used to enrich the flavor of the squash, but if you prefer not to imbibe, use apple juice or other fruit juice instead.*

2 small acorn or other round winter squashes, halved lengthwise and seeded
4 teaspoons vegan margarine
4 teaspoons sugar
4 teaspoons bourbon
¼ teaspoon ground allspice
Salt and freshly ground black pepper

1. Preheat the oven to 375°F. Lightly oil a 9 × 13-inch baking pan. Arrange the squash halves in the prepared pan, cut side up.

2. Into each squash cavity place 1 teaspoon each of the margarine, sugar, and bourbon. Sprinkle each with allspice and season with salt and pepper to taste. Cover tightly with foil and bake until tender, about 45 minutes. Serve immediately.

# yellow squash with corn, edamame, and dill 🅕

makes 4 servings

*Protein-rich edamame, or green soy beans, are widely available in supermarkets, both fresh and frozen, as well as in and out of the pod. This great-tasting and nutritious ingredient is more than just a trendy appetizer, as this recipe shows. It takes edamame and treats it like down-home lima beans in this variation on succotash.*

1 cup shelled fresh or frozen edamame
1 medium yellow summer squash, halved lengthwise and cut into ½-inch slices
1 cup fresh or frozen corn kernels
2 tablespoons olive oil
½ cup chopped fresh dillweed
1 teaspoon fresh lemon juice
⅛ teaspoon ground cayenne
Salt

1. In a medium saucepan of boiling salted water, cook the edamame until tender, about 10 minutes. Drain and set aside.

2. Steam the squash and corn until just tender, 3 to 4 minutes. Set aside.

3. In a large saucepan, heat the oil over medium heat. Stir in the dillweed, lemon juice, and cayenne. Add the cooked edamame, squash, and corn. Season with salt to taste. Toss to combine and simmer until hot, about 3 minutes. Serve immediately.

# roasted rosemary yellow squash and chayote

makes 4 servings

*My prolific summer crop of squash keeps me busy thinking of new ways to serve them.*

*Roasting brings out their natural sweetness and pungent rosemary makes an interesting change from the parsley or basil more often associated with these vegetables.*

2 medium chayote, peeled, pitted, and cut into ¼-inch slices
2 small yellow summer squash, halved lengthwise, seeded, and cut into ¼-inch slices
2 garlic cloves, minced
3 tablespoons olive oil
1 tablespoon chopped fresh rosemary or ½ teaspoon dried rosemary, crushed
Salt and freshly ground black pepper
1 cup ripe cherry or grape tomatoes, halved lengthwise

1. Preheat the oven to 425°F. Arrange the chayote and yellow squash in a 9 × 13-inch baking pan. Add the garlic, oil, and rosemary, and season to with salt and pepper to taste. Toss to coat.

2. Roast until the vegetables are tender, about 20 minutes, stirring once. Add the tomatoes and roast 15 minutes more. Serve immediately.

# zucchini sauté with sun-dried tomatoes, olives, and peppers 🅕

makes 4 servings

*Fast, easy, and loaded with Mediterranean flavors, this sauté is a great way to enjoy zucchini.*

2 tablespoons olive oil
4 small zucchini, cut into ¼-inch slices
2 garlic cloves, minced
Salt and freshly ground black pepper
¼ cup oil-packed sun-dried tomatoes, cut into ¼-inch strips
¼ cup kalamata olives, pitted and halved
2 tablespoons chopped fresh parsley
2 teaspoons fresh lemon juice

1. In a large skillet, heat the oil over medium heat. Add the zucchini, cover, and cook until softened, turning once, about 7 minutes.

2. Add the garlic and season with salt and pepper to taste. Cook 1 minute longer.

3. Stir in the sun-dried tomatoes, olives, parsley, and lemon juice and cook until hot, about 2 minutes longer. Serve immediately.

# zucchini walnut fritters

makes 4 to 6 servings

*Tender sweet zucchini unites with crunchy walnuts and the potato helps bring it all together in these crispy fritters. For extra flavor, you can add up to a teaspoon of your favorite minced fresh herb to the mixture, but I prefer letting the zucchini and walnuts shine on their own.*

1 medium zucchini, finely shredded
1 small potato, peeled and finely shredded
¼ cup minced green onion
¾ cup finely ground walnuts
2 tablespoons chopped fresh parsley
½ teaspoon baking powder
½ teaspoon salt
¼ teaspoon freshly ground black pepper
½ cup all-purpose flour, plus more if needed
Olive oil, for frying

1. Preheat the oven to 250°F. In a large bowl, combine the zucchini, potato, green onion, walnuts, parsley, baking powder, salt, and pepper. Stir in the flour, adding more if needed to make a thick batter.

2. In a large skillet, heat a thin layer of oil over medium heat. Scoop a large tablespoonful of the fritter batter into the hot oil. Add as many fritters as you can without crowding. Flatten the fritters with a spatula. Fry until golden brown on both sides, 6 to 8 minutes total. Remove the cooked fritters to a heat-proof platter and keep warm in the oven while you cook the rest. Serve immediately.

# roasted zucchini and tomatoes

makes 4 servings

*This is an adaptation of my mother's zucchini recipe that I've enjoyed since childhood. Instead of combining the ingredients on top of the stove, I cook them in the oven, giving the dish an added dimension of flavor that only comes from roasting.*

4 small zucchini, halved lengthwise
½ small yellow onion, chopped
2 garlic cloves, minced
4 ripe plum tomatoes, chopped
1 tablespoon olive oil
1 teaspoon dried basil
¼ teaspoon dried oregano
Salt and freshly ground black pepper
2 tablespoons minced fresh parsley

1. Preheat the oven to 400°F. Lightly oil a 9 × 13-inch baking pan. Cut the zucchini into ¼-inch slices and place in the prepared pan. Add the onion, garlic, tomatoes, oil, basil, oregano, and salt and pepper to taste, tossing to coat.

2. Roast, uncovered, until tender, stirring once about halfway through, 30 to 40 minutes.

3. Transfer to a serving bowl, toss with the parsley, and serve immediately.

# cornmeal-crusted fried green tomatoes 🅕

makes 4 servings

*For a delicious Southern-style treat, serve these spicy succulent tomatoes with the Remoulade Sauce (page 555). Green tomatoes are traditional and favored for their firm texture, although underripe red tomatoes could be substituted if they are firm enough to hold their shape when cooked. Cajun seasoning can be found in the spice section of any supermarket and usually contains a mixture of paprika, ground cayenne, onion power, and garlic powder, and sometimes thyme, oregano, or celery seed, among other spices.*

½ cup yellow cornmeal
½ teaspoon Cajun seasoning
½ teaspoon salt
¼ teaspoon freshly ground black pepper
3 or 4 firm green tomatoes, cut into ½-inch slices
Canola or grapeseed oil, for frying

1. In a shallow bowl, combine the cornmeal, Cajun seasoning, salt, and pepper. Dredge the tomato slices in the cornmeal mixture, turning to coat both sides.

2. In a large skillet, heat a thin layer of oil over medium-high heat. Add the tomato slices and cook until golden brown on both sides, turning once, about 8 minutes total. Serve immediately.

# panko-fried green tomatoes with peanut sauce 🅕

makes 4 servings

*This classic from the American South gets an Asian makeover with a panko crumb coating and a creamy peanut sauce. If you can't find panko, substitute regular unseasoned bread crumbs.*

¾ cup panko
3 or 4 firm green tomatoes, cut into ½-inch slices
3 tablespoons canola or grapeseed oil
Salt and freshly ground black pepper
3 tablespoons creamy peanut butter
2 tablespoons soy sauce
1 tablespoon fresh lemon or lime juice
1 teaspoon sugar
⅛ teaspoon ground cayenne

1. Preheat the oven to 250° F. Place the panko in a shallow bowl. Dip the tomato slices in the panko, turning to coat on all sides.

2. In a large skillet, heat the oil over medium heat. Add the tomato slices in one layer, working in batches if necessary. Season each tomato slice with salt and pepper to taste. Cook, turning once, until crisp on both sides, about 8 minutes total. Transfer to a heatproof platter and keep warm in the oven.

3. In a small saucepan, combine the peanut butter, soy sauce, lemon juice, sugar, and cayenne, stirring to dissolve the sugar and warm the sauce. Taste, adjusting seasonings if necessary. Add a tablespoon or two of water, if needed, for desired consistency.

4. Drizzle the sauce over the tomato slices and serve immediately.

# curry roasted vegetables

makes 4 to 6 servings

*To turn these fragrant veggies into a main-dish meal, add a can of chickpeas when you add the green beans and serve over freshly cooked basmati rice.*

2 large carrots, cut into ½-inch slices

2 medium parsnips, cut into ½-inch slices

1 medium russet potato, peeled and cut into 1-inch chunks

1 medium red onion, chopped

¼ cup olive oil

1½ tablespoons hot or mild curry powder

½ teaspoon salt

¼ teaspoon freshly ground black pepper

8 ounces green beans, trimmed and cut into 1-inch pieces

1. Preheat the oven to 425°F. Lightly oil a 9 × 13-inch baking dish and set aside.

2. In a large bowl, combine the carrots, parsnips, potato, and onion. Add the oil, curry powder, salt, and pepper. Toss to coat the vegetables.

3. Spread the vegetables in the prepared baking pan and roast until the vegetables are tender and browned, about 45 minutes.

4. While the vegetables are roasting, steam the green beans until tender, about 7 minutes. During the last 10 minutes of roasting time, add the green beans to the roasting vegetables and stir to combine. Serve immediately.

# versatile roasted vegetables

makes 6 servings

*The vegetables in this recipe were made to be slow-roasted—they become sweet and caramelized and amazingly flavorful. Here's the versatile part: You can add garlic or chunks of sweet potato or carrot. Omit certain vegetables or add different seasonings. Increase the tomatoes, and serve this over pasta as a chunky sauce or add sautéed seitan near the end and serve over rice.*

1 medium eggplant, halved lengthwise and cut into ½-inch slices

1 medium zucchini, halved lengthwise and cut into ½-inch slices

1 medium red bell pepper, cut into ½-inch strips

1 large red onion, cut into ½-inch dice

3 ripe plum tomatoes, cut into 1-inch dice

⅓ cup olive oil

½ teaspoon dried marjoram

½ teaspoon dried basil

½ teaspoon dried thyme

Salt and freshly ground black pepper

1 tablespoon shredded fresh basil leaves, for garnish

1 tablespoon minced fresh parsley, for garnish

1. Preheat the oven to 425°F. Lightly oil a 9 × 13-inch baking pan and set aside.

2. In a large bowl, combine the eggplant, zucchini, bell pepper, onion, and tomatoes. Add the oil, marjoram, dried basil, thyme, and salt and black pepper to taste. Toss the vegetables to coat. Transfer the vegetables to the prepared pan, spreading the vegetables in a single layer.

3. Roast the vegetables until tender and just beginning to brown, about 1 hour, stirring occasionally. Transfer to a large serving bowl and sprinkle with fresh basil and parsley. Serve immediately.

# balsamic braised vegetables

makes 4 to 6 servings

*The rich braising liquid permeates the vegetables as they cook, giving them a deeply flavorful intensity. To transform this into a main dish, add diced steamed tempeh to braise with the vegetables and serve over your favorite cooked grain. You can vary the vegetables used by the season—try it with winter root vegetables such as carrots, parsnips, and turnips.*

2 tablespoons olive oil

¼ cup diced celery

3 garlic cloves, chopped

⅓ cup balsamic vinegar

2 tablespoons pure maple syrup or agave nectar

1 tablespoon light brown sugar

2 tablespoons chopped fresh parsley

½ teaspoon dried oregano

½ teaspoon dried thyme

½ teaspoon salt

¼ teaspoon freshly ground black pepper

¾ cup water

1 medium red onion, cut into ½-inch dice

1 large carrot, cut into ½-inch dice

1 medium red bell pepper, cut into ½-inch dice

1 small eggplant, peeled and cut into ½-inch dice

1 medium zucchini, diced

12 small white mushrooms, lightly rinsed, patted dry, whole or halved depending on size

Salt and freshly ground black pepper

1. In a large saucepan, heat 1 tablespoon of the oil over medium heat. Add the celery, cover, and cook until softened, about 5 minutes. Add the garlic and cook 1 minute longer. Add the balsamic vinegar, maple syrup, sugar, parsley, oregano, thyme, salt, black pepper, and water and simmer for about 10 minutes or until sauce reduces slightly. Set aside.

2. In a large skillet, heat the remaining 1 tablespoon oil over medium heat. Add the onion, carrot, bell pepper, eggplant, zucchini, and mushrooms. Cover and cook to soften slightly, about 8 minutes.

3. Add the balsamic braising liquid. Cover, reduce heat to medium-low, and simmer until the vegetables are just tender, stirring occasionally, about 25 minutes. Uncover and cook 12 to 15 minutes longer to reduce the liquid. Taste, adjusting seasonings if necessary. Serve immediately.

# grilled vegetable skewers with charmoula sauce

makes 4 servings

*Charmoula sauce is a fragrantly herbal Moroccan sauce traditionally used to flavor fish dishes. In this recipe it is paired with a wide variety of vegetables, but I also like to use it for grilled tofu or portobello mushrooms. If using wooden skewers, soak them in water for at least 30 minutes before use to prevent burning.*

¾ cup coarsely chopped fresh parsley

¾ cup coarsely chopped fresh cilantro

3 garlic cloves, crushed

½ teaspoon ground coriander

½ teaspoon ground cumin

½ teaspoon sweet paprika

½ teaspoon salt

¼ teaspoon ground cayenne

3 tablespoons fresh lemon juice

⅓ cup olive oil

1 medium red bell pepper, cut lengthwise into 1½-inch squares

1 small eggplant, cut into 1-inch chunks

1 medium zucchini, cut into 1-inch chunks

12 white mushrooms, lightly rinsed and patted dry

12 ripe cherry tomatoes

1. In a blender or food processor, combine the parsley, cilantro, and garlic and process until finely minced. Add the coriander, cumin, paprika, salt, cayenne, lemon juice, and oil. Process until smooth. Transfer to a small bowl.

2. Preheat the grill. Thread the bell pepper, eggplant, zucchini, mushrooms, and tomatoes onto skewers and arrange them in a shallow baking dish. Pour about half of the charmoula sauce over the skewered vegetables and marinate at room temperature for 20 minutes.

3. Place the skewered vegetables on the hot grill directly over the heat source. Grill until the vegetables are browned and tender, turning once halfway through the grilling, about 10 minutes total. Transfer to a platter and spoon the remaining sauce over all. Serve immediately.

broiled vegetable skewers: Arrange the skewered vegetables on a broiler pan and place under the broiler, about 4 inches from the heat. Broil until cooked on the inside and browned on the outside, about 8 minutes total, turning once halfway through.

# chimichurri grilled vegetables

makes 4 servings

*Chimichurri is a garlicky herb sauce of Argentina that traditionally accompanies grilled meats, but it makes a great sauce for grilled vegetables as well. I like to serve these flavorful veggies on a bed of freshly cooked quinoa or coconut rice and black beans.*

2 medium shallots, quartered
3 garlic cloves, crushed
⅓ cup fresh parsley leaves
¼ cup fresh basil leaves

2 teaspoons fresh thyme
½ teaspoon salt
¼ teaspoon freshly ground black pepper
2 tablespoons fresh lemon juice
½ cup olive oil
1 medium red onion, halved lengthwise, then quartered
1 medium sweet potato, peeled and cut into ½-inch slices
1 large red or yellow bell pepper, cut into 1½-inch pieces
2 small zucchini, cut diagonally into ½-inch thick slices
2 ripe plantains, halved lengthwise, then cut in half horizontally

1. Preheat the grill. In a blender or food processor, combine the shallots and garlic and process until minced. Add the parsley, basil, thyme, salt, and pepper and pulse until finely minced. Add the lemon juice and olive oil and process until well blended. Transfer to a small bowl.

2. Brush the vegetables with the chimichurri sauce and place them on the grill.

3. Turn the vegetables in the same order you put them on the grill. Brush the vegetables with more of the chimichurri sauce and continue to grill until the vegetables are tender, about 10 to 15 minutes for everything but the plantains, which should be done in about 7 minutes. Serve hot, drizzled with the remaining sauce.

roasted chimichurri vegetables: Toss the onion and sweet potato slices with olive oil and place them in a 9 × 13-inch baking dish. Roast in a 400°F oven for 30 minutes. Add the remaining vegetables and the chimichurri sauce and toss to combine. Return to the oven and roast another 30 minutes or until all the vegetables are tender, turning once about halfway through, so the vegetables brown nicely all over.

# BREADS

## Yeast Breads

basic white bread

whole wheat raisin bread

three-grain bread

oatmeal-walnut bread

pesto potato bread

great garlic bread

sunflower artisan bread

rustic loaf with cured
black olives and rosemary

## Quick Breads

quick herb bread

irish soda bread
with golden raisins

cornbread

fired-up jalapeño cornbread

pumpkin bread with cranberries

chocolate chip banana bread

lemon-drenched
banana-macadamia bread

ginger-molasses bread
with blueberries

orange-date-walnut bread

apple "waldorf" bread

sunflower zucchini bread

carrot bread with cranberries
and walnuts

## Biscuits, Muffins, and Scones

baking powder biscuits

drop biscuits

moroccan-spiced
sweet potato biscuits

corn muffins

chive-flecked spud muffins

pb&j muffins

orange–chocolate chip muffins

cran-apple muffins

apricot-walnut scones

cherry-hazelnut scones

chocolate chip scones

blueberry-almond scones

rosemary scones

## Flat Breads

pesto foccacia

caramelized onion and
walnut focaccia

foccacia with sun-dried
tomatoes and black olives

foccacia with shallots,
figs, and basil

grilled porcini and
tomato-dusted garlic focaccia

chapati

za'atar-spiced flatbread

coriander-sunflower seed
flatbread

lemon-pepper flatbread

## Crackers

sesame crackers

whole wheat sesame crackers

fennel-scented flax crackers

walnut oat crackers

imply thinking about the fragrance and taste of homemade bread evokes a sense of comfort and well-being. Yet this ancient and basic "staff of life" is more often purchased at a store than baked at home. This, despite the fact that, although bread can be one of the most economical foods to make from scratch, a crusty loaf of "artisan" bread at the market can often set you back more than a few dollars. Still, most people opt for buying rather than baking, mostly for convenience.

For vegans, making bread can be more of a necessity. Purchasing ready-made bread can involve a lot of label reading because dairy, eggs, and other animal products are often present.

While most breads share the foundation ingredients of flour and water, an astounding variety can be created from those humble ingredients. In this chapter, you will find some tasty representatives, from yeast breads to quick breads, crackers to muffins, and flat breads to biscuits.

Yeast breads can be time-consuming to prepare because of the necessary kneading and rising steps, but they can also be the most satisfying. Perhaps equal to the great flavor and aroma of home-baked bread is simply the satisfaction of making it from scratch yourself.

If time isn't on your side, quick breads may satisfy your urge to bake in a fraction of the time. Whether sweet or savory, muffins,

biscuits, and scones can make wonderful additions to meals any time of day—or between meals with a hot cup of tea or coffee.

Rounding out the chapter is a selection of flatbreads and crackers that are surprisingly simple to make.

If you like to bake, then you should enjoy the variety of vegan baked goods in this chapter. And if you've never tried baking, these recipes are easy to follow and may just get you hooked.

Note: Most of the recipes call for all-purpose flour. If you'd like a more whole-grain bread, you can substitute spelt flour for all or part of the all-purpose flour, since it is provides the most similar loaves in texture while still being a whole grain. You can also use whole-wheat flour for part of the flour, which will result in denser loaves. There are, of course, numerous other flours that you might want to experiment with, such as those made from oat, rice, corn, soy, and more, each adding its own unique taste and texture to baked goods.

Note: The oven rack position used in the recipes should be the middle position unless otherwise specified.

# Yeast Breads

## basic white bread

makes 1 loaf

*This delicious and unpretentious bread conjures up childhood memories of the loaves my mother used to bake. Reconnect with your family traditions or start new ones. Try the bread with organic peanut butter and good (if not homemade) jam for a fabulous PB&J— or with any topping you like.*

1½ cups warm water
1 package active dry yeast (2¼ teaspoons)
2 tablespoons olive oil
2 teaspoons sugar
1½ teaspoons salt
4 cups all-purpose flour or bread flour

1. In a large bowl, combine ½ cup of the water with the yeast and stir until dissolved. Add the remaining 1 cup water, olive oil, sugar, salt, and 2 cups of the flour. Mix well.

2. Stir in enough of the remaining flour to make a soft dough. Turn the dough out onto a lightly floured surface and knead until smooth and elastic, about 5 minutes.

3. Place in a lightly oiled bowl, turning to coat the top. Cover with plastic wrap or a clean dish towel and let rise in a warm place until doubled in size, about 30 minutes. Test dough by poking it with your finger. It's ready if the indentation from your finger remains.

4. Lightly oil a 9-inch loaf pan and set aside. Punch the dough down and turn the dough out onto a lightly floured surface. Shape the dough into a loaf and place it in the prepared pan. Cover with plastic wrap or a clean dish towel and let rise in a warm place for 30 minutes.

5. Preheat the oven to 400°F. Uncover the dough and use a sharp knife to make 3 diagonal slashes across the top of the loaf. Bake for 15 minutes, then reduce the heat to 350°F and bake until golden brown, about 30 minutes. Cool on a wire rack for 30 minutes before slicing.

## bread storage tips

It is best to use home baked bread shortly after it is made, since it doesn't stay fresh for more than a day or so. Once bread is completely cool after baking, you can wrap the loaf well in plastic wrap.

If using within a day or two, bread can be stored at room temperature. Beyond that it will go stale quickly, or, if humid, it may develop mold. Refrigeration will cause bread to dry out quickly, but in hot weather, refrigeration is preferable to keeping it at room temperature for too long.

If not using the bread right away, it can be stored in the freezer. Breads freeze well and this is the best choice for storage longer than a few days.

To freeze bread, first wrap it in plastic wrap and then double-wrap it in foil. Frozen bread will keep well for a month to six weeks in the freezer. Thaw frozen bread at room temperature before using.

# whole wheat raisin bread

makes 1 loaf

*This wholesome dense loaf gets its subtle sweetness from molasses and, of course, the raisins and a touch of cinnamon. It makes excellent toast—try it toasted with a smear of vegan margarine. Spelt flour is also a good choice for this recipe since it has a nutty flavor similar to whole wheat.*

3 tablespoons dark molasses

1 package active dry yeast (2¼ teaspoons)

1½ cup warm plain soy milk

2 cups whole wheat flour

2 cups all-purpose flour

1¼ teaspoons salt

1 teaspoon ground cinnamon

1 cup regular or golden raisins

1. In a small bowl, combine the molasses and yeast. Add ¼ cup of the soy milk and stir until yeast is dissolved. Set it aside for 5 minutes.

2. In a large bowl, combine the wheat flour, all-purpose flour, salt, cinnamon, and raisins. Add the yeast mixture and the remaining 1¼ cups soy milk, stirring to form a soft dough.

3. Knead the dough for 5 minutes, then place it in a lightly oiled bowl, turning the dough to coat with oil. Cover with plastic wrap or a clean dish towel and let rise in a warm place until doubled in size, about 1 hour. Test dough by poking it with your finger. It's ready if the indentation from your finger remains.

4. Lightly oil a 9-inch loaf pan and set it aside. Punch the dough down and turn it out onto a lightly floured surface. Shape the dough into a loaf and place it in the prepared pan. Cover with plastic wrap or a clean tea towel and let rise in a warm place for 1 hour.

5. Preheat the oven to 350°F. Uncover the dough and bake for 45 minutes, or until the top is golden brown. During the last 20 minutes of baking time, cover loosely with foil.

6. Remove the loaf from the oven and set aside to cool for 5 minutes, then turn out onto a wire rack to cool for 30 minutes before slicing.

# three-grain bread

makes 1 loaf

*The sturdiness of wheat combines with mellow oat flour and subtly sweet cornmeal for a wholesome and flavorful bread. When recipe tester Edie Fidler tested this firm-textured bread, she commented that it had a similar texture to the German rye bread she enjoyed while growing up. This makes a great sandwich bread, but I also enjoy it warm from the oven with some vegan margarine and peach jam.*

1¼ cups hot water

2 tablespoons pure maple syrup

2 tablespoons olive oil

1¼ teaspoons salt

1 package active dry yeast (2¼ teaspoons)

1½ cups whole wheat flour

1½ cups oat flour

1 cup yellow cornmeal

1. In a large bowl, combine the water, maple syrup, oil, and salt. Let cool until warm (not hot) and add the yeast. Stir to combine, then set aside for 10 minutes.

2. In a separate large bowl, combine the whole wheat flour, oat flour, and cornmeal and stir

until well combined. Add about half the flour mixture to the liquid mixture, stirring to blend.

3. Work in the remaining flour mixture until combined, turn out the dough out onto a lightly floured surface. Knead the dough until it is smooth and elastic, about 8 minutes.

4. Place the dough into a large lightly oiled bowl, turning the dough to coat with oil. Cover with plastic wrap or a clean dish towel and let rise in a warm place until doubled in size, about 1 hour. Test dough by poking it with your finger. It's ready if the indentation from your finger remains.

5. Lightly oil a large baking sheet and set aside. Punch the dough down and turn it out onto a lightly floured surface. Shape the dough into a round or long loaf and place it on the prepared baking sheet. Cover with plastic wrap or a clean dish towel, set aside in a warm place, and let rise again for about 1 hour.

6. Preheat oven to 375°F. Uncover the dough and use a sharp knife to cut 3 diagonal slashes in the top of the loaf, about ¼ inch deep. Bake until golden brown, 40 to 45 minutes. The bread is done if it sounds hollow when tapped on the bottom. Cool on a wire rack for 30 minutes before slicing.

# oatmeal-walnut bread

makes 1 loaf

*Combine oats, maple syrup, and the added crunch of walnuts, and you have a cozy comforting loaf that makes a satisfying bread for breakfast or anytime. If you don't like nuts in your bread, just leave out the walnuts. When Tami Noyes tested this recipe, she reported:*

*"After making the same oatmeal bread recipe for nearly 20 years despite trying others, this one is taking its place. We loved this bread. The crust was perfect and the crumb was just the right texture."*

1¼ cups boiling water
½ cup old-fashioned oats
2 tablespoons vegan margarine
1¼ teaspoons salt
¼ cup pure maple syrup
1 package active dry yeast (2¼ teaspoons)
3¼ cups all-purpose flour or bread flour
½ cup finely chopped walnuts

1. In a large bowl, combine the boiling water, oats, margarine, salt, and maple syrup. Stir to combine, then set aside to cool to lukewarm. Add the yeast, then stir in the flour and walnuts and knead until smooth, about 5 minutes.

2. Place the dough in a lightly oiled bowl, turning the dough to coat with oil. Cover with plastic wrap or clean dish towel and let rise in a warm place until doubled, about 1 hour. Test dough by poking it with your finger. It's ready if the indentation from your finger remains.

3. Lightly oil a 9-inch loaf pan. Punch the dough down, then shape it into a loaf, and place it in the prepared pan. Cover the pan with plastic wrap or clean dish towel and let rise again for 45 minutes.

4. Preheat the oven to 375°F. Uncover and bake the bread until golden brown, 35 to 40 minutes. Cover loosely with foil if it begins to brown too quickly. After cooling in the pan for 5 minutes, remove the loaf from the pan and cool it on a wire rack for 30 minutes before slicing.

# pesto potato bread

makes 2 loaves

*This indulgent bread contains two of my favorite foods: fragrant basil pesto and mashed potatoes. Enjoying them in a loaf of fresh-baked bread is pure joy. Moist and flavorful, this bread needs no embellishment, although a brief dip in good olive oil adds to the decadence.*

1 cup plain soy milk

1 cup leftover mashed potatoes

3 tablespoons pesto, homemade (page 565) or store-bought

1 tablespoon olive oil

1½ teaspoons salt

1 teaspoon sugar

1 package active dry yeast (2¼ teaspoons)

¼ cup warm water

4 cups all-purpose flour or bread flour, or more if needed

1. In a large saucepan, heat the soy milk until hot but not boiling. Stir in the potatoes, pesto, oil, salt, and sugar, stirring until well mixed. Transfer to a large bowl and set aside to cool to room temperature.

2. In a small bowl, combine the yeast and the water, stirring to dissolve the yeast. Let the mixture stand for 10 minutes, then stir it into the potato mixture. Add about half the flour, stirring to combine. Work in the remaining flour to form a soft dough, then transfer to a lightly floured surface. Add up to ½ cup of additional flour, if needed.

3. Knead the dough until it is smooth and elastic, about 8 minutes, using additional flour as needed to keep the dough from sticking.

4. Place the dough in a large lightly oiled bowl, turning the dough to coat with oil. Cover with plastic wrap or a clean dish towel and let rise in a warm place until doubled in size, about 1 hour. Test dough by poking it with your finger. It's ready if the indentation from your finger remains.

5. Lightly oil a large baking sheet and set it aside. Punch down the dough and turn it out onto lightly floured surface. Knead the dough for 5 minutes. Divide the dough in half, shape into 2 round loaves, and place them on the prepared baking sheet. Cover the loaves with plastic wrap or clean dish towel. Set aside in a warm place and let rise again for 45 minutes.

6. Preheat the oven to 375°F. Uncover dough and use a sharp knife to cut 2 or 3 diagonal slashes in the top of each loaf. Bake until golden brown, about 35 minutes. The bread is done if it sounds hollow when tapped on the bottom. Cool on a wire rack for 30 minutes before slicing.

# great garlic bread

makes 2 loaves

*I adapted this recipe from one shared with me by recipe tester Toni Dalhmeier. With great garlicky flavor baked inside, it's an ideal bread for crostini and bruschetta. Just slice it, toast it, and add your favorite topping (page 35). As a variation, you can add 1 teaspoon of Italian seasoning to the dough or ½ teaspoon each of dried basil and oregano.*

4 garlic cloves

1 packet active dry yeast (2¼ teaspoons)

1 tablespoon sugar

¾ cup warm water

⅔ cup warm plain soy milk

¼ cup silken tofu, drained

1 tablespoon olive oil, plus more for brushing

1¼ teaspoons salt

½ teaspoon garlic salt

1 cup whole wheat flour

3 cups all-purpose flour or bread flour

1. Preheat the oven to 350°F. Roast garlic in a small ungreased baking dish until golden and very aromatic, about 15 minutes. Squeeze the garlic out of its skins and mash to a paste. Set aside.

2. In a small bowl, combine the yeast, sugar, and warm water and set it aside.

3. In a blender or food processor, combine the soy milk, tofu, the 1 tablespoon of oil, salt, and garlic salt and blend until smooth.

4. In a large bowl, combine the whole wheat flour and 2½ cups all-purpose flour. Add the soy milk mixture and the yeast mixture to the flours and stir to combine. Knead the dough for 10 minutes, sprinkling in as much of the remaining ½ cup all-purpose flour until the dough is smooth. The dough will be soft and sticky. Brush with the remaining oil, cover with plastic wrap or a clean dish towel, and let rise in warm place until doubled, about 1 hour.

5. Preheat oven to 425°F. Lightly oil a large baking sheet.

6. Divide the dough in half and shape into 2 long narrow loaves. Arrange the loaves on the prepared pan. Cover with plastic wrap or a clean dish towel and let the loaves rise again for 15 minutes. Uncover and use a sharp knife to cut 2 or 3 diagonal slashes in the top of each loaf.

7. Bake for 20 to 25 minutes, until golden brown. The breads are done if they sound hollow when tapped on the bottom. For added garlic flavor, when the bread comes out of the oven, brush the top of the loaves lightly with oil and sprinkle with a little garlic salt. Cool for 30 minutes on a wire rack before slicing.

# sunflower artisan bread

makes 1 loaf

*The rustic free-form shape (as opposed to the uniformity of a loaf pan) is a hallmark of an artisan bread. The most difficult thing about this hearty bread is not eating it fresh from the oven in one sitting.*

1¼ cups plain soy milk

3 tablespoons pure maple syrup

2 tablespoons olive oil

1 teaspoon salt

1 package active dry yeast (2¼ teaspoons)

3 cups all-purpose flour or bread flour

½ cup sunflower seeds

1. In a medium saucepan, combine the soy milk, maple syrup, oil, and salt and heat over low heat until lukewarm. Remove from the heat, stir in the yeast, and set aside.

2. In a large bowl, combine the flour and sunflower seeds. Add the yeast mixture and mix well to combine. Turn the dough out onto a lightly floured work surface and knead for 5 minutes.

3. Place the dough in a large lightly oiled bowl, turning the dough to coat with oil. Cover with plastic wrap or a clean dish towel and let rise for 1 hour. Test dough by poking it with your finger. It's ready if the indentation from your finger remains.

4. Lightly oil a baking sheet. Punch the dough down, then shape it into a loaf. Place the dough on the prepared baking sheet. Cover with plastic wrap or a clean dish towel and let rise again for 1 hour.

5. Preheat the oven to 375°F. Uncover and bake the bread until golden brown, about 40 minutes. During the last 20 minutes of baking time, cover the bread loosely with foil. Turn the loaf out onto a wire rack to cool for 30 minutes before slicing.

# rustic loaf with cured black olives and rosemary

makes 1 loaf

*As if the aroma of baking bread weren't enough, this one has the added fragrance of rosemary and olives to keep your mouth watering until it's time to dig in.*

1¼ cups plain soy milk

1 tablespoon dark molasses

1 tablespoon olive oil

1½ teaspoons salt

1 package active dry yeast (2¼ teaspoons)

1½ cups all-purpose flour or bread flour

2 cups whole wheat flour

2 teaspoons chopped fresh rosemary
    or 1 teaspoon dried

½ cup oil-cured black olives, pitted and chopped

1. In a medium saucepan, combine the soy milk, molasses, oil, and salt and heat over low heat until lukewarm. Stir in the yeast and set aside.

2. In a large bowl, combine the all-purpose flour and ½ cup of the wheat flour and mix until well combined. Add the yeast mixture and mix well.

3. Add the remaining 1½ cups of the whole wheat flour and the rosemary and knead

the dough for 3 minutes. Add the olives and knead just long enough to incorporate them into the dough.

4. Place the dough in a large lightly oiled bowl, turning to coat the dough. Cover with plastic wrap or a clean dish towel and let rise in a warm place until doubled, about 1 hour. Test dough by poking it with your finger. It's ready if the indentation from your finger remains.

5. Lightly oil a baking sheet and set it aside. Punch the dough down and turn it out onto a lightly floured surface. Shape the dough into a loaf and place it on the prepared baking sheet. Cover with plastic wrap or a clean dish towel. Set aside in a warm place and let rise again for 1 hour.

6. Preheat oven to 375°F. Uncover and use a sharp knife to cut 2 or 3 diagonal slashes in the top of the loaf. Bake until golden brown, about 40 minutes. Turn the loaf out onto a wire rack to cool for 30 minutes before slicing.

# QUICK BREADS

## quick herb bread
makes 1 loaf

*Herb breads are usually associated with yeast breads, so it's a pleasant surprise to make a rich flavorful bread that requires no kneading or raising time. For a more wholesome loaf, use spelt flour instead of white flour. You can change the herbs in this bread to suit your taste or to complement your meal—one idea is to substitute celery seed and dried dillweed for the basil, thyme, and marjoram.*

3 cups all-purpose flour
2 teaspoons baking powder
½ teaspoon dried basil
¼ teaspoon dried thyme
¼ teaspoon dried marjoram
½ teaspoon salt
¼ teaspoon freshly ground black pepper
1¼ cups plain soy milk
2 tablespoons olive oil

1. Preheat the oven to 350°F. Lightly oil a 9-inch loaf pan and set aside.

2. In a large bowl, combine the flour, baking powder, basil, thyme, marjoram, salt, and pepper, stirring to blend. Pour in the soy milk and oil and combine swiftly until well blended.

3. Transfer the dough to the prepared pan. Bake until golden brown and a toothpick inserted in the center comes out clean, about 40 minutes. Cool 20 minutes on wire rack before slicing.

# irish soda bread
# with golden raisins

makes 1 loaf

*This yummy round loaf is required eating on St. Patrick's Day in my house. Traditionally made with buttermilk, this vegan version combines soy milk and vinegar to create the acidic environment necessary for the baking soda to work its leavening magic.*

1½ cups warm plain soy milk

1 tablespoon cider vinegar

3¾ cups all-purpose flour

2 tablespoons sugar

1½ teaspoons salt

2 teaspoons baking powder

1 teaspoon baking soda

1 cup golden raisins

1. Preheat the oven to 375°F. Lightly oil a baking sheet and set aside.

2. In a small bowl, combine the soy milk and vinegar and set aside.

3. In a large bowl, combine the flour, sugar, salt, baking powder, and baking soda. Mix until blended. Mix in the raisins and the soy milk mixture to make a soft dough.

4. Turn the dough out onto a lightly floured work surface and knead for 1 minute, then shape into a round loaf. Place the loaf on the prepared baking sheet and flatten the loaf with your hands so that it is about 2 to 3 inches high. Use a sharp knife to cut an x-shaped slash into the top of the loaf.

5. Bake until golden brown and a toothpick inserted in the center comes out clean, about 40 to 45 minutes. Cool on a wire rack for 20 minutes before slicing.

## versatile quick breads and muffins

One of the great things about quick breads and muffins, besides their obvious deliciousness, is that the batter from each recipe can be used interchangeably.

As a general rule of thumb, one quick bread loaf recipe can make two mini-loaves (great for gift-giving) or a dozen muffins, and vice versa. Simply adjust the baking time accordingly: more time for (denser) breads, less time for muffins.

# cornbread

makes 1 loaf

*Cornbread is one of the most flavorful and versatile quick breads. It can be enjoyed any time of day, with or without embellishment, and served alone or as a mealtime accompaniment. I especially like to pair it with a pot of spicy chili. This is a basic cornbread recipe for cornbread purists. It has a higher ratio of cornmeal than flour for a deeper corn flavor and none of the add-ins of the recipe that follows—just good old-fashioned cornbread. (If you like sweet cornbread try the Corn Muffins, on page 408.)*

1½ cups warm plain soy milk
1 tablespoon cider vinegar
1½ cups yellow cornmeal
¾ cup all-purpose flour
2 tablespoons sugar
2 teaspoons baking powder
½ teaspoon salt
¼ cup olive oil

1. Preheat the oven to 375°F. Lightly oil an 8-inch square baking pan and place it in the oven while you prepare the batter.

2. In a small bowl, combine the soy milk and vinegar and set aside.

3. In a large bowl, combine the cornmeal, flour, sugar, baking powder, and salt. Stir in the soy milk mixture and the oil and mix well with a few quick strokes.

4. Remove the hot pan from the oven and scrape the batter into the hot pan.

5. Bake until golden brown and a toothpick inserted in the center comes out clean, about 30 minutes. Cool for 10 minutes. Serve warm.

# fired-up jalapeño cornbread

makes 1 loaf

*Unlike the simple and basic cornbread recipe, this one is dressed to the nines. Delicious bits of sweet and hot tantalize your taste buds as you eat this cornbread studded with corn kernels and bits of jalapeño, and sweetened with a touch of maple syrup. If you'd rather not get all "fired-up," simply eliminate the chiles.*

1 cup all-purpose flour
1 cup yellow cornmeal
2 teaspoon baking powder
1 teaspoon salt
1 cup plain soy milk
3 tablespoons pure maple syrup
1 cup fresh or thawed frozen corn kernels
¼ cup olive oil
¼ cup canned jalapeño, chopped

1. Preheat the oven to 375°F. Lightly oil an 8-inch square baking pan and set aside.

2. In a large bowl, combine the flour, cornmeal, baking powder, and salt and set aside.

3. In a separate bowl, combine the soy milk, maple syrup, corn kernels, oil, and chiles.

4. Add the wet ingredients to the dry ingredients and mix well with a few quick strokes.

5. Transfer the batter to the prepared pan and bake until golden brown and a toothpick inserted in the center comes out clean, about 30 minutes. Cool 10 minutes. Serve warm.

# pumpkin bread with cranberries

makes 1 loaf

*This lovely loaf has a mildly spiced pumpkin flavor with sweet-tart bursts of cranberry. Hulled pumpkin seeds or chopped pecans make a good addition to this gorgeous bread that's almost too pretty to eat. It makes a great hostess gift around the holidays—just wrap it tightly in plastic wrap after it's completely cooled and tie it with a pretty ribbon.*

2 cups all-purpose flour

1½ teaspoons baking powder

½ teaspoon baking soda

¾ teaspoon salt

1 cup canned solid-pack pumpkin

1 cup light brown sugar

⅓ cup canola oil

⅓ cup plus 2 tablespoons soy milk

1 teaspoon pure vanilla extract

1 teaspoon cinnamon

¼ teaspoon ground allspice

¼ teaspoon powdered ginger

¼ teaspoon ground nutmeg

⅔ cup sweetened dried cranberries

1. Preheat the oven to 350°F. Lightly oil a 9-inch loaf pan and set aside.

2. In a large bowl, combine the flour, baking powder, baking soda, and salt. Set aside.

3. In a separate bowl, combine the pumpkin, sugar, oil, soy milk, vanilla, cinnamon, allspice, ginger, and nutmeg.

4. Mix the wet ingredients into the dry ingredients. Fold in the cranberries and mix until just combined.

5. Transfer the batter to the prepared pan. Bake until a toothpick inserted in the center comes out clean, about 1 hour. Cool on a wire rack before slicing.

# chocolate chip banana bread

makes 1 loaf

*Testers agree that this is the best banana bread they have ever eaten. Use more or fewer chocolate chips according to your personal preference. I adapted this recipe from one shared with me by my friend, Ann Swissdorf, who uses leftovers to make a great French toast, although it's hard to imagine leftovers.*

1 cup all-purpose flour

¾ cup whole wheat flour

½ cup sugar

2 teaspoons baking powder

½ teaspoon baking soda

¼ teaspoon salt

3 ripe bananas

⅓ cup apple juice

1 teaspoon pure vanilla extract

3 tablespoons canola oil

½ to ¾ cup vegan semisweet chocolate chips

½ cup chopped walnuts

1. Preheat the oven to 350°F. Lightly oil a 9-inch loaf pan and set aside.

**2.** In a large mixing bowl, combine both kinds of flour, the sugar, baking powder, baking soda, and salt and set aside.

**3.** In a blender or food processor, combine the bananas, apple juice, vanilla, and oil and process until well blended.

**4.** Add the wet ingredients to the dry ingredients, then fold in the chocolate chips and walnuts, stirring gently until the flour is just moistened. Do not over mix.

**5.** Transfer the batter to the prepared loaf pan. Bake until firm and a toothpick inserted in the center comes out clean, about 50 minutes. Cool on a wire rack for about 20 minutes before slicing.

# lemon-drenched banana-macadamia bread

makes 1 loaf

*The sweet-tart lemony syrup adds sparkle to this banana bread and, along with the macadamias, helps to set it apart from the rest of the pack. When recipe tester Robin Dempsey served this bread to her husband, he called it "a flavor explosion." For a more traditional banana bread, omit the lemon syrup and swap out the macadamias for walnuts or pecans.*

2 ripe bananas

⅓ cup canola oil

1 teaspoon pure vanilla extract

2 cups all-purpose flour

¾ cup sugar

½ cup coarsely chopped macadamia nuts

1½ teaspoons baking powder

½ teaspoon baking soda

Zest and juice of 2 lemons

½ teaspoon salt

**1.** Preheat the oven to 350°F. Lightly oil a 9-inch loaf pan and set aside.

**2.** In a blender or food processor, puree the bananas. Add the oil and vanilla extract and blend until smooth. Set aside.

**3.** In a large bowl, combine the flour, ½ cup of the sugar, macadamia nuts, baking powder, baking soda, lemon zest, and salt. Fold in the banana mixture, stirring until just mixed.

**4.** Scrape the batter into the prepared pan. Bake until golden brown on top and a toothpick inserted in the center comes out clean, 35 to 40 minutes. Let cool in the pan on a wire rack.

**5.** While the bread is cooling, combine the lemon juice and the remaining ¼ cup sugar in a small saucepan and simmer over low heat, stirring, until the sugar is dissolved. Set aside to cool.

**6.** Use a metal skewer or toothpick to poke several holes in the top of the loaf. Pour the syrup over the top of the loaf and let it stand for 10 minutes before removing from the pan and slicing.

# ginger-molasses bread with blueberries

makes 1 loaf

*This moist, dark bread is a flavorful merging of the seasons with blueberries showing up in wintertime gingerbread. The secret, of course, is using dried or frozen blueberries, both of which are available year-round.*

1 cup warm soy milk
1 tablespoon cider vinegar
2 cups all-purpose flour
½ cup yellow cornmeal
⅓ cup sugar
1 tablespoon ground ginger
1½ teaspoons baking soda
½ teaspoon baking powder
½ teaspoon salt
½ cup dark molasses
½ cup fresh, frozen, or sweetened dried blueberries

1. Preheat the oven to 350°F. Lightly oil a 9-inch loaf pan and set aside.

2. In a small bowl, combine the warm soy milk and vinegar and set aside.

3. In a large bowl, combine the flour, cornmeal, sugar, ginger, baking soda, baking powder, and salt. Mix well.

4. Add the molasses and the soy milk mixture to the flour mixture and stir until the batter is just mixed. Fold in the blueberries and transfer the batter to the prepared pan.

5. Bake until firm and a toothpick inserted in the middle comes out clean, about 1 hour. Let cool slightly before removing from the pan, then continue to cool on a wire rack for 20 minutes before slicing.

# orange-date-walnut bread

makes 1 loaf

*Slightly sweet, with tasty bits of dates, orange zest, and walnuts, this light, moist loaf is the epitome of tea breads—and it's great with coffee, too. Try other nuts, if you like, such as almonds or pecans.*

1 cup fresh orange juice
¼ cup pure maple syrup
1 tablespoon finely chopped orange zest
½ cup chopped dates
2 tablespoons canola oil
2 cups all-purpose flour
1 teaspoon baking powder
1 teaspoon baking soda
½ teaspoon salt
½ cup chopped walnuts

1. Preheat the oven to 350°F. Lightly oil a 9-inch loaf pan and set aside.

2. In a small saucepan, combine the orange juice and maple syrup and bring to a boil. Remove from the heat, add the orange zest, dates, and oil, and set aside.

3. In a large bowl, combine the flour, baking powder, baking soda, and salt.

4. Add the orange juice mixture to the flour mixture, stirring until just combined. Fold in the walnuts, then transfer the batter to the prepared pan.

5. Bake until golden brown and a toothpick inserted in the center comes out clean, about 40 minutes. Cool in the pan for 10 minutes, then turn out onto a wire rack and cool completely before slicing.

# apple "waldorf" bread

makes 1 loaf

*Key players in a Waldorf salad—apples, walnuts, and raisins—are the stars of this flavorful quick bread. For a breakfast treat, try it toasted and spread with apple butter.*

2 cups all-purpose flour
1 cup sugar
1 tablespoon baking powder
1 teaspoon ground cinnamon
½ teaspoon ground allspice
½ teaspoon salt
⅔ cup apple juice or soy milk
¼ cup canola oil
1 teaspoon pure vanilla extract
1 large crisp apple, peeled, cored, and shredded
½ cup chopped walnuts
½ cup raisins

1. Preheat the oven to 350°F. Lightly oil a 9-inch loaf pan and set aside.

2. In a large bowl, combine the flour, sugar, baking powder, cinnamon, allspice, and salt. Set aside.

3. In a separate large bowl, combine the apple juice, oil, and vanilla. Add the apple, walnuts, and raisins, stirring to combine.

4. Add the wet ingredients to the dry ingredients, stirring until just blended.

5. Scrape the batter into the prepared pan. Bake until golden brown and a toothpick inserted into the center comes out clean, 55 to 60 minutes. Cool for 15 minutes before removing from the pan and cool for 30 minutes on a wire rack before slicing.

# sunflower zucchini bread

makes 1 loaf

*Nothing says summer like zucchini and sunflowers, which is why I decided to include sunflower seeds in this zucchini bread recipe.*

½ cup canola oil
1 cup sugar
2 cups grated zucchini, squeezed dry
¼ cup plain or vanilla soy milk
1 teaspoon pure vanilla extract
2 cups all-purpose flour
2 teaspoons baking powder
2 teaspoons ground cinnamon
½ teaspoon salt
½ cup sunflower seeds

1. Preheat the oven to 350°F. Lightly oil a 9-inch loaf pan and set aside.

2. In a large bowl, combine the oil, sugar, zucchini, soy milk, and vanilla.

3. In a separate large bowl, combine the flour, baking powder, cinnamon, and salt. Stir the wet mixture into the dry mixture until well blended. Quickly fold in the sunflower seeds, mixing well.

4. Transfer the batter to the prepared pan. Bake until the center springs back when lightly pressed and a toothpick inserted in the center comes out clean, 50 to 55 minutes. During the last 10 minutes of baking time, cover the loaf loosely with foil to prevent the top from getting too dark. Cool on a wire rack for 30 minutes.

# carrot bread with cranberries and walnuts

makes 1 loaf

*As moist but not as sweet as a carrot cake, this pretty bread is studded with bits of carrot along with cranberries and walnuts. Serve warm, spread with a little vegan cream cheese. If you can't bear to wait an hour for this bread to bake, transfer the batter into a greased muffin pan and bake for 20 to 25 minutes.*

2 cups all-purpose flour

2 teaspoons baking powder

1 teaspoon ground cinnamon

½ teaspoon ground allspice

½ teaspoon ground ginger

½ teaspoon salt

1 cup light brown sugar

¾ cup plain or vanilla soy milk

⅓ cup canola oil

1 teaspoon pure vanilla extract

1¼ cups finely shredded carrots

½ cup sweetened dried cranberries

½ cup chopped walnuts

1. Preheat the oven to 350°F. Lightly oil a 9-inch loaf pan and set aside.

2. In a large bowl, mix the flour, baking powder, cinnamon, allspice, ginger, and salt. Set aside.

3. In a separate large bowl, combine the sugar, soy milk, oil, and vanilla. Add the carrots, cranberries, and walnuts and mix until well combined.

4. Add the wet ingredients to the dry ingredients, stirring until just blended. Scrape the batter into the prepared pan.

5. Bake until golden brown and a toothpick inserted into the center comes out clean, about 1 hour. Cool at least 15 minutes before removing from the pan. Cool on a wire rack for 30 minutes before slicing.

# BISCUITS, MUFFINS, AND SCONES

## baking powder biscuits

makes about 12 biscuits

*Biscuits are easy to put together and they bake quickly. For tender biscuits, avoid overmixing. In addition to being a wonderful dinner companion (especially dinners involving gravies), these and other biscuits make a terrific accompaniment to soups. They also make good breakfast or brunch options, whether slathered with vegan margarine or topped with gravy.*

2 cups all-purpose flour
1 tablespoon baking powder
¾ teaspoon salt
⅓ cup vegan margarine
¾ cup plain soy milk

1. Preheat the oven to 450°F. Lightly oil a baking sheet and set aside.

2. In a large bowl, combine the flour, baking powder, and salt. Mix well. Use a pastry blender or fork to cut in the margarine until the mixture resembles coarse crumbs. Add the soy milk, stirring just long enough to form a soft dough.

3. Turn the dough out onto a floured work surface and knead gently until the dough just holds together.

4. Shape the dough into a ½-inch-thick circle, about 8 inches in diameter. Use a floured 2-inch biscuit cutter or the rim of a small drinking glass to cut the biscuits into rounds.

5. Arrange the biscuits on the prepared baking sheet, spaced about an inch apart. Reshape any leftover dough, cut into biscuits, and place on the baking sheet.

6. Bake until golden brown, 8 to 10 minutes. Serve hot.

## drop biscuits

makes about 12 biscuits

*Visually, these biscuits define "rustic"—but they taste great, have a wonderful texture, and couldn't be easier to make.*

1¾ cups all-purpose flour
3 teaspoons baking powder
½ teaspoon salt
⅓ cup vegan margarine
¾ cup plain soy milk

1. Preheat the oven to 450°F. Lightly oil a baking sheet and set aside.

2. In a large bowl, combine the flour, baking powder, and salt. Use a pastry blender or fork to cut in the margarine until the mixture resembles coarse crumbs. Add the soy milk, stirring just long enough to form a soft dough.

3. Drop the dough by the tablespoonful onto the prepared baking sheet and bake until golden brown, 8 to 10 minutes. Serve hot.

# moroccan-spiced sweet potato biscuits

makes about 18 biscuits

*Serve these colorful, fragrantly spiced biscuits with a Moroccan stew to mirror the exotic flavors, or serve them with more everyday fare to enliven the meal. These biscuits are easy to put together and they bake quickly. For tender biscuits, avoid overmixing.*

2 cups all-purpose flour

1 tablespoon baking powder

2 teaspoons sugar

1 teaspoon salt

½ teaspoon ground allspice

½ teaspoon ground coriander

¼ teaspoon ground cumin

⅛ teaspoon ground cayenne

1 cup mashed sweet potatoes

½ cup plus 1 tablespoon plain soy milk

¼ cup canola oil

1. Preheat the oven to 425°F. Lightly oil a baking sheet and set aside.

2. In a large bowl, combine the flour, baking powder, sugar, salt, allspice, coriander, cumin, and cayenne. In a medium bowl, combine the sweet potatoes, soy milk, and oil and blend well.

3. Add the sweet potato mixture to the flour mixture and mix lightly with a fork until just combined and the mixture forms a soft dough.

4. Turn the dough out onto a lightly floured surface. Roll the dough out until it is about ½ inch thick and cut into rounds with a floured 2-inch biscuit cutter or the rim of a small drinking glass. Arrange the biscuits on the prepared baking sheet. Reshape any leftover dough, cut into biscuits, and place on the baking sheet.

5. Bake until the biscuits are golden brown on top, 16 to 18 minutes. Serve hot.

# corn muffins

makes 12 muffins

*Corn muffins are terrific anytime, but I especially like to serve them when I'm making chili for a crowd because they're easier to handle than cornbread. This recipe produces muffins on the sweet side. If you prefer more savory muffins, reduce the amount of sugar. If you like them sweeter, add a bit more sugar.*

1½ cups yellow cornmeal

½ cup all-purpose flour

2 tablespoons sugar

2 teaspoons baking powder

½ teaspoon salt

1⅓ cups plain soy milk

3 tablespoons canola oil

1. Preheat the oven to 400°F. Lightly oil a 12-cup muffin tin or line it with paper or foil liners and set aside.

2. In a large bowl, combine the cornmeal, flour, sugar, baking powder, and salt. In a medium bowl, combine the soy milk and oil.

3. Pour the wet ingredients into the dry ingredients and mix until just moistened.

4. Spoon the batter into the prepared muffin tin. Bake until golden brown and firm to the touch or a toothpick inserted in the center comes out clean, 20 to 25 minutes. Serve warm.

# chive-flecked spud muffins

makes 12 muffins

*More than just a carb-lover's dream, these rich and flavorful muffins are also a great excuse to cook up extra mashed potatoes, which are needed to make the muffins.*

*Note: if you don't have mashed potatoes on hand, you can quickly cook potatoes in the microwave. When cool enough to handle, cut the potatoes in half and spoon them out of the skins into a bowl. Mash with a little soy milk and olive oil or margarine and season with salt and pepper.*

1¾ cups all-purpose flour

2 teaspoons baking powder

½ teaspoon salt

1 cup leftover mashed potatoes (see headnote)

½ cup plain soy milk

¼ cup canola or grapeseed oil

2 tablespoons plus 1 teaspoon minced fresh chives

1. Preheat the oven to 400°F. Lightly oil a 12-cup muffin tin or line it with paper liners and set aside.

2. In a large bowl, combine the flour, baking powder, and salt. In a separate large bowl, combine the mashed potatoes, soy milk, oil, and chives, stirring until blended.

3. Pour the wet ingredients into the dry ingredients and mix until just moistened.

4. Spoon the batter into the prepared muffin tin. Bake for 22 to 25 minutes, until golden brown and a toothpick inserted into the center of a muffin comes out clean. Let the muffins cool about 5 minutes. Serve warm.

# pb&j muffins

makes 12 muffins

*A sweet surprise of jam awaits inside these tasty peanut butter muffins for an intriguing interpretation of the classic PB&J.*

2 cups all-purpose flour

¼ cup sugar

1 tablespoon baking powder

½ teaspoon ground cinnamon

½ teaspoon salt

⅓ cup creamy peanut butter

3 tablespoons vegan margarine

1 cup soy milk

¼ cup pure maple syrup

1 teaspoon pure vanilla extract

¼ cup seedless raspberry jam or your favorite flavor

¼ cup finely crushed unsalted roasted peanuts

1. Preheat the oven to 400°F. Lightly oil a 12-cup muffin tin or line it with paper liners and set aside.

2. In a large bowl, combine the flour, sugar, baking powder, cinnamon, and salt. Use a pastry blender or fork to cut in the peanut butter and margarine until the mixture resembles coarse crumbs. Add the soy milk, maple syrup, and vanilla and stir until just mixed. Do not overmix.

3. Spoon the batter into the prepared muffin tin (the batter will be thick). Use a small spoon to make a "well" in the center of each muffin and spoon 1 teaspoon of jam into the center of each muffin. Sprinkle a light dusting of the crushed peanuts on top of each muffin.

4. Bake for 25 minutes, until golden brown and a toothpick inserted into the center of a muffin comes out clean. Let cool for 5 minutes. Serve warm.

# orange–chocolate chip muffins

makes 12 muffins

*The recipe for these pretty, streusel-topped muffins was adapted from one shared with me by fellow cookbook author Nava Atlas. These delectable muffins are a tasty way to get your vitamin C.*

STREUSEL

¼ cup all-purpose flour

¼ cup sugar

1½ tablespoons unsweetened cocoa powder

1 teaspoon cinnamon

2 tablespoons canola oil

1 tablespoon fresh orange juice

MUFFINS

2 cups all-purpose flour

1½ teaspoons baking powder

1 teaspoon baking soda

½ cup fresh orange juice

½ cup orange juice concentrate

½ cup vanilla vegan yogurt

1 tablespoon canola oil

1 cup semisweet vegan chocolate chips

1. Preheat the oven to 375°F. Lightly oil a 12-cup muffin tin or line it with paper or foil liners and set aside.

2. Make the streusel: In a small mixing bowl, combine the flour, sugar, cocoa, and cinnamon. Pour in the oil and orange juice, then stir together until the dry ingredients are moistened. Set aside.

3. Make the muffins: In a large bowl, combine the flour, baking powder, and baking soda and stir together. Set aside.

4. In a medium bowl, combine the orange juice, orange juice concentrate, yogurt, and oil and stir until blended. Add the wet ingredients to the dry ingredients. Stir together until thoroughly combined, then stir in the chocolate chips.

5. Spoon the batter into the prepared muffin tin. Sprinkle the streusel mixture evenly over the muffins.

6. Bake for 25 minutes, until golden brown, and a toothpick inserted into the center of a muffin comes out clean. Let cool for 5 minutes. Serve warm.

# cran-apple muffins

makes 12 muffins

*Fruity, moist, and delicious, these muffins are great for breakfast or as a snack. The cranberries look like little red jewels, making them especially appealing. If you're trying to get your kids to eat healthier treats, muffins like these make a great alternative to cupcakes and other sweets.*

2 cups all-purpose flour

1 tablespoon baking powder

1½ teaspoons ground cinnamon

½ teaspoon salt

½ cup sugar

¼ cup soy milk

¼ cup applesauce

2 tablespoons canola oil

1 large Granny Smith or other tart apple, peeled, cored, shredded

¾ cup sweetened dried cranberries

1. Preheat the oven to 400°F. Lightly oil a 12-cup muffin tin or line it with paper or foil liners and set aside.

2. In a large bowl, combine the flour, baking powder, cinnamon, and salt.

3. In a separate large bowl, combine the sugar, soy milk, applesauce, and oil and blend until

smooth. Stir in the apple and cranberries. Add the wet ingredients to the dry ingredients and stir until just blended.

4. Transfer the batter to the prepared muffin pan.

5. Bake until golden brown and firm to the touch or until a toothpick inserted into the center of a muffin comes out clean, about 25 minutes. Let cool for 5 minutes. Serve warm.

# apricot-walnut scones

makes 8 scones

*Scones are little more than fancy biscuits, but unlike their unassuming cousins, scones are usually slightly sweet and contain some sort of treasure, such as fruit or nuts. Whereas biscuits are usually served as part of a meal, scones are generally reserved as a treat unto themselves, served with tea or coffee.*

2 cups all-purpose flour

½ cup sugar

2 teaspoons baking powder

1 teaspoon baking soda

½ teaspoon ground allspice

½ teaspoon salt

½ cup vegan margarine, softened

⅓ cup chopped dried apricots

⅓ cup chopped walnuts

⅓ cup soy milk

1. Preheat the oven to 375°F. Lightly oil a baking sheet and set aside.

2. In a large bowl, combine the flour, sugar, baking powder, baking soda, allspice, and salt. Use a pastry blender or fork to cut in the margarine until the mixture resembles coarse crumbs. Mix in the apricots, walnuts, and soy milk, stirring until just blended. Do not overmix.

3. Transfer the dough to a lightly floured work surface and pat the dough into a 1-inch-thick circle. Cut the dough into 8 wedges and place them on the prepared baking sheet.

4. Bake until golden brown, about 20 minutes. Cool for 5 minutes. Serve warm.

# cherry-hazelnut scones

makes 8 scones

*I especially love the flavor of the dried sweetened cherries and crunchy hazelnuts in these scones, but feel free to substitute your favorite dried fruit and nut combination, such as raisins and walnuts or cranberries and pecans.*

2 cups all-purpose flour

½ cup sugar

2 teaspoons baking powder

1 teaspoon baking soda

½ teaspoon salt

½ teaspoon ground nutmeg

½ cup vegan margarine

⅓ cup plain or vanilla soy milk

1 teaspoon pure vanilla extract

⅓ cup sweetened dried cherries

⅓ cup coarsely chopped hazelnuts

1. Preheat the oven to 375°F. Lightly oil a baking sheet and set aside.

2. In a large bowl, combine the flour, sugar, baking powder, baking soda, salt, and nutmeg. Use a pastry blender or fork to cut in the margarine until the mixture resembles coarse crumbs. Add the soy milk, vanilla, cherries, and hazelnuts. Stir until just blended. Do not overmix.

3. Transfer the dough to a lightly floured work surface. Press the dough into a 1-inch-thick circle. Cut the dough into 8 wedges and place them on the prepared baking sheet.

4. Bake until golden brown, about 20 minutes. Cool for 5 minutes. Serve warm.

# chocolate chip scones

makes 8 scones

*There are some people who believe everything is better with chocolate, these scones included. See if you agree.*

2 cups all-purpose flour

¾ cup sugar

2 teaspoons baking powder

1 teaspoon baking soda

½ teaspoon salt

½ cup vegan margarine

⅓ cup plain or vanilla soy milk

1 teaspoon pure vanilla extract

½ cup vegan semisweet chocolate chips

1. Preheat the oven to 375°F. Lightly oil a baking sheet and set aside.

2. In a large bowl, combine the flour, sugar, baking powder, baking soda, and salt. Use a pastry blender or fork to cut in the margarine until the mixture resembles coarse crumbs. Add the soy milk, vanilla, and chocolate chips and stir until just blended. Do not overmix.

3. Transfer the dough to a lightly floured work surface and shape the dough into a 1-inch-thick circle. Cut the dough into 8 wedges and place them on the prepared baking sheet.

4. Bake until golden brown, about 20 minutes. Cool for 5 minutes. Serve warm.

# blueberry-almond scones

makes 8 scones

*If using fresh or frozen blueberries, be gentle when mixing the dough so the fruit doesn't get all mashed up, resulting in purple (albeit tasty) scones.*

2 cups all-purpose flour

½ cup sugar

1 tablespoon baking powder

1 teaspoon ground cinnamon

½ teaspoon ground ginger

½ teaspoon salt

½ cup vegan margarine

⅓ cup plain or vanilla soy milk

1 teaspoon pure vanilla extract

½ cup frozen, fresh, or dried sweetened blueberries

½ cup slivered almonds

1. Preheat the oven to 375°F. Lightly oil a baking sheet and set aside.

2. In a large bowl, combine the flour, sugar, baking powder, cinnamon, ginger, and salt. Use a pastry blender or fork to cut in the margarine until the mixture resembles coarse crumbs. Add the soy milk, vanilla, blueberries, and almonds, and mix until just blended. Do not overmix.

3. Transfer the dough to a lightly floured work surface and shape the dough into 1-inch-thick circle. Cut the dough into 8 wedges and place them on the prepared baking sheet.

4. Bake until golden brown, about 20 minutes. Cool for 5 minutes. Serve warm.

# rosemary scones

makes 8 scones

*These scones are made with fragrant rose-mary, although you could substitute any herb you prefer. Unlike sweet scones, these savory scones are meant to be enjoyed as the rich biscuits they are—as a mealtime accompaniment.*

2 cups all-purpose flour

⅓ cup sugar

2 teaspoons baking powder

½ teaspoon salt

⅓ cup olive oil

⅓ cup plain soy milk

1 tablespoon finely chopped fresh rosemary

1. Preheat the oven to 375°F. Lightly oil a baking sheet and set aside.

2. In a large bowl, combine the flour, sugar, baking powder, and salt. In a medium bowl, combine the oil, soy milk, and rosemary. Pour the wet ingredients into the dry ingredients, stirring until just blended. Do not overmix.

3. Transfer the dough to a lightly floured work surface and press the dough into a 1-inch-thick circle. Cut the dough into 8 wedges and place them on the prepared baking sheet.

4. Bake until golden brown, about 20 minutes. Cool for 5 minutes. Serve warm.

# FLAT BREADS

## pesto focaccia

makes 4 to 6 servings

*Focaccia is basically pizza dough baked with a simple topping, often just olive oil and salt, or in this case, pesto. Unlike pizza, which is a meal in itself, focaccia is generally served as an accompaniment (like bread) or as a snack.*

1 package active dry yeast (2¼ teaspoons)

½ teaspoon sugar

1¾ cups warm water

3 cups all-purpose flour

1 teaspoon salt

3 tablespoons olive oil

¼ cup basil pesto, homemade (page 565) or store-bought, room temperature

1. In a small bowl, combine the yeast and sugar. Add ¼ cup of the water and stir to dissolve. Set aside for 5 minutes.

2. In a large bowl, combine the flour and salt, stirring to blend. Pour in the yeast mixture, 2 tablespoons of the oil, and as much of the remaining water as needed to form a soft dough.

3. Turn the dough out onto a lightly floured surface and knead until smooth and elastic, about 3 minutes.

4. Place the dough in a large lightly oiled bowl, turning the dough to coat with oil. Cover with plastic wrap or a clean dish towel and let rise in a warm place until doubled in size, about 1 hour.

5. Preheat the oven to 400°F. Lightly oil a pizza pan or baking sheet and set it aside. Punch the dough down. Stretch out the dough into

continues on next page

a 12-inch circle and place it on the prepared pan. Spread the remaining 1 tablespoon of oil on top of the dough. Use your thumb to make indentations across the surface of the dough, then place it on the lower rack of the oven and bake until golden brown, about 20 minutes. As soon as you take the focaccia out of the oven, spread the pesto lightly across the top surface. Cool for 5 minutes. Serve warm.

# caramelized onion and walnut focaccia

makes 4 servings

*The rich topping of meltingly sweet onions and crunchy walnuts makes this a focaccia that deserves to be the center of attention. It's a sophisticated snack to serve to guests with a glass of crisp white wine.*

DOUGH

½ teaspoon sugar

1 package active dry yeast (2¼ teaspoons)

1¼ cups warm water

3 cups all-purpose flour

1 teaspoon salt

2 tablespoons olive oil

TOPPING

2 tablespoons olive oil

2 medium Vidalia or other sweet yellow onions, cut into ¼-inch slices

2 teaspoons dried thyme

Salt and freshly ground black pepper

¼ cup chopped walnuts

1. Make the dough: In a small bowl, combine the sugar and yeast with ¼ cup of the water, stirring to dissolve. Let stand for 5 minutes.

2. In a large bowl, combine 2½ cups of the flour and the salt. Stir in the yeast mixture, oil, and as much of the remaining water as needed until a dough is formed.

3. Turn the dough out onto a lightly floured work surface and knead until smooth and elastic, about 3 minutes, adding as much of the remaining flour as needed to make a smooth dough.

4. Place the dough in a large lightly oiled bowl, turning the dough to coat with oil. Cover with plastic wrap or a clean dish towel and let rise in a warm place until doubled in size, about 1 hour.

5. Lightly oil a baking sheet and set aside. Punch the dough down. Stretch out the dough into a 12-inch circle and place on the prepared baking sheet and set aside.

6. Make the topping: In a large skillet, heat 2 tablespoons of the oil over medium heat. Add the onions, cover, and cook, stirring frequently, until most of the moisture has evaporated and the onions are soft, about 20 minutes. Stir in the thyme and cook, uncovered, stirring, until the onions are browned, 15 to 20 minutes longer. Season with salt and pepper to taste and set aside.

7. Preheat the oven to 400°F. Spread the onion mixture evenly onto the dough and sprinkle with the walnuts. Use your thumb to make indentations across the surface of the dough, pressing the onions and walnuts into the dough.

8. Bake until golden brown, about 20 minutes. Cool for 5 minutes. Serve warm.

# focaccia with sun-dried tomatoes and black olives

makes 4 to 6 servings

*Intensely rich sun-dried tomatoes and tangy black olives give this focaccia high marks for great flavor and appearance. Cut into small wedges, it makes a great addition to a party buffet.*

1 package active dry yeast (2¼ teaspoons)
½ teaspoon sugar
1¾ cups warm water
3 cups all-purpose flour
1 teaspoon salt
2 tablespoons plus 2 teaspoons olive oil
½ cup oil-packed sun-dried tomatoes, cut into ¼-inch strips
¼ cup black olives, pitted and chopped

1. In a small bowl, combine the yeast and the sugar. Add ¼ cup of the water and stir to dissolve. Set it aside for 5 minutes.

2. In a large bowl, combine the flour and salt, stirring to blend. Pour in the yeast mixture, 2 tablespoons of the oil, and as much of the remaining water as needed to form a soft dough.

3. Turn the dough out onto a lightly floured work surface and knead until smooth and elastic, about 3 minutes.

4. Place the dough in a large lightly oiled bowl, turning the dough to coat with oil. Cover with plastic wrap or a clean dish towel, and let rise in a warm place until doubled in size, about 1 hour.

5. Preheat the oven to 400°F. Lightly oil a pizza pan or baking sheet and set aside. Punch the dough down. Stretch out the dough into a 12-inch circle and place it on the prepared pan.

6. Spread the remaining 2 teaspoons of oil on top of the dough and sprinkle with the tomatoes and olives. Use your thumb to make indentations across the surface of the dough, pressing the tomatoes and olives into the dough.

7. Bake until golden brown, about 20 minutes. Cool for 5 minutes. Serve warm.

# foccacia with shallots, figs, and basil

makes 4 to 6 servings

*With flavorful toppings like shallots, figs, and basil, this focaccia is a definite show-stopper. Instead of shaping it into a circle, you can make it in a rectangle and bake it on a baking sheet. The focaccia can then be cut into squares instead of wedges. The choice is yours.*

1 package active dry yeast (2¼ teaspoons)
½ teaspoon sugar
1¾ cups warm water
3 cups all-purpose flour
1 teaspoon salt
3 tablespoons olive oil
2 medium shallots, cut into ¼-inch slices
½ cup chopped figs
Salt and freshly ground black pepper
2 tablespoons shredded basil leaves

1. In a small bowl, combine the yeast and sugar. Add ¼ cup of the water and stir to dissolve. Set aside for 5 minutes.

2. In a large bowl, combine the flour and salt, stirring to blend. Pour in the yeast mixture, 2 tablespoons of the oil, and as much of the remaining water as needed to form a soft dough.

continues on next page

3, Turn the dough out onto a lightly floured work surface and knead until smooth and elastic, about 3 minutes.

4. Place the dough in a large lightly oiled bowl, turning the dough to coat with oil. Cover with plastic wrap or a clean dish towel and let rise in a warm place until doubled in size, about 1 hour.

5. Preheat the oven to 400°F. Lightly oil a pizza pan or baking sheet and set aside. Punch the dough down. Stretch out the dough to fit the pan and place it on the prepared pan.

6. In a large skillet, heat the remaining 1 tablespoon of oil over medium heat. Add the shallots, cover, and cook until soft, about 7 minutes. Spread the shallot mixture on top of the dough. Sprinkle with the figs and season with salt and pepper to taste. Use your thumb to make indentations across the surface of the dough, pressing the shallots and figs into the dough.

7. Bake until golden brown, about 20 minutes. During the last 5 minutes of baking, remove from the oven and top with the basil, then return to the oven to finish baking. Cool for 5 minutes. Serve warm.

# grilled porcini and tomato-dusted garlic focaccia

makes 4 servings

*This flavorful focaccia, redolent of garlic, porcini mushrooms, and sun-dried tomatoes, is a great mealtime accompaniment. Because focaccia is so delicious, it's hard to eat just one piece, so I like to serve it with a light meal such as a vegetable stew or main-dish salad. Instead of grilling, you can bake this focaccia in a 400°F oven for 20 minutes.*

3 sun-dried tomatoes (not oil-packed)

3 slices dried porcini mushroom

½ teaspoon sugar

1 package active dry yeast (2¼ teaspoons)

1¾ cups warm water

3 cups all-purpose flour

3 garlic cloves, finely minced

1 teaspoon salt

½ teaspoon garlic powder

Olive oil

1. In a spice grinder or high-speed blender, grind the tomatoes and mushrooms to a powder. Set aside.

2. In a small bowl, combine the sugar and yeast with ¼ cup of the water, stirring to dissolve. Let stand for 5 minutes.

3. In a large bowl, combine the flour, the garlic, ½ teaspoon of the powdered tomato and mushrooms, the salt, and the garlic powder. Stir in the yeast mixture and as much of the remaining water as needed to form a soft dough.

4. On a lightly floured work surface, knead the dough until it is smooth and elastic, about 3 minutes.

5. Place the dough in a large lightly oiled bowl, turning the dough to coat with oil. Cover with plastic wrap or clean dish towel and let rise in a warm place until doubled in size, about 1 hour.

6. Preheat the grill. Punch down the dough and stretch it out into a 12-inch circle. Brush the dough with oil on both sides. Sprinkle the top with the remaining mushroom and tomato powder, using your fingers to rub it into the dough.

7. Place the dough on a hot grill, seasoned side up, and cook until the bottom is nicely

browned, about 10 minutes. Turn the dough over and cook the other side for 5 minutes. Brush the top with more oil and serve.

## chapati

makes 4 servings

*Chapati are unleavened Indian flatbread made with whole wheat flour and toasted on a griddle. It makes a wonderful addition to an Indian meal such as the Chickpea and Vegetable Curry (page 258) or the Yellow Dal with Spinach (page 263). Delicious, tender, and soft when freshly made, chapati are best if eaten soon after they are made, as they can become a bit tough if reheated.*

1 cup whole wheat flour
1 cup all-purpose flour
1 teaspoon salt
1 tablespoon canola oil
¾ cup warm water
3 tablespoons vegan margarine, melted

1. In a large bowl, combine both flours, salt, oil, and water to form a soft dough.

2. Knead the dough until smooth, 3 to 5 minutes, then cover tightly with plastic wrap. Let the dough rest for 30 minutes.

3. Preheat oven to 200°F. Divide the dough into 8 equal pieces. Roll out each piece of dough on a lightly floured work surface into a circles about ⅛ inch thick.

4. Heat a lightly oiled griddle or skillet over medium heat. Add the chapati, one at a time, and cook, turning once, until golden brown on both sides, about 2 minutes per side.

5. Transfer the cooked chapati to a heat-proof platter and brush with the melted margarine. Cover loosely with foil and keep warm in the oven while you cook the remaining chapatis.

## za'atar-spiced flatbread

makes 4 flatbreads

*This flatbread makes a good accompaniment to Pomegranate-Infused Lentil and Chickpea Stew (page 260) or Double-Sesame Tofu with Tahini Sauce (page 292). Za'atar is a Middle Eastern spice blend made up of herbs, sumac (a berry), sesame seeds, and salt. The flavor is something like a mixture of marjoram, thyme, and oregano. Look for it in Middle Eastern markets or online.*

2 cups all-purpose flour
1 teaspoon salt
¾ cup water
Olive oil, as needed
2 tablespoons za'atar spice blend (see headnote)

1. In a large bowl, combine the flour and salt and stir in as much of the water as needed until the dough holds together. Knead until smooth, about 5 minutes. Cover with plastic wrap and set aside for 15 minutes.

2. Preheat the oven to 250°F. Divide the dough into 4 equal pieces. Lightly flour your hands and shape each dough piece into balls. Flatten the balls on a lightly floured work surface, then roll out into circles about ¼ inch thick.

3. Brush the top surface of the dough circles with olive oil, then sprinkle with the za'atar spices, using your fingers to rub in the spices so they adhere to the dough.

4. In a large skillet, heat a thin layer of oil over medium-high heat. Place a dough circle in the skillet and cook, turning once, until brown spots appear, about 3 minutes per side.

5. Remove the cooked bread to a heat-proof platter, cover with foil, and keep warm in the oven while you cook the rest. Repeat with the remaining dough and serve at once.

# coriander-sunflower seed flatbread

makes 4 flatbreads

*One of the things I like most about homemade flatbread—in addition to the great taste—is its versatility: you can alter the seasonings to complement your meal. For example, this version spiced with coriander might be served with a Moroccan tagine or other stew that also contains the same spice. If I were making a curry, I might instead add some curry powder to the bread to mirror those spices.*

2 cups all-purpose flour

1 teaspoon salt

¾ cup water

Olive oil, as needed

1½ teaspoons ground coriander

½ cup unsalted sunflower seeds

1. In a large bowl, combine the flour and salt and stir in as much of the water as needed until the dough holds together. Knead until smooth, about 5 minutes. Cover with plastic wrap and set aside for 15 minutes.

2. Preheat the oven to 250°F. Divide the dough into 4 equal pieces. Lightly flour your hands and shape the pieces into balls. Flatten them on a lightly floured work surface, then roll out into circles about ¼ inch thick.

3. Brush the top surface of the dough circles with olive oil, then sprinkle them with coriander and sunflower seeds, using your fingers to rub in the spice and seeds so they adhere to the dough.

4. In a large skillet, heat a thin layer of oil over medium-high heat. Place one of the dough circles in the skillet and cook, turning once, until brown spots begin to appear, about 3 minutes per side.

5. Remove the cooked bread to a heat-proof platter, cover with foil, and keep warm while you cook the remaining flatbreads. Repeat with the remaining dough and serve at once.

# lemon-pepper flatbread

makes 4 flatbreads

*Pungent lemon-pepper gives this sesame flatbread added punch, but the flavor is mellow enough to complement a variety of dishes.*

2 cups all-purpose flour

1¼ teaspoons salt

¾ cup water

Toasted sesame oil, as needed

¼ cup sesame seeds

1½ teaspoons lemon-pepper seasoning

1. In a large bowl, combine the flour and salt and stir in as much of the water as needed until the dough holds together. Knead until smooth, about 5 minutes. Cover with plastic wrap and set aside for 20 minutes.

2. Divide the dough into 4 equal pieces. Lightly flour your hands and shape the pieces into balls. Flatten them on a lightly floured

work surface, then roll out into circles about ¼ inch thick.

3. Preheat the oven to 250°F. Brush the top surface of the dough circles with the oil, then sprinkle them with the sesame seeds and lemon-pepper seasoning, using your fingers to rub in the seeds and seasoning so they adhere to the dough.

4. In a large skillet, heat a thin layer of oil over medium-high heat. Place one of the dough circles in the skillet and cook, turning once, until brown spots begin to appear, about 3 minutes per side.

5. Remove the cooked bread to a heat-proof platter, cover with foil, and keep warm in the oven while you cook the remaining flatbreads. Repeat with the remaining dough and serve at once.

# CRACKERS

## sesame crackers

makes about 2 dozen crackers

*Homemade crackers are easy to make and fun to serve, especially to guests, where they can be a real conversation-starter. How many people do you know who make their own crackers?*

1 cup all-purpose flour
2 tablespoons yellow cornmeal
1 teaspoon sugar
½ teaspoon baking powder
¼ teaspoon salt
2 tablespoons vegan margarine
2 tablespoons sesame seeds
3 tablespoons plain soy milk

1. Preheat the oven to 350°F. Lightly oil a baking sheet or line it with parchment paper and set aside.

2. In a large bowl, combine the flour, cornmeal, sugar, baking powder, and salt. Cut the margarine into the dry ingredients with a pastry blender or fork until the mixture resembles coarse crumbs. Add the sesame seeds and soy milk and stir until a dough forms.

3. Turn out the dough onto a lightly floured work surface and roll out to ⅛-inch thickness.

4. Use a floured 2-inch biscuit cutter or the rim of a small drinking glass to cut the dough into rounds. Roll out and cut the scraps to make additional crackers.

5. Arrange the crackers about ½ inch apart on the prepared baking sheet. Bake until the edges are lightly browned, about 12 minutes.

continues on next page

6. If you didn't use parchment paper, loosen the crackers from the baking sheet with a metal spatula as soon as they come out of the oven to keep them from crumbling. Cool on wire racks for 5 minutes. If not using right away, let crackers cool completely on wire racks before storing in a dry place in a tightly closed container where they will keep for 2 to 3 days.

# whole wheat sesame crackers

makes about 3 dozen crackers

*The whole wheat flour gives extra flavor and fiber to these tasty crackers. If you don't want to take the time to cut the dough into cracker shapes, you can simply score the rolled-out dough with a sharp knife and break them into squares after baking.*

1¼ cups whole wheat flour
½ cup all-purpose flour
¼ cup plus 2 tablespoons sesame seeds
1 teaspoon salt
⅛ teaspoon freshly ground black pepper
⅓ cup vegan margarine
⅓ cup water

1. Preheat the oven to 375°F. Lightly oil a baking sheet or line with parchment paper and set aside.

2. In a food processor, combine both of the flours, ¼ cup of the sesame seeds, salt, and pepper, pulsing to blend. Add the margarine and pulse to blend.

3. With the machine running, slowly add just enough of the water to form a dough.

4. Turn the dough out onto a lightly floured work surface and roll out until very thin (¼ inch or less).

5. Sprinkle with the remaining 2 tablespoons sesame seeds, rolling gently with the rolling pin to press the seeds into the dough.

6. Use a floured cookie cutter or pastry wheel to cut the dough into desired cracker shapes. Arrange the crackers on the prepared baking sheet and bake until crisp and golden brown, 12 to 15 minutes.

7. If you didn't use parchment paper, loosen the crackers from the baking sheet with a metal spatula as soon as they come out of the oven to keep them from crumbling. Cool on wire racks for 5 minutes. If not using right away, let crackers cool completely on wire racks before storing in a dry place in a tightly closed container, where they will keep for 2 to 3 days.

# fennel-scented flax crackers

makes about 2 dozen crackers

*Since fragrant fennel seeds are not only in the cracker dough but also sprinkled on top, these crackers have a wonderful flavor. The flax seed is a nutritional bonus. I like to cut these crackers into long rectangles and serve them with a salad containing raw fennel, to accentuate and complement the flavor even more.*

½ cup ground flax seed
¾ cup all-purpose flour
1 tablespoon fennel seeds
½ teaspoon salt
¼ teaspoon onion powder
⅛ teaspoon ground cayenne
½ cup plus 1 tablespoon water

1. Preheat the oven to 375°F. Lightly oil a baking sheet or line with parchment paper and set aside.

2. In a bowl, combine the ground flax seed, flour, about half of the fennel seeds, salt, onion powder, and cayenne. Stir in the water and mix until a dough is formed. Cover with plastic wrap and set aside to rest for 30 minutes.

3. Uncover and knead a few times to make a smooth dough, then turn out onto a floured board and roll out to about $1/8$-inch thickness.

4. Sprinkle on the remaining fennel seeds and remaining salt and press into the dough with the rolling pin.

5. Use a cookie cutter or pastry wheel to cut the dough into cracker-size shapes. Arrange the crackers on the prepared baking sheet and bake until crisp and golden, 12 to 15 minutes.

6. If you didn't use parchment paper, loosen the crackers from the baking sheet with a metal spatula as soon as they come out of the oven to keep them from crumbling. Cool on wire racks for 5 minutes. If not using right away, let crackers cool completely on wire racks before storing in a dry place in a tightly closed container, where they will keep for 2 to 3 days.

# walnut oat crackers

makes about 3 dozen crackers

*Flavorful rolled oats and crunchy walnuts ensure that these hearty yet delicate crackers will make a great snack all on their own. Pecans may be used instead of walnuts, if you prefer. For a nuttier flavor, toast the nuts before using.*

1¾ cups old-fashioned oats
⅔ cup chopped walnut pieces
¼ cup all-purpose flour
1 teaspoon baking powder
¾ teaspoon salt
Pinch freshly ground black pepper
Pinch sugar
¼ cup cold vegan margarine, cut into small pieces
¼ cup plain soy milk

1. Preheat the oven to 375°F. Lightly oil a baking sheet or line it with a sheet of parchment paper and set it aside.

2. Place the oats and walnuts in a food processor and process until finely ground. Add the flour, baking powder, salt, pepper, and sugar; pulse to combine. Add the margarine and pulse until the mixture resembles coarse crumbs. With the machine running, add enough of the soy milk until a dough forms.

3. Turn the dough out onto a lightly floured surface, roll out dough to $1/8$ inch thick.

4. Use a cookie cutter or pastry wheel to cut into 2-inch circles, squares, or other shape.

5. Arrange the crackers on the prepared baking sheet about $1/2$ inch apart and bake until lightly browned on the bottom, 12 to 15 minutes.

6. If you didn't use parchment paper, loosen the crackers from the baking sheet with a metal spatula as soon as they come out of the oven to keep them from crumbling. Cool on wire racks for 5 minutes. If not using right away, let crackers cool completely on wire racks before storing in a dry place in a tightly closed container, where they will keep for 2 to 3 days.

# DESSERTS

## COOKIES, BROWNIES, AND LITTLE BITES

chocolate chip cookies

peanut butter cookies

maple-walnut oatmeal cookies

chocolate-cranberry oatmeal cookies

almond shortbread cookies

sesame cookies

vanilla walnut cookies

pine nut cookies

chai spice cookies

molasses spice cookies

orange-scented coconut cookies

peachy thumbprint cookies

hula cookies

double chocolate brownies

chocolate coconut brownies

ginger-spice brownies

pineapple squares

better pecan bars

chocolate-almond bars

agave baklava

peanut butter and chocolate buckeyes

chocolate–peanut butter fudge

chocolate smoosh fudge

chocolate-avocado fudge

chocolate-banana fudge

chocolate-macadamia cheezcake truffles

chocolate–almond butter truffles

chocolate-covered peanut butter–granola balls

apricot-walnut balls

vegan white chocolate

## CAKES AND CHEESECAKES

vegan chocolate mousse cake

chocolate-rum coffee cake

magical mystery chocolate cake

spicy chocolate cake with dark chocolate glaze

vegan pound cake

banana-walnut cake

crazy for carrot cake

"sour cream" coffee cake

orange-coconut cake

spice cake with mango and lime

apple lover's cake

giant peanut butter–chocolate chip cookie cake

not-so-plain vanilla cheezcake

triple coconut cheezcake

chocolate swirl tofu cheezcake

pumpkin cheezcake
with cranberry drizzle

pomegranate cheezcake
with glazed pecans

lemon-lime teasecake

no-bake avocado cheezcake

three-flavor ice cream cake

hot banana ice cream cake

white cupcakes with variations

## PIES, TARTS, CRISPS, AND COBBLERS

mom's apple pie
with cranberries

pumpkin pie with a hint of rum

sweet potato pie

pecan pie

peach crumb pie

chocolate no-bake silk pie

white chocolate hazelnut pie

chocolate mint espresso pie

strawberry cloud pie

no-bake fresh fruit pie

cashew–banana cream pie

peanut butter–ice cream pie

banana mango pie

ginger-pear tart with
cranberries and walnuts

apple tart with walnut crust

two-berry cobbler

apple and pear cobbler

blueberry-peach crisp

quick apple crisp

banana-pecan strudel

pear crumble

## PUDDINGS AND PARFAITS

baked chocolate pudding

cashew chocolate pudding

chocolate-banana pudding

sunset fruit pudding

maple-baked rice pudding
with dried cranberries

coconut-pistachio rice pudding

forbidden black rice pudding

paradise pudding

banana-orzo pudding

avocado-raspberry parfaits

strawberry parfaits
with cashew crème

vegan tiramisù

indian pudding

sweet vermicelli pudding

chocolate and walnut farfalle

fresh cherry-vanilla
bread pudding

pumpkin-cranberry
bread pudding

chocolate bread pudding
with rum sauce

f = fast

## Fruit Desserts

granola-stuffed baked apples

pecan and date-stuffed
roasted pears

banana fritters with
caramel sauce

baked bananas
with a twist of lime

blushing poached pears

grilled orange and strawberry
skewers

rum-sautéed pineapple
and bananas with toasted
coconut and pecans

nellie's peachy melba

fresh fruit "sushi"

asian flavors fruit bowl

sweet polenta with grilled
pineapple and strawberry sauce

pineapple couscous timbales
with blueberry sauce

lime-macerated mangos

vegan dessert crêpes

suzette-inspired
ice cream crêpes

caramelized figs in tuiles

cherry clafoutis

pear gratin with
cranberries and pecans

strawberry kanten

suspended peach kanten

## Nice Creams, Sorbets, and Granitas

cherry vanilla nice cream

chocolate nice cream

coffee nice cream

ginger-coconut nice cream

strawberry sorbet

cranberry sorbet

mocha sorbet

orange granita

## Dessert Sauces and Frostings

chocolate sauce

fudgy chocolate sauce

caramel sauce

warm walnut sauce

blueberry sauce

pineapple-apricot sauce

summer fruit sauce

winter fruit sauce

grand marnier sauce

strawberry-mango sauce

fresh strawberry topping

vegan whipped cream

cashew crème

lemon-cashew crème

vegan chocolate ganache

"cream cheese" frosting

"buttercream" frosting

chocolate fudge frosting

chocolate peanut butter frosting

I t is fair to say that virtually all traditional cakes and cookies, and even pies, contain either eggs, butter, or milk—sometimes all three. Therefore, where you might be able to order a vegan meal at a mainstream restaurant, chances are you might have to skip dessert. Or at least wait until you get home to enjoy a homemade vegan treat.

While some people consider desserts made without eggs or dairy products unthinkable, the recipes in this chapter will prove them wrong. It's easier than you might think to make vegan versions of many desserts—all it takes is switching the animal products with plant-based ones. It's also possible to make desserts that simply highlight naturally vegan ingredients like fruit, nuts, flours, sweeteners, and spices. From puddings and pies to cheesecakes and cookies, vegan desserts are not only possible, but they're also delicious and easy to make.

Like in savory recipes, soy milk and other non-dairy milks effortlessly fill in for dairy milk and vegan margarine does an admirable job replacing butter in dessert recipes. There are a number of ways to replace eggs in desserts, depending on whether the eggs are used for leavening, moisture, or both. Egg alternatives include a commercial replacement powder or ground flax seeds, both of which are blended with water. Applesauce or pureed banana or tofu blended with a little baking powder (see page xxiii) also does the job well. (You get additional nutrients with these ingredients, too.)

For a vegan butter replacement, as of this writing you can't do better than Earth Balance brand vegan margarine. Earth Balance makes great tasting nonhydrogenated vegan margarines, shortening, and buttery spreads that are interchangeable with butter in cooking and baking. The variety I like best for baking is the Earth Balance vegan buttery sticks.

Beyond the obvious eggs, butter, milk, and honey, be aware that other ingredients used in baking can contain animal products, such as semisweet chocolate chips. Fortunately, there are a number of wonderful vegan chocolate chips available. My favorite brand is Tropical Source, but there are others. Even some mainstream chocolate companies, such as Ghirardelli, make dairy-free semisweet chocolate chips.

Sugar is a problematic ingredient for many vegans because cane sugar is sometimes filtered through a process that uses charred animal bones. For this reason, some vegans choose to eschew cane sugar in favor of beet sugar, which is not filtered with animal bones, though it is much more expensive. If you are concerned about the filtering process of your cane sugar, it's best to check with the individual company to find out what filtering methods they use. As of this writing, two companies that produce cane sugar without using bone char are Florida Crystals and Amalgamated Sugar Company. Some vegans avoid sugar for health reasons, since it is virtually devoid of nutritional value. Fortunately, there is a wide range of vegan-friendly granulated sweeteners available that can be used in place

continues on next page

# baking basics

1. **READ THE RECIPE:** Baking and dessert recipes often include special instructions such as bringing ingredients to room temperature or cooling certain ingredients before proceeding. It's important to know what to expect before diving into a recipe.

2. **MISE EN PLACE:** If gathering your ingredients ahead of time is a good idea when cooking, it's imperative when you bake. Be sure to have all your ingredients ready and measured out before proceeding with a recipe. You don't want to be up to your elbows in cookie dough when you realize you're out of vanilla extract.

3. **MEASURE AND PREHEAT:** Baking is more of a precise science than cooking. As such it requires accurate measurements and proper baking temperatures. Be sure to level ingredients in your measuring spoons and cups and preheat the oven before baking.

Speaking of ovens, if you're unsure about the accuracy of your oven temperature, consider getting an oven thermometer to verify it. Unless otherwise specified, all baking should be done on the rack in the center position of the oven for even baking.

4. **BAKING EQUIPMENT:** In addition to the usual mixing bowls, measuring cups and spoons, knifes, whisks, cutting boards, saucepans, and strainers, a kitchen equipped for baking should have a minimum of the following: 2 baking sheets, an 8-inch square baking pan, two 9-inch round cake pans, a 9-inch pie plate, a 12-cup muffin tin, a 9-inch springform pan, a 9-inch loaf pan, a wire cooling rack, a 9 × 13-inch baking pan, a rolling pin, and assorted rubber and metal spatulas.

5. **"GREASE" IS THE WORD:** When recipe instructions say to "grease" a baking sheet

of white table sugar as well as a number of liquid sweeteners that can be used instead of honey in desserts. (See page 429 for a list.)

As mentioned in the bread chapter, if you are sensitive to gluten, there are a number of flours available that may be substituted for the all-purpose or whole wheat flour in recipes. And of course, those who avoid soy can use any of the other dairy-free milks in recipes calling for soy milk.

Vegan desserts are also a great way to bridge the gap with any non-vegans in your family. While they might not jump at the chance to sample a bowl of tofu stew, I have yet to see anyone turn down a second piece of my vegan cheesecake (which also contains tofu). In fact, it has been my experience that making a chocolate and tofu dessert is a great way to introduce tofu to anyone for the first time. These desserts will appeal to people watching their or pan, you can use vegan margarine to lightly coat the pan. This can be preferable in recipes where the somewhat "buttery" flavor of margarine will be complementary. If you prefer, you can lightly oil a pan with vegetable oil or spray the surface with non-stick cooking spray. In the case of baking sheets, you also have the option of using parchment paper or a silicone baking mat instead of oil, margarine, or cooking spray. In the case of certain cookie recipes that call for an "ungreased" baking sheet, you can still line the baking sheets with parchment paper or a silicone mat for easy clean up. So when a recipe tells you to "grease" or "lightly oil" a pan, you can decide which method is right for you.

6. DONENESS TEST: Cakes and cupcakes (as well as quick breads and muffins) can be tested for doneness by inserting a toothpick in the center, which should come out clean or with just a few crumbs on it.

7. STORING: Everyone loves fresh baked goods and in many homes they disappear as quickly as they are made. However, when it comes to storage, not all desserts are created equal. Naturally, you will want to keep refrigerated anything that is serve chilled, such as cheesecakes and puddings. Cookies can generally be cooled completely on wire racks and then stored at room temperature in an airtight container.

8. PACKING: Homemade cookies make great gifts. Arrange them in cookie tins or other airtight containers. For best results, select sturdy cookies such as chocolate chip or spice cookies, rather than something messy, such as pineapple squares, or fragile, such as tuiles. If packing cookies in layers or rows, separate them with waxed paper.

cholesterol intake as well as those allergic to dairy products or eggs.

From wholesome and comforting Blueberry-Peach Crisp (page 471) and Maple-Walnut Oatmeal Cookies (page 430) to sophisticated Chocolate No-Bake Silk Pie (page 464) and Pomegranate Cheezcake with Glazed Walnuts (page 455), this collection of luscious desserts are sure to satisfy even the sweetest tooth in the house.

# Cookies, Brownies, and Little Bites

## chocolate chip cookies 🅕

makes about 2 dozen cookies

*The classic chocolate chip cookie is hard to resist. This one has no added embellishments—just the traditional drop cookie chock full of its eponymous bits of chocolate and, of course, made with vegan ingredients.*

1 cup vegan margarine, softened

¾ cup light brown sugar

2 tablespoons pure maple syrup

1 teaspoon pure vanilla extract

2 cups all-purpose flour

1 teaspoon baking soda

½ teaspoon baking powder

½ teaspoon salt

1 cup semisweet vegan chocolate chips

1. Preheat the oven to 350°F.

2. In a large bowl, cream together the margarine and sugar until light and fluffy. Stir in the maple syrup and vanilla and mix until smooth.

3. In a separate large bowl, combine the flour, baking soda, baking powder, and salt. Add the dry ingredients to the wet ingredients, stirring well to combine. Fold in the chocolate chips.

4. Drop the dough by the tablespoonful onto ungreased baking sheets. Bake until slightly browned around the edges, about 15 minutes. Cool for a few minutes before transferring to a wire rack to cool completely, about 20 minutes. When completely cool, store in an airtight container.

## sweet things

The use of sweeteners is such a personal issue to many people for various reasons. In the recipes in this book that require a dry sweetener, I use the term "sugar" unless a specific flavor or texture is required, then I will specify, for example, "light brown sugar" or "confectioners' sugar." If you choose not to use white table sugar, a list of alternative dry sweeteners is on the right.

Honey is not vegan, so it is not used in this book. Liquid vegan sweeteners include agave nectar, maple syrup, molasses, and brown rice syrup. Most of the recipes in this book requiring a liquid sweetener call for agave nectar or maple syrup. A list of liquid sweeteners is also on the opposite page.

NOTE: Dry and liquid sweeteners are not interchangeable in recipes.

# sweeteners

## LIQUID SWEETENERS

**agave nectar**—a naturally sweet, golden syrup, it is the nectar of the agave plant and an ideal substitute for honey.

**maple syrup**—the boiled sap of maple trees, maple syrup is a good substitute for honey, although it has a distinct maple flavor. Buy "pure maple syrup," not pancake syrup, which is mostly colored corn syrup.

**molasses**—this dark, thick liquid remains after the sugar-making process and is rich in iron and calcium. The bold assertive flavor and dark color of molasses makes it best for desserts where those qualities are a plus, such as spice cookies.

**brown rice syrup**—a mild-tasting, natural liquid sweetener made from rice, it can be used in place of honey, although it is a bit less sweet and has a deep wholesome flavor.

## DRY SWEETENERS

**cane sugar**—also known as "white granulated sugar," it is less expensive than beet sugar and therefore more widely available. Technically vegan, but if the matter of the filtration method is an issue for you, there are some brands available that do not filter with bone char. If unsure about a particular brand, contact the company.

**unbleached or natural cane sugar**—made from dehydrated sugarcane juice that is milled into granulated powder. It is interchangeable with granulated white sugar, although it is slightly darker in color and has a slight molasses flavor, so only use it in recipes where this is a welcome addition.

**beet sugar**—accounts for about half of the white granulated sugar produced in the United States. Virtually the same in taste and appearance as white cane sugar with the only difference being that beet sugar is never filtered through bone char. More expensive than white cane sugar, it is available in natural food stores and well-stocked supermarkets.

**brown sugar**—cane or beet sugar that contains some molasses. Used in cooking for its distinctive flavor. Unrefined cane sugar products such as Sucanat (sugar cane natural) also contain the distinctive molasses color and flavor and can be used interchangeable with brown sugar, but only if you finely grind it first in a spice grinder or high-speed blender so it will dissolve in the same way.

**confectioners' sugar**—also called "powdered sugar" or "10x sugar," it is finely ground white sugar combined with cornstarch and is mainly used in dessert recipes to make frostings and candies. There are vegan brands available (made with sugar that is not filtered through bone char). If you prefer to make your own, combine 1 cup of granulated sugar with 1 tablespoon of cornstarch in a high-speed blender and process for a minute or two until finely ground.

# peanut butter cookies

makes about 3 dozen cookies

*Peanut butter lovers will enjoy the rich pure flavor of peanuts in these cookies. For variety, you can substitute another nut butter, such as almond or cashew butter, or add $\frac{1}{2}$ cup of semisweet chocolate chips to the batter.*

¾ cup creamy peanut butter

½ cup vegan margarine

½ cup sugar

⅓ cup maple syrup

3 tablespoons water

1 teaspoon pure vanilla extract

2½ cups all-purpose flour

1 teaspoon baking powder

¼ teaspoon salt

1. In a large bowl, combine the peanut butter, margarine, sugar, maple syrup, water, and vanilla and mix until well blended. Add the flour, baking powder, and salt and stir well to form a smooth dough. Cover and chill until firm, about 1 hour.

2. Preheat the oven to 350°F. Roll out the dough on a lightly floured work surface to a ¼ inch thickness. Cut into shapes with cookie cutters or the rim of a small drinking glass. Use a metal spatula to transfer the cookies to an ungreased baking sheet.

3. Bake until lightly browned at the edges, 8 to 10 minutes. Cool the cookies slightly before transferring to a wire rack to cool completely. Store in an airtight container.

# maple-walnut oatmeal cookies

makes about 2 dozen cookies

*These old-fashioned favorites are loaded with the wholesome goodness of old-fashioned oats, walnuts, and maple syrup. Dried cranberries would make a good addition for their color, flavor, and nutrients.*

1½ cups all-purpose flour

1 teaspoon baking powder

⅛ teaspoon salt

1 teaspoon ground cinnamon

¼ teaspoon ground nutmeg

1½ cups old-fashioned oats

1 cup chopped walnuts

½ cup vegan margarine, melted

½ cup pure maple syrup

¼ cup sugar

2 teaspoons pure vanilla extract

1. Preheat the oven to 375°F. In a large bowl, sift together the flour, baking powder, salt, cinnamon, and nutmeg. Stir in the oats and walnuts.

2. In a medium bowl, combine the margarine, maple syrup, sugar, and vanilla and mix well. Add the wet ingredients to the dry ingredients, stirring to mix well.

3. Drop the cookie dough by the tablespoonful onto an ungreased baking sheet and press down slightly with a fork. Bake until browned, 10 to 12 minutes. Cool the cookies slightly before transferring to a wire rack to cool completely. Store in an airtight container.

# chocolate-cranberry oatmeal cookies 𝕗

makes about 2 dozen cookies

*Here's a cookie designed to please everyone in the house. A tasty oatmeal cookie studded with chocolate chips and sweetened cranberries covers most bases of a cookie-loving household.*

½ cup vegan margarine

1 cup sugar

¼ cup apple juice

1 cup all-purpose flour

1 teaspoon baking powder

½ teaspoon salt

1 teaspoon pure vanilla extract

1 cup old-fashioned oats

½ cup vegan semisweet chocolate chips

½ cup sweetened dried cranberries

1. Preheat the oven to 375°F. In a large bowl, cream together the margarine and the sugar until light and fluffy. Blend in the juice.

2. Add the flour, baking powder, salt, and vanilla, blending well. Stir in the oats, chocolate chips, and cranberries and mix well.

3. Drop the dough from a teaspoon onto an ungreased baking sheet. Bake until nicely browned, about 15 minutes. Cool the cookies slightly before transferring to a wire rack to cool completely. Store in an airtight container.

# almond shortbread cookies 𝕗

makes about 2 dozen cookies

*These mellow cookies pack a lot of delicate almond flavor and are, to me, the quintessential tea cookie. If you want them a little sweeter, sift with confectioners' sugar after the cookies have cooled for several minutes.*

1 cup slivered almonds

¾ cup vegan margarine

½ cup sugar

1 teaspoon pure vanilla extract

½ teaspoon salt

1½ cups all-purpose flour

1. Preheat the oven to 350°F. Grind the almonds in a food processor. Add the margarine, sugar, vanilla, and salt and process until well blended. Add the flour, $1/2$ cup at a time, pulsing to combine after each addition.

2. Press the mixture into a dough ball. Pinch off pieces about 1 inch in diameter and roll into balls. Flatten the balls and arrange them on an ungreased baking sheet, about 1 inch apart. Bake until golden, about 12 minutes. Cool the cookies slightly before transferring to a wire rack to cool completely. Store in an airtight container.

# sesame cookies

makes 3 dozen cookies

*I like to serve these thin not-too-sweet cookies to accompany a dish of vegan ice cream after a spicy Asian meal.*

¾ cup vegan margarine, softened

½ cup sugar

1 teaspoon pure vanilla extract

2 tablespoons pure maple syrup

¼ teaspoon salt

2 cups all-purpose flour

¾ cup sesame seeds, lightly toasted

Confectioners' sugar

1. In a large bowl, cream together the margarine and sugar until light and fluffy. Blend in the vanilla, maple syrup, and salt. Stir in the flour and sesame seeds and mix well.

2. Roll the dough into a cylinder about 2 inches in diameter. Wrap it in plastic wrap and refrigerate for 1 hour or longer. Preheat the oven to 325°F.

3. Slice the cookie dough into ⅛-inch-thick rounds and arrange on an ungreased baking sheet about 2 inches apart. Bake until light brown, about 12 minutes. Cool slightly and roll the warm cookies in confectioners' sugar. When completely cool, store in an airtight container.

# vanilla walnut cookies

makes about 2 dozen cookies

*I like to decorate these cookies by pressing a walnut half into the center of each cookie before baking.*

½ cup vegan margarine

¾ cup sugar

1½ teaspoons pure vanilla extract

2 tablespoons water

2 cups all-purpose flour

½ cup ground toasted walnuts

2 teaspoons baking powder

½ teaspoon salt

1. In a large bowl, beat together the margarine, sugar, vanilla, and water until well blended. Add the flour, walnuts, baking powder, and salt and stir well to form a smooth dough. Preheat the oven to 350°F.

2. Pinch off small pieces of dough and roll them between your hands into balls. Place the dough balls onto an ungreased baking sheet and press down to flatten to about ¼ inch thick.

3. Bake until lightly browned at the edges, about 15 minutes. Cool for 10 minutes on the baking sheet before removing to a wire rack to cool completely. Store in an airtight container.

# pine nut cookies

makes about 3 dozen cookies

*These crunchy cookies are light and not-too-sweet—perfect with tea or coffee or to serve alongside a dish of vegan ice cream for dessert.*

¾ cup pine nuts

1 cup vegan margarine, softened

¾ cup sugar

1 teaspoon pure vanilla extract

2 cups all-purpose flour

½ teaspoon salt

¼ teaspoon baking powder

1. Preheat the oven to 350°F. Finely grind ½ cup of the pine nuts and set aside.

2. In a large bowl, cream together the margarine and sugar until light and fluffy. Beat in the vanilla and set aside.

3. In a medium bowl, stir together the flour, salt, and baking powder. Add the flour mixture to the sugar-margarine mixture. Add the ground pine nuts to the dough, mixing well.

4. Drop the dough, 1 teaspoonful at a time, 2 inches apart, onto an ungreased baking sheet, pressing a few of the remaining ¼ cup pine nuts into the top of each cookie.

5. Bake until a light golden brown, 12 to 15 minutes. Cool on the baking sheet for 5 minutes before carefully transferring to a wire rack to cool completely. Store in an airtight container.

## chai spice cookies

makes about 2 dozen cookies

*The fragrant spices used to make the Indian spiced tea known as chai are also in these aromatic spice cookies. If you enjoy the flavor of chai, then this cookie is your cup of tea.*

2 cups all-purpose flour

2 teaspoons baking powder

2 teaspoons ground cinnamon

1½ teaspoons ground cardamom

1 teaspoon ground ginger

1 teaspoon ground cloves

1 teaspoon ground fennel seed

½ teaspoon salt

¾ cup vegan margarine

¾ cup sugar

2 tablespoons plain or vanilla soy milk

2 tablespoons agave nectar

2 teaspoons pure vanilla extract

1. Preheat the oven to 350°F.

2. In a medium bowl, combine the flour, baking powder, cinnamon, cardamom, ginger, cloves, fennel seed, and salt. Mix to combine well.

3. In a large bowl, beat together the margarine, sugar, soy milk, agave nectar, and vanilla until well blended. Add the flour mixture, stirring well to form a smooth, stiff dough.

4. Pinch off small pieces of dough and roll them between your hands into balls. Place the dough balls onto an ungreased baking sheet and use a metal spatula or a fork to flatten the cookies to about ¼ inch thick.

5. Bake until lightly browned at the edges, about 15 minutes. Cool on the baking sheet for 5 minutes before removing to a wire rack to cool completely. Store in an airtight container.

## molasses spice cookies

makes about 3 dozen cookies

*These flavorful cookies are wonderful with a cup of hot tea or coffee on a rainy afternoon.*

¼ cup vegan margarine

¾ cup sugar

½ cup dark molasses

2 tablespoons water, plus more if needed

3 cups all-purpose flour

1 teaspoon baking soda

2 teaspoons ground ginger

1 teaspoon ground cinnamon

½ teaspoon ground allspice

½ teaspoon salt

1. In a large bowl, cream together the margarine with the sugar until light and fluffy. Mix in the molasses and water. Set aside.

2. In a medium bowl, combine the flour, baking soda, ginger, cinnamon, allspice, and salt. Gradually add the dry ingredients to the wet ingredients, adding a small amount of additional water if needed to form a stiff dough.

continues on next page

3. On a lightly floured work surface, roll the dough into a log about 2 inches in diameter. Wrap in plastic wrap and chill the dough for 1 hour or longer.

4. Preheat the oven to 350°F. Cut the dough into thin slices about ¼ inch thick and arrange on an ungreased baking sheet. Bake until the edges are browned, about 8 minutes. Cool for 5 minutes on the baking sheet before removing to a wire rack to cool completely. Store in an airtight container.

# orange-scented coconut cookies

makes about 3 dozen cookies

*These gluten-free cookies combine the rich taste of pecans and coconut with the natural sweetness of dates and maple syrup, accented by fresh orange juice and warming spices. This recipe was shared with me by Christine Waltermyer of the Natural Kitchen Cooking School.*

1 cup chopped toasted pecans

1 cup shredded unsweetened coconut

1 cup brown rice flour

½ teaspoon ground cinnamon

⅛ teaspoon ground nutmeg

¼ teaspoon salt

½ cup dates, pitted and chopped

2 tablespoons sweetened dried cranberries

2 teaspoons fresh orange zest

½ cup fresh orange juice

¼ cup pure maple syrup

¼ cup coconut oil

1 cup orange marmalade

1. Preheat the oven to 350° F. Lightly oil a baking sheet and set aside. In a large bowl, combine the pecans, coconut, rice flour, cinnamon, nutmeg, and salt. Set aside.

2. In a blender or food processor, combine the dates, cranberries, orange zest, orange juice, maple syrup, and coconut oil. Blend until smooth.

3. Mix the wet into the dry ingredients until well blended to form a stiff dough.

4. With wet hands, shape the dough into small balls and place them on the prepared baking sheet. Flatten the cookies and make an indentation in the center with your thumb. Fill centers of cookies with a small spoonful of marmalade.

5. Bake the cookies until golden brown, about 10 minutes. Cool for 5 minutes on the baking sheet, then remove the cookies to a wire rack to cool completely. Store in an airtight container.

# peachy thumbprint cookies 🅕

makes about 2 dozen cookies

*I'm partial to the luscious flavor of peach in these cookies, but you can use whatever jam or fruit spread you wish—strawberry and blueberry are great. In fact, if you have a few different flavors open in the refrigerator, you could use some of each.*

1½ cups all-purpose flour
1 teaspoon baking powder
½ teaspoon ground cinnamon
¼ teaspoon ground allspice
¼ teaspoon salt
2 tablespoons vegan margarine, softened
¼ cup applesauce
½ teaspoon pure vanilla extract
½ cup confectioners' sugar, plus additional
    for dusting cookies
½ cup peach fruit spread or jam

1. Preheat the oven to 400°F. In a large bowl, combine the flour, baking powder, cinnamon, allspice, and salt.

2. In a medium bowl, whisk together the margarine, applesauce, and vanilla, then add the sugar and mix well.

3. Add the wet ingredients to the dry ingredients and mix to form a smooth stiff dough.

4. With lightly floured hands, roll the dough into 1½-inch balls and place them on an ungreased baking sheet about 2 inches apart.

5. Press your thumb into the center of each dough ball to make an indentation and fill it with ½ teaspoon of the peach fruit spread. Bake until golden, 12 to 15 minutes.

6. Remove from oven and cool on the baking sheet for 10 minutes, then remove to a wire rack and dust with confectioners' sugar. When completely cool, store in an airtight container.

# hula cookies

makes about 3 dozen cookies

*Recipe tester Melissa Ling shared this recipe with me. Though you could use any flavor jam or jelly, making them with pineapple, mango, or passionfruit gives the cookies a tropical feel, especially, Melissa says, if you eat them while swaying your hips.*

2½ cups all-purpose flour
½ teaspoon baking powder
1 cup vegan margarine
1 cup sugar
1½ teaspoons egg replacer beaten into
    2 tablespoons water (page xxiii)
2 teaspoons pure vanilla extract
Tropical fruit jam or jelly, such as mango,
    passionfruit, or pineapple

1. Preheat the oven to 300°F. In a medium bowl, combine the flour and baking powder and mix well. Set aside.

2. In a large bowl, beat together the margarine and sugar with an electric mixer until light and fluffy. Add the egg replacer and vanilla and beat on medium until smooth. Add the dry ingredients to the wet ingredients and beat on low until thoroughly combined. The dough should be firm.

3. Scoop the dough, 1 tablespoon at a time, and roll into balls. Place the dough balls on ungreased baking sheets, about 1 inch apart.

4. Use a thumb or the back end of a ¼ teaspoon measuring spoon to make an indentation in the center of each dough ball. Place ¼ teaspoon of jam in each indentation. Bake until golden brown, 22 to 24 minutes. Cool on the baking sheet for 5 minutes before removing to a wire rack to cool completely. Store in an airtight container.

# double chocolate brownies

makes 12 brownies

*These chocolaty confections are a brownie lover's dream—a dense fudgy texture and rich intensely chocolate flavor. I know one chocoholic who actually topped one of these beauties with a scoop of chocolate vegan ice cream.*

1½ cups all-purpose flour

¾ cup unsweetened cocoa powder

1 teaspoon baking powder

½ teaspoon salt

1¼ cups sugar

½ cup vegan margarine

¼ cup water

2 teaspoons pure vanilla extract

⅔ cup vegan semi-sweet chocolate chips

1. Preheat the oven to 350°F. Lightly oil an 8-inch square baking pan and set aside. In a large bowl, combine the flour, cocoa, baking powder, and salt. Set aside.

2. In a medium bowl, cream together the sugar and margarine until light and fluffy. Stir in the water and vanilla and blend until smooth. Add the wet ingredients to the dry ingredients, stirring to blend. Fold in the chocolate chips.

3. Scrape the batter into the prepared baking pan and bake until the center is set and a toothpick inserted in the center comes out clean, about 40 minutes. Let the brownies cool 30 minutes before serving. Store in an airtight container.

# chocolate coconut brownies

makes 12 brownies

*My husband, Jon, loves coconut almost as much as he loves brownies. Now he can enjoy them both at the same time. If you're not a fan of coconut, simply use another dairy-free milk instead of the coconut milk and omit the coconut extract and shredded coconut.*

1 cup all-purpose flour

½ cup unsweetened cocoa powder

1 teaspoon baking powder

½ teaspoon salt

1 cup sugar

½ cup canola oil

¾ cup unsweetened coconut milk

1 teaspoon pure vanilla extract

1 teaspoon coconut extract

½ cup vegan semisweet chocolate chips

½ cup sweetened shredded coconut

1. Preheat the oven to 350°F. Grease an 8-inch square baking pan and set aside. In a large bowl, combine the flour, cocoa, baking powder, and salt. Set aside.

2. In a medium bowl, mix together the sugar and oil until blended. Stir in the coconut milk and the extracts and blend until smooth. Add the wet ingredients to the dry ingredients, stirring to blend. Fold in the chocolate chips and coconut.

3. Scrape the batter into the prepared baking pan and bake until the center is set and a toothpick inserted in the center comes out clean, 35 to 40 minutes. Let the brownies cool 30 minutes before serving. Store in an airtight container.

# ginger-spice brownies

makes 12 brownies

*Warm spices combine with chocolate and walnuts for a luxuriously different batch of brownies. For a sophisticated dessert, serve these moist, spicy, and not-too-sweet brownies with poached fruit, like pears, or a scoop of vanilla vegan ice cream.*

1¾ cups all-purpose flour

1 teaspoon baking powder

1 teaspoon baking soda

½ teaspoon salt

1 tablespoon ground ginger

½ teaspoon ground cinnamon

½ teaspoon ground allspice

3 tablespoons unsweetened cocoa powder

½ cup vegan semisweet chocolate chips

½ cup chopped walnuts

¼ cup canola oil

½ cup dark molasses

½ cup water

⅓ cup sugar

2 teaspoons grated fresh ginger

1. Preheat the oven to 350°F. Grease an 8-inch square baking pan and set aside. In a large bowl, combine the flour, baking powder, baking soda, salt, ground ginger, cinnamon, allspice, and cocoa. Stir in the chocolate chips and walnuts and set aside.

2. In medium bowl, combine the oil, molasses, water, sugar, and fresh ginger and mix well. Pour the wet ingredients into the dry ingredients and mix well.

3. Scrape the dough into the prepared baking pan. The dough will be sticky, so wet your hands to press it evenly into the pan. Bake until a toothpick inserted in the center comes out clean, 30 to 35 minutes. Cool on a wire rack 30 minutes before cutting. Store in an airtight container.

# pineapple squares

makes 9 squares

*These moist, fruity squares taste just as I remember them from my childhood. They were one of several pickup desserts that my mother made during holidays. All I needed to do to veganize my mother's original recipe was to swap out the butter for margarine and use a nondairy milk.*

2 cups canned crushed pineapple, drained

½ cup plus 2 tablespoons sugar

2 tablespoons cornstarch

1 tablespoon fresh lemon juice

⅓ cup vegan margarine

1½ cups all-purpose flour

1 teaspoon baking powder

½ teaspoon salt

⅓ cup plain or vanilla soy milk

1 teaspoon pure vanilla extract

½ cup flaked sweetened coconut

1. Preheat the oven to 350°F. Grease an 8-inch square baking pan. In a large saucepan, combine the pineapple, 2 tablespoons of the sugar, cornstarch, and lemon juice. Cook over medium heat, stirring until slightly thickened, about 2 minutes. Set aside.

2. In a large bowl, cream together the margarine and the remaining ½ cup of sugar until light and fluffy. Add the flour, baking powder, and salt. Stir in the soy milk and vanilla and mix until crumbly.

*continues on next page*

3. Press about two-thirds of the dough mixture into the prepared baking pan. Mix the coconut into the remaining dough mixture and set aside.

4. Spread the pineapple mixture evenly over the bottom crust in the baking dish. Sprinkle the remaining dough mixture evenly on top of the filling and press gently.

5. Bake until the top is golden brown, about 30 minutes. Cool 30 minutes before cutting. Store in an airtight container.

# better pecan bars

makes 12 bars

*The reasons these pecan bars are "better" is because they use no butter—and also because of the swirl of chocolate that makes them even more scrumptious.*

1 cup all-purpose flour
1 cup light brown sugar, divided
½ cup plus ¼ cup vegan margarine, softened
1 cup pecan pieces
¼ cup pure maple syrup
⅓ cup vegan semisweet chocolate chips

1. Preheat the oven to 350°F. Lightly oil an 8-inch square baking pan and set aside. In a food processor, combine the flour, ½ cup of the sugar, and ½ cup of the margarine. Process to mix well.

2. Transfer the mixture to the prepared baking pan and press it firmly into the bottom. Bake for 12 minutes. Remove from the oven and set aside.

3. In a saucepan, combine the remaining ½ cup of sugar and the remaining ¼ cup margarine. Cook over medium heat, stirring constantly, until mixture boils. Add the pecans and maple syrup and boil for about 30 seconds, stirring constantly. Pour the mixture evenly over the crust.

4. Bake until the caramel layer is bubbly and the crust is lightly browned, about 7 minutes. Remove from oven and sprinkle with chocolate chips. Allow chips to melt slightly then drag a fork through them to swirl into the top. Cool slightly, then refrigerate to set the topping before cutting into bars. Store in an airtight container.

# chocolate-almond bars

makes 12 bars

*These rich and delicious bar cookies are easy to make and guaranteed to satisfy the sweet tooth in your house. Peanut butter and peanuts may be used to replace the almonds and almond butter, if you prefer.*

⅔ cup vegan margarine, melted
½ cup almond butter
1 teaspoon pure vanilla extract
½ teaspoon salt
1 cup sugar
2 cups all-purpose flour
1 cup vegan semisweet chocolate chips
¾ cup slivered almonds

1. Preheat the oven to 375°F. Lightly grease an 8-inch square baking pan and set aside. In a large bowl, combine the margarine, almond butter, vanilla, and salt. Add the sugar and stir until well blended. Add the flour and stir until well blended.

2. Fold in the chocolate chips and half of the almonds. Press the dough into the prepared pan. Sprinkle the remaining almonds over the top and press them into the dough.

3. Bake until browned, 25 to 30 minutes. Cool completely before cutting into bars. Store in an airtight container.

# agave baklava

makes 36 pieces

*Vegans who love baklava can rejoice—they can now enjoy their favorite phyllo treat thanks to this vegan version that replaces the butter and honey with margarine and agave nectar. Frozen phyllo dough needs to thaw in the refrigerator (not at room temperature) for at least 6 hours. If you thaw it at room temperature, the phyllo sheets will stick together. Cutting the phyllo dough into half sheets makes it easier to work with.*

2 cups finely ground walnuts
1 teaspoon ground cinnamon
1 cup sugar
1 (16-ounce) package phyllo dough
1 cup vegan margarine, melted
½ cup water
½ cup agave nectar
2 teaspoons fresh lemon juice
1 teaspoon pure vanilla extract

1. Preheat the oven to 350°F. Grease a 9 × 13-inch baking pan and set aside. In a medium bowl, combine the nuts, cinnamon, and ¼ cup of the sugar and toss to combine. Set aside.

2. Unroll the phyllo dough onto a work surface and cut the dough in half so the sheets fit in the baking pan. Cover the unused phyllo with a damp cloth to keep it from drying out. Take half the phyllo sheets and place 1 phyllo sheet at a time into the prepared pan, brushing with melted margarine before adding the next.

3. Sprinkle the nut mixture over the phyllo. Repeat layering process with the remaining phyllo sheets and melted margarine. Brush the top sheet with margarine.

4. Cut the pastry into 2-inch diamonds with a sharp knife. To do this, first make 3 evenly spaced cuts through the length of the dough, cutting through the layers to the bottom of the dish, resulting in 4 long rows. Then make 9 diagonal cuts through the shorter width of the dough. You should end up with 36 pieces of baklava.

5. Bake until crisp and golden brown, about 45 minutes.

6. While the baklava is baking, combine the remaining ¾ cup sugar and water in a small saucepan over medium heat and bring to a boil. Reduce the heat to low and stir in the agave nectar, lemon juice, and vanilla. Simmer until syrupy, about 20 minutes.

7. Remove the baklava from the oven and spoon the syrup over it. Let cool completely, about 1 hour, before serving. Store in an airtight container.

# peanut butter and chocolate buckeyes

makes about 2 dozen pieces

*Named for their resemblance to the nut of the buckeye tree (a brown orb with a beige dot), these tasty candies are easy to make and a staple for peanut butter and chocolate lovers everywhere.*

¼ cup vegan margarine, room temperature

1¼ cups confectioners' sugar

1 cup creamy peanut butter

1 teaspoon pure vanilla extract

8 ounces vegan semisweet chocolate chips

1. Lightly grease a baking sheet and set aside. In a large bowl, combine the margarine, sugar, peanut butter, and vanilla and cream together until well mixed.

2. Use your hands to roll the dough into small balls. Insert a toothpick into the top of each ball and place them on the baking sheet. Put them in the freezer to firm up.

3. Melt the chocolate chips in a double boiler or microwave.* Remove the peanut butter balls from the freezer and dip them into the melted chocolate, leaving the top circle of each ball uncoated.

4. Place the coated balls back on the baking sheet and refrigerate just long enough so they begin to firm up. Remove the toothpicks and smooth the tops to cover the holes left by the toothpicks. Return to the refrigerator to continue firming up, about 1 hour. Store in an airtight container.

*The microwave provides a quick and easy way to melt chocolate. Simply place the chocolate in a microwave-safe bowl and put it in the microwave for 15 seconds. Remove the bowl from the microwave and stir the chocolate. Repeat until it is melted.*

# chocolate–peanut butter fudge

makes about 36 pieces

*This decadent fudge tastes like homemade peanut butter cups, but without all the work. The hardest part is waiting for it to firm up so you can devour it.*

1 cup peanut butter, crunchy or smooth

1 cup vegan semisweet chocolate chips

3½ cups confectioners' sugar

1 teaspoon pure vanilla extract

1. Line an 8-inch square baking pan with enough waxed paper or foil so that the ends hang over the edge of the pan. (This will help you get the fudge out of the pan later.) Set aside. Place the peanut butter in a food processor and blend until smooth.

2. Melt the chocolate chips in a double boiler or microwave. In a large bowl, combine the confectioners' sugar, vanilla, peanut butter, and melted chocolate and blend until smooth.

3. Scrape the mixture into the prepared pan. Smooth the top of the fudge and refrigerate until firm and chilled, at least 2 hours.

4. Once chilled, grip the waxed paper edges, lift the fudge from the pan, and transfer it to a cutting board. Remove and discard the waxed paper. Cut the fudge into 36 pieces and serve. Cover and refrigerate any leftovers.

# chocolate smoosh fudge

makes about 16 pieces

*This super-easy chocolate confection reminds me of fudge on steroids. It was adapted from a recipe shared with me by Laura Yanne, who gave it its name because it gets smooshed into the pan. If you prefer not to add the splash of brandy or rum, use cranberry juice instead— the added liquid provides a smoother consistency, livelier flavor, and fudgier texture. For a variation, try making it with different nuts or dried fruit: almonds or pecans instead of walnuts and raisins or dried cherries instead of cranberries.*

1 (12-ounce) bag vegan semisweet chocolate chips

¾ cup shredded sweetened coconut

¾ cup chopped walnuts

½ cup sweetened dried cranberries

2 tablespoons brandy, rum, or cranberry juice

1. Line an 8-inch square baking pan with enough waxed paper or foil so that the ends hang over the edge of the pan. (This will help you get the fudge out of the pan later.) Set aside. In a medium saucepan, slowly melt the chocolate chips over low heat. Stir in the coconut, walnuts, and cranberries. Stir in the brandy, blending until smooth.

2. Scrape the mixture into the prepared pan. Press (smoosh) the mixture evenly in the pan and refrigerate until firm and chilled, at least 2 hours.

3. Once chilled, grip the waxed paper, lift the fudge from the pan, and transfer it to a cutting board. Remove and discard the waxed paper. Cut it into 2-inch pieces and serve. Cover and refrigerate any leftovers.

# chocolate-avocado fudge

makes about 36 pieces

*Making fudge with an avocado may sound unusual, but the avocado's creamy, buttery texture and mellow flavor are an asset to this rich and flavorful fudge. Most fun of all, no one will guess the "secret" ingredient— or that it is dairy-free.*

1½ cups vegan semisweet chocolate chips

2 tablespoons vegan margarine

¼ cup unsweetened cocoa powder

1 ripe Hass avocado, pitted and peeled

1 teaspoon pure vanilla extract

3 cups confectioners' sugar

½ cup chopped walnuts

1. Line an 8-inch square baking pan with enough waxed paper or foil so that the ends hang over the edge of the pan. (This will help you get the fudge out of the pan later.) In a medium saucepan, combine the chocolate chips and margarine and melt over low heat. Stir in the cocoa and set aside.

2. In a blender or food processor, puree the avocado. Add the melted chocolate mixture and process until smooth. Add the vanilla and about half of the sugar and process until incorporated. Add the remaining sugar, a little at a time, to form a stiff dough.

3. Fold in the walnuts, then smooth the mixture evenly in the prepared pan. Refrigerate until firm, at least 3 hours.

4. Once chilled, grip the waxed paper, lift the fudge from the pan, and transfer it to a cutting board. Remove and discard the waxed paper. Cut the fudge into small pieces, arrange, and serve. Cover and refrigerate any leftovers.

# chocolate-banana fudge

*If you like bananas dipped in chocolate, you'll love this fudge. Like most fudge, it's easy to make and extremely rich and it has that added flavor layer of banana to make it special.*

1 ripe banana
¾ cup vegan semisweet chocolate chips
4 cups confectioners' sugar
1 teaspoon pure vanilla extract

1. Line an 8-inch square baking pan with enough waxed paper or aluminum foil so that the ends hang over the edge of the pan. (This will help you get the fudge out of the pan later.) Set aside. Place the banana in a food processor and blend until smooth.

2. Melt the chocolate chips in a double boiler or microwave, then add to the pureed banana along with the sugar and vanilla and process until smooth.

3. Scrape the mixture into the prepared pan. Smooth the top and refrigerate until firm, at least 2 hours.

4. Once chilled, grip the waxed paper, lift the fudge from the pan, and transfer it to a cutting board. Remove and discard the waxed paper. Cut the fudge into small pieces and serve. Cover and refrigerate any leftovers.

# chocolate-macadamia cheezcake truffles

*Tiny orbs dense with chocolate, dusted in cocoa, nuts, or other finery, and often seated in gold foil cups, truffles are like the sophisticated and prosperous cousins of fudge. These particular truffles provide the added pleasure of cheesecake.*

2 cups vegan semisweet chocolate chips
1 (8-ounce) container vegan cream cheese
2 cups confectioners' sugar
2 tablespoons pure vanilla extract
1 cup ground macadamia nuts

1. Melt the chocolate chips in a double boiler or microwave.

2. In a food processor, combine the cream cheese, sugar, and vanilla and process until well mixed. Add the melted chocolate chips and blend until well mixed. Transfer the mixture to a bowl and refrigerate until chilled, at least 2 hours.

3. Roll the chilled the mixture into 1-inch balls and place them on an ungreased baking sheet.

4. Place the ground macadamia nuts in a shallow bowl and roll the chilled balls in them, turning to coat. Transfer the truffles to a serving platter, refrigerate for 30 minutes, and serve. Cover and refrigerate any leftovers.

# chocolate–almond butter truffles

makes about 24 truffles

*The mellow buttery flavor of almonds merges with rich chocolate for a sublime treat. Serve with coffee after a special meal or to make an everyday meal special.*

1 cup vegan semisweet chocolate chips

½ cup almond butter

2 tablespoons plain or vanilla soy milk

1 tablespoon pure vanilla extract

1 cup confectioners' sugar

2 tablespoons unsweetened cocoa powder

½ cup finely chopped toasted almonds

1. Melt the chocolate in a double boiler or microwave.

2. In a food processor, combine the almond butter, soy milk, and vanilla and blend until smooth. Add the sugar, cocoa, and the melted chocolate and blend until smooth and creamy.

3. Transfer the mixture to a bowl and refrigerate until chilled, at least 45 minutes.

4. Roll the chilled mixture into 1-inch balls and place them on an ungreased baking sheet.

5. Place the ground almonds in a shallow bowl and roll the balls in them, turning to coat. Place the truffles on a serving platter, refrigerate for 30 minutes, and serve.

# chocolate-covered peanut butter–granola balls

makes about 3 dozen pieces

*If your trail mix decided it wanted to become truffles, this would be the result. These chewy and tasty little balls pack astounding flavor and texture into a tiny package. Make a batch as a nutritious after-school treat for the kids.*

½ cup granola, homemade (page 521) or store-bought

¼ cup sugar

½ cup golden raisins

½ cup unsalted shelled sunflower seeds

¼ cup sesame seeds

1½ cups creamy peanut butter

2 cups vegan semisweet chocolate chips

1. In a food processor, pulse together the granola, sugar, raisins, sunflower seeds, and sesame seeds. Blend in the peanut butter a little at a time to form a smooth dough. Refrigerate until chilled, for several hours or overnight.

2. Form the mixture into 1-inch balls and set aside. Melt the chocolate in a double boiler or microwave.

3. Dip the balls into the melted chocolate and arrange on an ungreased baking sheet. Refrigerate until firm, about 30 minutes, and serve.

# apricot-walnut balls Ⓕ

makes about 2 dozen pieces

*Here's a great no-cook treat you can make quickly. These fruity-nutty confections look like little snow balls. If you're making a tray of truffles and other pickup sweets, these coconut-clad treats offer a delicious respite from chocolate—for those who require one.*

¾ cup dried apricots
2 cups toasted walnut pieces
⅓ cup confectioners' sugar
1 teaspoon pure vanilla extract
1 cup finely shredded sweetened coconut

1. Place the apricots in a heatproof bowl and cover with boiling water. Let stand for 10 minutes, then drain well and place in a food processor. Add the walnuts, sugar, and vanilla and pulse to chop, then process to blend thoroughly.

2. Use your hands to shape the mixture into 1-inch balls. Place the coconut in a shallow bowl. Roll the balls in the coconut, arrange on a platter, and serve.

variations: Mix and match dried fruit and nut combinations. Some ideas include dried mango with cashews, dried pear with pecans, or mixed dried fruit with mixed nuts.

# vegan white chocolate

makes about 1 cup

*I've always adored white chocolate, which isn't vegan (it's really not chocolate either, but that's another story). When I first went vegan, commercial vegan white chocolate was unavailable, so I had to develop my own recipe for those white chocolate cravings. Food-grade coconut butter and soy milk powder are available at natural food stores and online.*

½ cup food-grade cocoa butter
½ cup confectioners' sugar
2 tablespoons soy milk powder
2 teaspoons pure vanilla extract

1. Lightly oil a small baking sheet and set aside. In a medium bowl, combine the sugar and soy milk powder. Set aside.

2. Melt the cocoa butter in the top of a double boiler over medium heat. Once it is melted, stir in the sugar and soy milk mixture and cook, stirring constantly, until the dry ingredients are dissolved and the mixture is smooth and well blended. Turn off the heat. Mix in the vanilla, stirring until blended.

3. Scrape the mixture onto the prepared baking sheet and set aside or refrigerate to cool completely, about 1 hour. Break into pieces, then transfer to a tightly sealed container and refrigerate until needed. Properly stored, it will keep for 1 to 2 weeks.

variation: stir ½ cup of toasted slivered almonds into the warm mixture for a delicious vegan almond bark.

# Cakes and Cheezcakes

## vegan chocolate mousse cake

makes 6 to 8 servings

*Chocolate lovers take note: the rich and flavorful chocolate cake comes complete with a chocolate mousse filling and a chocolate ganache icing. If you truly want to gild the lily, you can top each slice with a dollop of Vegan Whipped Cream (page 501) or Cashew Crème (page 501).*

MOUSSE

1 (12-ounce) package firm silken tofu, drained

½ cup sugar

1 teaspoon pure vanilla extract

1 cup vegan semisweet chocolate chips, melted

CAKE

1½ cups all-purpose flour

1 cup light brown sugar

¼ cup unsweetened cocoa powder

1 teaspoon baking soda

¼ teaspoon salt

⅓ cup canola oil

1 tablespoon apple cider vinegar

1½ teaspoons pure vanilla extract

1 cup cold water

2 cups Vegan Chocolate Ganache (page 502), slightly cooled

1. Make the mousse: In a food processor, process the tofu until smooth. Add the sugar and vanilla and process until smooth. Add the chocolate and process until blended. Transfer the mixture to a medium bowl, cover, and refrigerate until needed.

2. Make the cake: Preheat the oven to 350°F. Grease a 9-inch round cake pan and set aside. In a large bowl, combine the flour, sugar, cocoa, baking soda, and salt and mix until blended. Stir in the oil, vinegar, vanilla, and water and mix well.

3. Scrape the batter into the prepared pan and bake until a toothpick inserted in the center comes out clean, 30 to 35 minutes. Set aside to cool for 10 to 15 minutes before inverting it onto a wire rack to cool completely before assembling.

4. Use a serrated knife to cut the cake in half horizontally, creating 2 layers. Frost the top of one layer with the mousse. Top with the remaining cake layer. Pour the ganache over the cake and refrigerate for 30 minutes, to cool before slicing.

# chocolate-rum coffee cake

makes 8 to 10 servings

*Sure, you can enjoy this cake with a cup of coffee, but the "coffee" in the title refers to the fact that brewed coffee, along with rum and chocolate, is part of the triumvirate of flavor-makers in this rich and potent cake. A light dusting of confectioners' sugar is all that is needed on top, although a dollop of Vegan Whipped Cream (page 501) spiked with a bit of rum couldn't hurt.*

½ cup unsweetened cocoa powder, plus more for dusting pan

1 cup vegan margarine

¾ cup strong black coffee

½ cup dark rum

1¼ cups sugar

2½ cups all-purpose flour

1 tablespoon baking powder

1 teaspoon baking soda

½ teaspoon salt

1 teaspoon pure vanilla extract

1. Preheat the oven to 350°F. Grease a 9 × 13-inch baking pan or a 3-quart Bundt pan and dust it lightly with cocoa.

2. In a medium saucepan, combine the margarine, coffee, and rum over medium heat, stirring to melt the margarine. Add the sugar and stir until dissolved, then remove from the heat and set aside to cool, about 15 minutes.

3. In a large bowl, sift together the flour, ½ cup cocoa, baking powder, baking soda, and salt. Set aside.

4. When the margarine mixture is cool, stir in the vanilla. Stir the wet ingredients into the dry ingredients, mixing until just combined.

5. Pour the batter into the prepared pan and bake until a toothpick inserted in the center comes out clean, about 45 minutes. If using a Bundt pan, cool in the pan for about 15 minutes before inverting it onto a wire rack to cool completely before dusting with confectioners' sugar or slicing.

# magical mystery chocolate cake

makes 8 to 10 servings

*This fascinating, densely fudgy "pudding" cake is one of the most popular naturally vegan cakes around. Though it is known by various names including "wacky cake," "three-hole cake," and "crazy cake," I call my version Magical Mystery Cake because of the inherent mystery of a moist chocolate cake made with no eggs or dairy. Serve dusted with confectioners' sugar (after it is completely cool) or serve slightly warm with a scoop of vegan vanilla ice cream.*

2 cups all-purpose flour

1 cup sugar

¾ cup unsweetened cocoa powder

1 tablespoon baking powder

¼ teaspoon salt

¾ cup plain or vanilla soy milk

¼ cup canola or other neutral oil

2 teaspoons pure vanilla extract

1 cup sugar

2¼ cups hot water

1. Preheat the oven to 350°F. Lightly oil a 9 × 13-inch baking pan. Set aside.

2. In a large bowl, combine the flour, sugar, ¼ cup of the cocoa, baking powder, and salt. Mix to combine and set aside.

3. In a medium bowl, combine the soy milk, oil, and vanilla. Pour the liquid ingredients into the dry ingredients and mix until blended. Spread the batter into the prepared baking pan.

4. In a separate medium bowl, combine the sugar, the remaining ¹⁄₂ cup of cocoa, and the water. Stir to blend, then pour the mixture over the top of the cake (do not mix). Bake until a toothpick inserted in the center comes out clean, about 45 minutes.

5. Cool in the pan on a wire rack to cool completely for 60 minutes before slicing.

# spicy chocolate cake with dark chocolate glaze

makes 8 servings

*Cinnamon and a touch of cayenne give this rich and chocolate confection a unique depth of flavor. If you eliminate the cayenne and the cinnamon, you will have a rich but more straightforward single-layer chocolate cake.*

CAKE

1¾ cups all-purpose flour

1 cup sugar

¼ cup unsweetened cocoa powder

1 teaspoon baking soda

½ teaspoon baking powder

1½ teaspoons ground cinnamon

¼ teaspoon ground cayenne

⅓ cup canola oil

1 tablespoon apple cider vinegar

1½ teaspoons pure vanilla extract

1 cup cold water

GLAZE

2 (1-ounce) squares unsweetened vegan chocolate

¼ cup plain or vanilla soy milk

½ cup sugar

2 tablespoons vegan margarine

½ teaspoon pure vanilla extract

Pinch ground cayenne

1. Make the cake: Preheat the oven to 350°F. Grease a 9-inch round cake pan and set aside.

2. In a large bowl, combine the flour, sugar, cocoa, baking soda, baking powder, cinnamon, and cayenne.

3. In a medium bowl, combine the oil, vinegar, vanilla, and water. Stir the wet ingredients into the dry ingredients, mixing until just combined.

4. Pour the batter into the prepared pan and bake until a toothpick inserted into the center comes out clean, about 30 minutes. Cool the cake in the pan for 10 to 15 minutes, then invert it onto a wire rack and let the cake cool completely while you make the glaze.

5. Make the glaze: In a double boiler, combine the chocolate and soy milk and cook, stirring constantly, until the chocolate is melted. Stir in the sugar and cook, stirring constantly, for 5 minutes. Remove from the heat and stir in the margarine, vanilla, and cayenne. Drizzle the glaze over the cooled cake. Refrigerate the cake to let the glaze set before serving.

# vegan pound cake

makes 8 servings

*The old rule was "a pound each" of flour, sugar, butter, and eggs—but rules were made to be broken. This versatile cake can be enjoyed plain or embellished in a number of ways. Try it with a scoop of vegan ice cream and a drizzle of chocolate syrup or berry coulis or top it with sliced fresh fruit and Vegan Whipped Cream (page 501) or Cashew Crème (page 501).*

2 cups all-purpose flour

1¼ cups sugar

1 tablespoon baking powder

½ teaspoon salt

1 cup drained soft tofu

½ cup plain or vanilla soy milk

¼ cup canola or other neutral oil

2 teaspoons pure vanilla extract

1. Preheat the oven to 350°F. Grease an 8-inch loaf pan and set aside.

2. In a large bowl, mix the flour, sugar, baking powder, and salt. Set aside.

3. In a blender or food processor, combine the tofu, soy milk, oil, and vanilla. Blend until smooth, then pour the wet ingredients into the dry ingredients and stir together until just combined. Do not overmix.

4. Scrape the batter into the prepared pan. Bake until the cake is golden and a toothpick inserted in the center comes out clean, about 40 minutes.

5. Let the cake cool in the pan for 10 minutes before removing from the pan to a wire rack to cool completely before slicing.

# banana-walnut cake

makes 8 servings

*This cake can be enjoyed as is or frosted with the tofu "Cream Cheese" Frosting on page 502. My favorite way to serve it, however, is drizzled with the warm Blueberry Sauce on page 498.*

2 cups all-purpose flour

2½ teaspoons baking powder

½ teaspoon ground allspice

½ teaspoon ground cinnamon

½ teaspoon salt

3 ripe bananas

½ cup plain or vanilla soy milk

¼ cup canola or other neutral oil

¾ cup sugar

2 teaspoons pure vanilla extract

½ cup chopped walnuts

1. Preheat the oven to 350°F. Grease an 8-inch square cake pan and set aside.

2. In a large bowl, sift together the flour, baking powder, allspice, cinnamon, and salt and set aside.

3. In a food processor or blender, combine the bananas, soy milk, oil, sugar, and vanilla and blend until smooth. Add the wet ingredients to the dry ingredients and stir until just moistened. Do not overmix. Fold in the walnuts.

4. Scrape the batter into the prepared pan and bake until a toothpick inserted into the center comes out clean, 35 to 40 minutes. Allow to cool in pan for 10 to 15 minutes before inverting it onto a wire rack to cool completely before slicing.

# crazy for carrot cake

makes 8 servings

*Carrot cake is a personal favorite and anyone who has tasted mine agrees that it's the best carrot cake they've ever had, vegan or not. It's a rich and flavorful cake without being cloyingly sweet, moist with sweet bits of carrot and cloaked in a luscious and creamy frosting. And what a decadent way to get your beta-carotene for the day. For a bit of crunch, add $\frac{1}{2}$ cup chopped walnuts. For an even richer "carrot" color, substitute carrot juice for all or part of the soy milk.*

2 cups all-purpose flour
2 teaspoons baking powder
1 teaspoon baking soda
2 teaspoons ground cinnamon
$\frac{1}{2}$ teaspoon ground allspice
1 teaspoon salt
1 cup sugar
$\frac{1}{2}$ cup plain or vanilla soy milk
$\frac{1}{2}$ cup canola or other neutral oil
$\frac{1}{4}$ cup pure maple syrup
2 teaspoons pure vanilla extract
2 cups finely shredded carrots
$\frac{1}{2}$ cup golden raisins
1 recipe "Cream Cheese" Frosting (page 502)

1. Preheat the oven to 350°F. Grease a 9-inch square baking pan and set aside.

2. In a medium bowl, mix the flour, baking powder, baking soda, cinnamon, allspice, and salt.

3. In a large bowl, combine the sugar, soy milk, oil, maple syrup, and vanilla, then add the wet ingredients to the dry ingredients. Stir in the carrots and raisins until just mixed.

4. Scrape the batter into the prepared pan. Bake until a toothpick comes out clean, about 45 minutes.

5. Let the cake cool in pan for 15 minutes, then invert onto a wire rack to cool completely. When completely cool, frost the cake with "Cream Cheese" Frosting.

# "sour cream" coffee cake

makes 8 to 10 servings

*I adapted this recipe from one shared with me by my friend Lori Kettler. A tube or Bundt pan will give it that classic "coffee cake" look, but you can also bake it in a 9 × 13-inch baking pan if that's what you've got.*

$\frac{3}{4}$ cup chopped walnuts
$1\frac{1}{2}$ teaspoons ground cinnamon
2 cups sugar
3 cups all-purpose flour
2 teaspoons baking powder
$1\frac{1}{2}$ teaspoons baking soda
Pinch salt
1 (12-ounce) package firm silken tofu, drained
2 teaspoons fresh lemon juice
$\frac{1}{2}$ cup canola or other neutral oil
$1\frac{1}{2}$ teaspoons pure vanilla extract
$\frac{3}{4}$ cup vegan margarine

1. Preheat the oven to 350°F. Grease a tube pan and set it aside.

2. In a small bowl, combine the walnuts, cinnamon, and $\frac{3}{4}$ cup of the sugar and set aside.

3. In a medium bowl, sift together the flour, baking powder, baking soda, and salt and set aside.

4. In a food processor or blender, combine the tofu, lemon juice, canola oil, and vanilla, and blend until smooth.

continues on next page

**5.** In large bowl, combine the margarine with the remaining 1¼ cups sugar and beat with an electric mixer on high until light and fluffy. Add the flour mixture and the tofu mixture and beat on low speed until blended. Increase the speed to medium, and beat for 3 more minutes.

**6.** Spread half of the batter in the prepared pan and sprinkle with half of the walnut mixture. Spread the remaining batter evenly over top and sprinkle with remaining walnut mixture. Bake until firm and a toothpick inserted in the center comes out clean, approximately 60 minutes. If using a tube pan, let the cake cool in the pan for 10 minutes, before inverting the pan onto a wire rack to allow the cake to cool completely. If using a 9 × 13 pan, let the cake cool completely in the pan.

# orange-coconut cake

makes 8 to 10 servings

*This is an updated and veganized version of ambrosia cake, which my mother occasionally made decades ago. In addition to decorating with shredded coconut, the original version was festooned with canned mandarin orange segments, which I never liked and used to pick off. Needless to say, I have omitted them from this version.*

## CAKE

3 cups all-purpose flour

1½ cups sugar

1 tablespoon baking soda

1 cup unsweetened coconut milk

¾ cup canola or other neutral oil

1 cup fresh orange juice

2 tablespoons fresh lemon juice

2 teaspoons pure vanilla extract

1 teaspoon coconut extract

## FROSTING

8 ounces vegan cream cheese, softened

⅓ cup vegan margarine, softened

¼ cup unsweetened coconut milk

2 cups confectioners' sugar

2 tablespoons orange zest

1 teaspoon pure vanilla extract

1 teaspoon coconut or orange extract

1 cup sweetened shredded coconut

**1.** Make the cake: Preheat the oven to 350°F. Grease a 9 × 13-inch pan and set aside.

**2.** In a large bowl, sift together the flour, sugar, and baking soda.

**3.** In a separate large bowl, combine the coconut milk, oil, orange juice, lemon juice, vanilla, and coconut extract and whisk well to combine. Quickly whisk the wet ingredients into the dry ingredients to combine.

**4.** Pour the batter into the prepared pan. Bake until a toothpick inserted in the center comes out clean, about 45 minutes. Let the cake cool completely in the pan on a wire rack, about 1 hour.

**5.** Make the frosting: In a medium bowl, combine the cream cheese, margarine, and coconut milk and cream together with an electric mixer. Add 1 cup of the sugar and beat well on low speed to combine.

**6.** Add the coconut extract, orange zest, vanilla, and remaining 1 cup sugar and continue to beat until the mixture is light and fluffy.

**7.** Spread the frosting on the cooled cake and sprinkle with shredded coconut.

# spice cake with mango and lime

makes 8 servings

*This moist and flavorful cake studded with succulent pieces of juicy mango is great on its own, but a swath of vegan "Cream Cheese" Frosting (page 502) makes it even better. For more mango flavor, substitute mango puree (available in specialty food stores) for the applesauce.*

1½ cups all-purpose flour
¾ cup sugar
¼ cup yellow cornmeal
1 teaspoon baking soda
½ teaspoon salt
½ teaspoon baking powder
½ teaspoon ground cinnamon
½ teaspoon ground allspice
½ teaspoon ground ginger
1 cup applesauce
⅓ cup canola or other neutral oil
2 teaspoons grated lime zest
2 tablespoons water
1 ripe mango, peeled, pitted, and chopped

1. Preheat the oven to 350°F. Lightly oil a 9-inch round cake pan and set aside.

2. In a large bowl, combine the flour, sugar, cornmeal, baking soda, salt, baking powder, cinnamon, allspice, and ginger and set aside.

3. In a medium bowl, combine the applesauce, oil, lime zest, and water, stirring to blend. Fold in the mango. Add the wet ingredients to the dry ingredients and mix to combine.

4. Pour the batter into the prepared baking pan. Bake until a toothpick inserted in the center comes out clean, 45 to 50 minutes. Let the cake cool in the pan for 10 minutes then invert onto a wire rack to cool completely before slicing.

# apple lover's cake

makes 8 servings

*This cake has several dimensions of great apple flavor, including fresh and dried apple, applesauce, and even a little apple juice in the glaze.*

2 cups all-purpose flour
2 teaspoons baking powder
¼ teaspoon salt
½ cup sugar
⅓ cup applesauce
1 Granny Smith apple, peeled, cored, and shredded
⅓ cup dried apples, finely chopped
2 tablespoons canola or other neutral oil
½ cup confectioners' sugar
2 teaspoons apple juice

1. Preheat the oven to 350°F. Grease an 8-inch square baking pan and set aside.

2. In a large bowl, combine the flour, baking powder, and salt.

3. In a medium bowl, combine the sugar, applesauce, fresh apple, dried apples, and oil. Add the wet ingredients to the dry ingredients and stir just until moistened.

4. Spread the batter into the prepared pan and bake until a toothpick inserted in the center comes out clean, about 45 minutes.

5. Remove from the oven and let cool in the pan for 15 minutes, then invert onto a wire rack to cool completely.

6. In a small bowl, combine the confectioners' sugar and apple juice and blend until smooth, then drizzle over the cake.

## giant peanut butter–chocolate chip cookie cake

makes 8 servings

*Is this a cake that thinks it's a cookie or a cookie masquerading as a cake? What really matters is that it tastes fantastic—whether you slice it like a cake or break off a piece at a time like a cookie.*

¾ cup creamy peanut butter

¼ cup pure maple syrup

½ cup light brown sugar

¾ cup plain or vanilla soy milk

2 cups all-purpose flour

1 tablespoon baking powder

½ teaspoon salt

¾ cup semisweet vegan chocolate chips

1. Preheat the oven to 350°F. Lightly oil a 9-inch round cake pan and set aside.

2. In a food processor, combine the peanut butter, maple syrup, sugar, and soy milk and process until blended. In a large bowl, combine the flour, baking powder, and salt. Add the flour mixture to the peanut butter mixture and pulse to combine.

3. Turn the dough out onto a lightly floured work surface and sprinkle with chocolate chips. Use your hands to fold the chips into the dough, then transfer the dough to the prepared pan, pressing it evenly into the pan.

4. Bake until golden brown and slightly browned along the edges, about 40 minutes. Let it cool in the pan for 10 minutes before removing to a wire rack to cool completely, about 45 minutes.

## not-so-plain vanilla cheezcake

makes 6 servings

*Non-vegans can't believe there's no dairy in this tempting cheesecake. While it is delicious unadorned, it's even better topped with blueberries, strawberries, or other luscious fruit. If fresh berries are out of season, top with a layer of blueberry or strawberry fruit spread. For best results, before spreading on the cheesecake, place the fruit spread in a small bowl and stir until smooth.*

1½ cups vegan graham cracker crumbs

¼ cup vegan margarine, melted

2 (8-ounce) containers vegan cream cheese, room temperature

1 (12-ounce) package firm silken tofu, drained and patted dry

1 cup sugar

1 tablespoon cornstarch

2 teaspoons pure vanilla extract

1. Bring all the ingredients to room temperature. Preheat the oven to 350°F. Grease the bottom and sides of a 9-inch springform pan. Place crumbs in bottom of the pan, add the margarine, and mix with a fork until blended. Press the crumb mixture into bottom and sides of pan and set aside.

2. In a food processor, combine the cream cheese and tofu and blend until smooth. Add the sugar, cornstarch, and vanilla and blend until very creamy.

3. Pour the filling into the prepared crust and bake for 45 minutes. Turn off oven and leave the cheesecake inside for another 10 minutes.

When done, edges should be golden and starting to pull away from sides of pan and center should be soft set.

4. Remove cake from the oven and cool at room temperature for 1 hour, then refrigerate at least 4 hours before serving. Keep refrigerated.

# triple coconut cheezcake

makes 6 servings

*I developed this recipe for my coconut-loving husband, Jon, who never met a coconut dessert he didn't like. With coconut in the crust, in the filling, and sprinkled on top, this cheesecake is among the top requested desserts in our house. Tofutti "Better Than Cream Cheese" is my favorite brand of vegan cream cheese and it's available at natural food stores and some supermarkets.*

1½ cups vegan vanilla cookie crumbs
1 cup toasted sweetened shredded coconut
¼ cup vegan margarine, melted
3 (8-ounce) containers vegan cream cheese
1 cup sugar
¼ cup unsweetened coconut milk
1 tablespoon cornstarch
1½ teaspoons coconut extract
½ teaspoon pure vanilla extract

1. Bring all the ingredients to room temperature. Preheat the oven to 350°F. Grease the bottom and sides of a 9-inch springform pan. Place the crumbs and ¼ cup of the coconut in the bottom of the pan, add the margarine, and mix with a fork to blend. Press crumb mixture into bottom and sides of pan and set aside.

2. In a food processor, combine the cream cheese, sugar, coconut milk, cornstarch, coconut extract, and vanilla and blend until smooth.

3. Pour the filling into the prepared crust and bake for 45 minutes. Turn off oven and leave the cheesecake inside for another 10 minutes. When done, edges should be golden and starting to pull away from sides of pan and center should be soft set.

4. Remove cake from the oven and cool at room temperature for 1 hour, then refrigerate at least 4 hours before serving. When ready to serve, sprinkle the top with the remaining toasted coconut. Keep refrigerated.

## toasting coconut

To toast coconut, preheat the oven to 350°F. Place ½ cup shredded coconut in a small baking pan and bake until light golden brown, stirring occasionally, 6 to 8 minutes.

# chocolate swirl tofu cheezcake

makes 8 servings

*As if a chocolate cheesecake weren't enough, this one also has swirls of peanut butter and banana for a richly decadent and very pretty dessert. A garnish around the outer edge of the top with chocolate curls or ground peanuts wouldn't be unreasonable.*

1½ cups vegan chocolate cookie crumbs

¼ cup vegan margarine, melted

3 (8-ounce) containers vegan cream cheese

1 cup sugar

½ cup plain or vanilla soy milk

1 teaspoon pure vanilla extract

1 ripe banana

⅓ cup creamy peanut butter

½ cup semisweet vegan chocolate chips

1. Bring all the ingredients to room temperature. Preheat the oven to 350°F. Grease the bottom and sides of a 9-inch springform pan. Place the crumbs in the bottom of the pan, add the margarine, and mix with a fork to blend. Press crumb mixture into bottom and sides of pan and set aside.

2. In a food processor, combine the cream cheese, sugar, soy milk, and vanilla and blend until smooth. Add the banana and peanut butter and process until smooth. Pour the filling into the prepared crust.

3. Melt the chocolate in a double boiler or microwave. With a circular motion, pour the melted chocolate into the filling and using a thin metal spatula or knife, swirl the fill-ing around to create a pattern. Bake for 45 minutes. Turn off the oven and leave the cake inside for another 10 minutes. When done, edges should be golden and starting to pull away from sides of pan and center should be soft set. Remove the cake from the oven and cool at room temperature for 1 hour, then refrigerate for at least 4 hours before serving. Keep refrigerated.

# pumpkin cheezcake with cranberry drizzle

makes 8 servings

*Dense and rich with spiced pumpkin flavor, this dessert is a natural for your Thanksgiving table. The gorgeous orange color, offset by the vivid drizzle of cranberry, makes a beautiful presentation—and it's big enough to serve a crowd.*

CRUST

1½ cups vegan graham cracker crumbs

¼ cup vegan margarine, melted

FILLING

2 (8-ounce) containers vegan cream cheese

1 (15-ounce) can solid pack pumpkin

1 cup light brown sugar

1 tablespoon cornstarch

2 teaspoons ground cinnamon

¾ teaspoon ground allspice

½ teaspoon ground nutmeg

TOPPING

⅓ cup cranberry sauce, homemade (page 571) or store-bought

1 tablespoon pure maple syrup

1 teaspoon melted vegan margarine

1. Make the crust: Preheat the oven to 350°F. Grease a 9-inch springform pan. Place the crumbs in the bottom of the pan, add the melted margarine, and mix with a fork to blend. Press the crumb mixture into bottom and sides of pan and set aside.

2. Make the filling: In a food processor, combine the cream cheese and pumpkin and process until blended. Add the sugar, cornstarch, cinnamon, allspice, and nutmeg and process until well blended.

3. Pour the filling into the prepared crust. Bake for 45 minutes. Turn off the oven and leave cheesecake in the oven for another 10 minutes. When done, edges should be golden and starting to pull away from sides of pan and center should be soft set. Remove the cake from the oven and cool at room temperature for 1 hour. Refrigerate for at least 4 hours.

4. Make the topping: In a blender or food processor, combine the cranberry sauce, maple syrup, and margarine and blend until smooth. Pour the mixture into a squeeze bottle or small pitcher and drizzle the over the top of the cheesecake. Keep refrigerated.

# pomegranate cheezcake with glazed pecans

makes 8 servings

*This is the one to serve guests to complete a special meal. The exotic, sweet-tart flavor of pomegranate is a delightful surprise in this sophisticated dessert. Glazed pecans make it even more elegant.*

1¼ cups vegan vanilla cookie crumbs
¼ cup ground walnuts
¼ cup vegan margarine, melted
3 (8-ounce) containers vegan cream cheese, at room temperature
1 cup sugar
2 tablespoons Pomegranate Molasses (page 261)
2 tablespoons pomegranate juice
1 tablespoon cornstarch
1 cup glazed pecans (page 6)

1. Preheat the oven to 350°F. Grease a 9-inch springform pan. Place the crumbs and the ground walnuts in the bottom of the pan, add the margarine, and mix with a fork to blend. Press crumb mixture into bottom and sides of pan and set aside.

2. In a food processor, combine the cream cheese, sugar, pomegranate molasses, pomegranate juice, and cornstarch and blend until smooth.

3. Pour the filling into the prepared crust and bake for 45 minutes. Turn off oven and leave the cheesecake in the oven for another 10 minutes. When done, edges should be golden and starting to pull away from sides of pan and center should be soft set. Remove from the oven and cool at room temperature for 1 hour.

4. Arrange glazed pecan halves on the top outer edge of the cheesecake. Refrigerate at least 4 hours before serving. Keep refrigerated.

# lemon-lime teasecake

makes 8 servings

*This lovely "cheesecake"-style dessert was developed by my friend Francis Janes, chef and former owner of Ambrosia, a vegan restaurant in Seattle. Delicious in its own right, this dessert is ideal to serve people with food sensitivities—in addition to being free of eggs and dairy, the cake contains no wheat or soy. Choose Meyer lemons when in season (usually January through March), as they are milder and less tart than the more common Eureka and Lisbon varieties. If you prefer an all-lemon version, substitute additional lemon juice for the lime juice.*

CRUST

¾ cup old-fashioned oats

½ cup brown rice flour

½ cup ground walnuts

1 teaspoon ground cinnamon

½ teaspoon salt

3 tablespoons pure maple syrup

¼ cup canola or other neutral oil

1 teaspoon pure vanilla extract

FILLING

1 cup millet

4 cups water

½ cup raw cashews

3 tablespoons fresh lemon juice

3 tablespoons fresh lime juice

½ cup agave nectar

2 teaspoons pure vanilla extract

1 teaspoon lemon extract

½ cup toasted sliced almonds, for garnish

1. Make the crust: Preheat the oven to 350°F. Grease a 9-inch springform pan and set aside.

2. In large bowl, combine oats, flour, walnuts, cinnamon, and salt and mix well.

3. In a small bowl, combine the maple syrup, oil, and vanilla and mix well. Add the wet ingredients to the dry ingredients and mix to blend.

4. Press the crust firmly into the prepared pan. Bake until lightly browned, about 10 minutes. Cool 30 minutes before filling.

5. Make the filling: In a large saucepan, bring the millet and water to boil over high heat. Cover, lower heat, and simmer until the water is absorbed and the millet is soft, about 50 minutes.

6. In a high-speed blender, combine the cashews, lemon juice, lime juice, agave nectar, vanilla, and lemon extract. Process until completely smooth, about 3 minutes.

7. Add the cooked millett to the cashew mixture. Blend for another 3 minutes, until creamy. Pour into the cooled crust.

8. Cool the filling and crust at room temperature for 30 minutes, then refrigerate. Chill for at least 4 hours before serving. Keep refrigerated.

9. Garnish with sliced almonds sprinkled around the perimeter and serve.

# no-bake avocado cheezcake

makes 8 servings

*This is the one to make when it's too hot to turn on the oven but you want that sweet, creamy satisfaction that only comes from a cheesecake. The avocado adds its buttery richness and cool green color to the filling.*

*When you use lime juice instead of lemon, the taste is reminiscent of Key lime pie.*

1½ cups vegan graham cracker crumbs

¼ cup vegan margarine, melted

2 (8-ounce) containers vegan cream cheese, room temperature

1 ripe Hass avocado, pitted and peeled

¾ cup sugar

1 tablespoon fresh lemon or lime juice

1 teaspoon pure vanilla extract

1. Grease a 9-inch springform pan. Place the crumbs in the bottom of the pan, add the margarine, and mix with a fork to blend. Press the crumb mixture into bottom and sides of pan and set aside.

2. In a food processor, combine the cream cheese, avocado, sugar, lemon juice, and vanilla and blend until smooth.

3. Pour the avocado mixture into the prepared crust and refrigerate for 4 hours until set. Keep refrigerated.

# three-flavor ice cream cake

makes 8 servings

*This versatile dessert makes a great impact with a minimum of effort. Two flavors of vegan ice cream are layered in a chocolate crust and topped with strawberry jam. Fresh strawberries and toasted almonds are used for garnish, but really, the sky's the limit in terms of both what flavor(s) of vegan ice cream you use and what kind of topping you garnish it with. Note: Any of the homemade vegan ice creams in this book, such as Cherry Vanilla Nice Cream (page 492) or Chocolate Nice Cream (page 494) can be used instead of commercial products.*

1½ cups vegan chocolate cookie crumbs

¼ cup vegan margarine, melted

1 quart vegan vanilla ice cream, softened

1 pint vegan chocolate ice cream, softened

1 (8-ounce) jar strawberry jam

1 cup toasted sliced almonds, for garnish

Fresh strawberries, for garnish

1. Grease the bottom and sides of a 9-inch springform pan and set aside. Place the crumbs in the bottom of the pan, add the margarine, and mix with a fork to blend. Press the crumb mixture into the bottom of the prepared pan and set aside.

2. Press the vanilla ice cream into the prepared crust, smoothing the top with a rubber spatula. Freeze for 2 hours to firm up.

3. Spread the chocolate ice cream on top of the vanilla, smoothing the top with a spatula. Freeze for 2 more hours to firm up.

4. When ready to serve, remove the cake from the freezer to allow the ice cream to soften slightly. Place the fruit spread in a small bowl and stir until smooth. Remove the sides of the springform pan. Spread the fruit topping on top of cake. Sprinkle with almonds and garnish with fresh strawberries. Store any leftover cake in the freezer.

# hot banana ice cream cake

makes 8 servings

*Bananas Foster is a favorite dessert of my husband, Jon, so I enjoy experimenting with new variations. I especially like making this "ice cream cake" version for company since it is made ahead of time and presliced, so there's no fumbling with an ice cream scoop while you're sautéing the bananas.*

1¼ cups broken vegan vanilla cookies
¾ cup pecan pieces
¼ cup plus 3 tablespoons vegan margarine
1 quart vegan vanilla ice cream, softened
¼ cup light brown sugar
3 to 4 firm bananas, cut into ¼-inch slices
¼ cup dark rum or ¼ cup pineapple juice

1. Grease the bottom and sides of a 9-inch springform pan and set aside. In a food processor, combine the cookies and ¼ cup of the pecans and pulse until finely ground. Melt the ¼ cup of the margarine and add to the crumb mixture. Pulse to combine and moisten the crumbs. Press the crumb mixture into the bottom of the prepared pan and set aside.

2. Press the ice cream into the prepared crust, smoothing the top with a rubber spatula. Freeze for 3 hours to firm up.

3. Remove the cake from the freezer, remove the sides of the springform pan, and cut the cake into 8 slices. Fasten the sides back onto the pan and return the cake to the freezer until ready to serve.

4. Remove the sides of the springform pan and place the frozen cake slices on 8 dessert plates and set aside. In a medium skillet, combine the remaining 3 tablespoons margarine, remaining ½ cup pecans, and sugar and cook over medium heat. Cook, stirring, until the sugar dissolves, about 1 minute. Add the banana slices and cook until slightly browned and softened but not mushy, about 1 minute. Carefully add the rum. Continue to cook the sauce until the alcohol mostly evaporates, 1 to 2 minutes.

5. Spoon the bananas and sauce over each of the cake slices and serve immediately.

# white cupcakes with variations

makes 12 cupcakes

*This most versatile of cupcake recipes can be prepared as is and topped with "Buttercream" Frosting (page 503) for a white-on-white approach or dressed up with one of the variations on the opposite page.*

¾ cup plain or vanilla soy milk
1½ teaspoons apple cider vinegar
1¼ cups all-purpose flour
1 teaspoon baking powder
¼ teaspoon baking soda
¼ teaspoon salt
¾ cup sugar
¼ cup canola or other neutral oil
1½ teaspoons pure vanilla extract

1. Preheat the oven to 350°F. Line a 12-cup muffin tin with paper or foil cupcake liners. Set aside.

2. In a small bowl, combine the soy milk and vinegar and set aside. In a medium bowl, combine the flour, baking powder, baking soda, and salt. Mix to combine.

3. In a large bowl, combine the sugar, oil, and vanilla. Stir in the soy milk mixture. Add the dry ingredients to the wet ingredients and stir until smooth.

4. Pour the batter evenly into the prepared tin, about two-thirds full, and bake until a toothpick inserted in the center of a cupcake comes out clean, about 20 minutes. Cool completely before frosting.

coconut: Use coconut extract instead of vanilla. Substitute unsweetened coconut milk for the soy milk. Use the coconut frosting variation of the "Buttercream" Frosting.

lemon: Use lemon extract instead of vanilla. Add 2 teaspoons of very finely grated lemon zest to the batter. Use the lemon frosting variation of the "Buttercream" Frosting.

spice: Add 1 teaspoon ground cinnamon and $\frac{1}{4}$ teaspoon each of allspice, nutmeg, and cloves or ginger to the batter. Add $\frac{1}{2}$ cup chopped nuts, if desired. Use the spice frosting variation of the "Buttercream" Frosting.

## more variations on a cupcake

A cupcake is to a cake what a muffin is to a quick bread. No, it's not the riddle of the sphinx—it just means that in the same way you can use virtually any quick bread recipe to make muffins, you can use most any 8- or 9-inch single layer cake recipe to make cupcakes. That opens up a whole world of cupcake variations, from the Spicy Chocolate Cake with or without the "spice" (page 447) to the Banana-Walnut Cake (page 448) or the Crazy for Carrot Cake (page 449). If you want to make cupcakes using a cake recipe with more volume, go ahead—you can use the remaining batter to make extra cupcakes or pour the leftover batter into small greased ramekins and make little individual cakes.

You can also experiment with variations of the White Cupcake recipe here. I've provided lemon, coconut, and spice variations, but there's no need to stop there. Check out the extract shelf of the spice section of your supermarket for flavor ideas. You can also mix and match frostings—how about chocolate cupcakes with orange frosting? Spice cupcakes with chocolate frosting? Coconut cupcakes with lemon frosting?

You can further embellish your cupcake masterpieces by festooning the top of the frosting with tasty bits of toasted coconut, chopped nuts, crushed candies, crushed cookies, chocolate curls, or candy sprinkles.

# Pies, Tarts, Crisps, and Cobblers

## mom's apple pie with cranberries

makes 8 servings

*I've always thought that there was no way to improve on my mom's apple pie filling—and then I added some sweetened dried cranberries. Next time, I may also add some chopped walnuts.*

CRUST

2½ cups all-purpose flour

½ teaspoon salt

1 teaspoon sugar

1 cup vegan margarine, cut into small pieces

⅓ cup ice water, plus more if needed

FILLING

6 Granny Smith or other tart apples

¾ cup sweetened dried cranberries

½ cup sugar

1 tablespoon fresh lemon juice

1 tablespoon cornstarch

1 teaspoon ground cinnamon

1 tablespoon vegan margarine

1. Make the crust: In a large bowl, combine the flour, salt, and sugar. Use a pastry blender to cut in the margarine until the mixture resembles coarse crumbs. Add the water a little at a time and blend until dough just starts to hold together, adding a little more water if needed. Divide the dough into two round disks and wrap them in plastic wrap. Refrigerate for 30 minutes.

2. Roll out one piece of the dough on a lightly floured work surface to about 10 inches in diameter. Fit the dough into a 9-inch pie plate and trim and flute the edges. Roll out the remaining dough for the top crust and set aside. Preheat the oven to 400°F.

3. Make the filling: Peel, core, and cut the apples into ¼-inch slices and place them in a large bowl. Add the cranberries, sugar, lemon juice, cornstarch, and cinnamon, and stir to mix well.

4. Spoon the filling into the bottom crust and dot with bits of the margarine. Place the top crust over the fruit and crimp the edges. Pierce several holes in the top crust with the tines of a fork.

5. Bake for 10 minutes, then reduce heat to 350°F and bake until golden brown, about 45 minutes. Cool on a wire rack before serving at room temperature, about 45 minutes.

## pumpkin pie with a hint of rum

makes 8 servings

*A splash of rum heightens the flavor of the spices in this autumn favorite but can be omitted if you prefer.*

CRUST

1¼ cups all-purpose flour

¼ teaspoon salt

½ teaspoon sugar

½ cup vegan margarine, cut into small pieces

3 tablespoons ice water, plus more if needed

**FILLING**

1 (16-ounce) can solid pack pumpkin

1 (12-ounce) package extra-firm silken tofu, drained and patted dry

1 cup sugar

Prepared egg replacement mixture for 2 eggs (page xxiii)

¼ cup pure maple syrup

1 tablespoon dark rum

1 tablespoon cornstarch

2 teaspoons ground cinnamon

½ teaspoon ground allspice

½ teaspoon ground ginger

½ teaspoon ground nutmeg

1. In a medium bowl, combine the flour, salt, and sugar. Use a pastry blender or fork to cut in the margarine until the mixture resembles coarse crumbs. Add the water a little at a time and blend until dough just starts to hold together. Flatten the dough into a round disk and wrap it in plastic wrap. Refrigerate for 30 minutes while you prepare the filling.

2. In a food processor, combine the pumpkin and tofu until well blended. Add the sugar, egg replacer, maple syrup, rum, cornstarch, cinnamon, allspice, ginger, and nutmeg, mixing until smooth and well combined.

3. Preheat the oven to 400°F. Roll out the dough on a lightly floured work surface to about 10 inches in diameter. Fit the dough into a 9-inch pie plate and trim and flute the edges.

4. Pour the filling into the crust. Bake for 15 minutes, then reduce the oven temperature to 350°F and bake for another 30 to 45 minutes, or until the filling is set. Let cool to room temperature on a wire rack, then chill in the refrigerator for 4 hours or longer.

## pie crust options

Most of the pie recipes provide instruction for making pie crust dough in a bowl, but there are other options:

**food processor pie crust:** To make your pie crust dough in the food processor, combine the flour, salt, and sugar in a food processor and pulse to mix. Add the margarine and process until crumbly, then add the water and process to form a soft dough, taking care not to overprocess.

**ready-made pie crust:** When you're pressed for time, you can substitute a ready-made vegan pie shell instead of making it from scratch.

**crumb pie crust:** A third choice is to use a crumb crust for your pie made with your choice of ground cookies or graham crackers or a combination of nuts, oats, and other ingredients. There are several crumb crust recipes provided in the cheesecake recipe section.

# sweet potato pie

makes 8 servings

*This Southern classic is a great reason to bake some extra sweet potatoes. It makes a nice change from the usual pumpkin pie.*

CRUST

1¼ cups all-purpose flour

¼ teaspoon salt

½ teaspoon sugar

½ cup vegan margarine, cut into small pieces

3 tablespoons ice water, or more if needed

FILLING

2 cups mashed sweet potatoes

1 (12-ounce) package extra-firm silken tofu, drained and patted dry

1 cup light brown sugar

Prepared egg replacement mixture for 2 eggs (page xxiii)

¼ cup pure maple syrup

1 tablespoon cornstarch

2 teaspoons ground cinnamon

½ teaspoon ground allspice

½ teaspoon ground ginger

½ teaspoon ground nutmeg

1. Make the crust: In a large bowl, combine the flour, salt, and sugar. Use a pastry blender or fork to cut in the margarine until the mixture resembles coarse crumbs. Add the water a little at a time and blend until dough just starts to hold together.

2. Flatten the dough into a disk and wrap in plastic wrap. Refrigerate for 30 minutes while you prepare the filling.

3. Preheat the oven to 400°F.

4. Make the filling: In a food processor, combine the sweet potatoes and tofu until well blended. Add the sugar, egg replacer, maple syrup, cornstarch, cinnamon, allspice, ginger, and nutmeg, mixing until smooth and well combined.

5. Roll out dough on a lightly floured work surface to about 10 inches in diameter. Fit the dough into a 9-inch pie plate and trim and crimp the edges.

6. Pour the filling into the crust and bake for 15 minutes. Then turn reduce the oven temperature to 350°F and bake for another 35 to 45 minutes, or until the filling is set.

# pecan pie

makes 8 servings

*This super-rich, nutty pie needs no embellishment, but adding a scoop of vanilla is hard to resist.*

CRUST

1¼ cups all-purpose flour

¼ teaspoon salt

½ teaspoon sugar

½ cup vegan margarine, cut into small pieces

3 tablespoons ice water, plus more if needed

FILLING

3 tablespoons cornstarch

1 cup water

¾ cups pure maple syrup

½ cup light brown sugar

½ teaspoon salt

2 tablespoons vegan margarine

1 teaspoon pure vanilla extract

2 cups unsalted pecan halves or pieces

1. Make the crust: In a large bowl, combine the flour, salt, and sugar. Use a pastry blender or fork to cut in the margarine until the mix-

ture resembles coarse crumbs. Add the water a little at a time and blend until dough just starts to hold together.

2. Flatten the dough into a disk and wrap in plastic wrap. Refrigerate for 30 minutes while you prepare the filling. Preheat the oven to 400°F.

3. Make the filling: In a small bowl, combine the cornstarch and the ¼ cup water and set aside. In a medium saucepan, combine the remaining ¾ cup water, maple syrup, and brown sugar, and bring to a boil over high heat. Boil for 5 minutes, then stir in the salt and the cornstarch mixture. Cook, stirring until the mixture thickens and becomes shiny. Remove from the heat and add the margarine and vanilla, stirring to melt the margarine. Add the pecans, stirring to coat.

4. Roll out the dough on a lightly floured work surface to about 10 inches in diameter. Fit the dough into a 9-inch pie plate. Trim the dough and flute the edges. Prick holes in bottom of dough with a fork. Bake until golden, about 10 minutes, then remove from the oven and set aside. Reduce the oven temperature to 350°F.

5. Pour the filling into the prebaked crust spreading evenly. Bake for 30 minutes. Cool on a rack for about 1 hour, then refrigerate until chilled.

# peach crumb pie

makes 8 servings

*Even though fresh local peaches are abundant in August, the hottest month of the year, I can't resist heating up the oven to bake a peach pie.*

1¼ cups all-purpose flour
¼ teaspoon salt
½ teaspoon sugar
½ cup vegan margarine, cut into small pieces
3 tablespoons cold water, plus more if needed
5 ripe peaches, peeled, pitted, and sliced
1 teaspoon vegan margarine
2 tablespoons sugar
½ teaspoon ground cinnamon

TOPPING
¾ cup old-fashioned oats
⅓ cup vegan margarine, softened
2 tablespoons sugar
1 teaspoon ground cinnamon
¼ teaspoon salt

1. Make the crust: In a large bowl, combine the flour, salt, and sugar. Use a pastry blender or fork to cut in the margarine until the mixture resembles coarse crumbs. Add the water a little at a time and blend until the dough just starts to hold together.

2. Flatten the dough into a disk and wrap in plastic wrap. Refrigerate for 30 minutes while you prepare the filling.

3. Preheat the oven to 425°F. Roll out the dough on a lightly floured work surface to about 10 inches in diameter. Fit the dough in a 9-inch pie plate and trim and crimp the edges.

4. Arrange the peach slices in the crust. Dot with the margarine and sprinkle with sugar and cinnamon. Set aside.

5. Make the topping: In a medium bowl, combine the oats, margarine, sugar, cinnamon, and salt. Mix well and sprinkle on top of the fruit.

6. Bake until the fruit is bubbly and the crust is golden brown, about 40 minutes. Remove from oven and cool slightly, 15 to 20 minutes. Serve warm.

# chocolate no-bake silk pie

makes 8 servings

*This gorgeous and sophisticated dessert is a chocolate lover's dream: the creamy texture of the filling and luscious flavor is incomparable. It is guaranteed to win rave reviews from family and dinner guests. Even better, it is easier to make than it looks and requires no baking.*

1¼ cups vegan chocolate cookie crumbs

¼ cup vegan margarine, melted

1 (12-ounce) bag vegan semisweet chocolate chips

¾ cup unsalted raw cashews

½ cup water

½ cup agave nectar

1 (12-ounce) package firm silken tofu, drained and patted dry

2 teaspoons pure vanilla extract

Chocolate curls, vegan whipped cream, or chopped toasted nuts, for garnish (optional)

1. Lightly oil the bottom and sides of a 9-inch pie plate or springform pan and set aside. In a food processor, combine the cookie crumbs with the melted margarine and pulse until the crumbs are moistened. Press the crumb mixture into the bottom of the prepared pan. Refrigerate until needed.

2. Melt the chocolate chips in a double boiler or microwave. Set aside.

3. In a high-speed blender, grind the cashews to a powder. Add the water and blend until smooth. Add the agave nectar, tofu, and vanilla and blend until smooth. Add the melted chocolate chips and blend until creamy.

4. Pour the filling into the prepared crust and refrigerate for at least 3 hours to firm up. When ready to serve, top with your garnish of choice, if using.

# white chocolate hazelnut pie

makes 8 servings

*This elegant pie makes a wonderful finish to a special meal. White chocolate isn't really chocolate and the kind you find in supermarkets isn't vegan. Although you can find vegan white chocolate for sale, mostly online, it can be expensive. A recipe is provided on page 444 to make it at home. If you prefer not to use Frangelico, leave it out and substitute 1 teaspoon of hazelnut extract.*

1½ cups vegan vanilla or chocolate cookie crumbs

¼ cup vegan margarine, melted

1 cup vegan white chocolate chips or pieces, homemade (page 444) or store-bought

½ cup unsalted raw cashews

¼ cup water

2 tablespoons Frangelico (hazelnut liqueur)

6 ounces extra-firm silken tofu, drained

¼ cup agave nectar

1 teaspoon pure vanilla extract

½ cup crushed toasted hazelnuts, for garnish

½ cup fresh berries, for garnish

1. Grease an 8-inch pie plate or springform pan and set aside. In a food processor, combine the cookie crumbs and margarine and pulse until the crumbs are moistened. Press the crumb mixture into the bottom and sides of the prepared pan. Refrigerate until needed.

2. Melt the white chocolate in a double boiler over low heat, stirring constantly. Set aside.

3. In a high-speed blender, grind the cashews to a powder. Add the water and Frangelico and blend until smooth. Add the tofu, agave nectar, and vanilla and blend until smooth. Add the melted white chocolate and process until creamy.

4. Spread the mixture into the prepared pan. Cover and refrigerate 3 hours, until well chilled. To serve, garnish with crushed hazelnuts and fresh berries.

# chocolate mint espresso pie

makes 6 to 8 servings

*If you're of the opinion that chocolate, mint, and espresso should constitute three of the basic food groups, then this luscious pie, developed by recipe tester Lisa Dahlmeier, is for you. Garnish with Vegan Whipped Cream (page 501) or chocolate curls, if desired.*

2 cups vegan chocolate cookies or mint-flavored chocolate sandwich cookies

¼ cup vegan margarine, cut into small pieces

1 (12-ounce) package vegan semisweet chocolate chips

1 (12.3-ounce) package firm silken tofu, drained and crumbled

2 tablespoons pure maple syrup or agave nectar

2 tablespoons plain or vanilla soy milk

2 tablespoons crème de menthe

4 teaspoons instant espresso powder

1. Preheat the oven to 350°F. Lightly oil an 8-inch pie plate and set aside.

2. If using sandwich cookies, carefully take them apart, reserving the cream filling in a separate bowl. Finely grind the cookies in a food processor. Add the vegan margarine and pulse until well incorporated.

3. Press the crumb mixture into the bottom of the prepared pan. Bake for 5 minutes. If using sandwich cookies, while the crust is still hot, spread the reserved cream filling over top of the crust. Set aside to cool, for 5 minutes.

4. Melt the chocolate chips in a double boiler or microwave. Set aside.

5. In a blender or food processor, combine the tofu, maple syrup, soy milk, crème de menthe, and espresso powder. Process until smooth.

6. Blend the melted chocolate into the tofu mixture until completely incorporated. Spread the filling into the prepared crust. Refrigerate for at least 3 hours to set before serving.

variations: For extra mint flavor, use chocolate mint cookies to make your crumbs. For mint flavor without crème de menthe, substitute 1 teaspoon of peppermint extract and increase the soy milk to 4 tablespoons. If you don't like the flavor of mint, omit the crème de menthe and add 2 teaspoons of vanilla extract instead and increase the soy milk to 4 tablespoons.

# strawberry cloud pie

makes 8 servings

*Sweetened silken tofu provides the cloudlike filling on which the red ripe strawberries recline.*

CRUST

1¼ cups all-purpose flour

¼ teaspoon salt

½ teaspoon sugar

½ cup vegan margarine, cut into small pieces

3 tablespoons ice water

FILLING

1 (12-ounce) package firm silken tofu, drained and pressed

¾ cup sugar

1 teaspoon pure vanilla extract

2 cups sliced fresh strawberries

½ cup strawberry preserves

1 tablespoon cornstarch dissolved in 2 tablespoons water

1. Make the crust: In a food processor, combine the flour, salt, and sugar and pulse to combine. Add the margarine and process until crumbly. With the machine running, stream in the water and process to form a soft dough. Do not overmix. Flatten the dough into a disk and wrap in plastic wrap. Refrigerate for 30 minutes. Preheat the oven to 400°F.

2. Roll out the dough on a lightly floured work surface to about 10 inches in diameter. Fit the dough into a 9-inch pie plate. Trim and flute the edges. Prick holes in the bottom of the dough with a fork. Bake for 10 minutes, then remove from the oven and set aside. Reduce the oven temperature to 350°F.

3. Make the filling: In a blender or food processor, combine the tofu, sugar, and vanilla and blend until smooth. Pour into the prepared crust.

4. Bake for 30 minutes. Remove from the oven and set aside to cool for 30 minutes.

5. Arrange the sliced strawberries on top of the pie in a decorative pattern to cover the entire surface. Set aside.

6. Puree the preserves in a blender or food processor and transfer to a small saucepan over medium heat. Stir in the cornstarch mixture and continue stirring until the mixture has thickened.

7. Spoon the strawberry glaze over the pie. Refrigerate the pie at least 1 hour before serving to chill the filling and set the glaze.

# no-bake fresh fruit pie

makes 8 servings

*This tasty pie, made with heart-healthy tofu and fresh fruit, looks too pretty to be so good for you. Vary the type of fruit on top (berries are good) according to what you like and what's in season. The amount of fruit you need will depend on how thin you slice it. The idea is to arrange sliced fruit decoratively on top of the pie. Small berries, such as blueberries or raspberries, can be used whole—for these you will need about 2 cups. The kind of fruit spread you use should complement the fruit.*

1½ cups vegan oatmeal cookie crumbs

¼ cup vegan margarine

1 pound firm tofu, well drained and pressed (page xiv)

¾ cup sugar

1 teaspoon pure vanilla extract

1 ripe peach, pitted and cut into ¼-inch slices

2 ripe plums, pitted and cut into ¼-inch slices

¼ cup peach preserves

1 teaspoon fresh lemon juice

1. Grease a 9-inch pie plate and set aside. In a food processor, combine the crumbs and the melted margarine and process until the crumbs are moistened. Press the crumb mixture into the prepared pie plate. Refrigerate until needed.

2. In the food processor, combine the tofu, sugar, and vanilla and process until smooth. Spread the tofu mixture into the chilled crust and refrigerate for 1 hour.

3. Arrange the fruit decoratively on top of the tofu mixture. Set aside.

4. In a small heatproof bowl, combine the preserves and lemon juice and microwave until melted, about 5 seconds. Stir and drizzle over the fruit. Refrigerate the pie for at least 1 hour before serving to chill the filling and set the glaze.

# cashew–banana cream pie

makes 8 servings

*I like to garnish this yummy pie with toasted coconut for added flavor or with roasted cashews to exalt the nuts in the filling, but you could also garnish with berries for a splash of color or chocolate curls—just because.*

1½ cups vegan vanilla cookie crumbs

¼ cup vegan margarine, melted

½ cup unsalted raw cashews

1 (13-ounce) can unsweetened coconut milk

⅔ cup sugar

3 ripe bananas

1 tablespoon agar flakes

1 teaspoon pure vanilla extract

1 teaspoon coconut extract (optional)

Vegan Whipped Cream, homemade (page 501) or store-bought, and toasted coconut, for garnish

1. Lightly oil the bottom and sides of an 8-inch springform pan or pie plate and set aside. In a food processor, combine the cookie crumbs and margarine and pulse until the crumbs are moistened. Press the crumb mixture into the bottom and sides of the prepared pan. Refrigerate until needed.

2. In a high-speed blender, grind the cashews to a powder. Add the coconut milk, sugar, and one of the bananas and blend until smooth. Scrape the mixture into a saucepan, add the agar flakes, and set aside for 10 minutes to soften the agar. Bring just to a boil, then reduce the heat to low and simmer, stirring constantly to dissolve the agar, about 3 minutes. Remove from the heat and stir in the lemon juice, vanilla, and coconut extract, if using. Set aside.

3. Cut the remaining 2 bananas into ¼-inch slices and arrange evenly in the bottom of the prepared pan. Spread the cashew-banana mixture into the pan, then refrigerate until well chilled. When ready to serve, garnish with whipped cream and toasted coconut. Store leftovers covered in the refrigerator.

# peanut butter–
# ice cream pie

makes 8 servings

*It is hard to find a dessert that is easier to make that is also as absolutely scrumptious and picture-perfect pretty. I like to make it in a springform pan because I think it makes a nicer presentation, but you can use a 9-inch pie plate if you prefer.*

1½ cups vegan chocolate cookie crumbs
¼ cup vegan margarine, melted
1 quart vegan vanilla ice cream, softened
2 cups creamy peanut butter
Vegan chocolate curls, for garnish

1. Lightly oil the bottom and sides of a 9-inch springform pan and set aside. In a food processor, combine the cookie crumbs and margarine and process until the crumbs are moistened. Press the crumb mixture into the prepared pan and press into bottom and sides of pan. Refrigerate until needed.

2. In a food processor, combine the ice cream and peanut butter, mixing until well blended. Spread the mixture evenly into the prepared crust.

3. Freeze for 3 hours or overnight. Bring the pie to room temperature for 5 minutes and carefully remove the sides of the springform pan. Sprinkle chocolate curls over top of the pie and serve.

# banana mango pie

makes 6 servings

*This tasty pie is not only delicious and healthful but it's also a great way to use a bunch of ripe bananas.*

1½ cups vegan vanilla cookie crumbs
¼ cup vegan margarine, melted
1 cup mango juice
1 tablespoon agar flakes
¼ cup agave nectar
4 ripe bananas, peeled and cut into chunks
1 teaspoon fresh lemon juice
1 fresh ripe mango, peeled, pitted, and thinly sliced

1. Grease the bottom and sides of an 8-inch pie plate. Place the cookie crumbs and the melted margarine in the bottom of the pie plate and stir with a fork to combine until until the crumbs are moistened. Press into the bottom and sides of the prepared pie plate. Refrigerate until needed.

2. Combine the juice and agar flakes in a small saucepan. Let it sit for 10 minutes to soften. Add the agave nectar and bring the mixture just to a boil. Reduce the heat to a simmer and stir until dissolved, about 3 minutes.

3. Place the bananas in a food processor and process until smooth. Add the agar mixture and lemon juice and process until smooth and well blended. Use a rubber spatula to scrape the filling into the prepared crust. Refrigerate for 2 hours or longer to chill and set up.

4. Just before serving, arrange the mango slices in a circle on top of the pie.

# ginger-pear tart with cranberries and walnuts

makes 8 servings

*Similar to single-crust pies, tarts are made in a special tart pan with a removable bottom that makes them pretty to serve and easy to cut. If you don't have a tart pan, you can make this in a pie plate and it will still be delicious. I've also made tarts in a springform pan, pressing the dough evenly with my fingers up the sides to achieve the desired result.*

### CRUST

1¼ cups all-purpose flour

1 teaspoon sugar

¼ teaspoon salt

½ cup vegan margarine, cut into small pieces

3 tablespoons ice water

### FILLING

4 to 5 Bartlett pears, peeled, cored, and halved lengthwise

½ cup sweetened dried cranberries

½ cup chopped walnut pieces

2 tablespoons fresh lemon juice

½ teaspoon grated fresh ginger

3 tablespoons sugar

1 tablespoon cornstarch

### TOPPING

½ cup all-purpose flour

⅓ cup sugar

½ teaspoon ground ginger

½ teaspoon ground cinnamon

½ teaspoon ground allspice

⅛ teaspoon salt

3 tablespoons vegan margarine

1. Make the crust: In a food processor, combine the flour, sugar, and salt and pulse to combine. Add the margarine and process until crumbly. With the machine running, stream in the water until the dough just starts to hold together, adding more water if needed. Do not overmix. Flatten the dough into a disk and wrap in plastic wrap. Refrigerate for 30 minutes.

2. Roll out the dough on a lightly floured work surface to about 10 inches in diameter. Fit the dough into a 9-inch tart pan or pie plate and flute the edges. Set aside. Preheat the oven to 400°F.

3. Make the filling: Cut the pears into ¼-inch slices and place in a large bowl. Add the cranberries, walnuts, lemon juice, ginger, sugar, and cornstarch and toss to combine. Set aside about 12 of the pear slices to top the tart.

4. Spread the remaining pear mixture in the prepared crust, arranging the reserved pear slices concentrically on top. Set aside.

5. Make the topping: In a medium bowl, combine the flour, sugar, ginger, cinnamon, allspice, and salt. Cut in the margarine with a pastry blender until crumbly.

6. Sprinkle the topping over the pears and bake until tender, about 45 minutes. Cool on a wire rack before serving.

# apple tart with walnut crust

makes 8 servings

*The mellow flavor and crunchy texture of the walnut crust is a perfect match for the sweet-tart apples in this tantalizing tart.*

CRUST

1 cup walnut pieces

½ cup pitted dates

½ cup old-fashioned oats

3 tablespoons vegan margarine

2 tablespoons sugar

FILLING

5 Granny Smith apples, peeled, cored, and halved lengthwise

2 tablespoons fresh lemon juice

3 tablespoons sugar

1 tablespoon cornstarch

TOPPING

¾ cup all-purpose flour

½ cup sugar

1½ teaspoons ground cinnamon

⅛ teaspoon salt

¼ cup vegan margarine

1. Make the crust: In a food processor, combine the walnuts, dates, and oats and pulse until finely chopped. Add the margarine and sugar and process until well mixed.

2. Grease a 9-inch tart pan or pie plate. Press the crust mixture firmly onto the bottom and sides of the prepared pan. Set aside. Preheat the oven to 400°F.

3. Make the filling: Cut the apples into ¼-inch slices and place in a large bowl. Add the lemon juice, sugar, and cornstarch and toss to combine. Set aside about 12 of the apple slices to top the tart.

4. Spread the remaining apple mixture in the prepared crust, arranging the reserved apple slices concentrically on top.

5. Make the topping: In a medium bowl, combine the flour, sugar, cinnamon, and salt. Cut in the margarine with a pastry blender until crumbly.

6. Sprinkle the topping over the apples and bake until tender, about 45 minutes. Cool on a wire rack before serving.

# two-berry cobbler

makes 8 servings

*Necessity was the inspiration for this recipe. Knowing we had fresh blueberries in the house, my husband requested a cobbler. Only problem was, there weren't enough blueberries. I took a chance and bulked up the filling with some whole-berry cranberry sauce. This version is now requested in its own right.*

3 cups blueberries

¾ cup sugar

1 tablespoon cornstarch

¼ cup water

1 cup canned whole-berry cranberry sauce

1½ cups all-purpose flour

½ teaspoon ground cinnamon

2 teaspoons baking powder

½ teaspoon salt

⅓ cup vegan margarine, melted

½ cup plain or vanilla soy milk

1. Preheat the oven to 375°F. In a saucepan, combine the blueberries, ½ cup of the sugar, cornstarch, water, and cinnamon, stirring to blend. Bring to a boil over high heat, then reduce heat to low, and stir gently until slightly thickened, about 5 minutes.

2. Remove the saucepan from the heat and stir in the cranberry sauce until well mixed. Spoon the fruit mixture into the bottom of a 9-inch square baking pan and set aside.

3. In a large bowl, combine the flour, baking powder, salt, and remaining $1/4$ cup sugar. Blend in the margarine and soy milk until a soft dough forms. Drop the dough by large spoonfuls on top of the fruit mixture. Bake until the fruit is bubbly and the top of the crust is golden brown, about 40 minutes. Serve warm.

variations: If there's no shortage of berries in your house, omit the cranberry sauce and increase the blueberries to 4 cups. You can also mix and match berries in this recipe, using 2 cups blueberries and 2 cups sliced strawberries, for example. Frozen berries can also be substituted for all or part of the filling. Instead of a cobbler, you can bake the filling in a pie crust as well.

# apple and pear cobbler

makes 6 servings

*Two favorite fall fruits, apples and pears, combine in this homey cobbler, an ideal dessert for a crisp autumn day. Wonderful on its own, it is heavenly served warm with a scoop of vegan vanilla ice cream.*

3 Granny Smith apples, peeled, cored, and shredded
2 ripe pears, peeled, cored, and cut into 1/4-inch slices
2 teaspoons fresh lemon juice
1/2 cup plus 2 tablespoons sugar
2 tablespoons cornstarch
1 teaspoon ground cinnamon
1/2 teaspoon ground allspice
1 cup all-purpose flour
1 1/2 teaspoons baking powder
1/4 teaspoon salt
2 tablespoons canola or other neutral oil
1/2 cup plain or vanilla soy milk

1. Preheat the oven to 400°F. Grease a 9-inch square baking pan. Spread the apples and pears in the prepared pan. Sprinkle with the lemon juice and toss to coat. Stir in $1/2$ cup of the sugar, cornstarch, cinnamon, and allspice, stirring to mix.

2. In a medium bowl, combine the flour, the remaining 2 tablespoons sugar, the baking powder, and the salt. Add the oil and mix with a fork until the mixture resembles coarse crumbs. Mix in the soy milk. Spread the topping over the fruit. Bake until golden, about 30 minutes. Serve warm.

# blueberry-peach crisp

makes 8 servings

*Since peaches and blueberries are both delicious and usually in season at the same time, they make ideal companions in fruit pies, cobblers, or crisps like this one.*

4 fresh ripe peaches, peeled, pitted, and cut into 1/4-inch slices
2 cups fresh blueberries
1 tablespoon cornstarch
3/4 cup sugar
2 teaspoons fresh lemon juice
1 teaspoon ground cinnamon
1/2 cup all-purpose flour
1/2 cup old-fashioned oats
3 tablespoons vegan margarine

1. Preheat the oven to 375°F. Lightly oil a 9-inch square baking pan and set aside. In a large bowl, combine the peaches, blueberries, cornstarch, $1/4$ cup of the sugar, lemon juice, and $1/2$ teaspoon of the cinnamon. Mix gently and spoon into the prepared baking pan. Set aside.

continues on next page

2. In small bowl, combine the flour, oats, margarine, the remaining $\frac{1}{2}$ cup sugar, and the remaining $\frac{1}{2}$ teaspoon cinnamon. Use a pastry blender or fork to mix until crumbly.

3. Sprinkle the topping over the fruit mixture and bake until the top is browned and bubbly in the center, 30 to 40 minutes. Serve warm.

# quick apple crisp

makes 6 servings

*When you want the flavor of apple pie without the bother of a crust, this quick crisp is the way to go. Enlist some help to peel the apples and it can be in the oven in minutes.*

5 Granny Smith apples, peeled, cored, and cut into $\frac{1}{4}$-inch slices
$\frac{1}{2}$ cup pure maple syrup
1 tablespoon fresh lemon juice
1 teaspoon ground cinnamon
$\frac{1}{2}$ cup all-purpose flour
$\frac{1}{2}$ cup old-fashioned oats
$\frac{1}{2}$ cup finely chopped walnuts or pecans
$\frac{2}{3}$ cup light brown sugar
$\frac{1}{2}$ cup vegan margarine, softened

1. Preheat the oven to 350°F. Lightly oil a 9-inch square baking pan. Place the apples in the prepared pan. Drizzle the maple syrup and lemon juice over the apples and sprinkle with $\frac{1}{2}$ teaspoon of the cinnamon. Set aside.

2. In a medium bowl, mix the flour, oats, walnuts, sugar, and the remaining $\frac{1}{2}$ teaspoon cinnamon. Use a pastry blender to cut in the margarine until the mixture resembles coarse crumbs. Spread the topping over the apples and bake until bubbly and lightly browned on top, about 45 minutes. Serve warm.

# banana-pecan strudel

makes 6 servings

*Inspired by the classic New Orleans dessert Bananas Foster, this dessert tastes as impressive as it looks (especially when nestled with a scoop of vegan vanilla or pecan ice cream), but it couldn't be easier to make thanks to using store-bought puff pastry. It is a boon to vegans that Pepperidge Farm puff pastry sheets, found in supermarkets everywhere, are vegan.*

2 tablespoons vegan margarine
$\frac{1}{2}$ cup light brown sugar
$\frac{3}{4}$ cup chopped unsalted pecans
3 ripe bananas, sliced
2 tablespoons rum or 1 teaspoon rum extract (optional)
$\frac{1}{2}$ teaspoon ground cinnamon
1 sheet frozen puff pastry, thawed
Sugar, for rolling and dusting pastry

1. In a large skillet, melt the margarine over medium heat. Add the brown sugar and stir to blend. Add the pecans and bananas and cook for 1 minute, stirring to coat. Add the rum, if using, and the cinnamon and stir to combine. Remove from heat and set aside to cool.

2. Roll out the puff pastry on a lightly sugared work surface to eliminate the creases in the pastry.

3. Spread the cooled banana mixture down the length of the pastry. Fold the sides of the pastry over the banana mixture and tuck in the ends, sealing the edges with your fingers.

4. Place the strudel on an ungreased baking sheet and cut a few diagonal slashes on top of the pastry with a sharp knife to allow steam to

escape. Sprinkle a little sugar on the top of the strudel and refrigerate for 15 minutes. Preheat the oven to 400°F.

5. Bake the strudel until golden brown, 35 to 40 minutes. Cool for 10 minutes. Use a serated bread knife to cut into slices and serve.

# pear crumble

makes 6 servings

*This is an easy flavorful dessert that can work in both a casual or more formal setting. For added impact, add some chopped pecans to the topping and serve it warm with a scoop of vegan vanilla ice cream.*

5 ripe Bartlett pears, peeled, cored, and cut into ¼-inch slices

½ cup sugar

2 tablespoons cornstarch

1 teaspoon ground allspice

½ teaspoon ground ginger

1 cup all-purpose flour

½ cup old-fashioned oats

1 cup sugar

½ cup vegan margarine, cut into small pieces

1. Preheat the oven to 375°F. Place the pear slices in a 9-inch square baking pan and sprinkle with the sugar, the cornstarch, ½ teaspoon of the allspice, and the ginger.

2. In a medium bowl, combine the flour, oats, sugar, and remaining ½ teaspoon of allspice. Use a pastry blender or fork to cut in the margarine until the mixture resembles coarse crumbs.

3. Spread the topping over the pears and bake until browned and bubbly, about 40 minutes. Serve warm.

# PUDDINGS AND PARFAITS

# baked chocolate pudding

makes 6 servings

*These little puddings are nice because you just pop them in the oven—no standing over the stove and stirring. Plus, they get baked in their own serving dishes, so they're easy and attractive to serve. A dollop of Vegan Whipped Cream (page 501) or Cashew Crème (page 501) is always welcome.*

1 cup sugar

1 tablespoon canola or other neutral oil

1½ cups plain or vanilla soy milk

1 teaspoon pure vanilla extract

1 cup all-purpose flour

½ cup unsweetened cocoa powder

2 teaspoons baking powder

¼ teaspoon salt

1. Preheat the oven to 350°F. Grease 6 individual oven-safe dessert ramekins and set aside.

2. In a medium bowl, mix the sugar and oil until well blended. Stir in the soy milk and vanilla and set aside.

3. In a separate medium bowl, combine the flour, cocoa, baking powder, and salt. Mix the dry ingredients into the wet ingredients until just blended.

4. Spoon the pudding into the prepared ramekins and bake until set, about 25 minutes. Let stand at least 10 minutes before serving. Serve warm or at room temperature.

# cashew chocolate pudding

makes 4 servings

*Of all the vegan chocolate puddings I've tasted and made, this one is my favorite, not only because it's easy to make but also because it has a rich depth of flavor. Spoon it into your prettiest clear dessert glasses (martini glasses are especially nice for this) and garnish with chocolate curls or perhaps, some Vegan Whipped Cream (page 501) and a few perfectly ripe berries. The key to getting a silky smooth pudding is grinding the cashews to a powder in a high-speed blender such as a Vita-Mix. Otherwise, you can grind the cashews a little at a time in a spice grinder.*

1 cup vegan semisweet chocolate chips
½ cup unsalted raw cashews
½ cup plain or vanilla soy milk
¾ cup firm silken tofu, drained
⅓ cup agave nectar or pure maple syrup
1 teaspoon pure vanilla extract

1. Melt the chocolate chips in a double boiler or microwave. Set aside.

2. In a high-speed blender, grind the cashews to a fine powder. Add the soy milk and blend until smooth. Add the tofu, agave nectar, and vanilla and continue to blend until smooth and creamy.

3. Scrape the melted chocolate into the blender. Process until completely incorporated with the cashew mixture.

4. Divide the pudding among 4 small dessert bowls or glasses and refrigerate 2 hours, until firm and chilled.

# chocolate-banana pudding

makes 6 servings

*This creamy pudding is the result of the happy merger of two great flavors: bananas and chocolate. The chocolate flavor is dominant but nicely accented by the mellow sweetness of the banana. Chopped peanuts add a wonderful crunch and extra dimension of flavor.*

8 ounce vegan semisweet chocolate chips
2 ripe bananas
¼ cup pure maple syrup
1 teaspoon pure vanilla extract
½ cup chopped unsalted roasted peanuts

1. Melt the chocolate in a double boiler or microwave. Set aside.

2. In a blender or food processor, puree the bananas. Add the maple syrup and vanilla and blend until smooth. Add the melted chocolate and blend until smooth.

3. Divide the pudding evenly among 6 dessert bowls. Refrigerate 2 hours, until well chilled. Garnish with chopped peanuts.

# sunset fruit pudding

makes 4 servings

*This creamy fruit pudding gets its name because its dazzling color reminds me of a particularly dramatic sky at sunset. Fresh and delicious, it couldn't be easier to make. If you're feeling especially ambitious, puree each fruit separately, then divide among four dessert glasses and swirl gently with a knife to resemble the streaks in a sky. Enjoy unadorned or garnish with toasted crushed nuts, chocolate curls, toasted coconut, or ripe red strawberries.*

1 ripe mango, peeled, pitted, and chopped
8 fresh ripe strawberries, hulled
2 ripe bananas

1. In a food processor, combine the mango, strawberries, and bananas and process until smooth.

2. Divide the fruit mixture evenly among 4 dessert dishes and refrigerate until ready to serve.

# maple-baked rice pudding with dried cranberries

makes 6 servings

*This simple and delicious recipe for the comfort food classic uses leftover cooked rice, so plan ahead next time you put on a pot of rice. Then, just combine all the ingredients, pop in the oven, and let the comforting fragrance waft through the house.*

2½ cups cooked rice
1½ cups plain or vanilla soy milk
⅓ cup pure maple syrup
3 tablespoons sugar
1½ teaspoons pure vanilla extract
½ teaspoon ground cinnamon
Pinch salt
⅓ cup golden raisins or sweetened dried cranberries

1. Preheat the oven to 350°F. Lightly oil a 9-inch square baking pan. Combine all the ingredients in the prepared pan, stirring until well blended.

2. Bake until hot, about 45 minutes. Serve warm or cold.

# coconut-pistachio rice pudding

makes 6 servings

*This luscious rice pudding was inspired by two of my favorite rice desserts: the sweet sticky rice of Thailand and Indian kheer, which is often made with pistachios and cardamom. Chopped fresh mango makes a good addition, whether stirred right into the pudding or spooned on top as a garnish—or a little of both.*

1 (13.5-ounce) can unsweetened coconut milk
½ cup plain or vanilla soy milk
½ cup sugar
2½ cups cooked jasmine or basmati rice
1½ teaspoons pure vanilla extract
1 teaspoon ground cardamom or allspice
⅛ teaspoon salt
½ cup unsalted shelled pistachio nuts, coarsely chopped
½ cup sweetened shredded coconut

1. In a large saucepan, combine the coconut milk, soy milk, and sugar and bring almost to boil, stirring to dissolve the sugar.

2. Add the rice, vanilla, cardamom, and salt and simmer over medium-low heat for 20 minutes, or until desired consistency is reached, stirring occasionally.

3. Stir in the pistachios and coconut and let cool. Cover and refrigerate until well chilled, 2 hours.

# forbidden black rice pudding

makes 8 servings

*Chinese black rice, also known as "forbidden rice," can be found in well-stocked markets and gourmet grocers. It has a nutty taste, faintly reminiscent of popcorn. Its deep purple color when cooked lends a dramatic touch.*

1 cup forbidden black rice

3 cups water

½ teaspoon salt

½ cup sugar

1 (13.5-ounce) can unsweetened coconut milk

1. In a large saucepan, bring the rice, water, and salt to a boil over high heat. Reduce heat to low and cover and simmer until tender, about 45 minutes.

2. Stir in the sugar and all but ½ cup of the coconut milk and return to a boil, then reduce heat to low and simmer, uncovered, stirring occasionally, until thick, about 30 minutes.

3. Remove from heat and set aside to cool to room temperature, stirring occasionally. Divide the rice pudding evenly among 8 dessert bowls, drizzle the remaining coconut milk over the top, and serve.

# paradise pudding

makes 4 servings

*This delicious pudding can only be described as ambrosial comfort food. I adapted it from a recipe shared with me by Peter Kumar, a talented chef and restaurateur from Virginia Beach, Virginia. Look for* suji *(semolina or cream of wheat) in Indian markets and specialty grocers.*

1 tablespoon vegan margarine

¼ cup unsalted roasted cashews

¼ cup golden raisins

1 cup suji (semolina or cream of wheat)

½ cup sugar

1½ cups pineapple, mango, or white grape juice

¼ cup pineapple chunks

¼ teaspoon ground cardamom

1. In a medium skillet, heat the margarine over low heat. Add the cashews, raisins, and suji and toast until fragrant, stirring frequently, about 5 minutes.

2. Stir in the sugar and pineapple juice and continue to cook, stirring constantly. Add the pineapple chunks and cardamom and continue to cook a few minutes longer, until it resembles a thick pudding.

3. To serve, divide the pudding evenly among 4 small dessert dishes. Serve warm or at room temperature or refrigerate until chilled, about 2 hours.

variation: For a different presentation, double the recipe and transfer the cooked pudding to a 9-inch springform pan. Smooth the top and refrigerate until chilled. Cut into wedges and serve with a mango puree.

# banana orzo pudding

makes 6 servings

*This yummy pudding made with orzo, the tiny rice-shaped pasta, makes an interesting change from rice pudding. For added banana flavor, just before serving, thinly slice an additional banana and stir it into the pudding or use to garnish the top of the desserts when spooned into individual dessert dishes.*

2 ripe bananas

1 cup plain or vanilla soy milk

½ cup sugar

1½ teaspoons pure vanilla extract

½ teaspoon ground cinnamon

Pinch salt

2½ cups cooked orzo

½ cup toasted sliced almonds

1. In a blender or food processor, combine the bananas, soy milk, sugar, vanilla, cinnamon, and salt and blend until smooth.

2. Transfer the mixture to a medium saucepan and bring almost to boil over medium-high heat, stirring to dissolve the sugar. Add the cooked orzo and simmer over low heat for 20 minutes, or until desired consistency is reached, stirring occasionally. Set aside to cool.

3. Transfer the pudding to a bowl, cover, and refrigerate until chilled. Garnish with almonds. Serve warm or cold.

# avocado-raspberry parfaits 🅕

makes 4 servings

*These colorful parfaits are creamy and delicious. They're also super-easy to make and quite festive looking. Nondairy whipping cream, such as Rich's brand, is available in well-stocked supermarkets. If unavailable, use a ready-made vegan whipped cream, available at natural food stores or make your own using the recipe on page 501.*

2 ripe Hass avocados, pitted, peeled, and chopped

½ cup plus 1 teaspoon sugar

3 tablespoons fresh lime juice

½ teaspoon pure vanilla extract

1 cup fresh raspberries, plus 4 for garnish

1 cup vegan whipping cream

¾ cup vegan granola, homemade (page 521) or store-bought

Fresh mint sprigs for garnish

1. In a blender or food processor, combine the avocados, ½ cup of the sugar, lime juice, and vanilla and process until smooth. Set aside.

2. Finely chop the 1 cup of raspberries and place them in a small bowl. Sprinkle with the remaining 1 teaspoon sugar and set aside.

3. In a large bowl, beat the whipping cream with an electric mixer on high speed until soft peaks form. Set aside.

4. To assemble, spoon a layer of the granola into each of 4 parfait or wineglasses. Add a layer of the avocado mixture, followed by a layer of the whipped topping. Top each with a layer of the raspberries. Top with a small spoonful of whipped topping and garnish with the reserved raspberries and mint. Serve immediately.

# strawberry parfaits with cashew crème

makes 4 servings

*This luscious dessert tastes like strawberry shortcake without the cake. I like to make this dessert in early summer when fresh ripe strawberries are at their peak. If you can find four perfect small strawberries, save them to garnish the tops of the parfaits. Since this pretty dessert is light yet satisfying, it makes an ideal finish to a big meal.*

½ cup unsalted raw cashews
4 tablespoons sugar
½ cup plain or vanilla soy milk
¾ cup firm silken tofu, drained
1 teaspoon pure vanilla extract
2 cups sliced strawberries
1 teaspoon fresh lemon juice
Fresh mint leaves, for garnish

1. In a blender, grind the cashews and 3 tablespoons of the sugar to a fine powder. Add the soy milk and blend until smooth. Add the tofu and vanilla and continue to blend until smooth and creamy. Scrape the cashew mixture into a medium bowl, cover, and refrigerate for 30 minutes.

2. In a large bowl, combine the strawberries, lemon juice, and remaining 1 tablespoon sugar. Stir gently to combine and set aside at room temperature for 20 minutes.

3. Spoon alternating layers of the strawberries and cashew crème into parfait glasses or wineglasses, ending with a dollop of the cashew crème. Garnish with mint leaves and serve.

# vegan tiramisù

makes 6 servings

*Tiramisù, the Italian "pick me up" dessert, has long been one of my husband's favorites, so it was a priority to veganize it. For decadence, add a layer of vegan whipped cream and chocolate curls.*

1 cup firm tofu, drained and pressed dry
1 (8-ounce) container vegan cream cheese
½ cup vegan vanilla ice cream, softened
1 teaspoon pure vanilla extract
⅓ cup plus 1 tablespoon superfine sugar
½ cup coffee, cooled to room temperature
3 tablespoons coffee liqueur
1 vegan pound cake, homemade (page 448)
      or store-bought, or other white or yellow cake,
      cut into ½-inch-thick slices
1 tablespoon unsweetened cocoa powder

1. In a food processor, combine the tofu, cream cheese, ice cream, vanilla, and ⅓ cup of the sugar. Process until smooth and well blended.

2. In a small bowl, combine the coffee, the remaining 1 tablespoon sugar, and the coffee liqueur.

3. Arrange a single layer of cake slices in an 8-inch square baking pan and brush with half of the coffee mixture. Sprinkle with half of the cocoa. Spread half the tofu mixture over the cake. Arrange another layer of cake slices on top of the tofu mixture. Brush with the remaining coffee mixture and spread evenly with the remaining tofu mixture. Sprinkle with the remaining cocoa. Chill 1 hour before serving.

# indian pudding

makes 6 servings

*Indian pudding, especially popular during colonial times, is a sturdy and wholesome dessert made with cornmeal and sweetened with molasses. It is an especially satisfying "comfort" dessert, served warm on a frosty evening. It can also be served at room temperature or even chilled. Fresh berries would make a lovely garnish. This pudding can also be baked in individual ramekins, although the baking time should be reduced by about half.*

3½ cups plain or vanilla soy milk

½ cup sugar

½ cup dark molasses

½ cup yellow cornmeal

½ teaspoon salt

½ teaspoon ground allspice

½ teaspoon ground cinnamon

¼ teaspoon ground ginger

1. Preheat the oven to 350°F. Grease a 2-quart gratin dish or 9-inch square baking pan and set aside.

2. In a large saucepan, combine the soy milk, sugar, and molasses over medium heat and cook, stirring, until blended. Slowly add the cornmeal, whisking to incorporate. Cook, stirring until thickened, 5 to 7 minutes. Stir in the salt, allspice, cinnamon, and ginger and remove from the heat.

3. Pour the mixture into the prepared pan. Bake until the center is set, about 1 hour.

# sweet vermicelli pudding 🅕

makes 4 to 6 servings

*Inspired by the northern Indian pudding known as* sevian kheer, *this sweet noodle pudding is traditionally made with sevian noodles—extremely thin strands similar to the thinnest Italian vermicelli. Sevian noodles can be found in Indian markets, where you can also find rosewater. Since sevian can be difficult to find, thin vermicelli noodles or angel hair pasta can be used instead and vanilla extract may be used to replace rosewater if it is unavailable.*

2 tablespoons vegan margarine

6 ounces sevian noodles, vermicelli noodles, or angel hair pasta

½ cup toasted slivered almonds

½ cup unsalted shelled pistachio nuts

2 cups plain or vanilla soy milk

1 cup unsweetened coconut milk

¼ cup sugar

¼ cup golden raisins

½ teaspoon ground cardamom

1½ teaspoons rosewater or pure vanilla extract

1. In a large skillet, heat the margarine over medium heat. Break the noodles into 2-inch pieces and add them to the skillet along with ¼ cup each of the almonds and pistachios. Cook, stirring, until the noodles turn golden. Do not brown.

2. Stir in the soy milk and coconut milk and bring to simmer. Add the sugar, raisins, and cardamom and simmer for 10 minutes.

3. Stir in the rosewater, then transfer to a serving dish and sprinkle with the remaining almonds and pistachios. Serve warm or at room temperature.

# chocolate and walnut farfalle f

makes 4 servings

*This comforting and unusual combination is inspired by Eastern European desserts that pair noodles, walnuts, and sugar. I used far-falle instead of other noodles for their whimsical (butterfly) shape and added some chocolate for good measure. The result is a dense and hearty dessert that it best enjoyed on its own as a snack or served after a light meal. To toast walnuts, place them on a baking sheet and bake in a preheated 350°F oven for 15 to 20 minutes, turning occasionally until toasted.*

½ cup chopped toasted walnuts
¼ cup vegan semisweet chocolate pieces
8 ounces farfalle
3 tablespoons vegan margarine
¼ cup sugar

1. In a food processor or blender, grind the walnuts and chocolate pieces until crumbly. Do not overprocess. Set aside.

2. In a pot of boiling salted water, cook the farfalle, stirring occasionally, until al dente, about 8 minutes. Drain well and return to the pot.

3. Add the margarine and sugar and toss to combine and melt the margarine.

4. Transfer the noodle mixture to a serving bowl. Add the nut and chocolate mixture and toss to combine. Serve warm.

# fresh cherry-vanilla bread pudding

makes 6 servings

*When fresh cherries are in season, I can't seem to get enough of them. If you have a cherry pitter—a neat little gadget that also pits olives—this recipe comes together quickly.*

4 cups cubed white bread
2 cups pitted and halved cherries
2 cups plain or vanilla soy milk
8 ounces soft silken tofu, drained
⅔ cup sugar
2 teaspoons pure vanilla extract
½ cup flaked sweetened coconut

1. Preheat the oven to 350°F. Grease a 9-inch square baking pan. Spread the bread cubes in the prepared baking pan. Sprinkle evenly with the cherries and set aside.

2. In a blender or food processor, combine the soy milk, tofu, sugar, and vanilla and blend until smooth.

3. Pour the liquid mixture over the bread and cherries, pressing the bread to saturate with the liquid. Sprinkle the coconut on top, pressing into the mixture. Bake until firm, about 45 minutes. Allow to cool 15 minutes and serve. Or refrigerate, 2 hours, to serve chilled.

**blueberry-banana bread pudding:** Substitute blueberries for the cherries and bananas for the tofu. Omit the coconut and add ½ teaspoon of cinnamon. Serve as is or drizzled with the Lemon Cashew Crème (page 502).

**pineapple-coconut bread pudding:** Use fresh or canned chopped pineapple instead of the cherries. Use unsweetened coconut milk instead of the soy milk.

# pumpkin-cranberry bread pudding

makes 6 servings

*This is a cozy, comforting dessert to have in the house during the holiday season. It's also delicious for breakfast or a midday snack. For a double-pumpkin punch, use leftover sliced pumpkin bread (page 402) in place of the whole grain or white bread.*

4 cups cubed whole grain or white bread

½ cup sweetened dried cranberries

½ cup shelled pumpkin seeds (pepitas)

1 (16-ounce) can solid-pack pumpkin

¾ cup light brown sugar

1 teaspoon pure vanilla extract

1½ teaspoons ground cinnamon

½ teaspoon ground allspice

¼ teaspoon ground nutmeg

½ teaspoon salt

2 cups plain or vanilla soy milk

1. Preheat the oven to 350°F. Grease a 9 × 13-inch baking pan. Press half the bread cubes, half the cranberries, and half the pumpkin seeds into the bottom of the prepared baking pan. Set aside.

2. In a large bowl, combine the pumpkin, sugar, vanilla, cinnamon, allspice, nutmeg, and salt. Slowly whisk in the soy milk until smooth and well combined.

3. Pour half of the pumpkin mixture over the bread and cranberries in the pan, pushing the bread pieces down beneath the pumpkin mixture to moisten them. Top with the remaining bread, cranberries, and pumpkin seeds, followed by the remaining pumpkin mixture.

4. Bake until firm, about 45 minutes. Set aside for 15 minutes and serve, or refrigerate for 2 hours to serve chilled.

# chocolate bread pudding with rum sauce

makes 6 servings

*While you could bake this pudding in a square baking pan and scoop it into bowls, I think it's more interesting to make it in a springform pan and slice it like a cheesecake.*

⅓ cup unsweetened cocoa powder

¼ cup applesauce

2 cups plain or vanilla soy milk

⅔ cup sugar

½ teaspoon ground cinnamon

Pinch salt

2 teaspoons pure vanilla extract

4 cups white bread, torn into small pieces

½ cup semisweet vegan chocolate chips

½ cup vegan margarine, softened

½ cup confectioners' sugar

2½ tablespoons dark rum

1. Preheat the oven to 350°F. Grease an 8-inch springform pan and set aside. In a large bowl, combine the cocoa and applesauce, stirring to blend. Stir in the soy milk, sugar, cinnamon, salt, and 1 teaspoon of the vanilla. Mix in the bread and chocolate chips.

2. Scrape the mixture into the prepared pan, pressing with your hands to spread evenly. Bake until set, about 45 minutes. Remove from the oven and set aside to cool on a wire rack.

3. In a large bowl, combine the margarine and sugar and beat with an electric mixer on high speed until incorporated, about 2 minutes. Add the rum and remaining 1 teaspoon of vanilla and beat on high speed for 3 minutes.

4. Remove the sides of the springform pan, cut the pudding into wedges and transfer to dessert plates. Spoon the sauce over the pudding and serve.

# Fruit Desserts

## granola-stuffed baked apples

makes 4 servings

*Sweet and crunchy granola makes a yummy stuffing for these baked apples. They remind me of an inside-out apple pie. Best of all, they smell good while baking and look pretty served in shallow dessert bowls.*

½ cup vegan granola, homemade (page 521) or store-bought

2 tablespoons creamy peanut butter or almond butter

1 tablespoon vegan margarine

1 tablespoon pure maple syrup

½ teaspoon ground cinnamon

4 Granny Smith or other firm baking apples

1 cup apple juice

1. Preheat the oven to 350°F. Grease a 9 × 13-inch baking pan and set aside. In a medium bowl, combine the granola, peanut butter, margarine, maple syrup, and cinnamon and mix well.

2. Core the apples and stuff the granola mixture into the centers of the apples, packing tightly.

3. Place the apples upright in the prepared pan. Pour the apple juice over the apples and bake until tender, about 1 hour. Serve warm.

## pecan and date-stuffed roasted pears

makes 4 servings

*Roasting brings out the flavor of the pears, giving them a more intensely delicious taste than you get from poaching. The pecan and date stuffing adds sweetness and crunch, making this a sophisticated autumn dessert. For a special presentation, arrange two stuffed pear halves on a dessert plate and nestle a scoop of vegan vanilla ice cream in between. Drizzle on a little Chocolate Sauce (page 497) or raspberry coulis (page 489) if desired.*

4 firm ripe pears, cored

1 tablespoon fresh lemon juice

½ cup finely chopped pecans

4 dates, pitted and chopped

1 tablespoon vegan margarine

1 tablespoon pure maple syrup

¼ teaspoon ground cinnamon

⅛ teaspoon ground ginger

½ cup pear, white grape, or apple juice

1. Preheat the oven to 350°F. Grease a shallow baking dish and set aside. Halve the pears lengthwise and use a melon baller to scoop out the cores. Rub the exposed part of the pears with the lemon juice to avoid discoloration.

2. In a medium bowl, combine the pecans, dates, margarine, maple syrup, cinnamon, and ginger and mix well.

3. Stuff the mixture into the centers of the pear halves and arrange them in the prepared baking pan. Pour the juice over the pears. Bake until tender, 30 to 40 minutes. Serve warm.

variation: Use apples instead of pears.

# banana fritters
# with caramel sauce 🅕

makes 4 to 6 servings

*If you don't want to take the time to make the caramel sauce, these yummy fritters are also delicious dusted with confectioners' sugar.*

3 ripe bananas, mashed

2 tablespoons pure maple syrup

2 tablespoons sugar

⅓ cup plain or vanilla soy milk

⅔ cup all-purpose flour

½ teaspoon ground cinnamon

¼ teaspoon salt

2 teaspoons baking powder

1 tablespoon vegan margarine, melted

Canola or other neutral oil, for frying

Caramel Sauce, homemade (page 498)
    or store-bought

1. In a large bowl, combine the bananas, maple syrup, sugar, and soy milk. Stir in the flour, cinnamon, salt, and baking powder, then mix in the margarine until well blended.

2. In a large skillet, heat a thin layer of oil over medium-high heat. When the oil is hot, carefully place spoonfuls of the banana mixture into the skillet. Do not crowd. Fry until golden brown on one side, then turn and fry the other side, about 6 to 8 minutes total. Drain the cooked fritters on paper towels.

3. Arrange the fritters on dessert plates and drizzle with caramel sauce. Serve warm.

variation: Use another fruit to replace the bananas: try 3 apples or ripe pears, peeled, cored, and shredded; or 2 ripe mangoes, peeled, pitted, and finely chopped.

# baked bananas
# with a twist of lime 🅕

makes 4 servings

*Flavors of Southeast Asia merge in this easy and flavorful dessert. It's delicious on it's own but absolutely ethereal served with Ginger-Coconut Nice Cream (page 495) or any brand of vegan vanilla ice cream. A channel zester is a tool with a small sharp blade designed to cut long strips of peel from citrus fruit.*

2 or 3 limes

3 tablespoons light brown sugar

⅓ cup water

4 ripe bananas

2 tablespoons vegan margarine

2 tablespoons crushed unsalted roasted cashews
    or peanuts

2 tablespoons shredded sweetened coconut

1. Preheat the oven to 350°F. Use a channel zester to remove 4 long strips of peel from the limes. Twist the strips and set aside to use as garnish. Juice and zest the limes to yield 2 tablespoons of juice and 1 teaspoon of fine zest. Set aside.

2. In a small saucepan, combine the sugar and water and bring to a boil. Reduce heat to low and simmer for 30 seconds, stirring to dissolve the sugar. Remove from the heat and add the reserved lime juice and zest. Set aside.

3. Cut the bananas in half lengthwise and arrange in a shallow baking dish (an oval gratin dish works well). Pour on the sugar syrup and dot with bits of the margarine. Sprinkle with cashews and coconut and bake for 20 minutes, basting occasionally. Serve garnished with the reserved lime twists.

# blushing poached pears

makes 4 servings

*I find that "poaching" the pears in the oven instead of on the stovetop is easier and the pears seem more flavorful, too. I've added a blush to the classic pear dessert poire belle-Hélène, because as delicious as it is, I think the traditional version is too muted. The touch of color to the pears, accented by fresh mint sprigs, livens things up.*

1½ cups cranberry juice

1 cup sugar

2 teaspoons pure vanilla extract

4 ripe Bosc or D'Anjou pears

4 scoops vegan vanilla ice cream

Chocolate Sauce, homemade (page 497)
　　or store-bought

Mint sprigs, for garnish

1. Lightly grease a 9 × 13-inch baking pan and set aside. Preheat the oven to 400°F. In a large saucepan, combine the cranberry juice and sugar over medium heat. Cook, stirring, until the sugar dissolves, then bring to a boil over medium-high heat. Continue to boil for 8 minutes, then remove from the heat and stir in the vanilla.

2. Peel the pears and cut them in half length-wise. Scoop out the cores with a melon baller and arrange in the prepared pan. Pour the cranberry syrup over the pears, turning to coat. Bake until just tender, but not falling apart, about 30 minutes.

3. Remove from the oven and cool to room temperature, then refrigerate until chilled.

When ready to serve, arrange 2 of the pear halves on each of 4 chilled dessert plates, spooning any remaining syrup over the pears. Nestle a scoop of ice cream on each plate. Drizzle each with the chocolate sauce and garnish with a mint sprig.

# grilled orange and strawberry skewers

makes 4 servings

*This easy and elegant dessert is great on its own, but you can up the ante by serving the skewered fruit with vegan vanilla ice cream and drizzling with chocolate sauce. If using wooden skewers, remember to soak them for 30 minutes before using.*

2 large navel oranges, peeled and cut into
　　1-inch chunks

8 large ripe strawberries, hulled

½ cup Grand Marnier or other orange-flavored
　　liqueur

1. Skewer the orange chunks and strawberries on 8 skewers, placing 2 or 3 orange chunks on each skewer, followed by 1 strawberry, and finishing with 2 or 3 pieces of orange.

2. Place the skewered fruit in a shallow dish and pour the Grand Marnier over the fruit, turning to coat. Set aside for 1 hour. Preheat the grill.

3. Grill the fruit skewers, brushing with the marinade, about 3 minutes per side. Serve the skewers hot, drizzled with the remaining marinade.

# rum-sautéed pineapple and bananas with toasted coconut and pecans

makes 4 servings

*From the yummy, multifaceted tastes of the tropics in this dessert, no one would ever know that it could be made at the last minute. Once you cut up the pineapple, or if you use fresh precut chunks, you could have this dessert on the table in about 15 minutes. Serve over vegan ice cream or pound cake—or both.*

¼ cup vegan margarine

½ cup sugar

½ pineapple, peeled, cored, and cut into 1-inch chunks

2 ripe bananas, cut into ¼-inch slices

¼ cup dark rum

2 tablespoons toasted coconut

2 tablespoons unsalted toasted pecans, coarsely chopped

1. In a large skillet, heat the margarine and sugar over medium heat. Cook, stirring, until the sugar dissolves, about 2 minutes. Add the pineapple and bananas and cook for 1 to 2 minutes. Carefully add the rum and simmer until the alcohol cooks off, about 2 minutes.

2. Spoon into 4 dessert dishes and sprinkle with coconut and pecans.

# nellie's peachy melba

makes 4 servings

*The original peach Melba dessert was created by Auguste Escoffier in honor of opera singer Nellie Melba. This version strays from the original mainly in its use of vegan ice cream.*

2 cups water

3 ripe peaches

1½ cups sugar

2 tablespoons plus 1 teaspoon lemon juice

1 cup fresh raspberries

4 scoops vegan vanilla ice cream

1 tablespoon sliced toasted almonds

1. In a large saucepan, bring the water to a boil over high heat and add the peaches. After 30 seconds, reduce the heat to medium, scoop out the peaches with a slotted spoon, and place them in a bowl of cold water. To the simmering water, stir in 1 cup of the sugar and 2 tablespoons of the lemon juice, stirring to dissolve the sugar. Reduce the heat to low and keep the water at a simmer while you remove the skins from the peaches.

2. Remove the skins from the cooled peaches and return the peaches to the simmering water for 8 minutes. Drain the peaches, then pit and slice them. Set aside.

3. In a small saucepan, combine the raspberries and the remaining ½ cup of sugar and heat over medium heat. Crush the berries with the back of a spoon to release the liquid, stirring to dissolve the sugar. Press the berries through a fine sieve into a bowl to remove the seeds. Discard the seeds. Add the remaining 1 teaspoon of lemon juice and set aside.

4. Scoop the vegan ice cream into clear dessert bowls and top with the sliced peaches. Drizzle with the raspberry sauce, sprinkle with almonds, and serve.

# fresh fruit "sushi"

makes 4 servings

*No raw fish in this sushi—only slices of luscious fruit on top of mounds of sweet rice. As much as I enjoy nourishing my guests with the food I cook, I also love entertaining them. This whimsical dessert does both and is especially fun if you use actual sushi serving pieces, from chopsticks to dipping bowls.*

1½ cups firm chilled rice pudding, homemade (page 475) or store-bought
1 ripe peach, halved, pitted, and cut into ¼-inch slices
2 ripe plums, halved, pitted, and cut into ¼-inch slices
Mint leaves, cut into ¼-inch strips
Strawberry Sauce, homemade (page 487) or store-bought
Chocolate Sauce, homemade (page 497) or store-bought

1. Use your hands to shape the rice pudding into small "sushi-shaped" ovals and set aside.

2. Place a thin slice of fruit on top of each of the rice ovals and arrange them on a sushi platter or individual sushi plates.

3. Lay a strip of mint leaf across the middle of the top of each piece and serve with small dipping bowls of strawberry sauce and chocolate sauce.

# asian flavors fruit bowl

makes 4 to 6 servings

*Serve this flavorful fruit mélange after an Asian meal. If you're fortunate enough to find fresh lychees, by all means use them in this salad. Otherwise, the canned variety will have to do. (Use a cup of sugar syrup with fresh lychees.)*

1 (8-ounce) can lychees, packed in syrup
Juice of 1 lime
1 teaspoon lime zest
2 teaspoons sugar
¼ cup water
1 ripe mango, peeled, pitted, and cut into ½-inch dice
1 Asian pear, cored and cut into ½-inch dice
2 bananas, peeled and cut into ¼-inch slices
1 kiwifruit, peeled and cut into ¼-inch slices
1 tablespoon crushed unsalted roasted peanuts

1. Drain the lychee syrup into a small saucepan and place the lychees in a large bowl and set aside.

2. Add the lime juice and zest to the lychee syrup, along with the sugar and water and heat over low heat until the sugar dissolves. Bring to a boil and remove from heat. Set aside to cool.

3. To the bowl containing the lychees add the mango, pear, bananas, and kiwifruit. Drizzle with the reserved syrup, sprinkle with peanuts, and serve.

# sweet polenta with grilled pineapple and strawberry sauce

makes 4 servings

*The polenta may be made a few days ahead and refrigerated until needed. Then, simply cut it into serving portions and finish on the grill or in the oven or on top of the stove.*

**POLENTA**

3 cups water

¾ teaspoon salt

1 cup medium yellow cornmeal

¼ cup sugar

3 tablespoons vegan margarine

1 tablespoon canola or other neutral oil

**TOPPING**

¼ cup sugar

2 cups hulled strawberries

1 teaspoon fresh lemon juice

1 pineapple, peeled, cored, and cut into
 ½-inch slices

1. Make the polenta: Bring the water to a boil in a large saucepan. Reduce the heat to medium, add the salt, and slowly stir in the cornmeal. Reduce the heat to low, stir in the sugar and margarine, and continue to cook, stirring frequently, until thick, about 15 minutes.

2. Spoon the polenta into a greased shallow baking dish and refrigerate until firm, at least 30 minutes. Preheat the oven to 375°F.

3. Cut the polenta into serving-size pieces and arrange them on a greased baking sheet. Brush the tops with the oil and bake until hot and golden brown, about 20 minutes.

4. Make the topping: In a food processor, combine the sugar, 1 cup of the strawberries, and lemon juice, and blend well. Transfer to a small serving bowl and set aside.

5. Preheat the grill. Cut the remaining strawberries into thin slices and set aside. Grill the pineapple slices on both sides until grill marks appear.

6. Arrange a serving of the polenta on each plate, place the grilled pineapple on top, drizzle with the strawberry sauce, and scatter the strawberry slices over all.

# pineapple couscous timbales with blueberry sauce

makes 6 servings

*This showy dessert is actually quite simple to make and very healthful. Timbales are made by packing various dishes into drum or thimble-shaped molds. The food inside is unmolded, plated, and surrounded by a sauce. If you don't have timbale molds, you can make this recipe using mini springform pans or mini tart pans.*

2 cups pineapple juice

1 cup couscous

½ cup crushed pineapple, drained

1 tablespoon light brown sugar

½ teaspoon ground cinnamon

Blueberry Sauce, homemade (page 498)
 or store-bought

1. Lightly oil 6 timbale molds and set aside. In a medium saucepan, bring the pineapple juice to a boil over high heat. Add the couscous, pineapple, sugar, and cinnamon. Reduce the heat to low, cover, and simmer until the juice is absorbed, about 5 minutes.

2. Press the couscous mixture into the prepared molds and refrigerate for at least 1 hour.

3. Unmold the timbales and place each on a dessert plate, surround with a pool of the blueberry sauce, and serve.

# lime-macerated mangos

makes 4 to 6 servings

*Macerating sliced fruit with sugar amps up their natural sweetness and concentrates their flavors while drawing out their juices to produce a luscious syrup.*

3 ripe mangos
⅓ cup sugar
2 tablespoons fresh lime juice
½ cup dry white wine
Fresh mint sprigs

1. Peel, pit, and cut the mangos into ¹⁄₂-inch dice. Layer the diced mango in a large bowl, sprinkling each layer with about 1 tablespoon of the sugar. Cover with plastic wrap and refrigerate 2 hours.

2. Pour in the lime juice and wine, mixing gently to combine with the mango. Cover and refrigerate for 4 hours.

3. About 30 minutes before serving time, bring the fruit to room temperature. To serve, spoon the mango and the liquid into serving glasses and garnish with mint.

variation: Use 3 cups of sliced strawberries instead of the mangos. Replace the lime juice with lemon juice.

# vegan dessert crêpes

makes 10 crêpes

*Crêpes are the versatile basis of many sophisticated desserts. You can serve them filled with sautéed fruit or vegan ice cream and top them with caramel sauce, chocolate sauce, or a fruit sauce. They can also be enjoyed for breakfast, wrapped around some Close to Cottage Cheese (page 514) and topped with sliced fruit.*

1⅓ cups plain or vanilla soy milk
1 cup all-purpose flour
⅓ cup firm tofu, drained and crumbled
3 tablespoons vegan margarine, melted
2 tablespoons sugar
1½ teaspoons pure vanilla extract
½ teaspoon baking powder
⅛ teaspoon salt
Canola or other neutral oil, for cooking

1. In a blender, combine all the ingredients (except the oil for cooking) and blend until smooth.

2. Heat a nonstick medium skillet or crêpe pan over medium-high heat. Coat the pan with a small amount of oil. Pour about 3 tablespoons of the batter into the center of the skillet and tilt the pan to spread the batter out thinly. Cook until golden on both sides, flipping once. Transfer to a platter and repeat with the remaining batter, oiling the pan as needed.

3. The crêpes can now be used in the recipes below or topped with your favorite dessert sauce or sautéed fruit. These taste best if used on the same day that they are made.

# suzette-inspired ice cream crêpes

makes 4 servings

*The ice cream crêpes can be filled and frozen a few days in advance.*

1½ pints vegan vanilla ice cream, softened
4 Vegan Dessert Crêpes (page 488)
2 tablespoons vegan margarine
¼ confectioners' sugar
¼ cup fresh orange juice
1 tablespoon fresh lemon juice
¼ cup Grand Marnier or other orange-flavored
    liqueur

1. Use a large knife to cut one pint of ice cream into quarters vertically (you can do this while the ice cream is still in the container). Peel away the container and discard it. Arrange one whole quarter and ¼ cup of the remaining ½ pint of ice cream end to end on a piece of plastic wrap, enclose it in the wrap, and use your hands to shape it into a log. Repeat with the remaining ice cream to make four logs. Roll each of the ice cream logs inside each of the crêpes. Once the crêpes are filled, freeze them for about 30 minutes to firm up.

2. In a small skillet, heat the margarine over medium heat. Add the sugar. Stir in the orange juice, lemon juice, and Grand Marnier. Simmer, cooking off most of the alcohol, about 2 minutes.

3. To serve, place the filled crêpes on dessert plates and spoon some of the orange sauce over each crêpe.

## ice cream crêpes with strawberries:

Make the ice cream crêpes as above. For the topping: Place 2 cups thinly sliced hulled strawberries in a bowl and sprinkle with 2 tablespoons superfine sugar. Cover and set aside at room temperature for about an hour. Sprinkle with 1 teaspoon fresh lemon juice and stir gently to combine. When ready to serve, place each of the filled crêpes on a dessert plate and spoon some of the strawberries and their syrup over top. Garnish with a dollop of Vegan Whipped Cream (page 501) and chocolate curls.

# caramelized figs in tuiles
makes 4 servings

*I adapted this elegant finish to an autumn or winter meal from a recipe shared with me by my friend Corey Portalatin-Berrien, an exceptional vegan baker. Tuiles (French for "tiles") are fancy waferlike cookies that add drama to any dessert.*

8 figs
4 cups water
3 tablespoons sugar

TUILES
¼ cup pure maple syrup
2 tablespoons dark molasses
⅓ cup vegan margarine
½ cup sugar
1 tablespoon brandy
1 teaspoon vanilla extract
1¼ cups all-purpose flour
½ teaspoon ground ginger
¼ teaspoon salt

RASPBERRY COULIS
1 cup raspberries
2 tablespoons sugar
1 tablespoon fresh lime juice

Vegan vanilla ice cream
¼ cup toasted slivered almonds, for garnish

1. Add the figs to a medium saucepan and cover with water. Cook over medium heat until the figs are soft, about 10 minutes. Set aside to cool slightly. Preheat the broiler. Lightly oil a baking sheet.

2. Stem the poached figs and cut into ¼-inch slices. Place the sliced figs on the prepared baking sheet and sprinkle the sugar over the figs. Broil until the sugar has begun to caramelize, 2 to 3 minutes.

continues on next page

3. Make the tuiles: Preheat the oven to 350°F. Generously grease a baking sheet and set aside. Alternatively, you could arrange parchment paper or Silpat on a baking sheet. In a large saucepan, bring the maple syrup and molasses to a boil over medium heat. Add the margarine and sugar and stir until dissolved. Remove from the heat and stir in the brandy and vanilla.

4. In a medium bowl, combine the dry ingredients, mixing well. Slowly add to the molasses mixture, stirring constantly. The final consistency should be a thick batter. Drop about 3 tablespoonfuls of the batter 3 inches apart onto the prepared baking sheet. Use a metal spoon to spread the batter into 4 thin, circular wafers. Bake for 12 minutes or until lightly browned.

5. Let cool for about 15 seconds, then, while still hot, loosen the cookies with a metal spatula and drape each wafer over a rolling pin to create a curved nest. Let the wafer harden, about 10 minutes. Store remaining batter in the refrigerator in a tightly covered container where it will keep for several days.

6. Make the raspberry coulis: In a blender, puree the raspberries, sugar, and lime juice. Press through a fine sieve to remove the seeds. Discard the seeds and set coulis aside.

7. Arrange a tuile in the middle of each of 4 dessert plates. Layer the caramelized figs over the center of each wafer, overlapping. Place a small scoop of the ice cream into the center of each wafer. Drizzle the raspberry coulis on top and garnish with almonds. Serve immediately.

# cherry clafoutis

makes 8 servings

*Clafoutis is a traditional French dessert from the Limousin region. It is traditionally made with cherries baked in an almost pancakelike batter. For this vegan version, keep the cherries, but skip the dairy and eggs used in the classic. If you don't want to use cherries, you can substitute blueberries, plums, or another favorite (soft) fruit. Note: frozen cherries can be used if fresh are unavailable.*

2½ cups pitted cherries
1 cup vegan vanilla yogurt
¾ cup plain or vanilla soy milk
½ cup sugar
2 tablespoons pure maple syrup or agave nectar
1 teaspoon pure vanilla extract
Pinch salt
1 cup all-purpose flour
2 teaspoons baking powder
2 tablespoons confectioners' sugar

1. Preheat the oven to 375°F. Grease a 10-inch quiche dish or pie plate. Spread the cherries in the bottom of the prepared dish and set aside.

2. In a large bowl, combine the yogurt, soy milk, sugar, maple syrup, vanilla, and salt and mix until smooth. Beat in the flour and baking powder until combined. Do not overmix.

3. Pour the batter over the cherries and bake until set, 40 to 45 minutes. Cool on a wire rack for 20 minutes. Just before serving, sprinkle with the confectioners' sugar. Serve warm.

# pear gratin with cranberries and pecans

makes 4 to 6 servings

*This is a very light dessert, since it's little more than sweetened and spiced fruit with nuts sprinkled on top. If you serve it from an actual gratin dish, it can look very elegant. This gratin tastes best served warm in dessert bowls topped with a scoop of vegan vanilla ice cream. Instead of pears, you can make this gratin with other fruits, such as ripe peaches, mangos, or plums. Apples are a good choice, although they may take a bit longer to soften, so allow about 10 minutes extra baking time.*

4 fresh ripe pears, peeled and cored

½ cup sweetened dried cranberries

½ cup sugar

½ teaspoon ground ginger

1 tablespoon cornstarch

¼ cup plain or vanilla soy milk

⅔ cup coarsely chopped pecans

¼ cup vegan margarine

1. Preheat the oven to 400°F. Lightly grease a 2-quart gratin dish or 9 × 13-inch baking pan. Cut the pears into ¼-inch slices and spread them in the prepared dish. Add the cranberries, sugar, ginger, and cornstarch and toss to combine. Drizzle with the soy milk. Sprinkle pecans on top and dot with the margarine.

2. Bake until the fruit bubbles in the center, about 20 minutes. Serve warm.

# strawberry kanten

makes 6 servings

*Kanten is the Japanese word for agar or desserts made with agar. Agar, a type of dried sea vegetable, is a vegan alternative to gelatin, which is made with animal products. Agar has no flavor and is easy to use. One of the best things about agar (aside from the fact that it is vegan) is that it sets at room temperature, unlike gelatin, which must be chilled to set. In addition, agar has a greater gelling ability than gelatin, so you need less. These directions are for agar flakes (the most popular form), but if you have powdered or bar agar, refer to package instructions. Typically, the proportions are 1 tablespoon of agar to 1 cup of liquid. Look for agar in natural food stores.*

2 tablespoons agar flakes

2 cups white grape juice

1 cup hulled strawberries plus more for garnish

1 tablespoon agave nectar

Vegan Whipped Cream, homemade (page 501) or store-bought, for garnish

1. In a medium saucepan, combine the agar flakes and 1 cup of the juice and let soak for 10 minutes.

2. In a blender or food processor, puree the strawberries with the agave nectar and the remaining grape juice. Set aside.

3. Bring the agar and juice mixture to a boil over high heat, then reduce heat to low and simmer, stirring frequently, until the agar is dissolved, about 5 minutes.

4. Cool the juice mixture slightly, about 15 minutes, then pour into the blender with the pureed berries. Blend briefly to combine.

continues on next page

5. Pour into a glass baking dish or individual glass dessert dishes and allow to cool in the refrigerator until the kanten sets up, about 30 minutes. If kanten was made in a baking dish, cut it into squares. Garnish with the additional berries and whipped cream and serve.

## suspended peach kanten

makes 4 servings

*If you don't plan on unmolding this shimmering creation, at least prepare it in a clear glass bowl to show off the suspended peaches to good effect.*

2 cups white grape juice

2 tablespoons agar flakes

1 tablespoon agave nectar

2 ripe peaches, halved, pitted, and cut into ¼-inch slices

1. In a medium saucepan, combine the grape juice and agar and bring to a boil over high heat. Reduce heat to low and simmer, stirring occasionally, until the agar is dissolved, about 5 minutes. Stir in the agave nectar and set aside.

2. Arrange the peach slices in a gelatin mold or clear glass bowl. Pour the juice mixture over the peaches and chill, uncovered, until firm, 1 to 2 hours.

# NICE CREAMS, SORBETS, AND GRANITAS

## cherry vanilla nice cream

makes about 1½ pints

*Although there are numerous varieties of wonderful vegan ice creams available in supermarkets and natural food stores, sometimes it's fun to make it yourself. I call my homemade dairy-free ice cream "Nice Cream." All you need is an ice cream maker and your favorite ingredients. For the creamiest results, use the thickest, richest nondairy milk or cream you can find. I generally use the nut-based MimicCreme brand dairy-free cream. I think homemade vegan ice cream tastes best shortly after it is made, so I prefer to make it in small batches. Arrowroot powder is used to help thicken the ice cream because it thickens at lower temperatures than other thickeners and also helps prevent ice crystals from forming in the ice cream.*

2 tablespoons arrowroot powder

3 cups thick dairy-free milk or cream (see page 493)

½ cup sugar

2 teaspoons pure vanilla extract

1 cup chopped pitted cherries

1. In a small bowl, combine the arrowroot with ½ cup of the milk and blend until smooth. Set aside.

2. In a medium saucepan, combine the remaining 2 ½ cups milk with the sugar and heat to a simmer, stirring to dissolve the sugar. When the mixture comes just to a boil, remove from the heat and add the arrowroot mixture, stirring constantly for a minute to thicken slightly.

## bases for vegan ice cream

Vegan ice cream can be made using a number of different bases that replace the dairy cream. In my Nice Cream recipes I simply call for "thick dairy-free milk or cream" to allow you to choose a base you prefer. Here are some options.

1. MIMICCREME—a thick nut-based nondairy cream product available sweetened or unsweetened and sold in aseptic containers. (Note: If using the sweetened variety, you can eliminate the sugar from the Nice Cream recipes).

2. CASHEW CREAM: Make your own cashew cream: Grind 2 cups unsalted cashews to a powder in a high speed blender, add 2 cups water, and blend until smooth and creamy.

3. UNSWEETENED COCONUT MILK: If making coconut ice cream, this is ideal, but you can use it in combination with other milks and ingredients as well to add richness (see #5).

4. THICK SOY MILK OR SOY CREAMER: Certain brands of soy milk are thicker than others and soy "creamer" is thicker still. Silk brand sells a soy creamer that is widely available in supermarkets.

5. A COMBINATION: To make 1 quart of Nice Cream you will need anywhere from 2½ to 3 cups of a base "cream" (plus added sweetener and other ingredients, depending on the flavor). It's perfectly fine to create your own base using a combination of ingredients. For example: If you have soy milk or other dairy-free milk that is on the thin side, combine it with some finely ground cashews, or some soy creamer, or both, in any proportion to equal the amount you need.

6. IN A PINCH: If all you have is a regular soy or other nondairy milk, you can use it. The results won't be as rich and creamy, but you will still have a flavorful frozen dessert.

---

Stir in the vanilla and let the mixture cool to room temperature, then refrigerate it until chilled, 1 to 2 hours.

3. Once the mixture is chilled, freeze it in an ice cream maker according to manufacturer's directions, adding the cherries near the end of the churning process.

4. When the mixture is finished churning in the machine, it will be soft but ready to eat. For a firmer texture, transfer to a freezer-safe container and freeze no more than 1 or 2 hours for best flavor and texture.

plain vanilla: Omit the cherries.

strawberry: Substitute 1 cup sliced strawberries for the cherries.

vanilla–chocolate chip: Omit the cherries and add 1 cup of vegan semisweet chocolate chips near the end of the churning process.

cherry vanilla–chocolate chip: Keep the cherries and add 1 cup of vegan semisweet chocolate chips near the end of the churning process.

# chocolate nice cream

1½ tablespoons arrowroot powder
3 cups thick dairy-free milk or cream (see page 493)
¼ cup unsweetened cocoa powder
¾ cup sugar
½ cup vegan semisweet chocolate chips
1½ teaspoons pure vanilla extract

1. In a small bowl, combine the arrowroot with ½ cup of the milk and blend until smooth. Set aside.

2. In a medium saucepan, combine the remaining 2½ cups dairy-free milk with the cocoa powder and sugar and heat to a simmer, stirring to dissolve. When the mixture comes just to a boil, remove from the heat and add the arrowroot mixture, stirring constantly for a minute to thicken slightly. Stir in the chocolate chips and let them sit in the hot liquid for a few minutes before whisking to combine thoroughly. Stir in the vanilla and let the mixture cool to room temperature, then refrigerate it until chilled completely, 1 to 2 hours.

3. Once the mixture is chilled, freeze it in an ice cream maker according to the manufacturer's directions. When the mixture is finished churning in the machine, it will be soft, but ready to eat. For a firmer texture, transfer to a freezer-safe container and freeze no more than 1 or 2 hours for best flavor and texture.

**mint chocolate chip:** Add ½ cup chocolate chips and ½ cup minced fresh mint leaves near the end of the churning process.

**double-chocolate:** Add ¾ cup vegan semisweet chocolate chips near the end of the churning process.

**peanut butter–chocolate:** Add ½ cup creamy peanut butter, a spoonful at a time while the freezer is still churning, to add streaks of peanut butter throughout.

**chocolate–rum raisin:** Soak 1 cup of raisins in ½ cup of hot rum. Allow to cool. Stir the soaked raisins into the ice cream near the end of the churning process.

# coffee nice cream

makes about 1½ pints

*If you like a deep coffee-flavored ice cream, use strong brewed espresso instead of coffee. To serve, garnish with a dusting of instant espresso powder or serve with a shot of hot espresso to add at the table. It's also quite yummy (and potent) served with a splash of Scotch.*

2 tablespoons arrowroot powder
2½ cups thick dairy-free milk or cream (see page 493)
¾ cup very strong coffee
½ cup sugar
1 teaspoon pure vanilla extract

1. In a small bowl, combine the arrowroot with ¼ cup of the milk and blend until smooth. Set aside.

2. In a medium saucepan, combine the remaining 2¼ cups milk, coffee, and sugar and heat to a simmer, stirring to dissolve the sugar. When the mixture comes just to a boil, remove from the heat and add the arrowroot mixture, stirring constantly for a minute to thicken slightly. Stir in the vanilla and let the mixture cool to room temperature, then refrigerate it until chilled, 1 to 2 hours.

3. Once the mixture is chilled, freeze it in an ice cream maker according to the manufacturer's directions. When the mixture is finished

churning in the machine, it will be soft, but ready to eat. For a firmer texture, transfer to a freezer-safe container and freeze no more than 1 or 2 hours for best flavor and texture.

# ginger-coconut nice cream

makes about 1½ pints

*If you can't find ginger juice or bottled pureed ginger, you can use grated fresh ginger, but you'll need to strain the mixture before freezing to remove the fibrous bits. This dessert is absolutely amazing served after an Asian meal such as a Thai stir-fry.*

2 tablespoons arrowroot powder
2 (13.5-ounce) cans unsweetened coconut milk
½ cup sugar
2 teaspoons ginger juice or pureed bottled ginger
2 tablespoons minced crystallized ginger
⅓ cup toasted sweetened flaked coconut, for garnish

1. In a small bowl, combine the arrowroot with ¼ cup of the coconut milk, blending until smooth. Set aside.

2. In a medium saucepan, combine the sugar, the remaining coconut milk, and the ginger juice and bring just to a boil. Remove from the heat and add the arrowroot mixture, stirring to thicken. Let the mixture cool to room temperature, then refrigerate until chilled, 1 to 2 hours.

3. When the mixture is chilled, freeze it in an ice cream maker according to the manufacturer's directions, adding the crystallized ginger near the end of the churning process. When the mixture is finished churning in the machine, it will be soft, but ready to eat. For a firmer texture, transfer to a freezer-safe container and freeze no more than 1 or 2 hours for best flavor and texture. Serve garnished with toasted coconut.

# strawberry sorbet

makes about 1 pint

*Lighter than ice cream and naturally vegan, sorbet makes a refreshing finish to a heavy meal. This sorbet is best made with ripe strawberries.*

½ cup sugar
½ cup water
2 cups hulled strawberries
2 teaspoons fresh lemon juice

1. In a medium saucepan, combine the sugar and water. Cook, stirring, over low heat until sugar is dissolved, about 3 minutes. Increase the heat to high and bring to a boil, then remove from the heat. Transfer to a heatproof bowl and refrigerate until chilled about 2 hours.

2. In a blender or food processor, combine the strawberries and lemon juice and blend until smooth. Add the cooled sugar syrup to the strawberry mixture and process until smooth.

3. Freeze the mixture in an ice cream maker according to the manufacturer's instructions. When the mixture is finished churning in the machine, it will be soft, but ready to eat. For a firmer sorbet, transfer to a freezer-safe container and freeze no more than 1 to 2 hours for best flavor and texture.

peach sorbet: Instead of the strawberries, use 2½ cups peeled and chopped ripe peaches.

mango sorbet: Instead of the strawberries, use 2½ cups peeled and chopped ripe mango; use lime juice instead of lemon juice.

# cranberry sorbet

makes about 1½ pints

*This sweet-tart sorbet can be enjoyed any-time, but I've found it to be a welcome and refreshing addition after Thanksgiving dinner, when everyone is too full for pie and wants to wait an hour or so before indulging in dessert. This gives you a little something to serve before everyone disperses.*

¾ cup sugar

1 cup cranberry juice

1½ cups fresh cranberries

2 tablespoons fresh orange juice

2 teaspoons orange zest

1. In a medium saucepan, combine the sugar, cranberry juice, and cranberries and bring to a boil. Cook, stirring, over low heat until the cranberries pop and sugar is dissolved, about 5 minutes. Remove from the heat and strain into a bowl. Stir in the orange juice and orange zest. Refrigerate until chilled, about 1 hour.

2. Freeze the mixture in an ice cream maker according to the manufacturer's instructions. When the mixture is finished churning in the machine, it will be soft, but ready to eat. For a firmer sorbet, transfer to a freezer-safe container and freeze no more than 1 to 2 hours for best flavor and texture.

# mocha sorbet

makes about 1½ pints

*Coffee and chocolate reprise their popular duet—this time in a cool sorbet, an ideal way to enjoy "coffee and dessert" after a big meal on a hot summer evening. A good-quality cocoa powder is crucial to the success of this sorbet.*

1 cup sugar

2 cups brewed coffee

1 cup water

¾ cup unsweetened cocoa powder

⅛ teaspoon salt

1 teaspoon pure vanilla extract

1. In a large saucepan, heat the sugar over medium heat until it begins to melt. Continue to cook, stirring often, until completely melted and caramelized.

2. Stir in the coffee and water and cook over medium-low heat until the sugar is completely dissolved, stirring often. Add the cocoa and salt and stir until dissolved.

3. Transfer to a bowl and set aside to cool, stirring occasionally, about 15 minutes. Stir in the vanilla and refrigerate until chilled, about 2 hours.

4. Once the mixture is chilled, freeze it in an ice cream maker according to the manufacturer's instructions. When the mixture is finished churning in the machine, it will be soft but ready to eat. For firmer sorbet, transfer to a freezer-safe container and freeze for no more than 1 or 2 hours for best flavor and texture.

# orange granita

makes about 3 cups

*A granita is fun and easy to make and ideal for those who don't own an ice cream maker because you don't need one. Just freeze the mixture in a shallow baking pan and stir periodically with a fork. Citrus granitas are especially popular in Italy.*

½ cup sugar

½ cup water

2 cups orange juice

1 teaspoon fresh lemon juice

1. In a medium saucepan, combine the sugar and water and bring to a boil. Cook, stirring, until the sugar dissolves. Remove from heat and set aside to cool, about 15 minutes. Stir in the orange juice and lemon juice, then pour the mixture into a shallow baking pan.

2. Cover and freeze until firm, stirring about once per hour, about 3 hours.

3. When firm, remove the mixture from the freezer and scrape it with the tines of a fork until fluffy. Spoon the granita into a container, cover, and freeze until serving time. The taste and texture of the granita is best if eaten within a few hours after it is made.

lemon-lime granita: In step 1, use 2 cups sugar and 2 cups water and add ¼ cup fresh lemon juice and 3 tablespoons fresh lime juice instead of the orange juice. Add 1 teaspoon each finely grated lemon and lime zest, then proceed with the recipe.

coffee granita: In step 1, substitute 2 cups of cooled coffee for the orange juice. Omit the lemon juice and proceed with the recipe.

green tea granita: In step 1, use ⅔ cup sugar and ⅔ cup water. Add 2¾ cups cooled strongly brewed green tea instead of the orange juice. Increase the fresh lemon juice to 2 teaspoons and proceed with the recipe.

# DESSERT SAUCES AND FROSTINGS

## chocolate sauce 🅕

makes about 1 cup

*This makes a basic rich chocolate sauce that is thin enough to drizzle with a spoon or from a plastic squeeze bottle. Use it to add your signature flourish to plated desserts for a fancy presentation.*

½ cup pure agave nectar or maple syrup

½ cup unsweetened cocoa powder

3 tablespoons plain or vanilla soy milk

1 teaspoon pure vanilla extract

1. In a small saucepan, combine the agave nectar and cocoa, stirring until well combined. Bring to a simmer over low heat, cooking for about 1 minute, stirring constantly so the cocoa does not burn.

2. Remove from heat and stir in the soy milk and vanilla, stirring until well blended. The sauce is now ready to spoon or drizzle on desserts. Store leftover sauce covered in the refrigerator for up to 3 days.

# fudgy chocolate sauce

makes about 1 cup

*Try this decadent sauce spooned over cake or a dish of vegan ice cream—serve the sauce warm for a hot fudge sundae.*

½ cup sugar
¼ cup unsweetened cocoa powder
1 tablespoon plus 1 teaspoon cornstarch
½ cup plain or vanilla soy milk
2 teaspoons pure vanilla extract

1. In small saucepan, combine the sugar, cocoa, and cornstarch, stirring until blended. Stir in the soy milk and cook over low heat, stirring constantly, until it comes to a boil. Continue cooking and stirring until thickened and smooth.

2. Remove from heat and stir in the vanilla. Serve warm. Store leftover sauce covered in the refrigerator for up to 3 days.

# caramel sauce

makes about 1 cup

*Delicious served warm or chilled, this versatile sauce can be spooned over pound cake or spice cake. It's also good with banana fritters or as a dipping sauce for fresh fruit.*

½ cup sugar
3 tablespoons water
1 teaspoon pure vanilla extract
¾ cup plain or vanilla soy milk

1. In a medium saucepan, combine the sugar and water and bring to a boil. Reduce the heat to low and simmer until it turns an amber color, about 8 minutes. Do not burn.

2. Remove from the heat and stir in the vanilla and soy milk. Simmer over low heat until it

thickens slightly, stirring constantly. Serve warm or chilled. Store leftover sauce covered in the refrigerator for up to 3 days.

**orange-caramel sauce:** Use lemon juice instead of vanilla extract, use ¼ cup orange juice and ½ cup soy milk instead of ¾ cup soy milk; add 1 tablespoon Grand Marnier or Cointreau near the end.

# warm walnut sauce

makes about 2 cups

*Don't let its wholesome ingredients fool you—this luxurious sauce adds scrumptious decadence wherever it settles, whether oozing over a scoop of vegan ice cream or dripping down the sides of a thick slice of pound cake. I've even had this nut-studded sauce show up on top of bread pudding and brownies.*

⅓ cup vegan margarine
1½ cups chopped walnut pieces
½ cup pure maple syrup

1. In a large skillet, melt the margarine over medium heat. Add the walnuts and cook, stirring constantly, until lightly toasted.

2. Remove from the heat and stir in the maple syrup, stirring until the nuts are well coated. Keep warm until ready to serve. Store leftover sauce covered in the refrigerator for up to 3 days.

# blueberry sauce

makes about 2 cups

*If you prefer a smooth sauce, pour the blueberry mixture into a blender or food processor and blend until smooth. If you have leftover sauce, use it on pancakes or waffles or vegan vanilla ice cream.*

2 cups fresh or frozen blueberries

⅓ cup sugar

½ teaspoon ground cinnamon

¼ teaspoon salt

2 teaspoons cornstarch

1 tablespoon fresh lemon juice

½ teaspoon pure vanilla extract

1. In a large saucepan, combine the blueberries, sugar, cinnamon, and salt. Mix well, crushing some of the blueberries with the back of a spoon to release the juice.

2. In a small bowl, combine the cornstarch, lemon juice, and vanilla until blended. Set aside.

3. Bring the blueberry mixture to a boil over high heat, then reduce the heat to low, stir in the cornstarch mixture, and simmer, stirring, for 3 minutes. Remove from heat to cool slightly before serving. Store leftover sauce covered in the refrigerator for up to 3 days.

# pineapple-apricot sauce

makes about 2 cups

*Enjoy this colorful fruity sauce over the pound cake on page 448 or on the Pineapple Couscous Timbales on page 487. It's also great as a dipping sauce for fresh fruit.*

1 cup dried apricots

1 cup water

1 cup unsweetened pineapple juice

1. In a medium saucepan, combine the apricots and water. Cover and bring to a boil over high heat, then reduce heat to low and simmer

for 20 minutes. Remove from the burner and set aside to cool, about 15 minutes.

2. Transfer the soaked apricots to a blender or food processor and process until smooth. Add the pineapple juice and process again.

3. If serving warm, pour the sauce back into the saucepan and heat until warm. If serving chilled, pour the sauce into a bowl and refrigerate until chilled, 1 hour. Store leftover sauce covered in the refrigerator for up to 3 days.

# summer fruit sauce 🌀

makes about 2 cups

*This vibrant sauce with blueberries and bits of fresh peaches makes a dazzling dessert when spooned over vegan ice cream, pound cake, or both. Vary the fruit according to personal preference and availability.*

1 tablespoon cornstarch

1 cup fresh orange juice

¼ cup agave nectar

2 tablespoons vegan margarine

1 teaspoon finely grated orange zest

2 ripe peaches, halved, pitted, and finely chopped

½ cup fresh blueberries

1. In a medium saucepan, combine cornstarch and orange juice. Add the agave nectar and bring to a boil. Reduce heat to medium and cook, stirring constantly, until thickened, about 5 minutes.

2. Remove from the heat and stir in the margarine and orange zest. Stir in the peaches and blueberries. Serve at room temperature or chilled. Store leftover sauce covered in the refrigerator for up to 2 days.

# winter fruit sauce

makes about 2 cups

*Use already mixed dried fruit or mix and match your favorite combination to create a luscious sauce that can be enjoyed over spice cake, vegan ice cream, or baked sweetened polenta sticks.*

1 cup water
1 cup dried mixed fruit
1 teaspoon fresh lemon juice
½ teaspoon ground cinnamon
¼ cup apple juice

1. In a large saucepan, combine the water, dried fruit, lemon juice, and cinnamon. Cover and bring to a boil over high heat. Reduce heat to medium and simmer for 20 minutes.

2. Remove from the heat and set aside to cool, 15 minutes, then transfer to a blender or food processor and process until smooth. Add the apple juice and process until blended. Return the sauce to the saucepan and heat on low until warm. Store leftover sauce covered in the refrigerator for up to 3 days.

# grand marnier sauce

makes about 1½ cups

*This luxurious sauce tastes good enough to drink—but try to resist and save it for your dessert. It's ideal to spoon over warmed crêpes or over your favorite cake and vegan ice cream combo for the ultimate in classy desserts.*

1 cup fresh orange juice
⅓ cup confectioners' sugar
1 teaspoon finely grated orange zest
½ cup vegan margarine, cut into pieces
¼ cup Grand Marnier or other orange-flavored liqueur

1. In a small saucepan, heat the orange juice, sugar, and orange zest over low heat, stirring, for 5 minutes.

2. Increase the heat and bring to a boil. Whisk in the margarine pieces, one or two at a time. When thoroughly blended, remove from heat and stir in the Grand Marnier and serve immediately. Store leftover sauce covered in the refrigerator for up to 3 days.

# strawberry-mango sauce

makes about 2½ cups

*Mango and strawberries are a magical combination—together they create a vibrantly beautiful sauce that is naturally sweet and can be used over cake and ice cream desserts or as a dipping sauce for fresh or grilled fruit.*

½ cup thinly sliced hulled strawberries
1 ripe mango, peeled, pitted, and chopped
¼ cup white grape juice
1 teaspoon fresh lemon juice

1. In a blender or food processor, combine the strawberries and mango and process until smooth. Add the grape juice and lemon juice and process until blended.

**2.** Serve at room temperature or chilled. Store leftover sauce covered in the refrigerator for up to 3 days.

# fresh strawberry topping
makes about 2 cups

*This topping is perfect in its simplicity, and perfectly ambrosial when made with juicy ripe strawberries. It adds vibrant color and flavor to many desserts, from vegan ice creams and puddings, to fruit, brownies, and cakes. I think it's especially wonderful spooned over a scoop Strawberry Nice Cream (page 493) that has been nestled against a slice of pound cake (page 448).*

2 cups thinly sliced hulled strawberries
1 tablespoon sugar

**1.** In a medium bowl, combine the strawberries and sugar, stirring gently to combine.

**2.** Set aside at room temperature for 30 minutes to allow juices to form. This sauce tastes best if served on the day that it is made.

# vegan whipped cream
makes 1 ½ cups

*There are a variety of ways to make vegan whipped cream. This is one of them. Another is buying it ready-made at a natural food store. Use this as you would any whipped cream, on virtually any kind of dessert. Note:*

*if you prefer a whipped topping made without soy, use the Cashew Crème recipe that follows, using rice or almond milk instead of soy milk.*

1 cup firm silken tofu, drained and patted dry
½ cup agave nectar or pure maple syrup
1 tablespoon canola or other neutral oil
1 teaspoon pure vanilla extract
Pinch salt

Place all ingredients in a blender and blend until smooth and creamy. Chill before using. Store leftovers covered in the refrigerator for 1 to 2 days.

# cashew crème
makes about 1 ½ cups

*This is my favorite of all the alternatives to dairy-based whipped cream because I think it has the most flavor. Use it in any of the ways you would use whipped cream—as a topping for fruit, pie, cake, and so on.*

1 cup unsalted raw cashews
¼ cup plain or vanilla soy milk
¼ cup pure maple syrup
1 teaspoon pure vanilla extract

In a high-speed blender, process the cashews until finely ground. Add the soy milk, maple syrup, and vanilla and process until smooth and creamy. Transfer to a bowl, cover, and refrigerate until chilled. Store leftovers covered in the refrigerator for 1 to 2 days.

# lemon-cashew crème

makes about 2 cups

*This lemony creamy topping is great over fresh fruit or cake—especially banana or spice cake. If you don't have a high-speed blender to grind the cashews, use a spice grinder and then transfer to a regular blender or food processor to continue with the recipe.*

1 cup unsalted raw cashews

⅓ cup pure maple syrup or agave nectar

¼ cup fresh lemon juice

1 teaspoon pure vanilla extract

1 cup firm silken tofu, drained and pressed (page xiv)

1 teaspoon grated lemon zest

1. In a blender, grind the cashews to a fine powder. Add the maple syrup, lemon juice, and vanilla and process until smooth. Add the tofu and lemon zest and process until smooth and creamy. Taste, adjusting seasonings, adding more sweetener or lemon juice if needed.

2. Transfer to a bowl, cover, and refrigerate until chilled, 1 hour. Store leftover sauce covered in the refrigerator for up to 3 days.

# vegan chocolate ganache ❶

makes about 2 cups

*This easy-to-make chocolate ganache makes a velvety smooth topping or filling for cakes or cupcakes.*

1½ cups vegan semisweet chocolate chips

½ cup thick dairy-free milk or cream (see page 493)

1 tablespoon vegan margarine

1. In a double boiler or small saucepan, combine the chocolate chips, milk, and margarine, and cook over low heat, stirring until melted and smooth.

2. Transfer to a bowl and refrigerate to set up a bit before using, about 30 minutes. The consistency should be thick but pourable. Store leftovers covered in the refrigerator for 2 to 3 days.

# "cream cheese" frosting ❶

makes about 2½ cups

*This frosting is famous for being the crowning glory of Crazy for Carrot Cake (page 449), but it's also great on the Banana-Walnut Cake (page 448). Look for containers of vegan cream cheese in natural food stores and well-stocked supermarkets.*

1 (8-ounce) container vegan cream cheese, softened

2 tablespoons vegan margarine

2½ cups confectioners' sugar

1 teaspoon pure vanilla extract

1. In a medium bowl, beat the cream cheese and margarine together with an electric mixer on high speed until well blended.

2. Add the sugar and vanilla, then beat until light and fluffy. Store leftovers covered in the refrigerator for up to 3 days.

## "buttercream" frosting
makes about 3 cups

*So what if this frosting doesn't contain dairy butter or cream? It's still creamy and buttery—and delicious! Use this versatile, all-purpose frosting to decorate cookies, cakes, and cupcakes. Try any of the variations below or come up with your own favorite flavor combination.*

1 cup vegan margarine
4 cups confectioners' sugar
2 tablespoons plain or vanilla soy milk
1½ teaspoons pure vanilla extract

1. In a large bowl, cream the margarine with an electric mixer on high speed until light and fluffy.

2. Add the sugar, soy milk, and vanilla and mix until thoroughly combined. Continue mixing for about 2 minutes, until the frosting is smooth and stiff. Store leftovers covered in the refrigerator for 3 to 4 days.

coconut: Substitute coconut extract for the vanilla and sprinkle the frosted cake with toasted coconut.

spice: Add ½ teaspoon of ground cinnamon and ½ teaspoon each of ground allspice, nutmeg, and cloves or ginger. Sprinkle the frosted cake with chopped nuts of choice.

lemon: Substitute lemon extract for the vanilla. Sprinkle the frosted cake with crushed Lemonhead candies.

## chocolate fudge frosting
makes about 3 cups

*This basic chocolate frosting recipe makes enough to frost a 9-inch 2-layer cake.*

3 cups sugar
1 cup plain or vanilla soy milk
4 ounces unsweetened chocolate
3 tablespoons pure maple syrup
⅓ cup vegan margarine
1 teaspoon pure vanilla extract

1. In a large saucepan, combine the sugar, soy milk, chocolate, and maple syrup and bring just to a boil over medium-high heat, stirring frequently. Reduce the heat to medium and continue to cook until the chocolate is melted, about 5 minutes.

2. Remove from the heat and add the margarine and vanilla. Let the mixture cool to room temperature without stirring, 15 minutes.

3. After the mixture is cooled, beat it until it is creamy and stiff enough for spreading on a cake. If it becomes too stiff, add a few drops of hot water and beat until creamy. Store leftovers covered in the refrigerator for 3 to 4 days.

# chocolate peanut butter frosting 🅕

makes about 3 cups

*This creamy rich frosting combines the popular flavor combo of chocolate and peanut butter. Use it to frost your favorite cakes and cupcakes.*

¾ cup creamy peanut butter

⅓ cup unsweetened cocoa

3 cups confectioner's sugar

1 teaspoon pure vanilla extract

⅔ cup thick dairy-free milk or cream (see page 493)

1. In a food processor, combine all the ingredients and process until smooth and creamy. If the consistency is too thick, add a little more milk, a tablespoon at a time, until the desired consistency is reached.

2. Use a rubber spatula to scrape the frosting into a bowl. Use immediately or cover and refrigerate for up to 3 days.

# BREAKFAST AND BRUNCH

## BREAKFAST CASSEROLES, FRITTATAS, AND MORE

garden scramble

soy sausage scramble

scrambled tofu
with chiles and salsa

potato-tomato frittata

roasted vegetable frittata

kiss my grits
breakfast casserole

two-tomato brunch casserole

spinach and mushroom strata

vegan eggs benedict

bountiful breakfast burritos

burritos benedict

mango morning quesadillas

couscous brunch cake
with fresh fruit

close to cottage cheese

## PANCAKES, WAFFLES, AND FRENCH TOAST

cranberry pancakes
with orange-maple syrup

spiced apple pancakes

ginger-pear pancakes

banana-blueberry pancakes

johnnycakes

maple-pecan waffles

pumpkin waffles
with cranberry syrup

lemon-kissed blueberry waffles

very vanilla french toast

french toast with
caramel apple topping

peanut butter and
banana–stuffed french toast

## CEREALS

granola

granola-infused oatmeal

cran-apple oatmeal

morning polenta
with a drizzle of maple syrup

breakfast bulgur
with pears and pecans

dawn's early couscous

## BREAKFAST SIDES

apple coffee cake

breakfast bran muffins

banana-walnut
breakfast muffins

two-potato hash

pan-fried spuds

hash brown potatoes

tempeh bacon

sesame-soy breakfast spread

breakfast parfaits

 = fast

nyone who thinks breakfast is defined by eggs and bacon may be pleasantly surprised with this delightful variety of delicious reasons to wake up in the morning. Just a simple swap of ingredients can allow you to enjoy many popular breakfast foods traditionally made with animal products, including a delicious Roasted Vegetable Frittata (page 509) and an amazing Vegan Eggs Benedict (page 511).

The recipes in this chapter range from hearty breakfast casseroles to luscious waffles, pancakes, and French toast, as well as tasty grab-and-go treats such as breakfast burritos, coffee cake, and muffins.

There is also a tempting selection of warming breakfast grain dishes such as oatmeal with granola and side dishes ranging from Two-Potato Hash (page 524) to easy homemade Tempeh Bacon (page 525).

If your morning tastes lean toward quick and easy, vegan breakfasts can be conjured by splashing dairy-free milk onto your favorite cold cereal or slathering almond or peanut butter onto whole-grain toast or bagels. For a selection of satisfying smoothies that are great at breakfast or any time of day, refer to the recipes in the Beverages chapter, page 527.

# Breakfast Casseroles, Frittatas, and More

## garden scramble

makes 4 servings

*Talented vegan chef Francis Janes served this wonderful tofu and vegetable dish for brunch at his former Seattle restaurant, Café Ambrosia. I tweak it a little every time I make it and you can, too—swapping in different vegetables, herbs, or spices according to your own taste.*

1 pound firm tofu, drained, crumbled, and squeezed dry
¼ cup nutritional yeast
1 teaspoon onion powder
½ teaspoon garlic powder
½ teaspoon ground cumin
¼ teaspoon turmeric
½ teaspoon salt
¼ teaspoon freshly ground black pepper
1 tablespoon olive oil
1 small red onion, minced
½ cup minced red bell pepper
5 cremini mushrooms, lightly rinsed, patted dry, and thinly sliced
1 medium carrot, shredded
1 tablespoon soy sauce
1 cup fresh or thawed frozen peas
4 cilantro or parsley sprigs, for garnish

1. In a large bowl, combine the tofu, nutritional yeast, and dry spices and mix well. Set aside.

2. In a large skillet, heat the oil over medium heat. Add the onion, cover, and cook until tender, about 5 minutes. Add the bell pepper, mushrooms, and carrot and cook uncovered about 5 minutes longer. Stir in the soy sauce.

3. Add the tofu mixture and stir until hot and well combined. Add the peas and stir to combine. Cook, stirring the mixture until it is hot and any excess moisture has evaporated, about 5 minutes.

4. Serve hot or warm plates and garnish with sprigs of cilantro.

## soy sausage scramble

makes 4 servings

*Why wait for the weekend to enjoy this delicious breakfast dish when it is easy to make and packed with protein? You can cook it the night before and reheat it in the morning. I like it best served with toasted bread, but it can be used as a wrap filling if you want to take your breakfast with you. If you're not a fan of vegan sausage, you can substitute chopped seitan seasoned with ground fennel seed and a touch of cayenne.*

2 tablespoons olive oil
1 small sweet yellow onion, minced
1 (12-ounce) package vegan sausage, chopped
1 pound firm tofu, drained, crumbled, and squeezed dry
1 teaspoon salt
¼ teaspoon turmeric
¼ teaspoon freshly ground black pepper

1. In a large skillet, heat the oil over medium heat. Add the onion, cover, and cook until softened, about 5 minutes. Add the sausage and cook until browned, 5 minutes.

2. Add the tofu, salt, turmeric, and pepper, stirring until well combined. Cook over low heat until liquid is absorbed, about 10 minutes. Taste, adjusting seasonings if necessary, and serve immediately.

The term "brunch" (breakfast + lunch) was first coined in 1895, connoting a time when the elite whiled away the better part of a Sunday over a table laden with food. These days, the tradition has evolved so that for many people relaxing on the weekend includes going to a restaurant for brunch.

Unless you have a vegan restaurant nearby, finding vegan options on the typical restaurant brunch menu can be a challenge.

What's the solution? Make the best brunch in town right in your own kitchen. No standing in line for a table, no crowded noisy dining rooms, and no expensive tab to pay—you don't even have to leave a tip! Best of all, you can have it your way: right down to your favorite pumpkin pancakes or blueberry waffles.

You can design your brunch to suit your lifestyle: a cozy and romantic table for two, a fun family get-together, or even an excuse for a party: invite some friends and serve it up buffet-style. It's a terrific way to entertain. Make it as casual or fancy as you like: serve juice from pitchers into wine glasses, put fresh flowers on the table. Make fresh-baked muffins and flavored coffees. Serve a fancy main dish such as vegan eggs benedict or go easy on yourself with a no-fuss oven-baked casserole or frittata. Set up a cereal bar for the kids or a smoothie bar for teens.

Whether simple or elaborate, make it fun. Plan ahead and be sure to delegate some of the work so you can enjoy the day, too.

## scrambled tofu with chiles and salsa

makes 4 servings

*Mild-tasting tofu is a perfect foil for the chiles and salsa, which can be mild or hot, according to your personal preference. Enjoy this dish with toast or spoon it into a tortilla for a zesty breakfast wrap.*

1 tablespoon olive oil

1 small red onion, minced

1 pound firm tofu, well drained, squeezed dry, and crumbled

½ teaspoon salt

⅛ teaspoon freshly ground black pepper

1 (4-ounce) can chopped mild or hot green chiles, drained

2 ripe plum tomatoes, chopped

½ cup shredded vegan Cheddar cheese (optional)

1 cup tomato salsa, homemade (page 567) or store-bought

1. In a large skillet, heat the oil over medium heat. Add the onion and cook until softened, about 5 minutes. Add the tofu, salt, and pepper and cook, stirring occasionally, until tofu is hot and the liquid is absorbed, about 8 minutes.

2. Stir in the chiles, tomatoes, and Cheddar, if using. Cook 5 minutes longer.

3. Divide the tofu mixture among 4 plates, top each portion with salsa, and serve.

# potato-tomato frittata

makes 4 to 6 servings

*This frittata begins with already cooked potatoes, so plan to make it when you have leftover baked or roasted potatoes on hand.*

2 tablespoons olive oil

1 small onion, finely chopped

2 cold baked or roasted potatoes, cut into
  ¼-inch slices

Salt and freshly ground black pepper

1 pound firm tofu, well drained

¼ cup nutritional yeast

1 tablespoon soy sauce

½ teaspoon baking powder

2 ripe plum tomatoes, cut into ¼-inch slices

1. Preheat the oven to 400°F. Lightly oil a 9- or 10-inch tart pan and set aside. In a large skillet, heat the oil over medium heat. Add the onion, cover, and cook to soften, about 5 minutes. Increase the heat to medium-high. Add the potatoes and season with salt and pepper to taste. Cook until the potatoes are nicely browned, about 10 minutes, turning the potatoes frequently. Transfer to a large bowl and set aside.

2. In a blender or food processor, combine the tofu, yeast, soy sauce, baking powder, ½ teaspoon salt, and ⅛ teaspoon pepper, processing until smooth. Mix the tofu mixture into the potato-onion mixture.

3. Spread the mixture evenly into the prepared tart pan. Arrange the tomato slices in a circle around the perimeter of the top of the frittata.

4. Bake until the center is firm and set, about 30 minutes. Let the frittata cool for 5 to 10 minutes before serving.

# roasted vegetable frittata

makes 4 to 6 servings

*This vegan version of the Italian omelet known as a frittata is especially flavorful because it is made with roasted vegetables. Roast your vegetables ahead of when you need them for easy assembly.*

2 tablespoons olive oil

1 medium sweet yellow onion, finely chopped

1 large Yukon Gold potato, peeled and finely chopped

1 small red or yellow bell pepper, finely chopped

1½ cups sliced white mushrooms

Salt and freshly ground black pepper

1 pound firm tofu, well drained and crumbled

2 tablespoons nutritional yeast

1 tablespoon soy sauce

½ teaspoon baking powder

1. Preheat the oven to 425°F. Spread 1 tablespoon of the oil in the bottom of a 9 × 13-inch baking pan. Arrange the onion, potato, bell pepper, and mushrooms in the pan and drizzle with the remaining 1 tablespoon of oil. Season with salt and pepper to taste and place in the oven. Roast until the vegetables are tender and slightly browned on the edges, about 20 minutes.

2. Lightly oil a 9- or 10-inch tart pan and set aside. In a blender or food processor, combine the tofu, yeast, soy sauce, and baking powder with ½ teaspoon salt and ⅛ teaspoon pepper, processing until smooth.

3. In a large bowl, combine the tofu mixture and roasted vegetables and stir to mix well. Transfer the mixture to the prepared tart pan, spreading the mixture evenly.

4. Bake until the center is firm and set, about 30 minutes. Let the frittata cool for 10 minutes before serving.

# kiss my grits breakfast casserole

makes 6 servings

*Much like polenta, grits are coarsely ground corn kernels. A favorite breakfast food of the American South, they're great in this flavorful casserole that can be assembled ahead of time and popped into the ovenwhen needed. Be sure to use quick-cooking grits, not instant grits.*

1¾ cups unsweetened soy milk

1¾ cups vegetable broth, homemade (page 141) or store-bought

Salt

1 cup quick-cooking grits

½ cup shredded vegan Cheddar cheese

2 tablespoons vegan margarine

1 cup cooked and chopped tempeh bacon (page 525) or vegan sausage

1 cup fresh or frozen corn kernels

1. Preheat the oven to 375°F. Lightly oil a 9 × 13-inch baking pan and set aside.

2. In a large saucepan, combine the soy milk and broth and bring to a boil over high heat. Add salt to taste (depending on the saltiness of your broth) and stir in the grits. Reduce the heat to low and cook, stirring occasionally, until the grits are thickened but not stiff. Turn off the heat and stir in the cheese, margarine, tempeh bacon, and corn.

3. Scrape the mixture into the prepared baking pan. Spread evenly, smooth the top, and bake until slightly puffed and golden brown, about 45 minutes. Serve immediately.

# two-tomato brunch casserole

makes 6 servings

*This satisfying make-ahead casserole, with fresh and sun-dried tomatoes, is great for breakfast or brunch, or even a light supper.*

6 ripe plum tomatoes

2 tablespoons olive oil

1 large sweet yellow onion, finely chopped

½ cup minced oil-packed sun-dried tomatoes

1 teaspoon dried basil

½ teaspoon ground fennel seed

¼ teaspoon ground cayenne

1 pound firm tofu, drained and crumbled

2½ cups unsweetened soy milk

Salt and freshly ground black pepper

1 loaf Italian bread, cut into ½-inch cubes

2 tablespoons vegan Parmesan or Parmasio (page 193; optional)

1. Cut 3 of the plum tomatoes into ¼-inch slices and set aside. Finely chop the remaining 3 plum tomatoes and set aside. Preheat the oven to 375°F. Lightly oil a 9 × 13-inch baking pan and set aside.

2. In a large skillet, heat the oil over medium heat. Add onion and cook until softened, about 5 minutes. Stir in the chopped plum tomatoes and the sun-dried tomatoes. Add the basil, fennel seed, and cayenne and cook for 5 minutes, stirring occasionally. Season with salt and pepper to taste and set aside.

3. In a blender or food processor, combine the tofu, soy milk, and salt and pepper to taste. Blend until smooth. Arrange the bread cubes in the prepared baking pan. Distribute the onion-tomato mixture over the bread and pour on the tofu mixture, using a fork to distribute evenly. Set aside for 20 minutes, or until the liquid is absorbed.

**4.** Top the casserole with the reserved sliced tomatoes. Sprinkle with Parmesan, if using. Bake until puffy and lightly browned, about 45 minutes. Let stand 10 minutes before serving.

# spinach and mushroom strata

makes 6 servings

*You can prepare this hearty layered breakfast casserole ahead of time. Simply assemble, cover, and refrigerate overnight—then bake and serve. Instead of the mushrooms and spinach, you can make the strata with sautéed zucchini and red bell peppers or substitute cooked chard or kale for the spinach. Chopped cooked or canned artichoke hearts make a good addition as well.*

2 tablespoons olive oil
1 large red onion, finely chopped
3 garlic cloves, minced
2 cups sliced white mushrooms
1 (10-ounce) bag fresh baby spinach
1 pound firm tofu, well drained
2½ cups unsweetened soy milk
1 teaspoon salt
¼ teaspoon ground cayenne
5 cups cubed French or Italian bread
1 cup shredded vegan mozzarella
¼ cup grated vegan Parmesan or Parmasio (page 193)
1 teaspoon smoked paprika

**1.** In a large skillet, heat the oil over medium heat. Add the onion, cover, and cook until softened, 5 minutes. Stir in the garlic, then add the mushrooms and cook, uncovered, until the mushrooms release their liquid, about 5 minutes. Add the spinach and cook, stirring, to wilt the spinach, about 3 minutes. Set aside.

**2.** In a blender or food processor, process the tofu with the soy milk, salt, and cayenne. Set aside.

**3.** Preheat the oven to 350°F. Lightly oil a 9 × 13-inch baking pan. Arrange half of bread cubes in an even layer inside the prepared pan. Spoon half of the spinach-mushroom mixture over the bread and pour half of the soy mixture on top. Sprinkle with half the mozzarella.

**4.** Repeat the layering with the remaining ingredients. Allow the mixture to rest until the liquid is absorbed, about 20 minutes.

**5.** Sprinkle the strata with the remaining soy mozzarella, Parmesan, and paprika. Bake until puffy and lightly browned, about 45 minutes. Allow to stand 10 to 15 minutes before serving.

# vegan eggs benedict

makes 6 servings

*My friend Tal Ronnen, a talented vegan chef, developed this spin on Eggs Benedict. To save time, make the Hollandaze Sauce (page 552) a day in advance and reheat before serving.*

1 pound extra-firm tofu, well drained
3 tablespoons all-purpose flour
1 tablespoon nutritional yeast
Pinch turmeric
½ teaspoon salt
¼ teaspoon freshly ground black pepper
1 tablespoon canola or grapeseed oil
6 slices vegan Canadian bacon or tempeh bacon, homemade (page 525) or store-bought
3 English muffins, split
1 tablespoon vegan margarine
1 large ripe tomato, cut into ¼-inch slices
Hollandaze Sauce (page 552)
2 tablespoons minced fresh parsley, for garnish

continues on next page

1. Cut the tofu horizontally into six ¼-inch slices. Using a 3-inch cookie cutter or ring mold, cut the tofu slices into circles, reserving the remaining tofu for another use.

2. In a shallow bowl, combine the flour, nutritional yeast, turmeric, salt, and pepper. Mix well. Dredge the tofu in the flour mixture and set aside.

3. In a large skillet, heat the oil over medium-high heat. Add the tofu and cook until golden on both sides, turning once, about 4 minutes per side. Remove from the pan and set aside.

4. In the same skillet, adding more oil if needed, cook the bacon until browned on both sides, about 2 minutes per side. Set aside.

5. Toast the English muffins and spread with the margarine. Place one muffin half on each of 6 plates. Top each muffin half with a slice of tomato, followed by a piece of tofu and a slice of the bacon. Spoon Hollandaze Sauce on top. Sprinkle with parsley and serve immediately.

## bountiful breakfast burritos 🅕

makes 4 servings

*These are breakfast burritos loaded with the "works." Fill large or small tortillas, according to your preference or what's on hand. Serve with extra salsa, if desired.*

1 tablespoon olive oil
¼ cup chopped green onions
1½ cups chopped fresh spinach
1 pound extra-firm tofu, drained and crumbled
1 teaspoon salt
¼ teaspoon freshly ground black pepper
1 ripe tomato, chopped

2 tablespoons drained chopped canned mild or hot green chiles
½ teaspoon chili powder
1 cup picante sauce
½ cup vegan sour cream, homemade (page 574) or store-bought
8 (6- to 7-inch) or 4 (10-inch) flour tortillas

1. In a large skillet, heat the oil over medium heat. Add the green onions and spinach and cook for 1 minute. Add the tofu, salt, and pepper and cook for 5 minutes. Stir in the tomato, chiles, and chili powder. Add ½ cup of the picante sauce and cook until hot, about 5 minutes. Keep warm over low heat.

2. In a small bowl, combine the remaining ½ cup picante sauce with the sour cream and stir to mix well. Spread a tablespoonful of the sauce onto each tortilla. Spoon ½ cup of the tofu mixture down the center of each tortilla. Carefully roll up tortillas and arrange on plates. Serve remaining picante-sour cream mixture on the side.

## burritos benedict

makes 4 servings

*If the more traditional vegan eggs benedict are too frou-frou for you, try this less fussy, burrito-style version instead. Be sure to make the Hollandaze Sauce (page 552) ahead of time so the flavors have time to blend.*

2 tablespoons olive oil
8 strips tempeh bacon, homemade (page 525) or store-bought
¼ cup chopped green onions
1 pound extra-firm tofu, drained and crumbled
1 tablespoon nutritional yeast
Pinch turmeric
½ teaspoon salt
¼ teaspoon freshly ground black pepper

1 ripe tomato, chopped

1 cup Hollandaze Sauce (page 552)

4 (10-inch) flour tortillas

1. In a large skillet, heat 1 tablespoon of the oil over medium heat. Add the tempeh bacon and cook until browned and crispy, 1 minute per side. Remove from the skillet, coarsely chop, and set aside.

2. In the same skillet, heat the remaining 1 tablespoon oil over medium heat. Add the green onions, tofu, nutritional yeast, turmeric, salt, and pepper. Cook for 5 minutes. Stir in the tomato and cook until the mixture is hot and well blended, about 5 minutes longer.

3. Spread about 2 tablespoonfuls of the Hollandaze Sauce onto each tortilla. Sprinkle each with one quarter of the chopped tempeh bacon. Spoon $1/2$ cup of the tofu mixture down center of each tortilla.

4. Carefully roll up the tortillas and place on a plate. Top each burrito with a spoonful of the remaining sauce. Serve immediately.

# mango morning quesadillas 🅕

makes 4 servings

*This fun and fruity dish tastes more like dessert than breakfast, but it's easy, quick, and a great way to start the day with protein-rich tofu and a serving of fruit. Instead of mangos, you can use peaches, pineapple, or other ripe fruit. Top with the Cashew Crème (page 501) for a luxurious finish.*

8 ounces firm tofu, drained and crumbled

$1/4$ cup agave nectar

$1/2$ teaspoon ground coriander

2 ripe mangos, peeled, pitted, and chopped

8 (6-inch) soft flour tortillas

1. In a blender or food processor, combine the tofu, agave nectar, and coriander. Process until smooth. Add the mango and pulse to combine. Set aside.

2. Preheat the oven to 425°F. Lightly oil a large baking sheet.

3. Arrange 4 of the tortillas in a single layer on the prepared baking sheet. Spread the tofu mixture evenly over the tortillas, covering the tortillas to within $1/2$ inch of the edge. Top with the remaining tortillas, pressing gently.

4. Bake until the tortillas are lightly browned, about 7 minutes. Transfer the quesadillas to a cutting board. Cut them into wedges and serve.

# couscous brunch cake with fresh fruit

makes 4 to 6 servings

*This is one of my favorite brunch dishes, especially when serving a crowd. It is delicious and satisfying. Best of all, it can be made ahead of time and it looks beautiful with fresh fruit cascading down around it. If you're putting it on the table whole rather than plating it, you can cut it and then top it with the fruit for easier serving.*

2 cups white grape juice

1 cup couscous

1 tablespoon sugar

$1/2$ teaspoon ground cinnamon

1 cup blueberries

2 ripe peaches, halved, pitted, and chopped

2 teaspoons superfine sugar

1 teaspoon fresh lemon juice

1. In a large saucepan, bring the juice to a boil over high heat. Add the couscous, sugar,

continues on next page

and cinnamon. Reduce the heat to low, cover, and simmer until the juice is absorbed, about 5 minutes.

2. Lightly oil an 8-inch springform pan. Press the couscous mixture into the prepared pan. Cover loosely and refrigerate for at least an hour.

3. In a large bowl, combine the blueberries, peaches, superfine sugar, and lemon juice. Stir to mix well. Set aside at room temperature for 30 minutes. To serve, cut the cake into wedges and top each slice with some of the fruit.

## close to cottage cheese

makes 2 cups

*Use this vegan cottage cheese any way you would use the dairy version: as a filling for crêpes (page 488); spread on bagels; or spooned into a bowl, topped with fruit and sprinkled with nuts.*

1 pound firm tofu, drained
1½ tablespoons fresh lemon juice
1½ tablespoons apple cider vinegar
2 teaspoons canola or grapeseed oil
1 teaspoon salt

1. Steam the tofu for 5 minutes. Set aside to cool.

2. Transfer half of the tofu to a blender or food processor. Add the lemon juice, vinegar, oil, and salt and process until smooth.

3. In a large bowl, mash the remaining steamed tofu with a fork until crumbly. Add the pureed tofu mixture and stir to combine.

4. Cover and chill for at least 1 hour before using.

# PANCAKES, WAFFLES, AND FRENCH TOAST

## cranberry pancakes with orange-maple syrup

makes 4 to 6 servings

*Cranberries add sparkle to these luscious pancakes made even better with a drizzle of warm maple syrup studded with bits of orange. Tempeh Bacon (page 525) makes a delicious accompaniment.*

1 cup boiling water
½ cup sweetened dried cranberries
½ cup maple syrup
¼ cup fresh orange juice
¼ cup chopped orange
1 tablespoon vegan margarine
1½ cups all-purpose flour
3 tablespoons sugar
1 tablespoon baking powder
½ teaspoon salt
1½ cups soy milk
¼ cup soft silken tofu, drained
1 tablespoon canola or grapeseed oil,
     plus more for frying

1. In a heatproof bowl, pour the boiling water over the cranberries and set aside to soften, about 10 minutes. Drain well and set aside.

2. In a small saucepan, combine the maple syrup, orange juice, orange, and margarine and heat over low heat, stirring to melt the margarine. Keep warm. Preheat the oven to 225°F.

3. In a large bowl, combine the flour, sugar, baking powder, and salt and set aside.

4. In a food processor or blender, combine the soy milk, tofu, and oil until well blended.

5. Pour the wet ingredients into the dried ingredients and blend with a few swift strokes. Fold in the softened cranberries.

6. On a griddle or large skillet, heat a thin layer of oil over medium-high heat. Ladle $\frac{1}{4}$ cup to $\frac{1}{3}$ cup of the batter onto the hot griddle. Cook until small bubbles appear on the top, 2 to 3 minutes. Flip the pancake and cook until the second side is browned, about 2 minutes longer. Transfer cooked pancakes to a heatproof platter and keep warm in the oven while cooking the rest. Serve with orange-maple syrup.

# spiced apple pancakes

makes 4 servings

*These fragrant pancakes are the ultimate in a comfort-food breakfast. What's not to like about a stack of tender moist pancakes with a topping that smells like apple pie? Instead of apples, you can substitute another fruit such as pears, plums, or peaches.*

3 tablespoons vegan margarine, melted

3 Granny Smith apples, peeled, cored, and cut into ¼-inch slices

4 tablespoons sugar

1 tablespoon fresh lemon juice

1½ teaspoons ground cinnamon

¾ teaspoon ground allspice

¼ cup pure maple syrup

1½ cups all-purpose flour

1 tablespoon baking powder

¼ teaspoon ground nutmeg

½ teaspoon salt

1½ cups soy milk

Canola or grapeseed oil, for frying

1. In a large skillet, heat 1 tablespoon of the margarine over medium heat. Add the apples, 2 tablespoons of the sugar, the lemon juice, $\frac{1}{2}$ teaspoon of the cinnamon, and $\frac{1}{4}$ teaspoon of the allspice. Cook, stirring, to soften the apples. Add the maple syrup and keep warm over low heat.

2. Preheat the oven to 225°F. In a large bowl, combine the flour, the remaining 2 tablespoons sugar, the baking powder, the remaining 1 teaspoon cinnamon, the remaining $\frac{1}{2}$ teaspoon allspice, the nutmeg, and the salt. Set aside.

3. In a medium bowl, combine the soy milk and the remaining 2 tablespoons margarine. Blend until smooth. Pour the liquid into the dry ingredients and blend with a few swift strokes.

4. On a griddle or large skillet, heat a thin layer of oil over medium-high heat. Ladle $\frac{1}{4}$ cup to $\frac{1}{3}$ cup of batter onto the hot griddle. Cook until small bubbles appear on the top, about 3 minutes. Flip the pancake and cook until the second side is browned, about 2 minutes.

5. Transfer the cooked pancakes to a heatproof platter and keep warm in the oven while cooking the rest. Serve topped with the apple mixture.

# ginger-pear pancakes

makes 4 servings

*These fragrant and delicious pancakes are the cure for a cold and dreary weekend morning. Another fruit, such as apple or peach, may be used instead of the pear.*

2 cups all-purpose flour
2 tablespoons sugar
3 teaspoons baking powder
½ teaspoon salt
2 cups soy milk
2 tablespoons vegan margarine, melted
1 teaspoon grated fresh ginger
1 teaspoon pure vanilla extract
1 ripe pear, peeled, cored, and chopped
Canola or grapeseed oil, for frying

1. In a large bowl, combine the flour, sugar, baking powder, and salt and set aside.

2. In a separate large bowl, combine the soy milk, margarine, ginger, and vanilla. Add the wet ingredients to the dry ingredients and blend with a few swift strokes. Fold in the pear. Preheat the oven to 225°F.

3. On a griddle or large skillet, heat a thin layer of oil over medium-high heat. Ladle ¼ cup to ⅓ cup of the batter onto the hot griddle. Cook until small bubbles appear on the top, about 3 minutes. Flip the pancakes and cook until the second side is browned, about 2 to 3 minutes longer.

4. Transfer the cooked pancakes to a heat-proof platter and keep warm in the oven while cooking the rest.

# banana-blueberry pancakes

makes 4 servings

*The mellow-sweet flavor of bananas is only surpassed by the dazzle of juicy blueberries in these scrumptious pancakes. Serving them with Blueberry Sauce (page 498) can make a good thing better.*

1 ripe banana, mashed
2 cups soy milk
2 tablespoons vegan margarine, melted
1 teaspoon pure vanilla extract
1½ cups all-purpose flour
½ cup quick-cooking oats
2 tablespoons sugar
3 teaspoons baking powder
1 teaspoon ground cinnamon
½ teaspoon ground allspice
½ teaspoon ground nutmeg
½ teaspoon salt
1 cup fresh blueberries
Canola or grapeseed oil, for frying

1. In a large bowl, combine the banana, soy milk, melted margarine, and vanilla, mixing well. Set aside.

2. In a separate large bowl, combine the flour, oats, sugar, baking powder, cinnamon, allspice, nutmeg, and salt. Add the wet ingredients to the dry ingredients and blend with a few swift strokes. Fold in the blueberries. Preheat the oven to 225°F.

3. On a griddle or large skillet, heat a thin layer of oil over medium-high heat. Ladle ¼ cup to ⅓ cup cupfuls of batter onto the hot griddle. Cook until small bubbles appear on the top, about 3 minutes. Flip the pancakes and cook until the second side is browned, about 2 to 3 minutes.

**4.** Transfer cooked pancakes to a heatproof platter and keep warm in the oven while cooking the rest.

# johnnycakes

makes 4 servings

*As a long-time polenta lover, I enjoy anything made with cornmeal and these popular New England cornmeal pancakes are high on my list. Serve with a slather of margarine and a drizzle of maple syrup. Johnnycakes can also be served as a savory side dish similar to corn fritters. Simply cut the sugar by half and add $1/2$ cup of thawed frozen corn kernels to the batter.*

1 cup yellow cornmeal
1 teaspoon salt
1 teaspoon sugar
1½ cups boiling water, plus more if needed
Canola or grapeseed oil, for frying

**1.** In a medium bowl, combine the cornmeal, salt, and sugar and mix well. Slowly stir in the water, mixing until smooth. Add up to 3 tablespoons of additional water if the mixture is too thick. Preheat the oven to 225°F.

**2.** On a griddle or large skillet, heat a thin layer of oil over medium heat, adding enough oil to coat. Drop large tablespoonfuls of the batter onto the hot griddle and cook until small bubbles appear on the top, about 5 minutes. Be careful not to burn. Flip the Johnnycakes and cook until the second side is browned, another 4 to 5 minutes.

**3.** Transfer cooked Johnnycakes to a heatproof platter and keep warm in the oven while cooking the rest.

# maple-pecan waffles

makes 4 servings

*If you ever needed an excuse to buy a waffle iron, this is it. For added enjoyment, mirror the warming flavor of maple syrup and crunchy pecans inside the waffles by topping them with more of the same. You can use the same batter to make pancakes, if they're more to your liking.*

1¾ cups all-purpose flour
⅓ cup coarsely ground pecans
1 tablespoon baking powder
½ teaspoon salt
1½ cups soy milk
3 tablespoons pure maple syrup
3 tablespoons vegan margarine, melted

**1.** Lightly oil the waffle iron and preheat it. Preheat the oven to 225°F.

**2.** In a large bowl, combine the flour, pecans, baking powder, and salt. Set aside.

**3.** In a medium bowl, whisk together the soy milk, maple syrup, and margarine. Add the wet ingredients to the dry ingredients and blend with a few swift strokes, mixing until just combined.

**4.** Ladle $1/2$ to 1 cup of the batter (depending on the instructions with your waffle iron) onto the hot waffle iron. Cook until done, 3 to 5 minutes for most waffle irons. Transfer the cooked waffles to a heatproof platter and keep warm in the oven while cooking the rest of the waffles.

# pumpkin waffles
# with cranberry syrup

makes 4 servings

*These delicious waffles are especially fun to make during the holidays when the family is home and lazy mornings afford the opportunity to linger over a special breakfast. The batter can also be used to make great pancakes.*

½ cup whole berry cranberry sauce
⅓ cup cranberry juice
2 tablespoons pure maple syrup
1 tablespoon vegan margarine
1¾ cups all-purpose flour
⅓ cup sugar
1 tablespoon baking powder
½ teaspoon salt
1 teaspoon ground cinnamon
½ teaspoon ground ginger
½ teaspoon ground allspice
¼ teaspoon ground nutmeg
1 cup soy milk
½ cup canned solid-pack pumpkin
2 tablespoons canola or grapeseed oil
1 teaspoon pure vanilla extract

1. In a small saucepan, heat the cranberries, cranberry juice, maple syrup, and margarine over medium heat. Cook, stirring, until hot and well blended, about 5 minutes. Keep warm over very low heat until ready to serve.

2. Lightly oil the waffle iron and preheat it. Preheat the oven to 225°F. In a large bowl, combine the flour, sugar, baking powder, salt, cinnamon, ginger, allspice, and nutmeg. Set aside.

3. In a separate large bowl, whisk together the soy milk, pumpkin, oil, and vanilla until well blended. Add the liquid ingredients to the dry ingredients and blend with a few swift strokes until just combined.

4. Ladle ½ cup to 1 cup of the batter (depending on the instructions with your particular waffle iron) onto the hot waffle iron. Cook until done, 3 to 5 minutes for most waffle irons. Transfer cooked waffles to a heatproof platter and keep warm in the oven while making the rest of the waffles.

# lemon-kissed
# blueberry waffles

makes 4 servings

*These light and flavorful waffles are a summertime treat. Remember to leave some lumps in the batter to keep the waffles tender. You can use the same batter to make pancakes.*

1½ cups all-purpose flour
½ cup old-fashioned oats
¼ cup sugar
3 teaspoons baking powder
½ teaspoon salt
1 teaspoon ground cinnamon
2 cups soy milk
1 tablespoon fresh lemon juice
1 teaspoon lemon zest
¼ cup vegan margarine, melted
½ cup fresh blueberries

1. Lightly oil the waffle iron and preheat it. Preheat the oven to 225°F.

2. In a large bowl, combine the flour, oats, sugar, baking powder, salt, and cinnamon. Set aside.

3. In a separate large bowl, whisk together the soy milk, lemon juice, lemon zest, and margarine. Add the wet ingredients to the dry ingredients and blend with a few swift strokes, mixing until just combined. Fold in the blueberries.

4. Ladle $\frac{1}{2}$ to 1 cup of the batter (depending on the instructions with your waffle iron) onto the hot waffle iron. Cook until done, 3 to 5 minutes for most waffle irons. Transfer the cooked waffles to a heatproof platter and keep warm in the oven while cooking the rest.

## very vanilla french toast

makes 4 servings

*Top with the Blueberry Sauce on page 498 or warm maple syrup mixed with $\frac{1}{2}$ teaspoon of vanilla extract added. Extra cooked French toast may be frozen, then popped into the toaster or microwave to enjoy later on. For a variation, "top with sliced fresh fruit or a warm fruit compote.*

1 (12-ounce) package firm silken tofu, drained
1½ cups soy milk
2 tablespoons cornstarch
1 tablespoon canola or grapeseed oil
2 teaspoons sugar
1½ teaspoons pure vanilla extract
¼ teaspoon salt
8 slices day-old Italian bread
Canola or grapeseed oil, for frying

1. Preheat the oven to 225°F. In a blender or food processor, combine the tofu, soy milk, cornstarch, oil, sugar, vanilla, and salt and blend until smooth.

2. Pour the batter into a shallow bowl and dip the bread in the batter, turning to coat both sides.

3. On a griddle or large skillet, heat a thin layer of oil over medium heat. Place the French toast on the hot griddle and cook until golden brown on both sides, turning once, 3 to 4 minutes per side.

4. Transfer the cooked French toast to a heatproof platter and keep warm in the oven while cooking the rest.

## french toast with caramel apple topping

makes 4 servings

*The caramel apple topping can be a secret weapon to rouse any late sleepers in your house—the fabulous aroma is hard to resist.*

½ cup plus 2 teaspoons light brown sugar
3 tablespoons vegan margarine
4 Granny Smith apples, peeled, cored, and cut into ¼-inch slices
½ cup pure maple syrup
1 cup soy milk
⅓ cup all-purpose flour
½ teaspoon ground cinnamon
1½ teaspoons pure vanilla extract
8 slices bread of choice
Canola or grapeseed oil, for frying

1. Preheat the oven to 225°F. In a large skillet, heat $\frac{1}{2}$ cup of the sugar over medium-low heat. Cook, stirring constantly, until the sugar melts and begins to caramelize. Add the margarine and continue stirring to blend. Add the apple slices and stir to coat. Add the maple syrup and simmer over low heat until tender, stirring occasionally, about 7 minutes. Remove from heat and cover to keep warm.

2. In a shallow bowl, whisk together the soy milk, flour, cinnamon, vanilla, and the remaining 2 teaspoons sugar. Dip the bread in the batter, turning to coat both sides.

continues on next page

3. On a griddle or large skillet, heat a thin layer of oil over medium heat. Place the French toast on the griddle and cook until golden on both sides, turning once, 3 to 4 minutes per side.

4. Transfer the cooked French toast to a heatproof platter and keep warm in the oven while cooking the rest. Serve with the apple topping.

# peanut butter and banana–stuffed french toast

makes 4 servings

*Inspired by Elvis's favorite sandwich, this thick and flavorful French toast is best made with a sturdy French or Italian bread. If you use the smaller French baguette, you'll need 16 slices, but if you use the larger Italian loaf, 8 should suffice. Serve warm, sprinkled with confectioners' sugar, fresh strawberries or sliced banana, and maple syrup. Almond or cashew butter can be used instead of peanut butter, if you prefer.*

1 ripe banana

½ cup creamy peanut butter

¼ cup light brown sugar

2 teaspoons pure maple syrup

16 slices French bread or 8 slices Italian bread, cut into ½-inch slices

1 cup soy milk

3 tablespoons all-purpose flour

1 teaspoon pure vanilla extract

2 tablespoons vegan margarine, plus more if needed

1. In a medium bowl, mash the banana. Add the peanut butter, sugar, and maple syrup, stirring to mix well. Preheat the oven to 225°F.

2. Spread 1 to 2 tablespoons of the peanut butter-banana mixture onto half of the bread slices, then top each with one of the remaining bread slices.

3. In a shallow bowl, whisk together the soy milk, flour, and vanilla. Place a sandwich in the batter. Let it soak for about 5 seconds. Turn the sandwich over and let it soak another 5 seconds. Repeat with the remaining sandwiches.

4. On a griddle or large skillet, melt the margarine over medium heat. Cook the stuffed bread slices until golden brown on both sides, about 4 minutes per side. Transfer the cooked French toast warm to a heatproof platter and keep warm in the oven while cooking the rest.

# CEREALS

## granola

makes about 8 cups

*Homemade granola is more economical than commercial brands and tastes better, too, because you make it fresh yourself and you can customize the ingredients, with different additions such as dried blueberries, cranberries, or goji berries in place of the raisins or using walnuts or pecans instead of almonds.*

5½ cups old-fashioned oats
1½ cups slivered almonds
½ cup shelled sunflower seeds
1 cup golden raisins
1 cup shredded unsweetened coconut
1 cup pure maple syrup
½ teaspoon ground cinnamon
¼ teaspoon ground allspice
Pinch salt

1. Preheat the oven to 325°F. Spread the oats, almonds, and sunflower seeds in a 9 × 13-inch baking pan and place in the oven for 10 minutes.

2. Remove from the oven and reduce the temperature to 300°F. Add the raisins, coconut, maple syrup, cinnamon, allspice, and salt and stir to combine.

3. Return the pan to the oven and bake for 15 minutes, or until the mixture is crisp and dry. Be careful not to burn.

4. Remove from oven and let cool completely, 30 minutes. Transfer to an airtight container and store in the refrigerator where it will keep for several weeks.

## granola-infused oatmeal

makes 4 to 6 servings

*Sure, you could sprinkle some granola on top of a bowl of oatmeal, but that's not the ideal. When you add the granola to the entire pot and let it sit, the granola softens up and its flavor permeates the oatmeal, giving it added layers of flavor. If you still want that crunch of granola on top, then go for it.*

4 cups water
1¾ cups old-fashioned oats
1 teaspoon ground cinnamon
¼ teaspoon salt
¾ cup vegan granola, homemade (page 521) or store-bought

1. In a large saucepan, bring the water to a boil over high heat. Reduce the heat to low, stir in the oats, cinnamon, and salt. Simmer for 5 minutes, stirring occasionally.

2. Remove from the heat and stir in the granola. Cover and let stand for about 3 minutes before serving.

## cran-apple oatmeal

makes 4 to 6 servings

*The sweet sparkle of apples and cranberries turns everyday oatmeal into a special treat. A sprinkle of toasted nuts and a drizzle of maple syrup on top make it extra-special.*

2 cups water
2 cups apple juice
2 cups old-fashioned oats
1 tablespoon light brown sugar
1 teaspoon ground cinnamon
¼ teaspoon salt
1 Fuji or Gala apple, peeled, cored, and shredded
¼ cup sweetened dried cranberries

continues on next page

1. In a large saucepan, combine the water and apple juice and bring to a boil over high heat. Reduce the heat to low, stir in the oats, sugar, cinnamon, and salt. Simmer for 5 minutes, stirring occasionally.

2. Remove from the heat and stir in the apple and cranberries. Cover and let stand for about 3 minutes before serving.

## morning polenta with a drizzle of maple syrup

makes 4 servings

*Long before polenta became the darling of the dinner table, it was known as porridge and served for breakfast. If you prefer your breakfast on the savory side, simply omit or reduce the amount of maple syrup.*

4 cups water
1 teaspoon salt
1 cup yellow cornmeal
2 tablespoons vegan margarine
¼ cup pure maple syrup

1. In a large saucepan, bring the water to a boil over high heat. Add the salt and whisk in the cornmeal. Reduce heat to low. Cook, stirring, until the water is absorbed, about 15 minutes.

2. Turn off the heat and stir in the margarine. Spoon into 4 bowls, drizzle with the maple syrup, and serve.

## breakfast bulgur with pears and pecans

makes 4 servings

*Bulgur is a nutty-tasting quick-cooking grain that is used to make tabbouleh. Here it is transformed into a hot and hearty breakfast cereal.*

2 cups water
½ teaspoon salt
1 cup medium bulgur
1 tablespoon vegan margarine
2 ripe pears, peeled, cored, and chopped
¼ cup chopped pecans

1. In a large saucepan, bring the water to a boil over high heat. Add the salt and stir in the bulgur. Reduce heat to low, cover, and simmer until the bulgur is tender and liquid has absorbed, about 15 minutes.

2. Remove from the heat and stir in the margarine, pears, and pecans. Cover and let sit for 12 to 15 minutes more before serving.

## dawn's early couscous

makes 4 to 6 servings

*Let the sun rise on a new kind of breakfast treat. Borrow some couscous from your dinnertime pantry, simmer it sweet with juice, and load it up with your favorite nuts and fruit. Flax seeds are highly perishable, so store them in the refrigerator in a tightly sealed container.*

3 cups apple juice or white grape juice
2 cups couscous
½ teaspoon ground cinnamon
Salt
½ cup sweetened dried cranberries or other dried fruit
⅓ cup chopped walnuts or toasted slivered almonds
1 tablespoon ground flax seed

1. In a large saucepan, bring the apple juice to a boil over high heat. Add the couscous, cinnamon, and salt to taste. Stir in the cranberries, cover, and turn off the heat.

2. Let the couscous stand for 10 minutes. Stir in the walnuts, sprinkle with the flax seeds, and serve hot.

# Breakfast Sides

## apple coffee cake

makes 6 to 8 servings

*This is a yummy weekend breakfast treat that is also great to include on a brunch table. Since it takes about an hour to bake, you might want to get up early to pop it in the oven—just don't fall back to sleep! If you want to dress it up a little, a light dusting with confectioners' sugar would be a nice touch.*

1 Granny Smith apple, peeled, cored, and shredded
1 tablespoon fresh lemon juice
1 cup soy milk
¼ cup canola or grapeseed oil
2 cups all-purpose flour
¾ cup sugar
1 tablespoon baking powder
1 teaspoon ground cinnamon
½ teaspoon salt

1. Preheat the oven to 350°F. Lightly oil a 9-inch square baking pan and set aside. In a medium bowl, combine the apple and lemon juice and toss well to coat. Stir in the soy milk and oil. Mix well and set aside.

2. In a large bowl, mix the flour, sugar, baking powder, cinnamon, and salt. Add the wet ingredients to the dry ingredients and mix to combine.

3. Pour the batter into the prepared pan. Bake until golden brown and a toothpick inserted in the center comes out clean, about 1 hour. Cool in the pan on a wire rack for 20 minutes before serving.

## breakfast bran muffins

makes 12 muffins

*Those seemingly virtuous bran muffins that entice you at neighborhood coffee shops are often loaded with butter, eggs, and too much sugar. Here's the real deal, vegan style— great bran flavor with a hint of orange, fiber- rich and not too sweet—so you can have a second one and not feel guilty. If your bran flakes are especially large, measure them out first and then crush them into smaller flakes.*

3 cups bran flakes cereal
1½ cups all-purpose flour
½ cup raisins
3 teaspoons baking powder
½ teaspoon ground cinnamon
½ teaspoon salt
⅓ cup sugar
¾ cup fresh orange juice
¼ cup canola or grapeseed oil

1. Preheat the oven to 400°F. Lightly oil a 12-cup muffin tin or line it with paper liners and set aside.

2. In a large bowl, combine the bran flakes, flour, raisins, baking powder, cinnamon, and salt.

3. In a medium bowl, combine the sugar, orange juice, and oil and mix until blended. Pour the wet ingredients into the dry ingredients and mix until just moistened.

4. Spoon the batter into the prepared muffin tin, filling the cups about two-thirds full. Bake until golden brown and a toothpick inserted into a muffin comes out clean, about 20 minutes. Serve warm.

# banana-walnut breakfast muffins

makes 12 muffins

*Here's everything you like about banana nut bread in cute little muffins. Muffins freeze well, so don't hesitate to make a batch on the weekend and freeze some for a tasty surprise later in the week.*

1 cup all-purpose flour

¾ cup whole wheat flour

½ cup sugar

2 teaspoons baking powder

½ teaspoon baking soda

¼ teaspoon salt

½ cup chopped walnuts

2 tablespoons ground flax seeds

2 ripe bananas, mashed

¼ cup apple juice

3 tablespoons canola or grapeseed oil

1. Preheat the oven to 350°F. Lightly oil a 12-cup muffin tin or line it with paper liners and set aside.

2. In a large bowl, combine the all-purpose flour, wheat flour, sugar, baking powder, baking soda, salt, walnuts, and flax seed.

3. In a medium bowl, combine the bananas, apple juice, and oil. Mix until well blended. Add the wet ingredients to the dry ingredients and stir just until the flour is moistened. Do not overmix.

4. Spoon the batter into the prepared muffin tin. Bake until golden brown, 20 to 25 minutes. Serve warm.

# two-potato hash  ⨍

makes 4 servings

*Visions of a Sunday morning hash breakfast often inspires me to add a few extra potatoes in the oven on a Saturday evening and I'm always glad I did. If you're not a fan of sweet potatoes, use all white potatoes instead. Thawed and chopped, frozen veggie burgers may be used instead of the seitan.*

2 tablespoons olive oil

1 medium red onion, chopped

1 medium red or yellow bell pepper, chopped

1 cooked medium russet potato, peeled and cut into ½-inch dice

1 cooked medium sweet potato, peeled and cut into ½-inch dice

2 cups chopped seitan, homemade (page 305) or store-bought

Salt and freshly ground black pepper

1. In large skillet, heat the oil over medium heat. Add the onion and bell pepper. Cover and cook until softened, about 7 minutes.

2. Add the white potato, sweet potato, and seitan and season with salt and pepper to taste. Cook, uncovered, until lightly browned, stirring frequently, about 10 minutes. Serve hot.

# pan-fried spuds

makes 4 servings

*Truly one of the most delicious options for breakfast is pan-fried potatoes, also known as home fries. For a variation, leave out the bell pepper if you like or add a splash of lemon juice and some oregano. These potatoes are a great accompaniment to a tofu scramble.*

3 tablespoons olive oil

1 small yellow onion, minced

1 small red bell pepper, chopped

3 leftover baked potatoes, peeled and cut into ½-inch dice

½ teaspoon sweet or smoked paprika

Salt and freshly ground black pepper

1. In a large skillet, heat the oil over medium heat. Add the onion, cover, and cook until softened, about 5 minutes.

2. Add the bell pepper and cook for 2 minutes to soften slightly. Add the potatoes and paprika and season with salt and pepper. Cook until nicely browned, turning occasionally, about 15 minutes. Serve hot.

# hash brown potatoes

makes 4 servings

*Unlike home fries, which can be made with cooked potatoes, hash browns are made with shredded raw potatoes and fried kind of like a large potato pancake. Serve with scrambled tofu and tempeh bacon for a hearty breakfast or brunch.*

2 tablespoons olive oil

1½ pounds russet potatoes, peeled and shredded (about 3 cups)

½ cup shredded sweet yellow onion

1 teaspoon salt

¼ teaspoon freshly ground black pepper

1. In a large skillet, heat the oil over medium heat. Add the potatoes, onion, salt, and pepper. Stir to combine, then press down with a spatula to form a cake. Cook until the potatoes soften and become golden brown on the bottom, about 12 minutes.

2. Loosen the potatoes from the pan with a spatula and flip them over onto a large plate. Slide the potatoes back into the pan to brown the other side, about 10 minutes longer. Serve hot.

# tempeh bacon

makes 4 servings

*The thinner you can cut the tempeh, the crisper and tastier the results. Liquid smoke adds a smoky flavor to the tempeh strips. Look for it in well-stocked supermarkets. In addition to making a hearty breakfast side dish for pancakes, waffles, and scrambles, these strips are ideal for making BLTs and other sandwiches.*

8 ounces tempeh

2 tablespoons canola or grapeseed oil

2 tablespoons soy sauce

½ teaspoon liquid smoke

1. In a medium saucepan of simmering water, cook the tempeh for 30 minutes. Set aside to cool, then pat dry and cut it into ⅛-inch strips.

2. In a large skillet, heat the oil over medium heat. Add the tempeh slices and fry on both sides until browned, about 3 minutes per side. Drizzle with the soy sauce and liquid smoke, being careful not to splatter. Turn the tempeh to coat. Serve hot.

## sesame-soy breakfast spread

makes about 1 cup

*This zesty protein-rich spread is a great way to turn a bagel or toast into a nourishing quick breakfast. Slather it on and you can be on your way.*

½ cup soft tofu, drained and patted dry

2 tablespoons tahini (sesame paste)

2 tablespoons nutritional yeast

1 tablespoon fresh lemon juice

2 teaspoons flaxseed oil

1 teaspoon toasted sesame oil

½ teaspoon salt

In a blender or food processor, combine all the ingredients and blend until smooth. Scrape the mixture into a small bowl, cover, and refrigerate for several hours to deepen the flavor. Properly stored, it will keep for up to 3 days.

## breakfast parfaits

makes 4 servings

*These pretty parfaits are like having dessert for breakfast. Kids love them and it's a great way to get the breakfast skippers in your house to change their ways. For a quick variation, substitute vegan yogurt for the banana-almond mixture in the recipe. Change the flavor by using peanut butter instead of almond butter, a chopped peach or plum to replace the blueberries, or dried blueberries, goji berries, or raisins instead of the cranberries. You can even include a layer of cooked oatmeal for a hearty addition. If you don't have parfait glasses, use wineglasses or small dessert bowls.*

2 ripe bananas

⅓ cup almond butter

2 tablespoons pure maple syrup or agave nectar

1¼ cups vegan granola, homemade (page 521) or store-bought

¼ cup sweetened dried cranberries

¼ cup chopped walnuts

¾ cup fresh blueberries

4 fresh hulled strawberries, for garnish

1. In a food processor or blender, combine 1 of the bananas with the almond butter and maple syrup and blend until smooth. Set aside. Slice the remaining banana into ¼-inch slices and set aside.

2. Spoon a layer of granola into 4 parfait glasses or small bowls. Top with a layer of the banana-almond mixture, followed by a sprinkling of cranberries and walnuts, a few slices of the reserved banana, and some blueberries.

3. Repeat the layering until all the ingredients are used. Top each parfait with a strawberry and serve at once.

# BEVERAGES

## SMOOTHIES AND BLENDER DRINKS

peanut butter and banana smoothie

tropical smoothie

stone fruit smoothie

smoothies in winter

strawberry-banana smoothie

fresh cherry smoothie

creamy orange smoothie

purple haze fruit smoothie

papaya paradise smoothie

favorite fruit smoothie

indonesian avocado smoothie

thick and creamy mocha shake

mango lassi

rosewater lassi

make-your-own almond milk

horchata

good green drink

## FESTIVE BEVERAGES

rum-spiked soy nog

sparkling pomegranate-lime punch

mulled cider

wassail-inspired punch

holiday cranberry punch

hot butter-free rum

## COFFEE, TEA, AND COCOA

soy latte

frozen soy cappuccino

hot coffee mocha

coconut-mocha iced coffee

orange and cinnamon–spiced coffee

thai-style iced tea

dairy-free chai

hot cocoa

## SPRITZERS AND COOLERS

cranberry-pomegranate spritzer

coconut-pineapple cooler

white grape–citrus spritzer

morning sunshine cooler

lemon-ginger refresher

🅕 = fast

This chapter presents a host of recipes for spritzers, coolers, and punch, which are intrinsically vegan, as well as smoothies, shakes, and other dairy-free blended drinks that will keep vegans, and others who want to avoid dairy, turning the pages.

The only equipment needed to make the recipes in this chapter is a blender, although if you are into juicing, you can certainly make your own juices to use in many of the recipes. I purposely avoided the inclusion of specific juicing recipes since I didn't want readers to feel they needed to buy any special equipment to use this book.

Juicing can be a world unto itself and is often espoused to maximize the nutrients available in vegetables and fruits to promote health, healing, and vitality. Certainly, many fresh fruits and juices are used to make the smoothies in this chapter and I would encourage anyone interested in juicing to investigate it further by reading some good books on juicing as well as researching the types of juicers available to determine what suits your lifestyle. There are different types of juicers, from centrifugal to masticating. Juicing can also be done with a high-speed blender, such as a Vita-Mix. The cost of the machines varies nearly as much as opinions regarding reliability, user-friendliness, and quality of the end result.

You will notice that the serving yields vary among the recipes and this should be taken into account when preparing them. For example, many of the smoothie recipes yield anywhere from one large serving to four small servings, depending on the volume created by the ingredients. Some people enjoy quaffing a smoothie from a large glass in the morning or as a snack, while others may prefer to divide the beverage among several smaller glasses to share with others. Punches and party drinks are measured in quarts rather than servings so you can decide how much to make depending on factors such as the size of your glasses and the other beverages being served.

Depending on what ingredients you use—from refreshing all-fruit concoctions, to rich delights made with chocolate and coconut milk—smoothies can be as healthful or as decadent as you like. Blend in a scoop of non-dairy ice cream, and you have a creamy vegan milkshake. Even the popular blended coffee and tea specialty drinks can be enjoyed vegan-style. Mocha latte anyone?

## SMOOTHIES AND BLENDER DRINKS

## peanut butter and banana smoothie 🅕

makes 2 servings

*If you normally skip breakfast, consider a cool and creamy smoothie to jump start your morning. Since bananas are rich in potassium and other nutrients and peanut butter is a good source of protein, this thick and delicious smoothie is a great way to start the day.*

2 cups chilled plain or vanilla soy milk
    or other nondairy milk
2 frozen ripe bananas, cut into chunks
⅓ cup creamy peanut butter

In a blender or food processor, combine all the ingredients and blend until smooth and creamy. Serve immediately.

## tropical smoothie 🅕

makes 2 to 4 servings

*This cool creamy smoothie is a refreshing taste of the tropics. This recipe makes a lot, so share the wealth.*

1 ripe mango, peeled, pitted, and cut into chunks
1 cup fresh or canned pineapple
1 ripe banana diced
1 cup pineapple juice, chilled
1 cup unsweetened low-fat coconut milk, chilled
6 ice cubes

In blender or food processor, blend mango until smooth. Add remaining ingredients and blend until slushy. Serve immediately.

---

### smoothie tips

○ Chill your ingredients before you start.
○ Keep a stash of bananas in the freezer. Cut peeled ripe bananas into chunks and store them in zip-top freezer bags. Use in smoothies to add creaminess, sweetness, and nutrition.
○ Use frozen berries or freeze fruit juice in an ice cube tray to thicken smoothies.
○ Make extra to store in the refrigerator for twice the smoothie with half the work—just be sure to shake or stir well before serving.
○ Add a tablespoon of ground flaxseed—it's rich in essential omega-3 fatty acids and is more digestible (and provides a better texture to the smoothie) when finely ground. You can add a bit of flaxseed oil, if you prefer.
○ Include some acai juice (available in supermarkets and natural food stores) for a delicious boost of antioxidants.
○ Enhance the flavor with a splash of vanilla or other extract.
○ Try different flavor options; swapping fruit juice, soy milk, almond milk, rice milk, or coconut milk for the liquid called for.
○ For a hot weather treat, pour your favorite fruit smoothie mixture into ice pop molds to make healthy frozen snacks.

## stone fruit smoothie

makes 2 servings

*Mix and match your favorite stone fruits when they are ripe and in season for a delightful blush of a smoothie.*

2 ripe peaches, halved and pitted

1 ripe plum, halved and pitted

1 ripe apricot, halved and pitted

1 cup chilled plain or vanilla soy milk
   or other nondairy milk

3 ice cubes

In a blender or food processor, combine all the ingredients and blend until smooth. Pour into glasses and serve immediately.

## smoothies in winter

makes 2 to 3 servings

*Because they are usually rich with fresh fruit, smoothies always seemed like a ritual of summer. Ever since I started making these amazing pumpkin concoctions, I now regularly enjoy seasonal smoothies beginning with the first chill of autumn and on through the winter. Make a double batch and serve it instead of eggnog at your next holiday gathering.*

¾ cup canned solid-pack pumpkin

1 frozen ripe banana, cut into chunks

⅓ cup pure maple syrup

1 teaspoon pure vanilla extract

1 teaspoon ground cinnamon

½ teaspoon ground nutmeg

2 cups chilled plain or vanilla soy milk
   or other nondairy milk

1. In a blender or food processor, combine the pumpkin, banana, maple syrup, vanilla, cinnamon, ¼ teaspoon of the nutmeg, and 1 cup of the soy milk. Blend until smooth. Add the remaining soy milk and blend until smooth.

2. Pour into glasses and sprinkle the tops with the remaining ¼ teaspoon nutmeg. Serve immediately.

## strawberry-banana smoothie

makes 2 servings

*If your strawberries are less than perfectly sweet, add the optional strawberry jam to amp up the strawberry flavor. Smoothies make a great after-school snack for kids: they're refreshing and satisfying without being too filling, and it's a great way to get them to eat fruit.*

1½ cups fresh hulled or frozen strawberries

1 frozen banana, cut into chunks

2 cups chilled plain or vanilla soymilk
   or other nondairy milk

2 teaspoons strawberry jam (optional)

In a blender or food processor, combine the strawberries, banana, soy milk, and strawberry jam, if using, and blend until smooth. Serve immediately.

# fresh cherry smoothie 🅕

makes 2 servings

*When fresh cherries are in season (and reasonably priced), I can't help but buy more than I think can ever use, and they're still somehow gone within a few days. This smoothie is one way to enjoy this luscious fruit. If cherries are unavailable, use blueberries or strawberries.*

⅓ cup unsalted raw cashews
1¼ cups chilled plain or vanilla soy milk
    or other nondairy milk
1 tablespoon pure maple syrup or agave syrup
1 teaspoon pure vanilla extract
1 cup fresh cherries, pitted

1. In a high-speed blender, grind the cashews to a fine powder. Add the soy milk, maple syrup, and vanilla, and blend until smooth. Add the cherries and blend until thick and creamy.

2. Pour into glasses and serve at once.

# creamy orange smoothie 🅕

makes 2 servings

*If you were a fan of those frozen orange Creamsicles, then you probably won't agree that this luscious smoothie serves two—you'll want it all for yourself.*

1½ cups chilled fresh orange juice
1 cup vegan vanilla ice cream
½ cup ice cubes

In a blender or food processor, combine all the ingredients, and blend until smooth and creamy. Pour into glasses and serve immediately.

# purple haze fruit smoothie 🅕

makes 2 servings

*Blueberries and dates combine with mango and banana to create a delicious fruity blend that is positively purple.*

1 cup fresh or frozen blueberries
1 fresh ripe mango, peeled, pitted,
    cut into chunks
2 dates, pitted and chopped
2 frozen ripe bananas, cut into chunks
1 cup chilled almond milk or other
    nondairy milk

1. In a blender or food processor, combine the blueberries, mango, and dates and blend until smooth.

2. Add the bananas and almond milk and blend until thick and creamy. Serve immediately.

## papaya paradise smoothie

makes 2 servings

*One sip of this refreshing tropical smoothie and you'll feel like you're in paradise. Best of all, in addition to its delectable flavor, this smoothie is loaded with healthful nutrients such as vitamin C and potassium. Be sure to freeze bananas for smoothies well in advance of making them so you have them on hand when the smoothie mood strikes. If fresh papayas are unavailable, you can substitute fresh mangos or use dried papaya that has been soaked in warm water for about 10 minutes to soften.*

2 fresh ripe papayas, peeled, seeded, and cut into
 ½-inch dice
2 frozen ripe bananas, cut into chunks
½ cup chilled pineapple juice
½ cup chilled unsweetened coconut milk (optional)
Fresh strawberries or pineapple chunks,
 for garnish (optional)

1. In a blender or food processor, combine the papayas, bananas, pineapple juice, and coconut milk, if using until well blended.

2. Pour into glasses and garnish with strawberries or pineapple chunks, if using. Serve immediately.

## favorite fruit smoothie

makes 2 servings

*Smoothies are as versatile as your imagination and the ingredients at hand. Try different combinations of fruit, juice, and other ingredients to come up with your own signature blend. This one, with mango,*
*strawberries, banana, and orange juice is one of my favorites.*

1 ripe mango, peeled, seeded, and cut into chunks
1 cup hulled fresh strawberries
1 cup chilled fresh orange juice
1 frozen ripe banana, cut into chunks

1. In a blender food processor, combine the mango, strawberries, and orange juice. Blend until smooth.

2. Add the banana and blend until thick and creamy. Serve immediately.

## indonesian avocado smoothie

makes 2 servings

*The popular Indonesian avocado drink known as alpokat is thick and satisfying, much like a creamy, mildly sweet milkshake. It may sound and look unusual, but after a sip or two, you may be hooked—I know I was. In Indonesia, the drink is made with dairy milk, but soy milk fills in just fine. Some traditional versions use no chocolate, which is my preference, but I've included the option of adding a layer of chocolate soy milk for you to decide.*

¼ cup sugar
¼ cup water
1 teaspoon instant coffee
2 ripe Hass avocados, pitted, peeled,
 and cut into chunks
1¼ cups chilled soy milk or other nondairy milk
1 cup crushed ice
1 cup chilled chocolate soy milk (optional)

1. In a small saucepan, combine the water, sugar, and instant coffee over medium heat.

Simmer, stirring, until the sugar is dissolved. Set aside to cool, about 15 minutes.

2. In a blender or food processor, combine the avocados, soy milk, reserved syrup, and ice and blend until smooth.

3. Divide between 2 tall glasses and top each with ½ cup of the chocolate soy milk, if desired. Serve immediately.

# thick and creamy mocha shake

makes 2 servings

*If you like the flavor of chocolate and coffee, you'll love this yummy shake. Be sure to plan ahead since you need to freeze your coffee into ice cubes to help thicken the shake.*

1 cup chilled plain or vanilla soy milk
    or other nondairy milk
1 cup strong coffee, frozen into ice cubes
⅔ cup vegan chocolate ice cream
2 tablespoons chocolate syrup
1 teaspoon sugar, or to taste
1 teaspoon pure vanilla extract

In a blender or food processor, combine all the ingredients and blend until thick and smooth. Pour into tall glasses and serve at once.

# mango lassi

makes 2 servings

*The delectable fruity yogurt drink known as a mango lassi can be found on the menu of most Indian restaurants. While much Indian cuisine is vegetarian, the fact that they often use dairy products such as yogurt can put many vegetarian items off limits to vegans,*

*including the luscious lassi. Now you can assuage your lassi cravings at home by using vegan yogurt, available at natural food stores and some supermarkets. You can use plain yogurt if you like, but I enjoy the extra flavor of vanilla or coconut.*

2 fresh ripe mangos, peeled and pitted
1½ cups vegan vanilla or coconut yogurt
½ cup chilled plain or vanilla soy milk
    or other nondairy milk
4 ice cubes
Ground cardamom, for garnish (optional)

1. In a blender, combine the mangos and yogurt in a blender and blend until smooth. Add the soy milk and ice cubes and blend until smooth and creamy.

2. Pour into glasses and sprinkle with cardamom, if using. Serve immediately.

# rosewater lassi

makes 1 or 2 servings

*Look for rosewater at Indian markets or gourmet grocers. This delicate and refreshing drink is utterly sublime served with a spicy Indian meal.*

1 cup vanilla vegan yogurt
½ cup rosewater
⅓ cup superfine sugar or agave nectar
½ cup chilled plain or vanilla soy milk
    or other nondairy milk
½ cup ice

1. In a blender or food processor, combine the yogurt, rosewater, and sugar and blend until smooth.

2. Add the soy milk and ice and blend until smooth and creamy. Serve immediately.

# make-your-own almond milk

makes 1 quart (4 1-cup servings)

*Almonds are super-nutritious nuts that can be made into a delicious creamy alternative to soy milk. Sure you can buy almond milk at the store (look for it next to the soy milk), but making it from scratch is a satisfying experience and more economical. It is also less sweet, since many store brands contain added sweeteners. When you soak the almonds overnight, they become softer and more digestible.*

1 cup raw almonds
4 cups water

1. Place the almonds in a bowl with enough water to cover and soak overnight.

2. Drain the almonds and place them in a blender with 2 cups of the water. Blend until smooth, then add the remaining 2 cups of water and blend until very smooth. Strain the almond milk into a bowl through a fine-mesh strainer or a colander lined with cheesecloth.

3. Refrigerate the almond milk in a tightly sealed jar. Properly stored, it will keep for 3 to 4 days. Shake before using.

# horchata

makes 4 servings

*This traditional Mexican drink made with rice is naturally dairy-free.*

1 cup long-grain white rice
⅓ cup sugar
2 cups boiling water
2 teaspoons pure vanilla extract
2 cups chilled rice milk or other dairy-free milk
Ground cinnamon, for garnish

1. In a blender or spice grinder, grind the rice to a powder and place it in a large heatproof bowl. Add the sugar, then pour the boiling water over the rice and sugar. Set aside at room temperature for an hour.

2. Pour the rice mixture into a blender or food processor and blend until smooth. Add the vanilla and rice milk and blend until smooth.

3. Strain the mixture through a fine-mesh strainer and serve over ice. Serve immediately sprinkled with cinnamon.

# good green drink 🅕

makes 1 or 2 servings

*This virtuous verdant beverage is downright salubrious—it also tastes great and is especially refreshing after a workout. The natural sweetness of the pineapple juice provides the perfect balance to the tartness of the watercress. Spirulina, a protein-rich supplement made from blue-green algae, adds a nutritional wallop. Add a chunk or spear of fresh pineapple for a lovely (and tasty) garnish.*

1 cup diced peeled cucumber

½ cup watercress

1 tablespoon spirulina (see headnote)

1 cup chilled pineapple juice

¾ cup ice

In a blender or food processor, combine all the ingredients and blend until smooth. Serve immediately.

## FESTIVE BEVERAGES

# rum-spiked soy nog 🅕

makes 4 to 6 servings

*Vegan eggnog is not only possible, it's also absolutely ambrosial. I usually start with about 3 tablespoons of rum per quart of soy milk, but usually end up adding another "oops" of rum after a taste or two. You can, of course, leave out the rum altogether if you prefer.*

1 quart chilled vanilla soy milk or other
    nondairy milk

1 cup vanilla vegan ice cream

1 tablespoon pure maple syrup

1 teaspoon pure vanilla extract

3 tablespoons dark rum, or more to taste

¼ teaspoon ground nutmeg, plus more to garnish

1. In a blender or food processor, combine all the ingredients and blend until smooth and creamy.

2. Pour into eggnog cups and garnish with nutmeg. Serve immediately. Alternatively, you can prepare the nog ahead of time and refrigerate until ready to serve. Just be sure to stir or whisk it well before serving.

# sparkling pomegranate-lime punch

makes about 2 quarts

*This pretty punch is sweet-tart and refreshing. The dazzling red color decked out with bright green lime slices makes it almost obligatory at holiday parties.*

2 cups pomegranate juice, chilled

2 cups white grape juice, chilled

1 (6-ounce) can frozen limeade concentrate, thawed

3 cups club soda or seltzer, chilled

1 lime, cut into ¼-inch slices

1. In a punch bowl, combine the pomegranate juice, white grape juice, and limeade concentrate.

2. Pour in the club soda and stir to combine. Garnish with lime slices. Serve immediately.

# mulled cider

makes 2 quarts

*Take the chill off winter with a steaming mug of apple cider. A simmering pot of cider does double duty at any cold-weather gathering—it cheers and warms your guests and it makes your house smell wonderful and inviting.*

2 cinnamon sticks, plus more for garnish

2 teaspoons whole allspice

2 teaspoons whole cloves

2 quarts apple cider

1. In a large saucepan, combine the 2 cinnamon sticks, allspice, and cloves. Add the cider and bring to boil. Reduce heat to low, cover, and simmer for 10 minutes.

2. Pour the cider through a strainer into mugs and garnish each with a cinnamon stick. Serve immediately.

# wassail-inspired punch

makes about 2 quarts

*The wassail bowl is a traditional British holiday punch made with ale, sherry, and spices. My version uses less ale and more juice, resulting in a kind of "wassail light."*

3 cinnamon sticks, broken into thirds

1 teaspoon whole cloves

½ cup light brown sugar

1 quart apple juice

2 cups cranberry juice

¼ cup fresh lemon juice

1 (16-ounce) bottle ale

¼ cup sherry or rum (optional)

1 orange, cut into ¼-inch slices

1. Enclose the cinnamon and cloves in a small piece of cheesecloth and tie it with kitchen twine. Set aside.

2. In a large saucepan, combine the sugar and apple juice and stir over medium-high heat to dissolve the sugar. Add the cranberry juice, lemon juice, ale, and spice bag. Reduce the heat to medium and simmer until hot, about 5 minutes.

3. Before serving, remove and discard the spice bag and add the sherry, if using. Garnish with orange slices and serve immediately.

# holiday cranberry punch

makes about 2 quarts (8 ½-cup servings)

*For a nonalcoholic version, use an extra one-half cup each of the cranberry juice, pineapple juice, and club soda to replace the wine.*

3½ cups chilled cranberry juice
1½ cups chilled white wine
1 cup chilled pineapple juice
3 tablespoons fresh lime juice
1½ cups chilled lemon lime seltzer or soda
1 lime, cut into ¼-inch slices

In a pitcher or punch bowl containing ice, combine all the ingredients except the lime slices. Garnish with lime slices. Serve immediately.

# hot butter-free rum

makes 2 to 4 servings

*Inspired by the potent classic hot buttered rum, this version digresses from the original in a number of ways, from the use of vegan margarine instead of butter to the tasty addition of apple juice and vegan vanilla ice cream. Warming, bracing, and delicious, this toddy is definitely for grown-ups, unless, of course, you leave out the rum.*

1½ cups apple juice
½ cup water
2 tablespoons light brown sugar
1 cup vegan vanilla ice cream
1 teaspoon vegan margarine
⅔ cup dark rum
½ teaspoon ground cinnamon
Cinnamon sticks, for garnish (optional)

1. In a large saucepan, combine the apple juice, water, and sugar and bring to a boil, stirring to dissolve the sugar. Reduce the heat to a simmer and stir in the vegan ice cream, margarine, rum, and cinnamon. Heat, stirring, until hot and well blended.

2. Pour into 2 large mugs or 4 small cups. Serve immediately, garnished with cinnamon sticks, if desired.

# Coffee, Tea, and Cocoa

## soy latte

makes 2 to 3 servings

*The classic latte goes vegan when you use soy milk instead of cow's milk.*

1½ cups soy milk
2 cups hot strong coffee
Sugar (optional)

1. Steam the soy milk using a milk steamer or heat it in a saucepan and whisk until hot and frothy. Do not boil.

2. Pour the hot coffee into cups or mugs. Add sugar, if using.

3. Top with the hot soy milk. Serve immediately.

## frozen soy cappuccino

makes 2 servings

*It's wonderful that many boutique coffee shops now include soy milk as an option for their blended coffee drinks—but they're still expensive. Save some cash and make them at home.*

¼ cup sugar
1 cup hot espresso or strong brewed coffee
1½ cups soy milk or other dairy-free milk
1½ cups ice cubes

1. In a heatproof bowl, combine the sugar and the hot espresso, stirring to dissolve. Refrigerate the espresso mixture until chilled, 2 hours.

2. In a blender or food processor, combine the chilled espresso mixture, soy milk, and ice and blend until smooth. Serve immediately.

## hot coffee mocha

makes 2 to 4 servings

*I like to serve this special coffee after a big meal when everyone is too full for dessert but wants coffee and just a touch of something sweet. Here it is—all in one cup. The serving yield will depend on the size of the cup or mug you use. Not that this tasty brew needs further embellishment, but adding a dollop of vegan whipped cream just before serving makes it oh-so-special.*

2 cups brewed coffee
1½ cups soy milk or other dairy-free milk
3 tablespoons chocolate syrup
½ teaspoon pure vanilla extract
Ground cinnamon

1. In a large saucepan, heat the coffee, soy milk, and chocolate syrup over medium heat. Cook, stirring constantly, until it is simmering. Remove from the heat and stir in the vanilla.

2. Pour into cups and top with a dash of cinnamon. Serve immediately.

## coconut-mocha iced coffee

makes 2 to 3 servings

*The only thing better than coffee and chocolate may be the addition of coconut milk. This sweet and creamy drink tastes like a decadent dessert and is less expensive than the ones you find at fancy coffee shops.*

2 cups strong coffee, chilled

¾ cup unsweetened coconut milk

¼ cup chocolate syrup

1 tablespoon sugar

1 cup ice cubes

Toasted shredded coconut, for garnish (optional)

1. In a blender or food processor, combine all the ingredients except the coconut and blend until frothy.

2. Pour into glasses and sprinkle with coconut, if using. Serve immediately.

# orange and cinnamon–spiced coffee

makes 4 servings

*This fragrant spiced coffee makes any occasion festive. It's an especially nice addition to a holiday brunch.*

¼ cup ground coffee

Zest of 1 orange

1 cinnamon stick, broken

4 cups water

2 teaspoons sugar

1. In the basket of a coffeemaker, combine the coffee, orange zest, and cinnamon. Add the water and brew the coffee.

2. Once the coffee is brewed, stir in the sugar and serve hot.

# thai-style iced tea

makes 2 to 3 servings

*As vegan-friendly as most Thai restaurants can be, it can be difficult to find one that serves vegan Thai iced tea. Now you can make it at home. Look for Thai tea (cha*

*Thai) at Asian markets. If unavailable, use black tea.*

3 cups hot brewed Thai tea (cha Thai) or black tea

½ cup light brown sugar, or to taste

3 cardamom pods, crushed, or 1 teaspoon ground cardamom

1 cup plain or vanilla soy milk or other dairy-free milk

1. In a large saucepan, combine the tea, sugar, and cardamom over medium-high heat. Simmer, stirring, until the sugar is dissolved. Remove from the heat and stir in the soy milk. Strain out cardamom pods, if using.

2. Pour the tea into a pitcher and refrigerate until chilled, about 1 hour.

3. Serve over ice in tall glasses.

# dairy-free chai

makes 3 to 4 servings

*Vegan chai lattes at the local coffee shop can be pricey. Now you can enjoy this fragrant drink at home at a fraction of the cost—and no waiting in line. Loose tea can be used to replace the tea bags, if you prefer.*

4 cups water

1½-inch piece fresh ginger, cut into ¼-inch slices

6 cardamom pods

1 cinnamon stick, broken into thirds

¼ teaspoon black peppercorns

¼ teaspoon whole cloves

3 tablespoons sugar

3 black tea bags

1 cup plain or vanilla soy milk or other dairy-free milk

½ teaspoon pure vanilla extract

1. In a saucepan combine the water, ginger, cardamom, cinnamon, peppercorns, and cloves

continues on next page

and bring to a boil over high heat. Reduce heat to low, cover, and simmer for 5 minutes. Add the sugar, stirring to dissolve. Add the tea bags and set aside to steep, about 5 minutes.

2. Strain the mixture into another large saucepan, discarding the solids. Add the soy milk and vanilla. Simmer over low heat, and serve hot. Otherwise, refrigerate until cold to serve chilled.

## hot cocoa  $2\frac{1}{2}$

makes 2 servings

*Hot cocoa is comfort in a cup. Enjoy it anytime you need a hug. Swapping soy milk for dairy milk makes it vegan. To turn this cozy beverage into a decadent treat, top with vegan whipped cream (page 501).*

2 cups plain or vanilla soy milk or other
    dairy-free milk
 tablespoons unsweetened cocoa powder
1½ tablespoons sugar
1 teaspoon pure vanilla extract

In a small saucepan, combine all the ingredients over medium heat, stirring with a wire whisk until hot, about 5 minutes. Do not boil. Serve hot in cups or mugs.

# SPRITZERS AND COOLERS

## cranberry-pomegranate spritzer

makes 2 servings

*This refreshing ruby-red spritzer looks gorgeous in a glass and is loaded with potassium and antioxidants. It makes a delicious and healthful alternative to sugary sodas when you crave a drink with fizz.*

1½ cups chilled cranberry juice
½ cup chilled pomegranate juice
½ cup chilled lemon-lime seltzer
Lime wedges, for garnish

1. Divide the cranberry juice and pomegranate juice between 2 tall glasses (with or without ice).

2. Top each with half the seltzer and garnish with lime wedges. Serve immediately.

## coconut-pineapple cooler

makes 2 servings

*Frozen banana adds creaminess to this tropical blender beverage. Add a splash of rum if you're so inclined.*

1 cup unsweetened coconut milk
1 cup pineapple juice
½ cup orange juice
1 tablespoon fresh lime juice

1 banana, cut into chunks and frozen
1 cup crushed ice
Fresh strawberries or pineapple chunks,
     optional garnish

In a blender or food processor, combine all the ingredients and blend until smooth and creamy. Serve immediately, garnished with fruit, if desired.

# white grape–citrus spritzer 🅕

makes 2 servings

*If you're trying to wean your family off soda, try this sparkling cooler instead.*

2 cups chilled white grape juice
1 tablespoon fresh lemon juice
1 tablespoon fresh lime juice
1½ cups chilled lemon lime seltzer
Lemon or lime wedges, for garnish

Combine the grape juice, lemon juice, and lime juice in a pitcher or divide between 2 glasses. Add the seltzer and serve at once garnished with lemon or lime wedges.

# morning sunshine cooler 🅕

makes 2 servings

*Three vibrant juices combine for a ray of sunshine in a glass. I was served a juice blend similar to this in Tuscany and have enjoyed this since my return as a reminder of the trip.*

*If you want to add some fizz, top it off with some seltzer.*

1 cup chilled fresh orange juice
1 cup chilled mango juice
½ cup chilled carrot juice
Ice cubes, for serving

Combine all the ingredients except the ice cubes in a pitcher. Place the ice cubes in 2 glasses, pour the juice mixture over the ice, and serve immediately.

# lemon-ginger refresher 🅕

makes 2 servings

*The combination of ginger and lemon makes this thirst quencher particularly refreshing. Ginger paste and ginger juice, available in supermarkets, are easier to use than fresh grated ginger because they don't contain the fibrous bits.*

1½ teaspoons ginger paste or ginger juice
     (see headnote)
3 tablespoons fresh lemon juice
2 cups chilled apple juice
Ice cubes, for serving

1. Combine the ginger paste and lemon juice in a pitcher and stir to blend. Add the apple juice.

2. Place a few ice cubes in 2 glasses, pour the juice mixture over the ice, and serve immediately.

# SAUCES, RELISHES, AND CONDIMENTS

## BROWN SAUCES

basic brown sauce

bordelaise sauce

madeira sauce

mushroom sauce

golden mushroom gravy

## TOMATO-BASED SAUCES

fresh tomato sauce

chunky fresh tomato sauce

roasted yellow tomato and pepper coulis

barbecue sauce

roasted tomato–red chile sauce

ranchero sauce

## OTHER SAVORY SAUCES

vegan white sauce

creamy cashew sauce

mornay-style cheeze sauce

hollandaze sauce

bearnaze sauce

watercress sauce

miso-tahini sauce

lemon-basil sauce

## NO-COOK SAUCES

remoulade sauce

tamarind sauce

vegan aioli

chipotle aioli

harissa sauce

coconut-peanut sauce

thai peanut sauce

tahini-lemon sauce

spicy mango sauce

mango-ponzu dipping sauce

piquant green olive sauce

maple-mustard sauce

ginger-soy dipping sauce

apricot and chile dipping sauce

sesame-scallion dipping sauce

nothin' fishy nam pla

vegan worcestershire sauce

## CHUTNEYS

mango chutney

fresh cranberry chutney

dried fruit chutney

green tomato chutney

pear and apple chutney

fresh mint and coconut chutney

ginger-peach chutney

## PESTOS

pesto presto

basil pistou

black olive and walnut pesto

spinach and almond pesto

fresh and sun-dried
tomato pesto

parsley and sunflower pesto

## SALSAS

fresh tomato salsa

spicy mango and red pepper
salsa

chipotle-tomato salsa

pineapple-papaya salsa

tomatillo salsa

salsa verde

## CONDIMENTS AND RELISHES

corn relish

spiced tomato and peach relish

artichoke, tomato,
and roasted pepper relish

ginger-papaya relish

triple cranberry relish

red pepper, mango,
and avocado relish

red onion and apple relish

pineapple-lime relish

indonesian chile sauce

fresh tomato ketchup

vegan mayonnaise

chipotle mayonnaise

mustard-chive mayonnaise

wasabi mayonnaise

tofu sour cream

cucumber raita

## MARINADES AND RUBS

ginger-soy marinade

garlic-herb marinade

lemon pepper marinade

teriyaki marinade

tamari-dijon marinade

pungent pineapple marinade

indian spice rub

southwestern spice rub

The term "sauce" comes from a word that means "to salt." At its most basic, a sauce is a liquid that has been flavored and thickened to enrich and complement certain foods.

It is believed that roux-based sauces (made with flour and fat) were first produced in Italy and brought to France via Catherine de Medici's cooks. Still, it is French cuisine that gets the credit for raising sauce-making to an art form, since it was eighteenth-century French chefs who developed and classified a handful of basic sauces from which numerous others are derived. The five main sauces of French cooking are called the "mother sauces" because they provide the foundation for making many other sauces. The mother sauces are: béchamel (a milk-based white sauce), velouté (a stock-based white sauce), espagnole (a stock-based brown sauce), hollandaise (an emulsified butter sauce), and tomato (a tomato-based sauce).

The right sauce can turn an everyday meal into a spectacular event—just knowing that dinner involves a red wine reduction, for example, tells guests that they're in for a treat. But when it comes to making sauces, people sometimes draw a blank. Some think they are too difficult or time-consuming to prepare and may rely on commercial products, which are unfortunately often loaded with sodium and other additives. Others fall into ruts, serving the same tired sauces again and again. And since many classic sauces contain animal products, some vegans may think those rich sauces must be forever banished from their menus.

This chapter solves all these dilemmas, and more, with a mouth-watering collection of classic and contemporary sauces, as well as marinades, rubs, relishes, and other condiments. In addition to the sauces in this chapter, you will find sauces in this book that are components of main dishes and other recipes, including pastas. You will also find a selection of salad dressings located in the salad chapter beginning on page 422. Dessert sauces can be found beginning on page 497.

While many of these recipes, such as salsas, dressings, and relishes, are naturally vegan, others, such as classic béchamel, hollandaise, and Mornay sauce, have been retooled to contain no animal products. As Julia Child once said, a sauce can be "anything you want it to be." And I want mine to be vegan.

# BROWN SAUCES

## basic brown sauce

makes about 2½ cups

*Inspired by the classic espagnole sauce, this rich brown sauce is so flavorful, you will be amazed at how quick and easy it is to make. Use this one for special meals such as the Stuffed Baked Seitan Roast (page 306) or Buttercup Squash Stuffed with Pistachio-Apricot Rice on (page 343).*

2 tablespoons olive oil
½ cup finely chopped yellow onion
½ cup finely chopped carrots
½ cup finely chopped celery
2 garlic cloves, minced
¼ cup all-purpose flour
2 cups vegetable broth, homemade (page 141)
 or store-bought, or water
¼ cup dry red wine
2 tablespoons tomato paste
1 teaspoon minced fresh basil or ½ teaspoon dried
1 teaspoon minced fresh thyme or ½ teaspoon
 dried
2 tablespoons soy sauce

1. In a large saucepan, heat the oil over medium heat. Add the onion, carrots, celery, and garlic. Cook, stirring, until softened and lightly browned, about 10 minutes.

2. Add the flour and stir constantly until the flour is absorbed into the oil. Cook for another minute and add 1 cup of the broth.

3. When the mixture thickens, stir in the remaining 1 cup broth, the wine, tomato paste, basil, thyme, and soy sauce. Stir until the mixture becomes smooth. Cover and simmer over low heat for 10 minutes.

4. Puree the sauce in the saucepan with an immersion blender or in a blender or food processor and return to the pot. Serve hot. If not using right away, cool the sauce to room temperature, transfer to a container, cover, and refrigerate until needed. Properly stored, the sauce will keep for 2 to 3 days. Reheat the sauce in a saucepan over low heat until hot.

## making sauces vegan

While many sauces and condiments, such as chutneys and salsas, are naturally vegan, there are many that are not. These are primarily the cream- and cheese-based sauces, sauces that call for beef or chicken stock, and sauces that are thickened with butter or eggs. Fortunately, those are easily veganized.

Perhaps the easiest ingredient switch is to use vegetable stock instead of beef or chicken stock. In cream sauces, soy milk and other dairy-free milks are used to replace dairy milk and cream. The classic butter and flour roux is easily veganized by using olive oil or a vegan margarine to replace the butter. Vegetable and bean purees, nut butters, and arrowroot and cornstarch slurries are other ways to thicken and enrich vegan sauces.

# bordelaise sauce

makes about 2½ cups

*This rich and flavorful sauce uses Basic Brown Sauce as its base and is made even more delicious with the addition of shallots and wine. It's great served over Seitan en Croute (page 314).*

1 tablespoon olive oil
¼ cup minced shallots
½ cup chopped white mushrooms
½ cup dry red wine
½ teaspoon minced fresh thyme or
    ¼ teaspoon dried
¼ teaspoon freshly ground black pepper
2 cups Basic Brown Sauce (page 545)

1. In a medium saucepan, heat the oil over medium heat. Add the shallots and cook until softened, about 5 minutes. Stir in the mushrooms and cook 1 minute. Add the wine, thyme, and pepper and simmer until the liquid is reduced by half.

2. Stir in the brown sauce and simmer until hot. Serve immediately. If not using right away, cool the sauce to room temperature, transfer to a container, cover, and refrigerate until needed. Properly stored, the sauce will keep for 2 to 3 days. Reheat the sauce in a saucepan over low heat until hot.

# madeira sauce

makes about 1½ cups

*This full-bodied brown sauce is made with Madeira, a luscious fortified Portuguese wine with a slightly sweet flavor. It is especially good served over the Seitan en Croute (page 314) but can transform even the simplest sauté of seitan slices into an extra special entrée.*

1 tablespoon olive oil
1 medium shallot, minced
¾ cup Madeira
2 cups vegetable broth, homemade (page 141)
    or store-bought
1 tablespoon soy sauce
1 teaspoon fresh thyme or ½ teaspoon dried
¼ teaspoon freshly ground black pepper
1 tablespoon arrowroot powder or cornstarch
3 tablespoons cold water
Salt

1. In a medium saucepan, heat the oil over medium heat. Add the shallot and cook until softened, about 4 minutes. Add the Madeira, broth, soy sauce, thyme, pepper, and simmer until reduced by about half.

2. Remove from the heat and strain the sauce through a mesh strainer. Discard the solids. Return to the saucepan and heat over medium heat.

3. In a small bowl, combine the arrowroot and water and mix until blended, then stir into the sauce, stirring constantly until the sauce thickens. Taste, adjusting the seasonings, adding a pinch of salt if needed. Serve immediately. If not using right away, cool the sauce to room temperature, transfer to a container, cover, and refrigerate until needed. Properly stored, the sauce will keep for 2 to 3 days. Reheat the sauce in a saucepan over low heat until hot.

# mushroom sauce

makes about 2½ cups

*This sauce adds rich mushroom flavor to sautéed seitan, tempeh, or veggie burgers, or recipes such as the Soy-tan Dream Cutlets (page 294) or the Chickpea and*

Vegetable Loaf (page 266). It's also great over mashed potatoes. To achieve a darker brown color, add ½ teaspoon of gravy seasoning liquid, such as Kitchen Bouquet or Gravy Master, near the end of cooking time. The recipe calls for regular white mushrooms, but you can substitute another variety, if you prefer.

1 tablespoon olive oil

2 tablespoons minced shallot

6 ounces white mushrooms, lightly rinsed, patted dry, and cut into ¼-inch slices

2 cups vegetable broth, homemade (page 141) or store-bought, or water

2 tablespoons soy sauce

1 tablespoon minced fresh parsley

1 teaspoon minced fresh thyme leaves or ½ teaspoon dried

Salt and freshly ground black pepper

2 tablespoons cornstarch

¼ cup water

1. In a medium saucepan, heat the oil over medium heat. Add the shallot and cook until soft, about 5 minutes. Add the mushrooms and cook 2 minutes longer. Add the broth, soy sauce, parsley, thyme, and salt and pepper to taste and bring to a boil.

2. In a small bowl, combine the cornstarch and water and mix until blended. Reduce the heat to low, whisk the cornstarch mixture into the sauce, and stir until it thickens, about 3 minutes. Taste, adjusting seasonings if necessary, before serving. Serve immediately. If not using right away, cool the sauce to room temperature, transfer to a container, cover, and refrigerate until needed. Properly stored, the sauce will keep for 2 to 3 days. Reheat the sauce in a saucepan over low heat until hot.

# golden mushroom gravy

makes about 3 cups

Chickpeas lend more than their golden color to this creamy sauce—they also add protein and are pureed and used to thicken the sauce. Studded with slices of juicy mushrooms, this sauce is good served over the Herbed Millet and Pecan Loaf (page 281), the Savory Amaranth Patties (page 282), or the Couscous-Chickpea Loaf (page 278).

1 tablespoon olive oil

⅓ cup chopped onion

1 cup cooked or canned chickpeas, drained and rinsed

1½ cups vegetable broth, homemade (page 141) or store-bought

1½ cups sliced white mushrooms

1 teaspoon fresh minced thyme or ½ teaspoon dried

1 teaspoon fresh minced savory or ½ teaspoon dried

1 teaspoon fresh minced sage or ½ teaspoon dried

Salt and freshly ground black pepper

1. In a medium saucepan, heat the oil over medium heat. Add the onion, cover, and cook until softened, about 5 minutes. Stir in the chickpeas and ½ cup of the vegetable broth.

2. Transfer the mixture to a blender or food processor and blend until smooth. Set aside. In the same saucepan, combine the remaining 1 cup vegetable broth with the mushrooms over medium heat and bring to a boil.

3. Reduce the heat to low and stir in the chickpea mixture, thyme, savory, sage, and salt and pepper to taste, stirring constantly to blend. Serve immediately. If not using right away, cool the sauce to room temperature, transfer to a container, cover, and refrigerate until needed. Properly stored, the sauce will keep for 2 to 3 days. Reheat the sauce in a saucepan over low heat until hot.

# TOMATO-BASED SAUCES

## fresh tomato sauce

makes about 1½ cups

*This smooth sauce is best when made with very ripe, flavorful tomatoes. Pale supermarket tomatoes just don't do it justice. Use this sauce to adorn fried polenta, grilled vegetables, or anything else that would benefit from fresh tomato flavor. Add chopped parsley or basil, if desired.*

1 tablespoon olive oil
1 medium shallot, chopped
2 garlic cloves, minced
5 ripe tomatoes, cored and quartered
Salt and freshly ground black pepper

1. In a large skillet, heat the oil over medium heat. Add the shallot and garlic. Cover and cook until softened, stirring occasionally, about 3 minutes.

2. Stir in the tomatoes and season with salt and pepper to taste. Cook until the tomatoes soften, about 10 minutes, then transfer to a blender or food processor and puree.

3. Strain the mixture through a fine-mesh sieve into a large saucepan. Discard the solids. Heat over low heat until hot. Serve immediately. If not using right away, cool the sauce to room temperature, then transfer to a container, cover and refrigerate until needed. Properly stored, the sauce will keep for 2 to 3 days. Reheat the sauce in a saucepan over low heat until hot.

## chunky fresh tomato sauce

makes about 2 cups

*This sauce captures all that is wonderful about fresh tomatoes and should only be made using tomatoes at their seasonal peak. Toss it with hot pasta, additional olive oil, and fresh basil for a quick and easy meal. It also makes a yummy topping for bruschetta.*

4 to 5 ripe tomatoes, cored
2 tablespoons olive oil
1 tablespoon minced fresh flat-leaf parsley
Salt and freshly ground black pepper

1. Cut an "x" in the bottom of the tomatoes and immerse them in a saucepan of boiling water for about 30 seconds to loosen the skin. Remove the tomatoes from the water and submerge them in a bowl of ice water. Peel the skin from the tomatoes, then cut them into wedges and remove the seeds.

2. Coarsely chop the tomatoes and place them in a medium bowl. Drizzle with the olive oil and sprinkle with parsley. Season with salt and pepper to taste and toss gently to combine. Serve at room temperature. This sauce tastes best used on the same day that it is made.

## roasted yellow tomato and pepper coulis

makes about 2½ cups

*This tantalizing sauce gets its wonderful full-bodied flavor from roasting both tomatoes and bell peppers, which are then pureed into a coulis, a term for a pureed sauce. The use of yellow vegetables and the touch of piquancy provided by the mustard and vinegar make this sauce an interesting alternative to hollandaise and is therefore especially good on the Vegan Eggs Benedict (page 541) or the Burritos Benedict (page 512). Use it to jazz up your favorite steamed, grilled, or roasted vegetables such as asparagus, cauliflower, or Brussels sprouts.*

3 ripe yellow tomatoes, cored

2 medium yellow bell peppers, halved

1 teaspoon Dijon mustard

2 teaspoons white wine vinegar

Salt and white pepper

3 tablespoons olive oil, plus extra for tossing

1. Preheat the oven to 300°F. In a large bowl, toss the tomatoes and bell peppers in olive oil, then transfer them to a baking sheet.

2. Roast the vegetables for 30 minutes. Turn over and roast for another 30 minutes. Remove from the oven and transfer to a blender or food processor, pulsing to chop. Add the mustard, vinegar, and salt and pepper to taste.

3. Slowly add the 3 tablespoons of oil, blending until emulsified. Strain through a sieve and discard the solids. Taste, adjusting seasonings if necessary. Serve at room temperature or transfer to a saucepan and heat over low heat until hot. If not using right away, cool the sauce to room temperature, then transfer to a container, cover, and refrigerate until needed. Properly stored, the sauce will keep for 2 to 3 days. Reheat the sauce in a saucepan over low heat until hot.

# barbecue sauce

makes about 2½ cups

*Use this recipe as a starting point to make your own barbecue sauce that you can tweak to your taste, adding more or less chile, sugar, or other ingredients.*

1 tablespoon olive oil

1 medium yellow onion, chopped

1 medium red bell pepper, chopped

2 garlic cloves, minced

1 or 2 jalapeños or other fresh hot chiles, minced

1 (14.5-ounce) can crushed tomatoes

½ cup sugar

¼ cup cider vinegar

½ teaspoon salt

¼ teaspoon dried oregano

½ teaspoon liquid smoke (optional)

1. In a medium saucepan, heat the oil over medium heat. Add the onion, bell pepper, garlic, and chiles. Cover and cook until softened, 5 minutes. Stir in the tomatoes, sugar, vinegar, salt, and oregano and cook, uncovered, 5 minutes longer.

2. Transfer the mixture to a blender or food processor and process until smooth.

3. Return the mixture to the saucepan and bring to a boil over high heat. Reduce heat to low and cook, stirring frequently until thick, about 20 minutes. Stir in the liquid smoke, if using. Serve hot. If not using right away, cool the sauce to room temperature, then transfer to a container, cover, and refrigerate until needed. Properly stored, the sauce will keep for 3 to 4 days. Reheat the sauce in a saucepan over low heat until hot.

# roasted tomato–red chile sauce

makes about 2 cups

*This versatile sauce is great over baked tofu, sautéed polenta, or Mexican Green Rice and Beans (page 271).*

8 ripe plum tomatoes, halved lengthwise
1 fresh red chile, seeded and chopped
2 garlic cloves, chopped
1 tablespoon olive oil
1 tablespoon balsamic vinegar
Salt and freshly ground black pepper

1. Preheat the oven to 400°F. Place the tomatoes cut side up on a baking sheet. Sprinkle with chile, garlic, oil, and vinegar. Season with salt and pepper to taste and roast until the vegetables are softened, about 30 minutes.

2. Cool the vegetable mixture slightly, then transfer it to a blender or food processor and process until smooth.

3. Strain the sauce through a fine-mesh sieve. Remove and discard the solids. Taste, adjusting seasonings if necessary. The sauce may be served at room temperature or heated in a saucepan over low heat and served hot. If not using right away, cool the sauce to room temperature, then transfer to a container, cover, and refrigerate until needed. Properly stored, the sauce will keep for 3 to 4 days. Reheat the sauce in a saucepan over low heat until hot.

# ranchero sauce

makes about 2½ cups

*This robust tomato-based sauce is especially delicious over polenta and can be used in the same way that you would use any salsa or tomato sauce.*

1 tablespoon olive oil
½ cup chopped yellow onion
1 jalapeño, seeded and minced
2 garlic cloves, minced
1 (14.5-ounce) can crushed tomatoes
1 (4-ounce) can chopped mild green chiles, drained
1 teaspoon ground cumin
½ teaspoon chili powder
¼ cup minced fresh cilantro

1. In a medium saucepan, heat the oil over medium heat. Add the onion, jalapeño, and garlic. Cover and cook until softened, about 5 minutes.

2. Stir in the tomatoes, green chiles, cumin, and chili powder. Simmer, uncovered, for 15 to 20 minutes to allow flavors to blend. Just before serving, stir in the cilantro. Serve immediately. If not using right away, cool the sauce to room temperature, then transfer to a container, cover, and refrigerate until needed. Properly stored, the sauce will keep for 3 to 4 days. Reheat the sauce in a saucepan over low heat until hot.

# OTHER SAVORY SAUCES

## vegan white sauce

makes about 3 cups

*Unsweetened soy milk and vegan margarine replace the milk and butter in this vegan interpretation of the classic white sauce known as béchamel. Toss with cooked pasta and vegetables for a creamy pasta primavera or use it as a base for vegetable-noodle casseroles such as the Pastitsio (page 226) or to top the Zucchini Walnut Fritters (page 386).*

¼ cup vegan margarine
½ cup minced shallot or onion
3 tablespoons all-purpose flour
1 tablespoon dry white wine
1 cup vegetable broth, homemade (page 141) or store-bought
2 cups unsweetened soy milk
Dash ground nutmeg
1 bay leaf
Salt and freshly ground white pepper

1. In a medium saucepan, heat the margarine over medium heat. Add the shallot and cook until softened, about 4 minutes. Do not brown.

2. Stir in the flour and cook, stirring, until the flour is absorbed. Stir in the wine, broth, soy milk, nutmeg, and bay leaf and cook, stirring until thickened, about 5 minutes.

3. Remove the bay leaf and discard. Transfer the sauce to a blender or food processor and blend until smooth, then return to the saucepan. Season with salt and pepper to taste and heat over low heat until hot. Serve immediately.

If not using right away, cool the sauce to room temperature, transfer to a container, cover, and refrigerate until needed. Properly stored, the sauce will keep for 2 to 3 days. Reheat the sauce in a saucepan over low heat until hot.

## creamy cashew sauce

makes about 3 cups

*This rich, flavorful sauce can be used in much the same way as you would use a béchamel or other white sauce. The taste and texture of raw cashews make them ideal for a vegan cream sauce. If cashews are unavailable, blanched almonds may be used instead. Toss it with cooked pasta, sautéed vegetables, and fresh herbs for a satisfying meal or spoon it over the Eggplant Fritters (page 367). Use this sauce to make the Fettuccine with Fresh Figs and Walnuts (page 211) or the Creamy Cashew Fettuccine with Mushrooms and Peas (page 221).*

1 cup unsalted raw cashews
2 tablespoons nutritional yeast
2 cups unsweetened soy milk, plus more if needed
Salt
Ground cayenne

1. In a blender, process the cashews to a fine powder. Add the nutritional yeast and 1½ cups of the soy milk and blend until smooth. Season with salt and cayenne to taste.

2. Transfer the sauce to a medium saucepan and heat over medium heat. Stir the sauce until hot, about 5 minutes. Add more of the soy milk if a thinner sauce is desired. Serve immediately. If not using right away, cool the sauce to room temperature, transfer to a container, cover, and refrigerate until needed. Properly stored, the sauce will keep for 2 to 3 days. Reheat the sauce in a saucepan over low heat until hot.

# mornay-style cheeze sauce

makes about 2 cups

*This creamy smooth sauce gets its cheesy flavor and color from nutritional yeast, with a little help from the lemon juice and mustard. It makes a wonderful topping for steamed vegetables and can be folded into cooked pasta for a zesty mac and cheese. It is also used in Baked Pasta Shells and Broccoli (page 224) and Cheezy Tomato Macaroni (page 225).*

1 tablespoon olive oil
½ cup chopped onion
1 cup vegetable broth, homemade (page 141) or store-bought
½ cup nutritional yeast
⅛ teaspoon turmeric
Salt and freshly ground black pepper
1 tablespoon cornstarch dissolved in 2 tablespoons water
2 teaspoons fresh lemon juice
½ teaspoon yellow mustard
½ cup unsweetened soy milk

1. In a small saucepan, heat the oil over medium heat. Add the onion, cover, and cook until soft, about 10 minutes. Stir in the broth and nutritional yeast, turmeric, and salt and pepper and simmer, stirring, until the mixture starts to thicken and bubble. Whisk in the cornstarch mixture and cook, whisking, for 1 to 2 minutes to thicken.

2. Transfer the mixture to a blender or food processor and blend until smooth. Add the lemon juice, mustard, and soy milk and blend until smooth. Taste, adjusting seasonings if necessary. Return the sauce to the saucepan and heat over low heat, stirring, until hot. If not using right away, cool the sauce to room temperature, then transfer it to a container, cover, and refrigerate until needed. Properly stored, the sauce will keep for 2 to 3 days. Reheat the sauce in a saucepan over low heat.

# hollandaze sauce

makes about 1½ cups

*Anyone who is familiar with a classic hollandaise knows it is an emulsion of egg yolks and melted butter. While it seems like this classic sauce would be a formidable challenge to veganize, I rather like the creamy lemony result in this recipe. Use it to make Vegan Eggs Benedict (page 571) or the Burritos Benedict (page 512). It's also especially good over steamed broccoli or roasted cauliflower or asparagus.*

¾ cup unsalted raw cashews
3 tablespoons nutritional yeast
½ cup hot water
3 tablespoons fresh lemon juice
½ teaspoon yellow mustard
½ teaspoon salt
⅛ teaspoon turmeric
Pinch ground cayenne
3 tablespoons vegan margarine

1. In a high-speed blender, process the cashews to a fine powder. Add the nutritional yeast, water, lemon juice, mustard, salt, turmeric, and cayenne and blend until smooth.

2. In a small saucepan, melt the margarine over medium heat and add to the cashew mixture. Blend until smooth. Serve as is or return the sauce to the same saucepan and heat, stirring, over low heat. If not using right away, cool the sauce to room temperature, transfer to a container, cover, and refrigerate until needed. Properly stored, the sauce will keep

for 2 to 3 days. Reheat the sauce in a saucepan on top of the stove over low heat.

# bearnaze sauce

makes about 1½ cups

*If you like the flavor of tarragon, you'll love this variation on béarnaise sauce, graced with a fragrant and flavorful reduction of white wine, tarragon, and shallots. It's good enough to eat with a spoon, but more appropriate to use it to adorn steamed, roasted, or grilled vegetables. Asparagus or broccoli are likely suspects, but it's also wonderful on the Roasted Brussels Sprouts (page 359).*

¼ cup dry white wine

¼ cup white wine vinegar

¼ cup minced shallots

3 tablespoons vegan margarine

¾ cup unsalted raw cashews

⅓ cup water

1 tablespoon fresh lemon juice

½ teaspoon salt

⅛ teaspoon turmeric

1 tablespoon minced fresh tarragon or 1 teaspoon dried

2 teaspoons minced fresh parsley

1. In a small saucepan, combine the wine, vinegar, and shallots and simmer over medium heat until reduced by half, 2 to 3 minutes. Add the margarine and continue to simmer until margarine is melted. Keep warm over low heat.

2. In a high-speed blender, grind the cashews to a find powder. Add the water, lemon juice, salt, and turmeric and blend until smooth.

3. Add the hot wine reduction mixture to the cashew mixture and blend until smooth. Add the tarragon and parsley and combine until just blended. Serve immediately. If you

prefer the sauce warmer, return to the saucepan and heat slowly, stirring, over low heat. If not using right away, cool the sauce to room temperature, transfer to a container, cover, and refrigerate until needed. Properly stored, the sauce will keep for 2 to 3 days. Reheat the sauce in a saucepan over low heat.

# watercress sauce

makes about 1½ cups

*This sprightly sauce features the vivid green color and peppery fresh taste of watercress. I especially like to serve it over simple baked potatoes or tofu or to toss with noodles, not just to add great flavor but also for the dramatic color contrast. Use it to top the Potatoes Stuffed with Fennel and Peas (page 342).*

2 tablespoons olive oil

2 tablespoons chopped shallot

1 garlic clove, chopped

1 tablespoon white wine vinegar

1 large bunch watercress

Salt and freshly ground black pepper

Water, if needed

1. In a small saucepan, heat the oil over medium heat. Add the shallot and garlic and cook until softened, about 3 minutes. Remove from the heat and stir in the vinegar. Set aside.

2. In a medium saucepan of boiling water, blanch the watercress for about 2 minutes. Run under cold water and drain well.

3. Transfer the watercress to a blender or food processor. Add the shallot mixture and process until smooth. Season with salt and pepper to taste. Add a small amount of water, a tablespoon at a time, if the sauce is too thick.

continues on next page

4. Return the sauce to the saucepan and heat over medium heat until hot. Serve immediately. If not using right away, cool the sauce to room temperature, transfer to a container, cover, and refrigerate until needed. Properly stored, the sauce will keep for 2 to 3 days. Reheat the sauce in a saucepan over low heat until hot.

## miso-tahini sauce
makes about 1⅓ cups

*Try this savory sauce over roasted or grilled vegetables, rice and beans, or baked tofu or tempeh.*

¼ cup tahini (sesame paste)
1 tablespoon mellow white miso paste
1 tablespoon fresh lemon juice
1 teaspoon soy sauce
1 cup water

1. In a small saucepan, combine the tahini, miso paste, lemon juice, and soy sauce and heat over low heat. Add the water a little at a time, stirring constantly, until smooth.

2. Cook until heated through, about 10 minutes. Do not boil. Serve immediately. If not using right away, cool the sauce to room temperature, transfer to a container, cover, and refrigerate until needed. Properly stored, the sauce will keep for 2 to 3 days. Reheat the sauce in a saucepan over low heat until hot.

## lemon-basil sauce
makes about 1½ cups

*This lively sauce, pungently redolent of garlic, lemon, and basil, can be used as a topping for sautéed or baked tofu or grilled or roasted vegetables. I especially like it over grilled portobello mushrooms and rice.*

2 tablespoons olive oil
3 medium shallots, minced
2 garlic cloves, minced
2 tablespoons capers
1 cup dry white wine
½ cup vegetable broth, homemade (page 141)
    or store-bought
3 tablespoons vegan margarine
2 tablespoons fresh lemon juice
2 tablespoons minced fresh basil

1. In a medium saucepan, heat the oil over medium heat. Add the shallots and garlic and cook until softened, about 3 minutes. Add the capers and cook for 1 minute.

2. Stir in the white wine and broth and simmer until the liquid is reduced by half, about 5 minutes. Stir in the margarine, lemon juice, and basil. Serve immediately. If not using right away, transfer to a container, cover, and refrigerate until needed. Properly stored, the sauce will keep for 2 to 3 days. Reheat the sauce in a saucepan over low heat until hot.

# No-Cook Sauces

## remoulade sauce

makes about 1¼ cups

*This zesty veganized remoulade is modeled after the Creole version of the classic French sauce. It is a natural accompaniment to fried green tomatoes and is also good as a condiment for veggie burgers. In Denmark, remoulade is a popular dip for French fries.*

¾ cup vegan mayonnaise, homemade (page 573) or store-bought
3 tablespoons ketchup
1 medium shallot, minced
1 tablespoon minced fresh parsley
1 tablespoon chopped capers
2 teaspoons finely chopped pickle
1 teaspoon Dijon mustard
½ teaspoon smoked paprika
1 teaspoon minced fresh tarragon or chervil or ¼ teaspoon dried
Tabasco sauce
Salt

1. In a medium bowl, combine the mayonnaise, ketchup, shallot, parsley, capers, pickle, mustard, paprika, and tarragon. Season with Tabasco and salt to taste, stirring to blend well.

2. Cover and refrigerate for 30 minutes before serving to allow flavors to blend. If not using right away, keep covered in the refrigerator. Properly stored, the sauce will keep for 2 to 3 days.

## tamarind sauce

makes about 1¾ cups

*Tamarind paste adds a sweet-tart flavor and gorgeous reddish-mahogany color to foods. It can be found in Indian markets and gourmet grocers and is often sold as a ready to use paste or in block form, which still contains fibers and seeds. If using tamarind in block form, soak the tamarind in the water for 15 minutes, then strain through a sieve to remove fibers and seeds before using.*

2 tablespoons tamarind paste
1 cup warm water, plus or more if needed
⅓ cup pitted dates
⅓ cup sugar
1 teaspoon salt
1 teaspoon ground ginger
½ teaspoon ground cumin
¼ teaspoon ground cayenne

1. In a blender or food processor, combine all the ingredients, and process until smooth. Taste, adjusting seasonings if necessary, and add more water if needed for desired consistency.

2. Transfer to a small bowl. If not using right away, cover and refrigerate until needed. Properly stored, the sauce will keep for 2 to 3 days.

# vegan aioli 🄵

makes about 1½ cups

*Aioli is a garlic-flavored mayonnaise that originated in Provence. It gets its name from the French word for garlic,* ail. *It makes a wonderful dip for raw vegetables and is particularly delicious drizzled onto grilled vegetables.*

½ cup slivered almonds

3 garlic cloves, crushed

⅓ cup water

½ teaspoon Dijon mustard

2 tablespoons fresh lemon juice

2 teaspoons agave nectar

½ teaspoon salt

⅛ teaspoon ground cayenne

⅓ cup olive oil

1. Place the almonds in a medium bowl. Cover with water and soak overnight.

2. Drain the soaked almonds and transfer them to a blender. Add the garlic, water, mustard, lemon juice, agave nectar, salt, and cayenne and blend until smooth and creamy.

3. With the blender running, stream in the oil, blending until the mixture thickens.

4. Transfer to a medium bowl. If not using right away, cover and refrigerate until needed. Properly stored, the sauce will keep for 2 to 3 days.

## chipotle aioli 🄵

makes about 1 cup

*This spicy interpretation of aioli adds a kick to fajitas or bean burgers. It's also good drizzled on rice and beans or grilled vegetables.*

2 canned chipotle chiles in adobo, chopped

1 garlic clove, chopped

½ teaspoon sugar

1 teaspoon salt

½ teaspoon smoked paprika

¾ cup vegan mayonnaise, homemade (page 573) or store-bought

2 tablespoons fresh lemon juice

3 tablespoons olive oil

1. In a blender or food processor, combine the chiles, garlic, sugar, salt, and paprika and process until finely minced. Add the mayonnaise and lemon juice and blend until smooth.

2. With the machine running, stream in the oil.

3. Transfer to a medium bowl. If not using right away, cover and refrigerate until needed. Properly stored, the sauce will keep for 2 to 3 days.

# harissa sauce

makes 1 cup

*This versatile hot sauce from Tunisia can be used to add flavor and heat to North African recipes such as the Moroccan Vermicelli Vegetable Soup (page 154) and the Moroccan Lentil and Chickpea Soup (page 164). Stir a small amount into vegan mayonnaise to make a lively condiment for veggie burgers.*

½ cup dried hot red chiles, seeded

2½ teaspoons caraway seeds

1½ teaspoons coriander seeds

3 fresh hot red chiles, seeded and coarsely chopped

3 garlic cloves, chopped

½ teaspoon salt

2 tablespoons olive oil

1 tablespoon white wine vinegar

¼ cup water

1. In a medium heatproof bowl, combine the dried chiles and enough boiling water to cover. Soak for 20 minutes.

2. In a small skillet, combine the caraway and coriander seeds over low heat and toast them until fragrant, stirring frequently, about 2 minutes. Do not burn. Remove from heat and grind in a spice grinder.

3. In a blender or food processor, combine the fresh chiles and garlic and process until smooth.

4. Drain the dried chiles and add them to the chile-garlic mixture. Process until smooth. Add the ground toasted spices and salt and process until well combined. Add the oil, vinegar, and water and process until smooth and well blended.

5. Transfer to a bowl. If not using right away, cover and refrigerate until needed. Properly stored, the sauce will keep for 3 to 4 days.

## coconut-peanut sauce
makes about 1½ cups

*This creamy and flavorful sauce is easy to make and can be enjoyed cold as a dipping sauce or heated and served over baked tempeh or tossed with noodles.*

½ cup creamy peanut butter
3 green onions, chopped
2 teaspoons grated fresh ginger
2 teaspoons minced fresh garlic
¾ cup unsweetened coconut milk
3 tablespoons soy sauce
2 tablespoons fresh lime juice
1 teaspoon sugar
⅛ teaspoon ground cayenne

1. In a blender or food processor, combine all the ingredients and blend until smooth.

2. If serving cold, use immediately. If serving warm, transfer to a saucepan and heat gently over low heat, stirring until warm. If not using right away, cover and refrigerate until needed. This sauce tastes best if used on the same day it is made.

## thai peanut sauce
makes about 1½ cups

*This all-purpose peanut sauce can be used as a dipping sauce or thinned with coconut milk and tossed with hot or cold noodles. The heat from the red pepper flakes will intensify the longer it sits, so less may be better, unless you really like it hot.*

½ cup creamy peanut butter
1 garlic clove, chopped
¼ cup soy sauce
3 tablespoons fresh lime juice
1 teaspoon light brown sugar
¼ to ½ teaspoon crushed red pepper, to taste
½ cup water

1. In a blender or food processor, combine all the ingredients and process until well blended. Taste, adjusting seasonings if necessary.

2. If serving as a dipping sauce, use immediately. If using as a noodle sauce, transfer the peanut sauce to a saucepan over low heat and stir in up to a cup of unsweetened coconut milk and heat until hot. If not using right away, cover and refrigerate until needed. Properly stored, the sauce will keep for 2 to 3 days.

## tahini-lemon sauce

makes about 1 cup

*This creamy tahini sauce is sensational spooned over baked marinated tofu or drizzled over kale, spinach, or rice and beans. This sauce is also delicious tossed with cooked noodles, but since it only makes 1 cup, you'll need to double the recipe in order to have enough to coat the noodles.*

3 tablespoons tahini (sesame paste)
1 teaspoon minced garlic
3 tablespoons fresh lemon juice
2 tablespoons soy sauce
2 tablespoons toasted sesame oil
⅓ cup water, plus more if needed
2 tablespoons minced fresh parsley

1. In a small bowl, whisk together the tahini, garlic, lemon juice, and soy sauce. Whisk in the oil and water. Blend well.

2. Stir in the parsley, adding more water, a tablespoon at a time, if the sauce is too thick. This sauce can be served at room temperature or heated in a saucepan over low heat until warm. If not using right away, transfer to a container, cover, and refrigerate until needed. Properly stored, the sauce will keep for 2 to 3 days. Reheat the sauce in a saucepan over low heat to warm.

## spicy mango sauce

makes about 1½ cups

*This luscious sauce can be used as a dipping sauce or as a spicy sweet accompaniment to the Grilled Seitan and Vegetable Kabobs (page 314).*

1 ripe mango, peeled, pitted, and chopped
1 teaspoon minced fresh ginger
1 teaspoon minced garlic
¼ cup water
¼ cup soy sauce
¼ cup mirin
¼ cup orange juice concentrate
1 teaspoon Asian chili paste

1. In a medium saucepan, combine all the ingredients and simmer over low heat to blend the flavors, about 15 minutes.

2. Puree the sauce in a blender or food processor. Taste, adjusting seasonings. Transfer the sauce to a medium bowl. It can be served warm or at room temperature. If not using right away, cover, and refrigerate until needed. Properly stored, the sauce will keep for 2 to 3 days.

## mango-ponzu dipping sauce

makes about 1¼ cups

*Ponzu sauce is a citrusy Japanese cooking liquid available in well-stocked supermarkets, Asian markets, and gourmet grocers. This dipping sauce is especially good served with fried tofu chunks or spring rolls.*

1 cup diced ripe mango
1 tablespoon ponzu sauce (see headnote)
¼ teaspoon Asian chili paste
¼ teaspoon sugar
2 tablespoons water, plus more if needed

1. In a blender or food processor, combine all the ingredients and blend until smooth, adding another tablespoon of water if a thinner sauce is desired.

**2.** Transfer to a small bowl. Serve immediately or cover and refrigerate until ready to use. This sauce is best used on the same day it is made.

# piquant green olive sauce

makes about 1¾ cups

*This versatile and vibrant sauce is wonderful over steamed or roasted vegetables—try it with cauliflower. It's also great on baked potatoes and can be used to dress salads or sliced raw tomatoes.*

½ cup green olives, pitted
2 tablespoons capers
2 tablespoons canned chopped mild green chiles
1 green onion, chopped
1 tablespoon chopped fresh parsley
3 tablespoons olive oil
½ cup water
Salt and freshly ground black pepper

**1.** In a blender or food processor, combine the olives, capers, chiles, green onion, parsley, and olive oil and process until smooth. Add the water, a little at a time, until you have a smooth sauce. Season with salt and pepper to taste.

**2.** Serve at room temperature. If not using right away, transfer to a bowl, cover, and refrigerate until needed. Properly stored, the sauce will keep for 2 to 3 days.

# maple-mustard sauce

makes about ¾ cup

*Use this easy and zesty no-cook sauce on veggie burgers or as a dipping sauce for baked or fried tempeh chunks.*

½ cup vegan mayonnaise, homemade (page 573) or store-bought
¼ cup Dijon mustard
2 tablespoons pure maple syrup
1 teaspoon balsamic vinegar
½ teaspoon Tabasco sauce (optional)

In a small bowl, combine the mayonnaise, mustard, maple syrup, vinegar, and hot sauce, if using. Stir until well blended. If not using right away, cover and refrigerate until needed. Properly stored, the sauce will keep for 2 to 3 days.

# ginger-soy dipping sauce

makes about 1 cup

*This yummy sauce has a light teriyaki flavor and can be used as a dipping sauce for spring rolls, dumplings, or fried tofu.*

1 tablespoon grated fresh ginger
2 teaspoons minced green onion
1 teaspoon sugar
½ cup soy sauce
¼ cup rice vinegar
¼ cup fresh orange juice

**1.** In a small bowl, combine the ginger, green onion, and sugar. Stir in the soy sauce, vinegar, and orange juice.

**2.** Set aside at room temperature for about 15 minutes before serving or cover and refrigerate until ready to use. Properly stored, the sauce will for 3 to 4 days.

## apricot and chile dipping sauce ⓕ

makes about 1 cup

*This spicy, sweet-tart sauce is not only gorgeous, but it's also delicious. Try it with spring rolls, dumplings, or fried tofu or tempeh chunks.*

4 dried apricots
½ cup white grape juice or apple juice
½ teaspoon Asian chili paste
½ teaspoon grated fresh ginger
1 tablespoon soy sauce
1 tablespoon rice vinegar

1. In a small saucepan, combine the apricots and grape juice and heat just to a boil. Remove from the heat and set aside for 10 minutes to allow the apricots to soften.

2. Transfer the apricot mixture to a blender or food processor and process until smooth. Add the chili paste, ginger, soy sauce, and vinegar and process until smooth. Taste, adjusting seasonings if necessary. Transfer to a small bowl. If not using right away, cover and refrigerate until needed. Properly stored, the sauce will keep for 2 to 3 days.

## sesame-scallion dipping sauce ⓕ

makes about ½ cup

*A natural accompaniment for spring rolls or dumplings, this fragrant sauce is also a great way to jazz up a vegetable stir-fry or baked tofu.*

3 tablespoons water
2 tablespoons soy sauce
1 tablespoon mirin
1 tablespoon minced green onions
1 teaspoon minced lemongrass
1 teaspoon grated fresh ginger
1 teaspoon toasted sesame oil
1 teaspoon sesame seeds

In a small bowl, combine the ingredients and mix well. If not using right away, cover and refrigerate until needed. Properly stored, the sauce will keep for 3 to 4 days.

## nothin' fishy nam pla ⓕ

makes about ¾ cup

*Fish sauce is a popular ingredient in Thai and Vietnamese cooking, where it is known as* nam pla *and* nuoc mam, *respectively. This fish-free version provides a similar depth of flavor as the original.*

1 garlic clove, minced
2 teaspoons light brown sugar
1 teaspoon ground dulse or kelp (optional)*
¼ cup fresh lime juice
¼ cup soy sauce
2 tablespoons water

In a small bowl, combine the garlic, sugar, and dulse, if using. Add the lime juice, soy sauce, and water, stirring to blend well. If not using right away, cover and refrigerate until needed. Properly stored, the sauce will keep for up to 5 days.

*Dulse and kelp are sea vegetables available in natural food stores, packaged in a dried form. If you can't find ground kelp or dulse powder, grind your own in a spice grinder.

## vegan worcestershire sauce ⓕ

makes about ¾ cup

*Traditional Worcestershire sauce contains anchovies and is therefore not vegan. A good commercial vegan Worcestershire sauce is The Wizard's brand, available online or in natural food stores. It's easy to make your own with this recipe that comes very close to the flavor of the original.*

½ cup cider vinegar
1 tablespoon dark molasses
1 tablespoon dark brown sugar
2 tablespoons soy sauce
1 teaspoon ground kelp or dulse
1 teaspoon tamarind paste
½ teaspoon onion powder
½ teaspoon dry mustard
½ teaspoon ground ginger
½ teaspoon salt
½ teaspoon black pepper
¼ teaspoon ground allspice
¼ teaspoon ground cayenne

1. Combine all the ingredients in a small saucepan and bring to a boil, then remove from the heat and allow to cool to room temperature.

2. Transfer to a jar or other container with a tight-fitting lid and store in the refrigerator. Properly stored, the sauce will keep for 1 month.

# CHUTNEYS

## mango chutney

makes about 2½ cups

*Making chutney is so easy and the rewards are so great that once you make your first batch you'll probably be as hooked as I am. This delicious chutney is nothing like the commercial versions you find in supermarkets, which can be drab-looking and overly sweet. This one is spicy-sweet, fresh-tasting, and has a beautiful golden color.*

½ cup golden raisins
½ cup sugar
½ cup water
¼ cup apple cider vinegar
1 tablespoon grated fresh ginger
⅓ cup minced shallot
½ teaspoon ground allspice
½ teaspoon salt
3 to 4 firm ripe mangos, peeled, pitted, and chopped
1 small dried hot red chile

1. In a large saucepan, combine the raisins, sugar, water, vinegar, ginger, shallot, allspice, and salt over medium heat and bring to a boil. Reduce heat to low and simmer, stirring occasionally, for 5 minutes.

2. Mix in the mangos and the chile and cook until the mixture thickens, stirring frequently, about 20 minutes. Cool to room temperature. Remove the chile and discard before serving. If not using right away, spoon the chutney into a container with a tight-fitting lid. Cover and refrigerate until needed. Properly stored, this chutney will keep for up to 1 week.

# fresh cranberry chutney

makes about 2 cups

*Serve this dazzling chutney in place of the same old cranberry sauce—your guests will definitely take notice. If you don't want that hint of heat, omit or cut back on the crushed red pepper.*

1 (12-ounce) package fresh cranberries
½ cup apple cider vinegar
½ cup sugar
1 teaspoon ground cinnamon
½ teaspoon ground ginger
½ teaspoon ground nutmeg
½ teaspoon crushed red pepper

1. In a large saucepan, combine the cranberries, vinegar, and sugar and bring to a boil. Reduce heat to low and stir in the cinnamon, ginger, nutmeg, and crushed red pepper.

2. Simmer until the mixture is thick, stirring frequently, about 20 minutes. Cool completely before serving. If not using right away, spoon the chutney into a container with a tight-fitting lid. Cover and refrigerate until needed. Properly stored, this chutney will keep for up to 1 week.

# dried fruit chutney

makes about 2 cups

*This particular recipe is a great first chutney to make, since it requires even less preparation than the others because it is made with dried fruit. If you keep the ingredients on hand, you can always be less than 30 minutes away from a fresh batch of chutney.*

1 cup water
¼ cup apple cider vinegar
¼ cup sugar
1 tablespoon grated fresh ginger
⅓ cup minced onion
1 small dried hot red chile
½ teaspoon salt
1 cup dried apricots, chopped
½ cup pitted dates, chopped
½ cup raisins

1. In a large saucepan, combine the water, vinegar, sugar, ginger, onion, chile, and salt and bring to a boil, stirring occasionally. Reduce heat to low and simmer for 5 minutes.

2. Stir in the apricots, dates, and raisins and simmer until thickened, stirring frequently, about 20 minutes. Cool to room temperature. Remove the chile and discard before serving. If not using right away, spoon the chutney into a container with a tight-fitting lid. Cover and refrigerate until needed. Properly stored, this chutney will keep for up to 2 weeks.

# green tomato chutney

makes about 2 cups

*The distinctive tart flavor and firm texture of green tomatoes give this sweet and savory chutney its unique appeal. If you don't grow your own tomatoes, this chutney (and the Panko-Fried Green Tomatoes on page 384) are good reasons to seek out green tomatoes at your local farmer's market or green grocer.*

5 firm medium green tomatoes

1 cup golden raisins

⅓ cup minced onion

¼ cup apple cider vinegar

⅓ cup sugar

2 tablespoons grated fresh ginger

1 small dried hot red chile

½ teaspoon salt

½ cup water

1. Cut an "x" in the bottom of the tomatoes and immerse them in a saucepan of boiling water for about 30 seconds to loosen the skin. Remove the tomatoes from the water and submerge them in a bowl of ice water. Peel, core, and chop the tomatoes and set aside.

2. In a large saucepan, combine the raisins, onion, vinegar, sugar, ginger, chile, salt, and water and bring to a boil over medium heat, stirring frequently. Cook for 5 minutes.

3. Reduce the heat to low and add the chopped tomatoes. Cook until the mixture thickens, 30 to 40 minutes, stirring frequently.

4. Cool to room temperature. Remove the chile and discard before serving. If not using right away, spoon the chutney into a container with a tight-fitting lid. Cover and refrigerate until needed. Properly stored, this chutney will keep for up to 1 week.

# pear and apple chutney

makes about 3 cups

*Firm fruits work best in chutneys since they retain some of their texture once the chutney is cooked, so pears and apples are a natural fit. Make this in autumn when apples and pears are plentiful and serve it to accompany hearty seitan, tempeh, or bean dishes.*

2 firm Anjou or Bartlett pears, peeled, cored, and chopped

2 Granny Smith or McIntosh apples, peeled, cored, and chopped

½ cup raisins

¼ cup apple cider vinegar

1 tablespoon grated fresh ginger

⅓ cup minced onion

1 teaspoon ground cinnamon

½ teaspoon salt

½ teaspoon ground allspice

¼ teaspoon ground cloves

½ cup apple juice

¼ cup sugar

1. In a large saucepan, combine all the ingredients and bring to a boil over medium heat. Reduce heat to low and cook, stirring frequently, until the mixture is thickened and the liquid is absorbed, about 20 minutes.

2. Cool to room temperature. If not using right away, spoon the chutney into a container with a tight-fitting lid. Cover and refrigerate until needed. Properly stored, this chutney will keep for up to 1 week.

# fresh mint and coconut chutney 🅕

makes about 1 cup

*Mint can sometimes take over the herb garden, but once you taste this chutney you may be glad for that. If you don't grow your own mint, it is readily available at supermarkets, farmer's markets, and specialty grocers. If fresh coconut is unavailable, substitute $^1\!/_4$ cup unsweetened shredded coconut blended with $^1\!/_4$ cup unsweetened coconut milk. This chutney is a natural with the Vegetable Pakoras (page 44) or the Potato Samosas (page 44), but it also adds sparkle to simple grain and bean pilafs.*

1 cup fresh mint leaves, packed
1 fresh or dried hot red chile
1 tablespoon fresh lemon juice
½ teaspoon salt
½ cup grated fresh coconut

1. In a blender or food processor, combine the mint, chile, lemon juice, and salt and process to a paste.

2. Add the coconut and process until blended. This chutney is best if used on the same day that it is made.

# ginger-peach chutney

makes about 2 cups

*When fresh juicy peaches are in season, I like to make the most of their all-too-short season by enjoying them in as many ways as I can—from breakfast to dessert. This chutney brings peaches to the dinner table. It's especially good as a tantalizing accompaniment to the Grilled Seitan and Vegetable Kebabs (page 314).*

6 firm peaches
1 cup golden raisins
1 cup sugar
¼ cup apple cider vinegar
3 tablespoons chopped shallot
2 tablespoons grated fresh ginger
½ teaspoon ground ginger
½ teaspoon crushed red pepper
1 teaspoon salt
½ cup water

1. Immerse the peaches in a saucepan of boiling water for about 30 seconds to loosen the skin. Remove the peaches from the water and submerge them in a bowl of ice water. Peel, pit, and chop the peaches and set aside.

2. In a large saucepan, combine the raisins, sugar, vinegar, shallot, fresh ginger, ground ginger, crushed red pepper, salt, and water and bring to a boil over medium heat, stirring frequently. Cook for 5 minutes.

3. Reduce the heat to low and add the chopped peaches. Cook until the mixture thickens, stirring frequently, about 30 minutes.

4. Cool to room temperature. Remove the chile and discard before serving. If not using right away, spoon the chutney into a container with a tight-fitting lid. Cover and refrigerate until needed. Properly stored, this chutney will keep for up to 1 week.

# PESTOS

## pesto presto 🅕

makes about 1½ cups

*This basic pesto recipe is quick, easy, and versatile. As well as using it on pasta, add it to salad dressings, soups, stews, and anything that could use some wonderful basil flavor. The optional miso paste adds extra saltiness that would normally come from the cheese in non-vegan pesto, but doesn't significantly change the texture. If you don't use the miso, you may want to add a bit more salt.*

3 garlic cloves, crushed
⅓ cup pine nuts
½ teaspoon salt
3 cups fresh basil leaves
1 teaspoon white miso paste (optional)
⅓ cup olive oil

1. In a food processor, combine the garlic, pine nuts, and salt and process to a paste. Add the basil and miso, if using, and process until pureed.

2. With the machine running, stream in the oil, blending to incorporate. If not using right away, scrape the pesto into a small container with a tight-fitting lid. Pour a thin layer of olive oil on top of the pesto. Cover tightly and refrigerate until ready to use. Properly stored, the pesto will keep for 4 to 5 days.

## basil pistou 🅕

makes about 1½ cups

*A pistou is the French version of a pesto, usually made without the pine nuts (or the cheese). It tends to be a bit looser and lighter than a pesto but can be used in the same ways. I especially like to add a spoonful to vegetable soups just before serving.*

3 garlic cloves, crushed
½ teaspoon salt
3 cups fresh basil leaves
½ cup olive oil

1. In a food processor, combine the garlic and salt and grind to a smooth paste. Add the basil and process until pureed.

2. With the machine running, stream in the olive oil, processing until well blended. If not using right away, scrape the pistou into a small container with a tight-fitting lid. Pour a thin layer of olive oil on top of the pistou. Cover tightly and refrigerate until ready to use. Properly stored, pistou will keep for 4 to 5 days.

## black olive and walnut pesto 🅕

makes about 1 cup

*Try this dark robust pesto tossed with a chewy bite-size pasta shape such as rotini. It's also great as an appetizer, spread on warm foccacia. The flavor improves if made a few hours ahead of when you need it.*

2 garlic cloves, crushed
½ teaspoon salt
1 cup Gaeta olives, pitted
¼ cup minced fresh parsley
¼ cup walnut pieces
2 teaspoons fresh lemon juice
½ teaspoon dried marjoram
¼ teaspoon freshly ground black pepper
¼ cup olive oil

continues on next page

1. In a food processor, combine the garlic and salt and process to a paste. Add the olives, parsley, and walnuts and pulse until coarsely chopped. Add the lemon juice, marjoram, and pepper and process until blended.

2. With the machine running, stream in the olive oil and process to a paste. If not using right away, scrape the pesto into a small container with a tight-fitting lid. Pour a thin layer of olive oil on top of the pesto. Cover tightly and refrigerate until ready to use. Properly stored, the pesto will keep for 4 to 5 days.

## spinach and almond pesto

makes about 1¼ cups

*Spinach can be used to make a vibrant green pesto when basil is scarce. While the pesto will not have the distinctive fragrance of a basil pesto, it will still be flavorful and the texture similar. Instead of almonds you can use pine nuts or walnuts, if you prefer.*

2 garlic cloves, crushed
½ cup almonds
½ teaspoon salt
2 cups fresh spinach leaves
½ cup fresh flat-leaf parsley or basil
⅓ cup olive oil

1. In a food processor, combine the garlic, almonds, and salt and grind to a paste. Add the spinach and parsley and process until smooth. With the machine running, stream in the olive oil, processing until well blended.

2. If not using right away, scrape the pesto into a small container with a tight-fitting lid. Pour a thin layer of olive oil on the top of the pesto. Cover tightly and refrigerate until ready to use. Properly stored, the pesto will keep for 4 to 5 days.

## fresh and sun-dried tomato pesto

makes about 2 cups

*Calling this a pesto may be a stretch to some, since it calls for no herbs or other greens, but because it is ground to a paste in the spirit of a pesto, I think it qualifies. Suffused with the rich savor of tomatoes, this flavorful sauce is good tossed with freshly cooked pasta. The warmth of the hot pasta will heat the pesto just enough to bring out the flavor and impart a wonderful tomato aroma.*

3 garlic cloves, crushed
4 ripe plum tomatoes, cored, halved, and seeded
⅓ cup oil-packed sun-dried tomatoes
⅓ cup pine nuts
½ teaspoon salt
Freshly ground black pepper
¼ cup olive oil

1. In a food processor, combine the garlic, fresh tomatoes, sun-dried tomatoes, and pine nuts and process to a smooth paste. Add the salt and pepper to taste and process until well blended.

2. With the machine running, stream in the olive oil and process to a smooth paste. If not using right away, scrape the pesto into a small container with a tight-fitting lid. Pour a thin layer of olive oil on top of the pesto. Cover tightly and refrigerate until ready to use. Properly stored, the pesto will keep for 2 to 3 days.

## parsley and sunflower pesto 🅕

makes about 1 cup

*Parsley replaces the basil and sunflower seeds stand in for the pine nuts in this unusual variation on the pesto theme.*

2 garlic cloves, crushed
½ cup shelled unsalted sunflower seeds
½ teaspoon salt
2 cups fresh Italian parsley leaves
1 teaspoon white miso paste (optional)
⅓ cup olive oil

1. In a food processor, combine the garlic, sunflower seeds, and salt and process to a smooth paste. Add the parsley and miso, if using, and process until pureed.

2. With the machine running, stream in the olive oil until well blended. If not using right away, scrape the pesto into a small container with a tight-fitting lid. Pour a thin layer of olive oil on top of the pesto. Cover tightly and refrigerate until ready to use. Properly stored, the pesto will keep for 3 to 4 days.

# SALSAS

## fresh tomato salsa

makes about 2 cups

*If you have fresh tomatoes, there's no excuse not to make fresh salsa. Once you taste it (and see how easy it is to make), you won't want to go back to the bottled stuff.*

5 ripe Roma or plum tomatoes, chopped
1 serrano chile, seeded and minced
¼ cup chopped red onion
1 garlic clove, minced
1 tablespoon minced fresh cilantro
1 tablespoon fresh lime juice
½ teaspoon salt

In a glass bowl, combine all the ingredients and mix well. Cover and set aside for 30 minutes before serving. If not using right away, cover and refrigerate until ready to use. This salsa tastes best if used on the same day it is made, but properly stored, it will keep for up to 2 days.

## spicy mango and red pepper salsa

makes about 2½ cups

*The appealing combination of sweet mango and red bell pepper with spicy hot jalapeño makes a ravishing salsa that looks as good as it tastes.*

1 ripe mango, peeled, pitted, and cut into ¼-inch dice
⅓ cup minced red onion
1 small red bell pepper, chopped
1 small jalapeño, seeded and minced
2 tablespoons chopped fresh parsley or cilantro
1 tablespoon olive oil
1 tablespoon fresh lime juice
Salt

continues on next page

In a glass bowl, combine all the ingredients, mix well, cover, and set aside for 30 minutes before serving. If not using right away, refrigerate until ready to use. This salsa tastes best if used on the same day it is made, but properly stored, it will keep for up to 2 days.

## chipotle-tomato salsa

makes about 2 cups

*The smoky heat of the chipotle chile makes this a salsa to be reckoned with. Serve with food or your favorite corn chips.*

2 ripe tomatoes, chopped
⅓ cup minced red onion
1 canned chipotle in adobo
¼ cup chopped fresh cilantro
2 tablespoons fresh lime juice
¼ teaspoon salt

In a glass bowl, combine all the ingredients, mix well, cover, and set aside at room temperature for 30 minutes before serving or refrigerate until ready to use. Properly stored, it will keep for up to 2 days.

## pineapple-papaya salsa

makes about 3 cups

*This yummy fruity salsa adds a colorful taste of the tropics to your table. It makes a great accompaniment to the Black Bean and Walnut Croquettes (page 268) or the Sesame-Crusted Seitan (page 309). It can have a transformative effect on veggie burgers or grilled vegetables.*

2 cups chopped fresh pineapple
1 ripe papaya, peeled, seeded, and cut into
    ¼-inch dice
½ cup minced red onion

¼ cup chopped fresh cilantro or parsley
2 tablespoons fresh lime juice
1 teaspoon cider vinegar
2 teaspoons sugar
¼ teaspoon salt
1 small hot red chile, seeded and minced

In a glass bowl, combine all the ingredients, mix well, cover, and set aside at room temperature for 30 minutes before serving or refrigerate until ready to use. This salsa tastes best if used on the same day it is made, but properly stored, it will keep for up to 2 days.

## tomatillo salsa

makes about 1½ cups

*Tomatillos look like small green tomatoes in papery husks. Raw tomatillos are on the tart side, so cook them first if you prefer a more mellow flavor. If fresh tomatillos are unavailable, you can substitute the canned variety. This is a flavorful chunky salsa that is especially good served over rice and beans. The capers add a tangy if unconventional note.*

5 tomatillos, husked and chopped
⅓ cup chopped sweet yellow onion
⅓ cup chopped fresh cilantro
1 small jalapeño, seeded and minced
1 tablespoon fresh lime juice
1 tablespoon whole capers, plus 1 teaspoon
    minced
½ teaspoon salt

In a glass bowl, combine all the ingredients, mix well, cover, and set aside for 30 minutes before serving or cover and refrigerate until ready to use. Properly stored, it will keep in the refrigerator for up to 2 days.

## salsa verde

makes about 1¼ cups

*This versatile green sauce may be made hot or mild to suit your tastes and can be used to flavor burritos, tortilla casseroles, or over rice and beans. It's also delicious over sautéed sliced polenta and, of course, makes a great dip for tortilla chips.*

4 or 5 tomatillos, husked and coarsely chopped
1 medium shallot, coarsely chopped
1 garlic clove, chopped
1 serrano chile, seeded and chopped (optional)
¼ cup fresh flat-leaf parsley leaves
¼ cup fresh cilantro leaves
1 tablespoon fresh lime juice
Pinch sugar
½ teaspoon salt
⅛ teaspoon freshly ground black pepper
¼ cup olive oil

1. In a food processor, combine the tomatillos, shallot, garlic, chile, if using, parsley, and cilantro and pulse until finely chopped. Add the remaining ingredients and pulse until well mixed, but still coarsely textured.

2. Transfer to a glass bowl, cover, and set aside at room temperature for 30 minutes before serving or refrigerate until ready to use. Properly stored, it will keep for up to 2 days.

# CONDIMENTS AND RELISHES

## corn relish

makes about 3 cups

*This zesty relish is actually more of a side dish, mainly because it's hard to eat just a small amount. If you want some heat, substitute a minced red chile for the bell pepper.*

1 tablespoon olive oil
1 medium red onion, chopped
½ cup minced red bell pepper
2 cups fresh or frozen corn kernels
½ teaspoon sugar
2 tablespoons fresh lime juice
2 tablespoons minced fresh cilantro
Salt and freshly ground black pepper

1. In a large skillet, heat the oil over medium heat. Add the onion and bell pepper and cook for 5 minutes. Stir in the corn and sugar and remove from the heat.

2. Cool completely, then transfer to a bowl and stir in the lime juice, cilantro, and salt and black pepper to taste. If not using right away, cover and refrigerate until needed. Properly stored, this relish will keep for 2 to 3 days.

# spiced tomato and peach relish

makes about 2 cups

*The recipe for this unusual and piquant relish was shared with me by friend and cookbook author Nava Atlas, who likes to serve it with Indian-style curries. It's also a good accompaniment to dishes such as the Macadamia Cashew Patties (page 119) or the Chickpea and Vegetable Loaf (page 266).*

1 tablespoon olive oil
1 medium onion, finely chopped
1 tablespoon pure maple syrup or agave nectar
1 pound ripe tomatoes, peeled and finely chopped
2 to 3 sweet peaches, pitted and cut into ¼-inch dice
¼ cup dark or golden raisins
2 teaspoons grated fresh ginger
½ teaspoon ground cinnamon
¼ teaspoon crushed red pepper

1. In a large saucepan, heat the oil over medium heat. Add the onion and cook until translucent, about 5 minutes. Add the remaining ingredients and bring to a simmer. Cook over low heat, covered, for 10 to 15 minutes, stirring occasionally. The tomatoes and peaches should be tender but not mushy.

2. Taste, adjusting seasonings if necessary, then simmer, uncovered, over very low heat for another 5 minutes. Transfer to a bowl and cool to room temperature before serving. If not using right away, cover and refrigerate until needed. Properly stored, this relish will keep for 2 to 3 days.

# artichoke, tomato, and roasted pepper relish

makes about 2½ cups

*This zesty Mediterranean relish is delicious served with foccacia or garlic bread. It's also delicious tossed with hot or cold cooked pasta. Use a jarred roasted pepper to save time, or roast your own using the directions on page 10.*

2 ripe Roma or plum tomatoes, chopped
1 jarred roasted red pepper, chopped (or see page 10)
1 (14-ounce) can artichoke hearts, drained and chopped
3 green onions, minced
1 tablespoon capers
2 tablespoons minced fresh parsley
½ teaspoon fresh or dried oregano
1 tablespoon olive oil
1 tablespoon fresh lemon juice
¼ teaspoon salt
Freshly ground black pepper

In a large bowl, combine all the ingredients. Set aside at room temperature for 30 to 45 minutes before serving. This relish is best if used on the same day it is made.

# ginger-papaya relish

makes about 2 cups

*This relish, with the pinkish orange blush of papaya, looks too pretty to pack such a flavor punch. It's great served as an accompaniment to jerk-rubbed grilled vegetables or seitan.*

1 large papaya, peeled, seeded, and cut into
   ¼-inch dice
1 small red onion, finely minced
1 teaspoon grated fresh ginger
Pinch salt
1 tablespoon toasted sesame oil
1 teaspoon black mustard seeds

1. In a large bowl, combine the papaya, onion, ginger, and salt and set aside.

2. In a small skillet, heat the oil over medium heat. Add the mustard seeds and cook a few seconds until they pop, then stir into the relish. If not serving right away, cover and refrigerate until needed. This relish is best if served on the same day it is made.

## triple cranberry relish

makes about 2½ cups

*Three layers of cranberry flavor combine to form a lively alternative to traditional cranberry sauce. Serve at room temperature or chilled.*

1 (12-ounce) bag fresh cranberries
1 cup sweetened dried cranberries
½ cup cranberry juice
⅔ cup sugar
1 teaspoon finely grated lemon zest

1. In a large saucepan, combine all the ingredients and bring to a boil. Reduce the heat to low and simmer until the sauce thickens, stirring occasionally, about 25 minutes.

2. Set aside to cool to room temperature, then transfer to a bowl to serve warm. If serving chilled, cover and refrigerate for 1 hour or until needed. Properly stored, this relish will keep for 3 to 4 days.

## red pepper, mango, and avocado relish

makes about 3 cups

*The vivid colors of this spicy-sweet relish are just a hint of the vibrancy of its flavor and texture. Since it's destined to steal the spotlight, serve it with simple grilled vegetables over rice. The combination of lime juice, ginger, and cilantro gives this relish a Southeast Asian accent, making it a good accompaniment to a noodle stir-fry. I've also spooned it onto lightly dressed lettuce and served it as a salad. It's also great with tortilla chips, like a salsa.*

1 ripe mango, peeled, pitted, and cut into
   ¼-inch dice
¼ cup finely minced red bell pepper
¼ cup finely minced red onion
1 teaspoon grated fresh ginger
1 small jalapeño, seeded and minced
2 tablespoons chopped fresh cilantro
2 tablespoons fresh lime juice
¼ teaspoon sugar
Salt
1 ripe Hass avocado

1. In a large bowl, combine the mango, bell pepper, onion, ginger, and chile. Add the cilantro, lime juice, sugar, and salt to taste. Stir to combine, then refrigerate for 30 minutes.

2. Just before serving, pit, peel, and cut the avocado into ¼-inch dice. Add it to the relish and stir gently to combine. This relish is best if used shortly after it is made.

# red onion and apple relish

makes about 1½ cups

*This thick, jammy relish is wonderful served with hearty seitan or tempeh dishes. It also works miracles on a veggie burger.*

1 tablespoon olive oil
1 medium red onion, finely chopped
⅓ cup sugar
1 Granny Smith or other crisp tart apple
3 tablespoons apple cider vinegar
Salt

1. In a saucepan, heat the oil over medium heat. Add the onion and stir in the sugar. Cover and cook, stirring occasionally, until the onion is soft, about 20 minutes.

2. Peel, core, and shred the apple and add it to the onion mixture. Stir in the vinegar and salt to taste and cook, uncovered, until the mixture is thick, about 20 minutes. Transfer to a bowl and set aside to cool to room temperature. If not using right away, cover and refrigerate until needed, then bring back to room temperature before using. Properly stored, this relish will keep for 2 to 3 days.

# pineapple-lime relish

makes about 2 cups

*This juicy fruity relish may look sweet, but the chile makes it spicy. Its tropical nature makes it a good fit for island-inspired meals such as spiced rubbed grilled tempeh and vegetables or to jazz up simple fare such as rice and beans.*

2 cups chopped fresh pineapple or 1 (14-ounce) can crushed pineapple, drained, juice reserved
2 tablespoons sugar

2 tablespoons fresh lime juice
Salt
3 green onions, minced
1 hot red chile, seeded and minced
8 fresh basil or mint leaves, finely shredded

1. In a saucepan, heat ¼ cup of the reserved pineapple juice over low heat. Add the sugar and cook, stirring, until the sugar dissolves. Remove from the heat, stir in the lime juice, and add salt to taste. Set aside to cool.

2. In a large bowl, combine the pineapple, green onions, and chile. Pour in the juice mixture and stir to combine. Stir in the basil and serve. If not serving right away, cover and refrigerate until needed. This relish is best if used on the same day that it is made.

# indonesian chile sauce

makes about 1 cup

*I like to put a small bowl of this spicy condiment on the table anytime I serve a stir-fried rice or noodle dish. That way, those who like to add a little heat can do so to suit their own taste.*

1 small red bell pepper, chopped
3 hot red chiles, seeded and chopped
1 teaspoon sugar
¾ teaspoon salt
3 tablespoons canola or grapeseed oil
1 tablespoon rice vinegar

1. In a blender or food processor, combine the bell pepper, chiles, sugar, and salt and process until smooth.

2. In a medium skillet, heat the oil over medium heat. Add the pureed chile mixture and cook, stirring, to mellow the flavor and remove the raw taste, 5 to 7 minutes.

**3.** Remove from the heat and stir in the vinegar. Transfer to a small bowl and set aside to cool to room temperature. If not serving right away, cover and refrigerate until needed. If properly stored, it will keep for up to 1 week.

# fresh tomato ketchup

makes about 2 cups

*Homemade ketchup is fun to make and even more fun to serve—it really adds a touch of class to fried potatoes or veggie burgers. This recipe is best made using a food mill to remove the skins and seeds from the tomatoes. Otherwise, the tomatoes must first be skinned and seeded and then the finished ketchup pureed in a blender or run through a sieve to achieve a smooth texture.*

1 tablespoon olive oil

½ cup chopped sweet yellow onion

¼ cup chopped celery

1 garlic clove, minced

3 pounds ripe plum or Roma tomatoes, cored and halved

⅔ cup sugar

1 teaspoon salt

½ teaspoon dry mustard

½ teaspoon sweet or smoked paprika

½ teaspoon ground allspice

¼ teaspoon ground cinnamon

¼ teaspoon ground cayenne

⅓ cup apple cider vinegar

**1.** In a large saucepan, heat the oil over medium heat. Add the onion and celery, cover, and cook until softened, 5 minutes. Uncover, stir in the garlic, then add the tomatoes and cook until the vegetables are soft, about 20 minutes.

**2.** Run the vegetable mixture through a food mill and discard the tomato skins and seeds.

**3.** Return the pureed vegetables to the saucepan. Stir in the sugar, salt, mustard, paprika, allspice, cinnamon, and cayenne. Cook, stirring frequently, until thickened, about 30 minutes. Stir in the vinegar and cook for 15 minutes longer. Taste, adjusting seasonings, adding a bit more sugar if too tart or a bit more vinegar if too sweet.

**4.** Set aside to cool to room temperature. Transfer to a container with a tight-fitting lid. Cover and refrigerate until needed. Properly stored, it will keep for up to 2 weeks.

# vegan mayonnaise

makes about 2 cups

*There are a number of commercial brands of vegan mayonnaise available that are delicious and convenient, such as Vegenaise, but this delicious and simple recipe may inspire you to make your own.*

1 (12-ounce) package silken tofu, drained

2 tablespoons apple cider vinegar

1½ tablespoons Dijon mustard

1 teaspoon sugar

½ teaspoon salt

⅛ teaspoon turmeric

⅛ teaspoon ground cayenne (optional)

**1.** In food processor or blender, combine all the ingredients and process until smooth and well combined. Taste, adjusting seasonings if necessary.

**2.** Scrape the mayonnaise into a container with a tight-fitting lid, cover, and refrigerate until needed. Properly stored, it will keep for up to 5 days.

# chipotle mayonnaise

makes about ½ cup

*The flavor of smoky hot chipotle chile is mellowed but not tamed by the mayonnaise, making it a spicy flavorful condiment to slather on sandwiches. I also like to use it to make a zesty potato salad or as a dip for fried green tomatoes.*

1 canned chipotle chile in adobo
½ cup vegan mayonnaise, homemade (page 573) or store-bought
1 teaspoon fresh lime juice
Pinch salt

1. In a blender or food processor, puree the chipotle chile. Add the mayonnaise, lime juice, and salt and blend until smooth.

2. Scrape the mayonnaise into a container with a tight-fitting lid, cover, and refrigerate until needed. Properly stored, it will keep for up to 5 days.

# mustard-chive mayonnaise

makes about ½ cup

*Dijon mustard and a snip of chives elevate a simple mayo to a sublime spread. It's great on grilled tempeh or seitan sandwiches with lettuce and tomato.*

½ cup vegan mayonnaise, homemade (page 573) or store-bought
1 tablespoon Dijon mustard
2 teaspoons minced fresh chives
Pinch salt

In a small bowl, combine the mayonnaise and mustard. Add the chives and salt and stir until well blended. Cover and refrigerate until needed. Properly stored, it will keep in the refrigerator for up to 5 days.

# wasabi mayonnaise

makes about ½ cup

*If you like the special heat of wasabi, you'll like this mayonnaise. It can be used like any other mayonnaise (but with a kick) and it's also terrific as a spread on vegetable sushi rolls.*

½ cup vegan mayonnaise, homemade (page 573) or store-bought
1 teaspoon wasabi powder
Pinch salt

In a small bowl, combine all the ingredients. Stir until well blended. Cover and refrigerate until needed. Properly stored, it will keep for 3 to 4 days.

# tofu sour cream

makes about 1½ cups

*Commercially produced vegan sour cream is widely available, but it is also easy to make a tasty version at home. Add some snipped chives and load onto a baked potato with abandon.*

1 cup silken tofu, well drained
2 tablespoons fresh lemon juice
2 teaspoons canola or grapeseed oil
2 teaspoons cashew butter or tahini (sesame paste)
¼ teaspoon yellow mustard
½ teaspoon salt

1. In a blender or food processor, combine all the ingredients and process until smooth.

2. Scrape the mixture into a container with a tight-fitting lid, cover, and refrigerate until needed. Properly stored, it will keep for 3 to 4 days.

## cucumber raita

makes about 2½ cups

*A raita is a popular condiment in India that is served with spicy meals for its cooling effect. Raitas are usually a combination of yogurt and chopped vegetables, fruit, or herbs. Cucumber raita is one of the most popular. Vegan yogurt is available in natural food stores and well-stocked supermarkets. Be sure to get plain, not flavored, to make this savory and refreshing Indian cucumber relish.*

1 cup plain vegan yogurt
1 medium English cucumber, peeled and chopped
1 tablespoon minced green onion
2 tablespoons minced fresh mint leaves
Salt

In a medium bowl, combine the yogurt, cucumber, green onion, and mint. Season with salt, to taste and stir to combine. Serve immediately. If not serving right away, cover and refrigerate until needed, but use within a few hours after making or the raita will become watery from the cucumber.

# MARINADES AND RUBS

## ginger-soy marinade

makes about ⅔ cup

*This easy and fragrant marinade is ideal for tofu that will be baked or used in stir-fries. The leftover marinade can be poured into a saucepan and thickened with a little cornstarch and water to drizzle over the baked tofu or added to the stir-fry.*

1 tablespoon grated fresh ginger
1 green onion, chopped
1 garlic clove, minced
2 tablespoons sugar
¼ cup soy sauce
2 tablespoons mirin
1 tablespoon rice vinegar
1 tablespoon toasted sesame oil

In a small bowl, combine all the ingredients. and mix until blended. If not using right away, cover and refrigerate until needed. Properly stored, the marinade will keep up to 5 days.

# garlic-herb marinade

makes about ¾ cup

*I like this marinade for grilled, broiled, or roasted vegetables. I use the remaining marinade as a basting sauce to keep the vegetables from drying out.*

4 to 5 garlic cloves, crushed
2 teaspoons minced fresh rosemary
1 teaspoon minced fresh thyme
1 teaspoon minced fresh savory
½ teaspoon salt
¼ teaspoon freshly ground black pepper
½ cup olive oil

In a small bowl, combine the garlic, rosemary, thyme, savory, salt, and pepper. Stir in the oil and set aside at room temperature for 1 hour before using. If not using within 1 hour or so, cover and refrigerate until needed. Properly stored, the marinade will keep up to 5 days.

# lemon pepper marinade

makes about ½ cup

*Ground coriander adds an exotic nuance to this lively marinade that works equally well on tofu, tempeh, or seitan.*

2½ tablespoons fresh lemon juice
2 tablespoons soy sauce
1 tablespoon sugar
1 teaspoon grated lemon zest
1 garlic clove, minced
1 teaspoon coarsely ground black pepper
½ teaspoon ground coriander
Pinch ground cayenne
2 tablespoons olive oil

In a small bowl, combine the lemon juice, soy sauce, and sugar, stirring to blend. Add the lemon zest, garlic, pepper, coriander, and cayenne. Whisk in the oil. If not using right away, cover and refrigerate until needed. Properly stored, the marinade will keep for 3 to 4 days.

# teriyaki marinade

makes 1 cup

*If you've seen the high price of baked teriyaki tofu at the market, then you'll be as eager as I was to start making your own. Pour this marinade over sliced tofu, marinate, and bake—and let the savings begin.*

2 garlic cloves, crushed
2 teaspoons grated fresh ginger
2 tablespoons sugar
½ cup soy sauce
2 tablespoons fresh orange juice
2 tablespoons rice vinegar
2 tablespoons toasted sesame oil

In a small bowl, combine the garlic, ginger, and sugar. Stir in the soy sauce, orange juice, rice vinegar, and oil, mixing until well combined. If not using right away, cover and refrigerate until needed. Properly stored, the marinade will keep for 3 to 4 days.

# tamari-dijon marinade

makes about ½ cup

*The assertive flavors of this marinade are ideal for tempeh, which absorbs it readily.*

2 garlic cloves
1 tablespoon Dijon mustard
2 tablespoons tamari soy sauce

2 teaspoons balsamic vinegar

1 teaspoon fresh lemon juice

¼ teaspoon ground black pepper

¼ cup olive oil

In a blender, combine all the ingredients and blend until smooth. If not using right away, cover and refrigerate until needed. Properly stored, the marinade will keep for 3 to 4 days.

## pungent pineapple marinade

makes about 1 cup

*If you don't have a fresh jalapeño, use about ¹/₂ teaspoon of crushed red pepper to give this marinade its kick.*

1 jalapeño, seeded and chopped

3 green onions, chopped

1 garlic clove, chopped

1 tablespoon sugar

¼ cup pineapple juice

2 tablespoons fresh or canned chopped pineapple

2 tablespoons soy sauce

2 teaspoons dried thyme

1 teaspoon ground allspice

¼ cup olive oil

In a small bowl, combine the jalapeño, green onions, garlic, and sugar. Stir in the pineapple juice, chopped pineapple, soy sauce, thyme, and allspice. Stir in the oil and mix well. If not using right away, cover and refrigerate until needed. Properly stored, the marinade will keep for 2 to 3 days.

## indian spice rub

makes about ½ cup

*Rub these fragrant spices into slices of extra-firm tofu, then cook and serve it to someone who says tofu has no flavor.*

¼ cup minced onion

1½ tablespoons hot or mild curry powder

1 teaspoon salt

¼ teaspoon freshly ground black pepper

¼ teaspoon ground cayenne

2 tablespoons canola or grapeseed oil

In a blender or food processor, combine all the ingredients and blend to a paste. Add a little more oil if mixture is too thick. If not using right away, cover and refrigerate until needed. Properly stored, it will keep for 3 to 4 days.

## southwestern spice rub

makes about ½ cup

*This rub is especially good on tofu or seitan, which can then be grilled or sautéed with some onion and bell peppers and cut into strips for fajitas.*

¼ cup minced onion

1 garlic clove, minced

1 tablespoon chili powder

1 teaspoon smoked paprika

½ teaspoon cumin

1 teaspoon salt

½ teaspoon ground black pepper

2 tablespoons olive oil

1 tablespoon fresh lime juice

In a blender or food processor, combine all the ingredients and blend to a paste. If not using right away, cover and refrigerate until needed. Properly stored, it will keep for 3 to 4 days.

# FAST RECIPES

QUICK AND EASY RECIPES THAT CAN BE READY IN 30 MINUTES OR LESS

# MENUS

## MENUS AND MENU PLANNING

Whether we realize it or not, whenever we cook, we plan a menu. Consider the almost unconscious pairing of soup and a sandwich, a salad and spaghetti, a stir-fry and rice. Finish with a few cookies on hand from the pantry, and your menu is complete.

For many of us, our day-to-day menu planning is based on what's in the fridge or pantry, or our particular mood. Time can also be a factor—sometimes we need something in a hurry; other times, we feel like cooking something more elaborate. The seasons come into play, too. In the winter, a hot and hearty soup or stew is the only thing that satisfies. During the summer months, ripe tomatoes, corn, and watermelon almost do the menu-planning for you.

The times when the most deliberate menu planning comes into play are for holidays, special occasions, and when company's coming. Those are the times when we put the most thought into what will be served: a birthday party, a holiday dinner, a meal for special company. If you're expecting a crowd, you will need to decide if you want to serve the food or offer it buffet-style. Once you factor in the time of day and number of people, you

have the information you will need in order to plan your menu.

On the following pages are some sample menus that will give you ideas on what to prepare for a variety of occasions. In several of the menus, suggestions are given for one or more starters, whether it be an appetizer, soup, or salad. You can decide if you want to include one, or two, or none at all. Some of the menus include "one-dish" entrées while others incude side dishes to complete the meal. In each case a dessert suggestion is provided, although you can always take short-cuts and serve a bakery-made dessert or simply scoop up some vegan ice cream.

For those occasions when you're invited to someone's home for dinner, you may need a different strategy. First, make sure your hosts are made aware in advance that you are vegan. At that time you should be ready to provide suggestions on how they can easily accommodate your needs. Depending on the situation, you may want to offer to bring along a dish that you have prepared yourself, such as a one-dish casserole that can be popped in the oven, or perhaps a hearty rice salad to serve at room temperature. This helps take the pressure off your hosts, and ensures that you'll have something to eat.

# MENUS

## ANYTIME MEALS

### Family-Style Dinner

My Kinda Meat Loaf (page 294) with
    Mushroom Sauce (page 546)
Mashed Potatoes and Greens (page 374)
Versatile Roasted Vegetables (page 387)
Magical Mystery Chocolate Cake (page 446)

### Kids' Favorites

Some-Kinda-Nut Burgers (page 120)
Broccoli Slaw with Apple and Walnuts (page 75)
Baked Mac and Cheeze (page 222)
Double Chocolate Brownies (page 436)

### Busy Night

Green-Green Guacamole (page 9)
Fajitas Without Borders (page 311)
Spicy Southwestern-Style Coleslaw (page 76)
Rum-Sautéed Pineapple and Bananas with
    Toasted Coconut and Pecans (page 485)

### Feed a Crowd

Hearty Minestrone Soup (page 145)
Red Chard and Baby Spinach Lasagna (page 215)
Great Garlic Bread (page 397)
Banana-Walnut Cake (page 448)

## SEASONAL MENUS

### Autumn

Mushroom Croustades (page 33)
Endive and Orange Salad with Toasted Pecans
    (page 65)
Brazilian Black Bean Stew (page 255)
Sweet Potato Pie (page 462)

### Winter

Roasted Vegetable Bisque (page 179)
Spinach Salad with Almonds, Fuji Apple, and
    Figs (page 55)

Millet-Topped Lentil Shepherd's Pie (page 266)
Chocolate Swirl Tofu Cheezcake (page 454)

### Springtime

Cucumber Cashew Soup (page 183)
Watercress, Fennel, and Avocado Salad with
    Dried Cherries and Macadamias (page 53)
Lasagna Primavera (page 218)
Apple Tart with Walnut Crust (page 470)

### Summer

Fresh Tomato Salad (page 65) with
    Oh-My-Goddess Dressing (page 99)
Crispy Tofu with Sizzling Caper Sauce (page 284)
Quinoa and Summer Squash Pilaf (page 279)
Strawberry Parfaits with Cashew Crème (page 478)

## GLOBAL CUISINES

### Italian

Classic Crostini (page 35) with Black and Green
    Olive Tapenade (page 9)
Leaf Lettuce and Grilled Radicchio Salad with
    Lemony Dressing (page 53)
Ziti with Abruzzese Vegetable Ragù (page 200)
Sweet Polenta with Grilled Pineapple and
    Strawberry Sauce (page 486)

### French

Mushroom-Walnut Pâté (page 24)
Caramelized French Onion Soup (page 149)
Spinach Salad with Orange-Dijon Dressing (page 55)
Seitan with Spinach and Sun-Dried Tomatoes
    (page 317) or Crispy Tofu with Sizzling Caper
    Sauce (page 284)
Chard and New Potato Gratin with Herbes de
    Provence (page 322)
Suzette-Inspired Ice Crème Crepes (page 488)

### Greek

Lemony Rice-Stuffed Grape Leaves (page 28)
Greek Goddess Salad (page 54)
Spinach, White Bean, and Pine Nut Strudel
    (page 332)
Agave Baklava (page 439)

## Mexican

Tempeh Taco Bites (page 37)
Chile-Lime Tortilla Soup (page 145)
Black Beans with Serrano "Aioli" (page 256)
Fired-Up Jalapeño Cornbread (page 401)
Spicy Chocolate Cake with Dark Chocolate Glaze
   (page 447)

## Middle Eastern Mezze

Back-to-Basic Hummus (page 10)
Baba Ghanoush (page 12)
Marinated Olives (page 20)
Couscous Dolmas (page 28)
Classic Tabbouleh (page 87)
Pecan and Date-Stuffed Roasted Pears (page 482)

## Moroccan

Moroccan Vermicelli Vegetable Soup (page 154)
Eggplant and Bell Pepper Salad (page 61)
Seitan with Dried Plums, Olives, and Capers
   (page 308)
Mango Sorbet (page 495)

## Indian

Potato Samosas (page 44)
Vegetable Pakoras (page 44)
Fresh Mint and Coconut Chutney (page 564)
Three Lentil Dal (page 264)
Indian-Style Pizza (page 137)
Paradise Pudding (page 476)

## Chinese

Steamed Vegetable Dumplings (page 42)
Hot and Sour Soup (page 152)
Vegetable Lo Mein with Tofu (page 234)
Vegetable Fried Rice (page 268)
Ginger-Coconut Nice Cream (page 495)

## Japanese

Miso Soup (page 152)
Avocado and Asparagus Sushi Rolls (page 30)
Soy-Glazed Tofu (page 283)
Edamame Donburi (page 263)
Green Tea Granita (page 497)

## Vietnamese

Sesame-Cilantro Scallion Pancakes (page 39)
Vietnamese-Style Noodle Soup (page 151)
Orange-Glazed Tofu and Asparagus (page 285)
Baked Bananas with a Twist of Lime (page 483)

## Thai

Mango-Avocado Spring Rolls (page 25)
Tom Yum (page 153)
Drunken Spaghetti with Tofu (page 240)
Thai Kale with Coconut Milk (page 372)
Forbidden Black Rice Pudding (page 476)

# SPECIAL OCCASIONS

## Picnic al Fresco

Muffaletta Sandwiches (page 116)
Roasted Potato Salad with Chickpeas and
   Sun-Dried Tomatoes (page 69)
Rainbow Slaw (page 74)
Better Pecan Bars (page 438)

## Casual Company Dinner

Roasted Chickpeas (page 5)
Romaine and Grape Tomato Salad with
   Avocado and Baby Peas (page 50)
Creamy Cashew Fettuccine with Mushrooms and
   Peas (page 221)
Blueberry-Peach Crisp (page 471)

## Thanksgiving Dinner

Tempeh-Pimiento Cheeze Ball (page 19)
Chestnut Bisque with Fresh Pear (page 176)
Buttercup Squash Stuffed with Pistachio-Apricot
   Rice (page 343)
Green Bean Bake with Crispy Leeks (page 370)
Pumpkin Pie with a Hint of Rum (page 460)

### Christmas Dinner

Artichoke-and-Walnut–Stuffed Belgian Endive
(page 23)

Seitan en Croute (page 314) with Madeira Sauce
(page 546)

Bourbon-Baked Squash (page 383)

Brussels Sprouts with Shallots and Dillweed
(page 360)

Fennel and Garlic Mashed Potatoes (page 375)

Mom's Apple Pie with Cranberries (page 460)

### Game Night

Tortilla Chips (page 5)

Fresh Tomato Salsa (page 567)

Spicy Chipotle Potato Quesadillas (page 32)

Beer-Marinated Seitan Fajitas (page 125)

Creole Rice and Red Beans (page 272)

Chocolate-Cranberry Oatmeal Cookies (page 431)

### Mother's Day

Cherry Tomatoes Stuffed with Whirled Peas
(page 22)

Asparagus Edamame Bisque (page 167)

Roasted Vegetable Strudel (page 333)

Avocado-Raspberry Parfaits (page 477)

### Father's Day

Baby Potatoes Stuffed with Roasted Bell
Pepper and Walnuts (page 33)

Grilled Seitan and Vegetable Kabobs (page 314)

Mediterranean Quinoa Salad (page 89)

Giant Peanut Butter–Chocolate Chip Cookie Cake
(page 452)

### Special Occasion Dinner

Mushrooms Stuffed with Spinach and Walnuts
(page 32)

Orange and Fig Salad with Walnuts and Dried
Cherries (page 98)

Pan-Seared Seitan with Artichokes and Olives
(page 309)

Rosemary Fingerling Potatoes with Caramelized
Shallots (page 376)

Chocolate No-Bake Silk Pie (page 464)

## PARTIES

### Children's Party

Personalized Trail Mix (page 6)

EBAP Pizza (page 130)

Roasted Vegetable Stromboli (page 134)

Three Flavor Ice Cream Cake (page 457)

### Appetizer Buffet

Asparagus Wrapped in Phyllo (page 31)

Basic Bruschetta (page 34)

Lentil-Pecan Country-Style Pâté (page 24)

Savory Artichoke Squares (page 38)

Cucumber and Green Olive Dip (page 14)

Sesame Pita Chips (page 4)

### Brunch Buffet

Roasted Vegetable Frittata (page 509)

Two-Potato Hash (page 524)

Blueberry-Almond Scones (page 412)

Banana-Walnut Breakfast Muffins (page 524)

Couscous Brunch Cake with Fresh Fruit
(page 513)

Blazing Sunset Salad (page 96)

### Dinner Buffet

Dazzling Vegetable Salad (page 57)

Herbed Millet and Pecan Loaf (page 281)

Roasted Vegetable Strudel (page 333)

Quinoa and Chickpea Pilaf with Orange
and Pistachios (page 279)

Zucchini Walnut Fritters (page 385)

Foccacia with Sun-Dried Tomatoes and
Black Olives (page 415)

### Dessert Buffet

Triple Coconut Cheezcake (page 453)

Double Chocolate Brownies (page 436)

Pineapple Squares (page 437)

Chai Spice Cookies (page 433)

Chocolate-Macadamia Cheezcake Truffles
(page 442)

# RESOURCES

Vegan resources abound, from dining guides, to nutrition information, to online ingredients and products. Below is a list containing just a sampling of the many resources currently available.

## SHOPPING

Pangea—www.veganstore.com
Cosmo's Vegan Shoppe—
    www.cosmosveganshoppe.com
Mail Order Catalog—www.healthy-eating.com
Food Fight Vegan Grocery—
    www.foodfightgrocery.com
Vegan Essentials—www.veganessentials.com
Ethical Planet—www.ethicalplanet.com
Herbivore—www.herbivoreclothing.com

## DINING

www.happycow.net
www.vegdining.com
www.vegguide.org
www.vegan.com

## MEDIA

VegNews Magazine—www.vegnews.com
Vegetarian Times—www.vegetariantimes.com
    (Note: not entirely vegan)
Vegan Magazine—www.vegansociety.com
    (member magazine of UK Vegan Society)

Vegetarian Voice—www.navs-online.org
    (member magazine of North American
    Vegetarian Society)
Animal Times—www.peta.org (member
    magazine of PETA)
VegFamily—www.vegfamily.com (an online
    magazine)

## ORGANIZATIONS:

American Vegan Society (AVS)—
    www.americanvegan.org
Farm Sanctuary—www.farmsanctuary.org
Farm Animal Reform Movement (FARM)—
    www.farmusa.org
People for the Ethical Treatment of Animals
    (PETA)—www.peta-online.org
North American Vegetarian Society (NAVS)—
    www.navs-online.org
United Poultry Concerns (UPC)—
    www.upc-online.org
Pigs Peace Sanctuary—www.pigspeace.org
Vegetarian Resource Group (VRG)—
    www.vrg.org
Compassion Over Killing—www.cok.net

## NUTRITION:

Physicians Committee for Responsible
    Medicine (PCRM)—www.pcrm.org
McDougall Wellness Center—
    www.drmcdougall.com
Eat to Live—www.drfuhrman.com
www.veganhealth.org

## RECIPES

www.vegcooking.com
www.vegsource.com
www.vegweb.com

## INGREDIENTS

### FLOURS/GRAINS

Bob's Red Mill—www.bobsredmill.com

### SPICES

Penzey's—www.penzeys.com

### NONDAIRY

Follow Your Heart—www.followyourheart.com
Teese—www.teesecheese.com
Tofutti—www.tofutti.com
Earth Balance—www.earthbalance.net
Nasoya—www.nasoya.com
Soya Too—www.soyatoo.com

## VEGAN "MEATS"

Tofurky—www.tofurky.com
Fieldroast—www.fieldroast.com
Gimme Lean—www.lightlife.com

## INFORMATION

www.vegan.com
www.goveg.com
www.vegan.org
www.supervegan.com
www.veganoutreach.org

# RECOMMENDED READING

Barnard, Neal, M.D. *Food For Life: How the New Four Food Groups Can Save Your Life.* New York: Three Rivers Press, 1994.

Bennett, Beverly Lynn, and Sammartano, Ray. *The Complete Idiot's Guide to Vegan Living.* New York: Alpha Books, 2005.

Campbell, T. Colin, and Campbell, Thomas M. II. *The China Study: Startling Implications for Diet, Weight Loss and Long-Term Health.* Dallas, TX: BenBella Books, 2005.

Davis, Karen. *Prisoned Chickens, Poisoned Eggs: An Inside Look at the Modern Poultry Industry.* Summertown, TN: Book Publishing Company, 1996.

Eisnitz, Gail A. *Slaughterhouse: The Shocking Story of Greed, Neglect, and Inhumane Treatment Inside the U.S. Meat Industry.* Amherst, NY: Prometheus Books, 2006.

Klaper, Michael, M.D. *Vegan Nutrition: Pure and Simple.* Summertown, TN: Book Publishing Company, 1999.

Lyman, Howard F., et al. *No More Bull! The Mad Cowboy Targets America's Worst Enemy: Our Diet.* New York: Scribner, 2005.

———. *Mad Cowboy: Plain Truth from the Cattle Rancher Who Won't Eat Meat.* New York: Scribner, 2001.

Marcus, Erik. *Meat Market: Animals, Ethics, and Money.* Ithaca, NY: Brio Press, 2005.

———. *The Ultimate Vegan Guide: Compassionate Living Without Sacrifice.* CreateSpace: 2008.

———. *Vegan: The New Ethics of Eating.* Ithaca, NY: McBooks Press, 2000.

Mason, Jim, and Singer, Peter. *Animal Factories.* New York: Three Rivers Press, 1990.

Masson, Jeffrey Moussaieff. *The Face on Your Plate, The Truth About Food.* New York: W.W. Norton, 2009.

Robbins, John. *The Food Revolution: How Your Diet Can Help Save Your Life and Our World.* Newburyport, MA: Conari Press, 2001.

———. *Diet for a New America.* Tiburon, CA: H.J. Kramer, 1998.

Stepaniak, Joanne. *The Vegan Sourcebook.* Lincolnwood, IL: Lowell House, 1998.

# APPENDIX

~~~~~~~~~~

## the new four food groups

| food group | servings | description | serving size |
|---|---|---|---|
| FRUIT | 3 or more servings a day | Fruits are rich in fiber, vitamin C, and beta-carotene. Be sure to include at least one serving each day of fruits that are high in vitamin C—citrus fruits, melons, and strawberries are all good choices. Choose whole fruit over fruit juices, which do not contain very much fiber. | • 1 medium piece of fruit<br>• ½ cup cooked fruit<br>• 4 ounces juice |
| LEGUMES | 2 or more servings a day | Legumes, which is another name for beans, peas, and lentils, are all good sources of fiber, protein, iron, calcium, zinc, and B vitamins. This group also includes chickpeas, baked and refried beans, soymilk, tempeh, and texturized vegetable protein. | • 1 cup cooked beans<br>• 4 ounces tofu or tempeh<br>• 8 ounces soymilk |
| WHOLE GRAINS | 5 or more servings a day | This group includes bread, rice, tortillas, pasta, hot or cold cereal, corn, millet, barley, and bulgur wheat. Build each of your meals around a hearty grain dish—grains are rich in fiber and other complex carbohydrates, as well as protein, B vitamins, and zinc. | • ½ cup rice or other grain<br>• 1 ounce dry cereal<br>• 1 slice bread |
| VEGETABLES | 5 or more servings a day | Vegetables are packed with nutrients; they provide vitamin C, beta-carotene, riboflavin, iron, calcium, fiber, and other nutrients. Dark green leafy vegetables such as broccoli, collards, kale, chicory, or cabbage are especially good sources of these important nutrients. Dark yellow and orange vegetables such as carrots, winter squash, sweet potatoes, and pumpkin provide extra beta-carotene. Include generous portions of a variety of vegetables in your diet. | • 1 cup raw vegetables<br>• ½ cup cooked vegetables |

*"Reprinted with permission of Physicians Committee for Responsible Medicine"*

Many of us grew up with the USDA's old Basic Four food groups, first introduced in 1956. The passage of time has seen an increase in our knowledge about the importance of fiber, the health risks of cholesterol and fats, and the disease-preventive power of many nutrients found exclusively in plant-based foods. We also have discovered that the plant kingdom provides excellent sources of the nutrients once only associated with meat and dairy products—namely, protein and calcium.

The USDA revised its recommendations with the Food Guide Pyramid, a plan that reduced the prominence of animal products and vegetable fats. But because regular consumption of such foods—even in lower quantities—poses serious health risks, PCRM developed the New Four Food Groups in 1991. This no-cholesterol, low-fat plan supplies all of an average adult's daily nutritional requirements, including substantial amounts of fiber. Be sure to include a good source of vitamin B-12, such as fortified cereals or vitamin supplements.

# protein content of common vegan ingredients

*(Source: USDA Nutrient Database)*

| beans (cooked) beans (1 cup) | protein grams | grains (cooked) grain (1 cup) | protein grams | tofu, tempeh, seitan, etc. product | serving size | protein grams |
|---|---|---|---|---|---|---|
| Adzuki | 17 | Amaranth | 28 | Tofu, Extra-Firm | 3 oz | 10 |
| Black Beans | 15 | Barley, pearled | 4 | Tofu, Soft or Silken | 3 oz | 7 |
| Black-eyed Peas | 13 | Kasha | 6 | Tempeh | 3.5 oz | 18 |
| Cannellini | 19 | Bulgur | 6 | Seitan | 3 oz | 18 |
| Chickpeas | 15 | Cornmeal | 3 | Tofurky Italian Sausage | 3.5 oz | 29 |
| Great Northern | 15 | Millet | 6 | Morningstar Farms Burger Crumbles | 1 cup | 21 |
| Kidney Beans | 15 | Oats | 6 | Boca Burger Original Vegan | 2.5 oz | 13 |
| Lentils | 18 | Quinoa | 8 | | | |
| Lima Beans | 15 | Rice, brown | 5 | | | |
| Navy Beans | 19 | Rice, white | 4 | | | |
| Pinto Beans | 15 | Rice, wild | 7 | | | |
| Soybeans | 29 | Spelt | 11 | | | |
| Split Peas | 16 | Couscous | 6 | | | |

# weight measurements

| u.s. | | metric |
|---|---|---|
| ¼ ounce | | 8 grams |
| ½ ounce | | 15 grams |
| ¾ ounce | | 21 grams |
| 1 ounce | | 28 grams |
| 1½ ounces | | 42.5 grams |
| 2 ounces | | 57 grams |
| 4 ounces | | 115 grams |
| 8 ounces | ½ lb | 225 grams |
| 16 ounces | 1 lb | 450 grams |

# volume measurements

| u.s. | | metric |
|---|---|---|
| ¼ teaspoon | | 1 milliliter |
| ½ teaspoon | | 2.5 milliliters |
| 1 teaspoon | | 5 milliliters |
| 1 tablespoon | | 15 milliliters |
| 1 fluid ounce | 2 tablespoons | 30 milliliters |
| 2 fluid ounces | ¼ cup | 60 milliliters |
| 8 fluid ounces | 1 cup | 240 milliliters |
| 16 fluid ounces | 1 pint | 480 milliliters |
| 32 fluid ounces | 1 quart | 950 milliliters |

## weights and measurements equivalencies

| | | |
|---|---|---|
| Dash | less than ⅛ teaspoon | |
| 1 tablespoon | ½ fluid ounce | 3 teaspoons |
| ⅛ cup | 1 fluid ounce | 2 tablespoons |
| ¼ cup | 2 fluid ounces | 4 tablespoons |
| ½ cup | 4 fluid ounces | 8 tablespoons |
| ¾ cup | 6 fluid ounces | 12 tablespoons |
| 1 cup | 8 fluid ounces | 16 tablespoons |
| 1½ ounces | 3 tablespoons | |
| 1 pint | 480 milliliters | 2 cups |
| 1 quart | 1 liter | 2 pints |
| 1 gallon | 3.75 liters | 4 quarts |
| 1 ounce | 28.35 grams | |
| 1 pound | 16 ounces | |

## temperature measurements

| degrees farenheit (°F) | degrees celcius (°C) |
|---|---|
| 212 | 100 |
| 275 | 135 |
| 300 | 150 |
| 325 | 165 |
| 350 | 175 |
| 375 | 190 |
| 400 | 205 |
| 425 | 220 |
| 450 | 230 |
| 475 | 245 |
| 500 | 260 |

## pan substitutions

| | approximate pan dimensions (inches) | approximate volume (cups) | approximate volume (milliliters) (ml) |
|---|---|---|---|
| ROUND | 8 × 1½ inches | 4 cups | 948 ml |
| | 8 × 2 inches | 6 cups | 1.4 liters |
| | 9 × 1½ inches | 6 cups | 1.4 liters |
| | 10 × 2 inches | 11 cups | 2.6 liters |
| SPRINGFORM | 9 × 2½ inches | 10 cups | 2.4 liters |
| | 9 × 3 inches | 12 cups | 2.8 liters |
| | 10 × 2½ inches | 12 cups | 2.8 liters |
| SQUARE | 8 × 8 × 1½ inches | 6 cups | 1.4 liters |
| | 8 × 8 × 2 inches | 8 cups | 1.9 liters |
| | 9 × 9 × 2 inches | 10 cups | 2.4 liters |
| | 10 × 10 × 2 inches | 12 cups | 2.8 liters |
| RECTANGULAR | 11 × 7 × 2 inches | 6 cups | 1.4 liters |
| | 13 × 9 × 2 inches | 14 cups | 3.3 liters |
| LOAF | 8 × 4 × 2½ inches | 4 cups | 948 ml |
| | 8½ × 4½ × 2½ inches | 6 cups | 1.4 liters |
| | 9 × 5 × 3 inches | 8 cups | 1.9 liters |
| MUFFIN | 1¾ × ¾ inches | ⅛ cup | 30 ml |
| | 2¾ × 1⅛ inches | ¼ cup | 60 ml |
| | 2¾ × 1½ inches | ½ cup | 120 ml |

# INDEX

🅕 = fast